CHOOSING EUROPE?

CHOOSING EUROPE?

The European Electorate and National Politics in the Face of Union

Cees van der Eijk and Mark N. Franklin

with

Johan Ackaert, Mário Bacalhau,
Pilar del Castillo, Roland Cayrol, John Curtice,
Panayote Elias Dimitras, Colin Knox, Tom Mackie,
Renato Mannheimer, Michael Marsh, Erik Oppenhuis,
Dolores O'Reilly, Hermann Schmitt, Marc Swyngedouw,
Lieven de Winter, Torben Worre, Colette Ysmal

Ann Arbor

THE UNIVERSITY OF MICHIGAN PRESS

Copyright © by the University of Michigan 1996
All rights reserved
Published in the United States of America by
The University of Michigan Press
Manufactured in the United States of America
∞ Printed on acid-free paper

1999   1998   1997   1996   4   3   2   1

A CIP catalog record for this book is available from the British Library.

Library of Congress Cataloging-in-Publication Data

Eijk, Cees van der.
    Choosing Europe? : the European electorate and national politics
in the face of union / Cees van der Eijk and Mark Franklin with
Johan Ackaert . . . [et al.].
        p.   cm.
    Includes bibliographical references and index.
    ISBN 0-472-10357-1 (hardcover : alk. paper)
    1. European Parliament—Elections, 1989. 2. European Parliament—
Elections, 1994. 3. Elections—Europe. 4. European Union.
I. Franklin, Mark N. II. Title.
JN45.E55 1996
324.94′0558—dc20   95-40961
                                                         CIP

This book is for Kitty and Diane

Contents

Part III. Comparative Perspectives: The Mainsprings of European Electoral Behavior, 1989 and 1994

Preface

Studies of Europe-wide elections are hard to organize, hard to fund, hard to conduct, and hard to write about, so this book has been a long time in the making. The project took so long that the subject of our investigations changed its name while we were still at work. In the pages that follow we refer to this entity as far as possible as the European Union (EU), except that in the context of past studies (including the first of our own two election studies) we call it the European Community (EC), which it then was.

This is a book about elections to the European Parliament and why they fail to adequately perform the functions which elections are generally expected to perform: legitimizing power, holding politicians accountable for how they use that power, and representing citizens' interests. It also explores the consequences of European elections, not just those relating to the governance of the European Union but also those relating to domestic politics in member states. It contains a detailed account of the 1989 elections to the European Parliament and their aftermath—an account which yields insights about European and other elections generally—and specific propositions that are tested on data from the European elections of 1994.

The book is based primarily on two large-scale voting studies, the first of which was conducted in all 12 countries that were members of the (then) European Community at the time of the European elections of 1989, and the second of which was conducted in the same countries following the elections of 1994. Because each country provided its voters with a different set of institutional, political, social and economic contexts within which their votes were cast, analysis of these data provides not only insights about European elections but also comparative insights about the way in which the act of voting is affected by contextual differences. Indeed, because three of these countries held national elections concurrently with European elections in 1989, one of the contextual differences we were able to investigate was the presence or absence of a concurrent national election. By taking account of electoral context in this way we could study voting behavior in general—not just at European elections. So while the book is primarily about the nature and consequences of xii

European elections, it also necessarily gives rise to propositions about the behavior of those European citizens who participated (and about the many who failed to participate) in those elections. These propositions are far more elaborated than any that have come from single-country studies, and yield new insights into the mainsprings of electoral behavior. In sum, to increase our understanding of European elections we have also had to increase our understanding of European voters, much of which is relevant to their behavior in other contexts too.

The book is addressed to a number of different audiences. First of all, it is a book for those interested in and concerned about the progress of European integration in general and the future of the European Union in particular. This group includes the citizens of member countries as much as European and national politicians, officials, journalists, and other professional (or student) observers, many of whom so often (and justifiably) lament the existence of a democratic deficit in the conduct of EU affairs. Secondly, the book is for those interested in the domestic politics of any EU member country, not just for the sake of insights regarding relationships between the European Union and its member states, but particularly for the sake of insights regarding the often unexpected (and largely unrecognized) consequences of European elections for national politics. Thirdly, this is a book for those who take an interest in voting and elections. It contains a wealth of information not only about the specific European elections of 1989 and 1994, but also about the implications of differences between national party systems, electoral systems, and other institutional, social and political factors that define the context within which an election takes place. Because of this, the book should also appeal to students of comparative politics generally, and to those who use the comparative method in other areas of the social sciences, since it vindicates Przeworski's and Teune's 25-year-old promise for the power of truly comparative research. Finally, the book should benefit social scientists interested in the methods of comparative survey research. In it, a number of innovative approaches have proved their worth for analyzing the large masses of data which the two election studies gave rise to. These methods hold out the prospect of facilitating major breakthroughs, not only by those involved in comparative research, but also by those involved in the conduct and analysis of voting studies within particular countries.

It was Karlheinz Reif's idea to study European elections by means of survey questions added as 'wagons' to the 'locomotive' of special Eurobarometer surveys, conducted in addition to the regular twice-yearly 'standard' Eurobarometer studies. As Head of the Survey Research Unit of the European Commission that organizes these studies, he could help bring the additional surveys into being; and his contacts from his years as a professor of political science enabled him to gather the team of scholars who eventually undertook the project. In his new position as an official of the European Union he could not take any more central role, though he faithfully attended meetings of the group and contributed far more than the intellectual underpinnings outlined in the second chapter of this volume.

A first meeting of the research group was conducted in Mannheim in 1987, organized by Reif's long-time associate Hermann Schmitt, and funded by the German Volkswagen Foundation. Further meetings, at which the questionnaires were designed and findings were ultimately discussed, were funded by the same Foundation, the Dutch National Science Foundation, the University of Mannheim, the French CNRS, and a consortium of Italian local governments. Other meetings were conducted in conjunction with conferences (the European Consortium for Political Research, the American Political Science Association) that collaborators attended for other reasons; and not a few were paid for out of our own pockets. We could not possibly have paid for all the necessary meetings privately, and we are most grateful for the contributions we received towards these costs.

Funding for the surveys of voters conducted in 1989 and 1994 was, understandably, even harder to obtain. For a variety of reasons it was not always possible or opportune to apply for money from the organizations that would have been most appropriate in the case of a smaller enterprise or a single country study. Nevertheless, for the 1989 study, the British Economic and Social Research Council provided the greater part of the money needed to pay for the last of the three waves of interviews. The other 1989 waves (and a part of the third wave) were paid for by selling articles to media throughout Europe that reported preliminary findings from the first two waves, and by a grant from the office of the French Prime Minister. Similar financial problems plagued the 1994 study. The failure of some organizations to provide anticipated funding meant that the study had to adopt a narrower focus than had been hoped. The cost of adding this 1994 study to a post-election Standard Eurobarometer 'locomotive' was largely born by The German National Science Foundation (DFG), with a smaller grant from its Dutch counterpart (NWO).

Additional funding to pay for research assistance and travel costs was also provided by the Dutch National Science Foundation during the interval between the two studies. We are especially grateful that one grant paid for the salary of an associate researcher who was later to become one of our co-authors. Without someone to work almost full-time on data management and analysis this book would have taken even longer to complete. With some 50,000 interviews in four waves over 12 countries these were certainly two of the largest academic election studies ever to have been conducted by sample survey methods, and problems of data management and analysis were daunting. We are grateful to the home institutions of all members of the research group, and particularly to the University of Amsterdam, for supplying the very considerable amounts of computer time needed.

This form of collaborative enterprise would not have been possible at all without the presence of what, during the course of the project, became known as the Internet. The electronic mail, file transfer and remote access facilities that today permit researchers to interact with colleagues worldwide as easily as with those at their own institutions made it possible for us to have genuinely collaborative relationships among scholars who do not often meet in person, and no book of this kind could even have been envisioned in any previous era.

It should be evident by now that the work does not fit the pattern either of a typical multi-authored book or of a conventional edited volume. It is a product of the sort of collaboration that has only recently become possible between comparativists (some of whom are also country specialists) and country specialists (some of whom are also comparativists). To put together the two necessary components of our research team we did not have to locate ourselves at an institution containing the necessary country specialists; we could find them wherever they happened to be—generally residing in the countries that they study. The large number of collaborators does not, however, imply a fragmentation of research interests. The two election studies were conducted as part of a single integrated research project with a single set of objectives. Moreover, the book itself is a product of extensive consultation and debate by electronic mail and in meetings conducted in seven countries on two continents. Despite this, errors doubtless remain. Because of the collaborative nature of this enterprise, responsibility for such errors must be shared, but not equally among all co-authors. Different members of the group bear different portions both of credit and of blame.

The title page distinguishes two levels of authorship—those primarily responsible for putting this book together, and all others. Over and above this distinction, there were in practice enormous differences between the contributions of different individuals, some of whom provided significantly more than their country expertise, making contributions that are felt throughout the volume. To a large extent differential responsibilities are reflected in the distribution of chapter authorships, but one name must be especially mentioned. Hermann Schmitt served as coordinator of the project. He also edited, with Renato Mannheimer, a special issue of the *European Journal of Political Research* which published initial findings from the 1989 election study. In his capacities as editor of that volume, as coordinator of the project, and in other ways as well, he made intellectual contributions that go far beyond the chapters and appendices he authored.

Other contributors who would otherwise be inadequately recognized include Pilar del Castillo, Roland Cayrol, Renato Mannheimer, and Colette Ysmal, all of whom participated in planning and funding both components of the project and were responsible for much more than their country chapters. Michael Marsh and Erik Oppenhuis joined the team after the 1989 survey had been fielded, but made enormous contributions to its analysis and interpretation, as well as to all aspects of the 1994 study. Of equal importance in contributing to the 1989 study was Manfred Kuechler, who participated fully in all its aspects until leaving the group in 1992. Non-contributors who deserve special mention include Wolfgang Hirczy who gave us detailed comments on a draft of the entire manuscript; Harold Clarke, Max Kaase, Oskar Niedermayer, Susan Scarrow and four anonymous referees who provided helpful suggestions and advice; Marcel van Egmond who prepared the camera-ready pages; and Loreen LeJeune and Christina Triezenberg who were fountains of knowledge on the subject of copy-editing and electronic manuscript submission. Colin Day was the most supportive commissioning editor any authors could hope to have.

For their support during the research and writing process, we are grateful to our partners, Kitty and Diane, who not only suffered our frequent absences, but who also offered house-room to co-authors with good grace.

Cees van der Eijk   Mark Franklin
Amsterdam   Houston and Strathclyde

September 1995

Part I

**Research Setting:
European Elections and
the European Voter**

CHAPTER 1

The Problem:
Representation and Democracy in
the European Union

Mark Franklin and Cees van der Eijk

The European elections of 1989 and 1994 straddle the period of agonizing reassessment that accompanied the creation of the European Union. In June 1989 the European Community (as it then was) stood comparatively high in popular esteem. The 'Single European Market' project, inaugurated in 1986, seemed likely to be completed on schedule by the end of 1992, and politicians were already talking of the next step in terms of a single currency and central bank. European voters mostly approved of the EC, felt that their countries had benefitted from membership, and would be sorry if the EC were to be scrapped. In Britain and Denmark—traditionally the two most skeptical members of the European Union—the proportions favoring the EC had passed 50 percent some years previously, and even the lowest approval rating in these countries was reassuringly high. Five years later the atmosphere was very different. Not only had approval ratings dropped considerably since 1989, but the intervening period had seen the virtual demise of the European Exchange Rate Mechanism, with devaluations relative to the German Mark in several countries, making the objective of a single currency and central bank seem further away than ever. Moreover, the process of ratifying the Maastricht Treaty of European Union had shown apparent evidence that the European project was in deep trouble at the grass roots (Dinan, 1994: 290). The treaty ultimately came into force on 1st November 1993, but what had been intended as a crown on the achievement of the Single European Market was instead perceived by many as a step too far (cf. Urwin 1995: 256–259). The self-confident European Community of 1989 had become a much chastened and self-questioning European Union by the time of the 1994 elections. What had earlier been identified by some as a 'democratic deficit' in the governing institutions of the EC was by now referred to by many as a 'crisis of legitimacy', arising from the way in which the European Union had been constructed without the active support of Europe's voters.

This is a book about those voters: the ones who cast their ballots (as well as the many who did not) at Europe-wide elections held in 1989 and 1994. It is also a book about European elections in general, their failure to function as proper mechanisms for directing and legitimating the conduct of European affairs—or even to present voters with clear choices regarding Europe—and the reasons for this failure. In it we investigate in depth the European elections of 1989, and derive from this study a series of propositions about European electoral behavior which should be applicable to all European elections and which we test using data from the very different elections of 1994. On the basis of these validated propositions we then proceed to make recommendations for reforms that might alleviate the problems of accountability and control that we identify.

The book is divided into three parts. In Part I we summarize the efforts made so far to understand European elections, and we develop a research design that can build on these efforts. In Part II we investigate the European elections of 1989 and their aftermath, country by country. The objective is to determine to what extent the elections were domestic rather than European events, and the nature of the domestic consequences of the elections in each country. In the third part we take a comparative perspective, building on the findings from Part II to develop a set of propositions that describe the European electorate and the manner in which that electorate functions in European elections. The propositions are of two kinds: (a) propositions about European elections and their effects on national and European politics and (b) propositions about voting behavior more generally—why people vote and what determines their voting choice. The second set of propositions is needed in order to rule out some of the reasons that might have accounted for European elections taking the form that they do, but in the process we do learn things about voters that could not have been learned from the study of national elections. In the final chapter of Part III we explore the reasons for the crisis of legitimacy that faces the European Union and suggest steps that might be taken in order to alleviate the problem.

In the remainder of this introductory chapter we first provide a brief description of those EU institutions that are relevant to our story, then describe the crisis of legitimacy that we believe those institutions face.

Democratic Institutions in the European Union

The institutions that govern the European Union are quasi-parliamentary in structure, but very different from those found in any parliamentary nation state. Since 1979, elections have been held every five years to a parliament which has a variety of powers common to national parliaments, such as the power to reject the budget. However, the European Parliament does not have the most important power associated with parliamentary government, since the executive of the EU is not directly affected by the balance of parliamentary representation of electoral forces. So European elections do not initiate a process of government formation, as they do in most parliamentary democracies.[1]

Indeed, the executive branch of the EU is itself a very odd creature. The civil servants who work in Brussels (often referred to as 'Eurocrats') are headed by a Commission of the European Communities (official parlance has not yet caught up with the existence of a single European community, much less a European Union). This commission consists of a team of 'Commissioners' who are selected from member countries according to a formula that gives one or two commissioners to each country (depending on size), and who are accountable to the European Parliament in the sense that the Parliament has to ratify their appointment and may in certain circumstances dismiss them. These commissioners function as heads of departments (called Directorates General in EU parlance) but they do not come together into a Cabinet with ultimate decision-making powers. Instead, major decisions are taken by a quite separate body known in some circumstances as the Council of Ministers and in others as the European Council, which consists not of Commissioners of the EC/EU but instead of ministers from the governments of member states who travel to Brussels and elsewhere from their respective capital cities to attend meetings as necessary. These meetings involve different sets of ministers on different occasions (ministers of agriculture to discuss agricultural matters, finance ministers to discuss the budget, and so on). These individuals are not in any way accountable to the European Parliament. Instead they are in principle accountable for their actions in EU decision-making to their own national parliaments in the same way as they are accountable for their domestic actions. This hybrid structure reflects the EU's origins in treaties between sovereign nation-states.

Though unlike most parliamentary executives, the Council of Ministers has some features in common with the German Bundesrat (the upper house of the German Parliament) which represents the governments of the German Länder (or states), though the Council of Ministers has much greater powers of executive decision-making. The governing bodies of the EU are in fact quite elaborate, with a judiciary, and with legislative and executive structures and procedures more complex than portrayed here. However, this degree of detail is sufficient for our purposes.

---

1 The 1993 Treaty of European Union established new procedures by which the Commission of the EU is to be installed on the basis of a vote by the European Parliament. This takes the EU a step closer to normal parliamentary practices, with potential consequences which we shall discuss in Chapter 21.

A Crisis of Legitimacy?

Proper democratic representation and accountability are associated with the notion of free elections. However, in order for elections to fulfil these functions, a number of conditions must be met which are not necessarily provided by the simple institution of elections *per se*. The logic of democratic elections presupposes that the political verdict of electorates can be construed as emanating from the political preferences of voters, preferences that are relevant to the decision-making arena concerned. If this condition is met, elections can be considered to simultaneously (1) legitimize power allocated by the elections (and therefore also to legitimize policies which may be devised with this power), (2) exert electoral control by subjecting powerholders from a previous period to retrospective evaluation (that is, by holding officeholders accountable) and (3) represent groups of citizens and their interests in the political process (thus showing sensitivity to their concerns). In order for elections to function in this way, a primary condition is that voters have some awareness of the political stance and record of candidates and parties in the arena under consideration. As a secondary condition, relevant media coverage of the arena in question is obviously of crucial importance.

We maintain that these conditions are lacking in the present day European Union. Voters have on the whole never been encouraged to develop preferences for different European policies that would permit them to choose among candidates and parties at the European level, and relevant differences hardly figure in popular media coverage of events in Brussels. Indeed, candidates and parties seldom put forward policies that differ in regard to Europe, and frequently do not put forward policies of any relevance to European affairs. By failing to take the opportunity to present voters with meaningful choices they also miss the chance to educate them about European affairs. This failure is primarily due to the fact that the parties that select candidates and put forward policies at European elections are not European parties but national parties, and these parties generally treat European elections as opportunities to test their own relative popularity in the national arena. Naturally, national elections offer even less of a forum for discussion of European matters. So neither in their choice of national governments (who compose the Council of Ministers) nor in their choice of Members of the European Parliament (who hold the Commissioners accountable) are voters given the opportunity to have any input to the conduct of European affairs. Instead, inputs to the European decision-making process are restricted to individuals and groups who have non-electoral routes (for example, interest group lobbying) for making their desires known.

We believe that this lack of proper democratic accountability and control in European affairs has produced the basis for a crisis of legitimacy that is now upon us. Since voters are not given the opportunity to choose the type of Europe they want to live in, the choices made on their behalf are subject to challenge at any time. Moreover, national and European leaders lack democratic guidance in choosing between the many possible courses of action they could take. The crisis of legitimacy stems from both in the rudderlessness of the present European Union and from the absence of an electoral connection between its citizens and its leaders, as we will explain in more detail in Chapter 21. The future course of this crisis cannot be anticipated, but we see it as endemic to the current structure of political representation within the European Community, and as being bound to continue in more or less acute form until that structure is changed or until the EC/EU settles for a form of union that is compatible with existing structures.

Electoral Representation in the European Union

Members of the European Parliament (as well as many professional observers of European integration) diagnose a democratic deficit in European representative institutions. To their eyes, this deficit often appears in terms of a lack of power on the part of the European Parliament to assert itself in relation to the Commission and (particularly) the Council of Ministers. This book proposes a quite different diagnosis.

The proposition we wish to put forward is that the democratic deficit felt by Members of the European Parliament actually results from the fact that European elections are fought primarily on the basis of national political concerns, rather than on problems relevant to the European arena. It is true that the European Parliament lacks certain powers in comparison with modern-day national parliaments; but what it lacks most is not power but a mandate to use that power in any particular manner. It lacks that mandate because of the way in which European elections are conducted. In this book we will exhaustively document this proposition by devoting a chapter to each of the countries that participated in the European elections of 1989. But first we must explain why the deficit we diagnose did not lead to a crisis of legitimacy many years ago.

The reason is that, at least until recently, voters have not generally been conscious of a democratic deficit in the conduct of Community politics. They still generally perceived their national governments to be the dominant actors in EC/EU politics as well as in national politics, which in their eyes makes the European Parliament (and hence European elections) largely redundant. The neglect of European policies by voters has benefitted national governments by providing them wide latitude in decision-making. As long as the use of this latitude was not met by popular opposition we could speak of a 'permissive consensus' regarding successive moves towards European unity.

The consequence of this permissive consensus has been that national parties could avoid the need to coherently address and articulate European policy concerns—often a difficult matter for parties whose origins lie in the aggregation of quite other sorts of interests and concerns. Instead of defending their participation in European decision-making on the grounds of fulfilling an electoral mandate, ruling parties have consistently defended such actions on the grounds that they have done their best to protect national interests, thus casting European politics as a zero-sum game between the member states (and undermining their efforts in other spheres to stress the positive-sum aspects of European integration). Sometimes, of course, their best is not enough, and unpopular consequences seem to flow from European developments. Governments are then tempted to blame 'Europe' for these consequences. But, to the extent that governments succeed in externalizing the blame, they merely cause themselves to appear ineffectual in relation to events in Brussels, displacing the crisis of legitimacy from the European to the national arena.

It is our understanding that, in this manner, the permissive consensus is eroding, faster in some countries than in others. Various developments have increased the salience and visibility of European policies to individual citizens but have not led to debates regarding the substantive direction that such policies should take. In the absence of choice regarding what kind of Europe is being built on their behalf, voters may well come to demand a choice as to whether Europe should be built at all. Any such demands can have unpredictable consequences for European countries, as was amply demonstrated by the Danish and the French referenda over the Maastricht Treaty and by Mr Major's difficulties with dissent within the ranks of the British Conservative Party.

A first priority in this book will be to show that these and other national political developments are indeed consequences of the failure of European elections to perform their proper functions.

What Is To Be Done?

How can this crisis of legitimacy be resolved? Many European parliamentarians and some other scholars and observers have suggested that enhancing the powers of the European Parliament would have the effect of increasing that body's visibility. If this happened, individual citizens would be able to see that their interests were indeed being represented. Other scholars and observers have countered, however, that effective representation can only occur by way of national governments and their membership in the Council of Ministers (see Chapter 21 for details of these debates). Members of this school of thought have strongly argued that strengthening the European Parliament would be the wrong solution and that instead the unanimity rule should be restored in the Council of Ministers, thus ensuring that no government would have to report to its citizens that their interests had been overridden. Members of yet another school of thought have argued that the nation state is too large an entity to be adequately represented at the European level, and asserted that the interests of (for example) Scotland or Catalonia would be better served if they were independently represented in a 'Europe of Regions'.

It seems to us that all of these solutions address the wrong problem. The crisis of legitimacy that we observe does not arise from lack of power by either national or European parliaments but from lack of appropriate articulation of interests in both arenas. Neither of the first two suggested solutions addresses this problem. Direct representation of subnational regions within the policy-making bodies of the EC might improve the representation of regional interests, but it would still leave those regions with the same problems in regard to other interests (feminist or environmental interests, for example) as existing EU members now experience. In order to resolve the current crisis the real problem must be addressed.

In this book we will first and foremost be concerned to amass the evidence needed to document what we take to be the real problem, which is that voters have not been asked to make choices about how Europe should develop. The forthcoming 1996 Inter-Governmental Conference is expected to consider these matters, but the very constitution of this body as a meeting of governments perpetuates the problem. Those governments have not armed themselves with mandates from their voters to reach any particular decisions in regard to the future of the European Union. Only by putting choices to voters can mandates be acquired. The IGC could indeed draw up a list of such choices, and governing parties could return to their countries to put those choices before their voters; but, on the basis of past experience, it seems likely that the conference will end with an agreement signed by governments.

Of course, providing voters with choices may sound straightforward but it is not. As this book will make clear, it involves major problems whose solutions are not obvious. As a secondary objective in this book we will make suggestions, based on our findings, for the shape that such solutions might take.

Other Research Objectives

The same problems that yield an unpredictable future for the European Union also have consequences for the domestic political systems of member states. That European elections do not function as proper mechanisms for ensuring accountability and control of European matters does not mean that they have no consequences. On the contrary, the very lack of European content to European elections frees them to carry a burden of (quite unanticipated) repercussions for the politics of member states. This book will map out the nature of these consequences and to show how, even leaving aside the desirability of reform for Europe's sake, domestic political considerations lead to the same conclusion.

Finally, the nature of European elections provides us with an unprecedented opportunity to investigate features of electoral behavior that had previously remained obscure. Our study of the nature and consequences of European elections will show that these events are neither really European nor really elections. Paradoxically this makes them unusually well suited to answering some fundamental questions about the voting act. Because European elections are not really European, the processes they display are national political processes. Because they are not really elections, they display these processes uncontaminated by the intrusion of political concerns that might dominate particular national elections. In such conditions we can undertake a truly comparative study of why people vote and why they vote the way they do.

Improving our understanding of the mainsprings of electoral behavior is not just a matter of academic interest. One reason why European elections are not European in nature might have been because voters in specific European countries are so different from each other that a single election could not be conducted across the countries of the European Union. In other words, the national orientation of European elections might be an inevitable consequence of the unreadiness of European voters for any other orientation. We will argue that no barrier of the kind exists to the conduct of proper European elections. European voters constitute one electorate, separated by the particularities of national politics. The right leadership proposing relevant choices would find the European electorate quite able to make rational and considered judgements regarding European affairs in proper European elections. The lack of such elections in the past is not because of the lack of a European electorate but because of the lack of Europe-wide parties and leadership. Indeed we will show in this book that it is the myopia of national party leaders and the rigidities of national party systems that create today's crisis of legitimacy in Europe.

CHAPTER 2

The Foundations:
Unanswered Questions from the Study of
European Elections, 1979–1994

Michael Marsh and Mark Franklin

We are not the first to suggest that European elections are neither really European nor proper elections. The fact that elections to the European Parliament are different from elections to national parliaments in EC/EU member countries has been evident ever since the very first of these Europe-wide elections were held in June 1979. Turnout in such elections is low, major parties generally do badly (compared to their performance in adjacent national elections) and small parties often do better than in national elections. Writing in the immediate aftermath of the 1979 European elections, Reif and Schmitt (1980) proposed a way of thinking about these elections that would account for their characteristics. This was to regard them not primarily as European but as pale reflections of national elections, presenting voters with hardly any stimulus for their vote choice other than their habitual national party context.

The Second-order Election Model

A national election in a European country, as in most parliamentary regimes, allocates seats within the national legislature to different parties and, in that way, determines the relative claims of each party to control the apparatus of government. To differentiate such elections from European elections, Reif and Schmitt coined the phrase 'first-order' elections. Other elections, such as those for local offices, are less important precisely because they play no role in deciding who governs the country.[1] In Reif and Schmitt's terminology, these are 'second-order' national elections: national in the sense that voters are driven by national political cues, even though such elections may involve only part of the country, and even though national power may not be at stake. In the same way, elections to choose a ceremonial head of state would also be

---

1 Few European countries have federal systems with substantive powers reserved to sub-national bodies, and even in those countries (notably Germany) that do have federal systems, the pre-eminence of the federal level over the states is evident.

'second-order' national elections.[2] But these second-order elections are characterized by the same party system and are fought by the same parties as first-order elections, something that makes the relationship between first-order and second-order national elections particularly interesting.[3] The most important distinction is that in second-order national elections "there is less at stake as compared to first-order elections" (Reif, 1985a:8). Seen in these terms, European elections are second-order national elections because no actual executive power is at stake. The political complexion of the European Commission is not affected by these elections, much less that of the national governments whose members make up the European Union's Council of Ministers. Indeed, even if the composition of the European Commission were affected by European elections, arguably those elections would remain second-order elections as long as national political concerns remained paramount in the minds of voters.

Reif and Schmitt's fundamental assertion is that outcomes of second-order national elections cannot be separated from those of first-order elections conducted in the same political system. Concerns which are appropriate to the first-order arena will affect behavior in second-order national elections, even though second-order elections are ostensibly about something quite different. In particular, what is important is "the political situation of the first-order arena at the moment when the second-order election is being held" (Reif, 1985a:8). This hierarchy has nothing to do with the sequence in which elections are conducted. It is entirely a matter of the relative importance of different political arenas, with the most important arena being 'first'. Nevertheless, second-order election outcomes are generally contrasted with prior first-order outcomes,[4] which may give the spurious impression that sequence is important in determining which election is 'first-order'.[5]

Reif and Schmitt develop several arguments on the basis of their premises. The first is that, because European elections are less important, citizens will

---

2 Elections in a Presidential system are harder to place. Reif says of France that Presidential elections are always first-order elections, as are Assembly elections except perhaps when they follow closely on a presidential election. The US case seems to illustrate a different pattern, with the mid-term Congressional elections generally being second-order elections.

3 Elections for entities like Dutch water-boards, which are non-partisan, are qualitatively quite different.

4 Subsequent first-order outcomes are not yet known at the time of the second-order election, and prior second-order outcomes are of no interest at the time of a first-order election.

5 In fact, the need to contrast European elections with national elections held at a different time is unfortunate and leads to many potential pitfalls. In this volume we try to overcome these problems by defining as a baseline for comparisons not a prior national election but a hypothetical one occurring at the same time as the European election (see below and Chapter 3).

be less inclined to turn out and vote.[6] The second is that, because there is less at stake, those who do vote may not behave in the same fashion as in a first-order election. In what way they might vote differently, of course, depends on the considerations motivating voters in first-order elections, but one consideration that is singled out by Reif and Schmitt is people's concern with choosing a government, or at least influencing the formation of one. A party preference in a first-order election based on this consideration would not necessarily carry over into a second-order election. Thus someone might vote for a small party in a European election but hesitate to do so in a national election for fear that the vote would be 'wasted'.[7] The first-order context itself may also influence behavior in the second-order election. For instance, governing parties may be adversely affected if their 'normal' supporters withhold their votes, so as to express disapproval of government performance to date, knowing that such a warning will not actually result in a change of government.

These arguments enable us to characterize hypothesized differences between European elections and national elections as follows:

— Turnout will be lower in European elections;
— Larger parties will do worse and smaller parties will do better;
— Incumbent national government parties will suffer losses.

Smaller parties are, of course, often new and frequently more radical than larger parties, leading to the subsidiary proposition that new and radical parties would tend to be advantaged in European elections (Reif, 1984a).

Most of these propositions have received at least preliminary validation in the context of individual European elections, and, in the case of turnout, all European elections up to those of 1989 (Reif, 1984a, 1985a; Niedermayer, 1991; Curtice, 1989). Table 2.1 summarizes the actual pattern found across all first-order and European elections during a period starting shortly before direct elections to the European Parliament were instituted in 1979 and ending in December 1994. On average, turnout is indeed lower, government parties do lose votes, and the party system does become more fragmented—indicating a movement from larger to smaller parties—compared with the previous national election. On the other hand, except in the case of turnout, the differences are not large; and in every case, including turnout, the standard deviation approaches or exceeds the mean, indicating that there is a great deal of variance unexplained

---

6 Moreover, fewer resources will be expended on them by parties and the media. How far these factors are also responsible for lower turnout is unknown.

7 Even in a country whose electoral system is highly proportional, a vote for a small party may still be wasted in this sense because that party has such a small chance of influencing events.

Table 2.1 Comparing Average Turnout, Support for Government Parties and Fragmentation Between European Parliamentary Elections and Prior National Election, 1976-94

	Prior National	European Parliament	Difference	Standard Deviation
Turnout (%)	81.7	63.2	18.5	15.2
Government Support (%)	48.6	43.1	5.5	7.5
Rae's Fragmentation Index	0.74	0.77	0.03	0.04

Sources: National election results from Mackie and Rose (1991; updated in the European Journal of Political Research (EJPR) 1990-) and and European election results from the collections by Mackie and Craig (1980, 1985) and Mackie (1991). 1994 materials supplied by the European Parliament Office in Dublin. Data on government was obtained from Woldendorp, Keman and Budge (1993), subsequent issues of EJPR and, most recently, press reports.

by these differences. In addition, we do not know how far the different features are interconnected. In particular, how far is the decline of government support due to the fact that governments tend to be made up of larger parties?

More importantly, the idea that voters might withhold their support from governing parties—or from whatever party they might have voted for if national political power had been directly at stake—as a means of expressing disapproval of their performance raises a whole host of questions that Reif and Schmitt do not address. Why do voters choose to comment on national politics in a European Election? Whose behavior might be affected by their disapproval? Under what circumstances might such a comment be most telling? The obvious answers to these questions would seem to be that voters might withhold support in a European election in order to affect the behavior of political parties and their leaders, particularly during the run-up to a national election when the public will be more focussed on national politics than at other times and parties will have stronger incentives to adapt their policy stances in the light of expressions of voter concern. If voters do this, then we would expect to see different voting patterns in European elections held shortly before national elections than in European elections held earlier in the national electoral cycle. In the immediate aftermath of a national election there would be no reason for voters to comment on the performance of a party, and voters could 'vote with the heart' in Reif and Schmitt's terminology (see below). As a national election came closer, however, we would expect the importance of the election as a means of influencing national politics to increase, and voting behavior to change as a reflection of voters' attempts to exercise influence. If this happens, then two questions arise: (1) in what way does voting behavior change in these circumstances, and (2) to what extent does this difference in behavior influence events? Specifically, to what extent are domestic political developments affected by European elections and the behavior of voters in those elections?

In the remainder of this chapter we will take a closer look at turnout and party performance in European elections, and at the consequences of these elections for the national and European arenas, enquiring to what extent the second-order model can help us understand these important matters, and to what extent European election behavior may illuminate behavior in other spheres.

Turnout: Who Votes?

We have already seen that fewer people vote in European elections than in national ones. Indeed, turnout is often even lower in European Parliament elections than in other second-order national elections (Reif, 1985a: Table 1.5). The lower turnout in European elections has been put down largely to the fact that Europe has had little salience with the public, and that the consequences of the election for policy-making in the EC/EU are hard to discern. Whilst this ties in with what we know about turnout at the national level—and helps explain why turnout in Britain, for instance, is even lower at European than in local elections—what does it tell us about the large variations in turnout that exist between countries and between one European election and the next? The important general question of why some people vote and others do not has never been answered satisfactorily (see Chapter 19 for a summary of the literature on this topic). European elections provide a research opportunity which can contribute to our understanding of the determinants of turnout, with possible spinoffs in other contexts.

Across the EC as a whole, turnout was highest at the European elections of 1979. The average was 68 percent, falling to 65 percent in 1984, 63 percent in 1989 and a mere 60 percent in 1994. In some countries it was consistently high in these elections—around 90 percent (thus vitiating any expectation of uniform low turnout in European elections)—and in others very low. Moreover the difference between national and European turnout varied from election to election even for particular countries. What accounts for this variation over time and between countries? One factor is clearly the presence of compulsory voting in some countries, which keeps turnout high even in European elections. Blumler and Fox (1982) argued that other key factors were positive views about Europe and politicization of the culture (which affects turnout through increased campaign activity). They note that lowest turnout in 1979, relative to the previous national election, was in Denmark; and take this to support their argument that a vigorous campaign could not overcome the negative impact on turnout of reservations about the EC in that country. Niedermayer

(1990) also examined the effect on national turnout of views about the EC (averaged for each country), together with the effect of electoral systems and concurrent national elections; but he concluded that much of the contribution to turnout was due to factors which have nothing to do with European concerns.

Most of the research on turnout has focussed on individuals and has arrived at similar conclusions. The first multivariate analysis carried out on a number of countries (six) indicated five important factors: party loyalties, education, age, campaign interest and exposure, and positive attitudes to EC affairs (Blumler and Fox, 1982: Chapter 5). The first three might be expected to predict turnout in most elections and the importance of the specifically 'European' route to participation was only indirect, influencing turnout by virtue of its effect on other factors like campaign interest and exposure. Blumler and Fox found little evidence for the independent importance of attitudes towards European institutions themselves, unlike Inglehart and Rabier (1979), who relied on bivariate analysis.

It should also be emphasized that positive views on Europe (at the individual level) do not merely predict turnout in European elections, they also predict it at national elections (e.g. van der Eijk, 1984a,b; van der Eijk and Oppenhuis, 1990; van der Eijk and Schmitt, 1991). Such attitudes tend to be part of a syndrome of support for elected institutions in general, which is in no sense peculiarly linked to Europe and European elections. The weakness of 'European' explanations was underlined further by Schmitt and Mannheimer (1991a) whose multivariate analysis put particular weight on a factor they called 'habitual voting'—the predisposition to vote in whatever sort of election was called.[8] This was linked to age, political interest and above all to party attachment. Other variables, such as those tapping interest in and perceived salience of the EC, had no independent effect. Schmitt and Mannheimer found that attitudes to the EC in 1989 were important only in Denmark.

What do all these results mean for the second-order election model as an aid to interpreting turnout in European elections? For Schmitt and Mannheimer, the identification of habitual voting ties in closely with the second-order election idea. In a low salience election people vote out of habit, or because of social norms, general political involvement or party attachment. Only in a high salience,

---

8 Habitual voting was defined operationally in terms of being able and willing to say how one would vote in a general election held 'tomorrow' or how one did vote in the previous one. Schmitt and Mannheimer say this is at least sufficient to define habitual voters, but this is so only if habitual voters by definition know who they are going to vote for. In fact, the measure seems to contain some elements of party attachment. The authors admit that not all of those caught by their definition are true habitual voters, but the error in some countries seems huge. In Britain, for instance, over 70 percent are defined as habitual voters by Schmitt and Mannheimer, but turnout in the European election was only 36 percent.

first-order election will other factors matter much. However, some of Schmitt and Mannheimer's best results in predicting reported turnout were obtained for Greece and Ireland, where concurrent national elections were held. In other words, habitual voting appeared to predominate in first- order elections too. Whilst this may be a valid conclusion, it indicates that the importance of habitual voting is not confined to second-order elections.

Taken together, the various findings regarding turnout do not seem to amount to very much. That turnout should be lower in a less-salient election is hardly an earth-shaking finding, and it brings nothing from the study of European elections to illuminate our understanding of what makes people vote in that or any other context. Instead, all the borrowing goes in the other direction: European election turnout has been explained on the basis of what we already know about national election turnout. As useful as this work has been, it has not taken advantage of the opportunity to use European elections as an exciting new laboratory in which to study the mainsprings of electoral participation.[9]

It is not as though there are no puzzles left in understanding why people vote. As set out in more detail in Chapter 19, the greatest puzzle is why, in country after country, turnout should be declining despite increases in the number of people sharing the characteristic most closely associated with high turnout—education. Equally, the two countries with lowest turnout (Switzerland and the United States) are among the highest in educational attainments. Clearly, what makes the biggest difference when comparing individuals within a country may not be the most important thing when considering differences between countries or changes over time. Because turnout in European elections can be measured simultaneously over a wide range of different conditions, such elections might well provide a suitable laboratory for unlocking these mysteries. Taking advantage of this opportunity is one major objective of the present volume.

Another objective is to identify the national consequences, if any, of European elections. As argued earlier, if behavior in European elections is different when they are held shortly before a national election, this would seem to imply that voters are attempting by their European votes to affect the national electoral arena. One way in which behavior might be different would be in terms of enhanced turnout.[10] We address this question with data from all European

---

9 In this respect the study of European elections differs from the study of congressional midterm elections in the United States, since those have been used as laboratories to investigate the nature of voting choice more generally (cf. Hinkley, 1981, Campbell, 1987).

10 Of course there might be other reasons for increased turnout. Finding that turnout is higher at European elections held shortly before a national election is perhaps a necessary but hardly a sufficient reason for supposing that voters are acting instrumentally; but see below.

elections which have, at the time of writing, already been followed by national elections. This gives us 36 cases (12 countries times 3 elections less 2 because Spain and Portugal did not elect representatives to the 1979–84 European Parliament, plus 2 because Germany and Greece had already at the time of writing had national elections following the European elections of 1994). Obviously we needed to control in this analysis for the presence of compulsory voting, since this is the major factor determining turnout.

Table 2.2 indeed shows a significant effect from time until the next scheduled national election in countries without compulsory voting, when a control for compulsory voting is in effect.[11] According to this estimate, among countries without compulsory voting turnout is reduced by over a quarter of a percentage point (–0.28) for each month prior to an expected national election that European elections are held.[12] This would correspond to a (for European elections) comparatively low level of turnout when national elections were recent, at the start of the electoral cycle, changing to a comparatively (for European elections) high level of turnout when national elections were imminent, at the end of the cycle some four or five years later.[13]

This finding goes a long way towards explaining why turnout in the same country can vary dramatically from one European election to the next. Only in Luxembourg have European elections always been held at the same point in the national election cycle (the two elections always occur concurrently in that country). A possible reason for increased turnout in European elections that occurred shortly before national elections might be a spillover from the national context, with people paying more attention to politics, and parties making more efforts to motivate their voters.[14] On the other hand, if some part of this variability were due to differences over the course of the electoral cycle in the suitability of European elections as vehicles for commenting

---

11   Table 2.2 does not report the results from a properly specified model of the determinants of turnout, so the effects of time until the next election should not be taken as definitive. In Chapter 19 the question of turnout is considered in much greater detail, but we shall find that, even in a fully specified model, the number of months until the next election retains a significant effect.

12   While it is true that in most European countries the election date is discretionary within margins fixed by law, nevertheless there will generally be widespread awareness of the increasing likelihood of an election being called in circumstances of government crisis or towards the end of the permitted period.

13   If we take recent and imminent national elections to be those falling within one year of the European elections, the difference found empirically is 9.6 percent, on average. It might have been the case that this effect reflected not high turnout before a future national election but low turnout after a past national election. Separate analyses (not shown) indicate that turnout is indeed lower than average (for a European election) during the 12 months following a national election; but the drop is smaller than the rise that occurs during the 12 months before a national election.

14   We will attempt to evaluate this interpretation in more detail in Chapter 19.

Table 2.2 Effect of Time until the Next National Election on Turnout 1979-1994
(N = 36)[a]

Variable	b	Beta	Significance
Months until the next national election[b]	-0.27	-0.21	.003
Compulsory voting	33.67	0.86	.000
(Constant)	59.45		.000
Variance explained		0.85	

a Three elections times twelve countries, less 2 for Spain and Portugal in 1979, plus 2 for Germany and Greece in 1994 (see text).
b Concurrent national elections are coded 0 on this variable.

on national politics, this would quite reverse the previous view that European elections merely reflect domestic politics. But to see whether this is happening we need to look at party choice.

Party Choice: Why Is It Different?

In the case of party choice, as in the case of turnout, European elections present phenomena in need of explanation but also offer opportunities for conducting enquiries that could not be conducted elsewhere. We will start with the opportunities. Just as researchers have not yet taken advantage of European elections to study turnout, so they have not yet taken advantage of these elections to study party choice; yet, as in the case of turnout, there are puzzles regarding party choice that cannot easily be solved from within individual national contexts. The most important of these puzzles relates to tactical voting.

Attempts to explain why people vote the way they do generally ignore the fact that large parties are advantaged by their very size. Only occasionally do we see analyses that attempt to take account of variations in tactical situations to explain why people would vote for a party other than their first preference in certain circumstances (for example, Franklin, Niemi and Whitten, 1994). Yet the choice between parties is clearly structured by the relative electoral strengths (sizes) of the parties concerned: other things being equal, a large party will be more attractive to voters because it is likely to have an impact on public policy, in contrast to a small party which (again, all other things being equal) is likely to have less influence.[15] The extent of this

---

15 'All other things being equal' is of course a condition that never holds. This, however, does not detract from the argument, but merely raises an empirical question as to how strong such considerations actually are.

structuring is hard to determine from within the confines of a particular political system; but a European election provides a perfect laboratory in which a large number of concurrent European elections produce an enormous number of parties of different sizes whose support can be analyzed simultaneously, thus making it possible to measure the impact of party size in multivariate analysis.[16] At the same time the impact of electoral systems and other differences between countries can also be taken into account as never before (see Chapter 20 for further discussion of this topic).

Turning to European elections as events which produce phenomena in need of explanation, we see an even less satisfactory picture in regard to party choice than we did in regard to turnout. Perhaps because there are more differences to be explained (one for each political party instead of just one for whether people vote or not), the disparity between European and national elections in terms of party choice seems less coherent. Nevertheless, as we have seen, party choice does appear to follow a different pattern in European Parliament elections, whether the comparison is with prior, subsequent or simultaneous national elections. This difference is never great, and sometimes it is very slight, but there is a difference to be explained.

It would seem that, with some exceptions, differences between European and national party choice are not due to differences between the choices (parties) on offer. It is true that many parties contest European Parliament elections as members of a wider transnational grouping, and their election literature may carry other names in addition to their own (in Ireland, for example, Fine Gael campaigns as part of the christian democratic group—the People's Party of Europe); but, as we already indicated, second-order national elections (including European elections) are fought essentially by the same parties that compete in first-order elections. The European groupings appear to have little significance for the way people vote. Transnational party activity was probably most extensive at the first elections in 1979, when EC funds were available for such activities, but voters appear to have paid little attention even then. There was little perception of the result of the election in transnational terms. Blumler and Fox (1982:66) revealed that about 50 percent of voters admitted they had no idea which party grouping had been most successful in Europe as a whole, and that even among those who claimed to have some idea there was considerable diversity of opinion.

More generally, we have seen that the results of party choice tend to benefit smaller parties disproportionately and that larger parties and those in

---

16   Reif (1984a) and Schmitt (1990b) mention tactical considerations as a reason why large parties do better in national elections than in European elections (see below) but they do not use this insight as an aid to understanding the mainsprings of party choice.

government generally suffer. Yet what determines which small parties benefit, which larger parties lose, and how much the government parties suffer? One idea put forward by Reif (1984a) and Schmitt (1990b) is that in European elections voters 'vote with the heart' by simply picking the most attractive party or candidate without regard to government formation. In national elections, by contrast, they vote 'tactically' to maximize the probability that their vote will affect the composition of government. The theory of voting with the heart would explain why some parties gain votes in European elections. These would be parties that the voter finds attractive for some reason but will not vote for in a national election for fear that the vote would be wasted (in the sense of not counting in the calculus of government formation—see footnote 7 above). The theory could also explain why large parties do badly, but the idea that government parties do particularly badly requires an auxiliary explanation. Research on second-order national elections in other contexts has revealed a 'punishment effect' (Erikson, 1988) which would be consistent with the idea that voters withdraw support from governing parties in second-order national elections. However, this idea is somewhat at odds with the idea of voting with the heart in second-order elections.

Reif himself (1984a, 1985a) suggested that punishment effects occur particularly in certain circumstances. Building on work by Tufte (1975) and Miller and Mackie (1973), he used some simple models to describe a popularity cycle between national elections, in which governments fall into disfavor soon after taking office but then recover as the next national election approaches; and European elections held at various times in the cycle reflect these trends. By implication, it could still be the case that in the vicinity of national elections voters would vote with the heart; though the idea of a popularity cycle rather suggests that at such times the result would be close to what would have happened in national elections. Reif's tests of these models were really no more than suggestive, since each was based on only a handful of cases, and there has as yet been no systematic attempt to compare the appropriateness of different statistical models across countries.

When we conduct the analysis suggested by Reif with a data set derived from all European elections to date, we find only partial confirmation for the cyclical model. Table 2.3 shows that a polynomial function involving position in the national election cycle together with the square of the same measure explains 18 percent of the variance in government popularity dropoff in European elections, where dropoff is defined as the difference between the percentage supporting government parties at the European election and the percentage supporting government parties at the previous national election.

Though the coefficients meet conventional levels of significance, the proportion of variance explained is not impressive, particularly given the

Table 2.3   Effect of Position within the National Election Cycle on Dropoff in Government Support 1979-1994 (N = 46)*

Variable	b	Beta	Significance
Cycle	-39.1	-1.67	.005
Cycle-squared	31.3	1.53	.009
(Constant)	3.5		.267
Variance explained		0.18	

* Four elections times 12 countries, less Portugal and Spain for the 1979-84 Parliament.

small N, and since we actually tested six different models in order to find one that performed this well, even these findings may easily be the result of capitalizing on chance.[17]

A major problem with Reif's model arises from our difficulty in saying how much support government parties would have received had the European elections been national ones. Evidently both our measure of dropoff and Reif's alternative measure of deviation from a linear trend (see footnote 17) involve the conflation of three different possible sources of reduced government support: (1) the temporal location of the election within the national election cycle, (2) the fact that it is a second-order national election, and (3) changes in the baseline from which any such cycle would operate.[18]

To the extent that we accept the presence of such cycles, and to the extent that European elections respond to the same forces as government popularity, Reif would have been correct in seeing such elections as no more than opinion polls. The important question from our perspective in this chapter, however, is whether indeed people do vote in a European election as they would have done in a national election held on the same day; and if not, why not? This question can only be directly addressed in a very few instances: those where concurrent elections were held for national and European parliaments, and in at least some of these cases it is clear that European and national behavior

17 Reif proposed that one try to explain not the measure of dropoff used here but the deviation in percentage votes for the government from a linear trend between the adjacent national elections. Such a formulation does not yield statistically significant findings with this larger dataset. A cubed function (also proposed by Reif) did not yield significant results with either formulation of the dependent variable. Moreover, if one eliminates elections that occurred simultaneously with national elections (as suggested by Reif) then the squared term fails to reach significance. Here such elections are coded as occurring at the end of the electoral cycle.

18 Such changes do not have to follow the linear trend that Reif assumes. Much information on the basis of opinion polls suggests that such changes in are not linear at all (see, e.g., MacKuen, Erikson and Stimson, 1989).

differs. Elsewhere, the same information can be deduced from opinion poll data in which individuals are asked both how they voted in a European election and how they would have voted had that election been a national one—questions that were in fact asked in 1989 and 1994 and which enjoy a prominent role in the present book. We will not further concern ourselves with the domestic political support cycle, which is arguably better studied country by country (Ladner, 1996).

Another significant problem with the analysis in Table 2.3 is a failure to differentiate losses to government parties that stem from the government popularity cycle from those that stem from party size, since government parties tend to be large parties which are also expected to perform badly in European elections. John Curtice makes this point to qualify his findings that all governments lost votes in 1989, arguing that "if the European elections were bad news for governments they were rarely good news for oppositions either" (1989:227). He tackled a similar problem in explaining the success in many European countries of green parties in the 1989 elections, asking explicitly how much their success was due to their ideological appeal and how much to their small size. He found that while there was a pronounced shift to smaller parties in 1989, most of this went to the greens. Other small parties, on average, actually did less well than in previous national elections. What is most striking about this result is that it demonstrates a pattern which cannot easily be accounted for in second-order terms, hinting at a need for a supranational rather than a merely national focus: another contribution the present volume seeks to make (see especially Chapter 18).

In order to properly evaluate these questions, we again face the problem of deciding what should be the standard against which to compare European election results. If support for individual parties is compared with support at previous national elections this ignores the fact that with the passage of time one would in any case expect changes in party support. If party support at European elections is compared with a linear trend between adjacent national elections this assumes that changes in party support should have been regular. Far preferable would be comparisons between support given to parties in European elections with support that would have been given to the same parties had the European elections been national ones. In Part II of this book and in Chapter 18 we focus on such measures.

But, before we turn to these investigations, it is important to place them in context of what we know about relevant aspects of voting behavior from studies of national elections. The difference between party choice in a first-order national election and party choice in a European election is evidently affected by a variety of factors which can be explored under the headings of partisanship, issue (and ideological) voting, and campaign activity.

Partisanship and Differential Turnout

Among various intellectual antecedents to Reif's development of the second-order election model is work done in the US on the well-known tendency of support for the party controlling the White House to decline in mid-term elections (for a brief review see Niemi and Weisberg, 1993:207–221). One explanation, known as the 'surge and decline' theory, was originally developed by Angus Campbell et al. (1960) who argued that the key lay in differential partisan mobilization. In a Presidential election independents and those who identify only weakly with a party are more likely to vote, and their party choice, made on the basis of short-term factors favoring one candidate over another, will have a big impact on the result. In a mid-term election, parties' efforts to bring out the vote are weaker, with the consequence that fewer people vote and the result is closer to a 'normal' one defined by the distribution of partisanship nationally. While this interpretation does not eliminate the contribution made by changes in an individual's party choice, it does highlight the importance of differential turnout. In a second-order election not only may fewer people vote, but those not voting may be drawn disproportionately from certain groups. Unfortunately, much American survey evidence does not support the 'surge and decline' theory, which has prompted James Campbell (1987, 1992) to formulate a revised theory, in which it is partisans who are most likely to absent themselves in the mid-term election. Not all partisans are equally likely to absent themselves and Campbell highlights the tendency of supporters of the party controlling the Presidency to provide more of the absentees (cf. Erikson, 1988). Meanwhile, independents can affect the result by changing their mind (from the previous election) in response to short term forces.

These findings stress the importance of distinguishing the effects of differential turnout from those of voters making different choices in European than in national elections. No study has yet tried to disentangle the effects of turnout and shifting party preference on the result of European elections across a number of countries—something done in this volume, using a technique pioneered in studies of Dutch elections for the European Parliament (van der Eijk, 1989; van der Eijk and Oppenhuis, 1990). Nevertheless, attention has been given to the differential abilities of different parties to get their supporters out to vote for them. The second-order election model (and the American research alluded to above) gives rise to several propositions relevant to this question. In particular it might well be thought that government parties and larger parties would prove to be less effective at mobilizing their supporters in a European election. Schmitt (1990b) has examined the ability of parties to get their normal supporters (those who say they feel close to, fairly close to, sympathize with the party) to the polls to support their party. His conclusions do not appear to fit second-order election predictions: governing parties were not less effective than others at mobilizing their voters, nor were big parties (those with above average proportions of supporters). Governing parties actually proved to be more effective than other parties, and big parties were as good, if not better, than small ones. By contrast, newer and more ideologically homogenous parties appeared to be less effective. However, Schmitt also discovered that in first-order elections the advantage to the larger parties is even more dramatic. So it is not that big parties do badly in mobilizing their voters at European elections so much as that they are very successful in national ones, underlining again the importance of strategic voting which will be investigated in detail in Chapter 18.

Issue Voting and Ideology

One reason why people might be expected to vote differently in European than in national elections derives precisely from the fact that they are European elections with an ostensible focus on the European arena. Though Reif and Schmitt, and others who focus on aggregate election outcomes, have stressed the apparent lack of European content in European elections, the question needs to be addressed with data from public opinion polls. Nevertheless, the second-order model put forward by these authors does have issue implications. At the very least, the issue preferences of voters and parties in European Parliament elections might be more closely aligned than in national elections because of the absence of the need for tactical voting.

It is true, almost by definition, that in a second-order election the most important issues will be those relating to the first-order arena. Blumler and Fox (1982) discovered that only a minority of voters could name any European issue that emerged in the 1979 campaigns, although the range of difference across countries here was considerable, with only 22 percent in Ireland compared with 62 percent in Denmark who could identify a European campaign issue. Nor was any common agenda apparent among those who identified issues, except in a national context (where there was often a high level of agreement around such issues as unemployment and inflation). Nevertheless, in Denmark (where EC membership itself was an issue), in Britain and Ireland (where the domestic implications of the Common Agricultural Policy loomed large) and in Germany (where people mentioned greater European cooperation and the absence of war) significant proportions of voters did identify European issues. What Blumler and Fox do not give us is any evidence that people voted differently because they were aware of European issues, or that the second-order arena actually mattered to voters.

Evidence presented by Manfred Kuechler (1991) appears to confirm the relative lack of salience of EC issues in the 1989 election. People were asked to rate issues as more/less important. They were given four purely European issues (political unification, agricultural surpluses, Turkish EC membership and the Single Market) and eight other issues. Less than 3 percent thought any of the European issues to be "most important", and less than 10 percent thought any of them to fall among the three most important ones. Of course, most policy areas now have a significant European dimension, but more research is necessary to show us the extent to which this complexity is actually perceived by voters.

In any case, it remains problematic how far such considerations matter in the electoral decision. 'Issue voting' is a hotly contested matter at the national level, let alone in European elections. Kuechler (1991) looked to see if people voted for the party they thought was most competent to deal with issues they thought most important. More than a third appeared to doubt all parties in this respect but most voters did think one party more competent than the others, and the votes of such individuals in 1989 tended to be for that party. This result, as Kuechler admits, proves nothing but it does hold out the possibility that European elections are about issues. However, the findings of another study (van der Eijk and Franklin, 1991:124), which focussed on the attitudes of parties and their voters towards European integration, underscored the fact that parties do not acquire votes on the basis of European issues.

The general failure of researchers to establish the significance of obvious European issues must lead to skepticism about how far such an approach can account for differences between national and European voting, but none of this research has actually ruled out such effects. Before we can state definitively that European elections have no European content we must be more sure of our ground. Establishing the lack of impact of European issues on European election outcomes is a primary preoccupation of the country chapters in Part II of the present volume.

One step in this direction has already been taken by van der Eijk and Oppenhuis (1990). Rather than employing issues, they suggest that party choice can be explained by self-reported ideology—the location on a left/right scale where people place themselves. On the assumption that in European elections voters use their hearts rather than their heads (because of the lack of strategic concerns), these authors suggest that ideology will predict party choice in a European Parliament election better than in a proximate national one, and they discover this to have been the case in 1989; but the implications of this finding have yet to be explored. Evidently some voters must be choosing different parties in the European election than they would have chosen in a national election, but what is the consequence of this? Do parties gain any lasting advantage from good European electoral performance, or is the result discounted by commentators as an aberration only to be expected of a second-order election? Answering this question is another of the purposes of the country chapters in Part II of the present volume.

Campaigns

The decision of voters to go to the polls and, once there, to pick one party rather than another, is in part determined by election campaigns. What happens in European parliamentary campaigns? How are they perceived by the voters? The short answer provided by most research is that European parliamentary election campaigns are much more low-key than those for general elections, and that—as we have already seen—their specifically European content is, with a few exceptions, unobtrusive. Blumler and Fox (1982:51) concluded that the 1979 campaigns "agitated few voters' pulses" and "were fairly easily avoided by those not wishing to become involved", while Winfried Schulz (1983:343) concluded that, despite national variations in content and dynamics,

> ...None of the campaigns enjoyed many of the qualities which could have attracted more attention and interest in them. The status of the participants was generally low, the election seemed to have little relevance, evaluative content was largely missing and possibilities for identification were scarcely apparent.

Interest was generally even lower in 1989 (Cayrol, 1991: Table 1.2) but not everyone was unmoved. Franklin (1991) discovered that campaigns did appear to mobilize voters along traditional socio-demographic lines. Cayrol (1983, 1991), when examining some of the socio-political contours of campaign involvement, found, not surprisingly, that there are common factors which predict campaign exposure across Europe: age, gender (male) and middle class status are all associated with greater involvement, although he noted (1991) that gender and class biases were less strong in 1989 than previously. Those least interested in the European election campaign were those who had no interest in a national election either.

Few voters claimed that the campaigns helped them decide how to vote. In 1989, about one in five voters claimed that TV coverage—the main source of information—helped show "where my party stands", a few more than those claiming simply that it was "boring" (Cayrol, 1991: Table 7); but supporters of different parties were not uniform on the merits of TV coverage. Twenty-five percent of extreme-right voters felt coverage helped them to place their party's views, but only 12 percent of extreme-left voters thought so, and 18 percent of green voters. Questions must be raised about the importance of such results, given the success of green parties in 1989, but there is as yet no analysis which places involvement explicitly in a second-order context, and relates it to dimensions like large/small, new/old, government/opposition parties, or to position of the European election in the national election cycle. Yet such an analysis could illuminate the functions of campaigns in first-order elections as well. Again this is something that will be attempted in the present volume, specifically in Chapter 18.

Consequences of European Elections

Elections in parliamentary systems are judged normally by their consequences for government formation, but European elections are unlike general elections in that they do not give rise to a government, even indirectly. Reif (1984a:253) suggests mischievously that they are in danger of becoming "third-order" elections "with barely more relevance than a public opinion poll". What then are their consequences? Are they so irrelevant?

Practical Consequences

The second-order election model implies that it is more likely that national politics will effect European elections than vice-versa, but this does not mean that European elections have no consequences. Evidently European elections do determine the personal and party composition of the European Parliament, and the policy concerns of its newly-elected members. These results of the elections may even be of considerable importance for the ensuing direction of European affairs—not least because of the Parliament's co-decisionmaking and budgetary powers. Nevertheless, they do not arise from conscious choice on the part of voters, who are seldom told what the policy preferences of parties are, except perhaps in national terms. The effects of European elections on the composition of the European Parliament thus flow in reality from patterns of candidate recruitment and the fact that elections are held, not from the choices made by voters. Meanwhile, the fact that European elections are in reality linked to the national arena gives them the opportunity to have national consequences which (unlike their European consequences) may, in many cases, indeed be the result of purposive decisions by voters.

Like national elections, European Parliament elections may have consequences for the organizations that fight them. Perceptions of their performance can affect future strategy and tactics. Some parties may gain the valuable resources of visibility and credibility in European elections that will help them in future campaigns in other political arenas. There is anecdotal evidence from particular national contexts that bears upon this question. It is conventional wisdom that European electoral success played a role in the rise of the Front National in France and was important to the early success of the German greens. Reif (1984a) notes that government coalitions may be strained by adverse results, and gives illustrations. Ideally, these qualitative assessments could be given a more systematic foundation: under what conditions will European Parliament elections have consequences for national politics? One reason why little progress has been made in answering this question might be that there have been few European Parliament elections to study, but another is surely the fact that most observations of these election are made in their immediate aftermath, almost too soon for many consequences to be clear. From a perspective of four Europe-wide elections, and greater hindsight, more systematic findings arise, as we shall see in the country chapters of Part II and in Chapter 18.

One indication that such investigations will indeed discover national consequences of European elections is the fact that European election outcomes are demonstrably connected to the outcome of subsequent national elections—indeed this connection appears to be rather closer than that to prior national elections (Marsh, 1995). This can be shown more definitively by building on the analysis already conducted of the cyclical nature of European election outcomes. If we take the equation responsible for the findings in Table 2.3, and use it to derive a residual variable which is the deviation of the European election from the previous national election, net of cyclical effects, this residual turns out to be a fairly powerful predictor of swing at subsequent national elections.[19] In other words, to the extent that European election outcomes are not simply reflections of the government popularity cycle (and we already pointed out that variance explained in that analysis was quite low), the deviation from what might have been expected on the basis of the cyclical model is a leading indicator of what will happen to government parties at the next national election, as shown in Table 2.4.

When government parties did better in the European election than would have been expected on the basis of the location of that election in the national election cycle, those same parties also did better at the ensuing national election. When they did worse than expected at the European election they did worse at the ensuing national election. Variance explained is higher than it

---

19 By using the supposed government approval cycle in this way we do not mean to endorse the view that there is such a cycle or that (if it exists) it is properly measured in this fashion. Pertinent reservations about the use of polynomial regression in this context have been set out in van der Eijk (1987). We do not, however, wish to engage in argumentation on this score in the present context, where it turns out to make no substantive difference whether we use the residual or the raw dropoff score as our independent variable.

Table 2.4   Effect of Residual from Expected Dropoff on Change in Support for Governing parties at the next National Election, 1979-1994 (N = 36)*

Variable	b	Beta	Significance
Residual from Expected Dropoff	0.61	0.61	.000
(Constant)	-3.67	1.53	.000
Variance explained		0.38	

* Less Portugal and Spain in 1979; plus Greece and Germany in 1994 (see Table 2.2).

was in the estimation of the cyclical effect itself, suggesting that European elections might actually be better predictors of subsequent national elections than they are consequences of prior ones.[20] In other words, it is at least as important to discover what consequences European elections have for national politics as the other way around. Moreover, the fact that European elections appear to have consequences for the balance of political forces in subsequent national elections raises again (far more forcefully than in the case of turnout) the question of whether voters are trying by their European votes to affect the national political arena—a question that will be a major concern in Part III of this book.

Normative Consequences

National elections, and party competition at those elections, are supposed to promote political participation and to legitimize state activity (cf. Ginsberg and Stone, 1986). Many politicians and commentators had hoped that European elections would increase awareness of EC institutions—particularly the parliament—and contribute to their legitimacy. Furthermore, such elections might have stimulated debate about issues on the EC's agenda, both constitutional and otherwise, and given some legitimacy to that agenda and the proposals for tackling it.

The low turnout, disappointing levels of interest, and the lack of European content in EC/EU election campaigns have disappointed such hopes. Few would claim that European elections have done much to redress the 'democratic deficit' which has attracted so much attention, especially in the wake of domestic battles over the Maastricht Treaty. Many expectations may have been unrealistic, based more on imagined features of national elections

---

20 Restricting the data to cases where the next national election occurred less than two years later increased the variance explained to 0.42 (though with an N of only 20). Of course this analysis is not based on a properly specified model and should be regarded as no more than suggestive. A full investigation of these matters is conducted in Chapter 18.

than upon the realities of those contests. In the same way that early students of national elections were appalled at how far voters deviated from the ideal of citizenship, so people may have expected too much of European Parliament elections. For instance, even if European issues were widely discussed during European election campaigns, and given much more priority than national issues, this would not mean that people would vote on the basis of those issues, any more than they do in national elections. Indeed, studies of the referenda held in various countries to ratify the Maastricht Treaty concluded that the outcome had little to do with voters' assessments of the questions supposedly at issue (Franklin, Marsh and Wlezien, 1994; Franklin, Marsh and McLaren, 1994; Franklin, van der Eijk and Marsh, 1995a,b). If such contests show little evidence of European content, why should we expect any more of European elections?

A critical analysis of European Parliament elections by Bogdanor (1989) focussed not on the electorate but on the sorts of choices offered by the national party systems. He asserts that voters are not provided with the opportunity to cast a vote which can be interpreted as a choice between different visions of the EC/EU. "Elections, if they are to be meaningful, must fundamentally allow for choice", but national party systems provide "an artificial superstructure unable to articulate the wishes of the electorate" (1989:214). Similar complaints have also been made about other second-order national elections, especially very parochial ones where, it is sometimes said, party systems are not relevant.

Bogdanor's conclusions have been put in perspective by van der Eijk and Franklin (1991) in a study already referred to in this chapter. Their finding of a considerable correspondence between the views of parties and those of party supporters on the subject of European integration led these authors to conclude that, whilst the elections provided no mandate for future developments, they could nevertheless be viewed as ex-post-facto endorsements of, and hence legitimation for, the institutions of the (then) European Community. Nevertheless, the deficiencies of the European electoral process in failing to provide a mandate for future policy directions are grave ones, and worthy of more attention than they have been given. Moreover, these deficiencies have to be seen in the context of the equivalent failures of first-order national elections to provide choices on European matters. This is a major topic for the final chapter in this volume.

Conclusions

Any review of the literature on European Parliament elections would have to conclude that Reif's and Schmitt's suggestion that these must be seen first and patterns to be found in the results—propositions which are supported by empirical evidence. Many studies, particularly those focussed on one national context, have noted how things like the low turnout or the swing against the government illustrate the normal pattern expected in a second-order national election, with the national arena affecting the outcome of the European election. But none of these observations have served to establish conclusively the lack of European content to European elections, and none have addressed the possible consequences of this deficiency for the future of the European project. An even more surprising failure of past studies has been the lack of any systematic attempt to enquire about the effects of European elections on the national political arena, or whether such effects as occur are the consequence of intentional behavior on the part of voters. This question leads to the subsidiary question, raised repeatedly in this chapter, of whether European elections perform the same functions (and whether voters behave in the same way) when these elections are held early in the national election cycle as when they are held during the run-up to a national election.

For all these reasons our understanding of European elections has not developed as it might have done from the foundations established by Reif and Schmitt. The chapters that follow are intended to remedy these deficiencies. In the process, some of them will also report investigations that use European elections as they have never before been used, as laboratories in which to investigate the mainsprings of individual voting behavior. But before we turn to these investigations we need to tie together our various research questions, and introduce the methods and measures that will be employed in answering them. These are the subjects of Chapter 3.

CHAPTER 3

The Research:
Studying the Elections of 1989 and 1994

Cees van der Eijk and Mark Franklin

Fifteen years of studying European elections have, as Chapter 2 has shown, left us with some quite well-substantiated knowledge about the nature of these elections, but also with many questions still in need of answering. This book attempts to address these questions on the basis of a research design that is outlined in the present chapter.

The major departure from previous studies is that this is the first to be based on public opinion poll data obtained from surveys explicitly designed to study voting behavior in European elections. Because these studies were primarily concerned to investigate the behavior of European voters, they were conducted in the context of all that we have learned from over fifty years of studying national elections in Western countries. We hope that this context will help us to disentangle the threads that appeared so hopelessly intertwined in Chapter 2, and that it will yield definitive answers to the questions about European elections that previous research has left unanswered. At the same time, the European electoral context is employed in this study as a laboratory for investigating questions about voting behavior that remain unanswered after all those years of national election studies in Western countries. In this chapter we summarize the objectives with which the research team approached the task of studying the European elections of 1989 and 1994, and the design of the resulting project. We begin by restating the research questions that were outlined in the first two chapters of this volume; and then move on to the research design that was adopted in order to confront these research questions—the design that underlies the country chapters of Part II.

What Can Voters Tell Us about European Elections?

Bringing together the research questions mentioned at various points in Chapters 1 and 2, we find that these amount to seven in all—three about European elections and four about European voters. Of those relating to European elections, the first asks

1. is a European election really European in nature?

We could refer to a European election as being really European on the basis of either of the following: (a) individuals may vote or fail to vote because of support for or opposition to the idea of unification or because of their attitudes regarding particular European policies; and (b) voters might vote for different parties in European than in national elections because of the salience in European elections of European concerns. If (as we suppose on the basis of past research) we find that European elections are not really European but simply reflect the balance of political forces in the national political arena of each country, then the question arises

2. why is the outcome different from that of a national election?

Differences between European election outcomes and those that might have been expected in a national election held at the same time might be the straightforward consequence of low turnout affecting different parties unequally, or they might be due to voters supporting parties in the European contest that are different from those they would have supported in a national contest. In either case, we will need to investigate the reasons for the different outcomes, and in either case we are led to ask a third important question

3. what are the consequences of the voting act for national politics?

The answers to this question do not relate to individual voters but to political systems as wholes. They might be of a similar nature in all countries, or might differ from country to country. Those who supported the institution of direct elections to the European Parliament hoped that these elections would serve to alleviate the lack of democratic control of Community decision-making, which had become an obstacle in itself to the process of further integration (see Jacobs, Corbett and Shackleton, 1992). In addition, it was widely hoped that direct elections at the European level would instill a sense of European citizenship into the populations of member countries. The development of such supra-national orientations was not only expected to provide further stimulus for the integration process, but also to cushion any popular dissatisfaction with problems that further steps towards European unification were bound to generate. Even if European elections did not determine the makeup of a European government, they could still call attention to concerns, preferences, ideals and views on European matters of the voters in member countries. In other words, it was widely expected that these elections would create a connecting link between citizens and policy-makers in the European Union.

Both of our first two central research questions deal explicitly with the nature of this link: what kind of an electoral connection (if any) is created between the European voter and the European Parliament, and how does it affect the legitimacy of European policies or the direction taken by European integration? Evidently these elections do have consequences in terms of the personnel and party composition of the European Parliament, and the programmatic orientations and attitudes of its newly-elected members. These results may even be of considerable importance for the ensuing direction of European affairs.[1] Yet we already suspect that the elections that bring these representatives into the European Parliament hardly provide democratic legitimation for their policies. As we saw in Chapter 2, the accepted scholarly view holds that voting in European elections is dominated by national concerns to the exclusion of European ones, so that the outcome in no way expresses a mandate to govern Europe in any particular fashion—one aspect of the so-called 'democratic deficit' in European elections. But even if we confirm this conventional wisdom, this will not mean that European elections have no consequences, which brings us back to our third research question.

Clearly, the very fact that the elections do not perform the functions normally expected of democratic elections has consequences for the future of the European Union. Moreover, the consequences of European elections for the domestic political process in member countries may be even more extensive. We saw in Chapter 2 that voters turn out in greater numbers when European elections are held closely before subsequent national elections, and that European election outcomes are leading indicators of subsequent national election outcomes—especially if the time gap between the two elections is small. The implication of these findings is that European elections do have consequences for domestic politics, and that these are consequences of purposive actions on the part of voters. Establishing what these consequences are, and whether they are indeed the consequences that voters intend, is a neglected facet of European electoral research. Implicit in the first three central questions addressed in this volume is the notion that European elections should not primarily be viewed as poor copies of the 'real thing' but rather as unique phenomena whose true consequences have yet to be assessed. Evidently, in addressing these questions, it is important to distinguish the relative importance of national as opposed to European concerns and preferences in the choices

---

1 These consequences cannot be evaluated on the basis of a study of voters alone, and so they will not concern us in this book. A component of the 1989 European election study that would have provided data about European parliamentary candidates was abandoned because of lack of funding. A component of the 1994 European election study that did study candidates will be reported upon elsewhere.

made by European voters, and to distinguish the relative importance of national as opposed to European consequences flowing from the electoral verdict(s), or lack of verdict(s). Such distinctions are illustrated in Figure 3.1.

Understanding the nature of European elections requires a variety of investigations, some of which are best done comparatively and some from the perspective of individual countries. The analysis of the input side of the diagram can only be addressed on a country-by-country basis. As far as the output side is concerned, the national consequences are also best dealt with at the national level; however, the European consequences can evidently only be dealt with from a transnational perspective. Moreover, any systematic features of the national consequences will have to be assessed comparatively. The bulk of this book is divided into two parts on the basis of these different levels of analysis, with Part II consisting of a number of country chapters and Part III of a number of chapters that take a comparative perspective on topics that can be dealt with only at the European level. There is another important difference between the chapters of Part II and those of Part III. The country chapters focus on one particular European election—the one conducted in 1989. The comparative chapters, by contrast, analyze data not only from 1989 but also from 1994. Effectively, our inquiry has three stages. In the first stage, in Part II, we investigate a particular European election country by country. From these analyses we derive a number of propositions which in Part III are elaborated in comparative perspective by putting together data from all 14 of the political systems that were separately analyzed in Part II. Finally, the insights we derive from both the country and comparative analyses of 1989 data are put to a particularly stringent test: they are used to try to explain the features of a quite different election, the one that was held in 1994. Most of these tests are comparative in nature and are thus conducted in the chapters of Part III; however, a postscript to Part II (Chapter 17) does consider the 1994 European elections from the perspective of particular countries, enquiring in what ways the insights developed in the country chapters might have to be changed or elaborated in the light of 1994 events.

Figure 3.1 Inputs and Outputs of European Elections

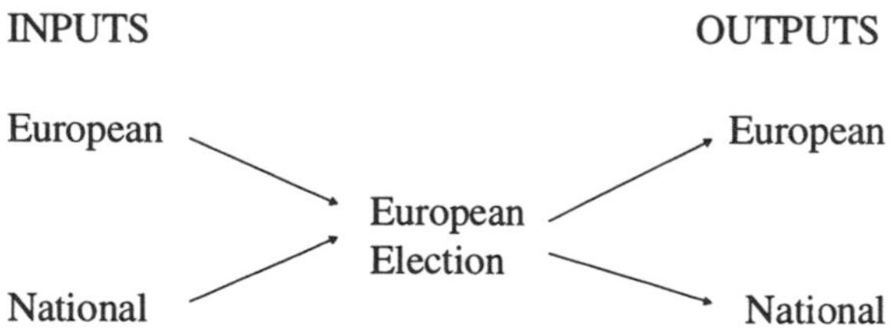

What Can European Elections Tell Us about Voters?

The other four research questions at the center of our concerns relate to voters. To the extent that we find no European complexion to a European election it might be true to say that the event consists of a number of national elections held simultaneously in countries that are members of the European Union. If this is so, the next question that has to be asked is whether there is anything about European voters (their myopia, ignorance, or lack of political motivation) that makes this inescapable, or must reasons for the national individuality of these contests be sought elsewhere? To answer this question we must focus on two questions which are much more specific:

4. why do people vote?

5. what makes them vote the way they do?

These questions have, indeed, been central to political science research since the dawn of voting studies, but they have virtually always been addressed from within the context of a single country. Our concern in this book is to discover how institutional, political and social contexts affect these two aspects of the voting act (see Beck, 1986, for an insightful plea for taking such contextual factors into account). Many features of national elections (for instance, the nature of the party system, the type of electoral system, the presence of compulsory voting, to name just three systemic factors often thought to be important)—are fixed features of elections within one country. So are political and social contexts. If systemic and contextual factors are important in determining why and how people vote, we would not know this from studying one country at a time. For all these reasons, we may ironically learn more about (national) electoral behavior from a European election study than from a series of national ones. Indeed, national elections, it can be argued, do not readily permit the disentangling of two major components of electoral motivation—policy concerns and strategic considerations. Voters may prefer certain parties on the basis of policy orientations, but hesitate to vote for those parties because they (the parties) are unlikely to be able to put their policies into effect. Potential voters may even fail to vote at all because they see no way in which their vote can contribute to a desired outcome.

Arguably, to understand the dynamics of turnout and party choice we need to be able to properly specify both sorts of concerns; but within a single country at a national election this is hard to do. At a European election, by contrast, we saw in Chapter 2 that strategic considerations are apparently modified, if not totally absent. In such an election we can try to evaluate the importance of strategic considerations by comparing turnout and party choice with what would have occurred had the election been a national one. We need to understand these differences in order to understand why European election outcomes differ from national election outcomes. Such an understanding will inevitably illuminate our understanding of voting behavior in national elections as well.

One of the things we might learn is that context makes a difference to how voters behave. To the extent that this context is specifiable in theoretical terms that are generally applicable to voters in all countries, we will have established that nationality is not the important thing, but rather the social, economic or political context within which the voting act takes place; and we will be able to make general statements about voters in European elections—statements that are not prefixed by lists of country names (cf. Przeworski and Teune, 1970). Depending on the exact nature of these statements, it might turn out that despite the segmented way in which European elections are currently conducted, Europe is in many ways already a single political system in which much the same political processes occur. Seen from that (cross-national) perspective, our questions about European voters give rise to a higher-order question:

6. *were the votes cast in 1989 and 1994 cast by one electorate or by many?*

If we find there is only one European electorate this will have profound implications for our interpretation of the nature of the democratic deficit in European elections. Such a finding would imply that differences observed between voters in different countries are a consequence of the different contexts in which those voters are placed (with different institutional arrangements and different social, economic and political stimuli) rather than of different reactions to those stimuli. Another party system, another electoral system, a new set of political issues, may be all that it would take to turn Dutch voters (for example) into Spaniards. If this is true, then we already have a single European electorate, hidden behind the particularities of national party politics. The existence of a single European electorate would color our understanding of the failure of these elections to center upon European themes or give rise to a European mandate. If the blame for this failure cannot be placed on insular and myopic voters, then responsibility for the democratic deficit in European elections must rest elsewhere: perhaps with parties and leaders who fail to present the voters with relevant stimuli. If Dutch voters could through the presentation of relevant stimuli have been turned into Spaniards, then why not into Europeans? In the concluding chapters of this book (Chapters 20 and 21) we will elaborate this idea. Of course, stimuli are only effective if they evoke responses.

Presenting European voters with European stimuli might not be enough to get them to change their orientations towards the European arena unless they were motivated to do so. This brings us to our final research question,

   7. *would European voters be motivated, in the proper circumstances, to direct the course of European politics?*

Only if the answer to this question is in the affirmative would we have reason to expect that voters would be responsive to relevant stimuli. Of course, this is not a question we will be able to answer definitively, because we do not observe proper stimuli being provided (except perhaps in Denmark—see Chapters 6 and 21). So in contrast to our other research questions this one must be approached indirectly, in terms of two necessary conditions for an affirmative answer (which might not turn out to be sufficient, but which are all that can be addressed from our present vantage point in history). These are (a) that voters have relevant perceptions about European affairs and (b) that they behave as though motivated to direct the course of policy-making. By relevant perceptions we mean that specific orientations and attitudes are inter-connected in a manner which is shared between individual voters and linked to the political discourse in their political systems. By motivation to direct the course of policy-making we mean that voters are not simply registering their identifications or behaving as though judging a beauty contest, but are voting in a politically instrumental manner that takes account of the constraints, limi-tations and possibilities of the specific context within which they find them-selves. These two preconditions, if present, should be all that are needed to ensure that the presentation of relevant stimuli will turn national voters into European ones. In the remainder of this chapter we introduce the research design established to answer these questions, and the common analyses it calls for that are reported in the country chapters.

The European Election Studies of 1989 and 1994

To study the 1989 European elections, three studies were fielded—the first two in conjunction with regular Eurobarometer surveys conducted in November 1988 and April 1989 and the third in conjunction with a special Euro-barometer conducted immediately following the June 1989 elections. In each of these waves, around 1,000 individuals were interviewed in each of the 12 countries of the (then) European Community (fewer in Luxembourg and more in the United Kingdom where a separate sample was drawn from Northern Ireland) yielding a total of some 36,000 interviews in three waves over 14 political systems (in addition to distinguishing Northern Ireland from Great

Britain, we also distinguish Flanders from Wallonia, since each of these Belgian regions has a separate party system). To study the 1994 European elections, about 13,500 interviews were conducted in a survey that followed the elections in June. This time we distinguished 15 political systems—looking separately at voters in the former East Germany as well as making the same distinctions in the United Kingdom and in Belgium as were made in 1989. The two projects are described in detail in Appendix A, so only their salient features are reported here.

The research questions underlying the 1989 and 1994 election studies did not call for panel designs. Our interests do not relate so much to the dynamics of individual choice as to the aggregate distribution of European versus national electoral concerns in June 1989 and June 1994. However, this does not mean that we could adopt a static (single time-point) design for studying each election. For one thing, we needed to be able to investigate the manner in which voters were made aware of the approach of a European election to see whether and to what extent they were reoriented to the European arena. Moreover, the 1989 study had to provide the means to calibrate its findings relative to findings about earlier European elections that were studied only at some remove from the actual events. Since no large-scale voter study was conducted either in 1979 or in 1984,[2] detailed information about vote intention and recall of voting choice in those elections was only possible on the basis of the regular Spring and Fall Eurobarometers conducted two months before and four months after the elections concerned, possibly resulting in contaminated findings. It was our aim, therefore, to sample the electorates of all member countries both before and immediately after the elections. For the elections of 1989 we used three time-points—late in 1988, in April 1989, and in June 1989.[3] Obviously, for each nation the three samples had to be selected by identical procedures (approaching random sampling as closely as possible) and had to allow statistical generalization to the entire electorate of each country.

---

2   In 1979 a European Election Study was conducted, initiated by Karlheinz Reif, but the mass survey component of this project was small. The project was particularly concerned with elites, campaigns and communications. Publications stemming from this project include a Special Issue of the *European Journal of Political Research* in 1980; Reif (1985a,b); Blumler and Fox (1982); Blumler (1984).

3   Given the usual time schedule for the Eurobarometer surveys (fielded in March/April and October/November of each year) and the timing of the European elections (June), it was virtually impossible to employ a regular Eurobarometer survey as the vehicle for a post-election study. Karlheinz Reif, the Director of the Eurobarometer surveys of the European Commission, was an active collaborator in the 1989 and 1994 European election studies (indeed, he originated the project—see Preface), and his willingness and ability to adjust the Eurobarometer schedule to suit the requirements of the European Election Studies was critical to the success of the project.

The decision as to timing was based upon the following assumptions. In late 1988 the electorates would be largely unaware of the upcoming European elections, and their choices and preferences would be determined mainly by factors arising from the national political arena. Consequently, this would provide a suitable anchor point and baseline for comparison. By the second time point, in April 1989, the upcoming elections would have become known to segments of the electorate, and triggered some thought and consideration. The third time point for interviewing was obvious: as soon as possible following the European elections, in order as far as possible to preempt memory distortion and decay. The 1994 election study involved one wave only, the major puzzle relating to turnout having been solved by the 1989 study (see below). It was fielded in conjunction with a special Eurobarometer conducted in June 1994, immediately after the elections. In this book we make little use of the 1989 pre-election waves of surveys, except in the present chapter which summarizes the most important findings.[4] A special issue of the *European Journal of Political Research*, January 1991, was largely devoted to studying the dynamics of opinion formation and mobilization at the time of a European election.

First Findings

Initial analyses of data deriving from the election study of 1989 resolved a number of questions that had plagued us and other scholars for many years, and opened the way to the research presented in the remainder of this book. In particular, the puzzle over whether participation in European elections was related to the extent of concern with European affairs was resolved in a quite intriguing manner that turned out to have implications for many facets of our study. The contradictory results of past studies in regard to the relationship between turnout and voters' concern and involvement with the EC/EU appear to have arisen because these studies were conducted at different times in relation to European elections (before or after, and with a greater or smaller time gap). In fact, it seems that when voters are asked about their vote in a European election they respond differently to this question when an election is somewhat hypothetical than at the time of the election. Seen from a distance, intentions to vote (and recall of having voted) appear to be related to pro-European attitudes. As the election approaches, however, and becomes less hypothetical, normal mechanisms appear to assert themselves. Actual turnout in European elections appears to respond to much the same forces as does turnout in national elections; and most voters in the European election could

---

4 We also use data from earlier waves in the construction of a variety of variables employed in our analyses of post-election data (see Appendix B).

be described as 'habitual voters' who participated in the elections just as they would have in national elections (Schmitt and Mannheimer, 1991a).

The importance of national concerns and national cues in what should have been a European election was found repeatedly in our early analyses. European elections are overwhelmingly treated as a means of demonstrating support for (and opposition to) national parties and their policies. One possible explanation for this is the fact that national party leaders exhort their followers to support the same parties in European elections as they support in national elections in order to further national political ends. Although our data are not ideally suited to testing this hypothesis, comparison of pre- and post-election responses using quasi-panel analysis suggests that this is indeed what happens (Franklin, 1991). Only a small number of those who vote fail to support the same parties in European elections as they would have done in national elections, putting to rest any suspicions that the small aggregate differences might have arisen from the canceling out of much more massive movements. Nevertheless, enough differences remain between national and European voting as to leave open the possibility that voters might have been induced to switch parties on the basis of issues considered salient in a European election that cut across the party lines established in national political discourse.

Although a detailed study of the issues that played a part in the European election campaign gave little support for this idea (Kuechler, 1991), the possibility could nevertheless not be totally eliminated, and remains a preoccupation in the present volume. This is what we turn to next, in the country chapters of Part II. Our expectation, based on previous research and our early analyses of all countries taken together, is that turnout and party choice in a European election will be explicable to a large extent on the basis of the same factors as turnout and party choice in national elections. The major differences we expect to find will be in the level of interest generated by parties and media (lower in European elections than in national ones), and in the absence of formal consequences for (national) government composition, which may have a variety of implications.

But while the confirmation of these expectations might appear unexciting, two features of the country chapters give them special importance for those interested in European politics. The first is the means we employ to compare European with national election outcomes. Understanding how European elections resemble national elections imparts a better understanding of what is involved in national elections in these countries. In particular, by computing the potential electorate of each party and the overlap between these potentials, we illuminate the nature of party systems and party competition in the countries of the European Union.

The second feature of the country chapters that gives them special interest is that they contain a detailed exploration of the actual consequences of European elections. Having definitively established what European elections are not, these chapters contain the first attempts to discover what they really are. Because several years had elapsed since the elections of 1989, authors of the country chapters in Part II were able to evaluate the consequences of these elections from a vantage point that allows their true meaning to be assessed. The country chapters deliberately fail to take account of the elections of 1994, for two reasons. In the first place, the consequences of a European election can only be thoroughly evaluated after the passage of enough time for these consequences to have become apparent. The most recent elections can thus never be as thoroughly evaluated as can earlier elections. In the second place, and more importantly, we wished our conclusions to be uncontaminated by data from 1994 so that we could use the 1994 elections, later in the book, as a venue for conducting critical tests of the general validity of our findings.

Measures and Methods

The country chapters focus particularly on the first three of the research questions that are central to this volume. To begin with, they assess how far the 1989 elections to the European Parliament were actually European in character—to what extent did issues relating to the European Community govern turnout and party choice. Secondly they investigate how the outcomes of these elections compare with what would have happened in national elections. Thirdly, they investigate the impact of these elections on national political processes (the importance of the elections for European political processes will be covered in Part III, along with the remaining research questions that focus on voting behavior). To give perspective on these investigations, the authors of the country chapters first needed to characterize the nature of the party system in each country. To yield comparability between countries they employed a common approach, which we will now describe.

Party Systems

Political parties can be described in a number of ways, and the country chapters will introduce the most important parties by means of a verbal characterization of their most salient political stances, ideologies, programs, and electoral success. Such descriptions can be invaluable in suggesting what parties stand for but, without some means of portraying the system's structure, can nevertheless fail to give an adequate account of a party system as a whole. A structure is determined by relations between elements. For this book, which focusses on voters and elections, the most relevant relationship is the degree to which various parties compete with one another for the support of voters.[5] Parties that look for votes among the same groups of people are obvious electoral competitors. The extent of this competition is easily established on the basis of answers to a set of simple survey questions (pioneered in the Dutch national election studies), one for each party, which probe the likelihood that voters will "ever" vote for the party in question. The responses range on a 10-point scale from "I will never vote for this party" to "I will certainly vote for this party at some time in the future".[6] In contrast to more usual questions about party preference, these questions allow voters to indicate whether there is more than just one party that is electorally attractive to them.

The use of these questions responds to one of the major problems in studying contemporary party systems: the fact that small parties have only a small number of people voting for them, so that analysis of why these votes are cast is hampered by the small number of respondents. By asking every respondent to rate all parties, we add to the information about those who prefer small parties information about those who do not prefer them. Having both sets of information enormously increases our ability to investigate the basis of party choice. In a manner that is described in Appendix B, the responses to the set of 'probability to vote' questions can be transformed into 'potential votes', and therefore also into a potential electorate (i.e., potential share of the vote) for each party. It will be clear that these potentials may sum to more than 100 percent, and will do so to the extent that voters say that there is more than one party for which they would 'ever' vote.[7] The size of the group of voters that

---

5 Note that this is not the same as competition for government power. Electoral competitors (at least in multi-party systems) are usually potential coalition partners, and often refrain from cutthroat competition with each other for votes, knowing that this may damage their collegial relations once in government. Nevertheless, the extent to which party leaders could attempt to poach each other's voters is an important feature of the party system even if they refrain from doing so.

6 The reference to the future is not meant to require special qualities of foresight from our respondents, but rather to serve as a projective device which allows them to express their view of the electoral attractiveness of each of the parties without being constrained by the restrictions of particular electoral systems, most of which stipulate that at any particular election one is allowed to vote for only a single party.

7 In a lot of ways these questions are similar to so-called thermometer ratings, where respondents are asked to indicate how 'warm' (sympathetic) or 'cold' they feel towards each party. The major difference between the thermometer ratings and the probability to vote questions is that the latter have been shown to relate to actual party choice in a much clearer and stronger fashion than the former (see Tillie, 1995, and also Chapter 20, Table 20.1, in the present volume). For a somewhat different set of objects, hypothetical or generic party types, similar probability to vote questions were asked in the Spring 1984 Eurobarometer. Analyses of these data were reported by, e.g., Inglehart (1990) and van der Eijk, Niemöller and Oppenhuis (1988). In these questions respondents were asked how likely it was that they would ever vote for a 'conservative', a 'christian

Table 3.1 Potential Electorates and Overlap Between Parties in a Hypothetical Party System (Cells contain percentages of the potential electorate of each column party that is shared by each row party)

	Party A	Party B	Party C	Party D
Party A	100	30	30	15
Party B	50	100	50	50
Party C	40	40	100	60
Party D	10	20	30	100
Size of Party's Potential as Proportion of the Electorate	30	50	40	20

belongs to the potential of two different parties can be assessed as well, by means of a procedure that is also described in Appendix B, and can be seen as the potential 'overlap' of the two parties and hence as a measure of how much they compete for the same votes. The results of these calculations will be reported within each country chapter in a table similar to Table 3.1, which contains a hypothetical example for a system consisting of four parties, labeled A, B, C, and D.

Table 3.1 shows first of all that parties in the hypothetical country indeed share the potential support of groups of voters. The sizes of the four parties' potential electorates (in the bottom row of the table) sum to 140 percent, indicating sizeable numbers of respondents who said that more than one party is a likely recipient of their vote. The earlier rows of the table show the manner in which these overlaps are patterned. For example, no less than 50 percent of the potential voters for party A can imagine voting for party B; looking down that column we see that party C is almost as attractive to the potential voters of party A, but a much smaller portion of A's potential voters considers party D attractive. Owing to the differences in parties' electoral strength (size), the table is not symmetrical across the diagonal. 30 percent of party B's potential support might vote for party A, whereas the corresponding figure for party A is 50 percent. Thus, the success of A in any election is very much dependent on the way in which voters who are attracted to both A and B make up their minds as to which of these two they will actually vote for.

We know from other research that the extent of overlap in the potential support for parties is often indicative of their similarity in the eyes of the voters (e.g. Budge and Farlie, 1977; Enelow and Hinich, 1984). Probably, in the example above, A and B have a lot in common, as have B and C; but A and D are much less similar. Quite often, parties that are strong electoral competitors

---

democratic', a 'communist' party etc., without equating these to actually existing parties.

represent similar interests, ideologies or political points of view, which explains why they are often political allies when it comes to decision-making, coalition formation, and the like. The pattern of overlaps shown in the table is of particular interest in providing immediate hints of an important characterization of party systems: the dimensions that structure electoral competition. If the parties can be ordered (as in the example above) in such a way that in each column the cell entries increase in size towards the diagonal and decrease when moving away from the diagonal, a single dimension dominates the electoral competition between parties.[8] If it is not possible to order them in this way then several dimensions of electoral competition operate simultaneously. The substantive nature of these dimensions can of course only be assessed from the characteristics of the various parties.[9]

In many countries, this structure appears to correspond closely with the position of parties on a left/right ideological spectrum. Therefore, the parties in the table are ordered from left to right, using the median positions of the respective parties on a left/right axis derived from questions that asked each respondent to place each party on a left/right scale measured from 1 to 10 (see Chapter 20 and Appendix B for further details of this scale). In the country chapters, for the sake of completeness, the table will contain this median position of each party, and also the size of the party's potential in terms of valid votes, in addition to the hypothetical coefficients shown in Table 3.1.

Differential Turnout and 'Quasi-switching'

One of our principal research questions concerns the degree to which the outcome of European elections in any country is the consequence of 'European' factors entering the calculus of voting choice. The relevant counterfactual in this regard is, of course, that voters' choices result from their orientations towards their national political systems. Quite frequently their orientations are taken from the result of the most recent national parliamentary election, for instance by commentators following a European election. This standard is rather unsatisfactory, however (as already shown in Chapter 2), since national political preferences might well have changed during the period since the

---

8 Minor deviations from a unidimensional pattern can, of course, also result from sampling errors. Only major deviations necessarily imply the co-existence of several different preference dimensions.

9 The logic of the argument implies that in principle the same should be true of the rows, but this will not always be the case in practice since each column is expressed as a percentage of a different amount, the size of the column party's potential electorate.

most recent national election—an event from the more-or-less distant past (cf. Anker, 1991).

To establish whether European elections had any European component calls for a comparison of the outcome with current (simultaneous) national party preferences. Those are directly available only where national and European elections were held on the same day—three countries in 1989 (namely Ireland, Greece and Luxembourg) and one in 1994 (Luxembourg). In all other cases we must construct a baseline from the results that a concurrent national election would have yielded. This is hard to do definitively, but we have attempted it on the basis of respondents' answers to questions concerning their current national party preference. In the process we have also invented a new piece of terminology, referring to those voters who indicate that they (would have) voted differently in a concurrent national election as 'quasi-switchers'. This term, comparable to the concept of 'split-ticket' voters in American elections, is not intended to imply change over time, but merely a contrast between voting preferences at the European and national levels. Even if we accept the resulting baseline uncritically, there is still another obstacle in the way of finding the quasi-switchers by comparing the national baseline with the European election results. In many countries turnout in the European elections is considerably lower than in other elections. As pointed out in Chapter 2, this might itself cause changes in party fortunes without anyone voting differently. To estimate the consequences we must compare party preferences of voters and non-voters in the European election. Only when this difference is taken into account can we find the true contribution of quasi-switching to the total impact (which we sometimes refer to as the 'second-order effect') of the different character of the European elections.[10] The assessment of these effects will be made in all country chapters in a similar fashion, reported in tables such as Table 3.2.

The fictitious example given in Table 3.2 shows a number of things. First of all, the difference between the result of the European election and that of a (hypothetical) concurrent national election (EE–NE, or the 'second-order effect') is limited in size: nowhere more than 5 percent of the valid vote. This is not to say that its political consequences are negligible or uniformly distributed. Parties B and C have done worse in the European election than they would have done in a national one. Parties A and D, however, have polled considerably better than they would have done in a national election. In comparison with their share of the vote, the losses of B and C are less dramatic than the gains of A and D. This illustrates a less than obvious feature of second-order effects that, although 'losses' to the large parties are evidently numerically

---

10   The calculation of turnout and quasi-switching effects is described in Appendix B.

Table 3.2 Hypothetical Effects of Turnout and Quasi–switching (Cell entries are percentages of the valid vote)

	Share of EE–vote	Share of NE–vote	EE–NE	Effect of Quasi–switching	Effect of Differences in Turnout
Party A	15	11	4	2	2
Party B	30	35	-5	-3	-2
Party C	45	49	-4	-7	3
Party D	10	5	5	8	-3

the same as 'gains' to smaller ones, a given absolute change means more to a small party than to a large one, which also implies that the potential consequences for party morale may be quite different. The way in which these differences between European and national election outcomes have arisen is not the same for the various parties in our hypothetical example. Two of the parties, A and C, benefitted from the lower than normal turnout, whereas B and D were comparatively less successful in mobilizing their potential followers. Apart from this turnout effect, the penultimate column of the table (labeled quasi-switching) shows to what extent there were any net effects of different party choice in the European election. In the fictitious table above we do see clear effects of quasi-switching—very negative for party C and very positive for party D, while parties A and B have been little affected. The motivations of these quasi-switchers, of course, still remain to be established empirically.

Assessing Individual-Level Influences on Turnout

One of the most important substantive questions to be addressed is whether or not, or to what extent, electoral participation is related to voters' substantive political interests or preferences. In other words, are specific groups (characterized by interests, ideological leanings, party preferences, issue-preferences, or opinions about European integration) over- or under-represented among those who vote? Of particular relevance to our investigation are suggestions which have linked the lower turnout that is normal at European elections to orientations, attitudes and evaluations regarding the European Union. To what extent, for example, particularly in those countries without a serious anti-European party, is low turnout the effect of hostility towards the EC/EU, as has frequently been suggested by political commentators? To what extent do people stay at home rather than vote because they do not see the relevance of the European Union and its institutions? This amounts to asking how far the interpretation by Schmitt and Mannheimer (1991a)—namely that electoral participation in European elections responds to the same influences as participation in national elections—is adequate.

These questions will be taken up in all country chapters by means of a common analysis. The object is to establish what kinds of variables help to distinguish between voters and non-voters. We start with variables known to be important for determining turnout in national elections. One can, for example, expect demographic and socio-economic background factors to be important in both contexts. Likewise, variables such as civic attitudes, political interest, and various indicators of political involvement which are not specifically related to the European Community can be expected to exert an influence in European elections similar to that in national elections.[11] One may even go further, and include in the analysis respondents' electoral participation in national elections, on the assumption that factors which may explain this and which have not been included in the analysis explicitly, have to be controlled for in an explanation of turnout in European elections before taking account of orientations and attitudes which are specifically related to the European Union. In order to avoid incorrectly attributing explanatory power, it is important to perform these analyses in such a way that more general and more distant causes of turnout are assessed before more proximate ones. Therefore, the analyses are performed in stages, in which blocks of variables are included in the following order:

1. Demographic and socio-economic background variables, such as age, gender, class, income, education, urbanization, religion, religiosity, and the like;
2. Generalized motivational and attitudinal variables not specifically related to European integration or the European Union but which have been found to be related to turnout in national elections—variables such as political interest, strength of party attachment, strength of political opinions, and the like;
3. Habitual voting (voted in the previous national election);[12]
4. Orientations, attitudes and evaluations pertaining to European integration and the European Union, such as EC-approval.

The rationale behind this sequence is that we should not consider the distinction between voting and non-voting in the European elections to be the consequence of European factors as long as pre-existing factors have not been included in

---

11 A full account of the influences we believe to be important in determining turnout in national and European elections is given in Chapter 19.

12 This of course subsumes blocks 1 and 2, but is included in order to tap additional factors missed in those blocks (see above).

the explanation. Some problems can arise in deciding which variables to include in each of the stages. As a case in point, consider questions about how far the work of the European Parliament affects respondents' lives. At first sight this question appears to concern European attitudes, orientations and evaluations. This becomes less evident, however, when we note that similar questions have been asked about national parliaments, regional assemblies, and municipal councils; and that responses to each question in this battery can be interpreted as arising from a single latent trait which is common to all of them and which can be interpreted as 'perceived importance of elected institutions' (see Appendix B and van der Eijk, 1984a; van der Eijk and Oppenhuis, 1990). This, however, robs the question of its specifically 'European' character. Therefore, it has been included (as one item counting towards a composite score measuring the perceived importance of elected institutions) in the second group of generalized political orientations.

The analyses of turnout to be reported in the country chapters consist of regressions of electoral participation, with stage-wise inclusion in the equation of the blocks of explanatory variables just listed. As shown in the (hypothetical) Table 3.3, the most important results from these analyses are not the regression coefficients but the (addition to) the percentage of explained variance, shown in the right-most column, effected by the blocks of variables as each is entered into the analysis. The results enable us to establish how much European issues and concerns add to an explanation of turnout once individual and domestic factors have been taken into account. In this table, as in other tables in this volume, we use the symbol R^2 synonymously with the expression 'variance explained' and present the coefficients as percentages—often, as in this case, rounded to the nearest one percent. In the hypothetical findings depicted in Table 3.3, the contribution to variance explained made by European attitudes is seen to be nil.

Assessing Individual-level Influences on Party Choice

Returning to the question of party choice, just as it is necessary to look at the individual-level concomitants of turnout effects, so it might have been thought necessary to look at the individual-level concomitants of quasi-switching. Had there been any sizeable (gross) effect of quasi-switching it would have been necessary to assess whether European orientations or other specific characteristics were involved. In fact the extent of quasi-switching was always found to be small, and attempts to analyze its concomitants generally inconclusive. Few country chapters report these findings.[13] Quasi-switching turns out to be a

---

13 Chapter 14 is an exception. It reports findings for the Netherlands that illustrate the sorts of

Table 3.3 Predictors of Turnout in a Hypothetical European Election (coefficients are percentages of variance explained)

	Total R^2	Increase in R^2
Demographics	3	
Civic Attitudes and (national) Political Orientations	12	9
Habitual Voting (did vote in previous national election)	22	10
European Attitudes	22	0

factor more interesting at the European level than at the national level of analysis, and it figures prominently in Part III of this volume—particularly in Chapter 18.

The absence in most member states of strong European effects on the election outcome led us to ask whether national political parties offer the voters of the member countries sufficient choice of different Europe-related policies and programs to permit the election to differ in any significant way from a purely national election. This question is addressed descriptively in the country chapters in order to determine to what degree we can blame political parties for this deficiency. Parties, after all, play a major role in shaping the nature of political debate, and it is partly up to them to offer the policy proposals that would enable a European election to differ in its content and orientations from a purely national election. When parties have indeed presented such proposals to the voters, then we need to take the next step and ask whether the proposals carry sufficient weight as to lead voters to diverge at all from domestic-national party preferences. In either case, the findings will have implications for the future development of the European Union—implications which will be taken up again in the final chapter of Part III.

The Effect of European Elections on National Politics

The analyses outlined above provide for each country an accounting of the extent to which the 1989 election had any European character, together with an evaluation of how far the outcome differed from what would have been seen in a national election. Having contributed in this way to an assessment of the first two research questions (whether the elections were really European and whether the results were different than they would have been in a concurrent

---

findings that might have been reported in other chapters too.

national election), the country chapters then turn to the third research question and ask what other consequences the elections may have had. This question is addressed by documenting the extent to which national politics were affected in each country by the very fact that a European election was held, the policy debates that took place, and the success or otherwise of parties as compared with their performance in previous national elections.

Despite the fact that elections to the European Parliament will certainly prove to have been not very European in most countries, it is clear that even in such countries they add an important date to the political calendar: an occasion when parties must take stock of their positions in regard to current issues, and present their positions for electoral approval. Since the election is ostensibly a European one, it may turn out that European issues come in this manner to affect domestic politics; but even without any such effects, the election can have consequences. Especially if the current national government and the political parties of a country treat the election as yielding endorsement or criticism, the result may affect government stability and party behavior in a number of ways.[14] Also, without the allocation of national executive power being formally at stake, the structural disadvantage that may afflict smaller and more radical parties at national elections is largely removed. Such parties can attempt to use European elections to improve their visibility and, in turn, their chances in subsequent national elections. Moreover, European elections may be seen as occasions for newly formed parties to test the waters of electoral competition. A respectable showing may boost the credibility of a new party, leading to enhanced performance in subsequent national elections. From this point of view, European elections may be seen as what is often referred to as the 'midwife assisting in the birth of new parties'. In these and other ways, elections to the European Parliament may have political consequences different from those envisioned by their original proponents.

Some of the other possible effects explored in the country chapters include consequences for government stability (particularly if there are dramatic changes in the votes given to coalition partners), consequences for the policy positions that parties may then assume (to capitalize on lessons from the European election), and consequences of all of this on public perceptions of party strengths and weaknesses. Effects of European elections may even include consequences for the party system, perhaps due to the fact that the rules for European elections may be more or less different from those of national elections. For example, the fact that the number of seats each country fills in

---

14 Even if party leaders try to insulate themselves from such endorsements and criticisms by claiming that the election is irrelevant, they may fail to the extent that newspaper and other commentators take a different view.

the European Parliament is always smaller than the number of seats in the national parliament enforces a threshold which will often be higher than customary in national elections. Moreover, the size and demarcation of constituencies will also differ. These differences may stimulate the formation of electoral pacts. Particularly interesting are cases where such collaborations continue after the European election, possibly even leading to party mergers. Finally, European elections may serve as a cause of dissension within existing parties. To the extent that such elections contribute to the politicization of issues which are not lined up with dominant domestic conflict dimensions, they may generate (or make manifest) divisions whose impact could extend beyond the European electoral context (possibly leading to splits and the emergence of new parties) and thereby affecting the future course of domestic politics. To the extent that European elections show potential for giving rise to unwanted repercussions for (domestic) parties and their leaders, the question also arises whether political actors have found any means of containing these repercussions and, if so, what these means might be. All of the questions addressed in the country chapters are also questions to which we will return in Part III of the book, once the findings about elections in specific countries have been detailed.

The Country Chapters

The chapters of Part II evaluate the European elections of 1989 country by country. In each chapter, authors start by describing the elections in national context, which involves describing the party system of the country and the salient political circumstances that characterized the election. In the process they present one of the common tables which are the same in all countries—the table showing the extent of overlap between parties, arranged so as to display the left/right ordering of parties. They move on to the question of turnout, and here present yet another of the common tables—one that indicates how far turnout can be explained by European as opposed to national issues and orientations. Finally they address the question of party choice, in which context they present a third table that is the same in all chapters—the table that evaluates the extent to which the election outcome in each country can be ascribed to differential turnout in European as opposed to national elections, and to what extent it can be ascribed to what we have called 'quasi-switching'.

The tables are not necessarily presented consecutively or even in the same order, but they are always present and always arranged in exactly the same fashion for ease of comparability between chapters. Because their layout and interpretation has been explained in the present chapter, authors were encouraged to simply refer to that explanation rather than repeating it in their own words. In all chapters the authors were encouraged to present additional tables that would elucidate the reasons for the election outcome and motivations for party choice. Inevitably these tables are not directly comparable across the country chapters. To the extent that our authors employ multivariate analyses, they always use OLS regression. Despite the fact that we often have dummy dependent variables (voted or not, chose to support some party or not) the use of probit analysis or logistic regression was ruled out mainly to ensure that findings would easily be communicated in as few pages as possible. A detailed comparison of findings based on OLS regression with findings based on other methods is to be found in Appendix B. To summarize the discussion there, all analyses employing OLS regression anywhere in this volume have been repeated using logistic regression, and any salient differences are noted in the chapters where they arise. The overwhelming majority of these analyses showed no salient differences with what had been found using OLS regression.

The final topic covered in each country chapter concerns the domestic consequences of the European elections. There is no common format to these discussions, since different authors are necessarily led to focus on different consequences. However, these discussions provide the basis for a comparative account in Chapter 17 (which also introduces findings from the 1994 European election study) that summarizes and systematizes the effects of European elections in preparation for the comparative analyses to be conducted in Part III.

Part II

National Perspectives:
The 1989 Elections and
their Aftermath

CHAPTER 4

Belgium:
An Electorate on the Eve of Disintegration

Johan Ackaert, Lieven de Winter and Marc Swyngedouw

The European parliamentary election of June 1989 was the first election after
a coalition change from a center-right to a center-left government that took
place in Spring 1988. It offered a choice of parties comparable to the one offered
at the 1987 general election. The opposition, particularly the liberals, tried to
use this election as a mid-term evaluation of governmental policy.[1] That policy
focused on institutional reforms intended to federalize the country into three
regions and three cultural communities, and consisted primarily of a major
transfer of competences from the national to the community level.[2] Economic
policies did not differ much from those pursued by previous center-right governments, but the new government did differ from its predecessor in its social
policies. The questions we will address in this chapter center on whether the
European election of 1989 did indeed serve as a mid-term evaluation of the
national government, and what consequences it had for domestic politics.
However, before turning to these questions we need to set the scene.

The present Belgian party system is characterized by extreme fragmentation.[3] The system started as a two party system in the 19th century, with the
catholic and liberal party opposed on the issue of the religious neutrality of
the bourgeois state.[4] After the breakthrough of the socialists at the end of the

---

1 Local elections in Fall 1988 could not serve this purpose as they cannot easily be compared
with general elections in Belgium, because of differences in parties on offer, candidates, issues,
etc.

2 This institutional reform was completed in July 1993. See also: Senelle (1990) and Alen
(1992). The reforms also included the installation of the Brussels Capital Regional Council to
become the legislative body for the Brussels region. It was elected for the first time through direct
elections held at the same time as the European elections.

3 Rae's index of party fragmentation in Parliament has fluctuated since the mid-sixties around
0.85 (Deschouwer, 1987). For the House elected in 1991 it amounts to 0.88.

4 For analyses of the Belgian system see Van Den Brande (1974); Lorwin (1966); Urwin (1970);
Heisler (1974); Hill (1974); Frognier (1974, 1976); Wirth (1977); Mughan (1979, 1983); Lijphart
(1981a,b); Huyse (1983); De Ridder and Fraga (1986); McRae (1986); Deschouwer (1987:75–
92); Dewachter (1987).

century and the emergence of the socio-economic left/right cleavage, the Belgian party system constituted a clear-cut example of Sartori's (1976) three-party type, until at least 1965. During this period the three traditional parties, christian democrats, socialists and liberals, alternately shared government offices in different coalition combinations. Although the relative strength of these parties varied considerably during the period, between them they received more than 90 percent of the total vote in most elections, in spite of the proportional representation system which was adopted in 1919. In the sixties and the seventies the number of parties represented in Parliament rose dramatically. Firstly, there was the breakthrough of the linguistic-regional-communautarian parties, the Volksunie in Flanders (VU), the Rassemblement Wallon (RW) in Wallonia, and the Front Démocratique des Francophones (FDF) in the Brussels region. These were so successful electorally that they had to be included in governing coalitions during the 1970s.[5]

The growing salience of the linguistic and regional cleavage, on which the success of the regional parties was based, divided the christian democrat, liberal and socialist parties internally. Each traditional party split into two organizationally and programmatically independent Flemish and francophone branches: the christian democrats into the Christelijke Volkspartij (CVP) and Parti Social Chrétien (PSC) in 1968, the liberals into the Partij voor Vrijheid en Vooruitgang (PVV) and the Parti Réformateur Liberal (PRL) in 1972, and finally the socialists into the Socialistische Partij (SP) and the Parti Socialiste (PS) in 1978.[6] Another wave of expansion of the party system occurred at the end of the seventies with the emergence of the ultra-Flemish nationalist and anti-migrant Vlaams Blok (VB), the poujadist Union Démocratique pour le Respect du Travail (UDRT), and the green parties (Agalev in Flanders and Ecolo in the francophone areas). Thus, by 1981, fourteen parties were represented in Parliament.

During the 1980s, the communists, the RW and the UDRT lost their last representatives in Parliament, thus reducing the number of parties in the system. However, the 1991 general election introduced the latest newcomers, the francophone extreme-right Front National and the libertarian Rossem. Hence, it is important to understand that in Belgium there are no longer any

---

5   In 1971, they obtained 22.3 percent of the national vote. The RW joined a governmental coalition in the 1974–1977 period, the VU from 1977 to 1978 and from 1988 to 1991, and the FDF from 1977 to 1980.

6   These linguistically homogeneous branches, once liberated from the electorally unprofitable politics of compromise within their former national parties, gradually took up most of the issues of the regional parties. During the first half of the 1980s the francophone traditional parties managed to reduce the electoral appeal of the FDF and the RW. The Volksunie started to decline at the end of that decade and at present it is looking for a new socio-political profile.

national parties—parties that present themselves in all thirty constituencies. All parties are homogeneously Flemish or francophone, and only present candidates in the Flemish or francophone constituencies, which explains the centrifugal dynamics of party competition on the communautarian conflict dimension (Sartori, 1976).[7] However, after the break-up of the traditional parties, none of the linguistic successors has ever joined a governmental coalition which did not also include their linguistic counterpart. As traditional party families are generally equally divided on linguistic issues, coalitions necessarily included the same kind of parties in the north and the south in order to keep policy distances on other conflict dimensions (socio-economic and denominational) as small as possible.

The analysis of party competition in the 1989 European parliamentary election confirms major tendencies revealed in recent analyses of the electoral markets in Belgium.[8]

Table 4.1a reveals the great overlap between the Flemish parties. The 'potential supporters' row sums up to 156 percent which means that most voters have strong preferences for more than one party. This confirms the high degree of fluidity of the Flemish party system which reached its peak in the 1991 general election (see Table 4.3a). The analysis of the potential of individual Flemish parties in the electoral market shows first that Agalev is the most popular alternative for the electorates of each of the other parties. In all parties, at least six out of ten voters would consider voting green in the future. This is not surprising given the general salience of ecological issues in postmodern politics, and the specific emphasis on this issue during the 1989 campaign. By contrast, the VU is the least popular alternative. Only one in four voters for the other parties would consider voting for the Flemish nationalists, while VU voters are most likely to consider voting for other parties. Their potential for losses was realized in the 1991 general election, reflecting that this party gradually lost its 'raison d'etre' after the major reforms toward federalization. As far as the traditional parties are concerned, the CVP has the largest potential. It should also be noticed that within each traditional party at least one out of three voters considered voting for each of the other traditional parties. This confirms the centripetal competition among traditional parties, as was recognized by analysts as well as by party strategists, at that time.

In spite of similar party profiles and historical background, the dynamics of the francophone party system are very different from those in the north of

7 With the exception of the bilingual Brussels-Halle Vilvoorde constituency in which all Flemish and francophone parties present candidate lists.

8 De Winter (1988, 1990); Swyngedouw and Billiet (1988); Swyngedouw, De Winter and Schulpen (1990); Swyngedouw (1992a,b,c).

Table 4.1a Potential Support and Overlap Between Parties in Flanders in 1989

	SP	Agalev	VU	PVV	CVP
SP	1.00	0.51	0.62	0.41	0.38
Agalev	0.71	1.00	0.78	0.59	0.57
VU	0.46	0.41	1.00	0.42	0.42
PVV	0.41	0.43	0.58	1.00	0.44
CVP	0.44	0.47	0.67	0.51	1.00
Pot. Support (% of Elect.)	29.5	41.3	21.7	29.6	34.2
Votes as % of Electorate	15.6	12.3	7.0	14.0	28.6
% of Valid Vote	18.5	14.5	8.3	16.5	33.7
L-R Median (1–10)	3.50	4.59	6.84	6.95	7.03

the country (see also Table 4.1b). Firstly, the general overlap in supporters is smaller, the sum of 'potential supporters' comes to 135 percent (this lower potential fluidity was reflected in the results of the 1991 general election). Secondly, the socialists not only have the largest proportion of potential voters but also their own electorate seems to be highly immune to competition from the other parties. This confirms the party's evolution towards a catch-all party (De Winter, 1993b).[9] Thirdly, the ecologists have much less support among the electorates of other parties than is the case in Flanders. However, as in Flanders, the regionalists of the FDF-RW draw the lowest electoral potential as well as the highest potential losses. Even more than in Flanders, the traditional parties in the francophone constituency have managed to reconquer the ground lost to the federalist parties in the 1970s.

In order to fully grasp the particularities of European elections in Belgium, one must underline the impact of the different rules which guide the European and general elections. In general elections, the 212 members of the Chamber of Representatives are elected by proportional representation from thirty multi-member constituencies. Parties in each constituency normally draw up lists which include a number of candidates equal to the number of representatives to be elected. They vary from two to thirty-three. However, the number of constituencies is reduced to only two for European elections; one Flemish and one francophone. The Flemish speaking constituency has 13 seats in the European Parliament, the francophone 11 seats. Voters living in the Dutch or francophone part of the country belong respectively to the Dutch or francophone

---

9 Unlike its Flemish comrades, the PS has not radicalized in the 1980s on left and postmaterialist issues.

Table 4.1b Potential Support and Overlap Between Parties in Wallonia in 1989

	PS	Ecolo	FDF/RW	PRL	PSC
PS	1.00	0.48	0.44	0.28	0.32
Ecologiste	0.35	1.00	0.69	0.50	0.43
FDF/RW	0.13	0.28	1.00	0.27	0.19
PRL	0.17	0.42	0.57	1.00	0.39
PSC	0.21	0.37	0.41	0.40	1.00
Pot. Support (% of Elect.)	41.3	30.2	12.3	25.6	26.3
Votes as % of Electorate	33.8	6.5	3.6	17.2	19.2
% of Valid Vote	42.1	8.0	4.5	21.4	24.0
L-R Median	2.68	4.96	6.30	7.31	7.45

constituency. Voters living in the 19 communes constituting the Region of Brussels Capital choose their constituency as they vote for a Flemish or franco-phone list (Van Den Berghe, 1979:8). As will be repeatedly shown later in the chapter, this dramatic difference in the size of the constituencies seriously affects electoral competition and the strategy and results of parties and their candidates.

Turnout

Turnout by Belgian voters at European elections is traditionally high. More than 90 percent of the electorate participated in the 1989 election, more than 80 percent cast a valid vote. This can be explained by the compulsory nature of voting in Belgium. In spite of this, turnout is lower in elections for the European Parliament than in other elections in Belgium. The average turnout in the six general elections in the 1977–1991 period was 93.9 percent and in the three local elections in the 1976–1988 period 94.2 percent, whereas the average turnout in the European parliamentary elections over the same period was only 91.4 percent. Hence, average turnout at European elections is roughly 2.5 percent lower than in general elections and about 2.8 percent lower than in local elections. Not only is turnout in European elections lower than in general elections, but so is the number of valid votes. Since 1976, the average valid vote in European parliamentary elections has been 89.4 percent, compared with 92.7 percent for the House, 91.8 percent for the Senate, 92.3 per-cent for Provincial Councils elections, and finally 95.6 percent at local elections.

There are several reasons for the variation in turnout and in blank and invalid voting between the different types of election. First of all, European parliamentary elections are organized at a time when nearly 200,000 Belgians are abroad on holiday. Secondly, voters do not perceive the institutions for which elections are held as equally important. Our data show that the national government is considered important by 87 percent of the Belgian respondents, followed by the national parliament (80 percent), local councils (74 percent), local executives (73 percent) and finally the European Parliament and the European Commission (both 66 percent). This difference in perception is reflected in the variation of turnout rates; the election for the least important institution mobilizes the least number of voters. Interest in the European Parliament among the electorate also seems to be low when judged by knowledge about European institutions. In Fall 1988 only 59 percent of Belgians knew about the existence of the European Parliament (in spite of the fact that there had already been elections in 1979 and 1984). That number increased to 65 percent in the Spring of 1989. This means that on the eve of the election, nearly one of three Belgians did not know what kind of institution they were voting for. Electors are also unaware of the distribution of competences between the different European institutions. Generally, they ascribe more power to the European Parliament than it really has. In addition, only 23 percent of the public was interested in the election campaign. Only three out of every ten voters watched television broadcasts related to the campaign (Swyngedouw et al., 1990).

Thirdly, there is little perceived difference between parties with regard to European issues: all parties and their electorates agree on the desirability of European integration (van der Eijk and Franklin, 1991). Given this lack of competition in policy terms, the campaign efforts of the different political parties are muted. The political parties declared after the election that they spent nearly 200 million Belgian Francs on their campaigns (Couttenier, 1990:213). This is much less than expenditure in the 1984 European parliamentary election, which reached 286 million BEF (Das, 1989:13). These sums are also lower than those for the preceding general election of 1987: about 970 million BEF (Das and DeWachter, 1991:27). Fourthly, domestic consequences of the European election were generally not envisaged. In fact, the coalition parties declared before the election that it would not have any effect on governmental policy. A final reason for abstentions and non-valid votes to be higher in European elections is that the electoral rules for European elections in Belgium tend to widen the social distance between candidates and voters.[10] As mentioned above, whereas general elections are organized in 30 multi-member constituencies, the European parliamentary elections are held in only two large constituencies. This reduces the chance that a voter would have had

---

10 The same can be seen for the differences in blank or invalid voting for the House and the Senate. There are fewer Senate seats and thus, in nearly half the cases, considerably larger constituencies. This results in more blank or invalid votes for the Senate (Ackaert et al., 1992:215).

Table 4.2a Predictors of 1989 Participation in the European Election in Flanders

	R^2	Added R^2
Demographics	0.07	
General Political Orientations	0.09	0.02
Habitual Voting	0.10	0.01
European Attitudes	0.11	0.01

Table 4.2b Predictors of 1989 Participation in the European Election in Wallonia

	R^2	Added R^2
Demographics	0.03	
General Political Orientations	0.08	0.05
Habitual Voting	0.10	0.02
European Attitudes	0.10	0.00

personal contact (or indeed any familiarity) with candidates, which lessens the chances of their casting a (valid) vote.

Tables 4.2a and 4.2b show the effect on turnout of different blocks of variables considered in the European Election Study. The predictive power of the equation is low; and European attitudes add virtually nothing to an explanation of electoral participation based on other (domestic) considerations. Habitual voting explains very little, which is largely the consequence of the high level of turnout in all kinds of elections in Belgium. The variance that is explained is—in Flanders as well as Wallonia—attributable to demographics and general political orientations.

Party and Candidate Choice

Tables 4.3a and 4.3b give the results of the general and European parliamentary elections in Belgium between 1978 and 1991. No statistical data exist to measure the gross shifts from one election to another covering the entire period.[11] Only net shifts between the parties can be calculated. The average

---

11 For partial comparisons (limited to Flanders) see Swyngedouw (1986); Swyngedouw and Billiet (1988); Swyngedouw, De Winter and Schulpen (1990); Swyngedouw, Billiet and Carton (1992).

Table 4.3a Results of Belgian Parties for the Elections of the House of Representatives and European Parliament Between 1978 and 1991. Flemish Parties

Year	CVP	SP	PVV	VU	Agalev	VB	Rossem
1978	26.1	12.4	10.4	7.0	0.2	1.4	-
1979 (Eur)	29.5	12.9	9.4	6.0	1.4	0.7	-
1981	19.3	12.4	12.9	9.8	2.3	1.1	-
1984 (Eur)	19.8	17.1	8.6	8.5	4.3	1.3	-
1985	21.3	14.6	10.7	7.9	3.7	1.4	-
1987	19.5	14.9	11.5	8.0	4.5	1.9	-
1989 (Eur)	21.1	12.4	10.6	5.4	7.6	4.1	-
1991	16.8	12.0	12.0	5.9	4.9	6.6	3.2

net shift for the general elections, as measured by the Pedersen index, amounts to 10.5; for the European parliamentary elections it is 15.4. However, if we compare the net shifts between, on the one hand, each European election since 1979 and, on the other hand, each preceding general election, the Pedersen index amounts to 10.2. Therefore, the larger net shifts between European parliamentary elections can be attributed largely to the greater time lapse between elections of this type. An additional explanation for the relatively large shifts between European parliamentary elections lies in the changes in the supply of candidates. The vote-catching candidates of the major parties at the European parliamentary elections rotate more than at the general elections. In 1979, for example, the CVP list was headed by party leader and former prime minister Leo Tindemans, who was at that time at the summit of his popularity. Nearly one in four Flemish voters voted for him. In 1984 the head of the Flemish christian democrat list was relatively unknown to the electorate and, as a consequence, the christian democrats lost badly. The return of Tindemans (Minister of Foreign Affairs since 1982) as head of the Flemish christian democrat list in the 1989 election again boosted the CVP vote.

The electoral fortunes of Flemish socialists in elections to the European Parliament run nearly opposite to those of the CVP. In 1979, the SP candidate list was headed by the new party leader Van Miert. He reached his peak of popularity only in 1984. As the leader of the Flemish socialist party he was the only candidate in 1984 with a high rank in national politics. Hence, in that year the Flemish socialists were the major winners. The replacement of Van Miert at the head of the list by the less known Galle in 1989 contributed heavily to the defeat of the SP. To conclude, the quality of the candidates on a list, particularly the quality of the candidate at the head of the list, is a factor not to be ignored in interpreting total shifts. This is reinforced by the electoral rules

Table 4.3b Results of Belgian Parties for the Elections of the House of Representatives and European Parliament Between 1978 and 1991. Francophone parties

Year	PSC	PS	PRL	FDF/RW	Ecolo
1978	10.1	13.0	6.0	7.3	0.6
1979 (Eur)	8.2	10.6	6.3	7.6	2.0
1981	7.1	12.7	8.6	4.2	2.2
1984 (Eur)	7.6	13.3	9.4	2.5	3.9
1985	8.0	13.8	10.2	1.2	2.5
1987	8.0	15.7	9.4	1.2	2.6
1989 (Eur)	8.1	14.5	7.2	1.5	6.3
1991	7.7	13.5	8.1	1.5	5.1

for European elections. As mentioned above, European elections are organized in two quasi-nationwide constituencies. This means that candidates' popularity is tested in terms of preference votes on a much larger scale than at general elections.[12] In fact, the number of preferential votes is traditionally higher in European elections (average 53.3 percent) than in the elections for the House (average 49.4 percent) or Senate (40.0 percent).[13]

However, the opportunities for testing one's national popularity which are offered by these much larger constituencies are not fully exploited. Many party leaders and high ranking-members of the party elites do not stand. Firstly, in contrast to past practices, candidates who present themselves in European elections while clearly intending to retain most interest in national politics are no longer much appreciated. Hence, a politician wanting to test his popularity by running as a candidate at a European election has to be willing to 'disappear' from the national political scene for some years and will not usually be considered for a cabinet position.[14] Secondly, the test is one which some politicians

---

12 In all elections there are two ways to cast a vote: a list vote (which means that one agrees with the order of the candidates on the list) and a preference vote (which means that one disagrees with the order and votes for a particular candidate on the party list).

13 Based on data from Das (1992:158), De Weerdt (1984:604) and Collinge (1990:17 and 22).

14 In the 1979 European election most parties stuffed their candidate list as much as possible with national party figures, even on the safe places on the list. Evidently, as cabinet positions became available to many of them in the following months or years, these resigned as MEPs and reentered national politics at a high level. See Dewachter and De Winter (1979); Verminck (1985). Since 1984, a position in the European Parliament has become incompatible with a post in the national parliament. Because nearly all Belgian ministers are recruited from the national parliament (De Winter, 1991), a seat in the European Parliament has become virtually incompatible with a cabinet post.

fear they will not pass. Given the variation in size between the multimember constituencies for the general elections (varying between two and 33 seats), the variations in party strength within them, and the fact that most prominent politicians present themselves in different constituencies, it is extremely difficult to compare MPs' personal popularity using general election preference votes. Hence, most prominent politicians can pretend that they are (one of) the most popular figure(s) in their constituency, with their main national competitors equally popular in their constituencies.[15] As the electoral system for the European Parliament provides for a much more objective testing ground of one's national popularity, many politicians do not participate in order not to lose face.[16] Therefore, since the 1984 European parliamentary election, most candidates are 'have been's' or 'would be's', rather than politicians hoping for a cabinet position in the near future.

The larger constituencies not only allow important candidates to test their popularity, they also facilitate the penetration of new parties in every remote corner of the country. When a party's low vote in general elections is due to an organizational weakness in many constituencies, European parliamentary elections give it an opportunity to overcome such organizational obstacles. For instance, the greens scored their first success at the 1979 European parliamentary election (Table 4.3). At the general elections in 1977 and 1978, they managed to present a list only in the Antwerp constituency, and failed to capture any seats. Since then, their results at European parliamentary elections have always been better than at the preceding general elections. This has also been the case in an even more spectacular way for the Vlaams Blok in the eighties. As these parties did present themselves in general elections first, European elections are not necessary to the emergence of the greens or the Vlaams Blok; however, these elections gave them much more visibility than general elections. Hence, one can conclude that European parliamentary elections have facilitated the breakthrough into the national party system of these newcomers.

Finally, citizens can experiment with their voting behavior without direct national political consequences as the European elections can be considered as of 'second-order' importance. European elections are even for voters of

---

15 For instance, the CVP backbencher Tant can pretend to be the most popular MP by capturing nearly 22 percent of the votes in the two member constituency of Oudenaarde in the 1991 elections (but only with 16,536 preference votes), while the liberal party president Verhofstadt scored 56,393 preferences votes in the 12 member constituency of Ghent (but with a 'penetration score' of only 14.7 percent.)

16 For instance, many leading PS politicians refrained from testing their popularity in the 1989 European elections, as the list included the highly popular outsider Happart, whose exceptional vote at the 1984 European elections left all mainstream candidates in the shade.

traditional parties an opportunity to express protest against governmental policy or the behavior of political elites, especially if no governmental crisis is expected in the event of large losses by the coalition parties. However, the shift in votes in 1989 did not just represent a one-time experiment, never to be repeated in elections that really mattered. On the contrary, the 1989 European parliamentary election was a prelude to what would happen two years later at the general election of 1991.

The Dutch Speaking Constituency

Comparing results with those of 1984, three winners and two big losers emerged from the European election of 1989 in Flanders.[17] The winners were the extreme right wing Vlaams Blok, the greens (Agalev) and, on a more moderate level, the christian democrats (CVP). The losers were the socialists (SP) and the Flemish nationalists (VU). As mentioned earlier, socialist losses can partly be explained by the absence of a popular leader as the head of the socialist list. Yet, the change at the top cannot explain the losses entirely: the socialists not only lost compared with 1984, they also did less well than in the general election of 1987. An additional explanation lies to the content of the socialist campaign. It was marked by themes like a 'social Europe', a 'green Europe' and 'speak Flemish, think European'. The last two do not belong to traditional socialist programmatic concerns. Budge and Farlie (1983) have suggested that electoral gains or losses can be related to the degree in which parties can make their (traditional) issues dominate the electoral campaign. Attempts to take over issues of other parties generally have negative effects. First of all, there is a problem of credibility. Secondly, such an attempt strengthens the position of the parties which are more credible on those issues. socialists tried to build up a 'green' image in the European election, and in consequence led the electorate to believe that environmental topics were the main issues of the election. In this way, the socialists strengthened the position of the Ecologists who are more credible in that area. Moreover, the coalition government did not make much impact in areas which are considered to be the socialists' topics: employment, pensions, and a just distribution of income and wealth. Furthermore, in a number of ways the socialists had failed to live up to their political aspirations, which had damaged the new, open, radical and dynamic image they had acquired in the beginning of the eighties.

Interpreting these losses and gains in terms of turnout effects and quasi-switching is a rather hazardous enterprise. Given the fact that the survey population has to be split between voters operating in the Flemish and the

---

17 Based on data from Fraeys (1979:411–426, 1984:587–601, 1988:3–24, 1989:551–564).

francophone party system, the number of respondents causing a particular turnout or quasi-switching effect are quite small.[18] Second, as Table 4.4 reveals, the turnout effects are small, particularly in the Dutch speaking constituency (all less than 0.5 percent, while in the francophone constituency they do not exceed 1 percent). The insignificance of turnout effects stems from the fact that with compulsory voting, differences in turnout between general and European parliamentary elections remain minimal, especially in Flanders. Hence, one can conclude that turnout effects are generally irrelevant to the explanation of parties' fate at the 1989 election.

Although the biggest loser in comparison with earlier elections was the socialist party, this party actually gained slightly in comparison with the votes it would have received in a concurrent national election held in 1989. This indicates that this party's mistakes had already affected the party's popularity in national politics before the European election.

The Flemish-nationalist party (VU) lost ground compared with the European election of 1984 as well as the general election of 1987; but again this party would have done even worse in a concurrent national election. The losses by the VU had been due largely to its participation in government. Firstly, this participation damaged its image as anti-establishment party and resulted in a transfer of votes to the greens. Secondly, the benefits (institutional reform) did not compensate for the costs (compromises) of this participation in the eyes of the radical Flemish nationalist electorate. A lot of them switched to the Vlaams Blok. By participating in government, the VU abandoned its role as a pressure party on the traditional parties. Thirdly, another part of the VU electorate returned to the traditional parties. Finally, the losses by the VU can be interpreted as the prelude of a more fundamental evolution. With the creation of a federal state the VU lost one of its major issues. Due to success, the party is losing its major raison d'etre. In fact, the relatively high quasi-switching score suggests that the VU's popularity in national politics was even worse than its already disastrous vote at the European election. The difference between these levels could be attributed to the relative popularity of the party's campaign for a Europe of the regions and the protection of Dutch-speaking and other linguistic minorities against the threats from European integration and standardization.

---

18 For a number of respondents it was impossible to determine unequivocally whether their constituency for national elections belongs to the Flemish or francophone area. These respondents have not been included in the analyses for Tables 4.4 and 4.5, owing to which the entries in the column "EE" deviate slightly from the official results of the two quasi-nationwide constituencies, which were reported in Tables 4.3a and 4.3b.

Table 4.4 Quasi–switching and Turnout Effects in the 1989 European Election in Flanders

	EE	NE	EE-NE	Quasi–switching	Turnout Effect
SP	18.4	17.6	0.8	0.5	0.3
Agalev	14.5	17.3	-2.8	-2.5	-0.3
VU	8.3	5.8	2.5	2.2	0.3
PVV	16.5	19.4	-2.9	-2.8	-0.1
CVP	33.7	30.6	3.1	2.6	0.5
Vlaams Blok	6.6	5.4	1.2	1.6	-0.4
Other	2.0	4.5	-1.5	0.7	-0.8

The Flemish ecologists (Agalev) were the major winner of the 1989 election in Flanders. They made progress relative to their vote in the European election of 1984 as well in comparison with the general election of 1987. The explanation is simple: other political parties labelled environmental problems as a main issue. The salience of this issue was boosted further by the preponderance of environmental problems and disasters in the daily news. The relatively high level of quasi-switching suggests that their popularity in national politics was even higher than that recorded at the European election. It is therefore surprising that this potential melted like snow in the sun at the following general election, when more than one third of their 1989 voters switched to other parties. Of course, in 1989 they were still the only protest party of the left, while later they had to compete with the libertarian list, Rossem.

The Vlaams Blok also made progress compared with the 1984 European parliamentary election and the 1987 general election. As mentioned above, the Vlaams Blok benefitted from the resistance of Flemish radical groups to governmental participation by the VU. Above all, the major reason for its victory lay in an increasing aversion of a part of the Flemish electorate (particularly socialist) to the presence of immigrants. Eurobarometer surveys have shown that, within Europe, the Belgian population displays the most hostile attitude towards foreigners from non-European Union countries.[19] In such a climate, a

---

19 About 62 percent think that the presence of those strangers is bad for the future of the country, 35 percent think that the rights of non-EU foreigners should be limited (this is the second highest in the EU). Anti-racist movements cannot reckon on much sympathy from public opinion either: more than one third disapproves of the actions of anti-racist movements (highest score in E), only 13 percent agree with those movements. The high level of negative attitudes towards foreigners in Belgium was later confirmed by the European Values Study. About 17 percent of Belgian respondents declared in that survey that they would not like people belonging to another race as neighbors. For Muslims this increases to 26 percent. In both instances these are the highest percent-

party like the Vlaams Blok that is able to politicize those xenophobic feelings is bound to do well at elections. Its positive quasi-switching score illustrates the opportunities European parliamentary elections offer for experimental voting, and the structural advantages that larger constituencies offer to organizationally weak single issue parties.[20]

The Flemish christian democrats (CVP) made slight progress compared with both the 1984 European election and the 1987 general election. As already mentioned, this progress can be explained largely by the comeback of vote catcher Leo Tindemans as the head of the CVP list. In fact, the relatively large positive quasi-switching score confirms that the popularity of the CVP in national politics was already on the road down, a point which was confirmed by its historic defeat at the 1991 general election.

The Flemish liberals (PVV) also improved their result compared with the 1984 European election. During the campaign they tried to cash in on the European image of the former member of the European Commission, De Clercq, and to use the election as a (negative) popularity test for the ruling government, from which they had been rather unexpectedly excluded in 1988. However, their success was far from brilliant. They lost votes compared with the general election of 1987 and the large negative quasi-switching figure indicates that their standing in national politics as the main opposition party was much better than was indicated by the vote they got in the European election.

The Francophone Constituency

The main winners in the francophone constituency were the greens (Ecolo), the socialists (PS) and the christian democrats (PSC). liberals (PRL) and the Brussels' francophone nationalists (FDF) lost. The greens (Ecolo) made enormous progress in comparison with the 1984 election and the 1987 general election (see Table 4.3b). Their success was due largely to the same factors which explain the success of the greens in the Dutch speaking constituency (Collinge, 1989:33). Their even greater popularity in national politics, as indicated by the

---

ages in the EU (Kerkhofs et al., 1992:239). See also Billiet, Carton and Huys who conclude: "...an impressive image of a broad circulation of negative conception, pictures, feelings and attitudes among the Belgians against foreigners... Those negative attitudes tend to have the upper hand. We can suppose that those ideas, sometimes even the misunderstandings and prejudices on which a party as the Vlaams Blok plays, are indeed dispersed in large segments of the population" (Billiet, Carton and Huys, 1990:119).

20 Until the end of the 1980s, the Vlaams Blok was organizationally well-developed only in the Antwerp constituencies, and experienced severe difficulties in composing candidate lists for general elections and in setting up campaign organizations in most of the other constituencies.

Table 4.5   Quasi–switching and Turnout Effects in the 1989 European Election in Wallonia

	EE	NE	EE-NE	Quasi–switching	Turnout Effect
PS	42.1	41.5	0.6	-0.4	1.0
Ecolo	8.0	10.2	-2.2	-2.5	0.3
FDF/RW	4.5	2.4	2.1	2.7	-0.6
PRL	21.4	20.9	0.5	1.5	-1.0
PSC	24.0	22.0	2.0	1.9	0.1
Other	0.0	3.0	-3.0	-3.2	0.2

relative large negative quasi-switching score in Table 4.5, was confirmed by their exceptionally good vote at the following general election.

The second winner in the francophone constituency was the socialist party (PS). Although internal quarrels about governmental participation and other matters led people to expect a defeat for the francophone socialists, they nevertheless made good progress compared to the 1984 European election. Their rather good result can be explained by the inclusion of dissident faction leader, J. Happart, as a socialist candidate. He won an enormous personal preference vote (Collinge, 1989:33).[21] The francophone christian democrats (PSC) also gained. They even realized a double success, improving on their 1984 European parliamentary election result as well as on their performance in the general election of 1987. The party was helped by popular local candidates and the popular figure of the Finance minister Maystadt (Collinge, 1989:33). The quasi-switching figure indicates, however, that its popularity in national politics was already suffering, a trend confirmed by losses at the subsequent general election. The francophone liberals (PRL) were the major loser. They lost votes in comparison with the previous European Parliament and with the more recent general election. Due to internal rivalries and leadership problems, the PRL did not present a real national leader in the francophone constituency. This poor result by the liberals even raised doubts about the future of 'neo-liberalism' (Collinge, 1989:34). In fact, the positive quasi-switching score indicates an even lower degree of popularity in national politics at this time, which was reflected at the subsequent general election. The FDF was the second loser. In spite of the fact that its candidate list included a former MEP of the greens, it lost nearly half of the support received in 1984. Its vote, however, approximates that of the FDF and RW combined at the 1987 general

---

21   As Happart had not then been sidelined, the party's national popularity resembles its support at the European parliamentary elections, as the very low quasi-switching score indicates.

election (Fraeys, 1989:555). Most likely, the start of the pacification between the two communities in Belgium and the solution of the 'Brussels problem', launched by the government installed in 1988, undermined the attractiveness of the linguistic-regional-communautarian parties. However, in spite of this decline in its relevance in national politics (as confirmed by the relatively large positive quasi-switching score), the party managed at the subsequent general election to consolidate the support won in the 1989 European parliamentary election and previous general election.

To conclude, the European election of 1989 can be regarded as a prelude to the general election of November 1991. In Flanders, this general election constituted an electoral earthquake, and a landslide for the extreme right. The socialists and christian democrats obtained their lowest post-war vote. liberals could hardly improve their positions. In Wallonia, all the traditional parties lost, thereby boosting the Ecologists (Fraeys, 1992:131–153). However, as we shall see, most party strategists and public opinion leaders did not see the writing on the wall after the 1989 election, and so returned to business as usual.

Effects of the Election

Governmental Policy and Issues

The effect of the European election on governmental policy was rather limited. The liberal opposition had labelled the election a test of the government's popularity, but in spite of an improvement over their showing in 1984, the liberals did not match their results at the 1987 general election. Thus, the test clearly backfired. Moreover, the acting prime minister announced before the election that his government would not consider a bad result as a disavowal of its policy. Of all the parties belonging to the majority, only the position of the VU was at stake. Its entrance into government in Spring 1988 was only its second experience of governmental responsibility. The first received a severe rebuke at the 1978 general election when the party lost one third of its votes. Hence, some feared that in the event of a new defeat, the pressure to leave the government would increase within the VU. Yet, in spite of the VU's losses, the anti-coalition tendency did not obtain the upper hand. The VU leaders decided to go on supporting the government, as the VU's support was necessary to maintain the 2/3 parliamentary majority constitutionally required to complete the institutional reform, a major objective of the government as well as of the party. One of the most important consequences of the election was the growing salience of the 'postmaterialist versus materialist' and the 'universal cultural openness versus particularist cultural closeness' cleavages in Belgian politics. The first cleavage pitted Agalev/Ecolo against CVP/PSC, PVV/PRL, SP/PS and VU/FDF. The second saw Agalev/Ecolo as the first pole and the Vlaams Blok as the other pole (Swyngedouw, 1992a,b,c). These cleavages became even more important than the religious one. Apart from anything else they focussed attention on the presence of immigrant workers in Belgium and dominated the campaign in the 1991 general election (Maddens, 1992:207), which yielded a victory for the Vlaams Blok. In this sense, there is no doubt that the European election provided the context for a breakthrough into Belgian politics of new issues which would later dominate electoral competition.

Internal Party Process

Losing elections traditionally causes the position of its leaders to be questioned (De Winter, 1993a:51; Maes, 1990:53). This happened after the European parliamentary election, particularly in the VU. In the months before the election, the party leader, Gabriels came under fire from different MPs of his party. The poor election results increased criticism of his political behavior. Two months later one of the 'founding fathers' of the VU, Coppieters, resigned from the party. He accused the leadership of not behaving like genuine Flemish nationalists. He demanded the resignation of the party leader and asked the party to withdraw its ministers from the cabinet but these demands were rejected by the party leaders.

In the Flemish liberal party (PVV) Neyts was replaced as party president by Verhofstadt only one week after the election, but this coup was arranged several months before the election. In addition, neither one of them stood in the European election. Hence, the return of Verhofstadt to the party presidency just after the European parliamentary election was entirely unaffected by their results. However, the results did have a rapid and profound impact on the party policy. On election night, Verhofstadt declared that his party would take a more hard-line position on the immigrant issue in Belgium, a policy change later endorsed by the party at large. This move was a reaction to the victory of the Vlaams Blok and the poor showing of the liberals.

There were no real consequences of defeat within the Flemish socialist party, the main loser. Most party leaders and bodies accepted the analysis of one of the senior leaders of that party, the Interior minister Tobback, who attributed the defeat to "a lamentable candidate list and a lamentable campaign". The socialists were convinced that, with better candidates and with a better programme, they would do better at a general election. When the 1991 general election proved to be just as disastrous, for the same reasons, it was clear that the socialist party had not seen "the writing on the wall" and had failed to adapt party strategy accordingly. The only impact of the European election on the SP was a weakening of the position of the New Left faction in the SP. The candidates of this small faction did poorly in 1989, largely because a very popular candidate did not run.[22] As the campaign of the SP focussed on a 'red and green' programme as supported by the New Left faction, the poor results of the party in general and of the New Left candidates in particular weakened the already marginal position of this faction within the party (De Winter, 1989).

Political observers focused particularly on the results of the socialist and christian democrat candidates within the francophone political parties. It was expected that the position of Deprez, the leader of the PSC, might be challenged in the event of bad results, in terms of preference votes or a general decline of the party list. As this did not happen he was able to remain in charge of his party. In the Parti Socialiste, the position of Spitaels, the party's strong leader, was not directly at stake. The only opposition to his absolutist grip on the party crystallized around the Walloon nationalist faction, led by Happart, and the vote for the latter was judged as an important indicator of the strength of this faction. Happart obtained more than one third of the socialist votes, and won even more preference votes than in the 1984 European election. This result could be taken to suggest that the party leader ought to change his policy of isolating that faction in the party leadership structure, something he had tried to do until then. In fact, since the 1989 European election, the party leadership has tried to placate this faction, by reintegrating some of its figureheads into the party executive and even into the national government.[23] Thus, in spite of the fact that the European election foreshadowed the major shifts in electoral support between parties that would be confirmed by the 1991 general election, party elites apparently learned very little from the European Parliament results in terms of party strategy and outlook, and the position of the leaders of the defeated party was not seriously challenged.

---

22 Their major candidate at the 1989 European parliamentary elections obtained only 5,000 preference votes. In the 1984 European elections, their candidate Ulburghs gained more than 20,000 preference votes. He wanted to stand again in 1989 but was not allowed to do so by party leaders, officially because of age limitation rules in the socialist party. Although Ulburghs joined the greens later (he was elected senator for Agalev in the 1991 national elections), we can assume that the greens acquired many of former Ulburghs voters.

23 The European elections had no consequences for the party system in terms of new forms of interparty collaboration, with two small exceptions. First, there was the temporary collaboration of small-left groups in the Dutch-speaking constituency. The list Regenboog (Rainbow) included candidates of the communist party, of the Trotskyite party (SAP) and some independent left-wing candidates. Rainbow obtained less than one percent of the vote in Flanders. The temporary electoral collaboration between the French-speaking regionalist party (FDF) and some ecologist candidates in Brussels did not do well either.

Conclusions

The role of European institutions in daily political life was not an issue in the 1989 election to the European Parliament. The interest of Belgian citizens in Europe is rather low. Europe does not divide the Belgians into pro and anti groups: most citizens, as well as the political parties, are in favor of Europe. The parties did not invest heavily in the campaign and domestic consequences of the European parliamentary election were generally not envisaged. In spite of the lack of European issues, turnout was high due to compulsory voting and only a little below the level at general elections. The main function of the European election thus was not an evaluation of parties' policies towards European integration and EC policy, but merely a mid-term test of the popularity of political parties and some politicians prominent in national politics. This is the effect of the particular electoral rules under which the country is divided in only two constituencies, allowing parties weakly organized at the constituency level to penetrate every remote corner of the country. Individual candidates can also test their popularity on a much larger audience. As governmental stability was not at stake, citizens were more likely to experiment in voting for single issue parties. In consequence, the 1989 European parliamentary election marked the breakthrough (but not the emergence) of the greens and of the extreme-right Vlaams Blok. The breakthrough of the latter and of the francophone greens was consolidated at the 1991 general election. The 1989 election presaged the further decline of the traditional parties in 1991, in particular that of the socialists. However, the main losers in 1989 did not take their warning to heart and continued with business as usual. The impact on their internal party politics was minimal. The election was the first sign of another increase in the fluidity of the Belgian electorate, especially in Flanders, where it continued to increase after the 1991 general election. Our analysis of the electoral market concluded that most of the parties seem to be able to win a substantial number of votes from other parties. Hence, abundant opportunities exist for ideological 'reprofiling' and realignment in order to achieve electoral successes. The dramatic further impact of the Vlaams Blok in 1991 provided confirmation that the immigration issue, first seen in the European election, maintains its place at the top of the political agenda.

CHAPTER 5

Britain:
Opening Pandora's Box

Mark Franklin and John Curtice

While Britain has twice been annexed by a European power (Rome in 54 BC, Normandy in 1066 AD) and for the first half of the present millennium had major territorial possessions on the mainland, the British have had mixed feelings about Europe ever since Queen Mary lost Calais. On the one hand Europe was close to hand and events taking place across the Channel could greatly affect daily life. On the other hand, having been ignominiously ejected, the British soon turned their attention to the larger world and, like many another bad loser, learned to cultivate a somewhat disparaging view of their continental neighbors. With the loss of empire in the years after World War II the importance of Europe to the British increased once again, but the British themselves were slow to respond. Keeping aloof when plans for a Common Market were first mooted, they belatedly recognized their error but, in applying late, gave the French the opportunity to reject them again—which de Gaulle did with gusto on the first two occasions that the British applied for membership.

Only with the departure of de Gaulle from the French political scene did British membership become possible; but the memory of rejection dies hard, especially when it reinforces feelings of estrangement from Europe that had become established over the previous five centuries. The perception that the cost of entry had been deliberately set high by those already in the club did nothing to ameliorate the situation, and British membership in the EU has never engendered the enthusiasm sometimes seen elsewhere in Europe. While attitudes towards the EU have gradually become more favorable and most Britons do now approve of EU membership, the majority probably regard it as no more than a necessary evil, to be limited as far as possible to technical matters that do not affect the British way of life.[1] British turnout in European elections held in 1979 and 1984 was the lowest in Europe (32 percent on both occasions, which was half the European average and 16 percent lower than in any

---

1 Note that all figures in this chapter refer to Great Britain only and exclude Northern Ireland. The election in Northern Ireland is discussed in Chapter 14.

other country), reflecting this estrangement and reinforcing the corresponding view held by other Europeans that Britain was only peripherally engaged.

In 1979 and 1984, European elections in Britain were prototypically second-order elections (Reif and Schmitt, 1980; Reif, 1985a) which stuck close to the result that might have been expected in a national election held at the same time (see Figure 5.1). Voters did not go to the polls in great numbers, but those that did used their vote to record their judgement on the domestic performance of government and opposition rather than about the future of Europe. Each party's share of the vote was within 7 percent of a trend line joining adjacent national elections.

However, the 1989 election was different. In that election the major parties were at least twice as far from such a trend line; indeed, Labour, the main opposition party won more votes than the Conservatives in a nationwide contest for the first time since 1974. Meanwhile one minor party (the Green Party) received 150 times the votes it might have expected on the basis of such a trend. At the same time, turnout was 4.5 percent higher in 1989 than at either previous European election.

In this chapter we will first of all examine why the 1989 election result was so different from earlier European elections in Britain. We will then examine the implications of the differences. Were European issues more important in the 1989 election and if so why? Did the election affect the course of British politics up to the 1992 general election and beyond? Above all, did the 1989 European election outcome in Britain provide any clues that might explain the

Figure 5.1 Votes Cast in National (solid lines) and European Elections (dotted lines) 1979–1992

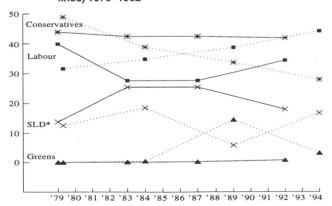

* Liberals in 1979; Social and Liberal Democrats in 1989 and 1992; Alliance of the Liberal Party with the Social Democratic Party otherwise.

unprecedented turmoil that accompanied the ratification of the Maastricht Treaty in the British parliament in 1993?

Why the 1989 European Election was Different

Three suggestions can be put forward to explain why the 1989 result was different. The first has to do with the timing of the election, the second with its European content (if any) and the third with its status as a second-order election.

As can be seen in Figure 4.1, the 1989 European election was the first to be conducted at any temporal distance from the preceding national election. In 1979 the two elections were conducted within a month of each other; in 1984 the European election occurred only a year after the corresponding national election. In 1989, by contrast, two years had elapsed since the previous national election—allowing time for opinions to shift, the government to fall out of favor, and typical mid-term forces to come into play.[2] But while this explanation might account for the poor showing of the incumbent Conservative government and the success of the main opposition Labour party, it certainly cannot account for the disastrous performance of the Liberal Democrats or the amazing breakthrough of the Green Party.

The second supposition, that the 1989 election was different because it was the first to address European issues, has clear attractions. The election occurred in the wake of unprecedented British activism on the European scene. Not only had Mrs Thatcher made the Single European Market a personal crusade on the basis that a free market in goods and services would reduce the role of the Brussels bureaucracy, but she had also taken a firm stand against further moves towards European integration, in opposition to some of her ministers and particularly in opposition to her predecessor as Tory leader, Edward Heath. During the months leading up to the European election, this conflict within the Tory party produced a series of headlines and kept European integration issues before the British public in an unprecedented fashion (Adonis, 1989). The greater interest shown in the election, as demonstrated by the higher turnout, might have been brought about by the heightened salience of Europe and the debate over the desirability of further moves towards unification.

This debate might also help account for Labour's success. For while Mrs Thatcher displayed her distrust of Brussels, Labour took a more pro-European stance than at any previous election (see below). And on the evidence of the polls it was Labour's stance which was the closer to public opinion (Adonis,

---

2 Ever since the mid-1950s, national governments in Britain have generally found themselves out of favor at mid-term (Norris, 1990).

1989:267). But if this explanation is correct it is difficult to see how we can account for the poor performance of the Liberal Democrat Party which had, in its various prior incarnations, been the most consistent defender of European union of any British party,[3] or the spectacular performance of the Greens (who were notably suspicious of Europe). So we cannot dismiss our third suggestion that, despite the higher turnout, the election was still predominantly a second-order election and that its outcome was determined by domestic issues rather than European concerns.

All three explanations thus provide promising leads, but each appears to have its limitations. Before we examine them more closely, however, we must say something about the British party and electoral systems and in particular identify how these differ from what we find in much of the rest of Europe.

The Context of the European Election

The British go to the polls in a political context that is unique in Europe. Firstly, Britain is the only EC country to employ single member districts with plurality voting. All other EC countries have some form of proportional representation in EC elections. Secondly, Britain is the only EC country with a so-called 'two party system'. Since the Second Word War all British governments have either been single party Conservative or Labour governments who, with the exception of only two relatively brief periods in the 1970s, have all had overall majorities in the House of Commons.

Indeed British politics have been dominated ever since 1924 by the Conservative Party (sometimes known as the Tories) whose origins go back to pre-democratic times, and the Labour Party which was founded in 1900 though it did not acquire its existing name until 1906.[4] No other party goes back even as far as the Second World War, although the Social and Liberal Democrats (formed by a merger in 1987 and now known simply as the Liberal Democrats) have as one of their components a Liberal Party that traces its origins to a party known as the Whigs in pre-democratic times. However, the other component of the Liberal Democrats, the Social Democratic Party (SDP), was formed as recently as 1982 in a split from the Labour Party. Although in the 1983 national election, the SDP and Liberals together came within 2.3 percent

---

3   The Social and Liberal Democratic Party was formed in 1987 from a merger of the previous Social Democratic Party and the former Liberal Party. The two parties had fought the elections of 1983 and 1987 in explicit alliance with each other that resulted in the nomination of only one candidate (either Liberal or SDP) in any one constituency.

4   In the previous national election, in 1987, these two parties won 376 and 229 seats respectively out of the 650 in the House of Commons.

of a tie with Labour for second place, the result was only close in terms of votes cast (26.0 percent to 28.3 percent), not of seats won (23 to 209). Further the Alliance (as it was then known) never again did even as well as in 1983. In 1987 it won only 23.1 percent of the vote (22 seats) while Labour secured 31.5 percent (229 seats). Meanwhile no other party has won seats all over Britain in recent years, though two nationalist parties (Plaid Cymru and the Scottish National Party) contest seats in Wales and Scotland, and won three seats each in 1987.

Though these were the only parties (other than Northern Irish parties) represented in parliament in 1989, they are not the only parties to have contested British elections. Since all that candidates need in order to stand is ten signatures and a £500 deposit (refundable if they secure 5 percent of the valid vote), British elections have always seen a smattering of eccentric and fringe groups contesting small numbers of seats. The most important of these have been the Communist Party which, while it never won more than half of one percent of the vote, did return two MPs to Westminster in 1945, and the Green Party (originally People, then Ecology) which first contested an election in 1974 and whose votes rose steadily in subsequent elections. Indeed the Greens overtook the dying Communists in 1979 and reached one third of one percent in 1987 (1.4 percent in the 133 seats contested).

European elections are conducted under the same rules and electoral system as elections to the national parliament. The only crucial difference is that there are far fewer constituencies—78 rather than 633. For smaller parties this has two (potentially countervailing) consequences. Since the major hurdle to a political party in fighting an election is raising the £500 deposit for each seat contested, it is much cheaper to run candidates in all European constituencies than in all national ones—less than £40,000 in a European election compared with over £300,000 in a national one. As we shall see, this cost difference was important for the Green Party because it meant that in 1989 it was able to field a full slate of candidates in a nationwide election for the first time ever. On the other hand, the smaller number of constituencies in a European election makes it even more difficult than it is in a national election for small parties whose vote is evenly spread geographically to win seats, while the winners' bonus in terms of seats won is also greater (Curtice and Steed, 1986).

While the mechanical differences between the situation in 1989 and that in 1987 may have been slight, the political differences were considerable. Britain's role in Europe has been one of the most divisive issues in British politics in the past twenty-five years. Although the Liberal Democrats are largely united behind a strongly pro-European position, both the Conservative and the Labour parties are divided between their pro- and anti-European wings. The consequent strains on party unity have revealed themselves on more than one occasion, such as the House of Commons vote on the original bill which enacted Britain's membership in 1972, the referendum on Britain's continued membership in 1975, and the decision whether or not to join the European Monetary Union—a decision eventually made in 1990. All of these issues saw significant backbench rebellions and/or serious internal divisions within the cabinet. So although the Conservative party had tended to be the more pro-European of the two major parties (it was a Conservative government which negotiated Britain's entry in 1972 while Labour argued in favor of leaving the European Community as recently as 1983) this was by no means certain to remain the case.

Indeed, by the time of the 1989 European election the two parties had clearly swapped sides. Excluded from power at Westminster, sections of the Labour movement (including not least the trade unions) began in the late 1980s to take a more favorable view of Brussels where the opportunities for influencing legislation on employees' rights and conditions appeared to be better than at home. Most symbolic of this change of mind was an invitation to Jacques Delors, President of the Commission, to address the annual Trades Union Congress (of which the vast majority of British trade unions are members) in the Fall of 1988. Indicative of the party's new tone in the 1989 European election was the emphasis it placed on the influence it could exert as a member of the Socialist group in the European Parliament. However, what made Europe increasingly attractive to the left—greater intervention in the operation of certain aspects of the market—also raised doubts about the future role of Europe in the minds of many of those on the Thatcherite free market wing of the Conservative party. Britain did not join the EC, so they argued, to have imposed upon it the kind of restrictions on business that the Conservative government had been busily discarding since 1979. Mrs Thatcher's Euro-skepticism was particularly fuelled by the draft European Social Charter—a component of the proposed treaty on European Union that was later to be known as the Maastricht Treaty—and the Conservative party manifesto was much concerned with the need to defend "national sovereignty" from the Eurocrats of Brussels. These arguments made clear the distance between Thatcherism and the Conservatives' nearest potential ally in the European Parliament, the Christian Democratic group; and the Conservatives' apparent isolation from the European political mainstream raised questions about how effective the party could be in the new parliament.

But even more damaging than the party's isolation was the extent of its internal divisions. The party's existing MEPs were for the most part much more enthusiastic about the process of European integration (and the prospect of joining the Christian Democratic group) than the party at Westminster. Further, Mrs Thatcher's anti-EC tone not only failed to command support from all of her ministers, but was attacked publicly by the party's previous leader, Edward Heath. The spectacle of the governing party tearing itself apart during an election campaign can have done little to enhance its standing with the voters (Adonis, 1989).

Moreover, the domestic background to the election was also not propitious for the Conservatives. Not merely did the election fall at the mid-point of the parliamentary cycle, when government popularity is (as we have already said) commonly low, but it was also a time of falling economic expectations, enhancing the probability of a vote against the governing party. Meanwhile, concern about the environment had risen to the top of the political agenda,[5] and the Conservatives' record on environmental protection was poor. Ironically, it was Mrs Thatcher herself who raised global warming to the top of the agenda by means of a speech in September 1988 that drew attention to the 'greenhouse effect'. In that speech and in some later addresses, Mrs Thatcher appeared to have been turned overnight into an environmentalist, using expressions and slogans straight out of the repertoire of green semantics; but since her party was poorly placed to benefit, this achievement was something of an 'own goal' (cf. Rüdig, Franklin and Bennie, 1993).

This rise in concern for the environment should have benefitted the Liberal Democrats, since the Liberal component of that party had been noted for its pro-environmental stance in earlier years; but the new party proved unable to capitalize on it. The merger with the Social Democrats had occurred less than two years previously, accompanied by much public wrangling, a change of leadership and serious disputes about what the party should be called. The result had been disastrous in the short term. Without name recognition or familiar leaders the new party's poll rating nose-dived, its predicament became the subject of political jokes, and few voters took it seriously(Denver,1992).

The same factors that hurt the Conservatives and the Liberal Democrats worked in the other direction for Labour and the Greens. After its disastrous electoral defeat in 1983, the Labour Party had made enormous strides towards jettisoning its more extreme socialist policies and was grooming itself for government. As the major opposition party it was the natural beneficiary of economic discontent. Moreover, despite still containing many anti-Europeans even in the party leadership, no schism became apparent during the campaign— partly because the social charter that was being attacked by Mrs Thatcher was something the whole Labour Party could agree on even if some were skeptical of Europe in other ways. On the other hand, the Labour party was not well

---

5   Gallup reported in June 1989 that the environment was cited as the most important problem by 14 percent of respondents, whereas normally the issue is barely mentioned at all (Rüdig et al, 1993).

positioned to take advantage of the new level of environmental concern. Distaste for nuclear energy and other environmental policies had been among the left-wing concerns that Labour had tried to distance itself from in jettisoning its socialist agenda; and the party found it hard to back-pedal on these initiatives in 1989.

Of all the parties that competed throughout Britain, only the Greens were unambiguously favored by the political situation during the European election campaign. Increased visibility (helped by free publicity from Mrs Thatcher) enabled it to capitalize as no other party could on the new level of environmental concern. Local elections held five weeks before the European elections saw the party win an average of 8 percent in the seats it fought, twice the figure in previous local elections (The Economist, 1989). With only 78 constituencies to find deposits for, the party could run candidates throughout the country for the first time—another source of free publicity. As we shall see, these factors are reflected in the findings of our study.

Among parties that campaigned less widely, the timing of the European elections was also highly favorable for the Scottish Nationalists. Already represented at Strasbourg by one MEP, Winnie Ewing (who had long-since made the far-flung Highlands and Islands constituency her personal fiefdom) the party had recently returned to the center stage of Scottish electoral politics, for the first time since the 1979 referendum on Scottish devolution, by winning the Glasgow Govan by-election from Labour in November 1988. Following the by-election, the party briefly registered one-third of the vote in Scottish opinion polls. Although the SNP could only realistically hope to gain one seat, the elections gave the party a chance to confirm its new found status which it did with over a quarter of the Scottish vote. In contrast, Plaid Cymru, the Welsh Nationalist Party, still showed no sign of breaking out beyond a Welsh-speaking enclave in the north and west of the principality.

The Opportunity Structure of British Partisanship

Table 5.1 displays the extent of overlap between British parties on the basis of our measures of 'probability to vote' discussed in Chapter 3. The Labour row in that table shows that, even though Labour regards itself (and is regarded) as the natural beneficiary of popular dissatisfaction with a Tory government, in fact the proportion of Conservatives who would ever consider voting Labour was smaller in 1989 than that of any other party. Less than thirty percent of Tories could imagine at some time voting Labour, whereas for supporters of other parties this figure was never less than sixty percent. Since dissatisfaction with the Tories is likely to have been felt far beyond this small segment, it seems likely that dissatisfaction with the government would not benefit Labour

Table 5.1 Potential Support and Overlap Between Parties in Britain in 1989

	Labour	Nat.	Greens	Lib.Dem.	Cons.
Labour	1.00	0.65	0.60	0.60	0.29
Nationalists	0.13	1.00	0.17	0.18	0.09
Greens	0.44	0.62	1.00	0.59	0.35
Liberal Democrats	0.35	0.52	0.46	1.00	0.30
Conservatives	0.28	0.42	0.45	0.49	1.00
Potential Support (%)	42.0	8.4	31.2	24.3	39.8
%Vote Elect	14.6	1.2	5.4	2.3	12.7
%Valid Vote	40.1	3.4	14.9	6.2	34.7
L-R median (1–10)	3.11	3.91	4.57	4.83	8.58

directly so much as indirectly by way of exchanges with other parties. Equally, we find that Labour voters are least likely to switch to the Conservatives. Indeed more generally we find that the British opportunity structure, as that of many other European countries, appears to be virtually unidimensional. When parties are ordered in terms of the propensity of their supporters to vote Tory, that order is replicated when we consider the preference of potential voters of various parties for Labour or Greens. Only the marginally greater willingness of Nationalists rather than Greens to support Liberal Democrats disturbs a perfect pattern in the rows.[6]

The opportunity structure shown in Table 5.1 also makes it clear that the Greens were best placed to benefit from dissatisfaction with other parties at the time of the 1989. The supporters of parties other than the Greens vary in how much they are prepared to support any particular party, with Conservative supporters least likely to defect and Liberal Democrats and Nationalists most likely; but in each case they placed the Greens either first or second among the parties that they could imagine voting for at some time. Above all, the Greens were placed above all other alternatives by supporters of both Labour and the Conservatives—the two parties with the largest number of supporters. The potential for a Green breakthrough in 1989 is very clear.

---

6 Viewed by column the disparities are greater, but this is because of the different sizes of parties upon which the comparisons are based, and especially the small size of the potential Nationalist vote. Given that Nationalist candidates do not contest any seats in England, it is not very surprising that many respondents in England, when asked to indicate the probability that they might vote 'Nationalist' indicated in practice that the probability was zero.

Switching and Quasi-switching

This opportunity structure is reflected in the reported origins of voters for those parties that gained support in the 1989 European elections. As shown in Table 5.2, only 0.4 percent of 1989 voters supported Labour while claiming to have previously voted Tory, whereas 2 percent of 1989 voters voted Green while claiming to have voted for Mrs Thatcher in 1987. Labour gained more votes from previous Liberal Democrats than from any other party, but the Greens won over the largest number of Liberal Democrats, gaining more voters from this small party than from the much larger Tories. The table also shows that almost a third of 1989 abstainers previously voted Conservative; but this is almost exactly in proportion to their share of the vote in the 1987 election, and suggests that whatever the reason for the poor Tory performance it was not brought about by Tory supporters staying at home.

We can check this supposition if we look at the differences between how our respondents voted in the European election and how they say they would have voted had the election been a national election. The findings are summarized in Table 5.3, which shows the extent to which parties gained and lost from quasi-switching and differential turnout in 1989 (see Chapter 3 for an explanation of these terms). There we see that the Tories were barely hurt at all by differential turnout, but did suffer quite considerably from quasi-switching. Labour, in contrast, was a clear beneficiary of differential turnout, but this advantage was lost through quasi-switching, and the party was left with about as many votes in the European election as it might have expected in a national election held at that time.

Table 5.2   Previous Vote (rows) of 1989 British Voters (columns) — Cells Contain Percent of all Voters

Total Percent	Cons.	Labour	Lib.Dem.	Greens	Other	Abst.	Total
Conservative	10.4	0.4	0.2	2.0	0.1	21.0	34.1
Labour	0.0	10.0	0.3	1.5	0.2	13.5	25.5
Alliance	0.3	1.3	1.7	2.2	0.2	8.2	13.9
Greens	0.0	0.0	0.0	0.6	0.0	0.3	0.9
Other	0.0	0.1	0.1	0.2	0.3	1.0	1.7
Too Young	0.1	0.5	0.0	0.2	0.1	6.5	7.4
Abstain	0.1	0.5	0.1	1.1	0.1	11.5	13.4
DK	0.1	0.3	0.2	0.3	0.0	2.4	3.3
Weighted N*	102	120	23	76	9	574	904

* Weighted to 1989 election result; percentages do not necessarily add to 100 because of rounding errors.

The clear beneficiaries of quasi-switching were the Greens. If the election had been a national election nearly half of their support would have melted away. The Greens' success in the election was thus very much a typical second-order election effect in which voters take the opportunity to experiment with small parties (Reif, 1984a). Even so, the results suggest that the Greens would still have done remarkably well had there been a national election in June 1989, polling something similar to the average 8 percent vote per candidate that they actually secured in the local elections in May. Meanwhile, although the Conservatives would not have done so badly had this been a national election, it is clear that Labour would still have gained a clear lead of more than 2 percent.

With these effects in mind, we need to look more directly at precisely what issues motivated voters. Earlier we suggested that both the state of the economy and the environmental issue could have been important. Alternatively, voters may have been expressing a more generalized mid-term dissatisfaction with the government. And given that voters did not vote exactly as they would have done in a national election, we clearly cannot yet dismiss the possibility that specifically European issues may have played some role. We now turn to some empirical tests of these propositions.

The Effects of Issues

We look first at why people bothered to vote at all. Table 5.4 makes it clear that whatever might have been responsible for the higher turnout in 1989, it was not the greater attention given in the months before the election to Britain's future in Europe. As has been found true in other EC countries, once the obvious predictors of the decision to vote in 1989 are taken into account (such as party identification, political interest, and whether the respondent voted in the 1987 national election), European attitudes add nothing more to variance explained.

Table 5.3   Quasi–switching and Turnout Effects in the 1989 European Election in Britain

	EE	NE	EE-NE	Quasi-switching	Turnout Effect
Labour	40.1	39.9	0.2	-4.3	4.5
Nationalists	3.4	2.5	0.9	0.9	0.0
Greens	14.9	8.5	6.4	7.9	-1.5
Liberal Democrats	6.2	8.6	-2.4	-1.7	-0.7
Conservatives	34.7	37.5	-2.8	-2.4	-0.4
Other	0.2	1.1	-0.9	0.2	-1.1

But what about the choice made by those who did turn out and vote? We have available to us indicators for each of the three possible domestic reasons we have suggested for the election outcome. We measure generalized protest against the government by identifying those respondents who said they had voted in order to 'warn' the government.[7] People's attitudes towards the economy are measured by their expectations about future improvements in the economy, while concern with the environment is measured by an index created out of two specific questions about the environment.[8] How well do these three issues help explain the pattern of party support?

First of all, we introduced each of these indicators into a regression analysis without including any other variables. We used as our dependent variable our respondents' reports of their probability of voting for each of the parties rather than their actual party choice because the former measures have more desirable statistical properties.[9] This produced a separate equation for the probability of voting for each party. In the case of the Conservatives and the Greens the variables account for as much as 9 percent of the variance,[10] and the direction of the associations for all parties are much as expected by

Table 5.4 Predictors of 1989 Participation in the European
          Election in Britain

	R^2	Added R^2
Demographics	0.07	
General Political Orientations	0.29	0.22
Habitual Voting	0.29	0.00
European Attitudes	0.29	0.00

7 Reif and Schmitt, 1980. Respondents were asked why they voted the way they did, and one of the options with which they were presented was that they had voted to send a warning to the governing party. A dummy variable was created to indicate respondents who chose this answer.

8 The index was created by combining respondents that picked out "the environment" in answer to a question about important problems facing the country, and those who said that the environment ranked first or second among important problems. The index was coded 1 or 2 for those who ranked the environment 1st or 2nd, and 3 for those who merely thought it important.

9 By employing the 'probability to vote' variables as dependent indicators of party choice we avoid two problems that would have arisen had we employed dummy variables derived from the party choice question. In the first place these dummy variables would be artifactually interrelated because they were derived from the same question, and secondly their dichotomous condition makes them strictly speaking unsuited to OLS regression analysis. The probability to vote questions suffer from neither of these defects, and we will see in Chapter 20 that they are good surrogates for actual voting choice in 1989.

10 They explain 6 percent of Labour voting choice but only 1 percent of SLD voting choice.

our suppositions. Conservative voters are supportive of the government and optimistic about the future of the economy. Labour voters are voting to warn the government and pessimistic about economic conditions. Green voters are pessimistic about the economy and concerned about the environment. SLD voters are merely pessimistic about the economy. But these findings ignore all other possible influences on voting behavior. A more rigorous test of the role of these domestic issues is obtained by including them in a more fully specified model. Unsurprisingly, the importance of other influences is quite clear. As Table 5.5 shows, the probability that someone will vote Conservative or Labour is strongly associated with their self-ascribed social class and, above all, their left/right self-placement.[11] Green voting is also clearly related to postmaterial values and to age, with young voters more likely to support the party than older voters.

At the same time the table still supports our argument that domestic issues played a role in the outcome. Even after taking all these other factors into account, voters who were pessimistic about the economy were significantly less likely to support the Conservatives and more likely to vote Labour. Equally we can see that those who wanted to send a general warning to the government were less keen on the Conservatives. But, as we had anticipated, these issues do not help us account for the success of the Greens whose support is instead related to concern about the environment. We thus have to make recourse to all of our suggested domestic explanations in order to account for the 1989 election result. Even then it is clear that our analysis has not succeeded in accounting for the spectacular failure of the Liberal Democrats.

Surprisingly, however, our analysis also shows that European issues were not without apparent influence. Opinions for and against the Social Charter were significantly associated with voting Conservative and Labour, adding 2 percent to variance explained for Conservative voters and 3 percent for Labour voters even when all the other variables had already been brought into the equation. This finding clearly reflects the stress that Mrs Thatcher had placed on her opposition to this component of the (proposed) Treaty of European Union, and the Labour Party's support for it.

Thus we cannot argue that the election outcome was entirely determined by domestic considerations. Of course, of all the debates about Europe, the

---

11 This variable alone accounts for 36 percent of the variance in Conservative voting and 29 percent of the variance in Labour voting. The lack of relationship between this variable and votes for the other two parties in the table does not mean that votes for those parties are not explicable in left/right terms. Voters for those parties tend to be centrally located on the left/right spectrum, and a variable that indicated extremity-centrality would pick them out quite well.

Social Charter is the one which fits most readily into the existing domestic battle between Conservative and Labour over the role of the government in guaranteeing minimum social conditions for all. Rather than introducing an entirely new issue into the British electoral battle, the debate about the Social Charter helped to intensify an existing national division. But even so, Table 5.5 shows that a European issue did become a part of the ongoing British party battle. Moreover, this was a very skewed issue in our data, with potential for doing the government a lot of damage. Fully 76 percent of respondents favored the Social Charter while only 13 percent opposed it. As the difference between opposition and support for the charter reduces the probability of a Labour vote by 9.4 percent (not shown), even controlling for all other variables,[12] this means that the issue could have contributed almost 6 percent (76 percent of 9.4 percent less 13 percent of 9.4) to the Labour vote—the equivalent of Labour's lead over the Conservatives (see Table 5.1). The European dimension to the election clearly cannot be ignored.

Table 5.5 Effects of Party Choice (Standardized Regression Coefficients)

	Cons	Labour	Lib Dem	Greens
Demographics/Identities				
Social Class	0.140*	-0.126*	-0.011	0.050
Age	0.088	-0.036	-0.069	-0.149*
Church Attendance	0.016	-0.042	0.142*	0.035
Home Ownership	0.121*	-0.088	0.003	0.018
Values				
Postmaterialism	-0.103*	0.047	0.053	0.133*
Left-right Position	0.489*	-0.454*	-0.052	-0.111
National Issues				
Warning the Government	-0.137*	0.089	0.091	0.108
Environmental Concern	0.040	-0.073	0.020	0.207*
Economic Conditions	0.143*	-0.112*	-0.034	-0.061
European Issues				
Social Charter	-0.125*	0.122*	-0.006	0.043
Total Variance Explained	0.476	0.392	0.062	0.178

* = significant at 0.05 level

12 The analysis upon which this estimate is based used the same independent variables as in Table 5.5 but a dummy dependent variable registering the presence or absence of a vote for Labour.

Domestic Consequences of the European Election

Elections are both a social process and a decision-making mechanism. The process of campaigning requires parties to furnish an appeal to the voters in order to mobilize their support. And the eventual choices that the voters make collectively determine who holds power. Both features can have consequences for a nation's politics. This is as true for a European as for a national election. Although in a European election real power is not at stake, the election result is reported by the media and discussed in terms of what it would have meant had it been a national election result.

The more transparent consequences are those that arise from the result of the election. In a national election the incumbent government or governmental coalition may be toppled from power; and even in a European election the ability of a party to continue in government may be threatened by a serious decline in its electoral support. But the process of campaigning and mobilization can be important too. Campaigns place the political parties under the public spotlight. Parties are required to take positions on the issues of the campaign. If these are new issues, the policy positions may be new ones and the election may be the first test of their impact upon a party's electoral credibility. Other issues may be ones upon which parties are internally divided. In such cases an election can be a threat to party cohesion and/or an important event in the battle to determine what party policy should be.

Indeed, so far as the 1989 European election in Britain is concerned, the process of campaigning was more important than the outcome for the future of British politics. By forcing Labour and the Conservatives to take public positions on the future of Europe, the election brought to public attention for the first time the fact that Labour was now more pro-European than the Conservatives. Labour was given the opportunity to educate its own electorate about its new policy. And by encouraging Labour to emphasize its links with the Socialist group in the European Parliament (not least because a Labour success aided by the electoral system was regarded as crucial to the overall strength of the Socialist group) the campaign played an important role in integrating the Labour party into European socialist politics. Meanwhile the divisions which were exposed in the Conservative party added to the tensions on the European issue which were to lie at the heart of Mrs Thatcher's eventual downfall—to which we will return.

But the outcome was not without its impact either, although in the event it proved to be short-lived. The immediate headlines surrounding the election focused on the apparent electoral breakthrough secured by both the opposition Labour party and the Greens. For the Greens the election result provided the oxygen of publicity. Although they had failed to secure any seats in the European

Parliament and were still unrepresented at Westminster, radio and television news and current affairs programs (which have an obligation to maintain political balance in their coverage) felt it incumbent on them in the months after the European election to include a representative of the Green party in many of their political discussions and news reports. The European elections certainly gained the Greens associate membership of the mainstream of British politics in the eyes of the journalistic community; and for good reason. The precedents of previous breakthroughs by small parties in European elections—such as the National Front in France in 1984 and the German Greens in 1979—indicated that European electoral success was commonly followed by national electoral success (Curtice, 1989). Further, in contrast to the Liberal Democrats, the party was clearly identified with a particular issue which had apparently grabbed the attention of the public. In addition, the election gave the party the opportunity to increase its organizational resources. The result produced a dramatic increase in party membership from 7,500 to 18,500. The financial as well as human resources which flowed from this appeared to give the party the means to fight every constituency at the next national election.

Meanwhile, the election result raised serious doubts about the long-term future of Britain's main third party, the Liberal Democrats. The result put the party back where the Liberal party had been at its nadir in the 1950s. Over-optimism at the time of merger coupled with lack of managerial control meant that the party was in severe financial difficulties. These difficulties could only be exacerbated by the loss of morale and membership which were threatened by its European election performance.

In the longer term, however, all the advantages that the election result brought the Greens appear to have been squandered to no avail. The party proved incapable of coping with the increased media interest in its affairs or in harnessing the enthusiasms of its increased membership. Heavily committed to the maintenance of internal democracy, it had eschewed the election of a single leader or granting too many powers to its national executive committee. With too much of its attention focused on its own (often lively) internal affairs, it proved incapable of seizing the political initiative (Rüdig, Franklin and Bennie, 1993). By the Fall its national opinion poll rating had fallen to 6 percent; and by 1991 it was at no more than 2 percent. Although it fielded 253 candidates in the 1992 general election they secured on average just 1.3 percent of the vote in the constituencies contested—almost identical to their 1.4 percent average vote in 1987 (Curtice and Steed, 1992). The Liberal Democrats in contrast climbed back up to 18 percent.

Labour's electoral success served similarly as a morale booster for the main opposition party. It was the first time Labour had outpolled the Conservatives in a nationwide election since the national election of October 1974.

At 40.1 percent of the vote, they passed the 40 percent barrier that had seemed to block them ever since the breakaway by the SDP in 1981. The result was taken at the time to suggest that after ten years in the political wilderness, Labour were once again deemed electable. Indeed, the election heralded a period of continuous opinion poll leads for Labour which only ended with the enforced resignation of Mrs Thatcher in the Fall of 1990. In the classic manner of a second-order election, the election provided the electorate with an opportunity to protest without toppling. But when faced with the decisive choice in 1992, Labour sank to a fourth heavy defeat. In contrast to the Greens, it is not clear to what extent the party itself can be blamed for this. More to the point are probably the actions taken by the Tories, in the wake of the European elections and of the events that followed, to put their house in order so as to be able to better deal with the Labour threat.

Which brings us back to the role of the European election in Mrs Thatcher's eventual downfall the following year. In November 1990 she narrowly failed to secure the votes necessary for victory in the first ballot of that year's annual leadership election in which she was challenged by Michael Heseltine, and she resigned soon afterwards. The European elections certainly did not lead directly to her defeat. It was heavy defeats in two parliamentary by-elections in the Fall of 1990, rather than the European election result, which ultimately stimulated serious concern about the party's electoral prospects amongst Conservative MPs. But the European defeat did remove some of the party's confidence in Mrs Thatcher's electoral invincibility and opened a period of continuous electoral unpopularity. Indeed she faced the first formal leadership challenge in November 1989 when the maverick backbencher, Sir Anthony Meyer, stood as a 'stalking horse' challenger to her leadership.

Most importantly, the exacerbation of tensions inside the Conservative party about Europe brought about by the European election campaign played an important role in the train of events which eventually led to Mrs Thatcher's downfall. For at the heart of the debate inside the government about Britain's relationship with Europe was the question of whether and when Britain should join the European Exchange Rate Mechanism. While Mrs Thatcher opposed joining the ERM, both her Foreign Secretary, Sir Geoffrey Howe, and her Chancellor, Nigel Lawson, were in favor. The issue was due to be raised again at the next European Council in Madrid just a fortnight after the European election. The European election result helped to undermine Mrs Thatcher's position and within days Howe and Lawson were to threaten resignation unless Mrs Thatcher announced at Madrid a clear timetable for Britain's entry into the mechanism (Thatcher, 1993:710–12 and 748–50). That threat was eventually defused, but resulted just a month later in Mrs Thatcher moving Howe from the Foreign Secretaryship to a less prominent post, thereby seriously embittering the already deteriorating relationship between them.

The government did eventually decide to join the Exchange Rate Mechanism in October 1990, but the inter-governmental discussions about European political and monetary union revealed further divisions in the Conservative government. Most crucially, Mrs Thatcher was left isolated at the 1990 Rome summit from which she returned in defiant mood with a ringing cry in the House of Commons of "No, No, No" to the prospect of closer European union. These comments finally precipitated the resignation of Sir Geoffrey Howe from the government and Howe then proceeded to deliver a stunning attack on Mrs Thatcher in his resignation speech in the House of Commons—a speech which decisively turned the tide against the Prime Minister within her own party.

So, as in the decision-making structure of the EC itself, inter-governmental discussions have had a greater impact on domestic British politics in recent years than either elections to or the proceedings of the European Parliament. But the European elections did play a role in triggering the sequence of events which eventually led to Mrs Thatcher's downfall. Whether Howe and Lawson would still have been emboldened to challenge Mrs Thatcher before the Madrid summit if the Conservatives had not done so badly in the European elections is not clear. That they did so certainly soured relations between Thatcher and Howe in a way that was to rebound devastatingly on Mrs Thatcher less than eighteen months later. And, of course, if Mrs Thatcher had remained leader of the Conservative party in the 1992 election, the outcome might have been very different.[13]

But the most important domestic consequence of the European election for Britain is only incidentally related to the electoral prospects of British parties. The failure of the campaign to provide voters with a clear choice for or against greater European unity (because the Tory split prevented that party from taking an unambiguously anti-EC stand) meant that a golden opportunity was missed to legitimate the steps taken since that time. If the election had been fought on this issue and the results had shown a clear majority in favor of further integration, then Mr. Major might have been spared the embarrassment of defeat on Britain's opt-out from the Social Chapter provisions of the Maastricht Treaty and the need to make an issue of confidence out of the ratification vote in July 1993—or the job of ratifying the treaty might have fallen to the leader of a different party. Alternatively, in the unlikely event that the

---

13 In the short run at least, Mrs Thatcher's removal resulted in a spectacular increase in Conservative support. Whether the change of leadership still benefitted the Conservatives by the time of the election is more debatable (see Crewe and King, 1994).

voters had backed Mrs Thatcher's repudiation of the moves later enshrined in the Maastricht Treaty, the question of ratification would presumably never have arisen, since the treaty in its actual form would not have been negotiated or signed.

Conclusions

The European election of 1989 was different from previous European elections in Britain for reasons that seem to have been both about Europe and about British domestic politics. Mrs Thatcher used the election as an opportunity for airing her views about the future course of European integration, and the resulting split in the Conservative Party made the election more salient than it would otherwise have been. While this does not appear to have been responsible for the rise in turnout, the specific debate about the Social Charter seems to have cost the Conservatives votes. In other respects, however, the election was very much a domestic affair. The brilliant performance of the Greens was attributable to a rise in environmental concern together with the inability of the Liberal Democrats to play their traditional role as the repository for protest votes following their disastrous merger. Meanwhile, voters who were pessimistic about the economy were more likely to vote Labour and less likely to support the Conservatives, while some appear simply to have wanted to give a general warning to the government. Exaggerating second-order effects magnified all three of these features of the European election—the extent of the Labour victory, the depth of the Liberal Democrat debacle and the brilliance of the Green surge; but all of these features would have been clearly visible (though more muted) even in a national election had one been held on the same day.

Unfortunately, Mrs Thatcher's attempt to spark a debate on the dangers of further European integration failed to register as such with the electorate, and there is no trace of any effect of opinions in this regard on either turnout or party choice. It was the split in the Conservative Party that was the most important feature of the 1989 European election, and arguably the most important legacy of the election was its contribution to publicizing that split and heightening the tensions about European policy within the government, tensions that were eventually to play a major role in Mrs Thatcher's downfall. That split, which continued to dog the Conservative party for the next four years, was not caused by the European election; but the election did provide a convenient point in the political calendar at which to register and possibly magnify the importance of European issues in British domestic politics. In doing so it served as a harbinger of political turmoil to come.

CHAPTER 6

Denmark:
Second-order Containment

Torben Worre

The introduction of direct elections to the European Parliament in 1979 produced a result very different from the familiar pattern of Danish national elections. The second election repeated this deviating pattern and, although a convergence was expected for the third European election in 1989, the result on the whole was little different from the first two. There thus exist two separate party systems in Denmark, one at the national level and one at the European level. The disparity between the two systems has to do with the influence of the European Community cleavage, which has no impact on party choice in national elections but influences voting behavior in European elections to a considerable extent.

The Danish Party System

The Danish party system is dominated by three traditional class parties originating in the last century: the Social Democrats (labor), the Liberals (agriculture) and the Conservatives (business). During recent decades their combined share of the vote has declined and a multitude of minor parties have received increasing though highly volatile voter support (see Borre, 1992). On the left wing, the Socialist People's Party is the only party with considerable and permanent support, while a number of small left wing parties (Justice Party, Communists, Left Socialists, Greens, Common Cause) have all dwindled into insignificance and lost their representation in parliament. In the Center there are three minor parties: the Radicals, the Center-Democrats and the Christian People's Party. They have few voters but considerable influence in the parliamentary process as the keys to majority coalition formation. Finally the Progress Party, a rather populist anti-establishment party, would, with regard to most issues, be located on the right. Of these minor parties, only the Socialist People's Party and the Progress Party have, at any time, reached the strength of medium size parties.

Table 6.1 shows the pattern of competition between Danish parties, as measured in terms of shared potential voters—those who would consider voting

Table 6.1 Potential Support and Overlap Between Parties in Denmark in 1989

	SPP	SD	Rad	CD	Lib	Cons	PP
Socialist People's Party	1.00	0.49	0.47	0.24	0.18	0.16	0.23
Social Democrats	0.77	1.00	0.71	0.46	0.33	0.35	0.37
Radicals	0.28	0.27	1.00	0.35	0.30	0.29	0.25
Centre Democrats	0.21	0.26	0.52	1.00	0.60	0.55	0.52
Liberals (Venstre)	0.18	0.22	0.52	0.71	1.00	0.67	0.57
Conservatives	0.17	0.24	0.52	0.68	0.69	1.00	0.60
Progress Party	0.19	0.20	0.35	0.49	0.45	0.46	1.00
Potential Support (%)	29.6	46.2	17.7	25.9	30.8	32.0	24.5
%Vote Elect	4.2	10.8	1.3	3.7	7.7	6.1	2.4
%Valid Vote	9.1	23.3	2.8	8.0	16.6	13.3	5.3
L-R median (1–10)	2.44	4.48	5.43	6.64	7.94	8.28	9.56

for several parties (see Chapter 3). It is apparent that all parties have a potential from two to six times greater than their actual support. Thus the Danish party system is highly competitive. It is also evident that the keenest competition occurs among neighbors on the basic left/right dimension: the Social Democratic voters are most attracted to the People's Socialist Party and the Radicals, while the Liberal voters are tempted by the Conservatives and the Center-Democrats. On the other hand every party has some competition from all other parties across the ideological spectrum, even the most distant ones.

The EC Cleavage

The Danish application for membership of the EC in 1961 was a matter of national consensus, supported by both government and opposition and by nearly all voters. But ten years later, as Danish entry was approaching, there was a surge of popular opposition to the EC. It was an unexpected, poorly organized, anti-establishment, grass-roots movement without support from any major political party or organization. Opposition to the EC was motivated by fear of erosion of Danish sovereignty and national identity, by resentment at centralization and bureaucracy, by doubts about the economic benefits, and by suspicion of involvement in great power politics.

Originally, only a few minor left-wing parties backed the opposition to Danish EC membership; but, before long, opposition flooded the established parties too. Organized anti-European factions appeared inside most parties and were especially strong among the Social Democrats and the Radicals.

Threatened by serious dissention on the most controversial issue of the period, the two parties accepted the official establishment of anti-European factions inside each of them and decided to leave the final decision to a referendum in order to isolate the European issue from the imminent general election.

During a long and passionate referendum campaign the opinion polls revealed a close race, but the result of the referendum of October 2nd 1972 was an impressive majority of 63 percent in favor of the EC. After Denmark's entry, however, support for the Community declined rapidly. During the rest of the 1970s opinion polls revealed an equal balance of opinion and during the early 1980s usually indicated a clear majority against the EC (Worre, 1993).

Widespread opposition to Danish membership of the EC and division inside several major parties has been the basis of a very reserved official Danish policy towards further European integration.[1] There are, however, considerable differences between the European policies of the Danish political parties. The most pro-European, or 'communitarian', attitudes occur among the four 'bourgeois' parties (Conservatives, Liberals, Center-Democrats, Christian People's Party). They did not rule out further integration as it was suggested in proposals for European union, although in practice their policies have been extremely pragmatic.

A more reserved group of parties consists of the Social Democrats, the Radicals, and, essentially, the Progress Party. These parties acknowledge Danish membership of the EC but in 1989 they wanted to preserve the Community in its current form and rejected further transfers of sovereignty. They were (and are) 'states rights' parties. According to the Social Democratic party manifesto in 1989, the party did not think that the development of EC policy was promoted by institutional changes or redistribution of powers between the institutions. It wanted the power of veto in the Council of Ministers to be preserved, and it rejected any supranational development of the EC towards a political union.[2]

Finally a group of parties are whole-hearted opponents of Danish membership of the EC. They are all left wing and all, except the Socialist People's Party, are very small. They combine opposition to the EC with opposition to NATO. The party manifesto of the Socialist People's Party states the following reasons for its fundamental rejection of the EC: its remote control weakens Danish democracy; its supranational and centralist structure is undemocratic; it is primarily an instrument for the interests of capitalism; and a supranational

---

1 For a history of Danish EC policy see: Birgit Nüchel Thomsen (1993).

2 This still stood as the party's official position in 1994. The Progress Party election manifesto of 1989 says: "The Progress Party cannot support the political union of the EC. The Progress Party considers the EC as primarily a free trade organization. The designation 'Europe of nations' expresses best the degree of integration acceptable to the Progress Party".

union precludes increased cooperation with the Nordic and other European countries. The strategy of EC opponents, backed by popular support in the opinion polls, has been to demand a new referendum on Danish membership, in which an anti-European majority in the electorate would prevail. Any steps towards a European union would have to be approved by a new referendum.[3]

Thus the original EC cleavage (for or against Danish membership of the EC) had by 1989 been supplemented by another (for or against European union) and the parties as well as the people were divided into three camps. This implied that the Center group of states-rights parties became decisive in European policy-making in Denmark. This group usually controlled about half the seats in the Danish parliament compared to one sixth for the EC opponents and the one third for the communitarian parties; and it could cooperate with either side depending on the issue.

Despite these differences in party policies, a Social Democratic minority government succeeded in maintaining a rather broad cooperation with regard to European policy for the first ten years of Danish membership. However, in 1982 a 'bourgeois' minority coalition government of the four pro-European parties took over. The parliamentary basis of the new government was a cooperation with the Radicals; but this party would not accept any commitment to support the government in matters of foreign policy. This gave the Social Democrat opposition an opportunity to separate the government from one of its supporting parties over EC questions and this happened in 1986, when a majority in parliament opposed the Single European Market. The government wanted to evade a major constitutional crisis over the EC but also to avert a general election on this issue. So the decision was referred to the voters in a referendum; and, despite the apparent majority against the EC, 56 percent of the electorate voted "yes" to the EC reform package. This referendum result put an end to discussion about Danish membership of the EC. Now the question of political union came into focus (Worre 1988).

Table 6.2 shows that the EC policies of political parties are reflected in the attitudes of their electorates to Danish membership of the EC, as expressed by their voting intentions in a new (hypothetical) EC referendum. Support for the Community is almost unanimous among voters of the bourgeois parties and opposition equally unanimous among the left-wing voters. The three states-rights parties are almost equally divided for and against the EC. These configurations have not changed much during the past decade.

The next section of the table presents the attitude of the party electorates to the form and degree of European integration, as expressed by a choice between

---

3 'For SF imod EF' (For SPP against EC). European election manifesto adopted by the executive committee of the SPP October 1988.

three options for European political cooperation.[4] Only a minority of 23 percent of Danish voters want any further integration involving a gradual transfer of powers to the Community. The communitarian approach is supported by half of the Liberal and Conservative voters but only by a minority among the smaller bourgeois parties and by 12 percent of the Social Democrats. The majority of Danish voters are in favor of preserving the status quo: cooperation among fully sovereign states with an unlimited right of veto. This 'states rights' attitude is held by a majority inside all of the pro-European parties and, in some of the minor bourgeois parties, by more than two thirds. Even within the Socialist People's Party nearly half opt for the status quo. Compared with the states rights perspective, only one fourth of Danish voters prefer an unconditional withdrawal, a slight majority inside the left-wing parties and a third of the Social Democrats, but very few bourgeois voters. Despite the dramatic EC cleavage in Danish politics there exists a rather broad consensus in the electorate in favor of the status quo; and this has been the case for at least ten years.

The difficulty of getting Danish acceptance of the constitutional changes that were proposed in successive treaties are due to this preference for the 'states rights' model. The debates on both the Single European Act (required to put the Single European Market into effect) of 1986 and the Maastricht Treaty of 1992 revealed differences of perception rather than of value: the supporters presented the reforms as minor accommodations implying minimal changes in the government of the EC, while opponents portrayed them as threats to Danish sovereignty. Fundamentally, both sides argued conservatively,

Table 6.2 The European Cleavage and the Danish Party System.
    Percentages, Parties Grouped by EC–policy

	Communitarian				States Rights			Anti–EC		
	Lib	Cons	CD	Chr	Rad	Prog	SD	SPP	Left	All voters
Vote in referendum on EC membership										
For EC	96	96	83	73	63	53	44	15	8	58
Against EC	4	4	17	27	37	47	56	85	92	42
Attitude to European integration										
Increase Integration	43	47	28	8	17	24	12	7	8	23
Preserve States Rights	53	51	69	83	69	52	54	41	19	52
Leave Community	4	2	3	8	14	22	34	52	69	25

4 The full wording of the options were: (1) The EC member countries should increasingly transfer powers to the EC and submit to the Community; (2) in the EC cooperation each member country should preserve full sovereignty and veto in EC decisions; (3) Denmark should leave the EC.

for the preservation of status quo, a cooperation based on extended states rights and only minimal supranational powers. An extension of these powers to cover the inner market or the environment was acceptable to many, but it had to overcome the suspicion that any transfer of power was a step towards federalism.

The 1989 European Election Campaign

The referendum on the Single European Market in 1986 seemed to have settled the question of Danish membership of the EC for good. Even the Socialist People's Party accepted that, henceforward, its role would be to influence decisions inside European institutions. "We shall make use of the EC whenever it serves a useful purpose, especially with regard to environmental issues", said the party's 1989 election manifesto. Its election slogan became 'Working Opposition'.

The Social Democrats had opposed the Single European Market because it limited Danish autonomy in the areas of the environment and the workplace. Now they pleaded for higher Community minimum standards in the same areas and even suggested the introduction of majority rule in this field. The government also had reservations with regard to the late phases of the Delors plan for an economic and monetary union. On the other hand, the bourgeois parties asserted that, with the Single European Market, there would be no need for further transfer of sovereignty for some time to come. "An interesting theme in five or ten years, perhaps; let us discuss it then", proclaimed the Prime Minister, Poul Schlüter. The formation of a new coalition government after the election of May 1988, including the 'states-rights' Radical party, emphasized the reserved Danish attitude to European union.

Thus Danish membership of the EC was no longer on the agenda of the 1989 European election campaign, and there was, for the first time ever, almost a consensus on Danish EC policy. During the election campaign this consensus on European matters encouraged a tendency among the parties to focus on domestic issues: a few weeks before the election the government presented a plan for a total restructuring of the Danish tax system. The Conservative election slogan was 'Vote the taxes down'. The Social Democrats presented an alternative tax reform plan and used its title as their election slogan: 'Get the 90s Going'.

Only two of the parties, the Liberals and the Center-Democrats, nominated leading party figures at the top of their electoral list. Most of the original MEPs retired after ten years of service and young and unknown politicians were nominated as top candidates. 'Kirsten Who' was what the 27-year old Social Democrat list leader called herself in response to reactions she had encountered during the first part of her campaign. The Radical and Christian Democrat ballots were headed by candidates aged 24 and 23 respectively. With these nominations, parties which had been torn since 1972 between supporters and opponents of the EC displayed their wish to bury the past and focus on that third of the electorate who had come of age during Danish EC membership.[5]

The campaign aroused little public interest. The parties concentrated their efforts on television, for decades the main electoral arena. Each party was given an evening of political broadcasting on the national channel but public attention was way below the level of general elections and even considerably below the previous European elections. Attention to other media declined, too. Far fewer read about the European election in newspapers and fewer discussed the election with family and friends. This decreasing interest finally manifested itself most convincingly in the level of turnout: only 46 percent of the electorate voted, 6 percent less than at the previous European election and only half as many as had voted in the previous general election.

Election Method

In European elections, unlike national ones, the whole of Denmark is one constituency. Since most of the candidates are relatively unknown local politicians, the personal votes tend to concentrate on a small number of well-known names at the top of the lists. As in other Danish elections, the election method used in the European election is proportional representation with list voting. However, as there are only 16 Danish seats in the European Parliament, a seat requires on average more than 6 percent of the votes cast. Most of the minor Danish parties are unable to pass this threshold (only five of the twelve parties participating in the national election of 1988). Therefore the European election law accepts electoral alliances, which are considered as one list at the first distribution of seats, but which, in a second stage, allot the seats won by the alliance to the parties involved. In this way votes for small parties are not necessarily wasted.

In the first European election two alliances were concluded, one between the four communitarian parties and one between all the anti-EC lists. But, in 1984, the pro-European alliance split in two, despite the fact that the four parties now belonged to the same coalition government. The two small partners were aware of the fact that the four-party alliance might leave them

---

5 For a report on the issues and campaign of the Danish European Election of 1989, see Worre(1989).

without any representation, while, in a two-party alliance, they would win at least one seat between them.

The three states-rights parties were ideologically quite different and they ran independently in the first two European elections, which in 1984 resulted in an under-representation of the Progress Party and the Radicals. In 1989 the Radicals had joined the government coalition with the two pro-European bourgeois parties. But, in order to underline its different EC policy, it concluded an electoral alliance with the main opposition party, the Social Democrats. This alliance did not win any seat for the Radicals, but it did gain an additional seat for the Social Democrats. Such an odd alliance was clearly meant to emphasize their joint 'states rights' policy.

The anti-EC alliance consists of the People's Movement and the left-wing parties. In 1979 there were three of those, ten years later reduced to one (the Socialist People's Party) because the minor parties abstained from running on their own candidates and contended themselves with recommending a vote for party members nominated on the People's Movement ticket.

In all three European Elections, coalition members have joined competing election alliances, apparently without any harm to government cohesion. Alliances seem now to be based less on considerations of similarity of policy than on calculations of election chances among the minor parties.

The European Party System

Unlike the situation in other European countries, direct elections in Denmark did not reproduce the distribution of party strength familiar from national elections. On the contrary, they gave rise to a strongly deviant pattern of results, which has now been confirmed at three consecutive elections (Worre 1987). The main reason for this difference is that a European election provides an opportunity to mobilize widespread opposition to the EC in the electorate. Among the political parties only the small left wing ones oppose membership of the EC and they are usually supported by only one-sixth of the electorate in national elections. But half of the electorate is against the EC, so the direct election offers a chance to appeal to the many dissidents inside the EC parties. As the left-wing parties have little appeal to most voters, each European election has included a special cross-party anti-European list, the People's Movement against the EC (originally organized to oppose the 1972 referendum). In European elections the aim of this movement has been to change the election into a kind of referendum, for or against the EC: "The European election is not a party affair but an opportunity to demonstrate the people's attitude to the EC", said the election manifesto. "It is important to underline that the Folketing today does not represent the people's attitude to the EC".[6]

As a cross-party single-issue movement, the People's Movement had no general policy and its MEPs were obligated to abstain from voting in the European Parliament in all matters that did not directly affect Danish membership.

Nomination to the People's Movement's ballot became a question of considerable tension inside the anti-European camp. At the first European election it was suggested that all the anti-EC parties should run their own ballots, while the People's Movement should nominate a ballot of independents and dissidents from the EC parties. In the end, however, the People's Movement decided to include members of the anti-EC parties, who were thus competing with their own parties. And, in the first European election, the Communists, realizing that they had little chance of winning a seat of their own, decided to call on their supporters to vote for the Communist candidate in the People's Movement ballot. In the following European election the Justice Party followed suit. In this way two very small parties, unable to pass the threshold for the national parliament, succeeded in getting outstanding party members elected as MEPs for the People's Movement. In the third European election all five minor left wing parties preferred to abstain from running on their own and limited their participation in the election to supporting their candidate nominated by the People's Movement, now mainly an umbrella organization of minor parties.

Table 6.3 shows the outcomes of the three European elections for each of the three party blocks, each compared with the results of the closest general election. It reveals considerable differences between the two kinds of election, differences which are persistent through time and which thus demonstrate the existence of two separate party systems, each with its distinct structure.

The general elections reflect the national Danish party system. This is not, of course, totally stable over a ten year period. But most of the changes, short term or lasting, are transmitted to the Euro-party system. Thus the doubling of the Conservative vote between 1979 and 1984 as a consequence of the 'prime minister effect,' was transferred to the European election (reflected in the row for the communitarian block in Table 6.3), and so was the simultaneous doubling of the Socialist People's Party vote. But, despite these changes in party strength, the Euro-party system preserves its distinctive character because it is usually the same kind of parties which are over- or under-represented in these

---

6 Quoted from 'Election platform of the People's Movement against EC' adopted by the national conference in Odense, October 28–29, 1978.

**Table 6.3   Results of European and Most Recent National Elections 1979–89.
Percentages of the Votes Cast; Parties Grouped by EC–policy.**

	1979			1984			1989			Avg.
	NE	EE	Ratio	NE	EE	Ratio	NE	EE	Ratio	Ratio
Communit.	30.8	36.5	119	42.8	42.6	100	37.8	40.6	115	111
States Rights	54.7	31.0	57	40.7	26.1	64	44.4	31.4	65	62
Anti–EC	14.1	32.5	230	16.3	31.3	192	17.8	28.0	161	194

elections compared with simultaneous national elections, and that is particularly true for blocks of parties.

A comparison of the election results over a period of time shows that the bourgeois parties generally do well in European elections. This is especially true of the two most committed pro-European parties, the Liberals and, in particular, the Center-Democrats, champions of Europeanism, who nearly double their vote compared to national elections (+95 percent in 1989, not displayed separately in Table 6.3). The Conservatives and the Christian People's Party, both considered more lukewarm on European matters, have varying results and no common pattern. All other states-rights parties suffer considerable losses in the European elections; on average the Socialist People's Party loses one fifth, the Social Democrats and the Progress Party one third, the Radicals nearly half of their usual vote. These poor outcomes have had a depressing and frustrating effect on the parties affected, which cover the whole ideological spectrum from left to right.

The most distinctive feature of the Euro-party system is the participation of the People's Movement against the EC, which (with 21 percent in 1979) was only one percent behind the biggest party in the first European election and only one per thousand from becoming the biggest party in 1984. It was generally expected that after the SEA referendum in 1986 the mission of the People's Movement would be over. In the pre-election wave of the European Election Study, fielded in April 1989, only 6 percent indicated an intention of voting for it. But on polling day 19 percent still voted for the People's Movement, an insignificant loss of 2 percent compared to the preceding European election.[7] Even in the previous European elections, the People's Movement had only emerged late in the opinion polls, the voters seeming not to be familiar with it until electioneering was well under way.

---

7 Of course this result should be viewed in the light of the fact that the Left Socialists, receiving 1.3 percent of the vote in the 1984 European elections, were not running on their own this time, but recommended a vote for the People's Movement.

A deviating European party structure is apparently related to the European policies of the parties, as is evident from Table 6.3. The bourgeois parties, with a clear communitarian line, have generally good results (this is especially true of the most committed pro-Europeans among them). The losers at the Euro-elections are the three parties with a reserved European 'states rights' policy; they generally receive less than two thirds of their usual vote. Finally, the anti-European lists are the big winners of the European elections, but this is entirely due to the participation of the People's Movement against the EC— the left-wing parties actually receive less than their usual vote.

A comparison over time reveals that, while the distinctiveness of the deviating European party system endures through the three elections, time has nevertheless brought some levelling: the under-representation of the states-rights parties has diminished, from 57 percent in the first to 65 percent in the last poll, while the over-representation of the anti-European block declined from 230 percent to 161 percent.

Turnout

The low turnout in European elections reflects the limited interest that attends them. The stakes are low and the voters are not yet very familiar with this new kind of participation. But, although interest and attention is much lower in European Elections than in national elections, it is generally the same political resources that influence turnout; their effect is just larger.[8]

Table 6.4 shows the combined influence on turnout of a variety of different types of variables. It reveals that the variation in turnout is explained mainly by demographics like sex, age and status (8 percent) and by civic attitudes and political orientations like political interest (another 17 percent), a relation very similar (though much stronger) to what is found in national elections. Non-voting in the last national election adds nothing to the explanation of abstention in the European election. Nor do European attitudes have any independent effect on turnout.

But political influences on participation should not be totally disregarded. A halving of the turnout can hardly affect all political parties equally. With the exception of the successful Center-Democrats, all parties in the European election attained only a fraction of the votes they would expect in

---

8 In national elections turnout ranges from 89 percent of the most interested to 83 percent of the little interested and 63 percent of those not interested at all, while in the European elections the corresponding participation is 80 percent, 47 percent and 27 percent. Among highly involved voters the turnout in European elections is 9 percent below the general level, among the least involved it is 36 percent lower.

Table 6.4 Predictors of 1989 Participation in the European Election in Denmark

	R^2	Added R^2
Demographics	0.08	
General Political Orientations	0.25	0.17
Habitual Voting	0.25	0.00
European Attitudes	0.25	0.00

national elections: the Liberals got 76 percent of their usual vote, the Conservatives, the Social Democrats, the People's Socialists about 40 percent, and the Radicals and the Progress Party only 31 percent and 24 percent respectively. Differences in turnout of those who would have supported each party in national elections, varying from 77 percent for the Liberals to only 32 percent for the Progress Party, evidently account for some of the decline in support.

The different ability to mobilize a party's potential voters is apparently connected to its European policy, as shown in Table 6.5. The divided and reserved 'states-rights' parties are able to turn out only 49 percent of the voters who might have voted for them in a national election, compared to 55 percent for the anti-European left wing and 61 percent for the communitarian bourgeois parties. But the attitude of the individual voter to the EC influences participation too. Supporters of the EC have always turned out in larger numbers than opponents: 5 percent more in 1989 and 8 percent more in 1984. This difference contributed to the over-representation of the EC-parties in European elections and accounts for the determined efforts of the People's Movement to mobilize EC opponents in order to get a more balanced representation of European Community attitudes.

Table 6.5 Turnout by EC Attitude and Party Preference. Percent Turnout in Each Group – Weighted; Parties Grouped by EC–policy

Attitude to EC	Communit. Parties	States Rights Parties	Anti–EC Parties	All Voters
EC supporter	66	58	47	54
EC opponent	39	49	64	49
Undecided	52	33	23	23
All voters	61	49	55	47

Turnout is thus affected by two political considerations: party preference and attitude to the EC. But these two forces interact; some voters agree with their preferred party on EC policy, others do not. In the first case the two influences converge to give voters unequivocal guidance, in the second case they become subject to cross pressure. Table 6.5 shows that voters who disagree with their party on EC policy have a substantially higher abstention rate than those who agree. EC supporters thus have a higher turnout than opponents in the bourgeois parties or the states rights parties, while the highest participation in the left wing parties is found among EC opponents. The two peaks of participation thus occur among bourgeois EC supporters (66 percent) and left-wing EC opponents (64 percent), while all cross-pressured groups have a turnout of less than 50 percent. This pattern is consistent over all the three European elections.

Party Choice

The difference between the result of a European election and those that would have occurred in a (hypothetical) simultaneous national election is the sum of two different influences: the effect of the lower turnout and the effect of 'quasi-switching' (see Chapter 3). Table 6.6 divides the difference between the two outcomes (hypothetical and actual) into the effects of the two influences. The turnout effect (loss above average due to lower turnout) hit the Progress Party in particular, and the Social Democrats and the Center-Democrats slightly, while the Liberals benefitted from the overall depressed turnout, because their supporters turned out to vote in above-average numbers.

Table 6.6 Quasi–switching and Turnout Effects in the 1989 European Election in Denmark

	EE	NE	EE-NE	Quasi-switching	Turnout Effect
Socialist People's party	9.1	15.6	-6.5	-6.9	0.4
People's Movement.against EC	18.9	0	18.9	18.9	0
Social Democrats	23.3	31.8	-8.5	-6.6	-1.9
Radicals	2.8	4.0	-1.2	-1.7	0.5
Center Democrats	8.0	4.9	3.1	3.3	-0.2
Christian People's Party	2.7	1.8	0.9	0.8	0.1
Liberals (Venstre)	16.6	10.7	5.9	1.9	4.0
Conservatives	13.3	15.0	-1.7	-2.8	1.1
Progress Party	5.3	11.7	-6.4	-2.5	-3.9
Other	0.0	4.5	-4.5	-4.4	-0.1

But most of the differences were caused by quasi-switching, which gives nearly all parties a net loss. Besides the People's Movement, whose 18.9 percent are all quasi-switchers, only the Center-Democrats got a major gain from vote switching, the Liberals and the Christian People's Party a limited one. Serious losses affect the Social Democrats and the Socialist People's Party, but the Progress Party, Conservatives and Radicals also lose severely as a result of switching. Thus the net differences in the parties' voting strengths are produced by numerous combinations of effects. Of the big winners the Liberals achieved their advantage predominantly from a turnout effect but the Center-Democrats exclusively from quasi-switching. Of the losers, the Progress Party suffered mainly from turnout effect, while the Social Democrats, the Socialist People's Party, the Conservatives and the Radicals lost due to quasi-switching, the three latter even having a slight gain from turnout effects, albeit far too small to balance the loss from quasi-switching.

EC Attitude and Party Choice

In other European countries voting in the European election is almost exclusively based on the usual party preference of the voters, but in Denmark the outcome is clearly also affected by attitude to the European Community. In national elections the Danish electorate usually gives only one sixth of the votes to the anti-EC left wing parties, although half of the voters are opposed to EC membership. Table 6.7 shows that there is a strong connection between EC attitude and party choice, even at national elections. EC supporters give nearly two-thirds of their vote to the bourgeois parties and the rest to the states rights parties. The anti-EC left-wing parties receive support exclusively from EC opponents, but get only 38 percent of the vote of those opponents while half of it goes to the states-rights parties and 13 percent to the bourgeois

Table 6.7   **Attitude to EC and Party Choice at National and European Elections. Percentages.**

Attitude to EC	Lib	Cons	CD	Chr	Rad	Prog	SD	SPP	Left	N
National Election										
EC supporter	22	34	5	2	6	6	21	4		418
EC opponent	1	5	2	1	6	8	36	32	9	289
European Election										
EC supporter	31	24	12	3	3	7	19	3	1	315
EC opponent	1	2	2	1	2	2	21	21	49	206

parties. This implies that nearly two-thirds of the EC opponents, equivalent to one third of the electorate, regularly vote in national elections for parties with which they disagree over EC policy. This has not affected their party preference, because the European cleavage has little salience in national elections. People do not vote for the small left-wing parties just because they are against EC. Party choice is decided by considerations of domestic politics and confidence, and most voters regard the EC as a settled matter. A preferred party is not necessarily preferred on all issues, as public opinion polls frequently reveal.

This difference between electorate and parliament is apparent from the results of the Danish referenda on the EC; but this difference also provides EC opponents with an opportunity to turn the European elections into a special event, a chance to mobilize the widespread opposition to the Community that exists even inside the pro-EC parties. From the beginning the EC-opponents justified their participation in the European elections with referendum-like arguments: "We want to offer an opportunity to the Danish people to send a delegation to the European Parliament which reflect the Danes' attitude to EC".[9] The participation of the People's Movement against the EC, without any other program than fighting the EC, stressed the referendum character of the poll.

This perspective was especially threatening to the Social Democrats, who proposed a very different conception of the European election as a poll that did not concern Danish EC membership (which was the prerogative of the national parliament) but whose aim was to influence European policies in the same direction as one wished to promote in national politics. Therefore, voters should stick to national party preferences. "The European election is a party affair", states the Social Democratic election manifesto, which ends: "A Social Democratic vote in the European election prepares the way for an open and red Europe". [10]

The result of the European election proves that the strategy of the EC opponents was quite successful: 70 percent of the voters opposing EC membership voted for an anti-EC list, half of them for the People's Movement and 21 percent for the Socialist People's Party, while Social Democrats were reduced to half of their usual strength and the Progress Party to 2 percent. The EC supporters, on the other hand, voted exactly as they did in national elections. This pattern duplicates what was seen during the first two European elections.

We demonstrated that the difference between the Danish party systems in national elections and European elections is the result of both differential turnout and party switching, and that the same forces are influencing both:

---

9 Quoted from the Justice Party election pamphlet of 1979.

10 Quoted from 'Et åbent Europa' (An Open Europe), the 1989 European election manifesto of the Social Democrats.

Table 6.8   Voting in European Elections by Attitude to EC and National Party Preference. Percentages.

	Bourgeois Party	States Rights	SPP	People's Movement	Non-voter	N
National Choice:						
Bourgeois Party						
EC Supporter	65	1			34	279
EC opponent	21	5		13	61	45
States Rights Party						
EC Supporter	8	49		1	42	149
EC Opponent	1	27	2	19	51	151
Anti-EC Party						
EC Supporter	8	4	31	4	53	42
EC opponent	1	1	26	35	36	122

national party preferences, attitude to the EC, and the incompatibility between the two. The combined effect of these variables is demonstrated in Table 6.8, which constitutes a kind of model of the nature of deviant Danish European election behavior. It shows, at the one extreme, that the consistently pro-EC bourgeois parties are able to keep 65 percent of their usual electorate through a combination of high turnout and lack of defection, while the less consistent states-rights parties are able to retain only 49 percent of their EC supporters. At the other extreme, the EC opponents of both camps cast no more than 21 percent and 27 percent of their vote in favor of their usual party because of the combined effect of the very low turnout and a heavy defection to the People's Movement. The Socialist People's Party is in agreement with its voters in opposing the EC, and consequently has a very high turnout, but the successful competition from the People's Movement does not leave it a larger share of their vote than in the other camps.

Consequences of the European Election

The first European election, which produced the strongly deviating Danish Euro-party system, proved at the same time that this party system had no effect whatsoever on domestic politics. Neither simultaneous opinion polls nor the general election which followed a few months later showed any sign of domestic impact from the massive voter migration in the European election; and the experience of the second and third European elections was the same. The 1989 election was influenced by second-order effects (e.g., a drop in support for the two government parties) but, as demonstrated above, these minor popularity shifts were surpassed by the structural effects of the EC cleavage, and they appear much more closely in the simultaneous opinion polls. The short life of the three-party coalition was hardly affected by the result of the European election.

The consensus tendency regarding EC policy observed during the election campaign, including an acceptance of EC membership and the internal market and agreement on the policies to be pursued inside the Community, made the EC cleavage less acute. But the European election result proved that there is still considerable polarization regarding the EC issue in the Danish electorate, even on this non-committal occasion. The expectations of an erosion of the Euro-party system were not met, although the result reveals a slight convergence. Since the 1986 referendum on the Single European Act opposition to EC membership has declined rapidly, while the integration cleavage has been at the top of the political agenda: the Maastricht Treaty on political and economic union was the subject of a third, passionately contested, referendum on June 2nd 1992, in which the European Union was rejected by a tiny majority of 50.7 percent of the votes cast (it was passed by a comfortable majority, in slightly modified form, a year later—see below).

That referendum underlined the reorientation of the EC cleavage from the membership issue to the integration issue. The People's Movement, spokesman of the old EC cleavage, has been subject to considerable internal tension over its future role. At the referendum of 1992 a number of new organizations were campaigning for a 'No,' the most outstanding being 'Denmark '92', under the slogan 'Europe yes, Union no'. Opinion polls taken at the time of the referendum show that although a majority rejected the Union, only 19 percent now want to leave the Community, less than ever before. After the referendum the moderate wing of the People's Movement (including three of its four MEP's) split off and joined the new anti-Union organizations to found the June Movement (named after the referendum month). While the rump People's Movement still wants to leave the EC, the June Movement accepts membership as a fact and wants to pursue a states-rights and anti-Union policy. The two movements are going to present competing lists in the next European election.

The rejection of the Maastricht Treaty made the future of Danish affiliation to the Community uncertain, but an agreement at the Edinburgh summit of the European Council in December 1992 permitted a number of Danish exemptions from the Union treaty, covering defence, currency and police powers, the three most tangible cessions of sovereignty in the treaty. Thus amended, the Union treaty was approved in a new referendum of May 18, 1993, by a majority of 56.8 percent. The Union treaty was at that time even supported by the Socialist People's Party, which felt that the Edinburgh agreements had complied with the party's criticisms of the Maastricht Treaty. But this change of policy did not have much impact on its voters, as 85 percent still voted no in the referendum (Nielsen, 1993).

The first three European elections in Denmark produced a separate, but rather stable European party system with a structure very different from the national system. The total reorientation of the European cleavages and the positions of parties and organizations will certainly imply a restructuring of this peculiar party system at the 1994 European election.

CHAPTER 7

France:
The Midwife Comes to Call

Colette Ysmal and Roland Cayrol

The European election of 1989 was the first that French politicians did not use solely for domestic political purposes. On the contrary, the main candidates attempted to speak more about Europe than about the policies of the President of the Republic or of the current Government. Nevertheless, as in 1979 and 1984, the election was marked by weak voter interest—evidenced by low voter turnout—and there is little evidence to suggest that voting preferences were much influenced by anything other than domestic considerations. European institutions remain remote and obscure for most French citizens and the electoral campaign barely helped in clarifying what the process of European integration is about.

A European election is in many ways quite different from other French elections. It is the only election which uses both national tickets and proportional representation.[1] Proportional representation increases the chances of election of a few members from each political stream;[2] while national lists and the limited number of seats to be filled (81) make it easier to find candidates. In consequence, the number of lists has continued to increase: 11 in 1979; 14 in 1984; and 15 in 1989. During the 1989 elections these lists represented not only the entire range of public opinion—from extreme left to extreme right— but also small groupings around individuals (such as those directed by Gérard Touati, Henri Joyeux, and Franck Biancheri) as well as pressure groups, such as the Hunting, Fishing, Nature and Traditions ticket led by André Goustat or that entitled "For the Defense of Animals in their Environment", a hitherto unknown group led by Arlette Alessandri.

Furthermore, the 1989 European election reflected the increasing disorder of the French party system which had stabilized by the end of the 1970s (Ysmal,

---

1 The legislative elections are by majority vote in two rounds in 577 districts; local elections (cantonales) also use majority ballot in two rounds; municipal elections use a mixed system (proportional and majority, but whose ultimate structure is majority). Finally, the regional elections use a proportional system, but within the constituency structure.

2 Election requires 5 percent of the votes cast.

1989; Borella, 1991): four large parties linked in pairs by political and electoral alliances, forming two very polarized blocks—one left and one right. The emergence of the National Front in 1984, and its ability ever since to maintain strong voter support, contributed to this increasing disorder. Since then, other groups have emerged and the traditional alliances between parties have collapsed.

In the 1989 elections there were as usual two small parties of the Trotskyite extreme left—Workers Struggle (Lutte Ouvrière) and the Movement for a Labor Party (Mouvement pour un Parti des Travailleurs) which formed a ticket called Europe for the Workers (Pour un Europe des Travailleurs). On the extreme right was the European Workers Party (Parti Ouvrier Européen). This formed the ticket For a Free France (Pour une France libre) which presented the themes of the National Front while at the same time promoting the European Community as the bastion of the 'west'. The Communist Party (PC), the Socialist Party (PS) and the National Front (FN) also presented their lists. The Communist Party, which is the oldest of the French parties, having been formed initially in 1920, has always espoused strict Soviet orthodoxy. It was the first political party founded under the Fourth Republic, and the most important of the leftist parties until 1978. Since the end of the 1970s, however, it has experienced a profound crisis, due principally to its break with the rest of the left (rupturing the Union of the Left in 1978) and its increasing opposition since 1984 to socialist governments.

The Socialist Party, founded in 1969 as successor to the old French Division of the Workers International (Section Française de l'Internationale Ouvrière—SFIO), originally tried to present itself as being very different from other European social democratic parties by promoting a "rupture with capitalism". However, its experiences in power between 1981 and 1986, and again after 1988, led it to readjust its economic policies in line with market economics, though moderated by the desire to maintain the benefits of the welfare state and to promote solidarity between social groups. As for the National Front, representing the "national right", it built its success on defending the French Nation and national identity, and its hallmark has become the permanent rejection of all immigration.

In contrast, European Renewal (Europe Rénovateurs), and the Greens (Europe-Ecologie) can be thought of as newcomers. The former, composed of Communist Party dissidents, is a result of the crisis within the Communist Party. Those who participated in the break criticized the PCF for its continued adherence to the Stalinist line, its operational structures and its anti-European position. As for the Greens, it was not the first time that they took part in elections.[3] It was, however, the first time that they participated at the European

---

3 The ecologists presented a candidate for the first time at the Presidential election of 1974.

level as an organized and institutionalized party since their foundation in 1984.[4] Their program's most well-known feature is an emphasis on the defense of the environment, but the party also attacks the 'productivist' logic of both left and right, and espouses the values of 'cultural liberalism', a French expression describing what is known elsewhere as postmaterialism (Inglehart, 1977).

The most important ruptures between traditional parties occurred within the moderate right with two simultaneous splits. The first broke up the alliance between the liberal parties (the Parti Radical and the Parti Républicain) and the Christian-Democrats (Centre des Démocrates Sociaux—CDS) which had existed since 1976 within the grouping called Union for French Democracy (Union pour la Démocratie Française—UDF). The second saw a split in the alliance which had endured since 1981 between this same UDF and the Rally for the Republic (Rassemblement pour la République—RPR) which followed the Gaullist tradition. In 1979, the UDF and RPR fought the European elections separately, the UDF led by Simone Veil (once president of the European Parliament), and the RPR led by Jacques Chirac. In 1984 the two parties formed a single ticket led by Simone Veil. Five years later Ms. Veil seceded from the group and won the support of most of its CDS members. One of the main reasons for her departure was that Simone Veil felt that she could not get the position she felt she deserved on the joint UDF/RPR ticket. At the same time, the antagonism between those who were strong supporters of Europe, namely the ex-President of the European Parliament (Veil) and the CDS, and those resisting greater European integration, namely the RPR, also played a role in the divisions. Finally, the CDS wished to affirm its unique Christian Democratic identity (its belief in the social market economy) and its greater liberalism in terms of law and integration of non-European immigrants, particularly as the UDF and RPR rallied behind Thatcherite liberalism and emphasized themes that seemed at times to echo National Front ideals in the areas of security and immigration. Thus the CDS saw the opportunity to line up behind a candidate who was not a party member and whose defeat, if it occurred, could not be directly attributed to the party, while at the same time minimizing the risk to their own forces.

It can thus be concluded that the candidatures at the European elections did not reflect the party structure which had existed during the 1988 national elections (presidential and legislative). Not only did the non-partisan lists receive 6.9 percent of the votes (see Appendix D) but there was apparently also a new

---

Since then, they have had a candidate at every Presidential election and a ticket at every European election. They have not, however, been very strongly represented at either the legislative or local elections.

4 The Greens/Ecologists had already presented a list at the municipal elections of 1989.

mutation of the party system. While the independent position of the CDS was unlikely to be sustainable at a national election, given the constraints of majority voting, the Greens (obtaining 10.6 percent instead of for instance 3.9 percent during the Presidential elections of 1988) appeared to be on the way to becoming a new force—the sixth important party alongside the PC, PS, UDF, RPR and National Front.

It was nevertheless from among these parties, in the throes of mutations and transitory alliances, that the electorate needed to choose in 1989. In fact, 90 percent of the electorate who cast votes, selected one of the six major forces in the structure: PC, PS, CDS,[5] National Front, the Greens and, finally, the union of the RPR with the rump of the UDF. With regard to the first five, the cleavage remains marked between the left and right, based on economic factors (from communist collectivism to the ultra liberalism of the National Front), social factors (from the maintenance of the welfare state supported by the PC and the PS, to social deregulation supported by the PR and the RPR, and demanded by the FN), and cultural factors (from postmaterialist values loyally upheld by the PC and the PS to the neo-conservatism of the FN).[6] On this dichotomous axis, the CDS and Simone Veil are centrally positioned.

On top of this structural dichotomy, a European wedge was superimposed within the party groupings. For instance, the National Front and the Communist Party are both very negative towards the European system, though for very different reasons. The former is opposed in the name of the Nation, menaced by both the European bureaucracy and the notion of integration, while the latter is opposed to the idea of a liberal or capitalist Europe. The PS and the CDS are most favorable to European union, while the RPR would like to slow the process of integration down, especially in relation to a common currency and the proposed frontier-free zone (associated with the Schengen Treaty). This is what led Valéry Giscard d'Estaing, who is known to be very favorable to European union, to moderate his stance on the subject. The ecologists are an exception to all this. European, but without any integrationist principles, they do not recognize, among other things, the *summa divisio* between left and right and claim to be neither one nor the other. They are, in the end, more economically liberal than the PS, and of course than the PC, as well as more liberal culturally, and in particular more open to the question of immigrants and their problems, than any other party. The electorate's perception of the party system as it was presented in 1989 largely confirms the structure and the

---

5 The list led by Simone Veil is not exactly a CDS list. Most of the CDS leaders supported her, but a few supported Valéry Giscard d'Estaing. Also, the ticket included a few people who did not belong to the CDS.

6 On the concept of neo-conservatism, see Minkenberg and Inglehart, 1990

position of the different parties within it as we have indicated. Based on the propensity of those interviewed to choose a party other than the one they voted for in 1989, Table 7.1 shows which parties share the same electorate and which have a specific clientele. On this issue, three comments can be made.

Firstly, the dominant feature is the overlap between parties.[7] The total of potential supporters is in fact nearly 190 percent. This does not mean, however, that all the parties or alliances are considered to be similar or unanimously attractive by the electorate; on the contrary, the competition between the parties remains determined by the left/right dimension. Parties which are similar in terms of their program, or their historical position on the French political scene, share the same electorate. On one side, the PC and the PS, despite their recent bad relations, represent two historical forms of French socialism and their electorates overlap somewhat. On the other side, the Centre and the Union again show considerable overlap, as is only logical since the parties of which they consist are allied both politically and electorally. The leftist parties are not very attractive to conservative voters and the conservative parties are even less so for leftist voters. Putting these shades of preference together we see a virtually uni-dimensional pattern in Table 7.1, with parties closest in ideological terms having greatest overlap in electoral terms.

Secondly, within this general framework, we do however see the centrist parties (the PS, the Greens, the Centre and Union) opposing the extreme parties (the PC and the FN). These last two are the ones which have the smallest

Table 7.1 Potential Support and Overlap Between Parties in France in 1989

	PC	PS	Ecol	CDS	Union	FN
PC	1.00	0.29	0.23	0.16	0.12	0.15
PS	0.76	1.00	0.66	0.50	0.40	0.32
Ecologiste	0.64	0.68	1.00	0.67	0.56	0.51
Centre (CDS)	0.28	0.34	0.44	1.00	0.67	0.49
Union	0.31	0.39	0.52	0.96	1.00	0.71
FN	0.17	0.13	0.21	0.31	0.31	1.00
Potential Support (%)	15.9	42.0	43.6	28.7	41.1	17.9
%Vote Elect	3.6	11.2	5.0	4.0	13.7	5.5
%Valid Vote	7.7	23.6	10.6	8.4	28.9	11.7
L-R median (1–10)	1.49	3.45	4.78	6.91	7.58	9.83

---

7 See Chapter 3 for a description of the 'probability to vote' measure.

potential electorates. The PC is the least attractive of the two parties in the eyes of the whole electorate. The situation is even more distinctive for the National Front. A large part of its potential electorate would gladly vote for the Union; however the opposite is true for voters of the Centre and Union, who are on average much less attracted to the FN. It can thus be deduced that ideological differences between voters who have maintained their confidence in the UDF and RPR and those who have moved to the National Front remain strong.

Finally, the case of the Greens is unique in many ways. On the one hand they have very few supporters of their very own, since their voters are attracted to most other parties except the PC and the FN. On the other hand they are the party with the largest potential electorate, in that they are rejected by very few. This leads to the question of the significance of an ecological choice for actual Green voters, and even more so for potential Green voters. The sympathy of the Green electorate to the PS, the Centre, and the Union explains the fact that, as it develops, the ecological party actually attracts voters from the left (especially from the PS) as well as the right. These voters are attracted most probably by the theme of environmental defense, but there are also some who wish to 'teach a lesson' to the traditional parties. It is remarkable that voters for the Greens in 1989 are particularly dissatisfied with the way in which democracy functions in France and feel almost unanimously that politicians are not "concerned with the problems of the French people".

Turnout

With only 48.7 percent voting, this election beat all records for low turnout in the entire history of French elections, with the single exception of the referendum of 1988 on the statute of New Caledonia (when the turnout was 36.9 percent). The severity of this result is apparent when compared to the average turnout for national or local elections (Table 7.2). It is clear that European elections are at the bottom of the hierarchy of elections, way behind presidential, legislative and even local elections.

Determinants of electoral participation

Table 7.3 shows the effects of different groups of variables on turnout. The decision whether or not to go to the ballot box, as has been shown by Schmitt and Mannheimer (1991a), depends very little on attitudes towards European issues—the advantages of belonging to the EC, whether or not integration should be accelerated, the extent of regret should the European Community be dismantled, or the positive or negative esteem in which the EC is held. Most

Table 7.2 Average Turnout at French Elections 1965–1989

Type of Election	%	N
Presidential Elections	82	5
Parliamentary Elections	77	7
Local Elections	67	13
European Elections	56	3

important seem to have been, on the one hand, the determinants traditionally related to political participation in general (interest in politics, strength of party links, and perceived importance of asserting political opinions) and, on the other hand, socio-demographic characteristics. With regard to the latter, age played a decisive role. It was in fact the young voters (18–35) who were least inclined to use the ballot boxes: only 29 percent of the 18 to 24 year-olds and 40 percent of the 25 to 34 year-olds said they voted, while 59 percent of the 35–49 age group and 64 percent of the 50+ age group did so. These statistics are in stark contrast to those obtained when asking if the individuals would vote in a national legislative election that was to take place tomorrow. The average participation level claimed for such an election is 77 percent, with little difference between the age groups: 74 percent of the 18–24 year olds, 77 percent of the 25–34 year olds, 81 percent of the 35–49 year olds, and 78 percent of the 50+ age group say they would vote.

These different variables provide an imperfect explanation for the level of participation in the elections. For a more complete picture, the nature of the election itself, or the way in which the election was perceived by the electorate must be understood. To do this we can follow the scheme provided by Lancelot (1968:150). Voters, according to Lancelot, participate more actively in elections when they perceive the political utility of their vote, which presupposes: (1) that the problems appear important to them, (2) that they have the possibility of choosing among several options and (3) that political competition influences

Table 7.3 Predictors of 1989 Participation in the European Election in France

	R^2	Added R^2
Demographics	0.13	
General Political Orientations	0.27	0.14
Habitual Voting	0.30	0.03
European Attitudes	0.31	0.01

the designation and orientation of political power. When viewed in this way the European elections constitute just about the least favorable conditions for participation because (1) Europe's problems are not at all, or very little known or understood, and thus cannot be perceived as important, (2) the programs of the various parties were quite similar as well as badly presented and (3) the complexity of European institutions and the lack of understanding of the functions of the Parliament do not give the electorate the impression that they are bestowing any form of power on those they elect.

These general characteristics were amplified in 1989 by three further factors which explain why there has been an increase in abstention in European elections from 39.3 percent in 1979 to 43.3 percent in 1984 and 51.3 percent in 1989. Firstly, the attraction of novelty was no longer present since this was the third European election. Secondly, and contrary to what had occurred in 1979 and 1984, the election campaigns were not at all focused on national issues, and no party leader attempted to use the election as a referendum on government policies. Lastly, and maybe most importantly, the elections came as the last of the largest number of elections conducted in rapid succession ever known in France: between May 1988 and June 1989, the French had voted six times. Surveys arranged by the CSA on the day of the European elections found that 50 percent of the abstainers had not voted because "there were too many elections", while 48 percent claimed that they were not well enough informed, and 44 percent said that they were "not interested in Europe".

Participation and the Strength of the Parties

The low participation level did not affect all parties uniformly, and mobilization differences were, as is shown in Table 7.4, quite significant. The turnout effect was strongly positive for the lists of the moderate right (those of the Centre and Union RPR-UDF) but negative for all other political forces. It does seem, according to the logic of second-order elections (Reif, 1985a; Reif and Schmitt, 1980; van der Eijk and Oppenhuis, 1990), that many voters wanted to give a 'warning' to the party in power, either by not voting or (more frequently) by actually voting differently than they would have voted in a (hypothetical) concurrent national election. Focussing purely on the column of turnout effects in Table 7.4 we see that the governing Socialist party was only marginally disadvantaged by the low participation level, whereas the Greens and the National Front were much more hurt by this effect. By referring to the principal determinants of the participation in the European elections (Table 7.3) we can propose a few hypotheses to explain these effects.

The first goes back to the voter's age and the difference between turnout of the different age groups in the European election and prospective turnout in national elections (see above). The strong positive turnout effect for the Centre and Union tickets stems from the fact that older voters, who traditionally choose the moderate conservative parties (Ysmal, 1990), vote in greater numbers than younger people. In this the situation is no different than in national elections, as the younger age group is more prone to vote for other parties. In contrast, the abstention of large numbers of young voters led to lower returns for the Greens in the European election and also, though less so, for the PS. Both of these parties normally do best amongst voters between the ages of 18 and 35. Amongst this age group, 75 percent of those who abstained in the European election but would have voted in a national election said they would have voted either Green or for the PS.

The reasons for the low participation rates in the case of the PC and the FN is more difficult to analyze because of the small numbers of people concerned as well as the very small differences observed in the surveys between the numbers of votes that would have been cast in national as opposed to European elections. The low turnout seems to be linked either to a lack of interest in European politics in general or to opposition to the European system itself. The former is more common amongst PC sympathizers, while the second is more applicable to those of the National Front. It appears, in effect, that while the position of Communist Party supporters on the scale of approval of the European system (Schmitt and Mannheimer, 1991a; van der Eijk and Oppenhuis, 1990) has no influence on their turnout, if they have little or no interest in European politics such supporters are less likely to turn out in a European election (more likely to turn out in a national election). The inverse, however, is true for the National Front, who would be able to mobilize highly anti-European voters in national elections, but not those who lack interest in European politics. Only more in-depth analyses on a larger sample could determine with any certainty which of these cross-pressures are most powerful.

Table 7.4   Quasi–switching and Turnout Effects in the 1989 European Election in France

	EE	NE	EE-NE	Quasi-Switching	Turnout Effect
PC	7.7	9.0	-1.3	-0.9	-0.4
PS	23.6	30.6	-7.0	-6.4	-0.6
Ecologiste	10.6	15.2	-4.6	-2.2	-2.4
Centre (CDS)	8.4	5.1	3.3	2.3	1.0
Union	28.9	26.7	2.2	-1.8	4.0
FN	11.7	9.9	1.8	3.3	-1.5
Other	8.9	3.5	5.4	5.7	-0.3

In conclusion, regardless of its determinants, it can be said that turnout had some effect on the results of the European elections and consequently on the distribution of seats. The stronger mobilization of the electorate in favor of the RPR-UDF ticket gave that group a bonus of 3 seats out of the 26 which it won.

Party Choice

Once the influence of the low participation rate has been analyzed, and its effects on the popularity of the various candidates or parties controlled, the question of whether there was an element of 'European specificity' in the distribution of the votes between the different parties or tickets can be assessed. The penultimate column of Table 7.4 shows that the differences between the European vote and the vote that would have been cast in a (hypothetical) concurrent national election are significant. On the one hand, the small parties belonging to the category 'others'—for instance, those of the extreme left or the Hunting, Fishing, Nature and Traditions movement—obtained unexpectedly high support (+6.4) compared to that which they would have obtained in a legislative election.[8] On the other hand, the Socialist Party received far fewer votes (–6.4) than it would have obtained in a national election. For the other groupings, the differences are less important, even if we take into account the fact that the National Front and the Centre did better in the European elections, while the Greens and the UDF/RPR coalition failed to maximize their potential support. Taking quasi-switching effects together with those of differential turnout, the overall effect was to benefit parties of the right at the expense of parties of the left (and especially the governing Socialists).

Overall, this difference between elections, as measured by the Pedersen (1979) index of volatility, affects about 25 percent of those electors who would have voted in the two elections. This percentage is not very different from that between successive pairs of national elections (25 percent for instance between the legislative elections of 1973 and 1978, 24 percent between the legislative election of 1986 and the Presidential one of 1988). However, one must bear in mind that the volatility measured here cannot arise from a real change in opinion through time but relates to differences in the circumstances of two types of election as viewed by voters at one point in time.

---

8 It should be taken into account that the Hunting, Fishing, Nature and Traditions ticket was not included in the list of possibilities presented to those interviewed when asked "if there was a General election tomorrow, which party would you vote for?"

Election Type, Voting System and Candidatures

The data presented thus far concerns, of course, different types of elections since, in France, 'national' elections are sometimes presidential and at other times legislative, both being different in context and geographic coverage. The Presidential election is the most decisive in the sense that the powers held by the President of the Republic are greater than those held by the National Assembly. The French people themselves consider the presidential vote to be the most important in their political system. Legislative elections have, since 1986, taken place in 577 districts while Presidential elections are held in only one. Thus the importance of the type of election, the voting procedures and the candidatures becomes clear. These factors are particularly important for European elections because completely different voting procedures are used, (see footnote 1), and the electorate considers them to be second-order elections.

The success of small parties or of 'theme-oriented' tickets appears to be a consequence of the electoral system. On the one hand, one-round proportional representation in one constituency permits such tickets to be national (contrary to majority balloting with two rounds in many constituencies, which requires a party to be sufficiently organized to be present everywhere). On the other hand, the voting system increases the fragmentation of the vote in so far as it liberates the voter from both strategic constraints (the so-called 'useful' vote) as well as from the influence of local leaders. In the case of a majority ballot with two rounds within a constituency framework, an elector's vote in the first round can be cast simply in order to prevent a particular candidate from entering the second round rather than on grounds of party affiliation. The vote is also affected by the personal qualities of the candidates, their understanding of the local context and their activities in the constituency (Ysmal, 1986; 1990). European candidates, even if running for re-election, are relatively unknown personally since they would have been elected on a national ticket and hold a very distant office elsewhere. As a consequence of these differences, strategic considerations are reduced, and circumstances encourage electors to vote "with their hearts rather than their heads" (Reif and Schmitt, 1980).

Such reasoning explains why votes for the ticket of the Centre, led by Simone Veil, would have been so much less in (hypothetical) concurrent legislative elections than in the European elections. A nationally recognized and appreciated personality,[9] and an ex-president of the European Parliament, Ms. Veil was undoubtedly able to profit from a popularity that her party does not

---

9 Simone Veil appears to be the most popular leader of all the parties of the right according to all measurements. Her popularity is in fact as great amongst those claiming to be on the left as it is among those on the right.

have. The CDS is a small party, badly organized and not nationally represented, which the majority of the electorate had never heard of, and for which they had never previously had the opportunity to vote (Ysmal, 1989). More significantly, the Centre ticket, which is not a part of the scheme of traditional alliances either within the UDF or between the UDF and the RPR, obtained votes from people who would normally have voted for one of those parties. Thus, the Centre's gains led to a deficit for the Union ticket led by Valéry Giscard d'Estaing. During legislative elections, however, where the power of alliances, strategic considerations (the union of the moderate right against both the left and the National Front), as well as the influence of incumbents all play a part, some of those who voted for the Centre in the European election would shift and vote again for the UDF/RPR coalition.

In the same way, the National Front gets better results at European elections thanks to the presence of Jean-Marie le Pen, who replaces less well known legislative candidates. The Communist Party, however, is slightly disadvantaged in a European election since it can no longer profit from the presence of its local notables (Mayors), who, ever since the intensification of the PCF crisis, have become more decisive than ever in sustaining what is left of the communist influence (Platone and Ranger, 1981; Courtois, 1988).

Second-order Elections

The voting system at the European election thus favored small parties and new tickets. Can this factor alone explain the differences between the 'European and (hypothetical) legislative results? An additional factor of potential importance is the second-order nature of European elections (Reif and Schmitt, 1980).

The absence of systematic figures on previous elections as well as the varying configuration of the candidatures makes it difficult to confirm the hypothesis that, as second-order elections, the European elections encouraged a more ideological vote or one that was, at least, more determined by left/right position. However, it seems likely that the benefits that we have seen accruing to small or new parties were magnified by the fact that the ballot does not determine the make-up of a future government. Above all, the difference between the results obtained by the Socialist Party in the European election and the results they would have obtained in concurrent legislative elections (7.0 percent) suggests that, in conformity with the predictions of Reif and Schmitt, the ruling party loses votes when electors wish to send a message to the Government, or to remind it of electoral promises that have not been kept, without removing it from power.

This pattern can be confirmed by comparing the results of the PS in the three European elections, with those obtained in preceding national elections

(Table 7.5). At European elections, the party loses vote share compared with national elections. Even though this data cannot show the evolution of public opinion between the different ballots, they do show that the difference between the European and national elections was much greater in 1984 and 1989 (–17.5 in 1984 relative to the legislative elections of 1981, and –11.2 in 1989 relative to those of 1986) than it had been in 1979 when the PS was not in power and could not be chastised for government failings (–2.8 in relation to 1978).

The extent to which the mobilization of the electorate favored a party can be measured by the conformity of party affiliation with votes for that party.[10] If the Socialist Party was victim of a protest during the European elections, then one should find that those who claim an affiliation with the Socialist Party (1) are less likely to vote for their party at the European than at the national level, and (2) that this propensity is stronger in their case than for supporters of other parties. Table 7.6 confirms this pattern. While 91 percent of those who claimed affiliation with the PS in 1989 said that they would vote for the Party in eventual legislative elections, only 74 percent said they would do so at the European elections—12 percent choosing the ecologists and 6 percent the Centre. The difference between the two votes is effectively bigger for the PS than for other parties. However, this second-order effect appears to be relatively limited in the sense that, with the exception of the National Front and the Greens who mobilize their electorate effectively regardless of the type of election, European elections also produce shifts in party sympathies for the Communist Party and the moderate right (Centre and Union), shifts which are obviously linked to the voting procedures and candidature systems in use.

Table 7.5 Results of the PS in European and Previous National Elections (Percentage of the Valid Vote)

	Year	PS	Difference EE and Most Recent NE
Parliamentary	1978	26.3	
European	1979	23.5	-2.8
Parliamentary	1981	38.3	
European	1984	20.8	-17.5
Parliamentary	1988	34.8	
European	1989	23.6	-11.2

---

10 The question was "Which party do you feel the closest to" followed by a list of parties.

Table 7.6 Difference Between European and National Party Choice for Identifiers of Each of the Parties

Party	% Identifiers Voting for Party They Identify With in National Elections	% Identifiers Voting for Party They Identify With in European Elections	N
PC	92.3	84.6	26
PS	91.0	73.8	149
Greens	90.6	87.9	33
Centre	81.8	50.0	22
Union	88.6	76.3	114
FN	95.2	95.5	22

European Issues

A third possible explanation for the results may come from the issues on which the elections were based, or on the fact that voter attitudes regarding Europe may have influenced the choice of candidates during the European vote, something which does not occur during national elections where only national political issues come into play. Such a hypothesis assumes, however, that, on the one hand, the voters have distinct attitudes on European issues and, on the other, that the parties or the competing candidates profess different opinions on this subject.

The electoral campaign did not really help clarify the issues surrounding the accelerating rate of European integration (Single European Act, Schengen Treaty, common currency or other such issues). Nor did it elucidate the powers of the European Parliament; nor even describe, whether accepted or not, what precisely was meant by 'European integration'. Despite this obscurity, there was at least a debate, in the sense that parties declared themselves to be either 'European', and were perceived as such by the public, or 'anti-European', or at least having serious reservations in this regard.

Three different tickets represented the diverse modalities of the anti-European stream. Firstly, the Communist Party, which did renounce its denunciation of the EC as a 'war machine' threatening the socialist heritage, nevertheless continued to criticize 'Liberal Europe' which supposedly favors only the power of money and is responsible for the unemployment of workers, who are sacrificed on the alter of profit maximization. Secondly, the National Front, using the theme (which is Gaullist in origin) of the Europe of Nations, opposed all transfers of sovereignty related to the Nation or its heritage (defense, currency, protection of national borders etc.), and also criticized the anonymous bureaucracy of Brussels which, without accountability or controls, could decide what each nation must do. Lastly, the Hunting, Fishing, Nature and Traditions list built its electoral appeal on the rejection of European rulings that concerned traditional hunting and fishing in certain French regions, and vigorously denounced the dangers of a centralized European state which does not respect regional distinctions.

The political debate was, however, more confused in the pro-European camp. At the institutional level, Simone Veil and the Centre ticket, who spoke of a "United States of Europe", were really the only group foreseeing a federal future with any clarity. Meanwhile, the PS, as well as the Greens and the Union, supported transfers of sovereignty and a single monetary policy. They all called for an extension of the powers of the European Parliament so as to improve democratic accountability and control. Finally, and unanimously, they all demanded that Europe have a social dimension. An especially attentive ear was required to distinguish the subtle differences between (a) the Socialist Party and the ecologists who, while supporting the Social Charter, slid into a critique of liberalism and a Europe responsive only to the laws of the market, (b) the centrists who wanted a "community charter of fundamental social rights", and (c) the Union RPR/UDF ticket which stubbornly reaffirmed their attachment to the "social ambition of Europe". Finally, Valéry Giscard d'Estaing's position appeared ambiguous because of his cohabitation with the RPR, a fraction which is very hostile towards any hints of federal ambitions and towards many of the proposed transfers of sovereignty.

As for the voters, their attitudes were not much different. Taking the index of general EC approval used by Schmitt and Mannheimer (1991a), 23 percent of the voters at the European election had negative attitudes towards Europe, while 17 percent were more or less neutral, and 60 percent were strongly for the European Community. If this data indicates substantial support for the European system, it must also be noted that the French people are in general more favorable to the principle of unification than to its practical and day to day application. While 86 percent of them claim to be "very much or to some extent for efforts being made to unify Western Europe", only 45 percent think that "France's membership in the European Community is a good thing"; and while 75 percent confirm that "the establishment of the Single European Market by 1992 is a very important issue", only 52 percent say that "France has on balance benefitted from being a member of the EC". Added to this ambivalence is a certain lack of real interest in the European system, and a very weak interest in the election campaign (Cayrol, 1991). These two factors help explain why European issues were not salient enough to permit the detection of different behavioral patterns in the European election as opposed to those in national elections. It is possible to compare the differences between the votes in the

European and legislative elections in relation to the position of the voters on the index of general EC approval. Generally speaking, voters opposed to the EC system were more likely to vote for anti-European parties in the European elections (PC, FN and the 'Hunters' ticket) than were those favoring the system, who overwhelmingly supported political parties well established in Europe. However, since these same differences would also have helped determine national partisanship, this factor does not necessarily indicate that European issues were an important factor in the distinctive outcome of the European election. In order to prove this, it would need to be demonstrated that the choice of party would have been different in the case of a national election, a demonstration made difficult by the differences in the candidacies that would have occurred at such an election and in the choice of candidates included in the survey.[11] The data show that the differences between elections are rather small, except in the case of the Socialist Party which mobilized its pro-European electorate quite ineffectively in the European elections.

In fact, European issues seemed to have only clearly helped the vote for the 'other' parties and candidates, namely the head of the Hunting, Fishing, Nature and Traditions ticket, who received the votes of people from all parts of the political spectrum who were opposed to Europe. For the other parties no such effect was observed

In conclusion, the choice made during the European elections seems to have been, in the first place, a consequence of voting procedures, the structure of the candidacies that it induced, and the freedom that it offered from the system of majority vote in two rounds that is used in other elections. To these differences must be added, at least for the Socialist party in power, a protest or warning vote. The hypothesis that the specific influence of European issues had an effect is verified only partially and incidentally.

Effects of the Elections

As in 1979 and 1984, the outcome of the 1989 European elections had important consequences on political life. However, unlike the two previous elections, the 1989 election had less of an effect on the relations between government and opposition than on the structure of the whole public debate.

The effects on relations between government and opposition, while not negligible, in fact appear limited. For the second time, the Socialist Party in power put on a mediocre performance. This did not, however, lead the opposition parties to question the legitimacy of the government. Nor did they demand early elections to reconcile the 'pays réel' (current political environment) with

---

11 Survey SOFRES for *Le Figaro*.

the 'pays légal' (actual constitutional constraints), as established by the presidential election of 1988 and the legislative ones which followed the re-election of François Mitterrand.

It is true that the situation in 1989 was profoundly different from that of 1984. In 1984, the low vote gained by the socialists corresponded to a record unpopularity of the President of the Republic and the Mauroy government; five years later, by contrast, François Mitterrand and the Prime Minister Michel Rocard were very popular, as in May 1989 62 percent and 65 percent respectively claimed to "have confidence in them to resolve the problems facing France today".[12] In consequence, after a nonpolitical electoral campaign, the voters put less emphasis on governmental issues. While in 1984 only 18 percent of those questioned claimed "not to have taken into account their attitude toward the government when voting", there were as many as 36 percent making the same claim in 1989. Thus, the percentage of voters who said they wanted either to "manifest their opposition to the government" or to "give them a warning" fell from 51 percent in 1984 to 36 percent in 1989.[13] In the end, the results obtained by the RPR/UDF alliance, led by Giscard d'Estaing, were quite mediocre, and did not justify the ex-President of the Republic or Jacques Chirac immediately presenting themselves as challengers to the government's majority.

The Disruption of the Party System

In reality, the major effects of the European election, just as in the case of previous European elections, were felt on the entire French party system. European elections have often been referred to as the 'midwife of new parties' and this is most apparent in France. In 1979, while the UDF and the RPR opposed each other on two separate tickets, the European election permitted the emergence and the structuring of a Chirac electorate which served as model for that which Jacques Chirac would reunite under his name during the Presidential elections of 1981 (Ysmal, 1986). In 1984, it was the National Front that made its appearance. Not only did it win 11 percent of the vote at its first attempt, but it also established a social and geographical base which would be reinforced with each subsequent election (Perrineau, 1989). In 1989, without even mentioning the minor tickets like that of André Goustat, it was the Greens who made a remarkable entry onto the political scene after fifteen years of marginalization in presidential and legislative elections.

12 Exit poll by IFOP. See 'Results of the European Elections', *Le Monde*, June 1989.

13 Exit poll by IFOP. See 'Results of the European elections', *Le Monde*, June 1989.

Of course the successes of these diverse political forces cannot be attributed only to voting procedures in European elections. The acquisition of large numbers of voters by parties that had until then remained small parties is obviously due either to specific partisan strategies (as in the case of the RPR in 1979) or to new demands by the electorate (such as with the FN and the Greens). At the same time, as was demonstrated by Lipset and Rokkan (1967), in order for new parties to establish their strategies, take advantage of the new demands and bring them into the political arena, it is also necessary to have a suitable political agenda and favorable voting procedures. This is precisely what European elections offer, both in the sense that they contain no real government issues, and also in the sense that the system of proportional representation permits the expression and representation of diverse minority opinions. In 1989, the disruption of the party system was at its maximum. Instead of the four political forces existing at the end of the 1970s, there were six political forces competing in elections with a chance of obtaining significant support. Thus, this European election, like its predecessors, encouraged a redistribution of power between forces within the French political system.

In 1989, the National Front was also a victim of the disruption since, compared with the Presidential elections of 1988, when it obtained 14.6 percent of the votes, it saw a deterioration of its influence. At the same time, while it did maintain a high level of support, the party became more institutionalized and thus had a greater influence in political debate. Though the party has been excluded from the national Parliament by the majority vote system since 1988, it asserts its presence in the European Parliament. Certain principal party leaders could thus claim the title of European deputy, which ensured simultaneously a good institutional image, a legal guarantee of immunity, and taxpayer support for party finances. Furthermore, it is from the success registered at European elections (confirmed at other elections but without any seats being won) that the FN became a strong force in the conservative camp, presenting the parties of the moderate right with a dilemma: either deal with the FN (join forces with the devil) or risk never gaining a majority.

The European elections came at a good time for the Greens. They were able to consolidate, at a national level, the success that they had—generally in medium-sized cities or large towns—in the municipal elections of 1989. The party of Antoine Waechter had until that point been marginalized and even ridiculed by a political class that was persuaded that the country would never succumb to the ecological disease. Of course, proportional representation and the second-order character of the ballot were, for them as for the FN, powerful allies. However, the fact that these elections took place within a European framework, and that the electoral campaign of 1989 was focussed on the future of Europe, were incontestably factors which favored the Greens. All the surveys indicate that voters who are sensitive to the theme of 'political renewal' are also—and French political leaders tend to forget this—strongly in favor of protecting the environment.

To the cases of the National Front and the Greens must be added that of the Centre. Since the beginning of the Fifth Republic the French political center, tugged between the left and right, has almost always leaned towards the right in legislative and Presidential elections. The majority vote system, and the bi-polarization that it creates, has not permitted the center to exist on its own and has constrained it to being no more than a part of the right. The European election of 1989 was a privileged though dangerous moment of autonomous existence. The Centre, with the Veil ticket, confirmed both its desire to affirm its individuality and its capacity to do so.[14] Meanwhile, this independence also demonstrated that, even at such a time, the Centre only has a weak electoral influence, confirming the reality of its situation within a political 'family' or ideology (Cayrol, 1989).

The Difficulties of Alliances

At any rate, this growth by the Greens, the National Front, the Centre and—tangentially—the small tickets apparently tends to modify French political debate. European elections served as a reminder of what can be forgotten during Presidential and legislative elections: that neither of the big political coalitions hold a majority of public support: neither, on the one hand, the UDF/RPR alliance (with 37.2 percent of the declared votes if the scores of the Giscard d'Estaing and Veil tickets are added) nor, on the other, the PS (with a total 33.5 percent for the PS, PC and extreme left combined). In order to govern the country with the true consent of a majority of the population, the RPR and UDF, like the PS are forced to reflect on their alliances.

For the RPR, and the dominating fraction of the UDF, this includes firstly making room for the centrists and in particular the CDS. The European elections reminded them that, even if the Centre has less electoral weight than it liked to believe it had, this alliance would be essential to winning future elections. It is thus sensible for the RPR to treat the CDS with enough respect so that they will not again go it alone with dreams of independence. A second and fundamental question, however, concerns the strategy to adopt with regard to the National Front. Should an alliance be accepted, even informally, with the extreme right, or should all links be refused in the name of moral and

---

14 In 1988, the CDS had formed its own group within the National Assembly (Union of the Centre) and, during the entire period of the Rocard government, had affirmed its independence from the RPR and the other groupings of the UDF by voting or abstaining on certain packages.

democratic values? Should the RPR attempt to reduce the power of the FN by tackling some of its themes, such as French identity, immigration and security, or should it avoid any slide towards the right? The first question was answered with a refusal to create any political or electoral alliances with the FN but the second has not been tackled, due primarily to internal divisions in both the RPR and UDF, which continue to hinder the development of common political positions related to future legislative and Presidential elections.

For the Socialist Party, the question of the Greens is obviously the most crucial, in the sense that the Greens recruit two-thirds of their voters from within the ranks of the left. Again, the issues are delicate. Should they or should they not believe in the permanence of the ecologists? In 1989 many socialist leaders still refused to. Is it possible to tame the party of Antoine Waechter by creating, along with strictly obedient Greens, a 'green and pink' tendency? Should electoral alliances with the Greens be promoted? Should the PS's program be made 'greener'? Should the idea of economic growth be completely abandoned, as well as that of nuclear energy, all for 10 to 11 percent of young voters?

The European elections of 1989 brought to light the issues and questions which would be at the center of political life in France until the decisive national legislative elections of 1993 and the Presidential ones of 1995, and brought about a sensible modification of the issues at the center of political debate.

The Emergence of Issues

The European elections evidently contributed to a revision of the themes about which political forces compete. The most immediate consequence of these results was the renewed debate on voting procedures to be used during the next legislative elections. Traditionally, as well as out of vested interest, since they seemed able to win the next elections, the UDF and RPR reaffirmed their preference for the two-round majority vote system. The National Front and the Greens, on the other hand, demanded the adoption of proportional representation for the legislative elections which, while eliminating the need to create alliances, guarantees them a parliamentary presence. The debate was most vivid within the PS and the Government. The socialists were, as always, divided between 'proportionalists' for whom the ballot must assure a true representation of public opinion, and partisans of the majority system, for whom efficiency and the creation of stable majorities are of the utmost importance. Yet the debate also dealt with two distinct visions of the future of the PS. The adoption of proportionality would signify that the party expected to maintain a maximum parliamentary representation at a time of lower public support; the maintenance of the majority method, on the other hand, would signify that the party was confirming its intention to assemble other political forces around it, in particular the ecologists.[15] The alliance between Michel Rocard and Laurent Fabius was created on this latter basis and was sealed three years later with the accession of Fabius to the post of First Secretary of the PS and the designation of Rocard as 'definite' candidate for the party at the Presidential elections foreseen for 1995.

The final, though probably the most important, effect of the 1989 European elections, was the considerable reinforcement of the importance of the European theme itself in French political debate. Because it was less centered on internal political issues than the preceding elections of 1979 and 1984, the vote of 1989 did not simply elect French representatives to the European Parliament but also opened a wider debate on the European system and its future. It is clear that Europe has become a more important theme in the eyes of militants, party leaders, and the electorate. The fact that attitudes to Europe did not directly affect voter choices or, in the case of the intention to vote in national elections, the distribution of votes between parties, does not imply that the voters were indifferent to the diverse visions of Europe that the political parties presented, or to what Europe could do for France and France for Europe. On the contrary, the voters hostile to Europe voted for anti-European parties while those who accept a political and economic Europe voted for parties who defended—even though obscurely—these positions. French domestic politics is now more in step with Europe.

In conclusion, it can be noted that the outcome of the European elections of 1989 takes on different faces depending on whether one is looking at Europe, at national political life, at the issues of concern, or at the behavior of the electorate. On the national scene, the 1989 elections, like the two preceding ones, contributed to the fragmentation of the party system and to electoral volatility. This result is due to the fact that a system of proportional representation is used rather than a majoritarian system, not to the intrinsic nature of the European elections themselves.[16] Of course, voting procedures do not create new electoral demands or new small parties or the increasing discomfort of the French with their political system, their parties and their leaders; but it does permit their expression within an election in which national power is not at stake. Furthermore, the effect of the proportional vote leaves its mark even

---

15 The issue was decided in March 1992 with the maintenance of the majority system.

16 Regional elections also function proportionally. The recent election of March 1992 showed some of the characteristics of European elections: multiplication of the number of lists on the ballot, increased electoral support for marginal parties or independent candidates, which never resulted in regional majorities, making the Regional Councils ungovernable. See Habert, Perrineau and Ysmal (1992).

when the election is over. On one hand the parties which emerged have been legitimized and tend to persevere, on the other hand, new partisan loyalties are created through the substitution of an 'opinion vote' for a 'Government vote'. Thus, the existence of European elections makes it more and more difficult to return to the constraints of the majority vote electoral system, and sows increasing disorder in French structures and loyalties.

CHAPTER 8

Germany:
A Bored Electorate

Hermann Schmitt

The German political landscape has changed dramatically since the Summer of 1989. The election to the European Parliament held at that time was the last country-wide election in West Germany before re-unification. It thus represents the last baseline for comparison with elections that followed unification, a fact which gives it special significance. At the same time the events associated with unification may well have overtaken possible national consequences which this European election would otherwise have had, and so may be seen as diminishing its political importance. In this chapter we will try to put this election into proper perspective—to identify its 'baseline character' as well as what may emerge as its lasting significance for German politics.

Background

Direct elections to the European Parliament have been identified as second–order elections (Reif and Schmitt, 1980). Characteristic of this type of election is the fact that its immediate arena-specific (i.e. European) political significance is less than its meaning for the primary (i.e. national) political arena. As a consequence, the outcome of such elections has been seen in the past, in Germany as elsewhere, to depend more on the overall political climate of the first-order political arena—and in particular on the popularity of the national government—than on the political climate in the European arena (Reif, 1985a).

In June 1989, when direct elections to the European Parliament were held in Germany for the third time, the domestic electoral cycle had just passed midterm. As is common at such times (cf. Dinkel, 1977), popular approval of the federal government was down, although improving again, according to the polls, after having passed the absolute bottom of its slump (Figure 8.1). Electoral prospects for the parties of the center-right federal government coalition were thought to be somewhere between very bad and disastrous.

Covering the full electoral cycle, Figure 8.1 illustrates the national political context of the 1989 European elections in greater detail. Hypothetical vote

**Figure 8.1 The Political Climate in the Federal Republic:
January 1987 — December 1990**

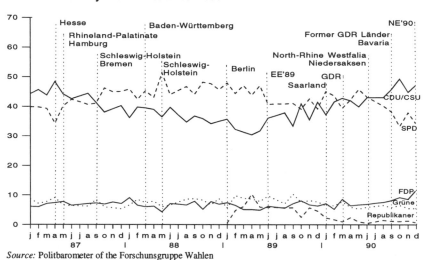

Source: Politbarometer of the Forschungsgruppe Wahlen

intentions ("if an election were to be held next Sunday") for the christian-democratic CDU/CSU, the major governing party, had declined almost continuously over a period of more than two years following the federal elections of January 1987. Support for the social-democratic SPD, the major opposition party, had increased during the same period, though to a lesser extent. The SPD was not able to benefit from all of the swing away from the government.

Three second-order national elections preceding the European ones had seen the federal government parties lose state and local power.[1] The gradual

---

1 Overshadowed by the Barschel Affair, the state elections of Schleswig-Holstein in June 1988 terminated an era of CDU dominance which had lasted almost four decades. Uwe Barschel, CDU-Prime Minister of Schleswig-Holstein, had misused his powers and committed suicide when the story was disclosed. A landslide SPD victory inaugurated a social democratic state government, and Björn Engholm (SPD) was elected Prime Minister. Six months later, the CDU and FDP experienced another "bitter defeat" (according to Helmut Kohl) when the CDU-FDP coalition government of Berlin lost its parliamentary majority and was replaced by a red-green Senate formed by the SPD and the Alternative Liste (the Berlin wing of the Grünen). It was in this election that the Republikaner, an extreme right and nationalist party founded in 1983 and contesting elections in West Berlin for the first time, polled an unexpected 7.5 percent of the vote. This right-wing breakthrough was mainly explained by the party's campaign emphasis on the immigration issue and the general shortage of suitable housing associated with it. (Incidentally, this breakthrough happened about three month after Franz-Josef Strauss suddenly died and left the West German far-right without a forceful and integrative leader). Losses sustained by the federal coalition parties were repeated in the Hesse local elections of March 1989. As in West

erosion of government support came to an end, according to the polls, in April 1989—about two months ahead of the 1989 European Parliament elections. After that the position of the CDU/CSU slowly improved again, and finally overtook the SPD in the Summer of 1990. Helmut Kohl and his government coalition won the first all-German Bundestagswahl (parliamentary elections) later that year by a comfortable margin.

Second-order elections are subject to the cyclical evolution of party support, while at the same time helping to shape that evolution.[2] However, their results are not totally determined by the national political climate. Arena-specific considerations can also have effects. The importance of these arena-specific factors varies between different sorts of second-order elections, and their weight in past European elections was not particular heavy. Still, there is some EC-specific background to the third European election in Germany that is worth mentioning.

The Federal Republic for years was among the most enthusiastic supporters of European integration in general, and of the European Community in particular. The announcement in the mid-seventies of direct elections to the European Parliament—and the actual conduct of those elections in 1979—caused an extraordinary increase in favorable attitudes towards the Community. However, soon after that first election, West Germans came to realize that their hopes had not materialized. Contrary to the expectations of many, the directly elected European Parliament was not able to determine the course of EC politics or to democratize the institutional arrangements of the Community. European euphoria which had reached a peak in Germany in 1979 was followed by widespread feelings of disenchantment with the Community.

During much of the following decade, Community politics had to cope with the 'Southern enlargement' (the admission of Greece, Spain and Portugal to full membership in the EC). It was only in the late eighties that the next 'grand design' of EC development—the completion of the single European market—once again brought the Community towards the center of the political

---

Berlin, both the left (SPD and Grünen) and the extreme right (NPD and Republikaner) were able to strengthen their positions, and a red-green Magistrat took over in the city of Frankfurt.

2 There is some dispute about whether the evolution of government parties popularity is indeed cyclical and how one should be able to demonstrate this empirically. Using weekly poll data on government parties' popularity, van der Eijk (1987) demonstrated that Dutch politics hardly reveals any imprint of an electoral cycle. He showed, moreover, that the usual polynomial regression approach to the phenomenon can be misleading due to existence of autocorrelated errors in the time series. However, as the Dutch situation is known from earlier research to constitute, within the European Community of the Nine, the only deviant case in this respect (e.g. Reif, 1985a:24ff), van der Eijk's work might be better understood as a further characterization of Dutch deviance than as a proof of the inappropriateness of the cyclical approach as such.

stage. This time, however, the West German public was among the more skeptical observers (Schmitt, 1989). Fears about detrimental effects were entertained on the left (regarding social dumping) and on the right of the political spectrum (regarding an uncontrolled influx of foreigners). Much like the popularity of the federal government, the European Community stood poorly in public opinion as the third European elections approached. Approval of EC-membership, a rough but quite sensitive indicator of generalized support for the European Community, was below the level reached ten years earlier, and well below the Community average at the time (Figure 8.2).

The actual result of the 1989 European election in Germany was not as catastrophic for the parties of the federal government as some observers had expected. The minor coalition partner, the FDP, managed to pass the five percent threshold and to regain representation in the European Parliament. Liberals as well as Christian-Democrats did register severe losses compared to the federal elections of 1987; but the corresponding gains did not go to the SPD or Grünen (Greens), who showed themselves unable to profit from the poor performance of the government parties. The most spectacular feature of the election was that the extreme-right Republikaner were able to secure, for the first time in a federation-wide election, over seven percent of the vote (see Table 8.1).

In marked contrast to most other EC countries, German participation in the 1989 European election was higher than in 1984. It reached 62.3 percent—a

Figure 8.2 EC Membership Approval in West Germany 1973–1990 Compared to Average Approval Rates in the Community (proportions are percent positive answers)

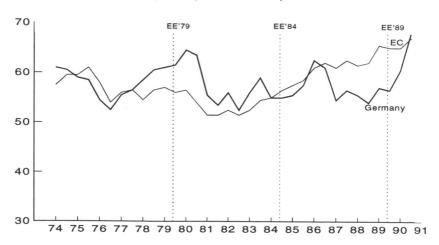

Moving average over two time points displayed. For Fall 1990 (EB34) the German findings are representative for the united Germany.
Source: Eurobarometer 1974–1991

level close to the 1979 election and considerably exceeding the 1984 result. However, while this elevated turnout figure did not fuel concerns about deficient support for the Community, neither was it high enough to put such concerns to rest.

Turnout

Turnout in European Elections

Voting is not compulsory in Germany. Hence, one of the distinctive features of European elections here is that turnout is low. And though participation was up in the 1989 European election compared to that held in 1984, it was still low compared to turnout in other German elections.

Over the last decade turnout in federal elections has fallen by 10 percent.[3] If one looks back as far as 1949, however, electoral participation in Bundestagswahlen does not show any particular trend and averages an unusually high 86 percent (see Table 8.2). The average turnout in West German local elections is about 10 percent lower, and is declining in most states. Next in rank-order are state elections (Landtagswahlen, which coincide with local elections in the city states of Berlin, Hamburg and Bremen) with an average participation rate of 72 percent over 131 elections. While state electoral participation is declining in some Länder (mostly in those with above-average participation

Table 8.1 The Third European Parliament Elections of June 1989: West German Results in Perspective

	NE'90	EE'89	NE'87	EE'84	NE'83	NE'80	EE'79
Grünen*	5.1	8.4	8.3	8.2	5.6	1.5	3.2
SPD	33.5	37.3	37.0	37.4	38.2	42.9	40.8
FDP	11.0	5.6	9.1	4.8	7.0	10.6	6.0
CDU/CSU	43.8	37.7	44.3	45.9	48.8	44.5	49.2
Republikaner	2.1	7.1					
Others**	4.5	3.7	1.4	3.7	0.5	0.5	0.8
Turnout	77.8	62.3	84.3	56.8	89.1	88.6	65.7

Note: NE = national elections (Bundestagswahlen); percentages of the valid 'second vote' are given here; EE = European elections; '-' = party did not compete.
* Combining for NE'90 West-German Grüne (3.9%, not represented in parliament) and East-German Bündnis 90 = Grüne (1.2%, represented).
** Including for NE'90 the PDS/Linke Liste (formerly SED; 2.4%, represented).

3 Considering turnout only in the 'old' FRG in the 1990 election.

Table 8.2 West German Electoral Participation: Federal, State, Local and European Elections 1949-1991

Elections	Mean	Trend	N
Federal Elections (Bundestagswahlen)	86.3	0.07	12
Local Elections (Kommunalwahlen)	75.6	-0.49	75
State Elections (Landtagswahlen)	72.2	-0.07	131
European Elections	61.6	-0.37	3

Note: For local and state elections, trend coefficients are averages of state-specific trends.

levels), it is on the rise in others, and there is no clear average trend. Turnout in European elections is lower still. Over the three elections held, an average of about 62 percent of those entitled to vote participated. In all three European election years, no turnout rate—whether in national, state or local elections— was below the European rate.

On the basis of turnout averages, then, European elections in West Germany clearly rank third, after federal elections in first place and local and state elections together in second place. Nevertheless, turnout differences between European elections and neighboring federal elections vary greatly according to the specifics of the electoral contests concerned.[4] This turnout difference was at an unprecedented minimum (15 percent) in 1989/90 when European election turnout was up, while participation in the following federal election was under 80 percent for the first time since 1949.

Mobilizing the 1989 European Vote

West German parties seem to have mobilized their final support at different times during the pre-electoral period. Between November 1988 and April 1989, as shown in our pre-election surveys, the SPD's share of prospective votes increased (from 24 to 29 percent of those entitled to vote), while the number of likely christian-democratic (CDU and CSU) voters stayed at about

---

4 Both the first and the third European elections were conducted in a year preceding a federal election, while the second was held the year after the 1983 Bundestagswahl. This might indicate that the mobilizing 'test-election' aspect, inherent in any second-order election, was less acute in 1984 and one is tempted to attribute the extraordinary low German turnout in this second European election to that difference. On the other hand, the federal elections of 1980 (Schmidt against Strauss) and of 1983 (plebiscite on FDP change of government coalition) were highly politicized and ideologically polarized. Those of 1987 (Kohl against Rau) and of 1990 (plebiscite on Kohl's unification policy) were far less closely contested, and the outcome of these elections was widely perceived to be a foregone conclusion (cf. Forschungsgruppe Wahlen, 1987; 1990b).

23 percent (see Table 8.3).[5] Our second pre-electoral survey was conducted exactly when public support for CDU and CSU reached its minimum. These parties' popularity recovered afterwards,[6] and so did their prospective votes in the European election. Our post-election survey shows the CDU/CSU share of votes considerably increased (from 22 percent in April to 27 percent in June), while the SPD evidently failed to mobilize additional support during the last weeks before the election. Two more parties were among the late mobilizers according to our findings: the Grünen on the left of the political spectrum, and the Republikaner on the far right. The Grünen were able to more than double their support between April and June (from 2.8 to 5.8 percent) and the Republikaner—hardly known in Fall 1988 and not yet coded separately

Table 8.3 The Evolution of European Vote Intentions and Reported Party Choice in Successive Waves of the European Election Study 1989 (percentages)

	Oct	Apr	Jun
Grünen	4	3	6
SPD	24	29	29
FDP	3	3	2
CDU/CSU	23	22	27
Republikaner	na	1	4
Others	1	1	2
Will/Did Vote Blank	1	0	1
Will/Did Not Vote	38	31	19
Don't Know	7	10	11
Respondents Aged 18 and Older	986	962	1135

na = not ascertained, base = entire adult population, voting or not.

5 These and the following analyses of the findings from our 1989 election study have been performed on the basis of samples (a) restricted to respondents aged 18 and older, and (b) weighted in order to improve representativeness according to a socio-demographic weighting routine provided by the fieldwork-institute EMNID. An adjustment of the parties' share of the vote according to the actual result (a 'political weighting') was not used, except for purposes of comparability with other chapters in the tables that all chapters have in common (Tables 8.4 to 8.6 in this chapter).

6 Among the reasons cited were a major cabinet reshuffle (April 13, 1989), the revision of government policies (Regierungserklärung of April 29, 1989), and the Gorbachev visit a few days before the European elections. The publicity surrounding the Gorbachev visit in particular—he was given an enthusiastic reception—might have contributed to the improvement of the image of the federal government.

from "others" in our October survey—almost tripled their prospective votes in the same period (from 1.4 in April to 3.9 percent in June).

The FDP, the other small party of the West German party system at the time, older than the other two and more centrist and less radical in the eyes of the voters,[7] was hardly able to gain additional support during the months before the election. This liberal party has made a political living out of its pivotal position in national (and frequently also in state and local) government formation when neither of the two major parties was able to muster an absolute majority in parliament. Much of its national electoral support is known to result from tactical voting: usually more than one in two 'second vote' FDP voters (and occasionally as many as 70 percent, as in the federal election of 1983) support with the 'first vote' the constituency candidate of one of the two major parties—and among these predominantly the candidate of the federal coalition partner (Forschungsgruppe Wahlen, 1990a:699).[8] Such considerations are irrelevant in European elections where each voter has just one vote, and where the FDP is not needed for any government majority. As a consequence, the electoral prospects of the FDP are systematically damaged in these electoral contests.

Due to characteristics of its core clientele—which typically belongs to the old middle and upper class, has some higher education, is rather well off, and shares a decidedly pro-European outlook—the FDP needs to invest less mobilization effort than other parties in getting 'their people' to the European ballot boxes. However, the main question for liberals has been whether this core clientele suffices to allow the party to pass the five percent hurdle applied in European (as in national and state) elections. Electoral algebra suggests that this is more easily achieved with lower overall mobilization;[9] and in June 1989 the rise in overall participation fell just short of the point that would have prevented German liberals from regaining representation in the European Parliament.

---

7 A popular view which might be doubted. Within the traditional cleavage structure of the West German party system, the small FDP occupies 'polar' positions on both the lay versus catholic and on the labor versus capital dimensions, and might therefore be understood to be the most 'extremist' of the traditional parties (cf. Schmitt, 1987b).

8 Federal electoral law provides voters with two votes: a first vote (Erststimme), with which they contribute to the election of a constituency candidate; and a second (Zweitstimme), which is given to party lists and determines the parliamentary strength of parties.

9 At first sight, this reasoning seems to be at odds with the observation that the FDP failed to pass the 5 percent threshold in 1984, when European turnout reached its lowest level hitherto. One must not forget, however, that the FDP had to reestablish a core of stable party support after its federal coalition change in 1982, which caused a good part of its 'social-liberal' leadership, its middle-level elite, and its rank and file to leave the party. This process was far from being completed by the Summer of 1984.

Changing Determinants of European Electoral Participation

Describing electoral mobilization is one thing, explaining individual turnout another. In what follows an effort will be made to explain the participation of individual Germans in the 1989 European elections. Determinants of electoral participation in 1989 are compared to those in 1979 to add some perspective to the result.[10] Dichotomous dependent variables measure intentions to participate as stated before each election and actual participation as reported afterwards.[11] Four groups of independent variables are considered in stagewise regression: social-structural characteristics, measures of political orientation (involvement), habitual voting (disposition), and European attitudes. Those indicators form two sets: an extended one that makes the best possible use of the survey data gathered in the framework of our 1989 election study; and a restricted one that incorporates only those variables also available for studying the 1979 European election.[12] The variables in the unrestricted set were introduced in Chapter 3, while indicators available for comparison between the two time points are presented here.

---

10 For the 1989 election, the second and third wave of surveys are employed, while the 1979 data are taken from Eurobarometer surveys number 11 and 12 which were conducted in April and October 1979. There is no 1979 survey equivalent to that which immediately followed the 1989 European election, but the regular October Eurobarometer (number 12) did ask questions about participation in the June elections. It is true that greater temporal distance could be expected to reduce recall accuracy, and thereby empirically blur the conceptual distinction between recalled behavior and behavioral intentions (Fishbein and Ajzen, 1975). On the other hand, one argument might mitigate this disadvantage. Vote choice in an election which is the first of its kind, as was the case with European elections in 1979, might not be forgotten as easily as that in other, more familiar elections. On this basis, in what follows we employ findings from the October 1979 survey as surrogates for what might have been found in a more immediately post-election study.

11 Variables measuring electoral participation were recoded to be dichotomies (respondent has participated versus not and don't know; respondent will certainly or probably participate versus all other replies). Both OLS and logistic regression techniques were applied in multivariate analyses. They generally arrived at the same results. OLS results are shown due to certain inconveniences regarding the presentation of logistic regression results.

12 Our use of a survey from October 1979 as a surrogate for an immediately post-election survey in 1979 is made plausible by comparisons (not shown) between the findings of the October 1989 EB32 and our June 1989 post-election study. For the variables that these two surveys have in common (more extensive than the restricted set, but less than the extended set mentioned in Table 8.4), the findings are very similar, giving us confidence that our October 1979 survey will also have yielded findings comparable to a June 1979 survey, had one been fielded. Of course the restricted set of variables is mainly restricted in terms of the richness of the first three blocks of predictors, which might help to accentuate the relative importance of the third block. However, this would be true in all four of the surveys we are comparing and should thus have no effect on the differences that we focus on in this section.

Social-structural characteristics in the restricted set include the age, gender, education, and religiosity of voters as well as the size of the community they live in. Conventional wisdom assumes that citizens situated in peripheral social categories will be less likely to vote. Accordingly it is the very young and the very old voters, the women, and the less well educated, who should turn out in smaller numbers. Overall, these expectations are hardly confirmed. Most social-structural traits are virtually unrelated to turnout, and the explanatory power of the others is far from impressive. Moreover, the effects found are hardly consistent over time. Proportions of variance explained with equivalent indicators range from 1 percent (recalled participation in Fall 1979) to 9 percent (participatory intention in Spring 1989). In general, social-structural contours of German participation in European elections were somewhat more pronounced in 1989 than ten years earlier (see Table 8.4).

The next block of variables in our restricted set consists of two measures of political orientation: party attachment and interest in politics (operationalized as the frequency of political discussion). Both indicators—but party attachment in particular—are known from previous research to be positively related to electoral participation. This is corroborated, though with two qualifications. The explanatory prominence of the two variables seems to vary with the timing of surveys (and thus with generic properties of the explanandum); both in 1989 and in 1979, political orientation variables contribute somewhat more to the prediction of recalled behavior (as established in post-electoral surveys) than to that of behavioral intentions (measured in pre-electoral ones). Second, the relative weight of the two components of this measure varies characteristically between the two elections (not shown). In 1979, when German parties still emphasized this electoral event quite strongly and included leading party figures as candidates (cf. Menke, 1985), party attachment was the major component in both intentions to participate and reported participation; ten years later, general political interest was a better predictor of pre-electoral vote intentions, while party attachment came to the fore in terms of recalled participation.

Next comes 'habitual voting', a 'block' made up of just one variable which is, moreover, measured by probably the most precarious indicator of all: the intention to participate in a forthcoming national election. Fortunately, two independent justifications for it can be given, one instrumental and the other substantial. The first has been introduced in Chapter 3 and refers to the sequence of blocks of variables included in multiple regression. From this perspective, its inclusion serves to account for all variation in the dependent variables other than that which is specific to the European election, and thus allows us to isolate the real impact of European orientations. The second justification refers to an explanation of turnout in the 1989 European elections which was proposed earlier and centers around the notion of habitual voting

(Schmitt and Mannheimer, 1991a). Empirical evidence found in that study supported the argument that people participated in the 1989 European elections because they are used to turning out on election day—more or less irrespective of the specific election at hand. In this previous study, participation in two elections different from the one in question was employed as an indicator of habitual voting, namely (reported) participation in the previous and (intended) participation in a forthcoming national election. Unfortunately, this composite indicator is not available over all four surveys under study here. Only one of its two highly correlated components can be put to use in our over time comparison. However, despite its presumed poverty, this single-item indicator can probably still give us some rough idea about how 'habitualized' German participation was in the first European election as compared to the third.

Irrespective of which election is analyzed, the additional explanatory weight of this variable is almost negligible regarding pre-electoral intentions to participate. However, its effect on reported participation differs between 1989 and 1979. While there is no difference between the contribution of this variable before and after the 1979 election, there is a substantial difference between the same two coefficients in 1989 (cf. Table 8.4). We read that as an indication that the character of participation in European elections has changed in Germany since the time of the first one. A more definitive sign is provided by the changing role played by European attitudes.

European attitudes are considered here in the form of two very basic scales, one measuring EC approval, and the other measuring awareness of the European Parliament. These scales are derived from dimensional (principal components) analyses of broadly comparable sets of indicators in the different surveys measuring respondents' attitudes towards European unification in

Table 8.4 Determinants of Electoral Participation (figures are R-squares and R-square changes from OLS regressions)

Timing of Survey:	Summer 1989 Reported		Spring 1989 Intended	Fall 1979 Reported	Spring 1979 Intended
Participation Indicators Used:	*Extended*	*Restricted*	*Restricted*	*Restricted*	*Restricted*
	R^2 Added R^2*	R^2 Added R^2**	R^2 Added R^2**	R^2 Added R^2	R^2 Added R^2
Social Structure	5	3	9	1	4
Political Orientation	27 22	11 8	15 6	11 10	11 7
Habitual Voting	31 4	25 14	16 1	14 3	14 3
European Attitudes	31 0	27 3	28 12	29 15	29 15

* This and the previous column display coefficients comparable with those in the equivalent tables of other country chapters.
** This and the previous column relate to 1989 responses but employ the restricted set of variables, for comparability with 1979.

general and towards the European Community and the European Parliament in particular. Earlier studies disagree about the explanatory weight, in the present context, of such European attitudes. Electoral research on the occasion of the first European election found turnout considerably related to a pro-European outlook (Inglehart and Rabier, 1979; Blumler and Fox, 1982), while later efforts to replicate those findings on the basis of our survey of 1989 participation failed in part. In 1989, pro-European attitudes were found to be substantially related to pre-electoral intentions to participate, but actual participation—reported after the event—was hardly predictable on the basis of European attitudes (Schmitt and Mannheimer, 1991a). A plausible conclusion from those observations was that the respective results of earlier studies should probably be considered as conceptual artefacts as they mistakenly took participatory intentions measured in pre-electoral surveys for the real thing, which is more closely approximated by recall in a survey conducted after the election. This, however, was probably a premature conclusion. At least in the German case, pro-European attitudes proved to be valuable predictors of both the intention to participate and reported participation in the first European election, while reported participation in the third is chiefly determined by other factors (see again Table 8.4).[13]

The character of German participation in European elections has been changing. When direct elections to the European Parliament were held for the first time, participation for many Germans still was a political statement, an expression of their support for a new and more democratic European Community. The third European election, by contrast, was just another boring second-order election—lacking the appeal of a path-breaking new step in the project of European unification.

Party Choice

Basic Structure

The basic form of the West German party system is straightforward: two cross-cutting cleavages—the religious and the class cleavage—structure the

---

13 Much the same pattern is shown if we employ the October 1989 Eurobarometer. Although the data are not entirely comparable, this strongly suggests that a June survey in 1979 would not have shown anything different from what is shown in the October 1979 survey. The finding does not necessarily call into question the earlier conclusion of Schmitt and Mannheimer that, in 1989, anticipated electoral participation was contaminated by European attitudes—merely the inference that electoral participation recalled after a long time lapse would be equally contaminated. Moreover, our interpretation of the findings stresses the lack of importance of European attitudes in 1989, suggesting that the effects from European attitudes in April 1989 were indeed spurious. Further research is evidently needed to clarify these relations.

vote. Over the past quarter century three main parties (or four, if we count the Bavarian CSU separately) have represented this basic cleavage structure in the Bundestag: Social-Democrats (SPD) on the labor side of the industrial conflict, Christian Democrats (CDU/CSU) on the church side of the religious conflict, and Liberals (FDP) occupying at once the most secular and the most capitalist (free market economy) position as is shown in Graph 3 (for more detailed expositions see Pappi, 1984; Schmitt, 1987b).

In the late seventies, during the second term of Helmut Schmidt's chancellorship, the party system entered a phase of acute failures in representation. Bürgerinitiativen (citizen action groups) and new social movements articulated their protest against the pragmatic Sachzwang-Politik of the governing SPD-FDP coalition under Helmut Schmidt—and notably against policies favoring high-risk technologies (e.g., nuclear plants), excessive consumption of natural resources and environmental destruction (e.g., an additional runway for Frankfurt airport), or military deterrence (e.g., medium-range missiles). These and other 'new politics' issues clearly constituted the political controversies of the time among the mass public (Baker et al., 1981) as well as among party elites (Schmitt, 1987a). Eventually, this 'new politics' dimension gained parliamentary representation in the form of the new party Die Grünen—in local and state assemblies first, in the federal Bundestag second, and in the European Parliament last.

Despite the fact that the Grünen obtained no representation in the European Parliament in 1979, it is of particular relevance in the present context that the conduct of the first direct election to the European Parliament encouraged and substantively supported the formation and consolidation of this new party. The German European election law acknowledges the candidature of political

Figure 8.3 The Basic Structure of the West German Party System

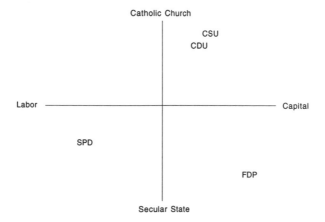

parties and "other political associations" (sonstige politische Vereinigungen). While this provision was originally introduced to enable the various groupings of the European Movement to participate in the elections, in the event it encouraged a variety of environmentalist and new-politics groupings to join forces and stand together for election as "Sonstige Politische Vereinigung Die Grünen". In the end, the Grünen failed to pass the five percent threshold in this first European election. However, their organizational consolidation was greatly supported by the system of government financial support for campaign efforts which granted them about 4.8 million DM (Menke, 1985). Three months later they first succeeded in gaining representation in a state parliament (Bremen), and achieved national political representation in the Bundestagswahl of Spring 1983.

By the end of the seventies, the structure of the West German party system had changed. A new dimension of party-political controversy had been added, which was initially largely independent of the old cleavage structure. However, the leadership of the Grünen increasingly aligned 'new politics' concerns with more traditional leftist positions or, in cleavage terms, with the interests of labor and the secular state (see Figure 8.3). This in turn caused a partial realignment of the party system as the Grünen started to attract more and more young and educated left-wing voters who would otherwise have had little choice but to join the Social-Democratic camp (Schmitt, 1990a; cf. Dalton and Rohrschneider, 1990 who see simultaneous dealignment and realignment processes at work). While not caused by the introduction of European elections in 1979, this change in the structure of the party system was greatly facilitated by it.

Ten years later, at the end of the eighties, a similar differentiation began on the right side of the political spectrum (Bauer and Schmitt, 1990). In 1989, the extreme-right wing party the Republikaner gained considerable electoral support in state and local elections as well as in the European election under study. It failed to enter the first all-German Bundestag which was elected in the Fall of 1990 (Table 8.1); yet one might doubt whether the European election of 1989 marked the peak of extreme right successes in post-war Germany (Schacht, 1991). The defeat of the Republikaner in the federal election of 1990 might turn out to be a transient phenomenon which should be attributed to the peculiarities of this unique 're-unification' election rather than to a decline in extreme-right support.[14] Extreme right successes in subsequent second-order

---

14 These elections are probably best understood as a plebiscite on chancellor Kohl's policy of "German Unity Now" with a more critical and skeptical position being taken by Kohl's competitor Lafontaine. This script left hardly any role for the Republikaner.

elections in West Germany,[15] and xenophobic excesses in both the East and the West of the country seem to support this view.

The Situation in 1989: Party Potentials and Floating Voters

Turning to the specifics of party choice in the 1989 European election, we find these more general properties of West German party competition at work. An instrument investigating the probability of individual party choice in European elections reveals that 85 percent of potential green voters were at the same time potential SPD voters. The recent realignment on the left of the party system finds its expression in this most substantial overlap of party potentials. Sizeable overlaps are also seen for the two other small parties: an impressive bi-directional overlap of potential FDP voters with the left (73 percent overlap with SPD) and the right (also 73 percent overlap with CDU/CSU), and a closeness of potential Republikaner voters to the CDU/CSU (62 percent overlap). Of the two youngest parties, the electoral attractiveness of the Grünen was more far-reaching than that of the Republikaner (see the 1st and 5th rows of Table 8.5).[16]

The two major parties—CDU/CSU and SPD—shared considerable parts of their potential electorate: more than four out of ten potential SPD voter could also imagine voting CDU/CSU, and nearly half the potential CDU/CSU voters might have voted SPD instead. Finally, the Republikaner were clearly not (yet?) as attractive an alternative to potential CDU/CSU voters as Die Grünen were to those of the SPD. Nevertheless, in the eyes of many voters the two major parties were, at the same time, both the polar opposites in the traditional party system and close competitors as well.

In Sartori's (1976) terms, this picture still highlights the centripetal traits of moderate pluralism, but it shows some signs of centrifugal competition and of increasing polarization. One was tempted, shortly after the European election, to predict an imminent alteration in the electoral climate. The advent of an extreme-right party, it was diagnosed, would cause the two major parties to concentrate more seriously than before on the integrity of their left (SPD) or right (CDU/CSU) wing—a process which would reduce the 'commonality' of the two major party alternatives (see Poguntke and Schmitt, 1990; Bauer and Schmitt, 1990). As far as we can see today, however, the contrary seems to

---

15 For example in the state elections of Bremen (September 1991) where the DVU polled 6.2 percent; in the state election of Schleswig-Holstein (April 1992) where they polled 6.3 percent; or in the state election of Baden-Württemberg (April 1992) where the Republikaner polled 10.9 percent.

16 The size of party potentials and overlaps depends on the specifics of their operational definition (see Appendix B). Schmitt (1989) uses a different definition which yields somewhat different results.

Table 8.5 Potential Support and Overlap Between Parties in Germany in 1989

	Grünen	SPD	FDP	CDU	Rep
Grünen	1.00	0.47	0.47	0.27	0.38
SPD	0.85	1.00	0.73	0.47	0.55
FDP	0.55	0.47	1.00	0.51	0.47
CDU/CSU	0.45	0.43	0.73	1.00	0.62
Republikaner	0.24	0.19	0.25	0.23	1.00
Potential Support (%)	27.1	49.0	31.4	44.7	16.9
%Vote Elect	5.2	23.0	3.4	23.3	4.4
%Valid Vote	8.4	37.3	5.6	37.8	7.1
L-R median (1–10)	2.44	3.64	5.65	7.34	9.62

have happened. Rather than taking good care of their respective ideological wings, the two main parties, CDU/CSU and SPD, moved towards rather than away from each other. In central policy areas they are probably as close together now as they have ever been. If a grand coalition government were to form after the Bundestagswahl of 1994, this would strengthen the new polar parties still further; and, at the time of writing, the prospect of such a coalition seems not unrealistic.

Party Choice in European and National Elections Compared

Is there a difference in German voting behavior between European and first-order national elections? Are there factors conducive to our understanding of the mechanisms of voting behavior which are more prominent in European elections than in national ones? And are there other factors which fail to impact the European vote while still being important for national party choice? Two rival hypotheses can be found in the literature. One of these assumes that in low stimulus elections long-term effects on vote choice such as party identification will outweigh short term effects (Campbell, 1966). The other stresses that second-order elections, due to the fact that national political power is not at stake, tend to reduce the decisional weight of long-term determinants in favor of the issues of the day (Reif and Schmitt, 1980; Reif, 1985a; Schmitt, 1990b).

One way to empirically approach an answer to these questions is to compare reports of electoral behavior in European elections with intentions regarding a hypothetical general election taking place 'tomorrow'. In doing so we can decompose the differences in proportions of the valid vote attributed to the various parties into the effects of different turnout levels as distinct from actual differences in the way people would vote in elections of each type (see Chapter 3 and Appendix B for an explanation of how this is done). Table 8.6 shows the result of such a procedure.[17]

According to Table 8.6, the European election results are very similar to the then existing national party preferences. The SPD appears to do a little worse as compared to (hypothetical) concurrent national elections, the CDU/CSU a little better, while differences for the other parties are much less and range below the margin of sampling error. Looking at the two components which bring about these differences we observe turnout effects to be particularly low, which is to be expected in view of the relatively high level of turnout of German voters in European elections: the group of European non-voters who could make a difference on the total results is just too small. Nevertheless, taking account of the effect of differential turnout emphasizes the surprising extent to which voters are failing to support the SPD simply because this is a European election—fully 2.6 percent of those who would have voted for this party in a national election failed to do so in the European election of 1989. The main beneficiary of this quasi-switching was Die Grünen. Other parties (and in particular the Republikaner) can be seen to have gained little from experimental voting or other second-order effects, while whatever small gains they did make were more than balanced by losses due to lower turnout. One should, of course, keep in mind that the method used to produce Table 8.6 is based on hypothetical and not on actual national party choice, which may possibly result in underestimating the amount of quasi-switching. The differences between the results of European and national elections could be read to suggest this, although here too a difficulty arises from the fact that elections held at

Table 8.6 Quasi-switching and Turnout Effects in the 1989 European Election in Germany

	EE	NE	EE-NE	Quasi-switching	Turnout Effect
Grünen	8.4	8.5	-0.1	1.2	-1.3
SPD	37.3	39.2	-1.9	-2.6	0.7
FDP	5.6	5.6	0.0	-0.1	0.1
CDU/CSU	37.8	36.4	1.4	0.2	1.2
Republikaner	7.1	7.4	-0.3	0.4	-0.7
Other	3.8	2.9	0.9	0.9	0.0

17 In the rest of this paragraph I report on the procedure proposed and the calculations provided by the primary authors of this volume.

different times bring into play the possibility of real changes in the electorate's party preferences occurring during the interval between the two elections.

The Domestic Consequences of the European Election

What were the effects of all this on the German political system? Immediately after the election, the CDU and (in particular) the CSU party elite launched an initiative to re-integrate the extreme right into their own rank and file. This was undertaken in a number of ways, including dismissing moderates from leading party positions,[18] the public espousal of extreme-right and nationalist positions,[19] and even inducing diplomatic affronts.[20] The aim of those activities was to prevent the Republikaner from achieving a comparable success in the Bundestagswahl of 1990. One might doubt whether this strategy would have worked; but it certainly would have had repercussions for German domestic politics and relations with other countries—repercussions directly attributable to the European election—had they not been quickly overshadowed by other events. In August and September of 1989 the breakdown of the German Democratic Republic began with the exodus of thousands of East German tourists via Hungary, and their occupation of West German embassies in Prague and Warsaw and of the West German mission in Berlin. The political agenda of the Federal Republic from then on was completely preoccupied with the process of German re-unification. Kohl's and his government's early and forceful policy of a rapid re-unification of the two countries appeased former dissatisfaction on the extreme right about his policies. The Republikaner in fact had no chance in the federal election of 1990. Nevertheless, their organizational consolidation, like that of the Grünen ten years earlier, will have been helped by the system of government financial support for campaign efforts; and their electoral success will certainly have helped their visibility, at least until it was overshadowed by later events.

---

18 At a CDU party conference in September, Heiner Geissler, a CDU moderate who served as the party's general secretary since 1977, was replaced by Volker Rühe, a conservative foreign policy specialist and vice-president of the CDU/CSU parliamentary party. The Bavarian CSU in particular had blamed its electoral setbacks on certain of Geissler's policies which it described as 'soft'.

19 Theo Waigel, federal minister of finance and leader of the CSU, caused considerable debate at home and abroad by stating that the German Reich had not ended with its capitulation in 1945, and that the lost territories in the east were still "part of the German question" since legally Germany still existed within its borders of 1937.

20 Shortly after the European election, Chancellor Kohl indefinitely postponed a visit to Poland that had been due in the middle of July. The decision to call off the visit compounded recent damage done to Polish-West German relations by statements by Theo Waigel.

But this overshadowing is not likely to persist. Public appreciation of Kohl's re-unification policy has been dwindling since 1990, notably so among citizens of the former GDR. At the same time, citizens are becoming more and more concerned about the further course of European integration—particularly in view of the monetary union projected in the Maastricht Treaty. These appear to be rather favorable conditions for the Republikaner to retain representation in the European Parliament in the fourth European election of June 1994, and to enter the Bundestag a few months later. If this happens, the European election of 1989 in Germany will be remembered as the second occasion upon which such an election helped in the establishment of a new political party.

Conclusion

What was characteristic of this third European election in Germany? The factual results need not be repeated in detail. There was a meager showing for the major governing party despite elevated turnout, the FDP regained representation in the European Parliament, and the Republikaner achieved representation there for the first time. These results aside, it appears that the most important features of this election were probably more psychological in nature. The lower levels of participation in the 1989 election on average, compared to 1979, and the increased importance of the usual social structural determinants of turnout, suggests that the European euphoria of 1979 has eroded with the passage of time, and with it the permissive consensus on which political elites used to rely in support of their efforts to unite Europe (see Chapter 21 for a more extended discussion of this topic). The European election of 1989 was seen by most Germans as just one more rather boring second-order election.

Boredom was only one pole in the Euro-psyche of German voters in 1989, if the most common. The other was fear, anger and protest. Not all Germans participating in the 1989 European election voted habitually; a good number of them appear to have voted very deliberately. These voters used the European parliamentary elections to voice their disapproval of the European Community on the one hand, and their opposition to and protest against the conduct of politics in general on the other (Schmitt, 1989). It was not the first time German voters had been provided with an electoral option that was critical of the European Community. Such options had been available in both of the two preceding European elections as well, but they were hardly chosen. What had changed in 1989 was not the candidature of the Republikaner but the mood of the Germans. This theme will be picked up in the third part of this book, notably in Chapter 18.

The mood was soon overshadowed by events associated with the re-unification of Germany, but we have indicated that there is every reason to suppose that it is still a reality that underlies German politics and that this reality will show itself in future elections. In that case, the third European election, in supporting the consolidation of the Republikaner much as the first sustained the emergence of the Grünen, will have served once again as a midwife attending the birth of a new party and thereby stimulating party system change.

CHAPTER 9

Greece:
A Confused Electorate

Panayote Elias Dimitras

Greece's restoration of democracy in 1974 opened the way to membership in the European Community of a country that, for most of its post-World War II history, had a two-and-a-half party system. After a transitional period in the late 1970s during which there was a near-dominant party system (Dimitras, 1992), the two-and-a-half party system reappeared in the 1980s. The two main families are the conservatives and the socialists, with the communists (the 'half' party) far behind in third place. Within each of these families one party is totally dominant: the conservative New Democracy (ND), the socialist Panhellenic Socialist Movement (PASOK), and the Greek Communist Party (KKE). Although the multitude of parties which contested the concurrent national and European elections and the very proportional electoral system employed for the first time in national elections in 1989 may have given the impression of a fragmentation of these families, the results actually confirmed the prognosis of experts that the two-and-a-half party system would survive the double contest intact.

Greece became a member of the European Community on 1 January 1981, and sent to the European Parliament a delegation appointed by the national parliament. That delegation was replaced by a directly elected one in October of that year when the first European elections (for Greece) took place in conjunction with national elections (Dimitras, 1984a). The second European elections took place in June 1984, without any concurrent national election, and were turned into a crucial national test by the main parties (Dimitras, 1984b). The third European elections were held in June 1989, again in conjunction with national elections, and the consequences were the same as in 1981 (Dimitras, 1989a). There was hardly any campaigning for the European election as in each case the concurrent national election was perceived to be critical, though with results that differed considerably between the two contests (the 1981 one brought PASOK to power and the 1989 one removed it).

Background to the 1989 Double Elections[1]

Since 1981 Greek politics have been dominated by PASOK which came to power that year after a landslide victory with 48 percent at the national elections in October, ousting ND which had governed Greece since the restoration of democracy in 1974. Moreover, along with the communist and other left parties, the global left dominated Greek politics with around 60 percent of the vote throughout the 1980s. Initially PASOK promised a profound, if not radical, transformation of Greek society, encapsulated in the 1981 campaign slogan "allaghi" (change). Four years later, having fulfilled a very satisfactory three-quarters of its 1981 pledges (Kalogeropoulou, 1989), and promising "better days" ahead, PASOK (with 46 percent of the vote) again won a comfortable majority of 5 percent over second placed ND in 1985. However, PASOK's 1985 campaign slogan turned out to have being deceitful in the light of the virtually immediate announcement of the most far-reaching austerity package that Greece had seen in normal times. These measures led to significant labor unrest and even to a split in the socialist union leadership, but neither was able to affect government policy. In the municipal elections of 1986, PASOK lost the country's three major cities because of the unwillingness of a sizeable minority of communist voters to vote socialist in the second ballot as would have been required (Greek Opinion, 1986). Although the austerity policy was largely successful, leading most economic indicators to move in the right direction, by mid-1988 ND and the other center-right parties still looked likely to exceed their 1985 performance by some 4 percent—a swing sufficient, if confirmed on election day, to deprive PASOK of victory to the benefit of ND.

Against this rather unfavorable (for PASOK) background, there erupted in the Fall of 1988 a series of scandals involving PASOK and its leader, the charismatic 69-year old Andreas Papandreou. First, when Papandreou took seriously ill and was rushed to London for examination and, eventually, delicate heart surgery, the Greeks discovered at his bedside his mistress, the 34-year old air stewardess Ms. Dimitra Liani, instead of his then wife of forty years, Ms. Margaret Papandreou. Although Mr. Papandreou was forced to announce his forthcoming divorce, stories from London continued to flow about Ms. Liani's and her friends' dominant role in Mr. Papandreou's decision-making at the expense of his former close associates and even his family. Nevertheless, in a country that is traditional but not puritan, and thus tolerates men's extramarital

---

1 This section draws heavily on my article about the 1989 European elections (Dimitras, 1989a). I am grateful to Butterworth, the publisher, for the use of some of the material published there.

affairs, the damage from this scandal was expected to be hardly noticeable by election day. A second scandal was more serious.

Just a few days before Mr. Papandreou's return from London, his government was obliged to appoint a special audit commissioner for the Bank of Crete, following convincing evidence of irregularities. Once in charge, the auditor accused the bank's owner, George Koskotas, of robbing his bank's funds to finance other projects; and he and some of his former associates responded with a series of allegations implicating the top PASOK leadership, including Papandreou, in receiving bribes amounting to billions of drachmas (1$ = 170 drs. in June 1989). In early 1989, hard evidence was produced of the deposit in a Swiss bank of $2 million in the name of Agamemnon Koutsogiorgas, who had been deputy prime minister and minister of justice at the time of an August 1988 law on bank confidentiality that favored Koskotas.

In any Western country such a scandal would have led to the resignation of the government. After all, Papandreou was at the very least politically accountable. However, just as in the case of his affair with Ms. Liani, Greece proved once more that, politically, it is not entirely a modern country. PASOK claimed that the Koskotas scandal was a foreign—perhaps even CIA—conspiracy to undermine it, and stressed Koskotas' early dealings with close associates and relatives of the ND leader, Mr. Constantine Mitsotakis. To many PASOK voters, these arguments appeared to be sufficiently convincing as to prevent their defection, thus minimizing the damage to the party's electoral prospects. To further minimize the possibility of the ND gaining an overall majority (further emphasizing the primitive flavor of Greek politics), PASOK followed conventional practice by governing parties in changing the electoral law to its own advantage (for the twelfth time in 20 parliamentary elections since 1926) from a reinforced proportional one to simple PR, thus bringing the rules for the national election into line with those that had from the time of Greece's accession to the EC been used in European elections.[2]

The Greek Party System in 1989

The use of simple PR, along with the persistently high number of undecided voters (as many as 20 percent-25 percent through early 1989), encouraged the defection from PASOK of a number of splinter parties and prompted many small parties to run separately instead of seeking refuge in the lists of large parties as in previous elections; so 23 parties ran in the national and 21 in the European election, the largest numbers ever. Nevertheless, it soon appeared

---

2 The European election system is actually even simpler than the one used in the 1989 national election (on these and other electoral systems see Dimitras, 1994).

that extreme proportionality (by Greek standards) was not leading to high fragmentation and that, as usual, there would only be three main contenders for most voters: ND, PASOK, and the Progressive Left Coalition. The latter was formed in early 1989 (in the wake of the 1988 scandals and the weakness of the various communist parties at the opinion polls) by KKE, the Euro-communist Greek Left, and various left and center-left splinter parties.

Table 9.1 shows the overlap between these and other parties in the Greek political system, and indicates a clear left/right spectrum; but one in which the total amount of overlap between parties (117 percent) is low in European perspective. The left/right structure is very clear looking down the columns (comparisons across rows are made more difficult by the different sizes of the parties): with two exceptions, coefficients are progressively lower as the distance between parties increases.

The first exception relates to the coefficients for the KKE-Interior-Renewal Left which are lower than the respective ones for the Coalition, although the former party's perceived left/right median is higher than the latter's. However, the difference between the two medians is very small (1.86 for KKE-I-RL as opposed to 1.72 for the Coalition) indicating that the two parties are perceived to have hardly any ideological differences. This is indeed the case, as the small KKE-I-RL is a splinter of the old KKE-I, whose majority formed the Greek Left and then joined the Coalition. This evolution led to the marginalization of the remaining KKE-I-RL, which could have also been considered to be slightly to the left of the Coalition, in which case the left/right continuity would have been preserved.

A similar account can be given of the second exception, the slightly lower, rather than higher, coefficients for the Democratic Renewal (DIANA),

Table 9.1 Potential Support and Overlap Between Parties in Greece in 1989

	LeftC	KKE-I-RL	PASOK	DIANA	ND	EPEN
Progr.Left Coalition	1.00	0.90	0.24	0.32	0.11	0.28
KKE-I–RL	0.33	1.00	0.12	0.23	0.07	0.26
PASOK	0.42	0.59	1.00	0.37	0.15	0.40
DIANA	0.19	0.37	0.13	1.00	0.28	0.60
New Democracy	0.21	0.35	0.16	0.88	1.00	0.82
EPEN	0.05	0.12	0.04	0.17	0.07	1.00
Potential Support (%)	20.3	7.4	35.5	12.1	38.0	3.4
%Vote Elect	11.2	0.5	28.3	1.1	31.7	0.9
%Valid Vote	14.3	0.6	36.0	1.4	40.4	1.2
L-R median (1–10)	1.72	1.86	4.82	7.85	8.77	9.96

when compared with the corresponding ones for ND. But DIANA, too, was a splinter of ND in 1985, and therefore the two parties can be thought of as having interchangeable positions on the left/right scale. So, in the end, the exceptions to the continuity of the coefficients do not challenge the clear left/right structure of the Greek party system shown by the data. There is evidently a considerable gulf separating the two extremes in Greek politics. If a line is drawn between PASOK as the right-most party of the left and DIANA as the left-most party of the right, we see that voters are much less likely to consider the possibility of a vote for parties 'on the other side' than for parties on the same side of this divide. We also see the strong loyalty of voters for the two major parties, ND and PASOK, who display considerably less overlap with the other parties than do the smaller parties' voters, being one-and-a-half time as likely to vote for their party than for any other party (see bottom row).

The Campaign

The 1989 campaign was centered on the national elections and there was hardly any debate related to the European election except for a few billboard posters and the fact that in many speeches politicians added towards the end one sentence asking for the voters' support in the European election too. Besides, unlike the situation in 1981, there was no separate arrangement for party television programs on the European elections. Parties were free to use the record 66.5 hours they were allocated as they wished, but chose to fill their time with monologues (usually from party rallies), well-directed interviews or, for the first time, five debates each involving five politicians (one each from PASOK, ND, the Coalition, DIANA and a different minor party each time) but not the parties' leaders. In any case these party programs had very low ratings, never exceeding 22 percent in the AC Nielsen Greater Athens diary surveys, but often falling as low as 5 percent or 6 percent for the major parties and 0 percent for the minor parties, whereas the election night returns had ratings of more than 50 percent.

The main reason for such a reaction to the special programs was that public opinion was generally fed up with the political parties' lack of substantial messages before and during the official campaign. Whereas the purging of public life from the scandals and those implicated in them was an important priority for many (especially conservative) voters, the political parties and their affiliated newspapers treated it as a near exclusive salient issue, concentrating their themes and headlines on it and neglecting the country's other equally pressing problems (economy, environment, education and—especially—drugs). Frequently, the campaign focused on serious but hard-to-prove allegations about the private lives of all political leaders, turning it into the dirtiest and most vicious campaign at least since 1974.

Turnout and Split Voting

Official turnout (which is supposed to be mandatory in Greece) at 85 percent in the 1989 European election, was high not only in terms of the standards set by other countries (See Chapter 19), but also (rather surprisingly) 0.4 percent higher than in the concurrent national election: in fact, it was the highest turnout ever recorded in a Greek election.[3] Less surprisingly, turnout in the European election of 1989 was 4.1 percent higher than in the 1984 European elections that did not have accompanying national elections to encourage participation, but also 3.4 percent higher than in the first (1981) European election which was held concurrently with a national election. On the other hand, the 1989 results resembled the 1981 ones more than the 1984 ones in that the smaller parties (i.e. all except ND and PASOK) received 7.1 percent more votes than in the concurrent national election (the respective figure was 12.5 percent in 1981); whereas in the 1984 European election the smaller parties won only 3.9 percent more votes than they had in the most recent parliamentary elections.

The lack of European content to the campaign is underlined by the fact that European attitudes add nothing to the explanation of turnout in Greece, which Table 9.2 shows to have been dominated by habitual voting, with very little impact from demographics and from civic attitudes and political orientations. The negligible difference between participation in the national and European elections does not leave any room for turnout effects, in contrast to

Table 9.2   Predictors of 1989 Participation in the European
            Election in Greece

	R^2	Added R^2
Demographics	0.08	
General Political Orientations	0.11	0.03
Habitual Voting	0.39	0.28
European Attitudes	0.39	0.00

---

3   Actual turnout is higher still—perhaps some 5 to 6 percent higher—in all elections, due to the presence on the voting lists of hundreds of thousands of registrations that should have been eliminated.

Table 9.3 Switching in the Concurrent 1989 Greek Elections

	EE	NE	EE-NE
Coalition	14.3	13.1	+1.2
KKE-I-RL	0.6	0.3	+0.3
PASOK	36.0	39.1	-3.1
DIANA	1.4	1.0	+0.4
ND	40.4	44.3	-3.9
EPEN	1.2	0.3	+0.9
Other	6.1	1.9	+4.2

the situation in most other EC countries. In Table 9.3, therefore, we give just the difference between votes in the European and national elections, which we will refer to as 'same day switching'.

Not surprisingly, the greater part of the same day switching occurred to the benefit of the smaller parties, unfortunately collected in the "other" category in our questionnaire—"unfortunately", because this hides the presence of three ecological parties (the two most important ones did not run in the concurrent national elections) which together polled 2.6 percent. The division of the green vote between three parties prevented any of them from winning the last European Parliament seat (it went to DIANA with 1.4 percent versus 1.1 percent for the Ecologists-Alternatives). However, their overall good performance led to a lasting ecological presence in Greek electoral politics. In any case, the swing in favor of the smaller parties conforms with 'second-order' expectations (Reif and Schmitt, 1980). The losers were the two larger parties, emphasizing the fact that their vote in the national election was amplified by strategic considerations. In the European election, where government power is not at stake, voters abandoned the two government contenders, ND in larger numbers than PASOK (3.9 percent versus 3.1 percent).

As we can see in Table 9.4, which underrepresents the swing away from the larger parties to the smaller ones, the main swings were 1.5 percent away from PASOK to the smaller parties and 1 percent away from ND to EPEN. Most of the swing to the smaller parties probably went to the ecologists, who have not been recorded separately in our survey. Moreover, an analysis of the switchers showed that, at least for some of them, their European party choice was the most rational one, while the respective national party choice was motivated by strategic voting: a similar conclusion was drawn from different survey data in the case of the 1981 concurrent election.

All of this emphasizes the time-bound nature of the 1989 elections. In the absence of a desire to punish an unreliable and scandal-ridden party, PASOK

Table 9.4 Split Voting Between Concurrent 1989 National and
European Elections in Greece (columns indicate
national party choice = 100%)

	ND	PASOK	Coal.	Other
EPEN	2	0	2	0
ND	95	1	0	0
DIANA	0	0	0	36
PASOK	0	94	4	3
KKE-I-RL	0	0	0	14
Coalition	0	1	90	4
Other	3	4	4	43

would have probably done better—as indeed it did in the November 1989 national election, just after Papandreou's indictment, and (even more so) in October 1993 with the financial scandal safely weathered (in fact even partially replaced by other scandals of the ND administration), Papandreou decently divorced and remarried, and ND having failed to turn around the left wing ideological majority of Greek voters. The Greek electorate in 1989 was a very confused electorate, disillusioned with the socialists on the one hand but not attracted by the only possible alternative, the conservatives, on the other. This is one reason why it took the Greeks three elections to definitely remove PASOK from power and replace it with ND in April 1990.

Domestic Consequences of the European Elections

Given the fact that these elections occurred concurrently with national ones, the impact of election day on domestic politics was the result mainly of the national election results. PASOK was removed from power but no one-party working majority took its place, forcing Greece to experience coalition governments for the following ten months, since the November 1989 election also failed to produce a working majority (Greeks having become fed up with unstable coalitions voted ND into power with just half the seats in April 1990). The European election results, on the other hand, affected the future of the smaller parties which considered the European election an 'easier' contest. One reason is the single constituency for the European elections, which makes it easier for small parties to run as they need to file just 24 candidates rather than the 100 or more needed in national elections. Another reason is the electoral system, which, in combination with the single constituency, makes it almost inevitable that one minor party, with a 1 to 2 percent share of the vote, will win the 24th seat and be represented in Strasbourg (this is why a 3 percent threshold has been introduced for the 1994 elections).

Turning to the impact of the European election results on the smaller parties, the extreme right lost its seat—a loss that precipitated its near disappearance from the electoral scene. On the other hand, DIANA's seat in the Strasbourg assembly helped the future life of that party, since, for example, parties represented in the European Parliament do have better access to the media during campaigns and, sometimes, to state-distributed campaign funds. Besides, the respectable score of the Ecologists-Alternatives led to the creation of a federation of ecological organizations with that name, which managed to elect one deputy at each of the following two national elections.[4]

As another consequence, the seat distribution within the Coalition had some delayed effects when dogmatic splits occurred. In the Fall of 1989 the hard left faction of the KKE split from the coalition, along with one Euro MP, to create the New Left Current (NAR), whose only significant political representation through 1994 was this one Euro MP. Then, in 1991, the majority of the KKE left the Coalition and bettered the latter's remnants in the 1993 election to win representation in the Greek parliament, while the Coalition was a victim of the new 3 percent threshold, leaving its two Euro MP's as its only representation after October 1993.

Finally, it is noteworthy that PASOK put onto its Euro-list some of its members implicated in the scandals, knowing well that their parliamentary immunity would not be waved in Strasbourg, unlike what would have happened in Athens, and saving them from court proceedings.

Conclusions

Apart from short-lived consequences for some minor parties—helped by the single district and shorter list in the European election—the European election of 1989 can hardly be said to have been of much importance in Greece. The fact that it not only coincided with a national election, but with a national election that ousted the incumbent government, meant that European voting choice was completely overshadowed by national political concerns. Perhaps surprisingly there were differences between the European and national outcomes, making it clear that at least some Greeks appreciated the different political stakes of the two electoral contests. These differences were in line with second-order election theory. In general, however, the voters were too confused by their national choices to have much attention to spare for another election of dubious significance.

---

4 In the longer term the effort appears to have been for nothing, as the federation had disintegrated by the time of the 1993 elections.

CHAPTER 10

Ireland:

An Electorate with its Mind on Lower Things

Michael Marsh

The most remarkable feature of the 1989 European Parliament elections in Ireland was that a general election was called to coincide with them. When the Fianna Fáil government decided that the combination of its high standing in the opinion polls and a defeat in the Dáil on a minor issue justified a general election, it ensured that when the Irish electorate were asked to consider the European Community and its future in the 1989 election for the European Parliament, voters would have their attention focused elsewhere. Their minds would not be directed upwards, to the great issues of creating a European Political Union, but to a less exalted need to elect an Irish government to deal with the public services and unemployment, and to elect some local TDs (members of the Irish Lower House of parliament, or Dáil) to obtain benefits for the constituency. The fact that the two elections were held at the same time had at least two fairly predictable consequences. Firstly, turnout in the European election was higher than it otherwise would have been, and secondly, if somewhat ironically, the publicity given to that election was markedly less than it would otherwise have been. Not so predictable was the partisan impact on the election outcome: would the coincidence of European and national elections help the major parties, help the minor parties, or would it make no difference?

The Irish party system is a little eccentric in the eyes of most Europeans. A critical feature in the development of the party system has been Ireland's relationship with Britain. The two largest parties grew out of the movement for national independence from Britain in the 1920s. Fianna Fáil (FF) and Fine Gael (FG) represented the anti and pro factions of a movement divided by the decision over whether or not to accept the 1921 Treaty which ended the war with Britain and established the Irish Free State in southern Ireland. In English, the parties appear as Soldiers of Destiny and Band of Gaels, terms conveying something of their civil war origins, but offering little enlightenment to those confused by the Irish names under which they are universally known. In recent years, the divisions between the parties have been economic and moral, as well as based on the national question, but differences have often been matters of style rather than substance. Fine Gael has been more liberal on moral issues in the 1980s, but a little to the right of Fianna Fáil on economic matters. Fianna Fáil subtitles itself The Republican Party, and with respect to the ongoing conflict in Northern Ireland is less conciliatory towards protestant opinion in that province than its rival. Both parties, when in government, have worked with the current instrument of British policy towards Northern Ireland, the Anglo-Irish agreement, despite Fianna Fáil's objections to it when in opposition. Fine Gael sits with the Christian Democrats in the European Parliament. Fianna Fáil sits with the Gaullists, though they would be equally at home with the Christian Democrats. The oldest party is the Labour Party, much smaller than the other two and for a long time the minor element in the two-and-a-half party system which characterized most of the period after 1951. It has always been very moderate in its ideology, only joining the international organization of social democratic parties quite recently, and it sits—when it gets the chance—with the socialist group in the European Parliament.

Two newcomers have recently extended the range of choice available to voters on the left and right of the system. An essentially Euro-communist party, the Workers' Party, challenged Labour from the left in the 1980s and gradually eroded its support in urban areas. Although the party's origins lay in the nationalist movement, north and south of the border, it has been as critical as any party of the role of the Provisional IRA in the ongoing conflict. Internal conflict within Fianna Fáil led to the launching of the Progressive Democrats (PDs) late in 1985 by dissident members of that party. While personality conflicts may have lain at the root of the split, the new party then set out to break the mould of Irish politics, and it occupies a sharply defined position in the political spectrum in contrast to the catch-all strategies of the major parties. Very progressive on social matters—to the extent of leaving all mention of God out of a draft constitution—it is right-wing on economic matters, and fits quite well into the Liberal group in the European Parliament.

The growth of these two new parties has greatly complicated the process of government formation in Ireland. An essentially political distinction had marked this process for over 40 years. Governments had traditionally been either single party Fianna Fáil, or coalitions of Fine Gael and Labour, and voters had taken this into account in their electoral behavior. Under the electoral system used in Ireland (for an explanation see Gallagher, 1986) those who voted for a party other than Fianna Fáil tended to express a clear secondary preference for other non-Fianna Fáil parties. As the non-Fianna Fáil alternative fragments, and as Fianna Fáil have found it ever harder to win an overall majority, governments have become harder to put together. After the 1987 election a minority FF administration depended upon this fragmentation for its existence, although Fine Gael had committed itself to support budgets as long as they embodied a sound economic philosophy—meaning a more tightly tied public purse. In an attempt to break out of this situation Fianna Fáil called an election in June 1989.

For the most part, inter-party policy differences can be mapped on two dimensions. The first of these is left/right, and the weight of expert judgement in recent years would place the Workers' Party at the left end of the Irish spectrum and the PDs on the right, with Labour, FF and FG between them. Two other dimensions dealing with Northern Ireland, and with social issues like divorce, abortion, and the role of the Catholic church in Irish society, tend to reinforce one another. On this dimension, FF is at the clerical and nationalist extreme and the Workers' Party at the other, with the PDs, Labour and FG between them. In 1989 there were also two other parties running that do not fit easily into this framework: Sinn Fein and the Greens. The former is the political wing of the Provisional IRA whose activities are largely focussed on Northern Ireland. While their main raison d'etre is a United Ireland, their electoral campaigns, particularly in areas away from the border, tend to emphasize local economic deprivations. The Greens, like Sinn Fein, were unrepresented in the Dáil or in local government, but the party went into the 1989 elections hoping for better things. Sinn Fein are extreme nationalists, yet quite secular, whilst the Greens are not easily placed on the left/right axis.

The above discussion reflects the perceptions of experts (some of which are summarized in Laver and Schofield, 1991:259; see also Laver and Hunt, 1992). Table 10.1 reveals something of the electorate's view of the party system. In indicating people's propensity to vote for parties other than their own, it

Table 10.1 Potential Support and Overlap Between Parties in Ireland in 1989

	SF	WP	Labour	Greens	PDP	FG	FF
Sinn Fein	1.00	0.30	0.22	0.22	0.18	0.13	0.13
Workers' Party	0.68	1.00	0.59	0.48	0.39	0.32	0.28
Labour	0.69	0.82	1.00	0.61	0.60	0.51	0.40
Greens	0.64	0.61	0.55	1.00	0.49	0.44	0.38
PDP	0.49	0.46	0.51	0.46	1.00	0.59	0.41
FG	0.51	0.54	0.62	0.60	0.85	1.00	0.54
FF	0.57	0.52	0.53	0.56	0.64	0.59	1.00
Potential Support (%)	11.0	25.2	35.3	31.9	30.0	43.2	47.5
%Vote Elect	1.5	5.1	6.3	2.5	7.9	14.4	20.9
%Valid Vote	2.3	7.6	9.5	3.7	11.9	21.6	31.5
L-R median (1–10)	1.40	2.31	3.32	4.62	6.84	7.65	7.86

shows which parties share much the same electorate and which parties have a clientele all of their own. The most obvious feature is the great overlap between parties. The potential supporters' row sums to far over 200 percent. This is a function perhaps of the proximity of many parties to one another, but also surely of the electoral system under which voters actually do vote for different parties on the same ballot paper. Evidently, most parties have a substantial electoral potential which few parties other than FF went even half way to realizing in 1989, despite the fact that over two-thirds of the voters turned out to vote.

For the others, Sinn Fein seems to be located on the left hand side of this spectrum, at least in as much as its supporters express a slight tendency to consider voting for parties of the left more than for those of the right, although the inclination is not a strong one. The Greens don't seem to fit in at all. Perhaps they really do represent a new dimension in politics, or perhaps they have not been around long enough yet for people to have much idea of what they stand for.

Turnout

The fact that as many as 68 percent of electors voted in the European Parliament election in 1989 is due to their coincidence with national elections. As Table 10.2 indicates, European elections have not historically attracted voters to the polls as effectively as other types of Irish elections. The first European elections in 1979 coincided with local elections and these probably helped to push turnout up to 64 percent. When the European elections occupied center stage in 1984 only 46 percent turned out. Without the added incentive of a general election, the 1989 European election would have probably seen the smallest turnout yet. In Spring 1984, 55 percent said they were certain to vote. Given that even this was an overestimate of the actual turnout, it seems possible that the 53 percent who said in April 1989 that they would certainly vote was also an overestimate. Had the Taoiseach (Prime Minister) Charles Haughey not

Table 10.2 Average Turnout at Irish elections 1965-1991 (percentages)

	Average Turnout	N
National Elections	74	9
Presidential Elections	63	3
Local Elections	61	5
EP Elections	59	3
EP Election Held in Isolation	46	1

chosen to seek a Dáil dissolution, turnout could have fallen even below the 1984 figure.

In 1989, the two elections tapped almost exactly the same electorates. All but 0.24 percent of those who made it to their polling station voted in both of the elections. There were, however, quite a large number of spoiled ballots in the European election—almost twice as many as in the general election—resulting in a difference of 1 percent in valid votes. This was less a result of deliberation than to some confusion about how preferences were to be specified over the two ballot papers.

Table 10.3 shows the effects of different blocks of variables on turnout (see also Marsh, 1991). Not surprisingly, European factors explain little about why people came out to vote. Demographic and general civic attitudes, plus the habit of voting in elections are what counts. This emphasizes, if it is necessary to do so, that it was the European election that benefitted from the mobilizing effects of the coincident national election, and not vice-versa.

In most of the other chapters in this volume, contributors examine the effect on party strength of a relatively low vote, relative to a (generally hypothetical) concurrent general election, which yields what has been called a 'turnout effect' (see Chapter 3). In Ireland, however, there was no such turnout effect; instead, people were mobilized to vote in the European election because of the coincidence of a general election. What we will look at here, therefore, is the effect of this mobilization. What difference did it make to party strength? In answering this question we cannot rely on reports of behavior. Those who voted in the European election also voted in the general election. Instead, we must depend entirely on how people said they would behave when questioned many weeks before the election and compare the party preference of those who said they are very likely to vote with the preference of those who said they were less likely to do so. To the extent that those who are less likely to vote were of a different partisan composition than those more likely to vote, it is plausible that the increase in turnout altered the result of the election. The April poll distinguished those who were certain to vote from those who would probably

Table 10.3 Predictors of 1989 Participation in the European Election in Ireland

	R^2	Added R^2
Demographics	0.12	
General Political Orientations	0.28	0.16
Habitual Voting	0.42	0.14
European Attitudes	0.42	0.00

vote and from those who would not. With 49 percent certain and another 32 percent probable, it is reasonable to suggest that the 68 percent who actually voted included almost all those certain and about half of those probable. Did those who would probably vote differ from those who would certainly do so? Table 10.4 shows the voting intention of those two groups.

The key contrast in this table is between line 1 (certain) and line 3 (certain and probable). Very crudely we can take line 1 as representing the preference of those who would have voted anyway, and line 3 as those who actually did so with the added motivation of a general election. What the table suggests is that even had all the probable voters turned out it would have made little difference to the result. Only in the case of the Workers' Party is there a distinct difference and the small number of cases there (14) means this is not significant.[1] There were a substantial number of undecided voters, particularly amongst the probables, who seem to have been disproportionately likely to be FG, FF or PD voters, judging by their national voting intention, but it would be unwise to read much into this as many of these may not have voted anyway. Much the same conclusions follow from a comparison of the national voting intentions of the certain as against the probable European voters, and from a similar contrast using a measure of the possibility that someone might vote for a particular party (see Table 10.1). On all these analyses it appears that there was very little partisan difference between those who said they were certain to vote and those who said they would probably vote in the European election.

There is really very little evidence then to indicate that the coincidence of a general election with the European election affected the result through an increase in the turnout. This is not to say that the result would have been the same had the general election not been held. The European campaign was

Table 10.4 Voting Intention and Intended Turnout*

	FF	FG	PDs	Labour	WP	Greens	Other	n
Certain	55.0	26.2	4.6	8.5	1.4	2.3	2.0	351
Probable	55.2	26.1	3.0	8.4	4.4	2.0	1.0	203
Certain and Probable	55.1	26.2	4.0	8.5	2.5	2.2	1.6	554

* Missing voting intention data excluded. Those who were not at least probable voters were not asked their voting intention.

---

1 The result of using a question tapping the probability that someone might vote for the Workers' Party gives an added weight to this exception, however. The question identified 54 Irish voters who said there was at least an 0.8 probability of supporting that party—9.1 percent of probable European voters as against 5.1 percent of certain European voters—so the Workers' Party may have gained slightly from the higher turnout.

completely overshadowed by that for the Dáil. It is possible that voting intentions would have been affected by a better publicized campaign with candidates least favorable to the EC, like Raymond Crotty, for instance, getting more publicity and support. Independents and small parties generally would have got more attention, perhaps to their benefit. Certainly many of the smaller parties and independent candidates claimed their campaigns were almost invisible, such was the glare from the publicity surrounding the general election. The weakness with this argument is that it assumes that the coincidence of Dáil and European elections helped the large, established, pro-EC parties. However, as we will see below, these parties actually did very badly, even by the standards of earlier European elections. It is hard to argue, given what we have shown above, that they would have done even worse without the benefit of the Dáil campaign.

Party Choice

Though almost everyone who voted in the general election also voted in the European election, the difference between the results of the two elections was considerable. The Pedersen index of volatility (Pedersen, 1979) measures the net difference in votes cast between two elections. Conventionally it is used to look at changes between pairs of national elections but it can equally well be used to compare a national and a European Parliament election held on the same day. It can take any value between 0 and 100 and when used to measure change between the two elections of 1989 it stands at 20, indicating that at least 1 in 5 voters voted differently in the two elections. This is dramatic. Only in a handful of instances in Europe has there been as large a difference as this between two successive national elections (Bartolini and Mair, 1990: Figure 3.1; see also Crewe and Denver, 1985), whilst the average figure for Ireland over the last quarter of a century is little more than a quarter of that. The biggest differences concern the largest two parties, with the Fianna Fáil vote down 12.6 percent on its general election figure and Fine Gael down 7.7 percent. With Labour remaining the same and the Workers' Party up only 2.6 percent, it was the other parties who reaped most of the benefits of the larger parties' failure in the European election. The PDs' vote was 6.4 percent higher, and the other small parties and independents collectively benefitted by 11.3 percent, with the Greens accounting for 3.7 percent of that. The result then was a swing of substantial proportions to the smaller parties.

All these figures, of course, are available from the election returns. The coincidence of the two elections and the lack of any turnout effect means that it is unnecessary to estimate the extent of quasi-switching between European and Dáil elections. The actual shift is apparent in the difference between the two sets of results. Table 10.5 shows the extent of the difference between the two elections.

How can this difference be understood? Three explanations are discussed here. Firstly, the importance of the different institutional context of the two elections, in particular the different constituencies and candidates. Secondly, the different degree of importance of the two elections with the European election being essentially a second-order contest (Reif, 1985a). Thirdly, reference is made to the specifically European dimension: are the results consistent with the thesis that the issues and cleavages are different in European elections?

Constituencies and Candidates

Dáil elections take place in 41 electoral areas, each choosing between 3 and 5 deputies with an average voter/seat ratio of roughly 1:21,000. European Parliament constituencies are only 4 in number. Again each elects between 3 and 5 members according to size but the ratio is something like 1:236,000. While the proportion of votes necessary to win a seat is no different in a 3 seat Dáil or European constituency, there is obviously a big difference in the number of votes required. We might expect this to help larger parties and hinder smaller ones, and particularly to hinder the independent candidates, who are more likely to lack the organizational resources to cope with the larger areas. However, this potential effect seems to have been quite overshadowed by another. In Ireland, the major consequence of the fact that the two elections were fought under a quite separate framework of constituency boundaries is that different candidates ran in each of them.

In Dáil elections, it is generally considered that there are two contributions to a candidate's vote: one is party and the other is personal. The latter derives from a number of attributes but essentially either stems from a perception that

Table 10.5 Comparison of 1989 European Parliament and Dáil Elections

	EP Election	General Election	Shift
FF	31.5	44.1	−12.6
FG	21.6	29.3	−7.7
Labour	9.5	9.5	0
PDs	11.9	5.5	6.4
WP	7.6	5.0	2.6
Greens	3.7	1.5	2.2
Others	14.1	5.1	9.0

the candidate can perform some particular service for the area or the voter, or is being rewarded for having done so. There is an important degree of parochialism in the political culture which makes it almost essential in Dáil elections that deputies be local people with strong roots in their constituencies. It is not clear how far this applies at the European level. To the extent that the aggregate national party vote is composed of these two elements it should not be surprising to find some significant differences between the Dáil and the European vote. We might expect far less differences between two successive Dáil votes as, across 41 constituencies and several hundred candidates, personal factors should balance out—although we do see wide variations in swings across constituencies. However, in the much more restricted competition of a European election, the candidate factor—whether it is more or less important— should produce results which are different to those of a Dáil election simply because the number of candidates is much smaller so there is less room for any canceling out process. Parties with candidates better than their average Dáil candidates should gain votes, and those with weaker candidates should lose them. So, which parties fielded the best candidates?

This question cannot be answered without some conception of what it is that makes a good candidate. Whatever the public might consider as the qualifications for a good MEP (King, 1981), it does seem as if the bigger scale of European politics means that the relatively close deputy-voter link which operates in Dáil constituencies is less important at election time. Certainly, someone with a high profile gained in national politics will probably outpoll someone whose claims to fame are essentially European. This was particularly obvious in the first European elections in 1979 when all five Fianna Fáil candidates who had been MEPs lost their seats to party colleagues whose experience was confined to Dáil elections, and across all parties only 2 of 8 former MEPs were elected compared with 8 of 9 former cabinet ministers. (Carty, 1981: Table III). In 1984, the very experienced Sean Flanagan (FF-EPD) was well beaten by his running mate Ray McSharry, a recent senior FF minister; and another incumbent, Noel Davern (FF-EPD), also lost out to another ex-minister new-comer. In 1989, Munster MEP Tom Raftery (FG-EPP) was beaten for a FG seat by John Cushnahan, former Northern Irish Alliance Party leader, a man admittedly making his debut in southern Irish politics but nonetheless someone who attracted much national publicity. While these are quite isolated instances, it is hard to find a good example where a senior party figure fails to take a seat, or loses a seat, while a more junior running mate with more European experience succeeds. Furthermore, some of the more striking successes by the smaller parties occurred where they ran high profile candidates. The strong PD performance was much assisted by the fact that senior party figures contested the election in Dublin, Munster, and Connacht-Ulster areas, although the worst vote of the Progressive Democrats, relative to the general election, was in Dublin. Similarly the strong showing in Dublin of Labour and of the Workers' Party can easily be attributed to candidate factors. Labour's deputy leader stood in Dublin, while the standard bearer for the Workers' Party was its leader, Proinsias De Rossa. Together these two attracted almost 29 percent of the vote, almost 8 percent more than their parties' general election vote in the area. Elsewhere, candidates of the two parties had much lower profiles. Amongst independents, T.J. Maher, former Irish Farmers Association leader and MEP since 1979, and Neil Blaney, now the longest serving TD, are people with a considerable reputation and standing. By common consent, Fianna Fáil and Fine Gael did not field a strong slate of candidates in that these included only one figure who had recently sat on the front benches for either party.

Naturally it is easier to identify quality, and the lack of it, in retrospect; but even before the results were in there was a feeling that Fianna Fáil and Fine Gael were not running strong vote-getting teams. The argument that a big name candidate is important for a party is supported by an analysis of those who voted differently at the European and Dáil elections. Those who switched were particularly likely to give as their reason for voting something unconnected to either the government or to the European Parliament (Keatinge and Marsh, 1990:143).

None of this should necessarily detract from the validity of European Parliament elections. The electorate is well within its rights to view big names, particularly former ministers, as being more competent to deal with European affairs and favoring them over the average MEP. Arguably, such people add to the importance of the Parliament. What the pattern does imply though, is that political status flows from the national to the European institution. It is difficult to think of any instance which demonstrates the possibility of the flow operating in the other direction.

Part of the increase in support for the smaller parties could be accounted for by the fact that it is easier in European elections to offer a candidate to all voters, or at least to more voters. It requires only 4 candidates to cover the country rather than 41. Fianna Fáil and Fine Gael ran candidates in all constituencies in both elections, but that is not true of the other parties. Thus the Greens ran candidates in 2 of the 4 European constituencies, compared with 12 of the 41 in the general election; the PDs, Labour and the Workers' Party each ran in all four as against 30/41, 28/41 and 21/41 respectively in the general election. SF ran in three constituencies compared with 12/41 in the Dáil election. Whilst 33/41 constituencies had at least one independent candidate in the general election, the general quality of candidates would have been much higher in the

European election. Three constituencies had at least one independent candidate whose name was widely known.

What difference did this greater coverage by the smaller parties make to the result? Table 10.6 gives the result of a simple simulation of the national election vote, based on the assumption that each party fielded the same number of candidates in the Dáil election as in the European election. The fact that the estimated Dáil vote is much closer than the actual Dáil vote to the European Parliament figure suggests that much of the increase in the Green, SF, and even the Workers' Party vote in the European election could be accounted for simply by the additional availability of those parties' candidates. The simulation is less convincing in cases where parties already ran candidates in at least half the constituencies since those left uncontested will have been those in which the party would have expected to do poorly. Hence the simulation considerably overestimates Labours actual performance. For different reasons the simulation drastically underestimates the actual success of PD and Independent candidates. This is probably due to the quality of candidates in both instances. Not only was their coverage more extensive in the European election, but also the parties (or groupings) were offering their better candidates in many cases.

A final point in favor of the candidate-centered explanation is that the quality of candidates goes some way towards explaining the particular pattern of gains and losses in the European Parliament election relative to the Dáil election in each of the four constituencies. In Dublin, where the two left candidates were the biggest names, it was the left who made the biggest gains. In Munster and Connacht-Ulster it was the strong independent and PD candidates who featured most prominently, whilst Leinster, which had probably the weakest field and no significant independent candidate, there was least overall change although the PDs made gains.

Table 10.6 Contribution of Increased Number of Candidacies to the Result of the European Parliament Election

	Labour	PD	WP	Greens	SF	Other
EP Vote	9.5	11.9	7.6	3.7	2.3	11.8
Dáil Vote	9.5	5.5	5.0	1.5	1.2	3.9
Estimated Dáil Vote*	12.2	6.2	8.7	2.5	2.6	4.8
Actual EP-Dáil Difference	0.0	6.4	2.6	2.2	1.1	7.9
Estimated EP-Dáil Difference	-2.7	5.7	-1.1	1.2	-0.3	7.0

* Dáil election percentage divided by the number of contested Dáil constituencies and multiplied by the number of constituencies contested in EP election

Second-order Elections

A second explanation for differences between national and European Parliament elections has been advanced by Reif (1985a), who argues that European elections have to be understood in national terms but differ from national ones in that they do not decide who shall form the government. Reif suggests that small parties will perform better because the composition of the government is not at issue; voters will pick whichever party is ideologically closest to them, rather than a party they realistically would like to see in government. He also suggests that the governing party will lose votes, especially at mid-term, and that turnout will be lower because the election is less salient. These last two predictions are clearly irrelevant here because of the concurrent elections.

It must be said that the first prediction works reasonably well, particularly with respect to independents. Reif's theory also offers an explanation of why quality candidates might be more important in a European election. Someone who wanted a government comprised of one or more established parties might well prefer an electable independent at a European election; and the Greens and even SF, seen as irrelevant in a general election, might also be a little more attractive when actual power was not at stake. But it is worth emphasizing that under the STV electoral system electors can vote for a candidate they like best but still indicate, by showing a second or third preference, that they would wish another candidate to be successful if their first choice is not elected. Votes are less easily wasted under such an electoral system.

Thus Reif's second-order election explanation offers some hints as to why independents did well, and the larger parties did poorly. It should also be mentioned that, relative to the previous Dáil election, both large parties also lost votes in 1984 (Fianna Fáil in opposition dropping 6 percent) but in 1979 Fine Gael (in opposition) gained 2.6 percent.

European Issues

The third source of explanations for the results are the issues in the two elections. Were they very different? To what extent do the particular European stances of the parties and candidates explain why some people voted differently in the two elections?

If European issues are to account for the changes, we should be able to observe three features of party and electoral behavior. First, voters should have salient attitudes on European affairs. Secondly, parties should have (or be perceived to have) different positions on those issues. Thirdly, the pattern of the cleavage(s) between parties should be different to that which operates in national elections: i.e., if voters vote on European issues alone that should lead to a different result. It is arguable that the first two features are not easily distinguished in the Irish case. Few voters see European issues as salient. Secondly, parties are fairly similar in their outlook and they do little to clarify their positions, or focus any debate on European issues. Indeed, parties have actually obscured their position on some European issues which might be electorally damaging. For instance, in 1984 the Christian Democrat group's views on Common Defence were conspicuous by their absence from Fine Gael's election manifesto, and some similar examples are discussed below.

On the third point, it seems clear that even to the extent that differences are salient, and that parties are perceived as representing different views, the relatively small anti-EC minority is best represented by a relatively small group of minor parties and Independents. Thus, even were voters to base their choice solely on European issues, it is not clear that the overall weight of the parties in the system would be very different from what they are in the national context.

The Voters

Irish voters are not all supportive of the EC. There are various pockets of opposition in particular institutions and social groupings. Crucial issues are sovereignty, neutrality, economic peripheralism and the rather liberal social ethos of the Community (Coakley, Holmes and Rees, forthcoming). The Single European Market (SEM) referendum that was held in Ireland in 1987, for instance, attracted a significant 'No' vote of 30 percent, and Eurobarometer polls consistently reflect the presence of some anti-EC feeling in Ireland. Moreover, the SEM referendum attracted only a 44 percent turnout, suggesting that EC support nationally is at best rather lukewarm. An index of European Approval constructed from the pre-election (April 1989) wave of our study points to some 6 percent opposed and a further 16 percent no more than neutral, 19 percent supportive and 53 percent strongly supportive. Although such data indicate broad support for the EC, they are less useful in showing us what sort of Europe people have in mind—if any. Is it one which simply emphasizes the economic opportunities (and hand-outs), or one which goes beyond that to stress a more positive integration, as outlined in the Social Charter, for instance? Should the EC deal with foreign policy and defence? The constitutional issues with respect to EC development are measured in the polls. There is still a great wariness, even opposition, to any defence pact (Marsh, 1992), a point used by opponents of the SEM, but there is widespread support for the European Parliament, the Single Market and the Social Charter. However, none of these issues featured at all prominently in the campaign in 1989. In our post-election survey, less than 5 percent of our respondents thought issues like European unification or completing the Single Market were amongst the three most important issues, let alone the possibility of Turkey's accession to the EC.

The Parties

One reason for this is that the parties have done little to popularize such issues. In the early days of Ireland's membership, the Labour party was opposed to the EC and campaigned against affiliation in 1973. Those days are long gone, although the party was virtually forced to stay out of the SEM referendum campaign in order to preserve a facade of party unity. The mantle of official opposition was taken up by the Workers' Party which campaigned against the SEM in 1987. The 'No' vote correlated at constituency level at .56 with the 1987 general election vote for the Workers' Party and .33 with the Labour vote (Gallagher, 1988). But even the opposition of the Workers' Party is now replaced by 'critical acceptance' (Coakley, Holmes and Rees, 1991). Their conference in Spring 1989 saw the party move away from many of its former orthodoxies in a spirit of 'perestroika'. Henceforth, the party claimed that it supported the EC and would work within its structures for democratic reforms.

Thus, in the 1989 European Parliament election, all the parties in the Dáil supported the EC. In practice, this meant little was said about it. European Monetary Union (EMU), for instance, was not mentioned in the manifestos put out by Fianna Fáil or Fine Gael. The Parliament itself—the extent to which its powers were adequate or should be increased—was not discussed by those parties. The opposition of Fianna Fáil's Gaullist allies to increases in European parliamentary powers, and the priority given to such increases by Fine Gael's allies in the Christian Democrat group were matters on which neither party felt the need to inform the electorate. Labour and the PDs did give the matter a little more manifesto attention, but only a little more, both calling for more power for the European Parliament. The constitutional matter of neutrality did surface but the main parties tended to avoid inconvenient debate, emphasizing Ireland's neutrality but not discussing the best response to the various inconsistencies in the maintenance of that position.

This is not to say that all parties adopted the same position on such issues. Fine Gael has traditionally been more federalist on Europe and more pragmatic on neutrality—although they were careful in 1989 not to let that pragmatism show (a 1988 party document espousing such pragmatism found no echo in the manifesto). The PDs occupy much the same position, but Fianna Fáil continued to stress the importance of the Council over the Parliament, for instance, and were at best lukewarm in their support for the SEM. They support the EC, but perhaps with more reservations about the directions integration might take. Labour and WP support integration but with very strong reservations over defence and security policies and concerns that the free-market emphasis does not become too strong. Real opposition, however, comes only from the fringes of the system in the shape of various independents, Sinn Fein and the

Green Party. There is some irony in the fact that the most European campaign in Munster was that of the anti-EC independent Joe Noonan, who even enlisted the help of German Green leader Petra Kelly in his search for those Irish voters who had voted against the Single European Market in the 1987 Referendum. A similar tendency was observable in all constituencies, with Sinn Fein particularly but also the Green party, as well as various independent candidates, employing a much more European focus on the issues.

European issues generally got recognition from candidates seeking to relate them to particular local problems: for instance, how tax harmonization would reduce problems associated with commerce over the border (see chapters on the elections in various constituencies in Hainsworth, 1992). As always, parties also emphasized their abilities to perform. Fine Gael's case, like Labour's, rested on its membership in one of the two largest groups within the European Parliament whilst Fianna Fáil claimed its relative size in an admittedly small group gave it much more leverage. Individual candidates, naturally enough, also tended to emphasize their personal achievements (and not only their European ones). Fianna Fáil also made much of its success in winning big money from the new Structural Fund, leaving their opponents able to do little more than complain limply about lack of consultation in drawing up the plans to spend it. Such claims reflect an extractive perception of Europe as a font of grants and benefits that some parties and politicians are better able to tap than others. There is little doubt that this vision is widespread, but perhaps little reason to suppose that the public perceptions of these abilities differ very much from perceptions of such abilities in a national context.

If votes are to be influenced by European concerns, it will be perceptions of party stances and not actual party differences which will matter. The findings of our (November 1989) first wave on the rankings of the various parties in terms of support for Europe are not entirely consistent with reality, and the shift of position by the Workers' Party after that poll could not be reflected in its results. The figures given by van der Eijk and Franklin (1991) indicate that the perception of party differences is quite pronounced, with Fianna Fáil, Fine Gael and the PDs close together on the pro-EC side while Labour is more central and the Greens (and particularly the Workers' Party) are well to the anti side. These perceptions are little influenced by respondents' views on the EC; and those who had little support for the EC shared the general viewpoint that the Greens and the Workers' Party had significant reservations about the Community. It is notable that each party's own supporters see their party as a little more pro-EC than does the electorate as a whole (van der Eijk and Oppenhuis, 1989: Table A19), perhaps reflecting the national norm that the EC is a good thing. In addition, each party's electorate appeared relatively supportive of the EC.

Anti-EC voters who wanted to express clear opposition would have to support one of the candidates from a minor party, or an independent. It is true that there was a drift of voters to those parties perceived as less supportive of the EC, with Labour in the center holding its vote. However, this does not explain the success of the PDs who should have lost a lot of votes on this interpretation. It also ignores the objective differences between the Workers' Party and the Greens, SF and some independents. In addition, not all independents were anti-EC. Certainly T. J. Maher was not an anti-EC candidate and, reservations on neutrality apart, nor was Neil Blaney.

National/European Differences
It seems probable that, were the only issue of the European Parliament election to be one of degree of support for the EC, the actual results would not differ hugely from national election results. Table 10.7 uses the question "Generally speaking, do you think Ireland's membership of the EC is a good thing, a bad thing, neither good nor bad?" and contrasts the distribution of voters' views on that question with the electoral strength of the different parties on the basis of two alternative assumptions (1) that Labour and the Workers' Party support is still only lukewarm and (2) that the Workers' Party and the Labour Party are both pro-EC parties. Independents were allocated as neutral in the Dáil election, and as appropriate in the European election. This exercise is not designed to suggest who voted for which party, only to emphasize that even if European issues were the sole factor in peoples' vote, the results would not have been very different. The Greens, SF and anti-EC independents could not have expected many more votes than they actually received. Even if neutral votes are added to anti votes, and Labour and WP are taken to be no more than neutral, we get

Table 10.7 Attitude to the EC and National Party Strength

	Pro	Neutral	Anti	(N+A)
Is EC a Good Thing?	72.4	14.0	13.6	(27.6)
National Vote(1)[a]	78.9	18.4	2.7	(21.1)
EP Vote(1)[c]	71.6	17.6	10.8	(28.4)
National Vote(2)[b]	93.4	3.9	2.7	(6.6)
EP Vote (2)[d]	89.6	0.6	10.8	(11.4)

a. FF/FG/PD pro, Labour/WP/Independents neutral, rest anti
b. FF/FG/PD/Labour/WP pro, Independents neutral, rest anti
c. FF/FG/PD pro, Labour/WP neutral, rest anti (Independents as appropriate)
d. FF/FG/PD/Labour/WP pro, rest anti (Independents as appropriate)

a figure only a little above the proportion of European voters who did not think the EC was a good thing. Possibly these survey ratings underestimate opposition to the EC since the 'No' vote in the 1987 referendum on the SEA was 30 percent, but the anti vote anyway was well short of that figure.

Finally on this point, it is worth noting that only 14 percent of Irish voters claimed that European rather than domestic issues decided their choice. Most of those voters chose one of the major parties, and a large proportion were pro EC. In addition, a majority of those claiming that European issues determined their vote stayed with the same party (Keatinge and Marsh, 1990). With at least 20 percent of voters changing their vote, this suggests that European issues were not decisive in most cases.

This discussion of explanations is somewhat inconclusive. However, it does seem clear that the second-order election theory does not provide convincing explanations of some of the results. Nor can the view that European issues affected the result significantly be easily sustained. The candidate-centered explanation is not easy to validate without clear definitions of candidate quality but does provide the most satisfying explanation of some of the patterns. Faced with different options, in effect, Irish voters made different choices.

Effects of the Elections

Whatever the reasons for them, immediate consideration of the results was almost completely overshadowed by the indecisive general election result and a developing crisis over the formation of the next government. Counting took place after the count for the national elections, and results were not known until two days after announcement of national results. Unlike 1979 and 1984, when the European elections occurred at mid-term, the coincidence of the two elections in 1989 makes it difficult to isolate the effects of performance in one of them. In general the European results amplified conclusions that might have been drawn from the national results. Fine Gael's disastrous showing underlined the fact that the party had made only small steps on the road back to their pre-1987 election status. Their 29 percent of the vote in the general election—a gain of 2 percent—still left them well short of their 37 percent in 1982. Fianna Fáil's failure to get even a third of the vote testified to the absence of realism in their aspirations to an overall majority. Most of the smaller parties confirmed the improvements in their fortunes evident in the general election. Only in the case of the PDs, who proved to be the biggest losers in the Dáil election and the biggest winners in the European Parliament election, was there a real reversal of fortunes. It is possible that this aspect of the result actually assisted in the resolution of the governmental crisis. The much needed boost to PD morale undoubtedly sustained that party in its determined bargaining with Fianna

Fáil, prior to the formation of the FF/PD government in July 1989. Possibly, too, it gave the party a little more public credibility in its stance of holding out for seats at the cabinet table as the price of its support. However, it would be hard to argue that the good European election result for the PDs was a necessary prelude to the successful outcome of their negotiations with Fianna Fáil.

When a party does not do well in elections, questions are always asked about the leader. The result of the 1979 European Parliament election was seen as a mid-term report on the Fianna Fáil government, and it came when the bills were being presented for all the electoral promises which had secured the party a famous victory in the 1977 election. It hardened critical opinion on the backbenches, and probably hastened the departure of the then leader, Jack Lynch, and the arrival of the new one, Charles Haughey—although Lynch had been intending to retire soon anyway. The level of support for Charles Haughey's FF in 1989 was considerably lower than it had been in 1979, but by then expectations had been depressed by the party's relatively poor showing throughout the 1980s. Concerns in the party after the election focussed more on the general election showing, and, even more, on the process of government formation. The result certainly further weakened Haughey's position but it was not something—once he was in government—that he could not survive. His eventual replacement early in 1992 owed little to the European election performance, which was simply one more indication of the obvious: that under Mr Haughey, Fianna Fáil were not going to win an overall majority.

Fine Gael had appointed a new leader, Alan Dukes, on the retirement of their old one, Garret Fitzgerald, after the 1987 election. Dukes persuaded his party of the need to support the economic policy of the FF government of 1987–1989, and this departure from the adversarial norms of Irish politics won him few friends within his party. His position was not strengthened by the indecisive general election result and the European vote confirmed many of his opponents in their belief that he was not the answer to the party's electoral problems. So the European election result was at least a factor in Duke's downfall after an even worse result for his party in the 1990 Presidential election. By contrast, the strong showing, particularly in Dublin, of Labour and the Workers' Party probably strengthened the position of their leaders, and certainly gave rise to renewed speculation about the imminent, if belated, rise of the Irish left.

Later elections, for the Presidency in 1990 (Gallagher and Marsh, 1991; O'Sullivan, 1991) and local elections in 1991 (Fitzgerald, 1992), can be seen to have confirmed trends apparent in the European elections. Fianna Fáil's performances have further emphasized its current electoral weakness, losing the Presidency for the first time, and giving way to numerous rainbow coalitions at local level. Fine Gael's slump has continued too. The parties of the left, the

Greens and the PDs have had rather more to crow about. These results all indicate the current weakness in the two largest Irish parties, which was evident in the European election, but not caused by it.

Just as the election has had little clear impact on parties, so its consequences for the party system are equally obscure. It helped all the smaller newer parties, and underlined in particular the potential of the Greens. However, their future success will owe far more to on-the-ground organization in the smaller Dáil and local election constituencies than their European election performance. The election showed they had come a long way since winning only 5242 votes (1.9%) in one constituency in 1984, but the Dáil election showed that equally clearly, and the seat won in the Dáil election had much more publicity value. The Green image projected during the Irish Presidency of the European Council in 1990, and the initial environmental program of the current government, may not be entirely unconnected with the apparently growing appeal of the Green party but again it would be hard to argue that the party's European election performance did any more than underline the message of the general election, or that even this message was any more than a single one of many things prompting the government to move in a slightly more environmentally conscious direction.

The unwillingness of parties to confront EC constitutional issues did not disappear after the election. The Irish Presidency of the EC passed off without any Dáil debate on the Irish position on the items then on the EC agenda; nor was this failure compensated by Irish MEPs contributing to the debate on those issues in the European Parliament. The draft Political Union Treaty was discussed only a few weeks before the Maastricht summit. When there have been developments within the parties on such issues since 1989, they have come about for quite different reasons. Thus the Gulf Crisis, and the decision of the Irish government to allow US planes to refuel on Irish territory, prompted the expression of some very clear differences between Labour and the Workers' party on one side, and Fine Gael and the PDs on the other, on the subject of Irish neutrality. Perhaps because of this general neglect, sharp conflicts on European issues have not been seen in the years since the 1989 elections.[2] However, Ireland's traditional neutrality—a legacy largely of the strained relationship with Britain—and the various implications of EC defence arrangements for that neutrality may yet cause considerable dissension.

---

2 The Labour party's problems over the Single European Market, when a largely pro-EC leadership compromised with a more anti-EC rank and file by keeping the party out of the campaign, resurfaced during the campaign for the Maastricht referendum in 1992. Labour's leader, Dick Spring, managed to put off a decision on the issue until the eve of the referendum when he called for a 'Yes' vote—but one in which conscientious objection would be permitted!

Conclusions

In the European election of 1989, Irish voters clearly had their minds on lower things. The national election distracted attention away from the European contest and ensured that, whatever the benefits for turnout, there would be little discussion of European issues. It was the national level, not the European level of government, that occupied the electorate. And to the extent that parties did campaign on European matters, they often dealt more with what Europe could do for Ireland than with what Ireland might do for Europe. When voters chose MEPs, national rather than European factors predominated.

Even so the election was not simply a muted echo of the Dáil election. The results were very different and in many respects amplified what the electorate was saying about the parties. We have argued that this difference cannot be attributed to specifically European concerns. Instead, it may best be accounted for by reference to personalities. The concept of second-order elections provides some theoretical grounding for this explanation, although by no means all of the results are entirely consistent with the predictions of the second-order model.

We also suggested that even if European issues had been critical, the outcome would have been very similar. Of course, if the parties treated elections as an occasion to fully inform the electorate on the possible options for future political development, the merits and disadvantages of parliamentary reform, and the potentialities of a new monetary policy, and were able to convince the media of the salience of these issues, then attitudes, and votes might change. Since national elections have yet to meet such idealistic hopes in respect to these issues, there seems little likelihood of European elections doing so.

CHAPTER 11

Italy:
Consulting the Oracle

Renato Mannheimer

In Italy, the 1989 European election coincided with a difficult and controversial government crisis. The shift of alliances within the factions of Christian Democracy had brought about the gradual isolation of the party secretary and premier, Ciriaco De Mita (a member of the left-wing faction) and the clear defeat of a political line in favor, at least in its declared program, of party renewal and institutional reforms. The party congress took place in February and De Mita was ousted from the position of party secretary. The deteriorating relationship between Christian Democracy and the Socialist Party and between the latter and the Republican and Liberal Parties led, during the PSI congress, to the withdrawal of Socialist ministers from the government and to the resignation of Ciriaco De Mita from the premiership on 19 May, which set off one of the longest crises in the history of the Italian Republic.[1]

Not only did this context of political crisis condition the European election campaign, but also the crisis itself was prolonged in expectation of the new balance of forces that would emerge from the election results.[2] What was forecast—and what the Socialists hoped for—was above all a growth in the Socialist vote, a collapse of the Communist Party and the consequent possibility of holding an early national election if the balance of forces so permitted (cf. Pasquino, 1990:55–6). The expectation that the Christian Democrat and Socialist share of the vote would increase at the expense of the PCI was

---

1 Besides the political aspect, it immediately emerged that the crisis was also institutional. After the secretary of the Republican Party, Giovanni Spadolini, had been given the task of sounding out the possibility of forming a government, the debate over the powers of the President of the Republic and the republican form of government intensified. The decision of the President, Francesco Cossiga, to entrust Spadolini with an exploratory role as a way to solve the crisis appeared to be "both a renunciation of the powers and duties of the President of the Republic and a supine acceptance of the partisan interests of the PSI and the DC and the subordination of the general public interest to a rapid solution to the crisis" (Pasquino, 1990:56).

2 The crisis was provoked by the opinion that the European election could act as "a true indicator of citizens' preference regarding the formation of the national government coalition". (Bardi, 1990a:39).

strengthened by the results of local elections in Sardinia on 11 June, a few days before the European election; but the European election itself—as a nation-wide surrogate for national elections—took an increasingly oracular aura as the day of the election approached.

Other events could have played a role in setting the 1989 European election within a truly European dimension and in awakening the Italian electorate's interest in it, but this did not happen. The approval of the European Single Market had led to an increase in the decision-making power of the European Parliament and to the mounting importance of the parliamentary majority in that body and, hence, the European vote. Also as a consequence of the single market, attention had been drawn to "a growing importance attached by an ever wider range of national parties to questions involving the Community and to alliances with political forces in other Member States" (Bardi, 1990a:2). Above all, the factor which could have been the most relevant in arousing the electorate's attention to European matters was the referendum on a treaty of European Union,[3] which—uniquely in Italy—was held in conjunction with the European election. Evidently, although these elements are important at the level of party political strategy, their importance was not really grasped by the voters, whether due to weak coverage by the press or because European questions have not yet been included in the parties' political communication with their own supporters, except in wholly generic terms. Above all, the focus on what the elections would reveal about the strength of national forces in the context of the prolonged government crisis, overcame all other perspectives.

The Political System

The Italian political system has been defined as a system of "extreme, multipolar and polarized pluralism" made up of a large number of political parties (Sartori, 1982). At the time of the 1989 European elections, the main pole was still occupied by Christian Democracy (DC), which lay at the center of the political continuum, while two secondary poles were occupied by the Communist Party (PCI) and the Italian Social Movement (MSI), opponents of the system on the extreme left and on the extreme right of the continuum respectively. Between these poles lay the other traditional Italian political parties. The so-called lay parties were the Liberal Party (PLI) to the right of the DC, and the Republican Party (PRI) and Social-Democratic Party (PSDI) to the left. The Italian Socialist Party (PSI), at one time close to the PCI, had for years been

---

3 Luciano Bardi points out, however, that the holding of the referendum at the same time "was not enough to underline the European significance of the election" (Bardi, 1990b:104).

moving more and more towards the center.[4] What we had, therefore, was a highly fragmented system with a wide ideological divergence between the two extreme poles.

Apart from the ideological aspect of the location of Italian parties between the extremes of right and left, there is a further important cleavage in the Italian political system: that based on religion. It does not take the form of a division between two different creeds but of the opposition between a lay and a confessional culture, where one party, Christian Democracy (DC), has a strongly religious nature. The opposition to the DC, which involved all the other traditional parties to varying degrees, found its most extreme form in the PCI. It and the DC were the two largest political forces. In certain regions, strong traditional cultural and political identities constituted networks of belonging that amounted to a highly structured socio-organizational fabric, which guaranteed a strong and widespread integration in terms of images of society, models of behavior and processes of socialization (cf. Capecchi et al. 1968:320). These subcultures, moreover, were thought to mark off sections of the electorate that were in part removed from the competitive arena of the parties since, due to subcultural 'belonging', voters in those subcultures always voted the same way (cf. Sartori 1982:279–80).

This picture had partially changed during the years leading up to the 1989 elections. First of all, the importance of the subcultures had declined considerably as Italian society was subjected to increasing modernization and secularization. The area of consensus of the traditional parties had diminished (and continued to diminish) to the benefit of new social actors, with the result that voters did not express any party preference (cf. Mackie, Mannheimer and Sani, 1992).

The ideological reference points for the new actors were different; the Greens and the Leagues had a much less clearly defined position on the left/right continuum. This has manifestly affected the structure of electoral competition, which had started to be shaped by new dimensions and were also fostered by the declining numbers of voters 'not in the market' because of subcultural identification.

An idea of the relationships between the different parties may be derived from the way in which the voters' perception of the political system is structured. Table 11.1 shows the propensity of the potential electorate of one party to

---

4 Other political forces at the time of the 1989 European election were the Radical Party (PR) and the Greens on the left of the continuum; Proletarian Democracy (DP) and the Anti-Prohibition League on the extreme left; the traditional regionalist lists, the South-Tyrol People's Party (PPST-SVP), the Val d'Aosta Union (UV) and the Sardinian Action Party (PSDA) at the center; the Lombard League and the other new leagues, which form a new right-wing opposition to the system.

consider the possibility of voting for another on the basis of the 'probability to vote' variables described in Chapter 3 of this book.

The first thing to note is the relatively high degree of overlap between the electorates of the different parties, even though none of the political forces comes close to being taken into consideration by half of the total electorate. The area of electoral competition has undoubtedly broadened due to the strong potential of the Greens, who despite being chosen by less than 5 percent of voters reach the same vote potential as the Communist Party.

The fundamental dimension that structures competition between the parties is essentially their position on the left/right continuum. Generally speaking, the further we move away from the political position of a party, the smaller its potential electorate becomes. There are, however, two elements that complicate this model. The Greens are an attractive alternative for the supporters of all the other political forces, obtaining high percentages of probable voters across the board. They are the only party which, by virtue of their limited ideological character and because they have a program focusing on themes that have only recently become political issues, does not compete in a precise political area but against virtually all the other parties.[5]

Table 11.1 Potential Support and Overlap Between Parties in Italy in 1989

	DP	PCI	PSI	Verdi	PSDI	PLIPRI	DC	MSI
DP	1.00	0.27	0.18	0.26	0.26	0.22	0.10	0.21
PCI	0.80	1.00	0.44	0.50	0.48	0.43	0.25	0.36
PSI	0.46	0.38	1.00	0.48	0.76	0.57	0.38	0.47
VERDI	0.74	0.47	0.53	1.00	0.60	0.61	0.38	0.48
PSDI	0.35	0.22	0.40	0.29	1.00	0.50	0.27	0.38
PLI-PRI	0.40	0.26	0.41	0.40	0.68	1.00	0.35	0.53
DC	0.37	0.30	0.54	0.49	0.74	0.69	1.00	0.54
MSI	0.23	0.13	0.20	0.18	0.30	0.31	0.16	1.00
Potential Support (%)	10.8	32.3	27.5	30.5	14.5	19.7	39.1	11.6
%Vote Elect	1.0	20.9	11.2	4.7	2.0	3.3	24.9	4.2
%Valid Vote	1.3	27.6	14.8	6.2	2.7	4.4	32.9	5.5
L-R median (1-10)	1.68	1.77	3.63	4.31	4.32	5.91	6.22	9.63

---

5 Although the greens attract considerable support across the entire spectrum of traditional parties, the strength of this support is not (yet?) sufficiently developed to make it the most attractive of all parties for many voters. For many it is their second or third choice, which accounts for the large differential between potential vote and actual vote in Table 11.1.

A further dimension can be derived from the relationship between Christian Democracy and the Socialist Party. They compete to a large extent with one another, and this applies especially to the Socialist electorate, which, of all the alternatives on offer, is most strongly inclined towards the DC. These two parties had for years been the most important in government coalition formation, and though they have their roots in areas that are ideologically different, they vie for the voters in the center, those that support the government majority.

Lastly, it is interesting to note that the Italian Social Movement (MSI) remained in a certain sense isolated, since it is the party that is least likely to attract the votes of the rest of the electorate.

The European Election of 1989

Elections for the European Parliament constitute a special type of consultation in which on the one hand the entire electorate is involved but, on the other, the institutional body concerned is unable to control the distribution of resources.[6] As a consequence, European elections are often seen as simply a way to measure and test the political mood of the country, and the election campaigns themselves generally focus on national concerns.

As is well known, a distinction is made at the theoretical level between first-order and second-order elections,[7] the latter having little influence on the effective balance of national political forces or on the composition of the government. European elections are thought for this reason to result in lower electoral turnout than national elections and a greater fluidity in voting patterns, with the possibility of voters opting at no risk for new or marginal political forces or for opposition parties. The fact that the composition of the government is not an important issue in the election campaign is sometimes supposed to favor the expression of a more ideological and less 'pragmatic' voting choice— especially since there is also no real inter-party conflict over important Community issues.[8] Indeed, there is a total lack of tension in Italian politics over European themes. The references that were made by commentators and

---

6 On the so-called 'democratic deficit' see Marquand (1979) and Weiler (1982).

7 For the application of the theoretical model of second-order elections to European elections see Reif (1984a:244–55); Reif and Schmitt (1980:3–44); Reif (1984a); and Reif (1985a). For Italy cf. Bardi (1990b) and Di Virgillio (1991) . See also Morlino and Uleri (1989:278).

8 Cf. Bardi (1990a) and Di Virgillio (1991:323–26). The resistance once put up by the Communist Party and the Italian Social Movement to the EC has now been entirely removed, for reasons both of international strategy involving the formation of an independent neutral area between the superpowers and of a strategy of alliances between the other political forces in Europe. Even in the Socialist camp, where there is potential opposition to European union in other countries, the Italian Socialist Party has always displayed a highly positive attitude towards the Community.

politicians, both during the election campaign and when analyzing the results, were always to national political issues. This is at least partly because the general attitude towards the Community is very favorable. Over 85 percent of respondents declare themselves in favor of unification and consider Community issues important. Almost 80 percent think it is a good thing to belong to the European Community, while 67 percent believe that Italy has benefitted from membership. Moreover, those who vote for the various parties display no major differences as regards approval of the European Community (van der Eijk and Franklin, 1991).

The Results of the Election

The expectations that had been generated by this election came only partially true in the results (see Table 11.2). The Socialists' hopes for a reduction of the gap between themselves and the Communist Party were not realized. Despite losing considerable ground compared to the 1984 European election, the PCI improved when compared to the previous national election, while the increase in the Socialist vote, though substantial compared to the 1984 European election, was only half a percentage point when compared to the most recent national election.

The decline of the PCI (from 33.3 percent, in 1984 to 27.6 percent in 1989 with a loss of 5 seats in the European Parliament) was, however, one of the most significant results. Other losers were the lay parties—the Social Democrats (PSDI), the Liberals (PLI) and the Republicans (PRI)—which taken together dropped from 9.6 percent to 7.1 percent;[9] and the Italian Social Movement (MSI), which lost one percentage point and one seat. There was no substantial change for the DC, the South-Tyrol People's Party (PPST-SVP), the Val d'Aosta Union list, the Sardinian Action Party (UV-PSDA), or Proletarian Democracy. The PSI, by contrast, grew from 11.2 percent to 14.8 percent, and gained 3 seats (winning 12 in all), thus contributing to the general advance of the Socialist lists in Europe. A further 8 seats went to forces that were presenting themselves for the first time at a European election: Green List (3.8 percent), Rainbow Greens (2.4 percent), Lombard League (1.8 percent), and Anti-Prohibitionists (1.2 percent).

Italy, therefore, was also affected by a phenomenon common to other Community countries: a growth in both the small and new lists and movements. These virtually doubled their support in Italy from 6.4 percent of the vote in

---

9 The leader of the Radicals, Marco Pannella, was in the 1989 election a candidate on a single list together with the Republicans, while other radicals were not on the lists of the PSDI, the Rainbow Greens and the Anti-Prohibitionists.

1984 to 12.1 percent in 1989,[10] at the expense of traditional opposition forces (as already noted) but also of government parties, whose vote declined from 57.4 percent to 54.8 percent.[11] Although it can be read as a characteristic feature of second-order elections, this tendency was already present in the preceding 1987 national election, in which the smaller parties had increased their share of the vote to 10.2 percent from 6.9 percent at the 1983 national election. Furthermore, the result of the referendum, in which the share of the vote in favor of a treaty of European Union reached 88.1 percent, moved in the same direction of a desire for change and a reduction in the traditional pattern of 'identification' and/or 'subcultural' voting for a party.

Table 11.2 Result of European and National Elections (Chamber of Deputies) 1979-1989 (Percentages)

Lists	1989 EE %	1989 EE Seats	1987 NE %	1984 EE %	1984 EE Seats	1979 EE %	1979 EE Seats
DC	32.9	26	34.3	33.0	26	36.4	29
PCI	27.6	22	26.6	33.3	27	29.6	24
PSI	14.8	12	14.3	11.2	9	11.0	9
MSI-DN	5.5	4	5.9	6.5	5	5.4	4
PLI-PRI-Fed	4.4	4		6.1	5		
PRI			3.7			2.6	2
PLI			2.1			3.6	3
PSDI	2.7	2	2.9	3.5	3	4.3	4
Fed. Green Lists	3.8	3	2.5				
DP*	1.3	1	1.7	1.4	1	1.9	2
Radical Party			2.6	3.4	3	3.7	3
Rainbow Greens	2.4	2					
Anti Prohibition League	1.2	1					
PPST	0.5	1	0.5	0.6	1	0.6	1
UV - PSDA	0.6	1	0.5	0.5	1	0.5	
Lombard League	1.8	2	0.5				
Other Lists	0.5	1.9	0.5		0.4		
Total	100.0	81	100.0	100.0	81	100.0	81

Source: ISTAT - Ministry of the Interior.
* The 1979 figure for Proletarian Democracy (DP) also includes that for the Party of Proletarian Unity.

---

10 If one considers the overall trend of European elections, one also notes, that the aggregate vote for the major parties decreased through the three elections, while the share of the vote for the small and new parties increased.

11 The growth of the right in the rest of Europe was not matched by the MSI in Italy.

A comparison between voting in the 1989 European election, at the 1987 national election, and voting intentions for the next national election help to clarify the significance of the European vote (see Table 11.3). Some features of the 1989 election cannot be put down to the particular context of the European election but are instead confirmed by the voting intentions for the next national election. The growth of smaller and newer parties is not in fact confined to the European election but is also found in the voting intentions for national elections. Rather than showing any difference from the other elections in Italy, the European vote is fully in line with the trends which previous elections, national and European, displayed.

The most striking fact is the percentage of blank ballots and abstentions, which was manifestly higher in the European election. Though only 4.3 percent said they would not have voted at a national election held on the same day,

Table 11.3 Declared Voting at 1989 European Election and 1987 National Election and Voting Intentions at Next National Election

Lists	National Election June 1987		European Election June 1989		Voting Intention Next National Election	
	n	%	n	%	n	%
DC	231	32.3	228	28.6	226	29.9
PCI	169	23.6	165	20.7	184	24.3
PSI	93	13.0	94	11.8	101	13.4
PSDI	17	2.4	17	2.1	19	2.5
PLI-PRI-Fed			30	3.8		
PLI	7	1.0			11	1.5
PRI	19	2.7			17	2.2
Radical Party	11	1.5			6	0.8
MSI	27	3.8	25	3.1	26	3.4
DP and Other Left*	16	2.2	10	1.3	16	2.1
Greens**	27	3.8	73	9.2	77	10.2
Other Parties	10	1.4			18	2.4
Lombard League			11	1.4		
Anti-prohibitionists			7	0.9		
Federalism			2	0.3		
Pensioners			3	0.4		
Blank	20	2.8	35	4.4	25	3.3
Not Voted	69	9.6	98	12.3	30	4.0
Total	716	100.0	798	100.0	756	100.0

Source: Post-electoral survey of the 1989 European Election Study (EES) in Italy
*In the European election only Proletarian Democracy (DP).
**In the European election Europe Greens and Rainbow Greens.

fully 9.4 percent failed to vote in the European election. This certainly suggests that the Italian electorate considered the European election to be less important.[12]

Turnout

The effective turnout of voters is considered particularly indicative in the case of European elections, both because it is generally used as a yardstick for the legitimacy and success of the European Community and because it can be used as an important factor in the interpretation of the character of the European vote. Turnout at this type of election is generally low in Italy as well as in the rest of the Community. In the 1989 European election Italy had the third highest turnout at 81.5 percent, behind Belgium and Luxembourg and just above Greece.[13] In the other eight countries, by contrast, levels of turnout were much lower, the average being 58.7 percent. On the whole, in the twelve Community countries turnout at European elections is around 60 percent compared to an average of 83.5 percent at national elections. It should be noted, however, that while the difference between turnout at national and European elections is about 23 percentage points in all the countries of the Community taken together, it is only 6 points in Italy. In Italy, therefore, although there is still a gap in turnout between the two different types of election, it is much narrower.

In order to explain the higher-than-average turnout in Italy at European elections, it must be remembered that there is a widespread perception of voting as a 'moral duty' (cf. Schmitt and Mannheimer, 1991a). However, the spread of a greater acceptability and 'legitimacy' of abstentionism has been noted, which is reflected in the lower turnout of recent years.[14] The percentage of Italians voting in the 1989 European election was lower than in the 1987 national election by 7.5 points. It was also lower in the previous two other European elections than in each preceding national election.

The reason for the lower turnout in European elections cannot be put down solely to the fact that the electorate views them as scarcely relevant, or

---

12   In order to evaluate these figures correctly, one has to take account of the number of respondents who failed to answer the question. Failure to vote is often concealed by failure to reply. In fact, on the question about European voting the percentage of non-responses is distinctly lower than in other cases (at the time of the interview it was the nearest event in both a temporal and psychological sense). In the question about the preceding national election non-response amounted to 25.2 percent, while for the question about future voting intentions this represented 21 percent of the sample. In the question regarding the 1989 European vote, non-response was only 16.6 percent.

13   In these countries voting is compulsory.

14   Cf. Mannheimer and Sani (1987:42–45), Di Virgillio (1991), Bardi (1990a,b)

that they are second-order elections—indeed, Table 11.4 shows no effect of European issues on turnout in Italy, just as in other countries of the European Union. On the other hand, a not inconsiderable factor is the difference between the electoral laws governing the two kinds of election. Polling stations are only open all day Sunday for European elections, whereas they stay open until 2 p.m. on Monday for national elections.[15] Furthermore, Italian citizens resident in other Community countries are allowed to vote. This has had the effect of artificially boosting the level of abstentionism due to the greater number of voters' certificates which are not handed in, because many emigrant voters have been counted twice as registered voters, both in their places of origin and in the Community countries where they now live.[16]

It should also be noted that the decline in turnout is not exclusive to European elections but, rather, a general trend affecting all elections from the end of the 1970s. The indifference towards European elections is not expressed, as one might suppose, in a greater number of non-valid votes. Comparison with the figures for national elections do not in fact show an unambiguous trend. There is not a particularly marked difference in the percentages of non-valid votes at European and at national elections, and the variations which do occur do not always have the same arithmetical sign. In the first two European elections, the number of blank and void votes was lower than in the preceding national election.

Table 11.4 Predictors of 1989 Participation in the European Election in Italy

	R^2	Added R^2
Demographics	0.02	
General Political Orientations	0.12	0.10
Habitual Voting	0.13	0.02
European Attitudes	0.14	0.00

---

15 See Bardi (1990b:107–110 and 1985:293–312). Another difference in the respective electoral laws works, in contrast, in two different directions. At European elections, the country is divided into only five constituencies, which are therefore much larger than at national elections. This makes it possible, on the one hand, to put forward well-known candidates in every constituency and attract the voters but, on the other, it prevents the blanket canvassing which is normally carried out in a more limited and easily controllable area.

16 Cf. Di Virgillio (1991:329–30). On the subject of abstentionism see also Mannheimer and Sani (1987: Chapter 3). The abstention rate among Italian voters resident abroad is much higher. At the 1989 election the abstention rate among such voters was 37.0 percent, at the 1984 election 41.7 percent and at the 1979 election 35.7 percent. However, the number of voters involved is very low: 612,642 in the last election, that is, 1.3 percent of the total Italian electorate.

Though settling at markedly lower levels than for national elections, the turnout of Italians at European elections does not seem to indicate substantially different voting trends, when also viewed in the light of the differences in electoral laws and the poorer performance of the other member countries (cf. Bardi, 1990:107–110). The decline in turnout is part of a general indifference to voting that has affected all elections in recent years.

At least in the case of Italy, the hypothesized lower turnout in a second-order election is debatable. Despite the fact that the turnout figures point in this direction, as seen above, the result of the vote matches perfectly with the national trend. The erosion of support for the government majority and other traditional parties to the benefit of small and new political forces are factors that had already been prefigured in the 1987 national election. The 1989 European vote anticipated the results of later elections to the Chamber and the Senate in April, 1992. In this last national election to have been held under the old electoral laws, the parties in the government majority and other traditional parties suffered heavier losses than ever before and the 'long wave' of the Socialist Party, the slow but constantly rising trend, now seems to be at an end. Hence, it is with this 1992 national election, even more than at the European election, that the vote appears to be one which is to a great extent freed from traditional 'identification' and 'belonging'.

Party Choice

The small effects of the European electoral context are confirmed by an analysis of the differences between parties supported in the European election and the parties respondents said they would have chosen at a (hypothetical) concurrent national election. In this analysis we distinguish between, on one side, the simple effect of the rate of turnout and, on the other, the effect of the type of election (quasi-switching). Table 11.5 shows, first of all, that there are in reality no marked differences between the two types of election, the biggest gap being a 1.5 percent loss to Christian Democracy, compared to the votes they would have received in a concurrent national election. The biggest differences are, however, to be attributed to the effect of the different turnout rates while the type of election explains very little.

Naturally, the two different factors are not distributed to the same extent among the various parties. In the case of the lay parties and Proletarian Democracy, the most important element is in fact the different type of election. But even in those cases, it seems very doubtful that one can speak of a specific European dimension to voting, of a different pattern in voters' political choices than at national elections. On the contrary, the Italian vote is relatively stable over time and little influenced by different contexts.

Table 11.5 Quasi–switching and Turnout Effects in the 1989 European Election in Italy

	EE	NE	EE-NE	Quasi-switching	Turnout Effect
DP	1.3	2.0	-0.7	-0.5	-0.2
PCI	27.6	28.8	-1.2	-0.4	-0.8
PSI	14.8	14.5	0.3	-0.3	0.6
Verdi	6.2	7.2	-1.0	-1.0	0.0
PSDI	2.7	2.8	-0.1	0.0	-0.1
PLI-PRI	4.4	3.8	0.6	0.8	-0.2
DC	32.9	31.7	1.2	0.8	0.4
MSI	5.5	5.0	0.5	0.4	0.1
Other	4.6	4.2	0.4	0.2	0.2

Voter Motivation

The position of the parties on European issues was not the only or main criterion adopted by electors in casting their vote. 47 percent of voters referred to the position of the parties on national issues as against 37 percent who held that European issues were important. Among the domestic motives for the way they voted, the majority of Respondents, 65.7 percent, took the existing government into consideration (Table 11.6).

These findings do make it seem as though European issues might have had some importance in determining the election result, in contrast to our earlier inferences on the basis of electoral outcomes. However, it can be ascertained that, while the variables relating to interest correlate—as is to be expected—with the 'European' motives behind voting, when effective knowledge of, and therefore concrete interest in, the Community is examined, the same relationship is weaker. Once again, the attention paid by Italians to the European Community appears to be mainly superficial, a generic declaration of interest that is not always backed up by a real involvement in, and true awareness of, Community issues.

European elections, therefore, appear to have little specific impact. They are not perceived as separate arenas of political competition. The way people vote is influenced above all by domestic political issues. Only the Greens show a greater interest in European issues and are perhaps the only parties among the small and new ones that have gained any advantage from European elections. In every other respect, it is improbable that these elections have acted as a 'midwife of new parties'. What we have is a phenomenon which, with regard to electoral behavior in Italy, should be seen above all to be related

Table 11.6 Voting Motivation at the 1989 European Election

In Deciding Who to Vote For, More Importance was Given to the Position of the Parties On:	%	%
National Issues	47.2	
of which: *By Voting I Wanted to Express:*		
Support for Government		26.4
Warning to Government		13.6
Opposition to Government		25.7
Did Not Consider Government		28.6
Don't Know		5.7
European Issues	37.1	
Don't Know	15.7	
Total %	100.0	110.0
n	859	405

Source: Post-electoral survey of EES'89 in Italy.

to local and national concerns, in part because the European electoral system works to the disadvantage of small parties.

Electoral Mobilization

An analysis of the evolution of voting intentions and declared voting at the 1989 European election in the three waves of the European election study shows that different behavior patterns took shape in the last few months before the election. The mobilization of the Green electorate, for instance, occurred above all in the period between the second pre-election survey in April 1989 and polling day on the 18th of June.

It is worth looking in more detail at the data of the April survey. In it, Christian Democracy recorded its lowest percentage while failures to reply were higher than in both the first pre-electoral and, understandably, the post-electoral surveys. One possible way of looking at these data is to see them as an expression of the difficult moment which Italian politics was going through during those months. It led to the government crisis of the 19 May with, on one side, the lack of confidence in the main government party (and the party of the outgoing premier) and, on the other, the increasing uncertainty of citizens as to how to vote. Likewise, the growing percentage of those opting for the Communist Party and, in contrast, the decline of the Socialists also underlines the loss of confidence in the government parties and the advance of the opposition.

European Elections as Indicators of National Trends

As we saw in Table 11.4, earlier in this chapter, voting behavior at preceding national elections is the variable that best explains turnout in European elections, together with the civic attitudes and political orientations of respondents, while European and socio-structural features play practically no role.[17] The latter generally have very little effect on Italian electoral behavior. The importance of past voting behavior and of turnout at preceding national elections exclude a 'European' orientation in the behavior of voters at the 1989 European election. The Italian electorate is constant in its focus on domestic issues, which continue to influence behavior also in a European context.

Rather than by a lack of interest in, or a feeling of hostility towards, the European Community, which—as seen above—is unlikely to be found within an overall favorable political context, effective turnout at European elections is determined by the same causes that make voters go to the polls at national elections. Whatever the particular motives for voting choice, the reference points are still chiefly the domestic political parties and the national government; and electors cast their vote with these actors in mind. The same, strictly national, terms of confirming or withdrawing confidence in the parties and the government propel the election campaign, and the election results are interpreted accordingly by the parties and the media. Moreover, the role of past voting experience shows that the habit of voting, going to the polls because that is what one has always done, is still an important factor in casting one's vote.[18]

For this reason, the high rate of turnout in Italy should not be read as a 'success' for the European Community, and its legitimacy in the eyes of the Italian electorate; paradoxically, it might turn out to be a symptom of a basic indifference on the part of the voters and of their inability to see European elections as something different from national elections.

The European Parliament is still seen in Italy to have very little relevance in terms of regulatory powers. Although, on the one hand, this permits a less sober attitude and greater 'irresponsibility' when voting, on the other hand it means that European elections are inevitably loaded with national political significance, to the extent that they have no distinct identity of their own. In this sense, the hypothesized consequences of second-order elections do not seem to materialize in Italy. Various aspects of the June 1989 European election, from the not excessive difference in rates of turnout to the results in apparent

---

17 By adding those who did not cast a valid vote to espondents who did not turn out, the incidence of 'non-voting' reaches 13.9 percent

18 See Schmitt and Mannheimer (1991a)

conformity with the national trend, rather than showing European elections to be less important elections which nonetheless have their own specific features, point to their convergence with national elections, thereby confirming in practice an interpretation in exclusively national terms.

The Domestic Consequences of the 1989 Election

Because the 1989 European election was treated by all concerned as an oracle, announcing what would have happened had it been a national election, the consequences of the European election were very much what they would have been had the election indeed been a national one. As stated earlier, the governing parties had hoped that the continuing decline in votes for the Communists would be to their advantage, and that evidence of increasing voter support would strengthen their hands in the continuing government crisis. In fact this did not happen. As we have seen, government parties lost votes in the European election compared to the previous election, although not as many as the Communists did. The main beneficiaries were the small and new parties.

So the European election result was not a vote of confidence in the government, which therefore did not call a national election as it might have done had the omens been more favorable; and the government crisis had to be resolved in a different fashion.

CHAPTER 12

Luxembourg:
Second-order Irrelevance

Cees van der Eijk and Hermann Schmitt

Luxembourg, the smallest of the member-states of the European Union, elects only six members of the European Parliament. Even with that small number, its citizens are still relatively over-represented in that Parliament, as is illustrated most tellingly by comparing its ratio of eligible voters to seats (approximately 200,000 per seat) to that of neighboring Germany, which had in 1989 the highest ratio in the EU (approximately 565,000 eligible voters per seat).[1] Although it is absolutely clear to the Luxembourgers that this small number of delegates renders moot the likelihood of their delegation decisively influencing European policies, this has not deterred them from continuously and consistently promoting the cause of European integration and calling for enhanced powers for the European Parliament.[2]

Luxembourg was one of three countries in which European and national parliamentary elections coincided in 1989. But whereas in Greece and Ireland the simultaneity resulted from the particular course of domestic political developments in the months immediately prior to June 1989, in Luxembourg this was not so. European and national elections in Luxembourg also coincided in 1979 and 1984, owing to the fact that the maximum term for the Luxembourg parliament is 5 years—the same as the fixed term of the European Parliament—while premature dissolution of the national parliament is a very rare phenomenon in Luxembourg politics. Consequently, until a conflict arises that is important enough to lead the government to dissolve the national parliament, national and European elections will remain 'wedded' to one another. Possibly even more than in other countries, this coincidence results in the national political

---

1 Exact figures on the size of the respective electorates in 1989 and the number of seats per country in the European Parliament are given in Appendix D.

2 This attitude on the part of the Luxembourg government is not, however, entirely shared by its population. In response to an often asked Eurobarometer question on whether the European Parliament should play a more important role than it does, Luxembourg samples since 1987 consistently show themselves less enthusiastic than any other national sample, except for Denmark and the United Kingdom (Eurobarometer 1993:141–147).

arena structurally overshadowing whatever 'European' matters otherwise might manifest themselves in the electoral contest.

What, if any, differences could one expect to see between European and national elections under these circumstances? At first blush, one might be tempted to expect no differences at all. As we shall see, however, the results of the two elections differ considerably. One reason for this is to be found in the differences between the electoral systems which are used in national and European elections. A second reason has to do with differences in the slate of parties and candidates participating in both contests. A third concerns differences in voters' motivations which spring from the different tactical situation in the two elections.

The Electoral System

In national parliamentary elections Luxembourg uses a special variant of proportional representation. The country is divided in four multi-member districts, each of which is represented by a number of seats proportional to its share of the electorate. In each of these districts, parties may present lists of candidates no longer than the number of seats contested in that district. The order of the candidates on the list has no special meaning and is sometimes just alphabetical. Voters cast as many votes as their are seats to be filled. Voters may distribute their votes over different candidates (which do not need to be of the same list), and can even cast more than one of their votes for a single candidate. Alternatively, voters may cast a list-vote. List-votes (which are equivalent to giving each candidate on the list one preference vote) count toward the total number of seats a party acquires, but are irrelevant in determining which of its candidates is elected, as that aspect is determined by the differences in the number of votes which have been cast for each of the candidates. In contrast to many other systems of proportional representation, this leaves parties powerless in determining (by the ordering of their list) which of their candidates will be elected. Of course, the real power of the parties lies in their right to decide whether or not to include a particular candidate on their list at all. After that it is entirely in the hands of the voters who will be elected. This system makes for a highly personalized kind of electoral politics which is reinforced by the division of the (very small) country in four districts.

The electoral system used for European elections in Luxembourg resembles the national one, yet differs in a number of ways which do make a difference. First of all, the country as a whole is one constituency, and each party may nominate more candidates (to a maximum of twelve) than the number of seats (six) to be filled. Here too, voters have, as many votes as there are seats, but they have to distribute their votes over different candidates (or cast a list-vote). They may not cast more than one vote for a single candidate.

One important consequence of the differences between the electoral systems for national and European elections is that, whereas parties may in national elections capitalize on the regional popularity of a candidate, in European elections they need to field candidates of national renown. Thus, the only nation-wide electoral arena that transcends regional and particularistic interests and issues is that of European elections, not that of national elections.

The Party System

The major European political movements of christian democracy, social democracy and liberalism dominate the Luxembourg party system. The Christian Social Party (CSV) is traditionally the largest party which has participated (as the leading party) in most post-World War II coalition governments. Ideologically it is clearly to the right of center, more so than its counterparts in Belgium, Germany and the Netherlands.[3] Traditionally, the second largest party in the country is the Socialist Workers' Party (LSAP), which belongs to the mainstream of European social democracy and maintains strong ties to the labor unions. Its strength is concentrated in the industrial areas in the south of the country, but the party had in recent decades to reorient itself from a blue-collar to a white-collar profile because of the greatly diminished importance of heavy industry. The third large party, which is of liberal hue, is the Democratic Party (DP). Originally a rather conservative party, it has successfully adopted a more centrist position since the late 1960s. For a brief period, under the leadership of Gaston Thorn in the 1970s, it led the national government in a coalition with the socialists; but, with the exception of the 1979 European elections, it has remained numerically the smallest of the three major parties.

In addition to the major parties, Luxembourg has several minor ones. Some of these belong to ideological traditions which are characteristic of many European countries, while the remainder are in general either single-issue parties or components of the lunatic fringe which occasionally registers some electoral success. Three ideological streams need to be mentioned. The Communist Party (KPL) was quite successful during the 1960s when it obtained more than 10 percent of the vote, but has declined considerably since then. The extreme-right is represented by the National Bewegong, and, historically, by a series of different parties which characteristically followed a rise-shine-decline

---

3 Compare the CSV's left/right position in the bottom row of Table 12.1, with the position of the major christian democratic counterparts in the surrounding countries, displayed in the analogous tables of Chapters 3, 7 and 12.

pattern of electoral success. The green movement is represented in Luxembourg by several parties, the most important of which are the GAP and the (break-away) GLEI. The first of these is more radical and is perceived to be a little to the left of the social democrats, whereas the GLEI is generally seen as consider-ably more centrist (see also Table 12.1).

In spite of the fact that all European elections have been held in conjunction with national ones, the same parties do not participate in each contest. In 1989 an important single-issue party in the national elections favored applying civil servants' generous rules for retirement pensions to everyone. This group obtained 4 seats in the 60 seat parliament, but it did not compete in the Euro-pean election, thus forcing a considerable number of voters to switch parties between the two simultaneous contests. Similar differences between the options open to the voters at European and national elections existed in 1979 (cf. Hirsch, 1985) and 1984 (cf. Hirsch, 1984).

The competitive relations between the various parties follow a pattern which conforms to that in countries with similar party systems. When considering the sum of the potential electorates of the various parties it becomes apparent that none of the parties can afford to take its votes for granted, even without taking into account the potential appeal of single-issue parties. Competitive relations are rather broad-ranging, meaning that there are no clear segments within which competition is fierce, but between which it is limited. On the contrary, each of the three mainstream parties, together with the two green parties, competes for votes with each of the others to a high degree. In all cases more than half (usually more than 60 percent) of the potential electorate

Table 12.1 Potential Support and Overlap Between Parties in Luxembourg in 1989

	KP	GAP	LSAP	GLEI	DP	CSV	Nat. Bew.
KP	1.00	0.38	0.21	0.36	0.24	0.19	0.58
GAP	0.75	1.00	0.44	0.80	0.50	0.36	0.68
LSAP	0.57	0.61	1.00	0.56	0.67	0.56	0.45
GLEI	0.71	0.81	0.41	1.00	0.46	0.35	0.79
DP	0.58	0.61	0.59	0.56	1.00	0.52	0.60
CSV	0.61	0.60	0.68	0.59	0.71	1.00	0.55
National Bewegong	0.48	0.29	0.14	0.33	0.21	0.14	1.00
Potential Support (%)	14.1	27.7	38.1	27.8	33.9	46.5	11.7
%Vote Elect	4.1	3.8	22.2	5.3	17.5	30.5	2.5
%Valid Vote	4.7	4.3	25.4	6.1	20.0	34.9	2.9
L-R median (1–10)	1.9	3.9	4.0	4.3	5.6	8.0	8.6

of one of these parties also belongs to other potential electorates. The relatively small potential following of the extreme parties (communists and National Bewegong) is also strongly attracted to other parties (as shown in the appropriate columns of Table 12.1)—although these parties themselves are not considered very attractive by the followers of more mainstream parties (as is reflected in the rows for the KPL and NB, respectively). The low degree of mutual isolation of the potential electorates of the Luxembourg parties indicates that most voters are potential switchers. It follows that seemingly minor factors, such as the appeal of particular candidates and the salience of local issues, may induce voters to make different choices in different (even if simultaneous) elections.

The extent to which the various parties are able to convert their potential support into actual votes differs greatly. Only the CSV, LSAP and DP manage to secure some 60 percent or more of their potential support. This reflects the fact that, where voters have to choose between different parties which they find sufficiently attractive on substantive grounds (ideology, issues, representation of cleavage groups), they also take into account party size (and hence the likelihood that it would be able to put its programs into practice), choosing a more powerful party rather than a weaker one if the degree of attraction on other grounds is not too dissimilar.[4]

Party Choice in European and National Elections

As discussed above, the different rules governing European and national elections, and the different options on offer in the two types of contest (together with the fact that voters are attracted to more than just one party) provide ample reasons for the results of European and national elections to differ. Table 12.2 gives, for all three European elections held so far, their results together with those of the simultaneous national elections. This table shows clearly that considerable differences exist between the results of concurrent elections. To a considerate extent, this is caused by the variety of lists which compete in national elections (in the table classified under the label "others", which also includes lists which do not compete in all four constituencies) but not in European elections. In all three election years, the category "others" gains considerably fewer votes in European elections. Nevertheless, an analysis of individual switching in the simultaneous national and European elections of 1989, based on data from the European election study (see Appendix A), shows that of all individual party switching, only about one third is linked to

---

4 This phenomenon is discussed in more detail in an analysis of party choice in Chapter 20 and, in other contexts, in Schmitt (1990b) and van der Eijk and Oppenhuis (1991).

the different availability of parties in both contests.[5] For the largest part, therefore, switching is not 'forced' upon voters but the consequence of their own choice—be it because of differential appeal of candidates in both contests, by the different tactical situations which these elections offer, or any other kind of reason.

The pattern of differences between simultaneous election results in all three years does not show the pattern often associated with second-order elections, namely that large parties lose votes and small parties gain (for a review of the literature on second-order elections, see Chapter 2). Whether or not this happens is clearly dependent on other factors, some of which may be election-specific. The largest party in the country, the CSV, was virtually unaffected by switching in 1979, negatively affected in 1984, but positively affected in 1989. The LSAP was hurt by switching in all three elections (although each time only to a limited extent), whereas the Liberal DP was in all three European elections a clear beneficiary of switching—in 1979 to a spectacular extent. The Greens, in spite of being fragmented between different lists, clearly benefitted from switching in the European elections.

No simple process or single factor is likely to give rise to this variegated set of differences. A 'mechanical' effect probably plays a role, but even this does not have to be singular. The likelihood of 'wasting' one's vote(s) on a small party, for example, is larger when only six seats are to be elected instead of 60 for the national parliament.[6] The existence of only one constituency

Table 12.2 Results of Simultaneous European (EE) and National (NE) Elections in Luxembourg, 1979, 1984 and 1989

	EE79	NE79	EE84	NE84	EE89	NE89	EE-NE '89
CSV	36.1	36.4	34.9	36.6	34.9	32.4	2.5
LSAP	21.7	22.5	29.9	31.8	25.5	26.2	-0.7
DP	28.1	21.9	22.1	20.3	20.0	17.2	2.8
KPL	5.0	4.9	4.1	4.4	4.7	4.4	0.3
Green*	–	–	6.1	3.7	11.3	7.5	3.8
Others	9.1	14.3	2.9	12.3	3.6	12.3	-8.7

* Comprising the results for all green lists. In 1979 Green tabulated with "Others"

5   A number of small parties, classified under "others", did compete in both contests, but gained even fewer votes in European elections than in national ones—most likely because voters could easily determine that, with only six seats to be elected, voting for some of the lists would be tantamount to throwing one's vote away.

6   Although political entrepreneurs probably anticipate the smaller chances of success by submitting fewer lists at European than at national elections.

instead of four may, on the other hand, be advantageous to small parties as a single campaign may require fewer resourcethan four. This factor may also be an advantage to large parties, however, as these can now run their most renowned politicians in a nation-wide election, whereas in national elections the charisma of people such as Gaston Thorn, Jacques Santer, Jup Weber or Colette Flesch can only be used in one of four constituencies.

Psychological factors may also play a role. The knowledge that no real (European or national) power is at stake may change the voters' calculus but, because of concurrent existence of the two elections, protest voting in the European elections makes little sense. These experiences from Luxembourg are too limited to disentangle all these possible effects, but they are sufficient to point to a wide variety of different, and possibly countervailing influences, the combined effect of which may be as much dependent on the idiosyncracies of the current situation as on structural features of the second-order election context.

Voting is compulsory in Luxembourg and reached in 1989 some 87 percent for both national and European elections. Consequently, in contrast to most other member states, the result of the elections is not partially a function of turnout effects. With such high turnout it is hard to explain differences between individuals in regard to whether or not they vote. As one would expect, given compulsory voting, demographic and socio-economic background variables are hardly at all related to electoral participation. Most of the explanatory power that can be derived from the variables introduced in Chapter 3 is found in general political orientations. The fact that turnout is the same for both kinds of elections makes it unlikely that specifically European factors would play a role in this explanation, as is attested to by Table 12.3.

Domestic Consequences of European Elections

In general, domestic politics in Luxembourg have been largely unaffected by European elections, in 1989 just as in the two previous ones. The outcome of

Table 12.3 Predictors of 1989 Participation in the European Election in Luxembourg

	R^2	Added R^2
Demographics	0.01	
General Political Orientations	0.10	0.09
Habitual Voting	0.12	0.02
European Attitudes	0.12	0.00

the elections could not, as in some other countries, be construed as a kind of mid-term evaluation of government performance or as an update of parties' standing with the electorate. The fact that national elections were held concurrently prevented this. Whatever disparities occurred between the results of the two elections, the relationships between national political parties were untouched by the European election result. Since more relevant measures were provided by the concurrent national elections, there was simply no possibility for perceiving the European election as an indicator of national trends, or as a hint of new developments on the domestic front, as was often the case in other member states of the European Union. In terms of the campaign too, European elections can hardly be expected to offer a platform for a public debate on issues left undiscussed in domestic politics. Again, the simultaneity of the two elections, in conjunction with the overbearing dominance of the national one, prevented this (cf. Hirsch, 1984, 1985; Hearl, 1989). Yet, in quite a different sense, European elections do have a domestic political impact. As stated earlier, the European elections are in Luxembourg the only nation-wide elections, transcending the boundaries of the four different constituencies in which national elections are held. Consequently, they are the only forum in which the popularity and electoral standing of individual politicians can accurately be assessed. The Luxembourg system of proportional representation is also highly personalized (see above). These two phenomena together make the European elections an excellent test for the personal popularity of candidates nation-wide. This subsequently proves to be important when the media focus their attention on politicians shown in the European elections to be popular. The resulting publicity has an independent effect on the political fortunes of such individuals. Although three European elections may be too few from which to generalize with any certainty, it may ironically very well turn out that, at the very time that national entities become increasingly less important in an integrating Europe, European elections in Luxembourg, by offering the only nation-wide competitive arena, contribute more to national than to European integration, which was their prime purpose in the eyes of many politicians and of large segments of the mass public.

CHAPTER 13

The Netherlands:
Small Party Evolution

Erik Oppenhuis

In the Netherlands the European elections of 1989 were dominated by national political issues and national parties just as were those of 1979 and 1984. Virtually all parties on offer were represented in the national parliament. Because of lack of disagreement between them on European affairs, their contest for votes could not but lead to appeals on national topics (Kok et al., 1985; van der Eijk, 1984a, 1989). A brief introduction to the peculiarities of the national political context will be given in this chapter.

The dominance of national concerns and the almost complete absence of any European content from the campaign is characteristic of what Reif and Schmitt (1980) have termed second-order elections. Such elections are supposed to be characterized by comparatively low turnout on the one hand and more expressive and experimental voting on the other. Possible explanations for low turnout, and hypotheses derived from the literature on second-order elections regarding party choice will be examined.

Although there seems to be little at stake in European elections, this does not necessarily imply that these elections are of no consequence. Two such consequences can be distinguished. Firstly, the result of a European election does affect the composition of the European Parliament. Secondly, as will be discussed in this chapter, the European election may have an impact on national politics to the extent that parties and politicians interpret the result as reflecting their national standing with the electorate. Three possible consequences of such interpretations can be distinguished:

- The outcome may strain relationships between government coalition partners, for instance when their respective electoral strengths changed unequally in comparison with the last general election;
- the outcome may give rise to changes in policy positions when it is interpreted as a warning to, or support for, government and its policies;
- the outcome may strain internal relations in a party, for instance because of poor election results.

Whether any of these political effects were felt in the Netherlands in 1989 will be discussed later in this chapter.

Another way in which European elections may have an impact on national politics is by promoting change in the party system. A well known hypothesis in the literature on party systems is that electoral thresholds serve to reduce the fragmentation of the party system (cf. Lijphart, 1984). The Dutch party system developed under a very low effective threshold of 0.67 percent of the valid vote. Owing to the fact that in the European Parliament only 25 seats are allocated to representatives from the Netherlands, the threshold in European elections becomes 4 percent. We will assess whether or not this has affected the behavior and performance of small parties in the Netherlands. However, before these questions can be answered, the Dutch political system will be briefly described.

The Dutch Political System[1]

The Netherlands has a multi-party system. During the post-war period, the number of parties represented in the national parliament ranged from 7 to 14. This comparatively large number can be understood as a consequence of a system of proportional representation with a low electoral threshold. Many of the parties are rather small, holding just a few seats, or sometimes only a single seat, in the national parliament. The major parties are embedded firmly in the European political traditions of social democracy (PvdA—the labor party), christian democracy (CDA) and liberalism (VVD, a rather conservative party, and D66, often characterized as left-liberal). None of these parties ever reached, or even came close to, a parliamentary majority. In consequence governments in the Netherlands are always coalition governments. The most common pattern is one in which the Christian Democrats form a government with either PvdA or VVD.[2]

In addition to the major parties, a variety of small parties also exist. These are of two types: parties that have managed to survive in parliament for more than a few years and those that have not been able to do so. Only the first type will be discussed here. This type includes a number of small parties to the left of the Labor Party, often characterized as 'small left' parties. These are the Pacifist Socialist Party (PSP), the Communist Party of the Netherlands (CPN), and the Political Party of Radicals (PPR), the last of which could be

---

1 For an extensive discussion of the Dutch political system see Daalder (1987).

2 The Christian Democratic party (CDA), or their most important predecessor the Catholic People's Party (KVP) has always been represented in the government since World War II. The Labor Party (PvdA) and right-wing Liberal party (VVD) were either coalition partner or opposition party, but have not participated together in government since 1952.

said to be a 'new left' party. Since June 1989 these parties have merged to form a new national political party: Green Left.[3] The right side of the political spectrum harbors three orthodox Christian parties (SGP, GPV and RPF) which are each related to one or other of various protestant dominations.[4]

Party Competition

To what extent do these parties compete with each other? Information about party competition in the Netherlands is provided in Table 13.1, where the parties are ordered according to their position on the left/right continuum. The overlap of potential support between parties is greater as parties are closer together on the left/right scale. Therefore one can conclude that party competition in the Netherlands is predominantly structured by the ideological left/right dimension. The most interesting exception can be found in the column of the orthodox Christian parties. Although the conservative liberals (VVD) are in left/right terms closer to them than the Christian Democrats (CDA), their overlap with the CDA is larger than that of the VVD (68 versus 50 percent overlap). This reflects the shared Christian identity of CDA and these orthodox parties.

A second conclusion that can be drawn from this table is that party competition in the Netherlands is intense. The sum of the potential support

Table13.1 Potential Support and Overlap Between Parties in The Netherlands in 1989

	GL	PVDA	D66	CDA	VVD	O.Chr
Green Left	1.00	0.34	0.41	0.17	0.24	0.42
PVDA	0.74	1.00	0.57	0.31	0.33	0.38
D66	0.76	0.50	1.00	0.40	0.59	0.52
CDA	0.44	0.36	0.55	1.00	0.67	0.68
VVD	0.36	0.23	0.48	0.40	1.00	0.50
Orthodox Christian	0.28	0.11	0.18	0.18	0.21	1.00
Potential Support (%)	18.0	38.8	33.4	45.6	27.4	11.7
%Vote Elect	2.8	14.5	3.3	16.3	6.4	2.8
%Valid Vote	6.0	30.7	7.0	34.6	13.6	5.9
L-R Median (1–10)	2.31	3.19	4.67	6.81	7.53	8.43

---

3 A fourth party, the Evangelical People's Party, had no seats in Parliament.

4 For a more detailed discussion of small parties in the Netherlands see Lucardie (1991).

for the various parties amounts to 175 percent, so parties are in competition for most of the votes available at each election.

Finally, some assessment can be made about the performance of each party in the European elections in terms of its success in mobilizing its potential support. It appears that the larger parties, PvdA and CDA, performed better than the other parties in the European elections of 1989, mobilizing around three quarters of their potential supporters. The worst performance was that of D66, which has an enormous potential support, but converted less than a fifth of it into votes.

The Context of the European Elections of 1989

At the time of the European elections, nine parties were represented in parliament. The government had been composed of CDA and VVD who had ruled together since 1977 (with a brief 18 month interlude for an unsuccessful CDA-PvdA-D66 coalition in 1981–82). This coalition fell apart in May 1989 because of internal strife in the VVD and because of the Liberals' frustration with their role in the coalition as a mere junior partner (Anker and Oppenhuis 1990). As a consequence, new national elections were called for September 1989. By then it was quite clear that the next government coalition would consist of the Christian Democrats and Labor, possibly with the center-left liberals (D66). It was in this context that the European elections of June 1989 took place.

Turnout in the 1989 European Elections

For the first time in Dutch history turnout in a nationwide election dropped below 50 percent. Even in other so-called low profile contests, such as provincial and municipal elections, electoral participation has never been that low. Figure 13.1 shows turnout levels for each of the different types of elections since the abolition of compulsory voting in 1970. Several conclusions can be drawn from this figure. Firstly, electoral participation is highest in national elections and lowest in European elections, while both regional and local elections have participation rates at an intermediate level. Secondly, within each category, the most recent election shows the lowest turnout. However, the decline in turnout is less steep between the last two European elections than between the last two elections for the other assemblies. It may be that turnout in the European elections is reaching its minimum. Thirdly, the drop in turnout levels between the last two elections for each type of assembly may reflect a general decrease in satisfaction with democracy, but this seems unlikely since turnout in national elections is still around 80 percent, which is amongst the highest in West European countries without compulsory voting.

Figure 13.1 Turnout for European, National, Regional and Local Elections Since 1970 (Percent)

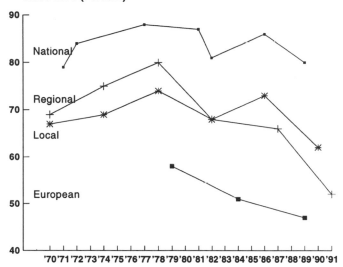

Why is turnout in European elections lower than in national parliamentary elections? To answer this question one should examine differences in electoral systems as well as individual characteristics that may affect electoral participation in the European elections. Many scholars have shown that differences in electoral systems affect the likelihood to vote (e.g. Wolfinger and Rosenstone, 1980; Powell, 1986; Jackman, 1987). Are there any differences between the electoral systems for European and for national elections? Most of the election rules and procedures are roughly identical for each election in the Netherlands. The only striking distinction between them is the difference in threshold which varies from 0.67 percent in national parliamentary elections to 4 percent in European elections. Could this difference in electoral threshold have caused the lower turnout? One can imagine that supporters of small parties are more inclined to stay at home if their party has no chance of winning a seat. However, in anticipation of this danger, the various small parties of the left and of the orthodox Christian right each constructed combination lists (i.e., electoral pacts) in 1989. Such tactics were intended to prevent their respective supporters from staying home. Thus enabling the small left and the orthodox Christian parties to win seats in European Parliament elections that they would not otherwise have secured.[5]

---

5 Party supporters in each block were not mutually antagonistic (van der Eijk and Niemöller, 1984).

Thus, low electoral participation in European elections cannot be explained on the basis of specific election rules and procedures. An explanation in terms of what the elections are about may be more fruitful. In this case the main question is to what extent do European attitudes and orientations contribute to the explanation of turnout in European elections? To address this question one has to take into account all the individual characteristics that affect turnout in national parliamentary elections. Table 13.2 shows the total R^2 and additional R^2 after including blocks of variables in the regression analysis. The variables in each block are described in Chapter 3.

This table shows that, after controlling for all factors that affect turnout in a national election, European attitudes and orientations do not make any additional contribution to the explanation of turnout in the European elections of 1989. This table also indicates that the failure to vote in European elections, as in national elections, is largely a matter of chance: only 28 percent of the variance can be explained by systematic factors.[6]

A Comparison with Previous European Elections

As mentioned above, the national government resigned just before the European election, announcing new parliamentary elections for September 1989. This turned the European elections into a dress-rehearsal for the general election three months later. In this respect the 1989 European elections were different from those in 1979 and 1984. To what extent did this alter the effect of EC-related variables in the explanation of turnout? Would the effect have been higher in other circumstances? Turnout in the 1979 and 1984 European elections was analyzed in order to assess whether or not the resignation of the government resulted in a situation in which the relationship between European factors and

Table13.2 Predictors of 1989 Participation in the European Election in The Netherlands

	R^2	Added R^2
Demographics	0.07	
General Political Orientations	0.28	0.21
Habitual Voting	0.28	0.00
European Attitudes	0.28	0.00

6 For similar conclusions with respect to national parliamentary elections, see Schram (1989) and Schmidt (1981,1983).

electoral participation was suppressed.[7] To a very large extent the results for 1979 and 1984 are similar to those for 1989, with European attitudes and orientations having hardly more explanatory power than in 1989.

Party Choice in the European Elections of 1989

This section addresses two questions related to party choice. Firstly, to what extent is the outcome of the European election different from what a hypothetical election for the national parliament would have yielded? Secondly, how can any difference between party choice in European elections and party preference in national elections be explained? Why do voters behave differently in European elections than they would have done in national elections?

Turnout Effects and Quasi-switching

The differences between the result of the European election and the outcome of a hypothetical concurrent national election are reported in Table 13.3. As was discussed in Chapter 3, two phenomena are responsible for these differences. One is a turnout effect, which caused some parties to suffer from the lower turnout while some parties gain. The other is quasi-switching, which occurs to the extent that voters supported a different party than they would have in a national election.

Table 13.3 shows clearly that both Labor (PvdA) and Christian Democrats (CDA) would have performed better in a national election than they did in the

Table 13.3 Quasi–switching and Turnout Effects in the 1989 European Election in The Netherlands

	EE	NE	EE-NE	Quasi-switching	Turnout Effect
Green Left	6.0	4.0	2.0	1.6	0.4
PVDA	30.7	31.9	-1.2	1.4	-2.6
D66	7.0	8.3	-1.3	-1.6	0.3
CDA	34.6	37.4	-2.8	-1.7	-1.1
VVD	13.6	11.9	1.7	-0.7	2.4
Orthodox Christian	5.9	4.4	1.5	1.0	0.5
Other	2.2	2.1	0.1	0.0	0.1

7 For this purpose, data from the continuous survey project of the University of Amsterdam (1984) and the 1979 European Election Survey (Blumler and Fox, 1982) were used. Neither of these studies contains all variables available for 1989, which renders the comparison a tentative one.

European election. However, the contribution of low turnout and quasi-switching to these disadvantageous results is remarkably different for each party. Labor (PvdA) lost a number of votes because of low turnout (minus 2.6 percent) but profited from quasi-switching (plus 1.4 percent). The Christian Democrats suffered marginally from low turnout but lost a number of voters due to quasi-switching (minus 1.7 percent). The other government party, the VVD (right liberals), also suffered slightly from quasi-switching, but it was more successful than other parties in mobilizing its adherents in the European elections (a gain of 2.4 percent). D66 lost quite some number of voters to other parties (−1.6 percent) and did not benefit from the low turnout level. The parties that benefitted most were Green Left and (to a lesser extent) the combination list of the small orthodox Christian parties. Both profited from low turnout as well as from quasi-switching. This favorable result can be attributed possibly to two phenomena. Firstly, as will be discussed below, there is not much at stake in European elections. Therefore voters may be more inclined to vote for small parties. Secondly, combination lists may be more appealing to the electorate than small parties operating independently.

Possible Causes of Quasi-switching

The remainder of this section focuses on causes of quasi-switching. Of course the results reported in Table 13.3 are net differences and underestimate the gross number of quasi-switchers. However, the total group of quasi-switchers is still small (11 percent of those who voted) .[8] No less than 89 percent voted exactly the same way as they would have done in a hypothetical national election. This is about what one would expect given the fact that the European election was dominated by national issues and conflicts so that party choice was based largely upon national party differences. European voting therefore differed only marginally from how people said they would have voted in national elections, had they been held at the same time.

Although it concerns only a small group, an interesting question is what are the reasons for quasi-switching. One explanation may be that in European elections some voters express their attitude towards the European Community in their vote, but this would require that parties offer a choice on European issues. van der Eijk and Oppenhuis (1989) have shown that, in the perception of Dutch voters, the political parties are hardly different in their positions on the European Community. All parties are perceived to be in favor, with VVD and

---

8 Owing to low turnout in the European elections this amounts to only 47 voters in the sample who report a different party choice for European and national elections.

CDA as the most outspokenly pro-European and the orthodox Christian parties as the least enthusiastic, although still positively inclined.

The fact that the parties vary only little makes it hard for voters to base their choice on attitudes for or against the European Community, but it does not preclude this entirely. Whether or not they do can easily be tested. If there is something like an 'anti-' or 'pro-' European vote, one would expect a greater congruence between a voter's attitude and the position of the party voted for in the European elections than between a voter's attitude and the preferred party in national elections.[9] This is not the case. The parties that voters support in the European elections are not more congruent with their own position on the European Community than the party they would have supported in a national election.[10] From this finding one may conclude that EC-related attitudes were irrelevant for those few quasi-switchers.

Other hypotheses about the causes for quasi-switching can be formulated on the basis of the theory of second-order elections suggested by Reif and Schmitt (1980) and Reif (1984a). The most important element is that in second-order elections there is not much at stake. The balance of power in the national parliament is not altered by the result of European election, nor does the composition of the government directly depend on it. Still, the concerns which enter the voter's calculus are national ones, even if the final choice lacks its usual consequences. This leads to a number of hypotheses about party choice in European (second-order) elections:

- Voting will be more experimental and expressive. Without fear of direct consequences (change of effective power position of parties, for instance) voters will be more inclined than otherwise to choose with their 'heart' rather than with their 'head'.
- Some adherents of government parties may want to express disapproval of government policies by voting for opposition parties, which they would hesitate to do if power were at stake.

The first hypothesis concerns the supposedly increased sincerity of the vote. The notion behind this is that voters may feel less need to take 'tactical'

---

9 The third wave of the European Election Study does not contain questions about party attitude towards the European Community. Therefore, it is necessary to impute aggregate results from the first wave. To this end the first-wave data were weighted so that the most important explanatory variables of party choice in The Netherlands—left/right self-placement, religion and church attendance—had the same distributions as in the third wave. The measures used to locate parties and voters in this area are described in Appendix B.

10 For a similar conclusion, from a somewhat different perspective, see van der Eijk and Franklin (1991).

considerations into account in elections that are less consequential. In a first-order election, by contrast, they might decide to vote for a large party rather than their preferred party because the strength of the former is more likely to affect the composition of a (coalition) government. This phenomenon usually works to the disadvantage of small parties (van der Eijk et al., 1986; Tillie, 1995). A well known perspective on Dutch voting is that it is predominantly determined in a Downsean manner by left/right (ideological) considerations (van der Eijk and Niemöller 1983, 1987). The foregoing reasoning suggests that this would be more pronounced in European than in national elections. This hypothesis is difficult to test empirically because most voters claim to have voted the same way as they would have in national elections. The small group of quasi-switchers gives ambiguous results. The party which they vote for in the European election is slightly closer to them in terms of ideological distance than the one they would have voted for in a national election: 1.45 versus 1.47 (on a 10-point scale); but this is too small a difference to convincingly support this hypothesis. Possibly our data underestimate the size of this difference, as the comparison does not involve actual behavior in a first-order election. A more relevant test would involve the comparison of reported vote in European elections with the same in national elections. Van der Eijk and Niemöller (1985) and van der Eijk and Oppenhuis (1990) have made such comparisons, which indicate that the propensity to vote at smallest distance is indeed somewhat more pronounced in European than in national elections.

A different elaboration of the hypothesis of experimental and expressive voting in second-order elections is that voters would be more inclined to support small or new parties. In none of the three European elections conducted in the Netherlands was a new party able to attract more than 0.5 percent of the votes. The higher effective threshold for representation in European elections makes the Netherlands a less amenable testing ground for new parties or political entrepreneurs than larger countries. In any case, the small number of quasi-switchers shows no unidirectional movement from big parties in national to small parties in European elections.

Finally, is there any evidence that some voters use the European election as an opportunity to express disapproval with the policies pursued by government parties? Were this to be the case one would expect that many quasi-switchers would vote for an opposition party in European elections yet maintain a national party preference for a government party. Table 13.3 provides some evidence for this on the aggregate level. The government parties lost 2.4 percent due to quasi-switching. This might be an indication of protest-voting against government policies. However, analyses at the individual level do not entirely support this interpretation. Although the combination of opposition vote in European elections and government vote in national elections occurs considerably more often than the reverse, the former cannot be interpreted as a protest against government policies, as most of the voters involved say that they approve of these policies. This leads to the conclusion that while some of the changes from government to opposition parties may be explained by disapproval of the governments record, most cannot.

Findings from the above analyses of party choice can be summarized as follows:

- Quasi-switching did not occur often. Only 11 percent of the voters would vote differently in a national elections than they did in the European elections.
- Anti- or pro-European attitudes are not related to quasi-switching.
- Dissatisfaction with government policies is only slightly related to quasi-switching.
- In European elections voters are slightly more likely to vote with the heart (i.e., at a smaller ideological distance) than in national parliamentary elections.

A Comparison with Previous European Elections

As was stated earlier, it seems that in the 1989 European elections the combination lists were more appealing to the electorate than independently operating small parties. If this is true then one would expect that the earlier European elections would not have been as beneficial to small parties as was the election of 1989. In 1979 all parties ran separate lists in the European election and it was clear that no small party would be able to obtain a seat in European Parliament. It is therefore unlikely that any of these parties would have obtained a better result than in a hypothetical concurrent national election. By 1984 both electoral coalitions were in place, but the small-left coalition had to compete with a party called the European Greens. One would expect therefore that the beneficial effects of quasi-switching found in 1989 would also have occurred in 1984 for the orthodox Christian combination list, but not for the small left combination since the latter suffered from competition.

The results found for 1979 and 1984 show a mixed pattern. In 1979, in the absence of any kind of electoral alliance, the outcome for the small left and orthodox Christian parties was not different from the hypothetical outcome in a national election. In 1984, the combination list of orthodox Christian parties did not seem to attract extra votes and the combination of small left parties suffered severely from the competition by the European Greens (due to quasi-switching they lost 1.2 percent to this party). So, instead of faring better, they fared worse. These comparisons provide some support for the supposition that combination lists were more appealing to the electorate, but further research on this phenomenon is needed before we can draw firm conclusions.

Combination lists meant that the 1989 elections were different from those of 1979. The elections were also different from the previous two European elections due to the fall of the cabinet two months earlier. This may have affected the degree of quasi-switching and turnout effects, especially for the government parties. Whether these effects for both government parties, CDA and VVD, can be attributed to the character of European elections or to the fall of the cabinet can be answered by examining the results for the (same) government parties in 1979 and 1984.

Government parties did much better in 1979 than in 1989. In 1989 they lost (in combination) 1 percent of their electoral support compared to a hypothetical national election, whereas in 1979 they gained 3.3 percent. The 1984 European elections showed no sizeable differences for the government parties between European voting behavior and national vote intention. With three different results in three European elections, we can draw no firm conclusions about the performance of government parties.

Domestic Consequences of the European Elections

The European Election as a 'Beauty Contest'

This section describes the context and domestic consequences of the European elections. Did the outcome strain the relationship between government coalition partners? Was it perceived as a vindication of, or warning to, the government coalition? Did it strain relations within parties that achieved a poor election result?

For reasons already discussed, the European elections of 1989 were generally perceived as a dress rehearsal for the September general election. Labor leader Kok tried explicitly to give the European elections the status of a nationwide opinion poll on the eve of parliamentary elections. However, once the results were known, most parties downplayed their significance. The low turnout was used to claim that the results could not be looked upon as fully representative of the Dutch electorate. Despite these reservations, the results were seen as pointers to the Second Chamber elections in September. The VVD looked on them positively, as their performance was better than had been predicted by opinion polls a few weeks earlier, and this gave them hope for September. Labor was disappointed in not becoming the largest party in the Netherlands.

The context was quite different in the previous European elections. In 1979 the election was dominated by the question whether or not the government coalition would still be able to claim majority support. The coalition had achieved a very small parliamentary majority in the 1977 national elections (49.8 percent of the votes yielding 77 seats out of 150). Labor Party leader Den Uyl made perfectly clear what the European elections of 1979 were about, namely an opportunity to express dissatisfaction with government policies and to show that the government was in fact a minority government (Kok et al. 1985). The results were disappointing for Labor, because the coalition gained 2.2 percent compared to the national election result in 1977. Instead of a warning, the election result was perceived to be an expression of support for government policies.

The 1984 elections were dominated by the question of whether or not the government would be punished for its policy concerning the placement of cruise missiles on Dutch territory. Just before the election the government decided to delay a final decision until November 1985, but both the VVD and the left parties considered this decision to be a firm step towards placement. As the Dutch electorate was perceived to be predominantly against, the European election was seen as an appropriate opportunity to express discontent with this government policy. Although the government coalition lost votes compared to the national elections of 1982 (winning 48.9 percent as against 52.4 in 1982) it would have still obtained a very slender majority of seats (76/150). The government was thus not punished as severely as the left opposition had hoped.

In general one may conclude that, in the Netherlands, European elections serve as large-scale opinion polls, giving an indication of the strength of different political parties. In 1979 and 1984 the European elections functioned as polls measuring the support for the government. In 1989 they were a dress-rehearsal for the Second Chamber elections later that year.

In none of the three direct elections to the European Parliament was the outcome such that it resulted in changes of party leadership or in strained relationships between coalition partners. Even when the result was disappointing for a particular party, the low turnout served as a face-saver. When almost half the voters do not vote, one can easily maintain that the outcome would have been different had a 'normal' turnout of some 80 percent been recorded.

Electoral Pacts in the European Elections

As already stated in the introduction, a high electoral threshold can reduce the fragmentation of a party system, so the comparatively high threshold in European elections could have affected the behavior of small parties in the Netherlands. This raises two questions that will be addressed below. First, did the formation of electoral pacts in European elections have any precursors on the national level? Second, did the formation of electoral pacts encourage or facilitate further cooperation? [11]

Green Left[12]

At the end of 1991 the constituent parts of Green Left merged into a new party. However, the formation of Green Left has been a long, time-consuming process. Only ten years before, during the first European elections, any kind of formal collaboration between the members of Green Left had been out of the question. At that time only the PSP was in favor of cooperation. The communists (CPN) were against, the EVP did not even exist and the PPR was at that time predominantly oriented towards the Labor Party (PvdA). In 1984 the situation changed and the small left parties succeeded in forming a combination list in the European elections.

To see whether this Green Left coalition had precursors on the national level, we will look at the development of electoral pacts in local and regional elections. These elections have characteristics in common with European elections: the threshold is much higher than in national elections, and they can be characterized as second-order elections, thus offering a good testing ground for the viability of electoral pacts.

Table 13.4 shows indeed that cooperation between the small left parties started in the early 1980s and then gradually developed to the point where Green Left existed as an electoral coalition in every province in 1991. A similar conclusion can be drawn when examining the development of small left coalitions in local elections, since 1970.[13]

---

11 This section is primarily based upon an analysis of major national newspapers (*De Volkskrant, Trouw* and *NRC*); chronicles of internal discussions and developments in political parties, as reported yearly in the publications of the Documentation Center for Dutch Political Parties (DNPP, 1978-1990); and party papers from the constituent parties of the electoral pacts discussed in the text (PPR, PSP, CPN, GPV, SGP, RPF).

12 Combination of small left parties that has had different names in different elections. In the European elections of 1984 the electoral pact was referred to as Green Progressive Agreement and their name on the ballot was just the combination of the proper names of the constituent parties. In the European elections of 1989 this electoral pact was labelled Rainbow Party, whereas in the national elections of September 1989, the same combination was named Green Left, the name which has remained in use since then. For the sake of clarity I will only refer to Green Left in the main text, although their official name was sometimes different.

13 The number of electoral pacts or combinations of PPR, PSP and CPN increased in municipalities larger than 20,000 inhabitants (N=166) as follows. 1970=4; 1974=13; 1978=24 and 1982=65. These figures show clearly that the number of electoral pacts in local elections

There are a number of plausible reasons for this increased propensity to cooperate. The first one is the failure of PPR and PvdA to form a combination list in the European elections of 1979 which was caused by the Labor Party's reluctance to give a PPR candidate an eligible place on the list. This helped to reorient the PPR from the PvdA towards the other small left parties. A second reason may be the participation of the Labor Party in a coalition-government with CDA and D66, from 1981–1982. The policies of this government produced great social unrest and the PvdA came into serious conflict with the unions.[14] This might have led to an increased tendency within the PPR to cooperate with the other small left parties, PSP and CPN. A final reason which may have increased the propensity to cooperate is the idea within the small left parties that cooperation in local and regional elections would bring electoral benefits. In any case it is clear that cooperation between small left parties preceded and possibly facilitated the coalition formed between these parties at the European election of 1984.

The European election of 1984 provided the first opportunity to find out whether such a combination would be appealing in a nationwide election. However, the result of these elections was not as promising as expected. The Green Left coalition succeeded in gaining seats in the European Parliament, but it obtained only 5.6 percent of the vote, which was not much more than the constituent parts had obtained during the national elections of 1982. Although the initiative was not rejected by the voters, the idea that a Green Left coalition would be more appealing than the separate parties appeared not to be valid. However, the psychological effect of the formation of a Green Left combination should not be underestimated. If we look again at Table 13.4 it is evident

Table13.4 Combinations Between Small Left Parties in the Twelve Provinces of the Netherlands (Provincial Elections).

Combinations	1978	1982	1987	1991
PSP/CPN		2		
PSP/PPR		3	5	
PSP/CPN/PPR		1	4	12
Total of Small Left Combinations	0	6	9	12

increased tremendously in the period 1978–1982 (de Jong and Verduyn Lunel, 1983).

14 The policies of Labor leader Den Uyl, especially with respect to sick-leave payments, encountered strong opposition (Anker and Oppenhuis, 1989).

that after 1984 the number of electoral pacts increased, since there were even more in the regional elections of 1987. Beside this numerical increase in combination lists another remarkable development can be noted. After 1984 the number of combinations in the regional elections in which both the communists (CPN) and the radicals (PPR) participated increased considerably. Whereas before 1987 this combination hardly existed (only in one province), in 1987 these combinations increased to four. Although it cannot be proven that the European election caused this willingness to work together, it is plausible that after the nationwide experience of the European elections of 1984, in which both the CPN and PPR participated as members of a larger Green Left coalition, it also became easier to cooperate in local and regional elections. This eventually led to the same pact in a national election, though for quite a long time there had been uncertainty as to whether this would happen. The acute pressure of early elections, caused by the government crisis, proved helpful to overcome hesitations and submit a single list of candidates in the general elections of September 1989 (Voerman,1990). Since then this electoral coalition has developed into a new party, replacing its constituent parts. Green Left is no longer merely a temporary alliance of PPR, PSP, CPN and EVP, but a merger of formerly independent parties.

Orthodox Christian Pact

Is there evidence of a similar process among the orthodox Christian parties? In 1979, before the first European elections, any kind of cooperation between the orthodox Christian parties was out of the question. The RPF phrased the anticipated consequences as follows:

> It is likely that the voice of the Reformation will be silent in the European Parliament.[15]

Undoubtedly the RPF was most sorry about this. They blamed the GPV for not working together and expressed the hope that in the next European elections there would be a party or a list named either Reformed Political Party or SGP/GPV/RPF. The GPV, the major opponent of electoral cooperation between the orthodox Christian parties, feared a loss of its own identity from participating in combination lists together with the SGP or the RPF. This attitude changed at the start of the 1980s. In a general conference in 1981 a small majority decided to attempt to establish electoral coalitions with both the SGP and RPF for regional and local elections in those areas where the GPV would not be able to win seats independently. However, one of the conditions for cooperation

---

15 As quoted in *Nieuw Nederland*, 1979/2:1.

was that, even in such situations, the constituent parties would conduct their own independent campaigns.

Table 13.5 shows that the results of this change of attitude were very visible, at least on the regional level. The number of electoral pacts between the orthodox Christian parties increased enormously from 1 in 1978 to 7 in 1982. One might infer that, by then, the fear of loss of identity was weakening. And, what is probably more important, these initiatives in forming electoral pacts were not rejected by the electorate.

After the experience with cooperation in a number of provinces in the 1982 regional elections, a combination list was formed in the European elections of 1984. As was the case with the formation of the Green Left, the cooperation started on the regional and local level and was extended to the European level in 1984. After participating in the European elections with a single list, the number of combinations of orthodox Christian parties increased even more and has now been established in every province. It seems plausible that cooperation in the European elections removed psychological obstacles in a number of provinces.

Although these parties work together currently on regional and supranational (European) levels, the SGP and GPV still emphasize strongly their own unique character. Whenever possible they announce that the appearance of orthodox Christian coalitions does not imply any abandonment of their independence. For this reason it is unlikely that the orthodox Christian parties will merge in the near future. Still, one might expect that in coming years the need for separate parties will diminish. The older members who founded SGP and GPV in 1918 and 1944 respectively, partly motivated by religious differences which have become less relevant, are slowly dying out. This process, together with the willingness of the RPF to work together with both SGP and GPV, provides grounds for the expectation that ultimately the cooperation between the orthodox Christian parties will increase and may eventually result in a new reformed political party.

Table13.5 Combinations Between Orthodox Christian Parties in the Twelve Provinces of the Netherlands (Provincial Elections).

Combinations	1978	1982	1987	1991
RPF/GPV/SGP		1	3	4
RPF/SGP	1	3	3	4
RPF/GPV		3	4	4
Total of Orthodox Christ. Combinations	1	7	10	12

Concluding Remarks

Failure to vote in European elections is, just as in national elections, largely a matter of random factors. Only twenty-eight percent of the variance in electoral participation in the 1989 European elections can be explained, largely by means of the same factors that influence electoral participation in national elections. European factors contribute only marginally to the explanation.

Due to quasi-switching, and to the fact that low turnout did not affect all parties equally, national elections (if these had been held at the same time) would have shown a different outcome from that in the European elections. Comparing the European elections of 1989 with those in 1979 and 1984 shows a general pattern which is related to the presence or absence of electoral coalitions on the left and orthodox Christian sides of the political spectrum. When existing small parties act together, they profit from both low turnout and quasi-switching. For this reason, collaboration among small left parties and among orthodox Christian parties has been stimulated by the existence of European elections. In both cases the cooperation started on the local and regional level and was extended to the supra-national European level. The small left parties have extended this cooperation still further by participating with one single list in the national parliamentary election of September 1989, and subsequently by a complete merger. The same may eventually happen with the orthodox Christian parties, though probably not in the very near future.

Furthermore, definitely no support has been found for the hypothesis that government parties perform worse in European elections. Whether the government parties lose or gain, compared to a hypothetical national election that might have been held at the same time, seems to be an election-specific matter.

Finally, there are indeed indirect effects from European elections on the national political arena. European elections serve as opinion polls measuring current support for parties. The fact that the government resigned in May 1989 therefore turned the June 1989 European elections into somewhat like a dress rehearsal for the general elections of September 1989.

CHAPTER 14

Northern Ireland:
Second-order Entrenchment

Colin Knox and Dolores O'Reilly

The inclusion of a chapter on Northern Ireland, an integral part of the United Kingdom, highlights the distinctive nature of Northern Ireland as a political entity at local, national and European elections. Its anomalous position within the United Kingdom in the 1989 European elections is demonstrated by the use of a PR electoral system—the Single Transferable Vote system—which is different from that used in the rest of the United Kingdom, and also by the absence of official candidates from mainland UK political parties. This chapter begins with a brief overview of politics in Northern Ireland and the particular features of the 1989 European elections. Turnout and party choice are specifically examined to see whether there were any 'second-order' influences (Reif, 1985) such as lower turnout, the promotion of smaller and/or new political parties or dissatisfaction with national government parties shown by a decline in their share of the vote.

Background

Since the partition of Ireland in 1921 (as a result of the Government of Ireland Act in 1920) and the creation of the Northern Ireland Parliament, almost all elections have centered on the nature of the state itself. Northern Ireland became a separate, albeit artificial, entity comprising six out of nine counties from the ancient province of Ulster. Its parliament at Stormont was modelled on Westminster and could legislate on a comprehensive scale with the major exceptions of war and peace, foreign trade and forms of taxation. The creation of a Northern Ireland parliament and the very limited involvement of Westminster in the affairs of Ulster until the late 1960s are testimony to a British position of extricating itself from the problems of the Irish. Throughout the lifetime of the Stormont parliament (1921–72) the Ulster Unionist Party held power without interruption and was accused of protecting the interests of Protestants by gerrymandering and discrimination in the areas of employment, policing, public housing and regional policy (Whyte, 1983). Discontent within the minority Catholic community was channelled into civil rights' demonstrations in 1968, which culminated in public disorder, internment, rioting, the involvement of British troops in 1969 and eventually the suspension of the Stormont parliament in March 1972. Since then a UK minister, the Secretary of State for Northern Ireland, has exercised 'direct rule' through the Northern Ireland Office. Various attempts to restore devolved government, reduce British involvement and create an atmosphere for accommodation between the two communities had met with little success by the time of the 1989 European elections.

A power-sharing Executive established in 1973 collapsed following a strike by Protestant workers. A constitutional convention elected in 1975 was dissolved after disagreement amongst its representatives. A constitutional conference took place in 1980 with the aim of transferring powers from Westminster to local elected representatives but failed to reach agreement. A rolling devolution initiative in 1982, aimed at the resumption of legislative and executive functions by a Northern Ireland Assembly, ended in 1986 without widespread cross-community support, having been boycotted by the Nationalist Social Democratic and Labour Party. The Anglo-Irish Agreement of 1985, which gave the Irish government a consultative role in specified affairs of Northern Ireland through an intergovernmental conference, met with implacable opposition from Unionists who perceived Dublin's involvement as thinly veiled joint sovereignty.

The mutual suspicion and distrust which have accompanied the litany of failed political initiatives find expression in voting patterns in Northern Ireland. The voting patterns of the rest of the United Kingdom in which tradition, social class and region play a large part are absent in Northern Ireland. The predominant voting cleavages in the province are religion and national identity which supersede all other alignments. Catholics are identified with the Social Democratic and Labour Party (SDLP) or with Sinn Fein—both of which stand for unification with the rest of Ireland—and Protestants are identified with the Ulster Unionist Party (UUP) or Democratic Unionist Party (DUP)—both of which defend the union with the United Kingdom. The Alliance Party occupies the middle ground appealing for moderation, compromise and maintenance of the link with Great Britain.

The Social Democratic and Labour Party, representing the majority of Catholics, was formed in 1970 "to organize and maintain in Northern Ireland a socialist party and to promote the cause of Irish unity based on the consent of a majority of people in Northern Ireland." Provisional Sinn Fein emerged in 1970, after the outbreak of civil disturbances when the republican movement split into Republican Clubs, whose military wings were the Official IRA, and the Provisional IRA (Provos). The Provos accused the Official movement of not defending Ulster Catholics at a crucial period and established Provisional

Sinn Fein as their political front in 1970. Sinn Fein contested elections from the 1982 Northern Ireland Assembly onwards, and this dual strategy of electoral and terrorist tactics was referred to as the 'ballot box and armalite' strategy.

The Ulster Unionist Party is the largest Unionist grouping in the Protestant community and is firmly committed to Ulster remaining within the United Kingdom. Its leader was also Prime Minister of Northern Ireland in the Stormont government (1921–72) up to the prorogation of Stormont. The Democratic Unionist Party was formed in 1971 by the Reverend Ian Paisley to promote traditional Protestant interests which he saw as being under threat. The party's aim is "to uphold and maintain the constitution of Northern Ireland as an integral part of the United Kingdom."

The Alliance Party was formed in 1970 as a center party aimed at moderate Catholics and Protestants and favors the constitutional link with Britain. Its primary objective is to secure a devolved government in Northern Ireland within the United Kingdom.

In the 1989 European elections, these five parties were joined by five additional candidates contesting an election for the first time. One was a Workers' party candidate, two were candidates using the label of the mainland Labour Party, though they were not official Labour candidates, one was a similarly unofficial Conservative candidate, and one was a candidate of the Ecology Party. Though these parties received few votes, we will be making reference to them at relevant points.

McAllister and Nelson (1979:279) have summarized the historic characteristics of the party system and electoral choice in Northern Ireland as follows:

- Parties did not share fundamental loyalty to the state: divisions between them were in fact based upon the question of its very existence;
- the electorate divided on religious rather than class lines—most Protestants voted Unionist and most Catholics Nationalist;
- stability did not result from the alternation of competing parties in government since Unionists held exclusive power;
- parties stood for one religious community, made no attempt to win votes from the other since such efforts were fruitless.

As shown in Table 14.1, while the potential vote of Ulster Unionists and Democratic Unionists overlaps significantly (at least 72 percent of those voting for one of these parties would consider voting for the other) there is little overlap between the potential vote for these parties and for the SDLP or Sinn Fein (no more than 14 percent would consider voting for these 'enemy' parties. Sinn Fein is equally exclusive in terms of the divide between its voters and those in the Unionist camp, however, the SDLP is somewhat less exclusive, and 23 percent of its supporters would consider voting for the UUP. Somewhat more surprising, at first sight, is the lack of overlap between the two anti-Unionist parties—no more than 21 percent of SDLP supporters would consider voting for Sinn Fein—but this has to be seen in context of the fact that Sinn Fein is the political wing of a terrorist organization whose actions are anathema even to many of those who support its political objectives.

Nevertheless, the table shows competition between parties for voters to be high. The size of the six parties' potential electorates sum to 148.5 percent, suggesting that a large number of respondents would envisage voting for more than one party at some stage in the future. A high 72 percent of UUP potential voters could vote DUP whilst 83 percent of the latter could vote UUP. This is indicative of intra-Unionist rivalry and a clear manifestation of the similarities between the two parties perceived by voters in such things as the combined opposition of the two parties to the Anglo-Irish agreement. Many DUP party activists complained that their relatively poor electoral showing in the 1987 general and 1989 local government elections had been a direct result of their loss of distinctiveness as a political party. For the rest, traditional battlelines are apparent. The Alliance Party demonstrates cross-party voting with 57 percent and 49 percent potentially voting UUP and SDLP respectively. The SDLP's nearest rivals are Alliance, Workers' party and Sinn Fein. Sinn Fein's rivals are the Workers' party and the SDLP. In general, therefore, both intra-Unionist and Nationalist competition is confirmed, with Alliance emerging as potentially

Table 14.1 Potential Support and Overlap Between Parties in Northern Ireland in 1989

	SF	WP	Lab	SDLP	All	UUP	Cons	DUP
Sinn Fein	1.00	0.38	0.26	0.21	0.13	0.03	0.15	0.04
Workers' Party	0.47	1.00	0.38	0.34	0.31	0.12	0.25	0.11
Labour	0.55	0.64	1.00	0.58	0.55	0.25	0.44	0.23
SDLP	0.44	0.58	0.58	1.00	0.49	0.14	0.24	0.12
Alliance	0.26	0.50	0.53	0.47	1.00	0.34	0.48	0.32
Ulster Unionist	0.11	0.33	0.40	0.23	0.57	1.00	0.71	0.83
Conservatives	0.30	0.40	0.42	0.23	0.47	0.41	1.00	0.41
Dem. Unionist	0.11	0.25	0.32	0.16	0.47	0.72	0.61	1.00
Potential Support (%)	11.6	14.5	24.4	24.4	23.6	39.9	23.2	34.5
%Vote Elect	4.4	0.5	0.3	12.3	2.5	10.7	2.3	14.4
%Valid Vote	9.1	1.0	0.7	25.5	5.2	22.2	4.8	29.9
L-R median (1–10)	1.28	2.28	2.76	3.82	5.02	7.55	7.78	7.93

attractive to both communities. Comparing the size of the party's potential with its actual vote as a proportion of the total electorate indicates that the Workers' party has most to gain from supporters of other parties while the DUP and SDLP have least to gain from such voters.

Clearly these figures have implications for the structure of party competition in Northern Ireland. Let us now turn to an examination of how this competition played out in the European elections of 1989.

The 1989 European Elections in Northern Ireland

The European elections took place on 15 June 1989, one month after the local council elections, in the single constituency of Northern Ireland to elect three MEPs. The stance of Northern Irish political parties towards Europe is broadly in line with Unionist/Nationalist divisions. On the one hand the SDLP and Alliance parties are strongly supportive of Europe (although Sinn Fein considers it irrelevant) while on the other hand the Ulster and Democratic Unionist parties have a negative view of the Community. The SDLP illustrated their support in their 1989 European manifesto which prioritized social, regional and environmental issues of Northern Ireland in Europe. The Alliance Party too, attempted to raise the profile of European issues in the campaign, pledging support for the Single European Act under its banner of "a Europe of free and caring citizens" (Hainsworth, 1990). The DUP, however, is highly suspicious of a European superstate with power residing centrally and the consequences of such an arrangement for the security and sovereignty of Northern Ireland. Despite such principled objections the DUP is intent on securing maximum EC funding for Northern Ireland and has been an outspoken critic of the United Kingdom government on the question of additionality. The UUP also has its reservations on Europe and resents Northern Ireland's political issues being debated in the European Parliament. The party is equally unhappy with attempts made by the SDLP and MEPs from Southern Ireland to foster a United Ireland stance under the guise of European integration. For their part Unionists counter with the claim that Irish independence is now an anachronism since links with Britain will be strengthened in a united Europe (Aughey, Hainsworth and Trimble, 1989).

The election campaign, to some extent, merged with that of the preceding local elections and attracted limited attention from the media. A free postal drop of election literature and the launch of the party manifestos provided candidates with limited exposure. The local TV network did not produce programs on the elections specifically or the European Parliament in general. As one observer put it: "In their poor coverage of the European campaign, the local broadcasting bodies fell far short of their frequently vaunted public service traditions" (Elliott, 1990:99).

Table 14.2 shows the results of the election, the main features of which were:

- The return of the major party representatives in the same rank order as 1984—DUP, SDLP and UUP respectively;
- the DUP and SDLP candidates (Paisley and Hume) were elected on the first count; the UUP candidate (Nicholson) was successfully elected on the second count with 86.3 percent of transfers from Paisley;
- although topping the poll for the third consecutive time, Paisley's percentage vote dropped by 3.7 percent compared with 1984 and Nicholson, the new UUP candidate, increased the party vote to its highest ever (22.2 percent) in European elections;
- the rivalry between the SDLP and Sinn Fein for the nationalist vote moved conclusively in favor of the SDLP with a decisive 3.4 percent increase in its vote and the lowest ever Sinn Fein percentage share— down from a high of over 13 percent in 1984;
- the Conservative candidate performed relatively well, compared with the Alliance Party, in spite of not having received the endorsement of UK Conservative Central Office; the Ecology/Green Party candidate had a respectable increase in vote (to 1.23 percent) and surpassed the Workers' party (1.05 percent); the two Labour candidates had a poor performance;
- six of the ten candidates lost deposits of £1000.

Hainsworth (1989:316) provides us with an overview:

The results were quite predictable and this tended to reduce interest in the election. Voting along traditional patterns and with a close eye to domestic concerns, the electorate returned three MEPs to represent mainstream Ulster Unionism (UUP, DUP) and constitutional nationalism (SDLP). Almost every four in five voters supported one of the successful candidates. Personality and precedent predominated.

Second-order Effects

Turnout

To what extent are predictions of lower turnout rates associated with second-order elections plausible in the case of Northern Ireland? Set against turnout rates for the first-order or parliamentary elections (1987 UK General election)

Table 14.2 The 1989 European Elections in Northern Ireland

	First Pref. No. Votes	Percent	1984 Percent Change	Transferred	Stage 2
DUP	160110	29.94	-3.7	-26407	133703
SDLP	136335	25.49	+3.4	–	136335
UUP	118785	22.21	+0.7	+22798	141583
Sinn Fein	48914	9.15	-4.1	+73	48987
Alliance	27905	5.22	+0.2	+728	28633
Conservatives	25789	4.82	–	+1082	26871
Ecology	6569	1.23	+0.9	+307	6875
Workers' Party	5590	1.05	-0.2	+78	5668
Labour R G*	3540	0.66	–	+120	3660
Labour '87	1274	0.24		+30	1304

Total votes: 540,254, Quota: 133,703, Turnout: 48.81 per cent
* Labour for Representative Government

and second-order local council elections (1985 and 1989) the 1989 European turnout rate of 48.8 percent is relatively low (see Table 14.3). Indeed compared with previous local, national and European elections turnout in the 1989 European elections is markedly low, although comparable with other European countries that do not have compulsory voting (Denmark, the Netherlands and France) and higher than Britain's 36.6 percent. Lakeman (1990) has suggested that within the United Kingdom, where two voting systems operate for European elections (plurality voting in Great Britain and PR in Northern Ireland), turnout is higher in Northern Ireland because of the PR system. Given the wider choice afforded by PR and the transparent link between votes cast and those elected, Northern Ireland electors are encouraged to use their vote. This is evidenced by the fact that 78.2 percent of the voters in the 1989 European election secured a candidate of their choice, compared with 47.1 percent in Britain (Wilder, 1990). This, however, would suggest quite different turnout rates within Northern Ireland for general elections to the UK parliament (plurality voting) and council and European elections (PR voting). There is no internal Northern Irish evidence available to support such an assertion—turnout rates in the last two general elections in Northern Ireland (1983 and 1987) were a high 72.9 percent and 67.4 percent respectively—though we shall see in Chapter 19 that comparisons with other countries make it appear that turnout in Northern Ireland was higher than it would have been in a European election without STV.

Apart from lower turnout rates expected in second-order elections, the share of the votes obtained by major political parties is also expected to decrease.

This was true of the UUP but not the DUP or SDLP between the 1987 General and the 1989 European elections. The relatively high DUP European vote can be attributed to a huge Paisley personality factor, his third time to top the polls in Northern Ireland. The low UUP vote may well be unconnected with the European nature of these elections, but rather may be due to a sense of alienation from the democratic process after the 1986 failure to get any results from the expression (in a UK by-election) of vehement opposition to the Anglo-Irish Agreement. The high SDLP vote was, in part, a personality vote; it was also assisted by stringent legal restrictions imposed on Sinn Fein, the SDLP's rivals (a media ban in 1988 on broadcasting direct statements by them or certain other organizations), and a reaction to the continuing violence of the IRA.

The main reasons for not voting in the European elections, in response to a direct question, are revealing. A significant 70.3 percent of respondents did not know or did not reply. Of the remaining 30 percent, lack of interest in politics and the European elections were cited as the key factors by 6.5 percent. A "foregone conclusion" achieved a 2.2 percent response which is somewhat at odds with the inevitability assertion. Of those who did vote in the European parliamentary elections, once again a significant proportion (48.6 percent) did not know why they had done so or did not reply to the question. A large percentage (37.7 percent) felt that the parties' domestic stance was much more important than its European stance. A mere 13.8 percent considered European matters to be important in relation to the party of their choice.

To elaborate on the differences between voters and non-voters it is insightful to examine their respective interests in European Community politics—in other words, was participation in the 1989 elections contingent

Table 14.3 Comparative Election Results in Northern Ireland (Percent)

	Euro 1979	UK 1983	Euro 1984	LG 1985	UK 1987	LG 1989	Euro 1989
UUP	21.9	34.0	21.5	29.5	37.9	30.4	22.2
DUP	29.8	20.0	33.6	24.3	11.7	18.7	29.9
Other Union.	7.3	3.1	2.9	3.1	5.3	3.8	-
Alliance	6.8	8.0	5.0	7.1	10.0	6.9	5.2
SDLP 24.6	17.9	17.9	22.1	17.8	21.1	21.0	25.5
Sinn Fein	-	13.4	13.3	11.8	11.4	11.2	9.2
Other Nat.	5.9	-	-	2.4	-	-	-
Workers' Party	0.8	1.9	1.3	1.6	2.6	2.1	1.0
Others	2.9	1.7	0.3	2.4	-	5.9	6.9
Turnout	56.9	72.9	65.4	60.1	67.4	57.4	48.8

Key: UK = UK General Elections, Euro = European Elections, LG = Local Government Elections upon interest in EC politics? A high 71 percent of respondents considered EC matters either very important or important for Northern Ireland's future, but it is hard to take this figure seriously when 63.8 percent show little or no interest in the politics of the EC. A priori, one would expect those who voted to be interested and conversely those not voting to exhibit little interest; but while bivariate analysis lends some initial support to this supposition, multivariate analysis shows that the bivariate relationships are due to the correlation of these attitudes to other (domestic) matters. As in other chapters, we conducted a multiple regression analysis of electoral participation with stage-wise inclusion of composite variables related to, first, demographics, then civic attitudes and general political orientations, then habitual voting (indicated by whether or not respondents had voted at the previous national election) and, finally, European attitudes (see Table 14.4).

This table shows that an amazing 51 percent of the variance in turnout can be explained in Northern Ireland by a combination of demographic characteristics (mainly education), together with civic attitudes and national political orientations, along with habitual voting. General political orientations provides the lion's share of this explanation with demographics adding some more and habitual voting characteristics adding very little. European attitudes, however, add almost nothing, confirming the lack of importance of EC matters in this election despite the stated importance of the EC to Northern Ireland.

The lack of media coverage was specifically singled out as contributing to a low turnout in the 1989 European elections. Some 27.6 percent of respondents were either very or quite interested in the election campaign with a further 33 percent a little interested. The most helpful source of information in making up the voter's mind was television. However, when asked to reflect on television coverage of the election campaign, respondents noted that it "told them nothing," was "rather boring" and left them "rather confused," in that order. Moreover, a mere 14.9 percent of those questioned suggested there was not enough time devoted to the European campaign on television. These results

Table 14.4 Predictors of 1989 Participation in the European Election in Northern Ireland

	R^2	Added R^2
Demographics	0.13	
General Political Orientations	0.43	0.30
Habitual Voting	0.51	0.08
European Attitudes	0.53	0.02

would suggest that no great demand existed for more coverage but, clearly, current reporting did little to assist voters in their choice of candidate. Of specific interest are the attitudes of voters and non-voters to the election campaign—illustrated in Table 14.5. There is a fairly weak association between voting and opinion on the amount of television coverage of the campaign (correlation 0.27). Those who voted were more likely to have felt that there had been too little coverage whereas those who had not voted were more likely to have felt that there had been too much. This suggests that those who were interested enough to vote were the only ones who would have liked more information. Again this casts doubt on the link between lack of media coverage and low turnout suggested by politicians involved in the election.

Party Choice

Changes in party choice in the European elections, as compared with previous first-order elections—the 1987 UK General election—can be summarized by a Pedersen index score of 29.5 indicating a high aggregate level of change. A comparison of the 1989 European elections with the preceding local council elections in 1989 and the European elections of 1984 results in index scores of 16.7 and 10.9 respectively. All three scores would appear, prima facie, to be surprisingly high for a country associated with traditional voting habits. If, however, the two main Unionist (UUP, DUP) and Nationalist (SDLP, Sinn Fein) parties are grouped, the scores drop to 11.6, 6.5 and 6.8 implying that a large proportion of the changes in party strength was due to intra-group volatility. The relatively high index score of 11.6 associated with the UK General '87/European '89 comparison might nevertheless indicate second-order influences involved in the improved vote share for the small Ecology/Green party and the emergence of the new Northern Ireland Conservative party. Such second-order behavior by voters might be indicated in the reasons they gave for having voted as they did. The election study data show that a small 4 percent of respondents "wanted to give a warning to the government" and the same

Table 14.5 Voters and Non-voters by Television Coverage of Campaign (Percent)

	DK, NA	Far Too Much	Bit Too Much	About Right	Not Enough
Did Vote	46.2	25.0	53.8	69.7	70.7
Did Not Vote	53.8	75.0	46.2	30.3	29.3
Total N	104	16	26	89	41

$X^2 = 20.74$, $p < 0.05$, Cramer's V = .27

percentage "wanted to express opposition to the government"—hardly conclusive proof of second-order behavior.

Table 14.6 reassesses this comparison in terms of differences between votes cast in the 1989 elections and those that respondents say they would have cast at a hypothetical national election held at the same time. It decomposes the changes into those attributable to differences in turnout and those attributable to differences in party support, out of those voting (what we call 'quasi-switching'—see Chapter 3).

The results illustrate a gain in votes for the DUP, SDLP and Sinn Fein at the European election (7.3 percent, 5.6 percent, 0.7 percent respectively in the third column of Table 14.6) and a decline in votes for all other parties, principally the Labour Party and UUP (down 7.2 percent and 3.5 percent respectively from what they would have received in a national election). In the case of those parties that performed better at the European election than the concurrent hypothetical national election, the contribution of low turnout and quasi-switching is different for each party. The DUP benefitted about equally from both whilst the SDLP profited to a large extent (5.1 percent) from low turnout but only marginally (0.5 percent) from vote switching. Sinn Fein suffered to a small extent from turnout (–0.4) but gained through quasi-switching (1.1). The Labour Party and the UUP both lost out because of low turnout levels(–3.6 percent Labour; –3.4 percent UUP) but, of the two, only Labour was much affected by quasi-switching. These figures hardly support the notion that small parties benefitted from the second-order nature of the elections. Conservatives actually did worse than they would in a national election held on the same day, and Labour did much worse. Of the smaller parties, only Sinn Fein (whom we have already characterized as the big losers of this

Table 14.6 Quasi–switching and Turnout Effects in the 1989 European Election in Northern Ireland

	EE	NE	EE-NE	Quasi-switching	Turnout Effect
Sinn Fein	9.1	8.4	0.7	1.1	-0.4
Workers' Party	1.0	1.4	-0.4	-0.3	-0.1
Labour	0.7	7.9	-7.2	-3.6	-3.6
SDLP	25.5	19.9	5.6	0.5	5.1
Alliance	5.2	5.4	-0.2	0.4	-0.6
Ulster Unionist	22.2	25.7	-3.5	-0.1	-3.4
Conservatives	4.8	7.3	-2.5	-1.6	-0.9
Democratic Unionist	29.9	22.6	7.3	2.9	4.4
Other	1.2	1.1	0.1	0.4	-0.3

election) did any better than they would in a national election. The big winners—the Democratic Unionists—benefitted from the fact that in a single constituency they could run their most popular candidate, which has more to do with the electoral system operating in a European election than with the fact that the election was a European one.

Finally we turn to the relationship between party choice and religion, the traditional Northern Irish cleavage. The conventional wisdom is that all elections—local, national and European—are fought in accordance with strict 'orange' and 'green' divisions. Did this apply to the 1989 Euro-voters?

Table 14.7 illustrates voting patterns and religious affiliation. The results capture the politics of extremes in Northern Ireland—no Protestants voting for the SDLP or Sinn Fein and no Catholics voting for the Ulster or Democratic Unionists. The bi-confessional Alliance Party attracted support from both religions. A significant correlation of 0.49 is indicative of the link between religion and party choice in Northern Ireland. Even more indicative was the transfer of surplus votes from the DUP leader. Over 86 percent (22,798) of his surplus votes went to the Ulster Unionist candidate, and the next highest recipient was the Northern Ireland Conservative candidate with a mere 4 percent.

Domestic Effects of European Elections

The domestic effects of the European elections are best described by issues which were prevalent in the 1979, '84 and '89 elections and their consequences. Within the broader context of the United Kingdom government the results of the three Euro-elections in Northern Ireland were only relevant in their reaffirmation of existing political differences evident at local and national level. With a strong Conservative government in power since 1979, Northern Ireland politicians could do little to destabilize or exert pressure for

Table 14.7 Party Choice by Religion (Percent)

	Catholic	Protestant	Others
UUP	0	24.7	12.0
DUP	0	20.5	0
Alliance	2.9	4.1	12.0
SDLP	31.4	0	4.0
Sinn Fein	14.3	0	0
Others/None	51.4	50.7	72.0
Total N	105	146	25

$X^2 = 133.85$, $p < 0.05$, Cramer's V = .49

change. The heralded closeness of the 1992 general election generated some debate about the role of Unionist politicians in a hung Parliament but, in the event, such a pivotal role did not materialize.

The three Euro-elections did, however, have consequences for the internal relations between parties. Because Northern Ireland is a single constituency of 3 MEPs, elections to the European Parliament are dominated by the personalities of the major political parties. European elections are therefore a microcosm of the ongoing intra Unionist and Nationalist contests fought by high profile politicians in each party. The election campaigns between Taylor and Paisley in 1979 and 1984, and between Paisley and Nicholson in 1989 reflect the DUP/UUP struggle to represent the majority community. Similarly Hume's campaign against Paddy Devlin (United Labour party) in 1979 and Danny Morrison (Sinn Fein) in 1984 and 1989 personifies the SDLP's claim to be the political voice of the minority community. The electoral vitriol generated in this way clearly had consequences for the relationship between parties. John Taylor's constant snipping at Paisley's parochial role and at his brand of extremism in Europe generated problems that had to be overcome when both parties formed a pact at the 1985 local government elections to "smash Sinn Fein" and subsequently to oppose the Anglo-Irish Agreement. In 1989, with the pact in place for 4 years and the DUP vote declining, resentment had built up between the two Unionist parties with a claim from DUP activists that their party had suffered from a loss of political identity. The 1989 local government elections and the European election saw a reversal in DUP electoral support though ambiguities in the pact reemerged over candidates in the 1992 general election campaign.

On the Nationalist side, the 1984 European election witnessed intense rivalry between Sinn Fein and the SDLP. The latter had suffered a decline in vote at the 1983 general election and the '84 European election vote enabled it to retrieve its electoral position—a trend which continued in the '89 European election. The consequence of this was to relieve the British government which had been alarmed at the level of Catholic support for Sinn Fein and its endorsement of the ared struggle. For all intents and purposes the 'threat' of Sinn Fein had been dismissed at the European level, but this was only of symbolic importance as the party's influence was much more problematic at local and national levels.

European elections have generated domestic discussions about the voting system in Northern Ireland. Elections to the European Parliament, the now defunct Northern Ireland Assembly and local councils take place under proportional representation (STV), whilst UK elections within Northern Ireland use majority voting. The European elections, however, highlight a specific anomaly in that members from Northern Ireland are elected differently from the remaining 78 members in Great Britain to the same European forum. This has resulted in a public debate about the integration of Northern Ireland within the United Kingdom by Unionists and arguments about fairer representation by Nationalists. The issue of PR surfaced in the 1979 European elections when Unionists claimed that both over-representation (relative to other member states) and the system of voting gave Catholics an unfair advantage and split the Unionist vote. This debate about PR resurfaced over elections to local councils in Northern Ireland. More recently mainstream British political parties (in particular, Labour and Liberal Democrats) in the run-up to the 1992 general election, have openly discussed the merits and demerits of changing to a system of proportional representation—a debate fuelled in part by the Northern Irish experience.

Finally, public debate in Northern Ireland has recently been influenced by the first phase of the 'talks process' between constitutional parties. Leaks from the discussions reveal that the SDLP suggested a form of government in Northern Ireland based on the European model. The proposals envisage an executive commission and a team of six commissioners, one appointed by the British Government, one by Dublin and one by Brussels. The local element would be supplied by three elected commissioners with an 85-member Northern Ireland Assembly whose powers, functions and structures would be modelled on the European Parliament. Reactions to the proposals from other parties have not been favorable, yet they are reflective of Hume's (SDLP) experience at the European level and were seen as a novel contribution to a largely sterile and intransigent debate.

Conclusion

In summary, although the low turnout in the 1989 European elections in Northern Ireland was almost certainly due to the lack of interest engendered by a second-order election, the other expected second-order effect—a decline in support for major political parties—was not evident. The high level of aggregate volatility across first and second-order elections seems to have resulted largely from intra-group competition in Unionist and Nationalist camps. Switching patterns in the European election have more to do with personality voting in the context of an altered electoral system than an expression of dissatisfaction on national or domestic issues.

As would be expected, the potential to vote for a different party is highest within rather than between Unionist and Nationalist blocs, which are delineated by religious differences. This lack of second-order effects on party choice is not particularly surprising in Northern Ireland's case. Mitchell (1991:77), for instance, has argued that "any attempt to analyze it [the party system] as a single unified political system makes it 'wildly deviant' by West European standards." Although local factors such as the inevitability of success for the 3 major parties, the closeness in time of the district council elections and disaffection following the Anglo-Irish Agreement were influential for both turnout and party choice in the 1989 European elections, the overriding concern which dominates all elections in Northern Ireland is the Union with the United Kingdom. Each order of elections, first or second, represents an opportunity to consolidate positions on the Union. The 1989 European elections provided yet another opportunity to pursue the same ends, and the fact that the opportunity was exploited to the fullest is what gives the election its flavor of second-order entrenchment.

CHAPTER 15

Portugal:
An Ephemeral Election

Mário Bacalhau

Portugal's restoration to democracy in 1974 opened the way to membership in the European Community eleven years later, at the same time as Spain; and the two countries both elected their first representatives to the European Parliament in special elections held in 1987. The European election of 1989 was thus the first opportunity for Portugal to participate in a Europe-wide election. Moreover, since the 1987 European election had been held at the same time as a national election which absorbed the total energies of candidates and voters, 1989 presented the Portuguese electorate with the first opportunity to participate in a contest focussed on European matters. In the event this opportunity was not taken, and the European election of 1989 took the form of merely a pale reflection of the appearance that a national election might have taken, had one been held at that time.

Background of the 1989 European Election

For an adequate understanding of the development and results of the European parliamentary elections in Portugal, two factors should be taken into account. First, Portugal only joined the EC in 1986. As a consequence, fewer elections for the European Parliament had been held in Portugal than anywhere else in the EC except for Spain, and the Portuguese electorate was poorly informed about the Community and the working of its institutions. Moreover, the period of membership—barely three years by the time of the 1989 European election— and the even shorter period during which the Portuguese Members of the European Parliament had occupied their mandates were not enough to ameliorate this. Parties, media and government institutions had by 1989 little experience with Europe and could offer little guidance or stimulus to the formation of an informed public debate on the ramifications of membership in the Community. Second, the new political regime, established after a military coup which toppled authoritarian rule on 25 April 1974, was in 1989 still growing in stability and strength. Membership of the European Community itself is believed to have been one of the main contributing factors to the modernization of Portugal's institutions into their present (pluralist democratic) form. Nevertheless, in a number of ways the present system is still finding its feet, most obviously in the case of the party system which in the course of the 1980s evolved from a highly fragmented to a semi-two-party system, with PS (socialists) and PSD (social democrats) as dominant parties.

The Party System

Portuguese politics is characterized by the existence of many parties while it is dominated by only a few of them. By far the most important are the Socialist Party and the Social Democratic Party, which occupy center-left and center-right positions respectively, as shown in the bottom row of Table 15.1, below. In 1987 the PSD gained a majority in Portugal's parliament, which allowed it to form a single-party government—in contrast to earlier cabinets during the 1970s and 1980s—with its party leader Cavaco Silva as Prime Minister. The Presidency had been occupied since 1986 by Mario Soares, the founder of the PS and former Prime Minister.

In addition to the PSD and PS a number of other parties are of relevance. The most important of these is the Communist Party (PCP) which generally polls more than 10 percent of the vote in Portuguese elections. It did not compete under its own name in the 1989 European elections, but as (the largest) part of an electoral coalition with a green faction, under the joint label of United Democratic Coalition (CDU). At the time of the 1989 European election most other parties had been reduced to more or less marginal positions owing to the sweeping victory of the PSD in the 1987 national parliamentary elections. The Democratic Renewal Party (PRD) of former President Eanes, had, after a strong parliamentary election result in 1985, fallen back to a mere 7 seats (out of 250) in 1987, and did not feel sufficiently strong to compete on its own in the European election, instead entering into an electoral coalition with the PS. The right-wing Center Social Democrats (CDS), an orthodox catholic party, had been reduced to 4 parliamentary seats in 1987. Various small left parties, such as the leninist-maoist UDP, have enjoyed no parliamentary representation since 1987. On the right, likewise, a number of small parties have been without parliamentary representation since 1987, some of which (like the monarchist PPM) did win seats in earlier parliaments. Their electoral prospects are generally perceived as very bleak.

The respective clienteles of the various parties do overlap to a considerable extent. Table 15.1, which has been constructed along the lines indicated in Chapter 3 and Appendix B, shows that ideologically similar parties are often also each other's electoral competitors. The most attractive alternative for the CDU is the PS: 60 percent of this Communist and Green potential vote

Table 15.1 Potential Support and Overlap Between Parties in Portugal in 1989

	UDP	CDU	PS	PSD	PPM	CDS
UDP	1.00	0.30	0.15	0.13	0.34	0.19
CDU	0.66	1.00	0.26	0.16	0.32	0.21
PS	0.76	0.60	1.00	0.58	0.82	0.62
PSD	0.58	0.30	0.49	1.00	0.84	0.78
PPM	0.43	0.18	0.20	0.24	1.00	0.40
CDS	0.47	0.23	0.30	0.45	0.81	1.00
Potential Support (%)	7.5	16.6	38.4	32.3	9.2	18.6
%Vote Elect	0.5	7.4	14.6	16.7	1.0	7.2
%Valid Vote	1.1	14.9	29.5	33.7	2.1	14.6
L-R median (1–10)	1.40	1.40	4.84	7.15	8.03	9.26

also belongs to the potential of the PS. The strongest overlap of the PS, on the other hand, is with the PSD (with the CDS as a less important, but still relevant electoral competitor); a preference that is reciprocated, since for PSD potential voters the PS is the most likely alternative (again with strong competition from the CDS). The potential support for small center-right parties such as the PPM is almost entirely shared with that of PS, PSD and CDS, which might make these small parties appropriate vehicles for occasional protest votes, but also into likely victims of the competition for the center by these major parties.

In addition to their competitive relations, Table 15.1 also displays the size of the actual support which these parties gained in the European elections of 1989 (expressed as percentages of the entire electorate, and of the valid votes) and the size of their potential support (expressed as a percentage of the entire electorate). The sum of the latter clearly shows that none of the parties can assume its votes to be beyond the reach of competitors, whereas the pattern of competition clearly displays three regions of competition: the struggle for the left vote (between CDU and PS), the struggle for the center (between PS, PSD and CDS), and that for the right vote (between PSD, PPM, PDC).

The Electoral System

In elections for the European Parliament "all Portuguese citizens registered in Portugal or in another member state of the European Community are entitled to vote ..." (art.3, Law no. 14/87 of 29 April). In general elections for the national parliament "all Portuguese citizens over 18 years of age are entitled to vote" and may be resident in any country as long as they are "listed on the electoral register" (Art.1, Law no. 14/79). In 1987, just 114,603 of the Portuguese abroad were registered voters and only 26.7 percent of them voted in the first European Parliament elections.

The main differences between the European Parliament and parliamentary electoral processes are the way in which candidates are put forward, the organization of electoral constituencies and the method of voting.

In general elections, "candidates are put forward by individual parties or by coalitions .. " (Art.21, Law no. 14/79). The electorate in divided into 22 constituencies (18 in Portugal, 1 for the Azores, 1 for Madeira, 1 for emigrants "in Europe", and 1 for those "outside Europe". The number of MP's for each constituency is proportional to the size of its electorate, except in the case of constituencies outside Portugal. The MP's "are elected from lists of names in each constituency, each voter having a single vote on the list". In elections for the European Parliament, candidates put themselves forward directly to the Constitutional Court, a politically independent institution responsible for the defence and application of the Constitution. The "electorate constitutes one single constituency, based in Lisbon, with one single electoral college" (Art. 2, Law no. 14/87).

In both European and general elections, representation is proportional and seats are distributed among the different lists in each constituency according to the d'Hondt system. Yet the two elections differ in the chances of representation for small parties. The substantial difference between the numbers elected to the two parliaments—24 to the European Parliament and 250 to the national parliament—effectively raises the threshold which has to be passed for representation, which works to the disadvantage of small groups and parties. Geographical distribution apart, about 330,000 votes are required to elect a Euro-MP, while approximately 34,000 are needed for a member of the national parliament. These two aspects of the electoral system may not make a significant difference to the overall distribution of votes cast, but candidates representing small political groups have much less chance of being elected in European Parliament elections than in general elections.

The difference between one or 22 constituencies is particularly significant as in Portugal distribution of ideological groups and, consequently, the electorate's partisan preferences, are concentrated in different geographical areas and constituencies. This is caused by important social and cultural differences between rural and urban areas, and between the developed coastal region and the underdeveloped interior. In a national election, groups or parties whose potential support is geographically concentrated have an advantage in the allocation of seats which they lack in the single constituency used in a European election. In principle, a countervailing tendency could be that it is more difficult for small parties to field 22 slates of candidates—one in each of the constituencies—than a single list in one constituency. Effects attributable to such a tendency can only be weak, however, because of the geographically concentrated following of the different parties referred to above.

The differences between the electoral systems and between the number of seats in national and European elections provides a clear incentive for political parties to engage in electoral coalitions or pacts, which was indeed what happened. In 1989, as indicated above, the Communists and Greens formed an electoral coalition (named CDU), as did the PS and PRD.

The European Elections of 1987 and 1989

Portugal officially joined the EC in January 1986, and held its first elections for the European Parliament in July 1987. These elections coincided with the general elections for the national parliament. The running of the campaign, the strategies adopted by the political parties, and the elections themselves were determined by the general elections. The most notable feature was the appearance of Lucas Pires as candidate, a charismatic and telegenic former leader of the CDS who enjoys broad cross-party esteem. Although the CDS endorsed his candidature, his campaigning was totally independent of the party machine and strategy. Turnout and the distributions of votes cast were roughly the same for both the general and European elections as is indicated by Table 15.2. The most notable difference between the results of the 1987 national and European elections concerned the CDS, which in the European election received more than 15 percent of the vote, as contrasted to a mere 4

Table 15.2 Election Results of European Elections (EE) in 1987 and 1989 and of National Elections (NE) in 1987 and 1991

	EE '87[a]	EE '89[b]	NE '87	NE '91[c]
PSD	37.4	33.7	50.1	50.4
PS	22.5	29.5[d]	22.3	29.3
PRD	4.4	_[d]	4.9	0.6
PCP/CDU	11.5	14.9[e]	12.2	8.8[f]
PPM	2.8	2.1	0.4	0.4
CDS	15.4	14.6	4.3	4.4
Others	6.0	5.2	5.8	6.1

Sources: a: Gallagher (1989); b: Appendix C; c: Goldey (1992)
d: electoral alliance of PS and PRD
e: CDU: electoral alliance of PCP and Greens
f: CDU-PEV: alliance of PCP, Greens and UDP and other small extreme left groups

percent in the national election. Indications are that the difference was mainly at the cost of the PSD. The personal stature of Lucas Pires is generally supposed to be the major factor in this difference.

Ideological confrontation during the 1989 campaign for the European election mainly took the form of all opposition parties attacking the PSD—which had an absolute majority in parliament—and the performance of its government. Consequently, the elections were seen by the main parties in terms of a referendum on the government and its achievements. The parties in opposition to the PSD centered their European Parliament election campaign on attacking the government's record for its first two years in office. The Prime Minister and PSD leader himself appealed to the electorate to vote for his candidates as "a way to express their confidence in the Executive". The Socialist Party's campaign slogan was "Let's change Portugal to win Portugal"—a reference to the possibility of a government defeat and changes at the next parliamentary elections. Its leaders proclaimed that on the 18th of June, the date set for the European Parliament elections, "the Portuguese have a unique chance to express their discontent with the government".

The Communist Party, the second largest opposition party, unleashed a campaign, backed up with documents, pictures and words, concentrating on corruption, diminishing salaries and deterioration of the environment and living standards caused by the PSD government. The main criticism of the CDS, the largest opposition party to the right of the PSD, was the way in which the government had handled nationalizations. It was outspoken about its belief that "[the PSD] had not encouraged development of true national power".

The electoral campaigns of the other eight small parties, most of them critical of EC membership, were also directed against the government, whether for its performance, or for its subordination of Portuguese to EC-interests, referred to as supra-nationalism and international capitalism.

The focus in the campaign on expressing either support for, or opposition to, the government is reflected in the results of a set of analyses that were conducted for the cross-national comparative chapters of this book. The analyses reported in Chapter 20 (Tables 20.2 and 20.3) show that, after ideological concerns which are the most powerful determinants of party choice, respondents' evaluations of the performance of the government was the next strongest factor in the choice which Portuguese voters made in the 1989 European elections.

Table 15.2 (above) presents the major results of the 1987 and 1989 European elections, to which is added, for reference purposes, the results of the national parliamentary elections of 1987 and 1991. It shows, first of all, a considerable difference between the results of the concurrent 1987 European and national elections. This difference is almost entirely concentrated in two parties: the PSD which polled about 14 percent less in the 1987 European election, and the CDS which obtained 11 percent more votes in the European contest. In comparison, the differences between the 1987 and 1989 European elections are much less pronounced. The PSD lost almost 5 percent in 1989, the PS and PRD together hardly improved on the sum of their separate 1987 results, the CDU gained some 3 percent (probably because of its alliance with greens which did not exist in 1987). The CDS lost about 1 percent of its share of the vote, but still did spectacularly better than in the 1987 national election, or, for that matter, in the 1991 national parliamentary elections. When looking at the two European and two national elections that took place in the 1987–1991 period, the CDS stands out as a special case, because it obtains in the European elections more than three times the proportion of votes it manages to get in national elections. In both 1987 and 1989 the personal charisma of Lucas Pires must be regarded as the most important contributing factor to this result.

To what extent can the outcome of the 1989 European election be interpreted as an adequate assessment of the then existing distribution of national party preferences? By comparing reported vote in the European election with the party people say they would have voted for if national elections had been held at the same time, we can answer this question (for details, see Chapter 3 and Appendix B). Table 15.3 shows the results, which lead to the following conclusions:

- although for most parties the differences is small between the result of the European election and that of a hypothetical concurrent national one, they are considerable for two parties, the PS and the CDS (see column EE-NE). Our data suggest that the PS would have done considerably better had a national contest been at stake, a finding which foreshadows the electoral gains which the PS was to make later, in the national elections of 1991 (see also Goldey, 1992). The CDS, on the

Table 15.3 Quasi–switching and Turnout Effects in the 1989 European Election in Portugal

	EE	NE	EE-NE	Quasi-switching	Turnout Effect
UDP	2.8	2.0	0.8	0.5	0.3
CDU	14.9	14.4	0.5	0.7	-0.2
PS	29.5	36.2	-6.7	-4.5	-2.2
PSD	33.7	33.6	0.1	-1.5	1.6
PPM	2.1	0.6	1.5	1.3	0.2
CDS	14.6	8.7	5.9	4.0	1.9

other hand, did much better in the European election than it would have in a national one held at the same time, a finding which makes the 1991 national election result for the CDS explicable, where, just as in 1987, it was unable to transcend a marginal performance. These differences for PS and CDS are both brought about by reinforcing effects of low turnout and of quasi-switching.

- for all other parties the separate as well as joint effects of depressed European turnout and quasi-switching are much less pronounced. Most noteworthy is that the governing PSD would have done about the same in a concurrent national election, although this would have been brought about by two different, countervailing effects. The PSD was more able than other parties to mobilize its potential supporters to turn out and vote (as is indicated by the positive effect in the turnout column). At the same time it lost this advantage because some voters who would have supported the PSD in a national election went for other parties in a European one (see the quasi-switching column).

Turnout

In addition to the distribution of votes cast for each candidate and party (which differs according to the type of election), abstention is an important feature of election results. Several reasons explain the changing behavior of the electorate in this regard: its perception of the election's importance in terms of power and government, the efforts put into the campaign by the parties (including their leaders and constituency parties), the parties' propaganda skills, and finally any personal contact or familiarity with the candidates. A combination of these factors contributes to the degree of ideological confrontation between the parties and candidates involved.

In spite of their efforts, the parties did not provide their candidates with the same back-up in terms of finance and personnel that they would have provided in national parliamentary elections. So, in addition to the distant nature of the European Community and the European Parliament, the lack of information about, interest in, and saliency of 'Europe', and lack of campaign expenditure were yet further reasons for the electorate's lack of interest in the campaign, and the subsequent low level of turnout. Without the benefit of concurrent national elections to boost the level of turnout, the second Portuguese elections to the European Parliament in 1989 saw the highest level of abstentions ever recorded for an election in Portugal.

The question remains, however, to which extent the causes for (low) turnout are to be sought in factors which affect electoral participation in national elections as well, or in factors having to do with European orientations or

Table 15.4 Predictors of 1989 Participation in the European Election in Portugal

	R^2	Added R^2
Demographics	0.04	
General Political Orientations	0.27	0.22
Habitual Voting	0.31	0.04
European Attitudes	0.31	0.00

evaluations of the course and consequences of European integration. As in other country chapters, an analysis of determinants of electoral participation can answer this question. Following the strategy described in Chapter 3, Table 15.4 shows the explanatory strength of various blocks of variables when accounting for differences in electoral participation. This table shows unequivocally that the factors which explain participation in the election are the same as those that normally play their role in national contests as well, and that European attitudes or evaluations bring no additional elements into the explanation. The conclusion therefore must be that the main reason for low turnout was the low saliency of the election, and that the level of turnout did not in any way express Portuguese feelings—be it negative or positive ones—regarding the process of European integration.

Domestic Consequences of the European Election

The European elections did not leave much of a footprint on the Portuguese political landscape. Neither did they contribute to any lasting changes in the party system, nor to the domestic political agenda. Of course, their timing made it difficult for them to exert whatever kind of lasting effects. The first European elections in Portugal, in 1987, coincided with national elections, and were thus completely overshadowed by domestic political developments. The reverberations of this realigning 1987 national election were still felt in 1989, which prevented the 1989 European election to serve to the same extent as it otherwise might have as a mid-term evaluation of the national government's standing with the electorate. The dramatic changes of 1987 in the domestic parties' strengths were not reversed, but represented a lasting turn towards a two-dominant party system. As in 1987, the results of the European election could not be taken to accurately portray the domestic popularity of various parties, because of the extraordinary vote-getting capacities of Lucas Pires. The governing PSD did lose somewhat when compared to 1987, but this was quite limited and was not perceived as a reversal of its support (which was quite correct, as witnessed by the subsequent national elections of 1991). All in all, 1989 came too soon after a national election (which had created a fundamental realignment of the Portuguese electorate and party system) to allow the European elections to act as catalyst for any new developments or initiatives. It is hardly a surprise that, under those circumstances, the election was an ephemeral affair.

CHAPTER 16

Spain:
A Dress Rehearsal for the National Elections

Pilar del Castillo

While Spain has been a full member of the European Community since January 1986, not until June 1987 were Spaniards called upon to elect their representatives to the European Parliament. Two years later they came back again to cast a vote in European elections. Spain's accession to the EC brought to an end a story which began more than twenty years earlier. The authoritarian character of General Franco's regime precluded Spain from applying for EC membership, but in the mid-sixties, in spite of political constraints, the so-called 'technocrats', a faction in the administration holding important positions in that period,[1] decided to seek at least a preferential economic agreement with the EC. At the same time the political groups in opposition to the regime also favored Spain becoming an EC member. For them the European flag would aid their struggle for a democratic political system; even the Communist Party, in contrast to most of its European counterparts, was in favor.[2]

Spain obtained the preferential economic agreement it had been seeking in 1970. Franco died in 1975 and, by 1977, with the calling for the first democratic elections, no political barriers any longer impeded a Spanish application for admittance to the EC. The Spanish Government formulated the petition in 1977 with the unanimous support of all parliamentary groups, but ten years of negotiations were necessary before Spain obtained membership. The strong pro-European attitudes shown by the elites had their correlate at the mass level; Spaniards also viewed integration with Europe in a very positive way (Lopez Pintor, 1982). In fact, pro-European attitudes at both elite and mass level have been a Spanish characteristic in Francoist as well as in democratic times.[3] It has been emphasized (Miguel Herrero, 1992) that membership of

---

1 This group, most of them linked to the religious organization *Opus Dei*, entered the government in the mid-fifties and contributed considerably to the planned economic and social and modernization which took place in the sixties.

2 The Communist Party supported the Treaty of Rome.

3 A high level of positive EC attitudes among parties and their electorates in Spain has also been shown recently by van der Eijk and Franklin (1991).

the EC acquired an aura, suggesting benefits in political, economic and social terms that were not questioned. This obstructed the development of a detached public debate on the costs and benefits for Spain of EC developments.

Because neither Spanish membership of the EC nor EC policies have been a matter of inter-party conflict,[4] it was easy to predict that European parliamentary elections in Spain would be dominated by national political issues. This chapter starts with a basic introduction to the Spanish party system and its evolution. Different explanations of the level of turnout in this election will be explored in the next section. In the third section party choice, will be analyzed from the perspective of second-order election theory. A final section will consider the impact of the European election results on national politics.

The Spanish Party System

Spain has a bicameral parliament, in which the lower house, the Congreso de los Diputados, has considerably more powers than the upper house, the Senado. The electoral system for the lower house, in spite of it being a system of proportional representation, strongly favors major parties. Actually it is one of those systems which produces a high deviation from proportionality (Gallagher, 1991), due to the combination of small districts (32 of the 52 districts have between 3 and 6 seats) and the use of the d'Hondt formula for translating votes into seats.

Since the re-emergence of democracy in 1977, the history of the party system can be divided into two different periods: 1977–1982 and after 1982.[5] The first was a period of moderate pluralism, with four significant parties, while the second is better described as a predominant party system, with the socialists as the predominant party.

The first democratic election of June 1977 shaped a moderate pluralistic party system. It was actually a four-party system, with a relatively low degree of

---

4 Controversies between the Government and opposition parties have only concerned the role of the Spanish national parliament in controlling the Government's contribution to decision making in the Council of Ministers. For party positions on European integration see (for the PSOE) Resolutions 32 of its Federal Congress, and (for the Partido Popular) that party's Programa de Gobierno: Politica Exterior y de Seguridad.

5 For an extensive discussion of both periods see Gunther, Sani and Shabad (1986); Linz and Montero (1986); Maravall (1981,1984). The 1993 national elections reshaped this party system, opening what will presumably turn out to be a third period which can be defined as an 'imperfect bi-party system'. Two major parties, PSOE and PP now share 74 percent of the total vote (ten points more than in the last national election). The difference in percentage of vote between these parties is 3.5 percent (previously 14 percent). On the other hand, the Center Party—CDS—got no parliamentary representation while the communists and nationalists retained more or less the same level of representation as in 1987.

polarization and centripetal orientations. Although a total of 12 parties obtained representation in Parliament, four nationwide parties shared 80 percent of the popular vote and 90 percent of seats in the Congress of Deputies. The major party was the Democratic Center Union (UCD), a center-right coalition of political forces (Hunneus, 1985; Gunther, 1986), which ruled alone from 1977 to 1982 as a minority government. The main opposition party was the Spanish Socialist Party (PSOE).[6] Much smaller in votes and seats were two minor but significant parties: to the right the conservative Alianza Popular—now renamed the Popular Party (PP)—and to the left the Spanish (Euro-) Communist Party (PCE). The intensity of the center-periphery cleavage in Catalonia and the Basque Country caused separate party systems to emerge in those regions. The Catalan one was slightly more fragmented than the national party system, whereas the Basque one was considerably more fragmented (Gunther, Sani and Shabad, 1986). Inter-party competition is predominantly centripetal and moderately polarized in Catalonia, while in the Basque area it is more polarized and shows centrifugal tendencies (LLera, 1985). The most important nationalist parties in those two regions are the Nationalist Basque Party (PNV) and Convergencia Uni (CIU) from Catalonia, the latter being an electoral coalition where the strongest partner is Convergencia.[7] Both the Basque and the Catalan groups are center-right parties.

The second democratic general election was conducted in March 1979 and was the first under the newly adopted democratic Constitution. It reaffirmed the party system which emerged in 1977. Three and a half years later, however, this party system broke down. The 1982 election result was an electoral landslide which brought about a deep realignment, increased the level of polarization and showed one of the highest levels of volatility in Europe in decades (Linz and Montero, 1986). The government party (UCD) was practically swept away (falling from 168 to 11 seats out of a total of 350). The former main opposition party, the PSOE, obtained 202 seats—an overwhelming overall majority. The conservative AP became the major opposition party (up from 9 to 107 seats). The Communist Party lost most of its seats (down from 23 to 4) and a new center party, the Center Democratic Union (CDS), founded by former Primer Minister Adolfo Suarez after his resignation in 1981, entered the political scene with a tiny parliamentary representation of just 2 seats. This pattern was

---

6 In the 1977 national election the Union de Centro Democratico got 33.4 percent of the vote and 165 seats while the Socialist Party (PSOE) obtained 28.1 percent of the vote and 118 seats. In the general election of 1979 the corresponding figures were 34.3 percent of the vote and 168 seats for the UCD and 30 percent of the vote and 121 seats for the PSOE.

7 The other partner is the group of christian democratic orientation, Union Democratica de Cataluna.

not substantially modified by subsequent general elections in 1986 and 1989. After 1989 the PSOE was one seat short of an overall parliamentary majority, but the PP had not much improved its parliamentary representation. Both the communists, at present forming part of a left coalition (IU), and the CDS had improved their parliamentary representation; but they remained far behind the two major parties (see Table 16.4). The 1982 realignment was not the consequence of dramatic changes in voter attitudes (Barnes, McDonough and Lopez Pina, 1986) but mainly due to the government party's (UCD) involvement after 1980 in self-destructive intra-party struggles (Gunther, 1986). Despite these changes at the national level, the regional party systems which had emerged in the first general election of 1977 in the Basque Country and in Catalonia have not substantially changed in more recent elections.[8]

Party Competition

Table 16.1 gives information on the competitiveness of the party system and the structure of electoral competition. The parties included are the four most important at the national level, ordered from the left to right, and the three main nationalist parties in their respective regions.

The first notable feature in Table 16.1 is that the sum of the potential electorates of the major parties does not even reach 100 percent. This illustrates a particular aspect of the relation between the Spanish electorate and the party system. Spanish voters are not enthusiastic about the options from which they can make a choice. The proportion of voters for whom no party is really attractive is higher than in any other country of the EC. This is reflected in the magnitude of the potential electorates (refer to Chapter 3 and Appendix B for the calculation of these). Van der Eijk and Oppenhuis (1991:62) report that the percentage of Spanish voters who rate their most attractive party less than 8 on a 10-point scale, which ranges from "I will certainly vote for this party at some time" (score 10) to "I will certainly never vote for this party" (score 1), is 33.2 percent—more than three times as much as the average (10.7 percent) in the other political systems of the EC. This is indicative of a (comparatively) high degree of alienation of the Spanish electorate from the existing party system. Such alienation notwithstanding, parties have to compete with one another for

---

8 A split from the Nationalist Basque Party increased the level of fragmentation in the Basque Party System. Three Basque nationalist parties currently exist, EuskadiKo EzKuerra, Eusko Alkartasuna (the breakaway faction of the PNV) and Herri Batasuna (ETA's legal arm). There is also one Adalusian nationalist party, PA, one Canarian nationalist party, AIC, two regional parties from the regions of respectively Aragon (PAR) and Valencia (UV), and one nationalist group from Galicia, BNG. Most of these have elected one or two deputies in each national election since 1977.

the share of the vote they eventually acquire. The structure of this competition reflects on the one hand the power of the left/right axis in Spanish politics, and on the other the unrelatedness of regional parties to that dimension. Looking at the four major national parties—IU, PSOE, CDS and PP—which are ordered from left to right in Table 16.1, we see that competition is more pronounced within the left and within the right bloc of parties than between them. More than two-thirds of potential IU voters belong to the potential electorate of the PSOE. The reverse percentage is lower because of the difference in size of these two parties but even so, the potential of the PSOE overlaps more with the IU than it does with right-wing parties. On the right side of the spectrum we see that CDS and PP, two parties of approximately equal potential size, each share more than half of the other's potential. The most centrist of these two, the CDS, is the one most likely to siphon off support from the PSOE, which is exactly as one would expect in view of these parties' position in left/right terms. Competition between the left and the right block of parties remains much lower than within each of the blocks.

For the regional parties we observe that their potential electorates overlap strongly with each of the major national parties, irrespective the ideological position of the latter. Party competition is significantly higher in Catalonia and also in the Basque Country; though the fragmentation of the party system (particularly among the nationalist groups) is much higher in the latter.

Table16.1 Potential Support and Overlap Between Parties in Spain in 1989

	National				Regional		
	IU	PSOE	CDS	PP	CIU	HB	PNV
IU	1.00	0.32	0.35	0.23	0.48	0.60	0.59
PSOE	0.69	1.00	0.51	0.40	0.52	0.47	0.66
CDS	0.37	0.25	1.00	0.56	0.51	0.43	0.59
PP	0.27	0.21	0.61	1.00	0.47	0.42	0.53
CIU	0.26	0.13	0.27	0.22	1.00	0.48	0.69
HB	0.10	0.04	0.07	0.06	0.15	1.00	0.29
PNV	0.17	0.09	0.16	0.14	0.37	0.51	1.00
Potential Support (%)	17.6	37.8	18.7	20.3	39.6*	13.2*	15.7*
%Vote Elect	3.3	21.5	3.9	11.6	15.7*	10.1*	10.6*‡
%Valid Vote	6.2	40.2	7.3	21.7	29.0*	22.1*	23.1*‡
L-R median (1–10)	2.13	4.14	5.91	8.39	5.53	1.21	5.25

* These figures pertain only to the respective regions of Catalonia (CIU, N=126) and the Basque Country (PNV, HB, N=66).
‡ The PNV participated in the 1989 EP elections under the electoral nationalist coalition CN.

Table 16.1 also reports the performance of each party in the 1989 European elections. The large parties at the national level, PSOE and PP, did considerable better than the smaller CDS and IU in converting their potential support into actual votes. However, some caution is needed in interpreting the performance of the Popular Party. Public opinion surveys in Spain commonly underestimate the support for this party.[9] To the extent that this occurs in our surveys too, it results in an underestimate of the size of the PP's potential electorate and thus in an overestimation of the ability of this party to mobilize that electorate in the 1989 European elections.

Turnout

Antecedents: The 1987 European Elections

In the first elections to the European Parliament, held in Spain in June 1987, participation was 68.7 percent. This placed Spain in sixth position among the members of the EC (on the basis of 1984 European election results for all but Spain and Portugal), a surprising result given the fact that the average rate of participation in Spanish first-order elections is quite inferior to that of most EC countries.[10] It is not unreasonable to assume that the high turnout in 1987 was caused by the fact that municipal and regional elections were conducted on the same day (del Castillo and Morán, 1989). As this factor was absent in 1989, it would have been reasonable to expect a significant drop in electoral participation compared to 1987. It would also have been reasonable to expect turnout to be one of the lowest in Europe, in view of participation patterns in other elections.[11]

Turnout in the 1989 European Elections

The first of these two expectations was confirmed but the second was not. Turnout in 1989 was 54.6 percent, a drop of fourteen points from the 1987 level. This, however, did not make Spain one of the least participant countries.

---

9 The Centro de Investigaciones Sociologicas, a public opinion research institution which is dependent on the government, conducts at least once a month a nationally representative survey in which vote intention is included. All such surveys show that, unlike other parties, a significant portion of the supporters of the Partido Popular (formerly Alianza Popular) are unwilling or reluctant to disclose their party preference.

10 A reason often given for low rates of electoral participation in Spain, particularly in the first years after the transition to democracy, is the preponderance of apolitical and anti-party attitudes which were fostered by the Francoist regime. For a detailed discussion on non-voting in Spain see Montero (1986 and 1990), Justel (1990), Astorkia (1992).

11 See Montero (1986).

Elsewhere too, electoral participation declined compared to 1984. Excluding countries that were conducting general elections on the same day and those that have compulsory voting, Spain ranked second out of seven. Turnout probably benefitted from the fact that Spain occupied the EC Presidency at the time, but this hypothesis cannot easily be tested given the absence of appropriate survey data.

As Table 16.2 shows, electoral participation in the 1989 European elections is substantially lower than in previous general and municipal elections, but not very different from turnout in some regional elections. Following the logic of the second-order elections thesis (Reif and Schmitt 1980), turnout can find itself affected when the electoral system notably diverges from the one applied to first-order national elections. In Spain the electoral rules for general elections and those for European elections differ in a number of important respects, which, however, do not easily explain the different levels of electoral participation. The electoral system for the European elections is, like the one regulating general elections, a proportional system of fixed lists, using the D'Hondt formula for the distribution of seats. But while in general elections there are 52 electoral districts, for European elections there is only one: the entire national territory. On the other hand, while for general elections there is a threshold of 3 percent in each electoral district, no minimum at all applies in European elections. The single district context forces regional parties, in regions with a small demographic size, to look for partners in other geographical areas with whom to ally themselves so as to win enough votes for a seat in the European Parliament. Those most in need of allies were the Basque

Table16.2 Turnout in Spain, 1977-1993 (percent)

Elections	77	79	80	81	82	83	84	85	86	87	88	89	90	91	92	93
European										69		55				
Lower House	79	68			80				71			70				78
Regional*																
13 Regions						64				72				62		
Basque		59					68		70				61			
Catalonia		62					64				59				54	
Galicia				55					57		59					58
Andalucia					66					71			55			
Municipal		60				68					70			63		

Percentages have been rounded up
* From a total of 17 regions, 13 held elections in the same year.

nationalist parties; and the more important of them did manage to form electoral coalitions with nationalist groups in other regions, in each of which they played the central role (Molins, 1989, 1992).

One could imagine that the loss of identity which resulted from such coalitions would have encouraged abstention among the supporters of the members of such pacts. This hypothesis is not confirmed. 91 percent of the voters who said they voted for the Basque Nationalist Party in the general election of 1986 declared that they voted in the 1989 European Parliament elections. Corresponding figures are 85 percent for the PP, 79 percent for the PSOE an 73 percent for the Catalan nationalists of CIU, all of which competed independently using their own symbols.[12]

As differences in electoral procedures do not seem to account for the low turnout in the European elections it is necessary to address other possible explanations. It is reasonable to explore the extent to which the specifically European dimension of these elections explains the low level of participation. Table 16.3 shows how much variance is explained by European attitudes and orientations of voters when they are added to an explanation which builds only on those variables which are usually taken into account for explaining turnout in national parliamentary elections (for the description of each block of variables see Chapter 3).

Two conclusions can be drawn from Table 16.3. First, European attitudes and orientations contribute hardly at all to an explanation of why people did or did not turn out to vote in the 1989 European elections. They do not even increase the variance explained by one percent. Second, the entire set of variables can account only partially for the variation in electoral participation: just 30 percent of the variance is explained (see Chapter 19 for further discussion of this point).

Table16.3 Predictors of 1989 Participation in the European Election in Spain

	R^2	Added R^2
Demographics	0.05	
General Political Orientations	0.16	0.11
Habitual Voting	0.17	0.01
European Attitudes	0.17	0.00

---

12 Centro de Investigaciones Sociologicas, Study 1817, June 1989; European post-election study.

Party Choice

Two questions regarding party preference in the European elections will be explored in this section. Firstly, how can the results of the European election in comparison to those of a hypothetical national election conducted at the same time be evaluated? Secondly, how can differences in party choice between national and European elections be explained?

Turnout Effects and Quasi-switching

Table 16.4 compares the result of the European election to a (hypothetical) simultaneous national election. The turnout effect gives information about the parties' differential ability to mobilize their voters in European and national elections while the data in the quasi-switching column show how many voters would choose different parties in one election than in the other (both dimensions are discussed in Chapter 3 of this book).

If we ignore for the moment the regional parties, CIU, PNV and HB, Table 16.4 clearly shows that all major nationwide parties apart from the PP would have done better in a national election than they did in the European election. Here, once again, conclusions concerning the conservatives (PP) have to be drawn with caution in view of the 'hidden' preference for this party whose support is commonly underestimated, as mentioned earlier.

The other three nationwide parties would have done better in a national election, but the contribution made to this difference by turnout and quasi-switching effects is different for each of them. As can be seen in Table 16.4, the parties on the left of the political spectrum suffered losses from quasi-switching whereas the parties on the right made modest gains from this

Table 16.4 Quasi–switching and Turnout Effects in the 1989 European Election in Spain

	EE	NE	EE-NE	Quasi-switching	Turnout Effect
IU	6.2	8.6	-2.4	-2.1	-0.3
PSOE	40.2	43.5	-3.3	-2.9	-0.4
CDS	7.3	8.4	-1.1	-0.5	-0.6
PP	21.7	18.7	3.0	2.2	0.8
CIU	4.3	4.4	-0.1	-0.1	0.0
HB	1.7	2.3	-0.6	-0.6	0.0
PNV/CN	1.9	0.9	1.0	0.7	0.3
Others	15.2	12.1	3.1	1.8	1.3

source. The socialists (PSOE) and the leftist coalition (IU) sustained losses of 2.9 and 2.1 percent respectively, due to quasi-switching, whereas the CDS lost only 0.5 percent because of quasi-switching and the PP gained 2.2 percent from switchers. In contrast to the effects from quasi-switching, the ability of parties to mobilize their own supporters is not related to their position on the left/right continuum. Most hurt by turnout effects is the CDS, with a loss of 0.6 percent. The result of the PSOE is also negatively affected by low turnout (0.4 percent) but this loss is small compared to that suffered from quasi-switching. The IU's slight loss from low turnout was 0.3 percent. The PP benefitted from the low overall level of turnout. It was the only party which profited from both quasi-switching and turnout effects.

Low turnout and quasi-switching did not affect the result of the nationalist CIU. For the Basque PNV one has to keep in mind that in the European elections they formed part of an electoral coalition together with other nationalist groups. In Table 16.4 a single row represents the PNV (as far as national elections are concerned) and the CN (for the European elections).[13] This group did better in the European election than it would have in a national election at the same time. This is caused mainly by quasi-switching, and is reinforced by a small turnout effect. HB, finally, lost votes in the European election due to quasi-switching.

Taken all together, fewer than 7 percent of Spanish voters engaged in what has been termed quasi-switching, which means that no less than 93 percent voted for the same party as they would have supported in a national election. The small size of the group of quasi-switchers prevents a detailed exploration of its causes at the individual level; but, given the fact that national elections were held only four months after the European one, a comparison of aggregate results in both elections may contribute to our insights on (quasi-)switching.

The 1989 European and National Elections Compared

Two months after the European elections the Prime Minister decided to call national elections, which took place on October 29th. As we will see below, this constitutes the main domestic consequence of the European elections in Spain. Table 16.5 reports the results obtained by the four major parties and the two main regionalist parties in both elections. A first conclusion is that the overall pattern of party strength is quite similar in both elections, which

---

13 Molins (1992) calculated that some 68 percent of the votes for the CN coalition can be attributed directly to the PNV. The other components of this electoral coalition were Coalicion Galega, Agrupaciones Independientes de Canarias and Partido Nacionalista de Castilla y Len. Because the PNV is by far the most important component of CN, they have been used as comparable entities in Table 16.4.

Table16.5 1989 European Elections and 1989 National Elections (Vote Percentage)

	IU	PSOE	CDS	PP	CiU	PNV
European Elections	6.1	39.5	7.1	21.4	4.4	1.9
National Elections	9.0	39.4	7.9	25.8	5.0	1.2
Difference (NE-EE)	2.9	-0.1	0.8	4.4	0.6	-0.7

underlines the small extent of quasi-switching commented upon above. But a different impact of quasi-switching and turnout emerges if the performance of specific parties in both elections are considered, rather than using the comparison derived from our post-electoral survey on European elections.

The most notable difference with respect to specific parties concerns the Partido Popular which gained an extra 4.4 percent of the vote in comparison to the European election. At first sight this may conflict with the interpretation of Table 16.4 which showed that the PP benefitted from both turnout and quasi-switching effects. This would lead to the expectation that this party would do worse, not better, in the national election of October 1989. The explanation for these seemingly incompatible results must be sought in the fact that at the European elections a party competed whose electoral support was obtained disproportionately at the expense of the PP but which could not be included in Table 16.4 because it was not separately evaluated in our survey. The somewhat tragi-comic Ruiz Mateos, a financier who has had to face various criminal charges and whose business holdings were expropriated by the government in 1983, was presented with the opportunity in the 1989 European election of gaining immunity by becoming a European deputy. His list got 3.85 percent of the total vote which was sufficient for two seats. Because of his extreme-right political orientation, the right wing of the PP constituted his main potential clientele.

Although we do not have sufficiently detailed survey data to substantiate this proposition, it seems quite plausible that most of those who voted for Ruiz Mateos in the European elections came from the PP and returned to it when a more 'serious matter' such as the national election took place (Ruiz Mateos' list competed then too, but got only 1.07 percent of the votes). This phenomenon accounts for most of the apparent discrepancy between the results of the two elections. In addition one has to keep in mind the problems mentioned earlier of survey bias in measuring PP support and, finally, the possibility that between the two elections minor changes in actual support for parties may have occurred. The communist coalition, IU, also did much better in the national elections than in the European one. This, however, is perfectly in line with expectations which can be derived from our estimate of turnout and quasi-switching effects: Table 16.4 showed that the IU would have done better in a national election held on the same day as the European election, and this apparently remained true four months later.

The analysis of turnout and quasi-switching effects would also lead to the expectation that the PSOE and CDS would do somewhat better in the national elections. For the CDS this expectation was indeed borne out (though not to the expected extent); for the PSOE it was not. For the third consecutive time the socialists won the general election but their share of the vote (39.4 percent) was almost indistinguishable from that in the European elections (39.5 percent). Why they did not do better in the October national election, as Table 16.4 implied that they would have, cannot be answered here; but one has, of course, to keep in mind that minor changes in political preferences may occur even during a four-month interval. Finally, the results for the regional parties in the national elections fit quite nicely with what might have been expected on the basis of the analysis of turnout and quasi-switching. The result for the Catalan CIU differed only marginally from that in the European elections, while the loss of the Basque PNV was exactly as large as the positive quasi-switching effect calculated with regard to the European elections.

Taken all together then, Spanish voters behaved in the 1989 European election very much the way they would have in a general election. The few voters who chose different parties immediately came back to their national preference in the general elections four months later. This is illustrated most clearly by the fate of two newcomers who seemed to do well in the European elections, but who returned to insignificance in the national election. One of these, the Ruiz Mateos list, has already been described. The other is the Greens. The overall vote for Green lists was 2.7 percent in the European election, a higher percentage than ever before obtained, and one which would have yielded one or possibly two European deputies were it not for the fact that this support was fragmented over four different lists.[14] In the general election of October, the two major Green parties (who obtained together 2.6 percent in the European elections) ran a combined list but nevertheless fell back to 0.8 percent. So the results of the national elections of October 1989 conform largely with the expectations which could have been formulated from the results of the European election on the basis of our analysis of turnout and quasi-switching effects.

---

14 The four green lists and their percentage of the vote are as follows: Green List (1.03 percent), Green Ecologists (1.02 percent), Green Party (0.37 percent), Green Alternative (0.30).

Domestic Consequences of European Elections

The Political Context

The 1989 European elections took place in a national political context which was one of the most turbulent since the socialists came to power with an over-whelming overall majority in 1982. The problems affected not only the government party but also the main opposition party, PP, and the center-right CDS.

For the socialists the European elections were the first electoral test following a severe confrontation between the government and the two main unions, the communist CCOO and the socialist UGT. Six months earlier, on December 14, 1988, both unions called a twenty-four hour general strike. The entire country was effectively paralyzed by this first general strike in more than seventy years. (The previous one, in 1917, had been called by the same socialist union, but then with the active support of the socialist party). The 1989 European elections were thus of great significance as a measure of possible erosion of popular support as a consequence of the general strike. It would also indicate what hope the party could have for retaining the overall parliamentary majority which had been renewed in 1986. The fact that the PSOE did relatively well in the European election played a significant part in the decision to call a general election.

The Popular Party had faced a leadership problem since the 1986 national election and the European election result also affected this. The founder of the party, Manuel Fraga, had decided to give up his position as leader of the party after the 1986 election because of his lack of success in improving the party's electoral standing. A new leader, Hernandez Manch, was appointed with Fraga's support in the aftermath of the 1986 general election. He was unable to solve the party's problems and after a series of internal crises Fraga returned as the party leader in 1988. The European election offered an opportunity to test the water for a new figurehead. A former Foreign Minister and ex-General Secretary of the Council of Europe, Marcelino Oreja, was appointed to head the list for the European election.

The European election was also quite crucial for defining the political strategy of the center-right party, CDS. Shortly before the election the party entered into a pact with the PP to unseat the socialist mayor of Madrid. This alliance was criticized by segments of the party and the outcome of the European election for the CDS would thus be of importance to an argument within the party on political strategy.

Thus, the European elections of 1989 were viewed by the main parties as an event with important domestic implications. This had not been the case with the European election of 1987, which took place only one year after a national election and which were overshadowed by simultaneous municipal and local elections. The PSOE and the PP in particular considered the 1989 election as a dress rehearsal for a general election, as is illustrated by the statement by the head of the PP list that the European parliamentary elections were like an American 'primary' election. The campaign was dominated absolutely by national issues despite efforts made by the heads of the lists of the two main parties (former Foreign Minister Fernando Moran for the socialists and Marcelino Oreja, ex-General Secretary of the Council of Europe, for the PP). Both heads of list had strong European backgrounds and insisted on emphasizing European matters, but their voices were drowned out largely by the messages of the national party leaders. Two issues in particular drew attention in the campaign: the general strike of December 1988 (a topic raised in particular by the communist coalition IU), and some cases of political corruption in the city council of Madrid.

Interpreting the Consequences of the Electoral Outcome

The results of the European elections were seen as favorable for the PSOE. They were interpreted as indicating that the general strike had been of, at most, limited importance to the voters; and the general view was that the socialists would be able to retain a parliamentary majority if a general election were to be called. Immediately after the election, the socialist prime minister refused to speculate on such an eventuality; but in September the Government announced that a general election would be held, justifying this by citing the need for renewed legitimation in the face of the consequences of the coming Single European Market. The 1989 general election did not give a new parliamentary majority to the PSOE (which would have been the third in succession). The party fell one seat short of such a majority, which could easily be made up for by parliamentary support from most of the Catalan and Basques nationalists, however.

The European election result for the PP, by contrast, was generally considered to be rather poor, in spite of the likelihood of a better showing in a general elections where the Ruiz Mateos list would be less able to siphon off support. Discussions regarding leadership changes began immediately, and at the beginning of September Jose M. Aznar, at that time President of the regional government of Castilla and Len, was appointed as party leader (and putative Prime Minister) in time for the coming national elections. The performance of the party in the 1989 national election was somewhat better than in either the European or the previous national elections, but not dramatically so. Still, the new leader was able to retain his position. This was facilitated by several factors. Firstly, the decline in the party's share of the vote was arrested;

secondly, although the percentage of votes was similar to that in the 1986 national election, the number of seats it won was slightly greater; and thirdly, for the first time the party's candidate out-polled the prime minister (heading the PSOE list) in the city of Madrid (but not in the province of Madrid taken as a whole). These factors, and the short period between his appointment and the election, enabled the new PP leader to remain in position and to gain the position of President of the party in April 1990. Since then a process of slow but unspectacular growth by the PP has set in, along with a move in its political stance towards a more centrist (center-right) position. This new stance helped the party to acquire a majority of the votes in the municipal elections in Madrid and to achieve very promising results in urban areas in the local and regional elections of 1991 (del Castillo, 1991). The next general election will show the extent to which the Popular Party has broken out of the stagnant position in which it previously found itself.

Finally, the poor results by the CDS in the European election, which were repeated in the general election of October 1989, were interpreted by the critics inside the party as a rejection by the electorate of its alliance with the PP in various municipalities, including Madrid. These pacts nevertheless continued. Two months after the general election the city government of Madrid was taken over by a coalition of PP and CDS, with a CDS politician as the new major of Madrid. But in other places, in some municipalities as well as in the national parliament, the CDS supported the PSOE. This confusing play of alliances did no good to the party's electoral standing. The damage was aggravated by the laziness and lack of political ambition of the CDS leader, former Primer Minister Adolfo Suarez, who neglected his political functions, and by the gradual improvement in the image of the PP. After serious losses in the municipal and regional elections of 1991 the fate of the party is unclear, and it has to decide whether to compete in future elections or to declare the dissolution of the party.[15]

When we review the various domestic consequences of the European elections, the first and most direct domestic effect was the decision by the government to call new parliamentary elections. Had the result of the European election been disappointing to the governing PSOE, national elections would not have been called earlier than necessary, but by being perceived as a positive 'dry run', the European election provided a green light in this respect. Other domestic effects of the European election were not particularly dramatic, they

---

15   The party President, former Prime Minister Afdolfo Suarez, resigned after his party suffered electoral disaster in the 1991 local and regional elections. The CDS won no parliamentary representation at all in many of the regions and it lost most of its city council members. In the end the party did present candidates in the 1993 national elections, but won no seats.

belong to the broad class of situations in which current political events (in this case the campaign for, and the results of, a second-order election) are used as political ammunition in ongoing debates and conflicts, within as well as between parties. In most of these instances, the European election and its results are 'just another brick in the wall', contributing to the way in which ongoing political processes unfold, but by themselves not decisive. They helped improve or undermine the positions of party leaders, but only within the parameters of their pre-existing strengths and weaknesses (though in one case the election provided a particularly useful means of evaluating a new party leader in circumstances where little was at stake). The same is true regarding their influence on the likelihood of possible alliances, their facilitation or obstruction of shifts in parties' general stance, and such.

At the same time it is important to indicate the effects the European election of 1989 did not have. It did not see the breakthrough of new political groups, parties, or issue concerns and did not stimulate a domestic political debate on the course of European integration and the position of Spain in that process.

Perhaps most importantly, in relation to the overall theme of this book, is the fact that in Spain two esteemed heads of list attempted to raise European issues in the European election but without any success. The reasons for the absence of European issues in these elections in Spain cannot thus be attributed to the fact that no-one mentioned them. European issues were raised, but gained no salience because the media paid more attention to national party leaders who were interested in publicizing different issues.

CHAPTER 17

The Dog That Did Not Bark:
The 1994 Elections in the Light of 1989

Cees van der Eijk, Mark Franklin and Tom Mackie

The accounts of the 1989 elections and their aftermath given in previous chapters confirm conventional wisdom in a number of ways. These were not real elections in which matters important in the European arena were the subject of debate and eventual decision. On the contrary, these were elections particular to each member country of the (then) European Community. Indeed, even the low turnout in these elections apparently was no reflection of European (or, more properly, anti-European) attitudes. The surprises in the country chapters relate not to the lack of European content in these elections, but to the extent of their domestic consequences. European elections have generally been viewed as being of little importance in either European or national terms, so the litany of domestic consequences seen in chapter after chapter of the second part of this book comes as something of a surprise. We will have more to say about these consequences later in the present chapter, when we look for equivalent consequences of the 1994 elections. But first we need to focus attention on the 'curious incident' of the dog that 'did nothing in the nighttime'.[1]

The fact that European elections have no European content is easily taken for granted, but it should not be. As is well known, the European Community (now the European Union) is a political entity which is not a nation state, administered by something which is not a real government, but which nevertheless at the time of the 1989 and 1994 elections directly affected important features of the lives of over 350 million people. Those people do live in countries with real governments, and national elections within those countries do involve discussion and eventual decision regarding important matters of public concern. But whole areas of relevance to daily life are not subject to direction by national governments because they fall under the control of the European Union. This is why elections to the European Parliament are held.[2]

---

1 This is a reference to a famous Sherlock Holmes detective story, 'Silver Blaze' (Conan Doyle, 1894), in which the main clue was something that was nearly overlooked because it did not happen. The point was that the dog should have barked.

2 We will see in Chapter 21 that the reverse argument can also be made, but for the moment we

That the elections of 1989 should have had no European content is hard to understand in the abstract, but perhaps easier to understand in more specific terms. After all, it could be argued that the unification of Europe happened somewhat behind the backs of the electorates of European countries, being largely a matter of accommodation between elites (Urwin, 1995; Sloot, 1992). Though referenda were held in various countries at the time of accession and later, the European Community still seemed to its citizens mainly concerned with removing the nuisance aspects of national boundaries. The fact that, by 1989, the EC had already taken major steps towards becoming a single European market, with eventual implications for ordinary citizens going well beyond those of previous decades, had at that time generated little attention, let alone controversy, in the national media that citizens depend on for their information.

In December 1991, however, in the Dutch town of Maastricht, the leaders of all the EC countries signed a 'Treaty of European Union' which formalized the achievements of the Single European Market and laid down steps towards further wide-ranging changes including the creation within a decade of a single currency and central bank. This treaty received much publicity, and, in case anyone should have missed its importance, the problems over ratification in France, Denmark, Germany and Britain filled major slots on prime-time television for days on end during 1992 and 1993[3]. By the time of the European elections of 1994 there should have been few Europeans unawakened to the fact that the future scope of the European Union had become a contentious issue. The first opportunity to see this new awareness manifest itself at the polls was in June 1994, and if ever a set of European elections were going to break the patterns of the past, it should have been these.

Despite this change of context, the European elections of 1994 followed very much the pattern of previous European elections. Party choice seemed, just like in 1989, to have been primarily motivated by domestic considerations. Indeed, there was no trace in 1994 even of the sort of common trend in favor of (or at the expense of) some particular kind of party, as was evident in 1989 when reference was made to a 'Green tide' (Curtice, 1989).

This lack of European concerns in the European elections of 1994 is the dog that did not bark. In the pages that follow we will document in more detail the fact that, despite the enormous change in context that had occurred between the two elections, fundamental features of the 1994 elections were quite similar to those of 1989. This lays the groundwork for the chapters of Part III which will address the question of why European elections do not perform the same functions for the European political system as people have

---

accept this common assumption.

3 See Urwin, 1995: 256–9, for an account of these problems.

become used to with national elections, and why this has remained true even after a major increase in the power and scope of the European Union. As elsewhere in this book, when we look at the political systems of the European Union altogether we distinguish between Britain and Northern Ireland, and also between Flanders and Wallonia in Belgium—in each case because the separate regions have different party systems.

1994: the General Picture

Turnout seemed in general to be low in 1994 (particularly when compared to national elections) and was down across the EU as a whole (60 percent, on average, compared to 63 percent five years earlier). However, as we shall see below, overall descriptions of Europe-wide turnout do not tell us very much: differences between countries are too large to permit a simple summary. As shown in Table 17.1 where countries are ranked according to change in turnout, turnout was up (when compared to the previous European elections of 1989) in Spain, Denmark, France and Flanders. On the other hand, a marked drop in turnout was registered in Italy, Greece, Luxembourg, and especially in the Netherlands, Portugal, Wallonia and Ireland. In the remaining countries

Table 17.1 Turnout and Turnout Change

Country	Electorate (millions)	Turnout (%) 1989	1994	Change
Spain	29.1	54.7	59.5	+4.8,
Denmark	3.3	47.4	52.9	+4.5
France	37.0	48.8	52.7	+3.9
Flanders	3.5	92.7	96.1	+3.4
Northern Ireland	1.3	47.5	49.8	+2.3
Britain	42.0	36.6	36.1	-0.5
Germany*	45.3	62.3	60.0	-2.3
Italy	45.6	81.4	74.8	-6.6
Greece	7.9	80.1	71.2	-8.9
Luxembourg	0.2	96.2	86.6	-9.6
Netherlands	10.7	48.8	35.6	-13.2
Wallonia	3.5	87.1	82.2	-14.9
Portugal	7.7	51.1	35.7	-15.6
Ireland	2.4	65.9	44.0	-21.9
Total electorate	239.5			
Weighted average		59.1	56.9	-2.2

* Only West Germany in 1989 and equivalent parts of the former West Germany in 1994.

(Germany, Great Britain and Northern Ireland) turnout was roughly of the same magnitude as in 1989.

Within each of these three groups of countries (distinguished according to whether turnout increased, decreased or remained about the same) there are great differences in the level of turnout, in 1989 as well as in 1994. At first sight, all these differences in level, magnitude of change and direction of change in turnout seem to display little structure. However, even without engaging in any formal analysis, a little contextual information goes a long way in making some sense out of the variations. As already discussed in Chapter 2, two major contextual factors are the presence or absence of compulsory voting and of concurrent national elections. Persistent differences between countries in level of turnout are clearly related to the presence of compulsory voting, which exists in Belgium, Italy, Luxembourg and Greece. Simultaneity of European and national elections helps account for the higher 1989 turnout of Ireland and Greece. Whereas in 1989 concurrent national elections were conducted in these countries, this was not the case in 1994. Yet, compulsory voting and concurrent national elections account for only part of the turnout differences. Neither of these two turnout-enhancing factors existed in the Netherlands in 1989, yet electoral participation in that country was much higher in 1989 than in 1994. Commentators attributed the decline to the fact that the 1994 European election was conducted only a few weeks after the election to the national parliament, whereas in 1989 the European election occurred in the run-up to a national parliamentary election. This suggests the potential relevance of the timing of a European election in the national electoral cycle (already suggested in Chapter 2).

According to observers in the various member states of the European Union, very little if any 'European' content was to be discerned in the campaigns or in the election results, just as had largely been the case in previous European elections.[4] The lack of European issues in the election was complemented, just as in 1989, by the fact that each national election seemed unique in its content and concerns. In Spain the dominant concerns centered on the scandals in which the reigning socialist government was embroiled; in Northern Ireland it was the recent invigoration of the peace process that overshadowed other matters; in Italy it was the confusion of the transition from the 'First' to the 'Second' Republic; and in France it was the jockeying for position among candidates within the left and the right in the run-up to the Presidential elections of 1995. Britain's European election was about crises of leadership within both major parties, while in Portugal the rivalry between President Soarez'

---

4 See, for example, the special issue of *Electoral Studies* (1994) for very brief characterizations of the 1994 European elections in the various member-states.

Socialists (PS) and Prime-Minister Cavaco Silva's Social Democrats (PSD) captured most of the attention. Even trans-national problems, such as the state of the economy or the environment only figured in forms that were fractured by the prisms of recent national politics.

In contrast to the previous European elections of 1989, no obvious Europe-wide evolution in the standing of any type of party could be discerned. Social-democratic parties lost votes in a number of countries (Belgium, Germany, the Netherlands and Spain) but gained votes elsewhere (Britain, Luxembourg and Portugal).[5] Christian-democrats lost ground (compared to 1989) in all three Benelux countries, but gained ground in Germany. Conservatives lost in Britain and Greece, but improved considerably in Spain. The share of the votes for Green parties went up in Germany, Ireland and Luxembourg, but fell, sometimes precipitously, in Britain, France and the Netherlands. Even the extreme-right did not manage to capitalize very often on the widespread mood of disappointment with the performance of national and European authorities in handling the trans-national issues of 1994: unemployment, migration and the environment. Extreme-right parties registered a small gain in Belgium, but also a small decline in France, and a disastrous result in Germany where the Republikaner were swept away.

All this diversity seems, at least at first sight, to invalidate any suggestion of a Europe-wide electoral response to the performance of European politics or to the new European realities of the mid-1990s: the advent of the European Union, the re-unification of Germany, the fall of communism, the greatly increased migration to the countries of the EU, and so on. Parties' electoral success, or lack thereof, seemed almost exclusively determined by the course of national political developments and events. Consequently, nowhere did parties, politicians or commentators use the 1989 European election results as primary points of reference when looking at the 1994 results, but instead referred to the outcomes of more recent national elections—or even of recent regional or local elections.

Reaffirming the Patterns of 1989

So far, our observations on the 1994 European elections are based on the information available to any informed spectator. However, as we were able to demonstrate for the European elections of 1989 (Chapters 4–16), the availability of survey evidence, in addition to election results, makes it possible to arrive at

---

5   In France the socialists performed poorly, but the separate lists of PS and MRG polled together more votes than their joint 1989 list, so that one cannot conclude that the major left-of-center tendency in France lost votes compared to 1989.

considerably deeper insights into the nature of these elections and the factors affecting turnout, party choice and parties' electoral performance. Such information also provides an opportunity to verify many of the insights and findings from our study of 1989, and to assess apparent developments. To take advantage of this opportunity we must first summarize what we have learned in the country chapters.

The purpose of the country chapters was to establish three things: whether European elections had any truly European content, how such elections differed in their results from national elections, and what were their domestic consequences. In regard to the first set of findings, our interest in 1994 is to see whether, and to what extent, there were any changes from 1989. The European elections of 1989 had virtually no European content; was that still true in 1994? Regarding the second set of findings, comparisons are a bit more complex, but still easily made. In all countries in 1989 outcomes of European elections differed not only from previous national elections (as was observed by other commentators) but also from what national elections held on the same day would have yielded (or did yield, in three cases). These differences were partly due to differential turnout, but more importantly to 'quasi-switching'— individuals voting differently in the European election than they did (or would have done) in a concurrent national election. The important question for 1994 is whether we see evidence of similar amounts of quasi-switching (particularly in relation to those of turnout-effects). If the amount of quasi-switching has changed, is the change linked to increases in European content?

With regard to the third set of findings, comparisons are rather more problematic, partly because European elections have a variety of domestic consequences (summarized below) and partly because some of the consequences that one might expect on the basis of our analyses of the aftermath of 1989 have not yet had time to fully manifest themselves. Therefore, at the time of writing (early 1995) it may be too early to arrive at the sort of considered assessments of the domestic consequences of the 1994 European elections that the country chapters of Part II have been able to supply regarding the elections of 1989.

In the remainder of this chapter we have two objectives. The first is to provide an inventory of findings from the country chapters, so as to see whether anything about the insights derived from 1989 are in need of revision on the basis of events in 1994. The second is to derive from this inventory a set of questions that still have not been answered on the basis of mere country-by-country analysis, even after studying two sets of European elections. Such questions might perhaps be answered at a higher level of analysis, where differences in institutional, political and social context from one country to another can be introduced as additional independent variables. For example, we have already suggested that variations in turnout from one election to the next may be accounted for by introducing the higher-level notion of the location of European elections in the domestic electoral cycle of different countries. Such an inventory of unanswered questions, coming as it does in a chapter that serves as a postscript to Part II, provides an introduction to the third part of this book, whose purpose is to answer them.

The European Content of European Elections

The question of the extent of European content of European elections was addressed in the country chapters of Part II in a number of ways. First, the authors of those chapters focussed on the degree to which electoral participation could be interpreted as emanating from attitudes, orientations and preferences of voters with respect to 'Europe'. This approach addresses frequently voiced concerns that low turnout in European elections might be indicative of lack of support for, or possibly even outright alienation from the European project (see especially Blumler and Fox, 1982). A second approach was to look at party choice, and see how the outcome of the European elections differed from what could have been expected in national elections conducted on the same day. To the extent that differences existed, and to the extent that these could not be attributed to depressed turnout, the question was whether or not they could be linked to the European (or anti-European) orientations of parties or voters. Thirdly, all the authors of the country chapters analyzed in a narrative fashion the nature of the political context of the elections, the campaign, the prevalent mood as to what was at stake, and the interpretation of the election results. In what follows we will pick up these same strands, starting with turnout.

Electoral Participation

Whether people turn out to vote or not, to the extent that we were able to explain it in the country chapters, was overwhelmingly determined by very much the same factors as those operating in national elections: social characteristics, general political orientations, and all those other variables that were referred to in the country chapters as 'habitual voting' (see also Chapter 3). Attitudes towards European integration hardly had any impact in 1989 on whether voters participated in the elections—despite enormous variations in the level of turnout and in affinities towards the European Union. The regression analysis of electoral participation in the various countries showed that nowhere did European orientations and attitudes add more than two percent to variance explained in turnout; so the low turnout in 1989 was not due to deliberate abstention on (anti-) European grounds. Replicating these analyses with data from the 1994 European Election Study, we find much the same thing. Indeed we find this even in the two countries (Greece and Ireland) where the presence of concurrent national elections in 1989 (but not in 1994) might have obstructed the manifestation of European effects. The relevant summary of the results from the country chapters together with the comparable new information for 1994 is displayed in Table 17.2.

The information in Table 17.2 is quite unequivocal in showing that low turnout in European elections generally has nothing whatsoever to do with the legitimacy or otherwise of EU institutions and policies.[6] So there must be other reasons for low turnout in European elections—reasons which also would have caused low turnout in national elections had those same reasons been present. The search for such reasons will be conducted in Chapter 19, where we will evaluate a properly specified model of turnout which takes account of systemic factors (such as compulsory voting and proportionality of the electoral system), political context (position in the electoral cycle, nature of the party system) and the individual characteristics of voters (education, political interest, and so on). Such a model will establish whether cross-national variations in turnout reflect the impact of different opportunity structures facing voters in different countries.

Party Choice

When it comes to party choice, we again saw virtually no European effects in 1989. In Britain a European issue had political implications, but this was because

Table 17.2 Additional Variance Explained in Turnout by 'European' Attitudes of Voters

Country	1989	1994	Country	1989	1994
Britain	0.00	0.01	Italy	0.00	0.00
Denmark	0.00	0.01	Luxembourg	0.00	0.00
France	0.01	0.00	Netherlands	0.00	0.00
Flanders	0.01	0.00	N. Ireland	0.02	0.01
Germany*	0.00	0.02	Portugal	0.00	0.00
Greece	0.00	0.00	Spain	0.00	0.01
Ireland	0.00	0.00	Wallonia	0.00	0.01

* See note to Table 17.1

6 This is despite the fact that with a 1994 survey that lacked the richness of indicators of general explanatory factors available in 1989 we could not expect to explain as much variance on the basis of clearly non-European factors. This will have left more variance unexplained, some of which might have been picked up by measures of pro-European attitudes. As can be seen, this hardly happened.

it had been 'domesticated' into the ongoing (national) party battle. In France, the energetic efforts of some candidates and parties to discuss European matters met with no response from an electorate that, for lack of previous public debate on such matters, had no suitable frame of reference. The vote choices of Frenchmen and women appeared hardly at all to be affected by these debates. In Spain, a similar attempt to discuss European matters, on the part of certain prominent candidates for the European Parliament, was shouted down by national party leaders who feared possible contamination of an election that they wanted to use as a bellwether to tell them the likely consequences of calling an early national election. In Italy, the avowed attractions of using the election as a bellwether were such as to cause a domestic political crisis to be 'put on hold' while the outcome of the European elections was awaited. In these two countries the election itself played an important role in the overt actions of politicians, and in this perverse sense one might say that a European stimulus had effects. In other countries of the (then) European Community (except for Denmark), even this cannot be said and voters made largely the same choices as they did in national elections. Only in Denmark did European matters get an airing that appeared genuinely designed to wean voters from their normal national party allegiances in order to take a position on European matters. Elsewhere, such quasi-switching as occurred could not be linked by authors of the country chapters to European issues.

Table 17.3 shows the incidence of quasi-switching in both 1989 and 1994. Differences in party choice in the European election from what would have occurred in national elections are somewhat more frequent in 1994 than they were in 1989. Averaged across the various political systems, no less than 82.7 percent of the voters supported in 1989 the same party as they would have supported in national elections; the corresponding figure for 1994 is 80.0 percent. This average, however, masks important differences between countries.

Table 17.3 Quasi-switchers as a Percentage of All Voters in the European Elections of 1989 and 1994.

Country	1989	1994	Country	1989	1994
Britain	13.0	16.0	Italy	19.7	20.7
Denmark	35.4	42.9	Luxembourg	15.0	14.3
Flanders	15.6	16.5	N. Ireland	13.7	19.4
France	27.2	40.8	Netherlands	12.4	19.6
Germany*	11.8	14.2	Portugal	9.7	12.7
Greece	8.1	12.4	Spain	22.2	12.5
Ireland	28.7	23.8	Wallonia	10.3	20.0

* See note to Table 17.1.

In Denmark more than 35 percent of the voters in 1989 were quasi-switchers, a number that grew in 1994 to almost 43 percent. In Ireland, the respective percentages were 29 percent in 1989 and 24 percent in 1994. France and Spain constitute outliers in terms of change, with quasi-switching virtually doubling in France (from 27 to 41 percent), while being virtually halved in Spain (from 22 to 12 percent). On the other hand, quasi-switching is a relatively rare phenomenon in Greece and Portugal. The country chapters of Part II have given us some clues as to the origin of these contrasts between systems. The Danish system is the only one where parties that do not compete in national elections offer themselves in European elections, and voting for such parties is not regarded as defecting from 'normal' national allegiances. In Greece and Portugal, the high degree of domestic party polarization between two dominant parties leaves less opportunity for voters to engage in quasi-switching without voting for a party that normally would be considered an opponent.

Aggregate Effects of Quasi-switching

In 1989, small parties did better and large parties did worse than they would have done in national elections. In 1994, the same is true. In both years this reflects predominantly the effect of quasi-switching while turnout effects are quite muted. Table 17.4 shows the correlations of parties' electoral strength with the magnitude of turnout effects and quasi-switching, as well as with the combined effects of these two processes.[7] The table shows a strong overall connection between party strength and performance in the European elections, with a combined correlation of about −0.4 (indicating that smaller parties gain, whereas large parties lose vote shares in comparison to concurrent national elections). The last two columns of the table show that this is largely due to the advantages they gain from quasi-switching, which are only partially offset by the small (and not statistically significant) positive effects of differential turnout.

Table 17.4 Correlations (Pearson's r) between Party Strength, Turnout Effects and Quasi-switching, 1989 and 1994.

Election year	Combined Effect	Quasi-switching	Turnout Effect
1989 (n = 95)	-0.37	-0.45	+0.14*
1994 (n = 86)	-0.41	-0.49	+0.05*

* Not significant at p=.05.

---

7 Party strength is measured by the votes that would have been received in a national election.

These effects, however, do differ considerably from country to country, as we will see in the next section of this chapter. Understanding these differences again requires a perspective beyond that of the countries themselves—a perspective in which contextual effects can be taken into account. Such an analysis can also tell us whether we are dealing with separate national electorates whose electoral choices are idiosyncratic to particular countries, or whether we are dealing with a single European electorate whose approach to electoral decision-making is essentially similar across the countries of the European Union. This question will be addressed in the context of a more elaborate analysis of the foundations of voting choice, in Chapter 20, where we inquire whether nationality plays any role in electoral decision-making once other effects have been taken into account. The same chapter will address the motivational basis of party choice, with the same objectives as our Chapter 19 analysis of the motivational basis of turnout differences (see above).

Despite the lack of European content and dominance of national factors, European elections nevertheless yield outcomes that differ from those of national elections. In Chapter 2 we asked whether these differences were simply due to differential abstention in an election considered less important by most voters. In the country chapters we found, in general, that the effects on party performance of low turnout are small in comparison with those of quasi-switching, laying to rest the possibility that differences between European and national election results were entirely bound up with differences in turnout. As shown in Table 17.5, the same is true of 1994.

In this table we assess the magnitudes of the overall differences between the outcomes of the European elections with those which concurrent national elections would have yielded (or, in some countries, did yield). These differences have been disaggregated into their two constituent parts—the net effects of selective turnout and those of quasi-switching. In the cases where concurrent national elections did occur, differences in turnout between these two simultaneous elections were negligible, so that there are no effects of differential turnout and the entire overall difference is due to quasi-switching.[8] Table 17.5 shows that the combined effects of turnout and quasi-switching are in many cases minor, but in a quarter of the 28 elections depicted there, they rise above 10 percent, which is generally considered to be far from negligible. These figures illustrate why European elections, when interpreted as bellwethers of parties' domestic electoral standing, can sometimes generate powerful reactions from politicians and commentators, with important domestic political consequences.

---

8 The index used to summarize the different outcomes, the so-called Pedersen Index (Pedersen, 1979) sums the absolute differences in vote share over all parties and divides the resulting sums by 2.

Table 17.5 Overall difference (Pedersen Index) between the distribution of votes in the European election and in a (usually hypothetical) concurrent national election

	Combined effects		Turnout effects		Quasi-switching	
	1989	1994	1989	1994	1989	1994
Britain	6.1	5.0	3.7	3.6	8.4	7.5
Flanders	7.2	5.5	1.6	0.6	5.3	5.3
Denmark	28.8	32.6	6.1	8.6	24.9	28.4
France	12.8	19.1	5.2	2.2	11.3	19.3
Germany[a]	2.3	4.4	2.0	2.6	2.7	5.5
Greece[b]	6.9	3.5	n.a.	1.2	6.9	2.5
Ireland[b]	20.3	9.3	n.a.	7.4	20.3	7.9
Italy	3.0	5.2	1.3	1.1	2.2	6.1
Luxembourg[b]	9.4	2.6	n.a.	n.a.	9.4	2.6
Netherlands	5.3	14.3	3.7	9.8	4.0	7.1
N. Ireland	13.8	10.3	9.3	4.7	5.6	8.6
Portugal	6.7	10.4	4.0	4.1	6.0	7.4
Spain	7.4	5.3	1.3	2.8	6.1	2.7
Wallonia	5.2	9.1	1.6	1.2	6.1	10.0

a See note to Table 17.1.
b Where concurrent national elections occurred, turnout effects are not applicable (n.a.).

But the table also suggests the possible instrumental basis of differences between European and national elections. Insofar as the outcome of European elections differs from the outcome that would have occurred in a concurrent national election, this appears to be largely because voters actively choose to make it so.[9] Evidently this suggestion is in need of confirmation in analyses designed for this purpose (see Chapter 20). The figures in Table 17.5 are country averages which mask considerable differences between the parties in any particular country—witness the tables on quasi-switching and turnout effects in the country chapters. Which particular factors lead some parties to benefit and others to be disadvantaged could not easily be established in those chapters, owing to the comparatively small number of parties in each of the countries. Across all the countries of the European Union, however, we have many times as many parties—perhaps enough to disentangle various effects, such as being in government or in opposition, being small or large, moderate or extreme, and so on. Such an analysis requires a Europe-wide approach and will be undertaken in Chapter 18.

---

9 As is evident from the fact that quasi-switching effects are generally larger than turnout effects.

Domestic Consequences of European Elections

We have seen that, in a number of ways, European elections have had notable domestic political consequences. In the Netherlands, these included the merger of small political parties, with lasting domestic consequences; in Germany they contributed to the change from a 2.5-party system to at least a 4-party system; in France 20 years of hard-fought consolidation by blocks of parties seems to have been put into reverse. These consequences were often attributed by authors of the country chapters to differences in the electoral rules under which European elections are fought. But not all of the consequences of European elections are of this kind. We saw that in Britain the 1989 election laid the basis for the fall of Mrs Thatcher; in Germany it led the CDU/CSU to a turn to the right (with concomitant consequences for policy towards migration and other matters); in Spain a national election was called because the outcome of the European election was deemed propitious; in Italy a political crisis was prolonged until the election was over. Many other consequences, large and small, were enumerated in the country chapters. Such consequences are the result of changes in opportunity structure and incentives for voters and political elites, brought about by the context and outcomes presented by European elections.

Turning to the elections of 1994, it is still at the time of writing (Spring 1995) too early for definitive statements about their consequences. Nevertheless, even at this early date some consequences are apparent. In Greece, there was a cabinet reshuffle soon after the elections which was widely attributed to the disappointing showing of the government; in Italy, the PDS had expected to do well, and the failure of this expectation led to the resignation of that party's secretary-general the day after the European elections (this also happened in the case of two minor parties which had expected to perform better); in France his very poor showing ended Michel Rocard's prospects of being nominated by his party as its Presidential candidate; in Spain (as in Britain) the European elections confirmed (and contributed to) the shakiness of Prime Ministerial leadership. On the other hand, in the Netherlands a surprising resurgence of the Christian Democratic party (which had only a month before lost over a third of its seats in national elections) had no apparent effects in revitalizing party morale—an anomaly that will be explained in Chapter 18.

One Electorate or Many? Unanswered Questions for Part III

These disparate consequences make it seem as though the electorates in the different countries of the European Union are reacting in quite different ways to the stimuli presented at a European election. If the voters in one European country really are so very different from those in another this might be one reason why European issues are not presented to them for their consideration and approval. National political leaders might have understood the limitations of their voters well enough to know that there would be no way in which a single verdict could emerge, so that keeping European issues off the political agenda—even in European elections—might be a rational (if not very satisfactory) solution to inherent limitations of an integrated Europe.

Such national specificity would indeed bode ill for the prospects of European elections ever being able to render an intelligible electoral verdict over matters of European policy. Yet we should not be too quick to read such national specificity into the findings of Part II. After all, we have seen that variations in election outcomes seem to be related to the position of European elections in the domestic national election cycle. Furthermore, we have seen the commonality of factors such as the benefits that small parties enjoy. At a higher level of analysis, where country characteristics and country-specific electoral contexts themselves become variable attributes of electoral context, we can address this question by controlling for such variables.

In Part III of this book we will first of all evaluate the possibility that the electorates in different countries of the European Union have different, nation-specific, approaches to making electoral choices. We start in Chapter 18 by focussing on how parties fare in these elections when compared to national contests, and try to explain differences in party performance in general terms that are valid across all countries of the European Union. We then move in Chapter 19 to focus on individual voters, and try to explain individual and aggregate turnout variations in equally general terms. Finally, in Chapter 20 we turn to the appeals made by individual parties to individual voters, and try to explain the differing responses to those appeals. These chapters develop models of behavior that aim for maximum generality. To the extent that they are successful they avoid the need to use either party or country names in descriptions of electoral behavior, just as they do not require the names of individual voters; and to the extent that these models are successful in this respect we will know that there are no inherent differences between the electoral responses of individuals living in different countries. In that case, the lack of European content in European elections will not be explicable in terms of the intrinsic diversity of European electorates. If, on the other hand, we are not able to construct models which apply equally to the voters of all European countries, it will follow that European elections cannot yield an intelligible Europe-wide verdict.

The models to be developed in Chapters 18 to 20 will attempt to provide specifications of why and how people vote, and these models should hold true beyond the one election that we primarily investigate in this volume. Applying these findings to countries outside the boundaries of the European Union is beyond the scope of what is possible in a single book, but we can evaluate our findings by using them to model features of the elections of 1994; and doing so is a second purpose of these chapters. To the extent that we find the same processes operating in 1994 as in 1989, despite the enormous differences in context that resulted from the signing and ratification of the Treaty of European Union, we will be confident that our findings are applicable to European elections in general—not just to those of 1989.

A final purpose of these Europe-wide analyses is to systematize the consequences of European elections for national politics in the EU member states—consequences which could only be suggested anecdotally in this chapter and in the earlier chapters of Part II. These consequences have real implications not only for the future of the European project but also for the well-being of individual member countries. Most of these implications arise from unintended consequences of European elections. Whether such consequences can be avoided is, of course, contingent upon the results of our analyses in Chapters 18 to 20. On the basis of those results, the final chapter in this volume will address the question whether European elections can be made into better instruments for bringing the preferences of European voters to bear on the governance of their Union.

Part III

Comparative Perspectives: The Mainsprings of European Electoral Behavior, 1989 and 1994

CHAPTER 18

The Party Context:
Outcomes

Erik Oppenhuis, Cees van der Eijk and Mark Franklin

Dominant throughout the chapters of this book, as well as in many other writings about European elections, is the theme that these elections are primarily national political contests. They are fought by national political parties and politicians, mainly over national problems, concerns and issues. Media focus and information are likewise directed towards national political arenas. Where they do not coincide with national elections, European elections are predominantly perceived as 'beauty contests', perhaps providing indications of what would have happened in a 'real' (first-order) election. Nevertheless, the chapters of Part II have established that European elections also have consequences for national politics. As should be evident from Chapter 17, these consequences are quite large in number and are not of the kind that proponents of European elections had in mind (e.g., Vedel, 1975; Tindemans, 1976). Many of the consequences we observe hinge on the attention given by politicians and commentators to the apparent success or failure of individual parties. The trouble is that these observers assume that European elections perform as indicators of what national elections would have yielded. Yet we have seen that voters behave differently in European elections, with consequences for the performance of political parties. What is it about the European election process that causes parties to do better or worse in comparison with the performance that might have been expected had the elections been national ones? Can we find underlying themes that will permit us to systematize these findings? Such is the purpose of the present chapter.

European Elections as Markers

European elections evidently serve as markers of party strength which are important until they are replaced or become obsolete. Until that happens they contribute to the cognitive maps which help people (politicians, journalists, citizens) to understand the world and determine their own behavior in it. Elections—even second-order elections—can be particularly important as markers because they clarify the political opportunity structure within which politicians and parties operate; that is, the opportunities and constraints for behavior which the environment places on them. As markers, the results of European elections will often replace earlier markers set by earlier elections. To the extent that the new markers manifest changes in party standing, European elections define new strategic and tactical situations for political actors which may change the future course of events.

Markers relating to the (changed) strength of parties also affect future media interpretations of current events—for example which news will be highlighted and which politicians will be invited to comment. Formerly obscure parties may thus be propelled into the limelight—as happened to the British and French greens, and the German Republikaner—which will alter their capacity to influence the electorate, with possible consequences for future elections. Voters, finally, also may take note of markers of party strength, particularly when their choice is affected by what generally are referred to as 'strategic' considerations. Of course there are many other markers of party strength (such as opinion polls), but election results acquire special importance because of the democratic ethos in Western societies, and because the official and impartial character of elections may give even second-order national elections the appearance of a 'trial run' for subsequent first-order elections.

In addition to providing markers of the electoral strength of parties, elections may also be used as markers of the electorate's mood. This hinges, of course, on the extent to which a certain interpretation of election results becomes dominant (irrespective of its validity). If voters are perceived to have swung to the left, or acquired ecological concerns, all parties will be affected by this perception, at least until it is overtaken by events.

In all these respects European elections can serve as catalysts or facilitators for developments that might well have occurred in other ways. However, there is one important aspect of European elections that is not so readily duplicated: they serve as opportunities for experimentation with policies, personnel and alliances which may show the viability of developments that would never have been tried in circumstances where more was at stake.

In the present chapter we will focus on European elections as markers of parties' electoral strength, and the consequences of treating them as such. In this context, the nature of the effects to be expected from a particular European election will depend above all on questions of timing: whether a European election is held in tandem with a national election, and, if not, how much time has elapsed since the most recent national election and how far in the future the next national election is expected to be. If a national election immediately precedes a European election (or occurs concurrently) the results of the European election will not count for much because a better marker exists.

To the extent that European election results are taken seriously as markers, parties that did well in the elections will be advantaged in comparison with those that did poorly. Both types of outcome occurred in one country or another in 1989, and we have seen their consequences explored in the country chapters of Part II. We also saw that the markers are frequently inaccurate as indicators of what would have happened had the election been a national election, since European election results are everywhere subject to turnout and quasi-switching effects. What we have not yet seen is a Europe-wide analysis of the circumstances in which (and the extent to which) particular parties are advantaged or disadvantaged by such effects. These are topics to which we now turn.

Circumstances Which Benefit Particular Parties

In what sorts of circumstances do particular parties do poorly in European elections, and in what sorts of circumstances do they do well? Is there anything systematic about the types of parties that do well or badly? Are there any circumstances which are particularly propitious (or otherwise) for particular parties? Answering these questions will permit us to evaluate the extent to which observers (voters, politicians, journalists) may be misled if they take the election outcome as a marker of parties' current domestic electoral strength. In the country chapters of Part II we have seen that the results of a European election differ in detail from what a national election would have yielded—or, in the few countries where concurrent national elections did take place, that results differ as between those two simultaneous electoral contests. Such differences arise from the combined effect of two different processes. First of all, there is the net effect of what we termed quasi-switching: voting for a different party in the European election than would have been supported in a national election held at the same time. Secondly there is the effect of the different (generally lower) turnout that European elections register compared to national elections. The separate and joint effects of these processes have been reported country by country, but in this chapter we will look at them from a cross-national perspective. Such a perspective will enable us to address a number of hypotheses that have been expressed in the literature about European elections: for example, that small, extreme and non-governing parties benefit. The comparative approach will also enable us to evaluate a possible explanation, commonly alluded to (and already described in detail in Chapter 2), to the effect that these differences occur because less is at stake in European elections than in national elections.

Some country chapters presented evidence that small parties benefit from institutional features of a European election—most importantly the smaller number of constituencies benefitted parties that lacked financial resources and personnel to compete nation-wide in a national election.[1] Little mention was, however, made of the strategic context of a European election where control of the apparatus of government is not at issue. Small parties can expect to benefit from this factor as well as from any mechanical advantage accruing from differences in the application of electoral rules; but within a single country it is hard to disentangle these two sources of advantage to small parties. In this chapter we will try to make the distinction in practical terms.

In the country chapters of Part II, the format in which turnout and quasi-switching effects were presented was, naturally, tied to each specific national context. In this chapter, we will present much the same information, but in a different form as we try to discern the circumstances in which parties gain or lose from quasi-switching and turnout effects. Our initial approach will be to use a crude typology of party families to which we add information on parties' strength and their status as government or opposition parties. This will allow us a first, predominantly descriptive, look at these phenomena. Then we will attempt to model the differences in magnitude of quasi-switching and turnout effects by way of multivariate analyses in which we can assess whether the differences we observe are explicable in terms of general concepts or whether we have to resort to country and party names.

A Descriptive Approach

An obvious way in which parties differ is in terms of their different kinds of ideological 'families'. Following the classifications by Müller-Rommel and Pridham (1991) and by Gallagher et al. (1992) we may distinguish, for example, between christian democratic, social democratic, green, extreme left, extreme right, and 'other' parties. For each such group of parties, we can establish how well their members fared in the 1989 European elections. As a case in point, Table 18.1 shows these results for the group of social democratic parties. These parties are named according to normal conventions in each country (by name or by initials) and the countries are designated (as they will be in many of the tables of Part III) by the first three letters of their names. These abbreviations are generally obvious, but it is worth mentioning that 'Net' stands for The Netherlands, 'NIr' for Northern Ireland, 'Fla' for Flanders and 'Wal' for Wallonia. These last two are regions of Belgium which, as elsewhere in Part III of this book, we treat separately since each of them has a separate party system. All fourteen of our political systems appear in this table, since social democracy is represented everywhere—something unmatched by any

---

1 The smaller number of European mandates, however, in comparison with the number of seats in national parliaments, implies a countervailing disadvantage: more votes are needed to get a seat.

Table 18.1 Quasi-switching and Turnout Effects for Social–Democratic Parties in Europe, 1989

Political System	Party Label	EE-NE[a]	Quasi-switching	Turnout Effect	Percent in EE	Gov't Party
Den	Soc.Dem	-8.5	-6.6	-1.9	23.3	No
NIr	Labour	-7.2	-3.6	-3.6	0.7	No
Fra	PS	-7.0	-6.4	-0.6	23.6	Yes
Por	PS	-6.7	-4.5	-2.2	29.5	No
Spa	PSOE	-3.3	-2.9	-0.4	40.2	Yes
Gre	PASOK	-3.1	-3.1	*	36.0	Yes
Ger	SPD	-1.9	-2.6	0.7	37.3	No
Net	PVDA	-1.2	1.4	-2.6	30.7	No
Lux	LASP	-0.7	-0.7	*	25.5	No
Ire	Labour	0	0	*	9.5	No
Bri	Labour	0.2	-4.3	4.5	40.1	No
Ita	PSI	0.3	-0.3	0.6	14.8	Yes
Wal	PS	0.6	-0.4	1.0	42.1	Yes
Fla	SP	0.8	0.5	0.3	18.4	Yes
NIr	SDLP	5.6	0.5	5.1	25.5	No

a Difference between votes in European elections and votes that would have been cast in a national election.
* Turnout effect negligible because of concurrent elections

of our other ideological families. The table includes, in addition to country and party names, first the overall second-order effect—the difference between the party's performance in the European elections of 1989 and an estimate of what the same party's performance would have been in a concurrent national election (EE–NE). The parties have been ranked on this criterion, so that we start with the parties whose electoral strength in a national election was understated by the European election, and progress through those whose national electoral strength was increasingly overstated. Next, the table shows the two components of this difference, the net effects of quasi-switching and of turnout differences. Finally, the table presents for each party its share of the valid vote in the European elections and whether or not it was included in the national government at the time of these elections. Table 18.1 shows that, despite the electoral strength of social democratic parties, only about half of them were in government in 1989, as indicated in the final column of the table. When looking at the difference between the European election result and those of concurrent national elections, we see that, for this group as a whole, negative effects in the 1989 European elections outweigh positive ones. However, this was for different reasons in different countries since the effects of quasi-switching and turnout are quite often out of phase. government status (in the final column of the table) is evidently no more of a shield against adverse quasi-switching or turnout effects for these parties than it is a guarantor of positive effects.

Similar tables were constructed for the other party families, but are not displayed here because all of them were just as inconclusive in terms of identifying the forces affecting party performance as was Table 18.1 for the social democrats. On average, christian democratic parties fared well in the European elections, at least when compared to their national political standing. Extreme left parties, on the other hand, like the social democrats, appear to have done poorly by this standard. For most party groups, however, no general tendency was apparent, with some of their members doing considerably better, some considerably worse, and some about the same as they would have done in a national election. This is even true of the one party family often singled out as having fared well Europe-wide in 1989: the Greens, whose electoral success Curtice (1989) referred to in terms of a 'Green tide'. Nowhere is a clear relationship between parties' government or opposition status on the one hand and their electoral performance on the other discernible from a mere visual inspection of tables like Table 18.1.

In general, of course, it is difficult to grasp the simultaneous consequences of these and other possibly relevant factors, such as parties' stance on European integration, their ideological leanings and extremity, the occurrence of simultaneous national elections, or the timing of European elections relative to national ones. In order to assess more systematically the nature of such relationships, we have to move to a multivariate analysis. Such an analysis will also permit us to assess empirically the worth of hypotheses which propose that government parties and large parties in general will do comparatively poorly in European elections, while ideologically extreme and small parties will benefit from a second-order national election context (for these hypotheses and a discussion of research on them, see Chapter 2).

Multivariate Analysis of Quasi-switching and Turnout Effects

In the analyses that follow we will attempt to explain differences between the parties in the European Community for each of three different phenomena in turn. First we look at the overall difference between parties' shares of the vote in the European election on the one hand and their share in (usually hypothetical) concurrent national elections on the other. We will refer to this difference as the 'second-order' effect. Second we look at the component of this difference which is the (net) effect of differential turnout. Finally we consider the remaining component, quasi-switching. As independent variables we will employ a number of party characteristics which have been proposed as relevant in previous theoretical or empirical work on second-order elections (see Chapter 2) some of which are the same as those employed in the previous section. The first of these is parties' strength, which is operationalized in terms of a party's national electoral strength at the time of the European election.[2]. Our second explanatory phenomenon is parties' ideological position. This yields three independent variables: the median position on a 10-point left/right scale assigned by voters to a party,[3] the extremity of a party (defined as the difference between the median position of the party and the median position of the electorate, both measured on 10-point scales), and the extent of agreement in voters' perceptions of a party's position on the left/right continuum.[4] As another aspect of a party's position we included its degree of support for European integration (see van der Eijk and Franklin, 1991). Whether a party was a member of a national government in June 1989 yields another dichotomous independent variable. We also included the degree to which each party is subject to electoral competition from other parties (see Appendix B and also van der Eijk and Oppenhuis, 1991; Tillie, 1995; Oppenhuis, 1995). Finally, we employed a set of dummy variables characterizing each party in terms of its belonging to one of the following party families: christian democratic, social democratic, green, extreme left, extreme right, and 'other'.

In addition to these characteristics of parties, we also took into account differences in the systemic and contextual situation within which each party had to compete for votes. These include:

- the presence of compulsory voting,
- the presence of concurrent national elections,
- the number of parties in the political system,
- the proportionality of the country's electoral system, operationalized in terms of the votes/seats ratio (see Chapter 19),
- the range of positions which parties occupy with respect to European integration,
- the dimensionality of the party system (see Chapter 19),
- the importance of the European electoral arena to the electorate of each country,[5]

---

2 See Chapter 3 and Appendix B for how this was estimated.

3 The interpolated median is used rather than the average, because the former is less affected by centripetal biases which are caused by measurement error and random responses around the centroid of the distribution.

4 For a description of this measure, see Appendix B.

5 This was operationalized in two ways: (1) the average difference in response to questions on the importance of the national and the European Parliaments, and (2) the difference in turnout between the European election and the most recent national election.

- the degree of electoral competitiveness in the political system, operationalized in terms of the proportion of the electorate which was subject to intense electoral competition,
- the proportion that was not attracted to any of the competing parties, and, finally,
- the importance of this particular European election as a marker for the domestic strengths of parties, operationalized in terms of the time elapsed since the most recent national election.[6]

These contextual variables cannot be expected to directly explain much of the variance in the dependent variables as they are constants for the various parties within each political system and of necessity negative second-order effects (or quasi-switching or turnout effects) for one party are compensated by positive effects for other parties in the same system. However, some of these systemic and contextual factors may interact significantly with party characteristics, allowing us to assess the possible consequences of differences in political context on the effects of such characteristics.

Treating as one case each party in each country that participated in the 1989 European elections (and for which we have data) provides 95 cases, which is a large number when compared to the number of parties in any single country. It is, however, few enough to yield potential statistical problems in the multiple regression analyses we intend to use, particularly when many independent variables are to be assessed for their possible contribution to an explanation. This is even more true when simple diagnostic tests reveal the existence of severe interaction effects between explanatory and contextual variables. The relationship, for example, between the effect of quasi-switching and parties' strength differs considerably in countries where national elections were held concurrently with European elections and those where they were not (the respective variance explained is 0.27 and 0.09). To avoid capitalizing on chance, the analyses reported below were conducted separately for different selections of explanatory variables and interaction terms.[7] All results were tested for stability by repeating the analysis after removing the worst-fitting cases, and the prediction equation was modified when the outcome of this test was unsatisfactory. Below we only report the final results of these analyses.

---

6   All of these variables are described in detail in Appendix B, and the rationale for many of them is further discussed in Chapter 19 where they play a more important role.

7   Care was also taken not to specify combinations of interaction effects that effectively resulted in the fitting of coefficients to single observations, which is a potential danger with only 14 political systems to provide different contexts.

What variables account for differences between the European and national electoral performance of parties that was documented in the chapters of Part II? The variable of greatest importance turns out to be party strength, which works independently as well as in interaction with two systemic variables: the presence or absence of concurrent national elections, and the time elapsed since the last national election. Table 18.2 summarizes the results. This explanation is a rather weak one, accounting for only 27 percent of the variance in second-order effects taken as a whole. Nevertheless, we shall see that the implications for party performance are considerable. In interpreting the effects of particular variables it is important to bear in mind that interaction terms have been defined in such a way as to minimize multicollinearity with the party-level variables from which they are derived.[8] The interaction terms indicate that large parties are particularly hurt when the most recent national elections were held less than approximately two and a half years before the European elections.[9]

These interactions may seem complicated, but actually they have a very straightforward interpretation. It is as if voters realize that the possible domestic political consequences of deviating from the party they would vote for in a

Table 18.2 Regression of Differences between European and National Electoral Standing of European Political Parties (n=95)

Independent Variable	b	Beta	Sig.
Strength of Party (% of votes cast)	-0.22	-0.74	0.0000
Strength of Party Interacting With:			
Concurrent National Elections	-1.94	-0.52	0.0003
Time Since Last National Election	1.99	0.47	0.0006
Constant	3.03		
R Square	27.1%		

8 Interaction terms have been defined as the product of the (standardized) independent variable (strength) on the one hand and deviations (in the form of z-scores) from the mean of the contextual variable (or, when the latter is dichotomous, +1 and −1) on the other. For the rationale behind this procedure, see, e.g., Jaccard, Turrisi and Wan (1990).

9 Negative deviations on the time elapsed variable multiplied by positive b-coefficients turn into negative effects for large parties, but into positive ones for small parties, as those have a negative deviation score for strength. In the extreme case in which the most recent national elections were conducted concurrently with the European elections, the interaction term has a positive value for large parties (positive score on strength multiplied by +1 for the presence of concurrent elections) which is multiplied by a negative coefficient to yield a negative effect for large parties (and the reverse for small ones).

national election are smallest when national elections are held concurrently, or only shortly before the European election. In such circumstances voters evidently feel free to use their vote experimentally or expressively. A large party stands (on average) to lose in that situation almost 10 percent of the vote share it would have acquired in a national election.

What about the two component parts which together make up these second-order effects: the consequences of quasi-switching and (low) turnout? Can they be explained by the same factors? Visual inspection of the descriptive information presented in Table 18.1 (and of similar tables, not shown, for other party families) suggested that these two components do not necessarily move in step. This is confirmed by regressions on both, performed in the same way as the regressions reported above. Analyzing turnout effects yields very little. Only strength has a weak (positive) effect (significant only with a confidence level of .10), and the explained variance amounts to no more than 4 percent.[10]

We will see in Chapter 19 that the act of electoral participation contains a large random component, and in the present context this random component prevents us from modelling the effects of turnout which seem quite idiosyncratic to particular parties. Whether a party benefits from or is hurt by the poor turnout in a European election can hardly be explained by its strength, and not at all by its ideological stance, its policy positions, or its government status (either alone or in interaction with elements of the political context of the election). The effects of depressed turnout on parties' vote shares appear largely random, which implies that the contribution they make to second-order effects will also be largely random. When we turn to quasi-switching, therefore, we would expect to be focussing on the more explicable component of the second-order effects; and the extent of quasi-switching indeed appears to be much more highly structured. The results of the analysis are summarized in Table 18.3, where we explain fully 47.4 percent of the variance in quasi-switching. The first part of the equation mirrors what we found for the combined effects of quasi-switching and turnout taken together, in terms of the impact of strength of party and the interactions of strength with concurrent national elections and time elapsed since the last national election (cf. Table 18.2). Were we only to include these variables in the equation we would explain 38 percent of the variance. We do find, however, additional effects which are related to the

---

10 By adding a series of interaction effects of strength with contextual factors, variance explained can be increased to approximately 15 percent but the specific interaction terms that accomplish this effectively fit individual parties (outliers) without generating better predictions for other parties. Restricting the analyses to the countries without compulsory voting, where turnout effects may be more pronounced and possibly more structured, does not alter the resulting picture.

Table 18.3 Determinants of Quasi–switching among European and National Electoral Standing of European Political Parties (n=94)

Independent Variable	b	Beta	Sig.
Strength of Party (% of votes cast)	-0.18	-0.67	0.0000
Strength of Party Interacting With:			
Concurrent National Elections	-2.24	-0.65	0.0000
Time Since Last National Election	2.31	0.65	0.0000
Ideological Extremity of Party Interacting With:			
Concurrent National Elections	-0.52	-0.34	0.0037
Time Since Last National Election	0.50	0.36	0.0014
Electoral Competitiveness With Other Parties	7.07	0.25	0.0261
Constant	-1.08		
R Square	47.4%		

ideological extremity of parties. Extremity by itself does not have significant effects, but its interactions with concurrent national elections and time elapsed since the most recent national election are significant, and increase the variance explained to 44 percent. The b-coefficients indicate that extreme parties benefit most from quasi-switching when the European election takes place quite some time after the most recent national one and that centrist parties benefit most when a European election takes place soon after a national election. The more closely a European election follows a national election, the less the advantage to extreme parties, which may even turn into a disadvantage when the interval is rather brief. When the interval is zero because of concurrent national elections, this has an extra negative impact on extreme parties' net effects from quasi-switching, and an extra positive impact on centrist parties.

At first sight, the consequences of interactions with strength and with extremity appear to contradict one another; yet they do not. What they imply is that during or shortly after national elections (when the results of European elections are least relevant as markers) there is more quasi-switching, and this tends to benefit smaller parties at the expense of larger ones. The main beneficiaries in such a period are, however, small parties which are not ideologically very extreme. When the time interval between a European election and the previous national one becomes larger (so that the outcome of the election is more likely to serve as a marker of parties' current domestic electoral standing) the differential advantage of small over large parties diminishes.[11] At the same time more extreme parties will benefit more than centrist ones from

---

11   This is indicated by the first three components of the equations reported in Tables 18.2 and 18.3.

whatever advantages small parties enjoy.[12] This interaction was masked in Table 18.2 by the random element contributed by turnout effects.

In addition to these factors, there are other differences between parties that affect the prevalence of quasi-switching. It is not entirely surprising that the parties most affected are those that share a large part of their potential vote with other parties and are, hence, subject to intense party competition. Differences between parties in this regard which have not yet been accounted for by other variables contribute yet another three percent to explained variance. By itself, this effect is not of much substantive interest—one might even consider it somewhat tautological in this context. It is of importance, though, in replacing effects that might otherwise accrue to other variables. Taking these various regression findings together, it is clear that the effects reported in Tables 18.2 and 18.3 are essentially the same, but that the former were somewhat obscured by the overlay of what turn out to be the (largely random) effects of depressed turnout. Looking specifically at effects on quasi-switching, parties' strength comes forward as the most important factor, with ideological extremity close behind. How, precisely, these two factors affect parties' gains or losses due to quasi-switching is strongly conditioned by how closely European elections follow national ones, as governed by the limiting condition of concurrent national elections.

The Sources of Small Party Gains

In this chapter we have stressed the strategic factors that lead party strength to be so strongly related to second-order effects.[13] In the country chapters of Part II, however, another factor was repeatedly singled out: the nature of the electoral system. European elections advantage small parties for a variety of mechanical reasons.[14] The most important of these is the smaller number of

---

12 As centrist and extreme parties differ in the sign of their value on the (z-scored) extremity variable, the two interactions of extremity with contextual factors work in opposite ways for them.

13 In Chapter 20 we will demonstrate the existence of strong strategic considerations related to party strength at the level of individual party preferences.

14 This favorable effect for small parties does not exist everywhere. In countries like the Netherlands (see Chapter 13), the smaller number of European compared to national representatives to be elected makes it impossible for some small parties to acquire any seats in the European Parliament, in spite of the fact that they usually are represented in the national parliament. To the extent that this causes such small parties not to compete at all, this negative (mechanical) effect of minor changes in the rules of the game does not show up in our data and analyses presented above. To the extent that they compete as part of electoral pacts or combination lists, they share, on average, in the advantages that accrue to small parties in European elections.

constituencies in European as compared to national elections, which requires a lower level of resources (in money and personnel) to effectively mobilize their potential vote on a nation-wide scale. On the basis of our findings we are now in a position to tentatively evaluate the relative importance of these two types of effect. This evaluation becomes possible because the strategic situation turns out to be affected by temporal factors, whereas logically the benefits to small parties that were purely mechanical should not be affected by matters of timing. Our coefficients also distinguish between two types of advantage bestowed by strength: a general effect which is felt in all European elections (no matter what their temporal distance from the most recent national election) by all small parties (no matter what their ideological complexion) and a particular effect felt by certain small parties depending on temporal and ideological considerations. Unfortunately, the parallel is not perfect. While it is logically implausible that mechanical advantages would be apportioned according to temporal and ideological considerations, it is quite likely that the strategic differences that benefit small parties would have both a general and a particular component. On this reasoning, the total effect of quasi-switching can be broken down into three components, as follows:

Quasi-switching = Mechanical + Fixed Strategic + Variable Strategic

Of these, only the variable strategic effect is separately identifiable because it occurs in interaction with time and ideology. The fixed strategic effect would benefit small parties no matter what their ideological complexion or the time elapsed since the previous national election, and might be zero. The mechanical effect would be the remainder. Decomposing quasi-switching into these components is not possible on the basis of our investigations in this chapter. Nevertheless, the estimates that we computed in the previous section for the effects of strength in interaction with time and ideology provide what is effectively a lower bound for strategic effects: they measure the extent of strategic effects if the fixed component were to be zero. To the extent that the fixed component is greater than zero, total strategic effects will be greater still. Further apportionment of effects as between fixed strategic and mechanical considerations is not straightforward and will depend on all sorts of factors that are beyond the scope of the present chapter; some of these were explored in Chapter 10 where Michael Marsh attempted to estimate the mechanical advantage bestowed on small Irish parties by the nature of the electoral rules governing European elections in Ireland.

The effects that are definitely strategic can be viewed as consequences deriving from the absence in European elections of the advantage that large parties enjoy when national power is at stake. This lower bound for strategic effects is two-thirds of the total components of quasi-switching, according to coefficients in Table 18.3.[15] These findings might seem to contradict the findings of country chapters that stressed the mechanical reasons for quasi-switching. In point of fact, however, they should rather be regarded as fruits of the comparative method. Strategic effects are not nearly so obvious when viewed from within each country as they are in comparative perspective. Only the presence of 14 political systems enabled us to discover the strategic interactions that have provided the center piece of this chapter, and it is only in comparative perspective that we can see the true importance of strategic relative to mechanical effects.

Replicability of the Findings

The findings detailed above were obtained from quasi-switching and turnout effects evident in the European elections of 1989. These effects might be unique to that election, or might in other ways have been the result of capitalizing on chance in the context of so many possible independent variables together with such a small number of cases. One way to increase the reliability of the findings would be to pool our 1989 data with data from the European elections of 1994. However, at the time of writing (Spring 1995), the survey data for the 1994 European elections have not yet been coded in sufficient detail to make this sensible. In particular, the votes cast for many small parties have been reported under the heading 'other'.[16] Since a critical aspect of our findings relates to small extreme parties, many of which are as yet unidentifiable for 1994, pooling the data will add noise without adding information—reducing the variance we will be able to explain and perhaps completely masking the effects we identify in 1989.[17] The same problem prevents us from using 1989 coefficients to 'predict' 1994 findings, as we do in later chapters.

---

15   The sum of the (absolute) beta weights seen in Table 18.3 for effects that occur in strategic interaction is 2.00, out of a total for all beta weights of 2.92. Using the logic pioneered by Donald Stokes (1974) this implies that two-thirds of the explained variance should be ascribed to effects that occur in strategic interaction and cannot therefore be benefitting small parties as a class.

16   Leaving out the 'other' parties (whose exact strength and extremity cannot be gauged since we do not know their individual identities) we find that the parties represented in our 1994 data on average lose 12 percent of the vote shares they would have gained in national elections in 1994, whereas the average loss due to quasi-switching should be zero if all competing parties are accounted for (in 1989, with many fewer parties still classified as 'other', the average loss is 3 percent).

17   In practice, the 1989 findings are reflected in such a pooled dataset, but with much less clarity; and in an analysis of 1994 data alone, the effects of time since the most recent national election, in interaction with strength and extremity, still show themselves as important, explaining some 31 percent of the variance in 1994 quasi-switching.

Our inability to replicate our 1989 findings with data from 1994 does not, however, mean that our 1989 findings are uncorroborated. We saw in Chapter 17 that the effects of quasi-switching benefit small parties more in 1994 than in 1989 (Table 17.4). In Chapter 19 we will see that position in the domestic electoral cycle has a strong influence on turnout, in 1994 as well as in 1989, in line with expectations that arise from the findings in this chapter. Above all, a pseudo-experimental situation was provided by the sequence of European, national and local elections that occurred in the Netherlands in 1994, with national elections following closely on local elections and being in turn followed closely by European elections. Expectations deriving from this chapter lead us to particularly expect votes for extreme parties in second-order elections that closely precede national elections, but not in second-order elections that closely follow national elections. That pattern of changing fortunes for extreme parties is precisely what was observed in the Netherlands in 1994 (van der Eijk, 1995) with extreme parties doing well in the local elections but not in the European elections.

Types of Second-order Elections: Voting with Heart and Boot

The difference between the share of the vote that parties get in European elections, as compared to (actual or hypothetical) concurrent national elections, turns out to vary in a fashion that is not at all random; and although in most cases the magnitude of these differences is rather small in percentage terms, occasionally they are far from trivial (see the tables of quasi-switching and turnout effects in the country chapters). In such cases European elections will be particularly misleading as markers, presenting a distorted picture of parties' national electoral strength. When voters and politicians base their later behavior on such markers, they may indeed be badly misled. Ironically, the likelihood that politicians would be misled depends in part on how much attention they pay to the results. When European elections are held concurrently or very shortly after national elections, they are more or less 'throw-away' elections. The marker set by the national election has not yet lost its plausibility, and is therefore not replaced. In such circumstances, European election outcomes cannot be expected to have political consequences.[18] Apparently voters are aware of this, because these are the electoral situations in which sincere

---

18 A case in point is the fate of the Dutch Christian Democratic party (CDA) in 1994. In the national elections of May 1994 this party obtained 22.2 percent of the vote, compared to 35.3 percent in the previous national election of 1989. Only a month later, in the European elections of June, the CDA obtained 30.8 percent of the vote. This remarkable bounce-back was universally discounted (even by the CDA itself) as not reflecting 'true' electoral preferences which had manifested themselves only a month before in the national elections.

voting seems most prevalent.[19] Under these circumstances extremist parties get no particular electoral advantage.

Contrasting strongly with this situation is the one in which a European election is conducted at a considerable temporal distance from the previous national election, possibly with the next national election already in sight.[20] In this situation the marker set by the previous national election has become obsolete, and politicians will regard the results of the European election as a new indicator of their own and other parties' electoral strength. Voters apparently sense this—presumably as a result of media coverage and the way in which politicians approach them during the campaign. In this circumstance voters have an incentive to behave strategically but in a sense of the word 'strategic' that is quite different from what we see in national elections, where large parties are advantaged by their strength. The strategic situation in such a 'marker-setting election' is characterized by an apparent lack of consequences for the allocation of power on the one hand and by the attentiveness of politicians and media on the other. In this circumstance, strategic voting may take the form of what is generally referred to as 'protest voting', benefitting radical small parties in particular. Knowing that politicians are attentive to the results while no actual power is at stake, some voters apparently take the opportunity (in the phrase of the British football hooligans) to 'put in the boot'.

This is one of the perverse consequences of the lack of focus in European elections on matters relating to the European project. In Britain and Spain in 1989, where the European elections were taken seriously by media and politicians as pointers to the possible outcome of a forthcoming national election, domestic consequences were palpable, as was shown in Chapters 5 and 16. In Greece, Luxembourg and Ireland, by contrast, European elections that occurred in conjunction with national elections could aptly be characterized as 'throw-away' elections. We will discuss the unintended effects of European elections on domestic politics in more detail in Chapter 21.

Our findings differ from those of previous analysts in a particularly crucial respect. In this chapter we defined quasi-switching and turnout effects as contributing to the difference between results of concurrent but different electoral contests, and we took the joint effects of these phenomena as amounting to second-order effects. Most other analysts have until now defined second-order effects as the difference in a party's share of valid votes seen in a European as

---

19 We judge these votes to be sincere because the strategic advantages that large parties enjoy in national elections are at a minimum.

20 To judge from evidence presented in certain country chapters, this is particularly so when the government has freedom to call an early national election in the light of the European election outcome.

compared to the most recent national election. By adopting this latter definition, however, they obfuscate the situation by including in their second-order effects any changes that may have occurred in the electorate's domestic party preferences since the last national election. Such changes are then combined in an unknown fashion with the net effects of quasi-switching and differential turnout. Only by assuming some of these terms to be zero can this knot be untangled; but, as we have demonstrated by estimating these various effects, such assumptions do not hold.

When contrasting our findings with the expectations that might be derived from second-order election theory (see Chapter 2 for a review of the main tenets of that theory) we find them supporting some of those expectations but not others. The hypothesis that larger parties are negatively affected by second-order elections is clearly supported: party strength is the most important factor conditioning the difference between European and national electoral performance. On the other hand, we found no support whatsoever for the notion that government parties in particular stand to suffer from such effects. The corollary of adverse effects for large parties is that smaller ones do rather well in second-order contests. The idea, however, that more radical parties in particular reap these fruits was not unequivocally supported by our findings: whether or not this happens depends on the location of the European election in the domestic electoral cycle, the period between two adjacent national elections. When European elections fall early in this cycle, the lack of incentive to cast a protest vote means that it is not so much extreme as moderate small parties that gain the most.

So the most important implication of our findings for second-order election theory appears to us to be this non-uniformity of effects due to their dependency on contextual factors. The presence of concurrent national elections, and the time difference between national and European ones, are crucial influences not only on the magnitude, but even on the direction of the effects of strength and ideological extremity. With the exception of Reif's (1985a) analysis of the location of a European election in the domestic political cycle, little attention has previously been given to such contextual dependencies.[21]

---

21 Reif's conception of the electoral cycle is quite different from ours. His view is that governments suffer unpopularity at midterm, and the cycle consists in a swing away from government support in the months following a national election, followed by a swing back towards government support as the next election approaches. This is, of course, an idealized view of what would happen in the absence of real changes in government party support. Reif sees European elections occurring at different points in this idealized cycle as displaying the popularity of parties at that point. Our view is quite different, since our concern is with the extent to which European elections will be viewed by parties and other political actors as markers for real changes in support for government (and other) parties, and the consequences that flow from their interpretation of the outcomes in this light.

This is not to say, however, that all second-order effects are contingent. Only about two-thirds of the contribution to quasi-switching is dependent on temporal and ideological considerations. Fully one-third is not conditional to these strategic factors, and much of this remainder may be ascribed to the mechanical effect of the different rules that apply in European compared to national elections. Nevertheless, contextual dependencies appear to dominate the difference between national and European election outcomes. The most important of these that we have isolated relates to the different motivational forces that are associated with different strategic situations. In first-order national elections voters vote with the head—this is the context in which rational forethought is most apparent and in which rationality implies taking into account the power of parties to put their programs into effect. In second-order European elections two different contexts can occur. In throw-away elections, where better markers of party strength exist, voters vote with the heart—this is the context in which sincere voting is most apparent. Finally, in marker-setting ' by the outcome but political power is not (or is not perceived to be) directly at stake, some voters vote with the boot—this is the context in which protest, frustration, and anger are most tellingly expressed.[22]

Discussion

By supplying an opportunity to 'put in the boot', European elections might seem to provide no small service to national political systems, reducing the amount of sclerosis that they might otherwise suffer. If all elections were first-order elections, electorates might hesitate to give vent to anger and frustration or to experiment with new parties because of the possible consequences of giving power to less preferred alternatives or even to untried elites. European elections provide opportunities on this score that are superior to those provided by other second-order elections. Municipal and regional elections by definition incorporate multiple contests (irrespective of how much those contests might be dominated by national concerns) so that they always retain some degree of differentiation which is absent when representatives are elected to a single body. European elections are the only second-order elections that are fought on a nation-wide scale in each political system that is part of the European Union, and as such they constitute the best available stand-ins for national

---

22 This extraordinary finding goes more than a little way towards explaining the surprising 1992 outcomes of Maastricht Treaty referenda in France and Denmark. There voters were more than normally aware of politicians' attention to the result, and could more than usually be sure of a hearing when they registered their protest. But the protest they registered apparently concerned their unhappiness with domestic circumstances, not their unhappiness with the Maastricht Treaty, as we shall see in Chapter 21.

elections. Without European elections to act as safety valves, it would be just that little bit more likely that anger and frustration would increase to the point at which voters might become heedless of practical consequences in their desire to 'throw the rascals out' at a national election. Moreover, by providing an arena in which new parties can compete for favor and existing parties can experiment with new policies and leaders, European elections also widen the opportunities for political competition—possibly leading to a long-term improvement in the alternatives on offer to voters and in the match between these alternatives and voters' concerns.[23]

Taken together, what this amounts to is a sort of lubrication of the wheels of national electoral politics—or more properly a reduction in the inertia that is otherwise so characteristic of parliamentary regimes.[24] Seen from these perspectives, the consequences of European elections for national politics go far beyond those stressed earlier in this chapter, of providing markers that may be misleading. Even protest votes can have benign consequences if they lead to more attentive representation of voters' concerns. So European elections, despite their nuisance value for political parties, may have some positive consequences for the quality of democracy in member states.

Nevertheless, these perhaps beneficial consequences of European elections hardly serve to counterbalance their undesirable consequences in two areas. In the first place, by being treated as markers for the domestic political standing of parties, attention is diverted from the arena that European elections are supposed to serve. In the second place, even within the national arena, the mistaken assumption that these elections truly reflect the national standing of parties can potentially lead party leaders to miscalculate their reactions to European election outcomes. There is no guarantee that, when voters protest, the identity of the party they vote for is a reflection of the nature of their concern, so reacting to that protest will not necessarily please the voters and may well damage the country. We consider these matters in greater detail in Chapter 21.

---

23 For this reason, European elections have often been referred to as the midwife assisting at the birth of new parties. These elections also seem able to accelerate the demise of political leaders and perhaps also (although this was not observed in our study) of political parties.

24 Some reasons for this inertia are discussed in Chapter 21.

CHAPTER 19

The Institutional Context: Turnout

Mark Franklin, Cees van der Eijk and Erik Oppenhuis

As discussed at some length in Chapter 2, turnout at European elections is lower than in national elections (even where compulsory voting keeps it high) but its actual level is also strongly related to the position in the national election cycle at which a European election occurs. Elections occurring early in the cycle (within a year of the previous national elections) show turnout that is lower by 10 percent or more than elections that occur when the next national election is close (within a year). In Chapter 2 we puzzled over whether this variation might be due to a 'spillover' effect whereby the approaching national election created a context of greater political excitement in which it was easier for parties to mobilize their voters, or whether people might be responding to the fact that votes cast shortly before a national election were more likely to influence the national political context. Preliminary evidence hinted at just such an instrumental motivation, since European election outcomes constitute leading indicators of national election outcomes. Evidence from Chapter 18 reinforces this suggestion. We have just seen how protest votes increase when a national election is in prospect, presumably because the increased attention paid by national politicians and commentators at such times makes protest voting worthwhile.

Despite these two sources of circumstantial evidence, it is still not clear that variations in European election turnout reflect differences in the motivations of voters rather than merely uneven mobilizing efforts of parties and other opinion leaders. Evidently, there may be elements of both mechanisms at work. However, it is important for us to discover whether voter motivation plays any part because of our interest in assessing how the electorates of different European countries may respond to new political circumstances. The final research question listed in Chapter 3 asked whether European voters could be motivated to adapt to a more European party system posing more European choices. If we find that voters go to the polls purely out of loyalty, habit and duty, then it will be unlikely that they will be induced to adapt their electoral behavior to changes in the institutional framework of the European Union. On the other hand, to the extent that we find enough voters who appear by their behavior to be trying to affect the course of political events, then reforms aimed at increasing the political significance of European elections will appear more practical. Of course the feasibility of such reforms also depends on the answer we find to another of our primary research questions: do European voters constitute one electorate or many? Even if they would respond to new motivations, the stimuli might have to be different in each member country. Only if people vote for largely the same reasons in each country do we really have the prospect of changing the character of European elections.

Our interest in the determinants of turnout does go beyond a desire to see whether European voters might be induced to embrace developments making European elections both more properly European and more properly elections. As mentioned in Chapter 2, there are unanswered questions regarding turnout that might be answered by employing European elections as laboratories in which decisions made by individuals about whether to cast their vote can be analyzed in contextual perspective. These unanswered questions, however, are precisely the ones that need to be posed in order for us to address our own primary research questions.

The Turnout Puzzle

After more than half a century of careful research, it was still possible for Brody (1978) to refer to turnout as a 'puzzle'; and fifteen years later that puzzle is still largely unresolved. In particular, while we know much about why some people vote while others do not (Campbell et al., 1960; Verba and Nie, 1972; Kim, Petrocik and Enokson, 1975; Wolfinger and Rosenstone, 1980; Crewe, 1981) and why certain countries or regions see higher turnout than others (Merriam and Gosnell, 1924; Tingsten, 1937; Matthews and Prothro, 1963; Kim, Petrocik and Enokson, 1975; Wolfinger and Rosenstone, 1980; Powell, 1980, 1986; Jackman, 1987), we have almost no way of explaining the decline in turnout that has occurred in the United States and Europe in recent decades (Teixeira, 1992:39; Flickinger and Studley 1992:1). This decline has occurred despite widespread increases in that socio-economic characteristic—educa-tion—which is most strongly connected to turnout at the individual level.

One problem with past studies is that they have not incorporated predictors that can change very much between one election and the next, while turnout itself has changed quite dramatically. Variables like the proportionality of the electoral system or the presence of compulsory voting are effectively constants in most countries, while variables like educational attainment can only change with the maturing of new generations of better-educated individuals. In general it seems clear that what Milbrath and Goel (1977) call 'facilitative' factors, which would include all the variables listed above, do not vary enough over time to account for observed changes in electoral participation, let alone the slow decline in turnout. We are thus driven to focus on the other class of factors identified by these authors: what they call 'motivational' factors (see also Verba and Nie, 1972; Hirczy, 1992).

In this chapter we try to show the importance of motivational factors in determining differences in turnout both within and between countries, and over time. We do so by studying electoral participation across and within the countries that took part in the third EC-wide elections to the European Parliament in 1989. Our findings are then checked by testing the expectations that derive from them on data from the European elections of 1994. If the importance of relevant sorts of motivational factors can be demonstrated in this way, this will enable us to conclude that European voters are indeed influenced by the desire to affect the conduct of public affairs. Moreover, if these motivational factors account for country differences, we will additionally know that we are dealing with one electorate not many. The findings may also help solve Brody's 'puzzle'.

European elections might at first sight appear to be poor venues for studying turnout. As explained in Chapter 2, such elections are generally regarded as 'second-order' national elections which, just like many local and regional elections, lack salience. However, exactly this low-key character of EU elections yields a number of important advantages. Turnout is generally low, maximizing the variance of the variable of prime interest.[1] Moreover, since at each election some countries hold national (first order) elections on the same day as European elections (three in 1989, one in 1994), the difference between the two types of election becomes a matter for empirical investigation rather than an impediment to research.[2]

Though the EC/EU had 12 members at the time of the 1989 and 1994 European elections, we distinguish, as elsewhere in this book, 14 different political systems, treating separately the samples from Great Britain and Northern Ireland, and dividing the Belgian sample into Flanders and Wallonia since each of these regions has a different party system.[3]

---

1 When we aggregate these data and talk about country-level findings we try to refer to 'turnout' whereas when talking about individual-level findings we try to refer to 'electoral participation'. However, for the sake of convenience when making statements that refer to both levels we will refer occasionally to electoral participation as 'turnout'.

2 The timing of first-order elections in Europe is seldom set by a fixed electoral calendar but more often by domestic political circumstances, though there is always a limit on the maximum time that can elapse between such elections.

3 A separate sample from the former East Germany that was drawn in 1994 is ignored in this chapter, as elsewhere, because it does not yield comparability with the 1989 study.

Average turnout in these political systems did vary considerably in the two elections. Table 19.1 shows it ranging from around 36 percent to around 96 percent at each election.[4] Yet the within-country variation associated with differences between individuals was far greater. In a one-way analysis of variance of electoral participation by country, only 15.5 percent (in 1989) and 14.0 percent (in 1994) of the individual-level variance can be explained even by the large country differences seen in Table 19.1, leaving between 84 and 86 percent of the individual-level variation to be explained on other grounds.

In what follows, before trying to account for individual-level variations in electoral participation, we will first explain as much as possible of the country-level variance on the basis of institutional and contextual differences between countries.[5] In the process we will see to what extent, when country names are replaced by these more theoretically interesting concepts, we can account for observed country differences.

Table 19.1 Turnout in European Elections by Political System, 1989 and 1994

Political System	Election Year 1989	1994	Political System	Election Year 1989	1994
Denmark	47.4	52.9	Italy	81.4	74.8
Flanders	92.7	96.1	Luxembourg	96.2	86.6
France	48.8	52.7	Netherlands	47.5	35.6
Germany	62.3	50.0	Northern Ireland	48.8	49.8
Great Britain	36.6	36.1	Portugal	51.2	35.7
Greece	80.1	71.2	Spain	54.7	59.5
Ireland	68.3	44.0	Wallonia	87.1	82.2
Average Turnout (N=14)				65.3	60.7
Variance Explained by Country Differences				15.5	14.0

4 Country samples were weighted in the following fashion. First party preference was weighted to reflect official returns (van der Eijk and Oppenhuis, 1991). Next, the distribution of voters and non-voters was weighted to reflect official turnout. Finally, all samples were weighted to an equal size of 750 (yielding a grand total of 10,500 weighted cases—approximately the same as the number of unweighted cases in our EC-wide dataset once respondents with missing data on the dependent variable had been removed). This last step allowed us to optimally assess effects of systemic differences, particularly those between the smaller and the larger member states.

5 Efforts to productively combine different surveys into a single, amalgamated dataset are often thwarted by differences between surveys in content, question wording and question format. The questionnaires of the European election study, however, were identical in the different member states of the EC, apart from unavoidable differences in party names, etc., and the need to use different languages for their administration.

Research Design

Our focus in this chapter on predictors of turnout that can change quite markedly from election to election leads us to look, as already explained, particularly at contextual factors that have motivational consequences. Such factors have been investigated before, and we will employ many measures taken from earlier studies in order to properly assess the adequacy of our own additions. Indeed, the literature suggests so many variables as to yield potential problems of over-identification (particularly since some of them pertain to political systems, of which we only have 14) unless we adopt a strategy to reduce their number.

The procedure we adopted involved three strategies.[6] The first was to distinguish primary from secondary concerns. Putative causes that flow directly from our theoretical concern for evaluating the motivational basis of voting choice are considered first. Other concerns are secondary, and concepts related to those concerns are only evaluated for inclusion once controls for primary concepts are in force. The second strategy was to group together systemic variables that represented alternative indicators of the same concept. From each such group that indicator was chosen which yielded maximum variance explained. The third strategy was to adopt a stagewise procedure in which institutional characteristics were considered first, then social and political context, and finally individual characteristics. By only considering for inclusion contextual characteristics that added to the variance explained by institutional characteristics, we take advantage of our understanding of causal sequence. Institutional factors could not be the result of social or political context, so there is no point in allowing those contextual variables to share the variance explained by institutions. By forcing them to pass the strong test of actually adding to the variance explained by institutional factors, we reduce the likelihood that chance correlations with institutional differences will lead them to be included among the country-level variables. When we came to the point of selecting individual-level variables, the same procedure ensured that we did not add variables whose effects were already accounted for by other variables earlier in causal sequence. The three strategies worked in tandem to keep to a minimum the number of variables to be included in the final model, without reducing the number of variables that would be given the opportunity to show their importance.

Our choice of variables was thus made in stages, starting with systemic characteristics, continuing with social and political context, and ending with

---

6 We could not employ conventional stepwise or backward elimination techniques because systemic and compositional effects might then be replaced by individual-level effects simply because of the greater variability of individual-level measures.

individual characteristics. At each stage, independent variables were selected from among groups of alternative measures (if any) on the basis of variance explained, and residuals from each stage were used as the dependent variables for analysis at the next stage. We must stress, however, that this procedure was used only for variable selection and not for model evaluation. The effects of all variables in an equation were estimated simultaneously, after the selection had been made.[7]

In the pages that follow we first enumerate in more detail the various influences on electoral participation that we can evaluate with our data, and then turn to our actual analyses, leading to a discussion of the implications of our findings for understanding variations in voter turnout.

Systemic And Contextual Determinants Of Turnout

How can we conceptually differentiate the member states of the EU so as to avoid the need for proper names when trying to explain turnout? Previous theorizing has suggested a plethora of variables (cf. Powell, 1980, 1986; Crewe, 1981; Jackman, 1987; Blais and Carty, 1990; Crepaz, 1990) to which we add even more. All these variables, however, fall into a small number of obvious classes, as follows:

Institutional context
What are the rules of the game? Two aspects have generally been stressed. The first is the nature of the electoral system, most obviously whether it employs plurality voting (Britain), Single Transferable Vote (STV—Ireland and Northern Ireland) or List System proportional representation (PR—elsewhere). In addition, there are variations in thresholds for representation (caused either by the sizes of electoral districts, the number of seats to be filled, or by imposed restrictions), possibilities for apparentement, and sundry other differences all of which translate into the proportionality of outcomes (votes/seats ratio) which we therefore use as the first of our independent variables.[8] An alternative formulation was in terms of electoral system type, distinguishing plurality from STV from PR systems.[9] The second institutional aspect that we take into account is

---

7 Clearly, stagewise analysis yields coefficients that are different from those produced when all effects are computed simultaneously.

8 This measure has been operationalized not in terms of the European elections themselves, but in terms of the most recent national election: the systemic context in which voters were socialized and to which they have become accustomed.

9 In European elections we only have one example of plurality voting which occurs in Britain. This was treated as the base category and not given a dummy variable. Northern Ireland is an STV system in European Elections, and was coded as such along with the Irish Republic. Other

whether compulsory voting is in effect (in Flanders, Wallonia, Greece, Luxembourg and Italy) or not (elsewhere). We expect that more proportionality, by increasing the predictable consequences of the voting act (cf. Blais and Carty, 1990), will lead to higher turnout; while a legal requirement to vote will evidently do the same. As a subsidiary concern we noted whether the election was held on a Thursday (Denmark, Great Britain, Ireland, Northern Ireland, the Netherlands and Spain) or on the following Sunday (elsewhere). It has several times been suggested (see, for example, Crewe, 1981) that Sunday voting will reduce the costs of electoral participation.

Social context
A number of social phenomena may affect turnout and party choice. These are mainly aggregate-level versions of individual-level variables that we will return to below, in which the process of aggregation takes the form of finding averages or proportions for each EC country. The idea is that people may be affected by the character of the society in which they live even if they do not share a dominant characteristic. These aggregations include the composition of the electorate in terms of education, age, and the size of groups defined by traditional (class, religion) and hypothesized (materialist/postmaterialist) cleavages.

Political context
Domestic political events and processes in the member countries of the European Union determine the political context within which European elections are fought. As we already argued in Chapter 18, the mere fact that European elections are to be seen as second-order national elections does not mean that they are all equally unimportant. On the contrary, the specific domestic context in which a European election is held may on some occasions turn a European election into a highly significant political event in terms of national politics, for example because it might trigger national elections (as happened in Spain in 1989). Overriding all others is the question whether a national election was held concurrently with European elections. If so, the national election will have been one with direct consequences for the allocation of power to govern the country, and turnout at the European election will have been artificially inflated because those voting for domestic political reasons will in general also have voted in the concurrent European election (Reif and Schmitt, 1980; Reif, 1984a; see also Chapters 4, 9, 11 and 12). Even in the absence of concurrent national elections, however, we can expect a second feature of the national political context to be important. The position in the national electoral calendar

---

countries were coded as PR.

occupied by the European election will determine how much attention is paid to it by politicians and commentators (see Chapter 18).[10] This position can be measured in a number of competing ways—by dummy variables indicating whether or not national elections are imminent or took place recently, and by time elapsed since the most recent national election and time left (benefitting from hindsight)[11] until national elections were due. A further contextual variable is the strength of the linkage between parties and the social groups traditionally supporting them. Strong links between political parties and identifiable social groups were found by Powell (1980) to provide a context within which parties could mobilize their voters to turn out. Though this linkage has been declining in importance in most European countries in recent decades (Franklin et al., 1992), Franklin (1991) still found it played a role in determining party choice in the 1989 European elections, so there is reason to suppose that it might still play a part in mobilizing turnout as well.[12] As a subsidiary concern, we also evaluated the extent of approval of the European Community for possible effects on turnout.[13]

Options from which to choose
Once we had explained as much variance as possible on the basis of the variables discussed above, we turned to the supply side to see whether the nature of the choices on offer made any difference to turnout. It has been suggested

---

10 We would have liked a more direct measure of the 'domestic political importance' of a European election, but in the absence of an indicator such as the money expended by parties and candidates compared to that spent in surrounding national elections (a figure which, for a variety of reasons, is exceedingly hard to obtain reliably) the location of the election within the domestic electoral cycle is the best surrogate.

11 Although hindsight is needed for us to code this variable, this does not mean that within the countries concerned a national election will have been unexpected. While in most European countries the election date is discretionary within margins fixed by law, nevertheless there will generally be widespread awareness of the increasing likelihood of an election being called in circumstances of government crisis or towards the end of the permitted period.

12 The variable was measured by regression analysis of left voting with class and religious variables using the same procedure (and the same variables) as in *Electoral Change* (Franklin et al., 1992). The variance explained was then used as a country-level variable. There is some question as to whether the same procedures yield comparable findings in different kinds of elections. However, it has always been argued that European elections should be regarded as 'second-order' national elections (Reif and Schmitt, 1980; Reif, 1984a, 1985a) and in Chapter 20 we will show that the links between social groups and political party support are the same in European as in national elections, just as is the case for other kinds of links between voters and parties.

13 Although the country chapters found no such effects, logically effects could still be found over Europe as a whole. The variable is the average score on a cumulative scale containing items indicating approval of European integration and the EC (Treiber-Reif and Schmitt, 1990; van der Eijk and Oppenhuis, 1990). For details, see also Appendix B.

(Andersen, 1979; Schattschneider, 1960) that the greater the number of parties, the more competitive the party system and the more satisfied voters report themselves to be with the choices on offer, the more likely voters are to find a choice that appeals to them and the more likely they are to vote. Variables bearing upon these considerations were as follows:

a. the number of parties competing for seats in the European Parliament in any particular country, which primarily reflects the breadth of choice offered to the electorate;[14]

b. the competitiveness of parties (how far the same voters are likely to support more than one party) determines whether parties must compete for voters that other parties are also trying to woo. We expect competition to generate extra incentives for party leaders to mobilize their potential voters;[15]

c. the simplicity of the space within which party choices are made, operationalized in terms of the variance explained by the first two principal components in a factor analysis of the probability to vote questions described in footnote 15—the assumption being that decision costs are smaller when the options are clearly structured along a few dimensions;

d. the adequacy of representation (the extent to which the set of competing parties caters to the political preferences of the electorate) indicated by 1 minus the proportion of the electorate for whom no party scored above average in the probability to vote questions described in footnote 17; and

e. the variety of policy positions offered with respect to European integration. Although European elections are mainly about domestic politics, they at least purport to relate to the European one. By far the most important question in that arena is how far European integration should be pursued. The amount of choice on this question is indicated by the range of positions taken by political parties (van der Eijk and Franklin, 1991). Greater choice should, once again, raise the average benefits of voting.

---

14 The operationalization in terms of number of parties participating in the European election was the least equivocal of several possibilities, including effective number of parties (requiring a choice between different ways to measure this), or number of parties in national elections (requiring arbitrary decisions as to which ballot options to count or disregard).

15 Cf. Powell (1980:19). This is the first of three measures that are based on the 'probability to vote' questions that were introduced in Chapter 3 and extensively employed in the country chapters of Part II. The first of the derived variables measures the extent to which individuals gave above-average scores to more than one party (see Chapter 20 for more details; also see van der Eijk and Oppenhuis, 1991). This value will be larger as voters report a greater likelihood of voting for more than one party and smaller when they would never think of voting for more than one party.

Individual-Level Determinants Of Turnout

All of the above considerations are implemented at the systemic level, as indicators of differences between countries that could affect average turnout. Of course, many of them could not have been coded without individual-level data from which to derive the aggregate figures, and many of the individual-level counterparts of the aggregate characteristics might also relate to the likelihood of turning out to vote. People might vote not only because they live among highly educated people, but because they themselves are highly educated (indeed, this is the more usual way in which such variables have previously been employed). Because we have no shortage of degrees of freedom at the individual level, we did not need to concern ourselves with the number of individual-level variables employed in our analysis, and could spread our net widely among those suggested in past research as being important.

Just as education may be considered both an element of social context and an individual characteristic of voters, so it is for other social context variables. Thus we include as individual-level variables all those whose aggregate-level equivalents have already been mentioned above. Added to these were individual-level socio-demographic characteristics commonly found in analyses of electoral participation: income, gender, and group memberships (Campbell et al., 1960; Verba and Nie, 1972; Kim, Petrocik and Enokson, 1975; Wolfinger and Rosenstone, 1980; Parry, Moyser and Day, 1992).[16]

Turning to the effects on turnout of being motivated to pay attention to political phenomena, we coded political interest on the basis of various behavioral and attitudinal indicators (attention to newspapers and TV, interest in news about the campaign, and other such variables—see Appendix B). In addition, we included a specific measure of campaign mobilization: a dichotomous variable indicating whether coverage of the campaign helped our respondents in any way when it came to choosing which party to support.[17]

There is some question whether party identification functions in the same way in Europe as in the United States (Budge, Crewe and Farlie, 1976; Thomassen, 1976; van der Eijk and Niemöller, 1983). Nevertheless, identification with a political party is consistently reported to be a powerful predictor of electoral participation. In our analyses we use an indicator of affective attachment to a political party, which was the closest available alias for party

---

16 The actual analysis of demographic effects was performed country by country for reasons explained below.

17 Three variables in our survey were relevant to this measure which was coded 1 if the respondent was helped to make up his mind, shown where his party stood, or had European issues elucidated by the campaign. Otherwise it was coded 0.

identification (but see Katz, 1985, for a critique of this measure). In order to specifically tap more unambiguously instrumental motivations, we also include a measure of the extent to which the choices on offer match the needs of each individual. A variable referred to as 'appeal of best choice' expresses the strength of preference for the best-liked party.[18]

Interaction Effects

The attempt to simultaneously investigate effects on turnout that derive from country and individual differences requires us to be very sensitive to the possibility of interaction effects. Evidently, in a country where turnout is virtually universal there will be little opportunity for individual-level differences to play any role (see Hirczy, 1995). The corollary is that only in countries where turnout is not perfect can we expect to find much in the way of individual-level effects. To the extent that systemic and compositional influences determine turnout they will thus limit the extent to which individual-level influences can do so, and interactions between variables measured at different levels will be inevitable. This mechanical limit to the effects of individual-level variables— often known as a 'ceiling' effect—is automatically taken into account by analysis procedures such as probit or logit; and using such an analysis would 'solve' this problem. However, such analyses, by so efficiently taking account of ceiling effects, make it hard for us to observe their occurrence. We thus use OLS regression in preference so as to understand the substantive implications of the ceiling and other effects we observe. However, in order to guard against the possibility of being misled by specification errors, we also compute the effects by means of logistic regression.[19]

A different type of interaction might arise because individual-level effects of particular variables are different in different countries. In some, campaign mobilization may play a more important role; in some, party identification may be paramount; and so on. If there are significant differences between countries then our estimation of individual-level influences on turnout will be subject to specification error when all countries are taken together, requiring the use of interactions between individual-level independent variables and dummy variables representing specific countries to account for these differences. The method we used to search for such terms is detailed below. However, some of the possible differences between countries are not relevant to our current

---

18   The value of the highest score given by each individual to any party when asked for the probability (on a scale of 1 to 10) that they would 'ever' vote for that party (see footnote 15).

19   See Mitchell and Wlezien (1995) for an assessment of the competing claims of logistic regression versus probit analysis when studying turnout.

concerns. For example, the precise nature of demographic effects will vary according to the manner in which social distinctions have become politicized or intertwined with other factors affecting electoral participation.[20] Much the same is true of variations in the effects of components contributing to political interest, which will have been mediated by such matters as television coverage and communications infrastructure.

In order to avoid becoming entangled in differences in the relationships between these independent variables deriving from the existence in different countries of different processes involving demographic effects and political interest, we estimated these effects separately in each country. From these analyses we derived a set of predicted values of electoral participation (in statistical parlance, the y-hats from the analysis of these variables in each country) which could be used in the overall analyses to replace demographic effects and the effects of political interest.

Contextual Effects

The first steps in our analysis investigate the context of the voting act. We have seen (Table 19.1) that turnout varies from country to country. Indeed, fully 15.5 percent of the variance in turnout at the individual level is accounted for by country differences in 1989. To what extent are these differences due to country-level features that we can specify? Because of our causal perspective, we start with systemic factors, then add factors pertaining to the social context, and finally add factors specific to the political context of a particular election. Our procedure is to report the variables entered in each context and then display the combined effects of all contextual variables. There is no reason to display coefficients for the interim models since these change as fuller specification is achieved.

Of the systemic factors, three variables proved important: compulsory voting, proportionality of the electoral system (votes/seats ratio), and Sunday voting. With these variables in place, no social context variables added appreciably to the variance we could explain without them. Finally, the domestic importance of the European elections was clearly a significant matter, as hypothesized. Of the various ways in which we operationalized this concept, time until the next national election turned out to be the most powerful.[21]

---

20 Many demographic effects are of no theoretical interest (for example, the effect of urbanization on turnout will to a great extent be dependent on transportation infrastructure in rural areas). Other differences are sufficiently intricate as to demand more discussion than can be given here. The specific differences between countries in terms of these variables are analyzed elsewhere (Oppenhuis, 1995).

21 Despite expectations to the contrary, the approach of the next election turns out not to be a

In Table 19.2 we display the effects of these variables in terms of coefficients calculated both at the level of the political system (N = 14 analysis) and at the individual level (n = 10,500 analysis). At the level of the political system, the dependent variable is turnout, and the coefficients in that part of the table relate to the increment in percentage turnout (on a scale of 0 to 100) that we observe consequential upon various factors. At the level of the individual, the dependent variable is voted or not, and the coefficients in that part of the table relate to the probability (on a scale of 0 to 1) that particular individuals will have voted in given circumstances. Of course, by mathematical necessity in the case of countries weighted to the same n (see footnote 4), the effects of the various factors in the two analyses are identical (except for rounding errors) once the conversion of probabilities to percentages has been made—the left-hand set of b's are 100 times the right-hand set. The regression weights in the beta columns of the table, however, are not equivalent since they are affected by the amount of unexplained variance: much greater in the case of the n=10,500 analysis which counts individual-level variability as unexplained (so far). The table shows that with four variables we can explain almost 92 percent of the variance in system-level turnout. No other contextual variable from among those we could have included adds even one-tenth of one percent

Table 19.2 Regression of Electoral Participation on Systemic Characteristics in an EC-wide Analysis of the 1989 Elections

Independent Variables	N=14		n=10500	
	b	Beta	b	Beta
Systemic				
Compulsory Voting	26.08	0.667	0.264	0.264
Sunday Voting	9.35	0.245	0.093	0.096
Proportionality	0.46	0.133	0.005	0.053
Political				
Time until Next National Election *	-0.30	-0.236	-0.003	0.093
Constant	17.77		0.180	
Variance Explained	0.918		0.142	

* Coded 0 in the case of concurrent national elections.

step-function, but a gradually increasing effect. This variable is a more powerful predictor than time since the previous national election, probably because, with different lengths of Parliamentary terms, the critical run-up period would have to be coded differently in terms of time since the previous election.

to this total of variance explained.[22] Our principal findings are quite interpretable. Judging from the regression weights in the beta columns of the table, compulsory voting has by far the strongest effect with the other three variables having between a quarter and a third of the impact of compulsory voting.

The effects we measure in the columns headed b enable us to estimate the level of turnout corresponding to various combinations of systemic and political characteristics.[23] Strikingly, the possible values encompass virtually the whole range of turnout rates up to a maximum of 99.8 percent which one would expect in a system with perfect proportionality, compulsory voting, and Sunday voting with a concurrent national election (which is synonymous with zero time until the next national election). Scholarly caution limits the range over which we can realistically model our findings to little more than the range actually seen in the countries we investigate, but this runs from 36 to 96 percent; and at 96 percent turnout there is very little individual-level variance left to analyze. So it is clear that real world variations in systemic and political context do define the extent to which individual characteristics matter: individual-level effects can only occur to the extent that contextual effects permit.

It not only matters which variables are included in the equation of Table 19.2 but also which variables are missing. Remarkable at first sight is the fact that electoral system characteristics such as PR and STV add nothing to an explanation based on the votes/seats ratio. At second sight this is less surprising, however. Only two countries have STV and only one has plurality voting; all others have party-list PR systems in European elections. The internal diversity (thresholds, apparentement, etc.) among all these other countries means that there is not a clear contrast between them and either STV or plurality systems. Moreover, the distinguishing feature of plurality voting (the likelihood of a wasted vote) is already captured by our measure of proportionality in a more general way than a mere contrast between plurality, STV and PR affords. Less surprising is the absence from Table 19.2 of a variable indicating concurrent national elections. The effect of this variable is very strong until we take account

---

22 Many of the coefficients listed in Table 19.2 fail to reach conventional levels of statistical significance in the N=14 analysis (though the level of significance in the n=10,500 analysis is high—see Table 19.3). Despite high variance explained, the small N in the country-level analysis raises the question of whether our findings capitalize on chance. This problem will be addressed when we investigate the replicability of these findings in other elections (see below).

23 This can be done by multiplying each of the characteristics of an actual or hypothetical political system by the appropriate regression effect (b) from Table 19.2, and then adding up the results of these multiplications, together with the constant term. Except for proportionality (and time until the next national elections, which is measured in months), independent variables are all dichotomies measuring the presence (1) or absence (0) of some characteristic. The measure of proportionality ranges from 0 to 100 with a maximum (in our data) of 99.8.

of time until the next national election, which evidently incorporates its effects. Much more remarkable is the fact that no social context variables are included. Countries with elderly populations, highly unionized populations, or more highly educated populations do not display higher turnout, despite the fact that these characteristics at the individual level clearly distinguish between those who vote and those do not. Moreover, 'supply side' factors determining the options from which voters can choose make no difference in this universe of countries.

Residual Country Effects

We saw in Table 19.2 that the between-country variance in turnout that we can explain by means of systemic and contextual effects was 91.8 percent. With an N of 14, this is an impressive result (see Powell, 1986, and Jackman, 1987, for similar analyses that explain less variance with about the same number of countries and more independent variables unless country dummies are included). Nevertheless, there might be room within the variance left unexplained for residual country effects to prove significant. If the explanatory variables identified in Table 19.2 had failed to capture all of the relevant differences between our 14 systems, these would manifest themselves in significant residuals for various countries. Such residuals would, in the absence of specified variables, only be 'explained' by proper names of countries (represented by dummy variables). To the extent that country residuals prove significant, the possibility of finding additional systemic or contextual influences will remain open.

Given the N=14 findings, it will come as no surprise to discover that the residual effects of country in such an analysis are small. Three countries showed deviations from expected turnout that were significant at the .05 level (no other residual effect was even significant at the .1 level). Observed turnout in Greece is some 12 percent lower than would have been expected from its systemic and political characteristics; turnout in Flanders and Ireland is some eight percent higher. An explanation for these deviations can be found in Chapter 9 in which Panayote Dimitras explains how Greek turnout is under-estimated by some 10 percent because of administrative problems in maintaining the electoral register. When this error is taken into account by adapting the turnout value for Greece and re-estimating the equation (yielding a smaller constant term) not only does Greece lose its status as an outlier, but so too does Flanders (and variance explained in the analysis from which the residual is computed rises to 0.95). Only Ireland retains a significant residual in this analysis, for reasons that cannot readily be determined. For most countries turnout expected in 1989 on the basis of systemic and political characteristics is within four percent of the actual turnout recorded in 1989—despite the fact that this turnout varies from 36 to 96 percent (see Table 19.1).

Individual Influences

In the final stage of our investigation, individual characteristics of voters are used to explain remaining differences in electoral participation. Here we focus on the variance that was unexplained by systemic and political context variables in the n=10,500 analysis of Table 19.2. However, this stage followed a succession of analyses which sought to identify interactions with system-level variables, as follows.

First, an EC-wide regression analysis was run to establish which individual-level variables merited further consideration. Having found these variables, the residuals from the analysis were saved and the file split by country, after which the saved residuals were regressed on the same independent variables as had already been used in the Europe-wide analysis that generated the residuals. Significant effects indicated interactions: the strength of the effect of the individual-level variable was different in a particular country than Europe-wide. If the sign and size of such country-specific effects corresponded to country differences in systemic variables, interaction effects could be specified and included in a new analysis of individual differences, avoiding the possibility of specification errors, as discussed earlier in this chapter.

The most important outcome of this investigation of interactions was that it found nothing but ceiling effects. The effects of individual characteristics do depend on how much space is left for such characteristics to play a role after institutional and political contexts have defined the overall level of participation; but, apart from this, European countries do not differ from one another in the way in which turnout is determined.[24]

Table 19.3 reinforces the aggregate findings presented in Table 19.2. The systemic and contextual measures retain their effects in this more fully specified analysis; the added individual-level characteristics are statistically speaking orthogonal to them. Most of these new effects are consistent with findings reported in literature referred to earlier in this chapter. The likelihood of voting is greatest among those with an interest in politics, who found the campaign helpful in making a choice among the parties on offer, who found among those parties at least one that was very appealing (see footnote 18) and with which they could identify. Socio-demographic characteristics are also of clear importance. Elsewhere (Oppenhuis, 1995) it has been shown that this variable encapsulates mainly the effects of age and education, with age operating in a curvilinear fashion.

---

24 The same conclusion holds when we employed measures of socio-demographic effect and political interest that were calculated over all countries at once. Though when used in a Europe-wide analysis the overall variables explained about 5 percent less variance than the tailored measures, for no country was the difference statistically significant.

Table 19.3 Regression of Electoral Participation on Individual Characteristics, Controlling for Systemic and Compositional Effects, in an EC-wide Analysis (n=8978)

	b	Beta	Sig. T	Logistic Effect*
Independent Variables				
Political Interest	0.107	0.225	0.000	0.125
Socio-demographic Effect	0.091	0.190	0.000	0.097
Appeal of Best Choice	0.023	0.099	0.000	0.042
Campaign Mobilization	0.083	0.078	0.000	0.122
Party Attachment	0.025	0.052	0.002	0.041
Interactions with Systemic Effects				
Compulsory Voting with				
Political Interest	-0.043	-0.089	0.000	ns
Campaign Mobilization	-0.028	-0.061	0.000	ns
Appeal of Best Choice	-0.016	-0.033	0.000	ns
Controls for Systemic and Compositional Effects				
Compulsory Voting	0.253	0.227	0.000	0.289
Time until Next National Election	-0.003	-0.107	0.000	-0.003
Sunday Voting	0.097	0.102	0.000	0.126
Proportionality	0.003	0.036	0.000	0.003
Constant	0.003		0.451	
Variance Explained (pseudo R^2)	0.356			(0.319)

*The difference of proportions in participation predicted by the estimated equation when each variable in turn is increased one unit above its mean, while keeping all other variables at their mean values (ns = not significant).

Because of intricate variations from country to country which we have no space to unravel here, the relative importance of the different components of our composite measure of political interest is also investigated elsewhere (Oppenhuis, 1995); but in all countries this measure is effectively one of attentiveness. Turning to campaign mobilization, the most important component is the success of political parties in communicating to the electorate their political or ideological stance.

A great many other variables do not enter the equation at all, even when very relaxed criteria for significance are applied. Postmaterialist value orientations, for example, do not figure in the explanation. Particularly noteworthy is the fact that EC-related attitudes, preferences and orientations play no significant role in the explanation of electoral participation in European elections, in contrast to the findings of some earlier, less elaborate studies.[25] This underscores

---

25 For a more detailed discussion of how the erroneous conclusion (that EC-related attitudes,

again the conclusion drawn by many analysts (see Chapter 2) that what we are dealing with are second-order national rather than European elections, and validates our use of these data to reach general conclusions about turnout.

Our search for interaction effects found them only with compulsory voting.[26] This most powerful systemic effect, when present to raise the level of turnout, reduces the effects of three of the most powerful individual-level variables correspondingly. Because our coding of interaction terms as −1,+1 (rather than 0,1 dummies—see footnote 26) requires that they either be subtracted from individual-level influences (where absent) or added to these influences (where present) their effect is twice as great as their magnitudes in Table 19.3. Thus the weight of political interest ranges from 0.136 in the presence of compulsory voting (0.225 − 0.089) to 0.314 in the absence of compulsory voting (0.225 + 0.089),[27] making it by far the most powerful of the effects we measure in the absence of compulsory voting. The effects of campaign mobilization and of the appeal of party are equally dependent on the extent to which systemic forces leave space for them to operate. It is also important to note that some interaction effects that might have been expected were not found in practice. In particular, there is no interaction between time until next national election and campaign mobilization, which suggests a lack of 'spillover' on turnout from the added excitement and salience of politics during a national election or the run-up to such an election. Campaigns, indeed, appear to perform much the same role whatever the importance of the election concerned.

Turning to the logistic regression effects (created by finding the difference of predicted proportions in turnout when each variable is increased by one unit above its mean value while keeping all other variables at their mean values) we see that these differ little from their OLS counterparts. In the case of coefficients where interactions were present in the OLS findings, equivalent logistic effects are greater because they incorporate the interaction effects that are separately computed in OLS regression.[28] In the case of other coefficients

---

values and orientations do positively affect turnout) was reached, see Schmitt and Mannheimer (1991a) and van der Eijk and Schmitt (1991).

26 Interaction terms come from multiplying by 1 data values that occur in the presence of compulsory voting and by −1 data values that occur in the absence of this condition. Interaction terms constructed in this way are not customary (more usual is to multiply by 1 and 0) but have useful properties, particularly in reducing the multicollinearity that would otherwise occur with the terms from which they derive (cf. Jaccard, Turrisi and Wan, 1990).

27 Since the interaction effects are all negative, we have to bear in mind that subtracting a negative means addition. The weight of each variable in the equation is given by the coefficients in the column headed beta. Also known as the 'standardized regression coefficient', it gives the effect of each variable on a scale that is comparable across all variables.

28 The similarity between the logistic effects and the b-coefficients is even clearer when for the

the OLS and logistic equivalents are very close to having the same values. We would not have been led to any different conclusions about the relative influence of institutional, contextual or individual effects on turnout by employing logistic regression in lieu of OLS regression, despite the strong ceiling effects we observe. But the OLS analysis has the advantage, in the context of the present research design, of explicitly demonstrating the consequences of such ceilings for the effects of individual-level characteristics. Manifestly, as a system approaches perfect turnout there is less and less room for individual-level effects, and this oft-ignored truism is evident in our findings.

Accounting for the Decision to Vote

In the analyses reported above we have looked at electoral participation in the member-states of the European Union at the aggregate and individual levels during the 1989 elections for the European Parliament. In line with the findings of other researchers, the variance explained at the individual level is not particularly impressive; yet it was the variance explained by an analysis that employed most of the kinds of independent variable suggested by other researchers as affecting turnout. One possible reason for a level of variance explained that can only be described as moderate was already suggested in passing in Chapter 18: failure to vote is only partially the result of a considered decision, and is also very much subject to random factors. These might have to do with illness and other family crises on the one hand and politically peripheral factors on the other, such as vagaries of the weather and the differential appeal of TV programming. Nevertheless, the explanatory variables in Table 19.3 account for the quite different probability of voting among different categories of individuals (which can be modelled from the b coefficients shown there),[29] setting the parameters within which random factors may play a role. Our earlier search for residual country effects suggested that there is little room for improving our findings at the systemic level. Indeed, the small deviation of most countries from a level of turnout explicable on the basis of

---

latter an EC average is calculated of the strengths of the various effects in different countries. Thus the b of political interest is 0.107, to be increased by .043 (the b of the interaction) where no compulsory voting exists, and to be decreased by the same amount elsewhere. In the 10 countries without compulsory voting the effect of political interest is thus .150 (.107 + .043), while elsewhere it is .064 (.107 − .043). The average of these 14 values (10 times .150 plus 4 times .064) is .125, the exact magnitude of the logistic effect.

29 See footnote 23 for an explanation of how to do this. The units employed for measuring independent variables in this table are either the same as in Table 19.2 (see footnote 23), the same as that of the dependent variable (in the case of socio-demographic and campaign effects), or as described in footnotes 17 and 18.

their institutional and political context leaves little room for any other country-specific effects on turnout.[30] However, there is still the question whether important variables have been omitted at the individual level. In particular, if we omitted variables that tap habitual and myopic dispositions, such omissions might put our conclusions into question.

From one perspective it might seem that all of the variance unexplained so far should be considered available to be explained by effects as yet unspecified, but if chance really does play a large role in determining who will not vote when turnout is not perfect, then it may never be possible to identify these effects. Moreover, it is important to be aware that not all of the variance that is unexplained by regression analysis need be considered random or idiosyncratic. Regression analysis suffers from a number of drawbacks when employed with dummy dependent variables and among these deficiencies is an arbitrary limit on the amount of variance that can be explained; this is generally well short of 1.0, and results from distributional characteristics of the dependent and independent variables.[31] So the space left for additional factors to play any role is probably quite limited in practice. One indication of the limited possibilities of attributing unexplained variance to omitted variables can be found in the country chapters of Part II of this book. In the country-specific explanations of turnout presented there, electoral participation in previous elections (referred to as 'habitual voting') was used as a way to account for all kinds of omitted variables of lasting relevance.[32] The extra explanatory power derived from this indicator was negligible in most countries. The same conclusion is reached when we replicate our findings using data from a quite different election (see below).

Instrumental Motivation as the Dominant Force

Looking again at the variables included in Table 19.3, we may ask what they tell us about the kind of factors which induce citizens to use their vote rather than staying home. In terms of the traditional distinction between facilitative

30 Though when additional variance is injected into the country-level data by introducing changes in turnout from one election to the next, additional variables might still prove important.

31 The upper limit of 1.0 in variance explained could only be reached if all independent variables had the same distribution as each other and as the dependent variable. Calculating the attainable maximum is complex and was not attempted here; but as an example of the sort of ceiling found in practice, the attainable maximum for the variance in party choice explained by social class in Britain in 1964, using six independent dichotomies, was under 0.4 (Franklin, 1982). A different set of independent variables would of course yield a different attainable maximum.

32 The term 'habitual voting' was used by Schmitt and Mannheimer (1991a) because omitted variables indicated in this way would have to be ones that were not specific to any particular election.

and motivational factors only one of the independent variables is unambiguously facilitative in character: Sunday voting. Virtually all others are primarily motivational. This is even to a large extent true for the socio-demographic effect. As stated earlier, about half of the effects of this composite measure are those of education (the other half is largely due to the effects of age, which are no doubt mainly facilitative). We see education, contrary to Milbrath and Goel (1977), mainly as a motivational factor, enhancing participation by imbuing people with a participatory value system. The motivational character of political interest, campaign mobilization, party attachment and appeal of best choice is obvious. The systemic and contextual variables of proportionality and time until the next election in our view also represent motivational factors: their effects hinge on voters' desire for their vote to have political influence. Whenever circumstances diminish the possibilities of it doing so, the motivation to turn out diminishes accordingly. High proportionality, by ensuring that votes are more directly translated into parliamentary seats, enhances the predictable consequences of the voting act and helps create the circumstances for purposeful behavior. Time until the next election is, as explained earlier, the best proxy at hand for what one could see as the political importance of an election, also a factor whose effect can only be understood in motivational terms.

Having identified many of the explanatory factors from Table 19.3 as motivational does not yet tell us what kind of motivations we are dealing with. In view of the research questions elaborated in Chapter 3, the distinction between instrumental and affective motivations is of crucial importance, since the latter primarily reflect the desire to express with one's vote an identification with groups or organizations. If voting were largely a matter of affirming loyalties acquired in childhood, there would be little reason to hope for motivated voter responses to new opportunities to affect the course of political (and especially European) events. However, party attachment is the only factor in Table 19.3 which can easily be interpreted as affective rather than instrumental in nature. With the exception of compulsory voting, all other factors identified as motivational are instrumental in nature: they rest on the desire to contribute by one's vote to the chances of securing a desired political outcome.[33]

Adding up the importance of instrumental motivations (political interest, appeal of best choice, campaign mobilization, time until next election and proportionality) we find that their combined weight in the absence of compulsory voting is 0.637.[34] This is nearly double the 0.344 which can be ascribed

---

33   The status of compulsory voting is hard to define in terms of this distinction, since it is neither affective nor instrumental in terms of political motivation.

34   Campaign effects may, of course, include exhortations to voters to show their loyalty; but even if all of these effects were indeed of that nature (which is unlikely) this would only account

to facilitative factors and affective motivations in this situation, some of which (socio-demographic effects, for example) no doubt incorporate an instrumental component. In the presence of compulsory voting, the total weight of instrumental effects is reduced to 0.271; but the low extent of instrumental effects in this circumstance should not be taken to imply that 'on average' instrumental motivations fall somewhere between these limits. To the contrary, the importance of instrumental motivations is shown uniquely when they are not attenuated by compulsory voting (note that in the equation of Table 19.3 only instrumental motivations are affected by the presence or absence of this factor).

Modelling Turnout In Other Elections

Another way to assess the degree to which we have been successful in describing the factors that determine the level of turnout is to see how accurately coefficients derived from our study of the 1989 elections permit us to model behavior in other elections, particularly those of 1994. In 1989, a European election brought to the polls in above average numbers those who were well-educated, in the prime of life, interested in politics, attached to their parties, and touched by the campaign—especially if the election was an important one and the country was one where voting was relatively easy and where political forces appeared relatively responsive. Indeed, we have in Table 19.3 precise estimates of how much each of these factors contributed in 1989 to determining the likelihood that someone would vote. If these coefficients do as good a job of predicting which individuals cast their votes in 1994 as does a prediction based on 1994 coefficients, this will provide independent validation for our findings (and, therefore, also for the primacy of motivational factors).

The mechanics are straightforward enough. Having weighted our 1994 data in precisely the same manner as our 1989 data, and coded the variables in the same way, we first conduct a regression analysis which duplicates as nearly as possible on 1994 data the analysis reported in Table 19.3, and use the resulting coefficients to derive a prediction of whether people will report having voted.[35] We then make a similar prediction for each individual in the 1994 dataset by using the coefficients from Table 19.3 instead of the 1994 coefficients. The two predictions are virtually identical, correlating with each other at the level of 0.94; and this despite the fact that individual countries saw quite different levels of turnout in the two elections, as shown in Table 19.1.[36]

---

for a small part of the effects of such motivations.

35 In statistical parlance, this amounts to obtaining the y-hats from the regression analysis conducted on 1994 data.

36 In fact the two analyses for 1989 and 1994 cannot be precisely identical, since our 1994 data

A more interesting (though only partial) validation of the findings can be obtained by seeing to what extent we can correctly estimate overall turnout, country by country, in elections other than those conducted in 1989 on the basis of coefficients from the analysis of 1989 data reported in Table 19.2. In this exercise we do not have to restrict ourselves to using the 1994 elections for validation purposes. All the country-level independent variables are available for earlier European elections too, so we can validate our N=14 findings by estimating turnout in each country that elected representatives to the 1979–84 Parliament or the 1984–89 Parliament as well as in those that took part in the elections of 1994, yielding 40 cases for replication (14 political systems for two elections and 12 political systems for one election, since Spain and Portugal did not send representatives to the 1979–84 Parliament). When we employ the same procedure as used above, the two sets of country-level predictions correlate at the level of 0.99. Clearly it makes no difference whether we use coefficients from our analysis of 1989 or coefficients from all elections except for 1989: the predictions are effectively identical.

Assessment

In the European elections studied here, participation can be characterized with just three systemic variables, one contextual phenomenon, five individual-level variables and three interaction terms. Considering the plethora of variables suggested in past research, this winnowing down of the field of causal factors is quite remarkable, and is due primarily to the fact that we have employed multivariate analysis in the context of a causal framework that selected additional variables only if they added to the variance explained by others occurring earlier in causal sequence. No doubt the inclusion of intervening variables (such as those having to do with the mobilizing efforts of parties) would add to the richness of our understanding of causal processes, but only at the expense of parsimony. In summary, turnout is high in political systems where voting is compulsory or where votes are translated into seats with a high degree of proportionality,[37] though turnout can also be raised by other means. Sunday

---

has fewer variables upon which to base our prediction—only one indicator of political interest and no indicators of campaign effect. So the variance explained in 1994 is less than in 1989 (0.243 instead of 0.354). Nevertheless, the result of using 1989 coefficients for those variables that both years have in common hardly affects the variance we can explain (0.223 instead of 0.243). As fit-maximizing procedures such as regression unavoidably capitalize on chance, it is almost impossible to imagine improving on the success of this replication which is much the same as would have been obtained by randomly splitting a dataset consisting of 21,000 individuals in half and replicating the analysis on both halves.

37 Of course there is some question as to whether compulsory voting reflects existing norms as

voting helps, but more important is the question of whether political power is at stake (indicated in our data by the presence of concurrent national elections). Where effects that stem from systemic characteristics still leave room for individual differences, by far the most potent predictors of electoral participation are political interest, campaign mobilization, and the suitability of available political choices.

Taking these effects together, our initial expectations appear to have been confirmed. Leaving aside compulsory voting, turnout seems above all to be affected by voters' feelings that they can with their vote contribute to desired political outcomes. This requires on the one hand predictability of the political consequences of an election result, and on the other hand the availability of parties that voters value positively. Proportionality enhances the predictable consequences of a voter's choice, which are also more apparent as national elections approach. Where such contextual characteristics leave any room for individual variation, the quality of communications between parties and voters makes up the bulk of the difference. The three variables involved are political interest, campaign mobilization and the appeal of the most attractive party. So in countries where publicly induced motivation is lacking and electoral participation is consequently imperfect, private motivation (where present) fills the gap so that attentive publics vote while inattentive publics are less likely to do so. The fact that very much the same processes have been found to operate at the individual and systemic levels helps to validate the findings at both levels.

In reaching this conclusion we also contribute to the validation of findings from other studies that focussed particularly on institutional effects (especially Powell, 1980, 1986; and Jackman, 1987). What our own study adds is (1) evidence of the importance of political context; (2) evidence that systemic and contextual effects override the effects of individual characteristics so that the latter are only important where the former permit; and (3) a picture of how systemic and individual-level influences interact when both are present. But more important than any of these findings is our stress on the primacy of instrumental motivations, particularly those associated with the political importance of elections.

If we generalize these findings beyond the political systems included in our study, the implication is that low turnout countries probably suffer from a lack of immediately apparent consequences flowing from the voting act. In

---

well as causing such norms, but pseudo experiments conducted in the Netherlands (where compulsory voting was removed in 1970), Austria (where it was introduced in one province and abandoned in others during the 1980s) and elsewhere have allowed Hirczy (1992:164–193) to establish that the very presence of the law does make a difference of between 5 and 35 percent (depending on pre-existing turnout levels). Cf. Hirczy, 1994.

Switzerland, the government has for 40 years consisted of a coalition of the same parties in proportions that do not change with changing election outcomes, so the consequences of the voting act in federal elections are hard to discern, just as they are in European elections. In the US, the ability of candidates to actually deliver on campaign pledges is dependent on so many factors other than their own electoral success as to virtually cut the link between the vote and its potential consequences—a small step from elections to the European Parliament where there is no link to cut (see Chapter 21 for further discussion of the European implications of this point).

To the extent that we can account for virtually universal turnout within some political systems in terms of characteristics that might be achievable elsewhere, we demonstrate the potential potency of electoral engineering. While it is unlikely that the systemic and contextual characteristics we have isolated would be the only ones determining turnout in countries not included in our study, the very fact that country differences account for such large turnout differentials suggests that institutions and political context should be the first things to be addressed when attempting to manipulate electoral participation. Our findings also imply that the country level should be the one we first turn to when we try to understand the puzzle of declining turnout in Western countries—including many that are not members of the European Union.

In this context, our findings do suggest a change in the basis of European electoral participation that has almost certainly taken place during the past 30 years and which might well contribute towards resolving this puzzle in Europe and perhaps elsewhere. Powell's (1980) analysis found effects from group linkages that are absent in our 1989 findings. In *Electoral Change* (1992) Franklin and others showed that the strength of such linkages has indeed declined throughout Europe over the past 30 years. This change alone might account for much of the turnout decline that has taken place in Europe over that period, but exploring this possibility goes beyond the remit of the present chapter.

Returning to the research questions that this chapter set out to answer, our findings show that voters do go to the polls because of a desire for political influence. Moreover, there is no evidence of different processes at work in different countries. There is scant evidence of voters who go to the polls purely out of habit, loyalty or a sense of duty, despite the fact that variables that would have indicated such motivations were given every chance to show themselves.

On the basis of these findings we feel confident that many European voters would indeed adapt to changes in their political and social circumstances that served to increase the importance of European elections. A new party system, new issues that became politicized, above all a clear relevance of European elections for the allocation of power and thereby for the direction of European policy-making, would not leave them unmoved. Of course, we have yet to see whether European issues would have the same meaning in different countries of the European Union and whether party choice is as flexible in the light of changing circumstances as turnout appears to be (two topics for the next chapter); but, at least on the basis of evidence presented here, the situation looks promising. There is no reason to doubt that proper European elections, fought by European parties on European issues and deciding the allocation of power within the European Union would quickly turn the Dutch (and the French and the British, and all the rest) into Europeans. The reasons for the crisis of legitimacy described in Chapter 1 do not appear to lie in the fact that European voters are unthinking and unresponsive in the face of variations in (and changes to) the political context within which they find themselves at the time of an election. Nor do they appear to flow from myopic parochialism on the part of voters from particular countries. Quite to the contrary: the enormous differences in turnout that we observe from country to country within the European Union, and from election to election (including national elections) within those countries, seem to be almost entirely due to the operation of specific cues to which voters respond; and voters in all countries of the European Union respond to these cues in the same ways. Though our conclusions in this chapter relate only to turnout, evidence is mounting that, behind the particularities of politics in individual countries, European voters already constitute a single electorate, at least in terms of their responses to the forces we have been concerned with in this chapter.

CHAPTER 20

The Strategic Context:
Party Choice

Cees van der Eijk, Mark Franklin and Erik Oppenhuis

In Chapter 19 we saw that, to a large extent, differences in turnout from one country to the next can be explained by variations in systemic characteristics and in the political and social context of individual voters. This means that what is particular about countries are their systemic and contextual characteristics, not the way in which people react to these characteristics. Can the same be said about party choice? Do voters choose between parties on similar grounds in different countries, or have they been socialized into culture-specific modes of expressing their interests, hopes and fears at the ballot box? When it comes to party choice, are we dealing with one European electorate or many?

This way of phrasing the question emphasizes that the answers we seek would not invoke proper names, either of countries or of parties, as part of the explanation of variations in party choice. Just as we did in Chapter 19, we will here try to replace proper names of countries and of parties with meaningful variables that can be expected to account for differences in the manner in which voters make their choices when they go to the polls.

Another finding in Chapter 19 was that voters are sensitive to the context in which an election is conducted. We tentatively concluded from this that a stronger focus in European elections on 'visions of Europe' from which voters could choose would not leave them unmoved. In the present chapter we hope to confirm this finding by establishing that party choice is also sensitive to contextual and other factors that voters react to in an instrumental fashion.

Party Choice in European and National Elections

We start from the observation, derived from the country chapters of Part II, that in most countries of the European Union party choice in European elections is very similar to that in national elections. The frequency of what we have dubbed quasi-switching (voting for a different party in the European elections than one would have voted for in a national election held at the same time) is in most countries limited (see also Table 17.3). Where it does occur, it seems to flow largely from differences in the strategic situation: voters in different circumstances attach different weights to considerations relating to the allocation of government power and the expression of protest (see Chapter 18). So far, however, we have seen no indications that the substantive considerations that people bring to bear on their choice are different in European from those in national elections.[1]

From one perspective this might be disappointing. European elections are—apart from depressed turnout—not that special or different from national elections, and in particular do not have much European content (although this does not mean that they have no consequences for European or national politics—see chapters 17, 18 and 21). On the other hand this very similarity to national elections provides us with a golden opportunity to engage in a genuinely comparative analysis of party choice—the sort of analysis which usually is not possible on the basis of national election studies. Such studies generally fail to be strictly comparable for at least three reasons: (1) the timing of elections differs, both in terms of the place they occupy on the calendar as well as in terms of the political occurrences leading up to an election (fall of cabinet, scandal, etc.); (2) there are distinct national traditions of what is and what is not included in national election studies;[2] and (3) to the extent that national election studies do contain information about the same theoretical constructs, the way in which these are operationalized is often quite different.[3] Our study does not suffer from any of these problems.

In spite of the fact that the number of variables in our dataset is somewhat limited when compared to national election studies, those concepts that we have measured exist in very comparable terms. This provides us with a unique opportunity to comparatively evaluate a number of theories about party choice. This opportunity is important in two ways. In the first place it enables us to confront some major theoretical questions about the foundations of voting choice in a way that can be valuable to political scientists who have no interest in European elections per se. More importantly, it enables us to come to grips

---

1 These observations are even valid for Denmark, despite the support given in that country to the People's Movement Against the EC (see Chapter 6), since support for that party, which competes only in European elections, turned out to be very predictable in terms of national party choice.

2 Cf. Franklin, Mackie, Valen et al. (1992), who found only 8 social structural variables in common across studies conducted in 16 countries.'

3 Thus, Franklin, Mackie, Valen et al. (1992) found left/right self-placement to have been measured in all countries but not in comparable terms; and Budge, Crewe and Farlie (1976) found great difficulty in comparing even as narrow a concept as party identification across any large number of countries.

with the primary concern that we have in this chapter: of determining whether, when it comes to party choice, we are dealing with one European electorate or many.[4]

Traditional Approaches to the Comparative Analysis of Party Choice

Comparing party choice between different countries, each having its own particular party system, can be done in various ways. One common approach is to employ a typology of 'party families' which is supposedly valid across countries. Gallagher et al. (1992), for example, distinguish in the countries of Western Europe between christian democratic, social democratic, liberal, communist, extreme right, new left, green, secular conservative, agrarian, and 'other' parties. This results in one uniform system of party families replacing the particular party systems of each country. The next step is then to establish to what extent the choice of voters for one or another member of this set of party families can be explained by the same factors in different countries. Useful as such approaches are for generating ideas about what is common or different in various systems, they leave us with a problem caused by unavoidable arbitrariness in the classification of specific parties. First of all, which types are to be distinguished? Are, for instance, secular conservative parties (such as the British Conservatives) and christian democratic parties (such as the German CDU) to be distinguished as separate types or not?[5] Second, a typology assumes differences between types which exceeds those within types. It is not easy to assess the empirical validity of such assumptions, and expert judgements might vary. The problem is particularly acute when several competing parties from one country are classified as belonging to the same type (the Italian PSI and PSDI both as social democratic, the Dutch VVD and D66 both as liberal, etc.), or when markedly different parties from different countries are grouped together (e.g. the British Conservative Party, the Gaullist RPR, the Irish Fiánna Fáil, and the slightly Poujadist Progress Party in Denmark are all members of the secular conservative family in the classification of Gallagher et al.).

This is not the only typology employed by researchers. Dichotomous distinctions in particular have been a popular way of avoiding some of the

---

4 In fact, just as in Chapters 18 and 19, we distinguish 14 different electorates in the analyses that follow, since Northern Ireland has a party system quite different from that of mainland Britain and is consequently treated as a separate political system, as are Flanders and Wallonia for analogous reasons.

5 In this context, one may note that even if one were to employ the European parliamentary party groupings this would not solve the problem, as parties may, and occasionally do, change group membership. See, for example, the discussion in Chapter 5 on the membership of secular conservative parties in party groupings in the European Parliament.

above-mentioned problems. In this approach, one type of party (greens, communists, christian democrats, or extreme right, for example) is contrasted with all others in order to assess the cross-national (dis)similarities between their followers. Such a rationale underlies the well-known Alford-index (Alford, 1963) which purports to measure the extent of class voting by calculating the proportion voting for parties considered to be 'working-class parties' among working-class as compared to non-working-class respondents. Needless to say, dichotomous distinctions cannot escape the limitations inherent in typologizing. Dichotomies can even compound the problem by defining as one of the sides of the dichotomy a very heterogeneous 'type' defined only by being not part of the other type (green or social democrat, for example) which is supposed to be rather homogeneous. Such a strategy runs the risk of failing to reflect actual differences between parties merely because of the lack of homogeneity in one type.

A second kind of solution to the problem of comparing voter choice in different party systems starts out by identifying a single criterion on which to characterize individual political parties, leaving aside all other aspects which may characterize them. The most frequently used characteristic in this tradition has been the position of parties in a left/right spectrum (Inglehart and Klingemann, 1976; Castles and Mair, 1984; van der Eijk and Niemöller, 1987; Franklin, Mackie, Valen et al., 1992). This approach avoids unequal heterogeneity when the distinction is used in a dichotomous fashion (left versus right); when it is used as a scale it avoids the problem of arbitrary classification. These advantages, however, are only gained at the cost of assuming that all other characteristics of parties can be ignored as irrelevant to the explanation of party choice—an assumption which, notwithstanding the acknowledged importance of the left/right distinction in many political systems, is frequently contested.

A New Approach to the Comparative Analysis of Party Choice

The approach that we will employ in this chapter avoids both the problems of ad-hoc classification and of focussing on only a single characteristic to distinguish parties from one-another. It does so by employing as a dependent variable the electoral attractiveness of a political party (we will refer to this variable as party preference), a characteristic which can be measured for all parties, irrespective of their particular traits and irrespective of the political system in which they are located. As already explained in Chapter 3, respondents to the 1989 European Election Study were asked, "Please tell me for each of the following how probable it is that you will ever vote for this party in general elections?" after which they were presented with the names of virtually all parties in their political system.[6] These questions yielded a set of variables, one for each party contesting the European elections, measuring on a scale of 1 to 10 the likelihood that the respondent would vote for the party concerned.

The open-ended reference to "ever" in the question is intended to function only as a projective device which encourages respondents to express the extent of their current preference for each party, without being constrained by the restrictions of the ballot which in most countries allows only a single party to be chosen (i.e., which allows only a so-called ipsative expression of preference).[7] Because respondents were asked to evaluate all parties, even those they had not supported in the European elections, we have a score from each respondent for virtually every party that contested the elections in that respondent's country.

In the analyses to be conducted in this chapter this measure of party preference is the phenomenon to be explained, the dependent variable. Such a dependent variable does require the use of an innovative research strategy which will be described in detail below; but at this point it is mainly important to note that its use avoids the problems enumerated earlier. By employing this variable we avoid the need to arbitrarily classify parties in one or another category of a typology, or to focus on any specific characteristic of parties to the exclusion of others. Two additional advantages should also be mentioned. First of all, this variable avoids a problem in the analysis of actual party choice which arises from the (sometimes exceedingly) small numbers of respondents who voted for small parties, as all respondents are asked these questions for all parties in their system. Second, and substantively much more importantly, these variables allow more valid causal propositions than can be made from analyzing actual party choice. Explanatory statements of party choice imply intra-individual comparison of parties which, in multi-party systems, cannot be observed when using actual party choice. A theory that states, for example, that post-materialism is an important determinant of party choice implies that voters evaluate all parties on the basis of such value

---

6 "All" parties has to be understood as all parties which were deemed sufficiently important to be included in the question. In general this included all parties represented in the (national) parliaments, as well as those which, on the basis of contextual knowledge (such as opinion polls) could have been expected to gain such representation in a national election held on the same day. The number of parties about which this question (sometimes referred to as the 'probability to vote' question) was asked ranged from a low of 5 in Germany to a high of 10 in France, Italy and Portugal. The complete list of 105 parties covered by this set of questions is given in Appendix B.

7 Some electoral systems allow the expression of multiple preferences. One can think of STV, the German dual ballot system, and the Luxembourg system of multiple votes with panachage. As the analysis in this chapter will show, however, the probability to vote questions pose no special problems in these cases. To say whether one would ever vote for a party does not require the respondent to distinguish between the various methods by which he or she might do this.

orientations. The attribution of actual party choice to this specific factor can only be supported by evidence showing that the second-best party in this respect is also the respondent's second choice, that the party which is evaluated as worst is the last one to be chosen. This is impossible to assess empirically when analyzing actual choice, since that relates only to a voter's first choice.[8] From the responses to the 'probability to vote' questions, however, we can immediately derive a person's second, third and following choices. Consequently, our use of responses to 'probability to vote' questions gives a much firmer empirical basis to explanatory propositions about determinants of party preference than actual party choice does.

A few objections to this approach might be raised. First of all, the probability to vote question which we used asked about national elections, even though it was posed in the context of a European election study. This is not much of a problem however. Assessing national vote intention at the time of a European election rather than at the time of a national election no doubt reduces election-specific national forces that might color the vote in particular countries at particular times; but this might be an advantage when our objective is to discover what determines national vote choice in general terms.[9] A more serious objection could be that we substitute the explanation of party preference (which may be seen as electoral attractiveness of parties) for what was originally to be explained, actual party choice. This objection would, however, only be valid if the party that respondents actually voted for were often different from the one to which they gave the highest score. In fact our whole approach rests on the assumption that respondents do vote for the party to which they give the highest probability to vote score. Only on this basis can we confidently interpret the second-highest score as a voter's second choice, and so on.

Table 20.1 shows that our assumption is well-founded by indicating the extent to which actual party choice can be deduced from the probability to vote variables. As can readily be seen, except in Flanders the transformation

---

8 Tillie (1995) demonstrates that it is indeed quite possible to commit causal mis-attributions if only actual party choice is available. Of course, in strict two-party or two-candidate contests this argument does not hold, because then, but only then, the complete rank order of preferences is known by knowing which is first.

9 In the first wave of the European Election Study, we asked the same set of probability to vote questions, but specifically focussing on European elections. As our study is not a panel study, the data from the various waves cannot be combined at the level of the individual respondent and therefore we limit ourselves in this book to the analysis of the data from the third wave, which was conducted immediately after the elections of June 1989. A large number of analyses have, however, been performed to assess whether responses to these questions are different or have to be interpreted differently when asked about European rather than about (hypothetical) national elections. The findings from these analyses are unequivocally negative.

Table 20.1 Percentage Voters Voting for the Party with the Highest Probability to Vote

	Fla	Wal	Den	Fra	Ger	Bri	Gre	Ire	Ita	Lux	NIr	Net	Por	Spa
Percentage	82.0	92.1	97.2	86.8	94.1	92.8	96.1	92.2	91.3	87.7	88.3	96.1	89.8	91.2
n[a]	422	278	744	725	891	720	714	704	729	235	202	789	598	555
Number of Parties[b]	5	6	7	10	5	6	6	7	10	7	9	9	10	8

a The percentages are based on voters who said that in a national election they would vote for a party included among the probability to vote questions.
b N of parties for which the 'probability to vote' question was asked.

gives percentages of 86 percent or more (the average for Belgium as a whole is 86.3 per cent), with an average of 91.2 percent for all countries taken together. These party preference scores are indeed very accurate reflections of actual vote intentions. The consequence is that by analyzing the former we can arrive at valid conclusions about the latter.[10]

In the sections that follow we will first introduce our independent variables and the design of the analyses to be conducted. Next we will report these analyses for each country separately. Finally we will combine the results of these country-specific analyses to permit a cross-national investigation of the main questions facing us in this chapter, namely whether we are dealing with one European electorate or many and to what extent European voters seem able to adapt to changes in political context.

Theories of Party Choice: The Selection of Explanatory Variables

A relatively small number of different mechanisms have been proposed as underlying the choice between parties. Our data enable us to evaluate a number of the most widely espoused of these—including social cleavage theory, new politics theories, ideological voting, issue voting, government evaluations, EC/EU evaluations—as follows.

---

10 Many other analyses can be performed to demonstrate that the replacement of actual party choice with this specific set of preference scores for each of the parties is justified. The most important of these is an unfolding analysis which demonstrates that the scores on the probability to vote questions can be understood to emanate from the same latent factors for all parties; hence that the origins of this score for the party which one actually voted for are the same as for all other parties. Such validating analyses have been reported in great detail by Tillie (1995).

Social Cleavage Theory

The idea that membership in groups defined by social cleavages underlies voting choice is a venerable one, dating back to the earliest academic voting studies (Lazarsfeld, Berelson and Gaudet, 1944; Berelson, Lazarsfeld and McPhee, 1954). The definitive theoretical elaboration of how such group memberships came to underlie party choice in Europe was made by Lipset and Rokkan in their seminal 'Cleavage Structures, Party Systems and Voter Alignments' (1967) in which the origins of European political parties were traced to the lines of social cleavage that underlay political divisions at the time of the introduction of mass suffrage. Lipset and Rokkan also proposed that, at the time at which they were writing, party systems were essentially 'frozen' in the mold of those (often by then vestigial) social divisions. This 'freezing hypothesis' as it has come to be called was confirmed by Rose and Urwin's (1970) study of the 22 countries that have since become known as the 'Rose-Urwin Universe'. Since the mid-1960s it has become clear that social divisions have weakened and declined in their influence on party choice throughout Western Europe and, indeed, beyond (Dalton, Flanagan and Beck, 1984; Franklin et al., 1992); but though the influence of social divisions has declined almost everywhere, that decline has nowhere progressed so far as to render these cleavages entirely irrelevant (Franklin et al., 1992: Chapter 19). The most important cleavages in European systems are generally considered to be religion and class. In our data, these two cleavages are represented by measures of respondent's occupation, education and unionization (as alternative measures of class location); and of church attendance and denomination (as alternative measures of religion).

New Politics Theories

The weakening of traditional social cleavages in determining partisanship has opened the question of whether these cleavages are in the process of being replaced by new ones. Particularly with the emergence of 'new' political parties in many countries, it has become fashionable to propose that these parties must receive support from 'new' social movements defined by some 'new' social cleavage, although there is considerable disagreement about the nature of this supposed cleavage (Inglehart, 1971, 1977, 1984; Offe, 1984, 1985; Cotgrove and Duff, 1980; Cotgrove, 1982; Kitschelt, 1988; Müller-Rommel, 1989; Rüdig, 1990; Betz 1990; Poguntke, 1992). By far the most frequently suggested candidate for new cleavage status is the division originally proposed by Ronald Inglehart between voters whose values were primarily materialist and those whose values he saw as 'postmaterialist', centering upon quality of life and self-actualization rather than upon material well-being. Some of those proposing the existence of new political values and movements do not link these primarily to cleavages which demarcate social groups but rather to new issues that have arisen in recent years to challenge the primacy of the issues that were linked to traditional social cleavages (Dalton, 1984; Bürklin, 1987; Rüdig, 1990). Irrespective of which of these two views is more appropriate, both use similar distinctions in people's value orientations to make their point, and these values are commonly indicated by the materialism/post-materialism distinction. Although the utility of such distinctions as an explanation for party choice has been questioned by many scholars including ourselves (van der Eijk, Franklin, Mackie and Valen, 1992; see also Clarke and Dutt, 1991), it nevertheless remains a concept that is so widely employed by political scientists that we could hardly ignore it as long as we have the means to measure it. Our data contains the standard Inglehart battery of questions that supposedly classify respondents into materialist, mixed and postmaterialist categories.

Ideological Voting

Social cleavages and (by some accounts) new political movements are supposed to condition voting choice by calling into play the loyalties towards 'in-groups' that are effectively part of childhood socialization. Group members are assumed to have interests in common that 'go without saying', so that an electoral victory by the group can be relied upon to bring political outcomes that further the interests of group members. What those interests might be does not have to be explicitly specified.

In contrast to these theories of voting choice based on group loyalties, so-called 'rational choice' theories propose a political world in which voters choose among candidates or parties on the basis of campaign promises and other signals that explicitly relate to (expected) policy outcomes and to the preferences of voters as between alternative packages of policy outcomes. Alternative sets of policy proposals (put forward by different candidates or parties) are often contrasted along more general dimensions, sometimes referred to as ideological in nature, sometimes as 'super issues' (Inglehart, 1984) or political schema (Conover and Feldman, 1984; Kerlinger, 1984). The assumption is that voters are able to characterize not only parties or candidates in such terms, but themselves as well. The choice between parties can then be viewed in terms of a comparison by each voter of the parties in the light of his or her own position. Exactly how this comparison is made is a matter of debate among theorists (Downs, 1957; van der Eijk and Niemöller, 1983, 1987; Fuchs and Klingemann, 1989; MacDonald et al. 1991). Although such a theory can be applied in terms of various ideological dimensions, the most promising one is the left/right spectrum.

Although Downs (1957) originally intended this type of rational choice theory to apply primarily to the American situation of two competing political parties, it can be generalized to handle multiple parties in two ways. When several parties propose different packages of policies, the differences between the parties can often be adequately represented by placing them at different points between far left and far right. Sometimes a second or even third dimension may be deemed necessary in order to adequately represent the differences between parties, but in the European context it has generally been asserted that a single left/right dimension is the only ideological one that is required (Barnes and Kaase, 1979; van der Eijk and Niemöller, 1983; MacDonald et al., 1991). In the questionnaires that were employed in the 1989 European Election Study, voters were asked to place both themselves and the parties of their political system on a left/right scale. This information will be used to generate appropriate independent variables.

Issue Voting

Theories of ideological voting are related to those of issue voting. The latter differ from ideological theories only in failing to take the step from policy proposals to ideological differences. Rather than comparing one's own position to that of parties in terms of ideology, one does so for positions defined in terms of specific issues. Most surveys show clear correlations between issue preferences and evaluations of parties' issue positions on the one hand and the actual choice of voters on the other. Some analysts have concluded from this that electorates do use issues as criteria for choice. Others argue, however, that the observed relationship can largely be explained by other factors which influence both choice and issue preferences (relevant summaries of the debate can be found in Converse, 1975; Smith, 1989; Dalton and Wattenberg, 1993; see also Kuechler, 1991). Theoretically, the debate centers on the level of voters' information and sophistication and on the integration ('constraint') of their opinions and preferences. Empirically, it hinges not so much on bivariate correlations, but on causal interpretations of such correlations when other variables are also taken into account.

In this chapter we will not engage in explicit causal analysis, yet we will assess the strength of a number of issue concerns from both multivariate and bivariate perspectives. From our data we use voters' views on the salience of 12 issues; that is, their own views on how important or unimportant these issues were in their choice between parties. The set of 12 contains four general issues which were politically relevant in all member countries of the Community: unemployment, stable prices, arms limitations and environmental protection. An additional four were issues common to all countries, but specifically geared to the EC/EU context: political unification of the Community, agricultural surpluses, Turkish membership in the EU, and the creation of the Single European Market. Finally, four issues were country-specific ones chosen on the basis of advice from country experts, representing the most important matters of political debate in each country at the time of the election. In a later section of this chapter we will describe how we arrive at a measure of 'issue voting' from the indicators which we have at our disposal.

Government Performance

To some extent, issue preferences can be encapsulated in (or substituted by) the evaluation of government performance. Elections can be used by voters to register their approval of the performance of their government, or their lack of approval for its failures. When satisfied, they may be expected to support the parties in government; when not, they vote for the opposition. Such a simple scheme is, of course, most applicable in countries where single-party government is the norm. In systems characterized by coalition government the basic rationale of expressing by one's vote an evaluation of the performance of the government is also applicable, although the form it takes may be more difficult to assess. One could argue that, because no governmental power is at stake in European elections, it does not make sense to explain party choice on the basis of evaluations of government performance. Yet, on the other hand, the view of European elections as second-order national elections (see Chapter 2 of this book) suggests to the contrary that they would be ideal vehicles for the expression of such evaluations. To what extent these evaluations are related to party choice can be established by means of respondents answers to the question, "Do you approve or disapprove of the (national) government's record to date." Just as in the case of issue voting, we will focus on the explanatory power of this consideration without engaging in any explicit causal analysis to sort out whether evaluations of government performance cause party choice or reflect it.

Evaluations of the European Community

Although from the voter's perspective no government power is at stake in European elections, the very fact that they took place may have offered voters an opportunity to express in their party choice their approval or disapproval of the way in which the Community has developed. Elsewhere (van der Eijk and Franklin, 1991) we have shown that in many countries of the Community the major political parties differ little from one another in terms of the positions they take regarding the future course of European integration, so that voters have little opportunity to base their choice on such considerations. To the extent that real differences do exist between parties, we found that on average voters' positions in regard to European integration do correlate with those of the parties they support. In this chapter we will see whether this relation still exists when the analysis is performed on the level of individual voters rather than in aggregate terms. The relevant measure in our data is the score given by respondents on a uni-dimensional scale registering approval for the current extent of European integration (three items) and for further integration (one item).[11]

Other Theories

It is important to note that the perspectives outlined above are only a subset of those that have been proposed in the literature to explain voting choice. The most prominent theory which will not be represented in our analyses in this chapter is party identification theory (Campbell et al., 1960), which posits that voters support the party with which they most closely identify. This theory was developed primarily to explain voting choice in the United States, and considerable difficulty has been found in applying it to the European context (Budge, Crewe and Farlie, 1976; Thomassen, 1976; van der Eijk and Niemöller, 1983; Heath and MacDonald, 1988; Franklin, 1991). Even in the United States questions have been raised about the theory since the late 1970s (Achen, 1979; Page and Jones, 1979; Fiorina, 1981; Franklin, 1984; Asher, 1988; Dalton and Wattenberg, 1993). Nevertheless, the concept is still widely employed as a shorthand predictor of voting choice (Schmitt and Holmberg, 1995) or as a reference point in a causal model that incorporates reciprocal effects on the vote (Page and Jones, 1979; Franklin, 1985). The current debates over party identification theory hinge, even more than those over other perspectives, on the merits of different causal models, some of which require panel data (which our study does not provide) and which are anyway beyond the level of complexity that we can address in the present chapter. The simple finding that claimed identification with a party adds to the statistical explanation of voting for that party would contribute little to the debate on party identification theory, and would help us equally little in answering what is the main research question before us in this chapter: whether voters in different countries express their substantive interests, hopes and fears at the ballot box in similar ways.

---

11 Appendix B describes the separate items and the construction of the index.

Design of the Analyses

The Dependent Variable

As indicated above, the dependent variable for our analyses is the electoral preference of voters for each of the political parties in their country, which is expressed in a score ranging from 1 (no likelihood of supporting the party) to 10 (strong likelihood). These preferences would normally be represented in a data matrix as different variables, one for each party, which would not readily lend themselves to being analyzed simultaneously. Yet it is not sufficient to analyze these variables one by one. It would not do conceptually, because what we are looking for are determinants of party preference in general rather than a specific model for one party or another. It would also not do for another reason: we mentioned earlier that one of the major advantages of the use of these non-ipsative party preferences is that they bring into sight inter-party variation in the attractiveness of parties needed for valid explanatory statements about the nature of party choice. Analyzing these preferences one by one, however, would lose this (individual-level) inter-party variation, as such a design focusses exclusively on the variation between individuals (intra-party variation). An adequate analysis of these scores requires a research design in which inter- and intra-party variance is accounted for simultaneously. This can be realized by rearranging the original data into a so-called stacked form (Brown and Halaby, 1982; Stimson, 1985)—viewing each preference score given by a voter as a separate 'case' to be explained. In this way, each respondent is represented by a number of 'cases' in the stacked dataset, as many as the number of parties for which he or she gave a preference score.

The procedure is illustrated by Figure 20.1. The stacked dataset can be analyzed in the same way as any ('normal') rectangular data matrix. The dependent variable is the preference score for each political party in turn; appropriate identifiers allow characteristics of individual respondents and parties to be added as independent variables. Such a stacked data matrix allows us to examine the dependent variable using familiar and straightforward methods of analysis, such as regression.

Using the form of a stacked data matrix makes it possible to transcend insights bound to particular parties by replacing proper names of parties by theoretically and empirically meaningful variables which characterize them. Thus we might include typological descriptors (such as liberal or not) as independent variables in order to assess whether party choice for such parties was distinctive—enabling us to investigate what had to be assumed in the case of some alternative approaches (see above). To the extent that we can

Figure 20.1 The Construction of a 'Stacked' Data Set

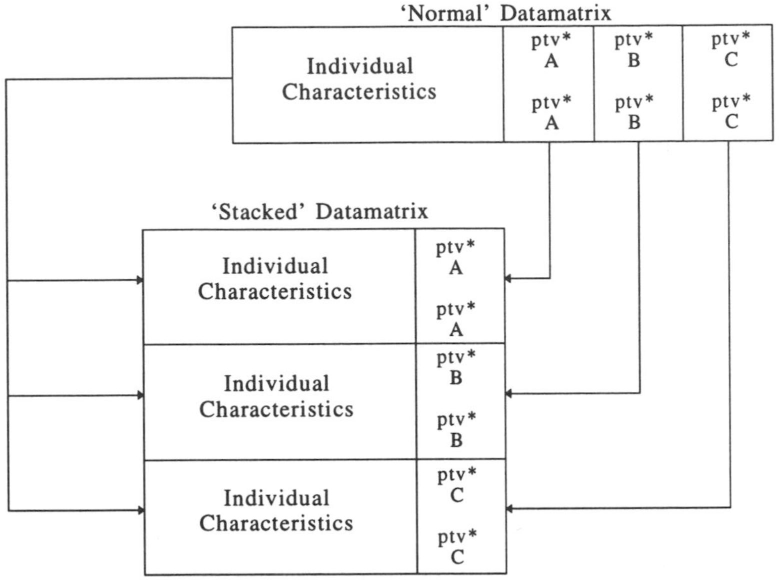

'Normal' Datamatrix

Individual Characteristics	ptv* A	ptv* B	ptv* C
	ptv* A	ptv* B	ptv* C

'Stacked' Datamatrix

Individual Characteristics	ptv* A
	ptv* A
Individual Characteristics	ptv* B
	ptv* B
Individual Characteristics	ptv* C
	ptv* C

adequately specify the distinctive nature of different parties we arrive at more general knowledge about the determinants of party preference than traditional analysis designs permit.

This strategy can also be extended to encompass different political systems: we just combine the stacked datasets from various countries into one single data matrix, in which one single variable represents party preference for all respondents over all parties in all countries.[12] Just as we did in Chapters 18 and 19, we will, where possible, replace proper names of countries by variables which characterize them. In this way we can address the major questions of this chapter: whether we are dealing with many different electorates, or just one. To the extent that a single European electorate exists, there will be no need to enter country names as variables in the explanation of party preference.

---

12 Obviously, these ways of arranging a data matrix yield one which contains a very large number of 'cases': the sum over all countries of the number of respondents in each country times the number of parties for which the probability to vote question was asked. After deleting missing data (but before weighting—see below), this dataset contains more than 51,000 'cases'.

As before, we will use (multiple) regression methods to determine the effects of explanatory variables on these preference scores.[13] Careful analysis of residuals will enable us to assess the need for interaction effects or for the introduction of additional explanatory variables. But before the analyses can be performed, we first have to decide how to represent the independent variables in the regressions.

The Independent Variables

We have already enumerated the theories of party choice that can be included in our analyses. These are: social cleavages (class and religion), the 'new politics' dimension (represented by materialist/postmaterialist orientations), left/right ideology, the relative salience of 12 issues, evaluation of government performance, and approval of European integration. There are two ways in which independent variables can be constructed to represent these theories. The first applies only to left/right ideological orientation and will be discussed first, the other method applies to all other theories and will be discussed next.

In our post-election survey we asked respondents to indicate, on a scale from 1 (left) to 10 (right) where they perceived each of the various parties in their political system to be located, as well as their own most preferred position on this dimension. This information allows, for each combination of respondent and party (i.e., each 'case' in the stacked dataset), a measure to be constructed which indicates how suited that party is to the ideological orientation of that respondent. The literature suggests two different ways to do this: the distance approach and the directional approach. The first belongs to the class of Downsean models of party choice. Parties and voters are assumed to occupy positions in a (generally one-dimensional) space, and the preference of voters for parties is postulated to be a function of proximity: the smaller the distance, the larger the preference. In terms of ipsative party choice this results in Downs' well-known smallest-distance hypothesis: voters vote for the party which is nearest to their own location. In non-ipsative situations such as this one, distance is the factor that explains preference.

The directional approach, pioneered by Rabinowitz and MacDonald (1989) suggests that positions of parties on a continuum (such as the left/right one) are to be interpreted as intensities of political convictions which can be characterized by either pole, and where the midpoint of the scale indicates no preference for either pole. The substantive nature of beliefs held by, for

---

13   In contrast to Chapter 19, there will be no need to employ logistic regression in tandem with OLS regression, since our dependent variable is not a dichotomy and nor do we expect threshold and ceiling effects in the case of variables that are not percentages of the same total.

instance, center-left and more outspokenly left people is not different, but the intensity with which they hold these opinions is. According to this approach, that party is best suited for a voter which yields the highest product of individual and party deviation from the neutral middle point of the scale.[14] We have operationalized ideological factors in both ways (left/right distance and left/right directional fit). For both we expect that, to the extent that these ideological orientations are relevant in the explanation of party preference, clear correlations will be found with party preference. As we will report below, they are; but in multivariate analyses we present only the results of the distance measure as it yields in all political systems of the European Union more explanatory power than the directional measure.[15]

The procedure applied to left/right orientations cannot be used in the same way for the other independent variables. The reason for this is that we cannot unequivocally characterize the various parties in a political system in terms of these factors. As an example, we may consider religion. A similar procedure as used for left/right requires us to indicate for each voter in turn whether each of the parties is more or less suitable for them, supposing that their own religious beliefs were the only factor determining their preference for parties. In some countries this may be possible (provided there is sufficient contextual information—see for example van der Eijk, Niemöller and Tillie, 1986; Tillie, 1995). In general, however, it will not be fruitful to follow this path, for reasons aptly summarized by Gallagher et al. (1992:104) who state that:

---

14 The directional model is particularly suited for multidimensional situations, in which positions of both individuals and parties on a number of different dimensions (for example issue-dimensions) are to be combined into a single measure of 'fit' between voters and party positions. We cannot apply the model in this fashion, as our data contain voters' perceptions of party positions only for the left/right continuum. Yet the directional approach has been suggested as a general alternative to distance models, and can therefore also be applied in one-dimensional situations.

15 The difference in R2 between equivalent models using the distance or the directional operationalization of left/right ideology ranges in our 14 political systems from 0.01 to 0.17, always in favor of the distance measure. The average difference is 0.09. Readers familiar with the directional model might remark that this model has not been implemented adequately as our analyses do not include a 'penalty' for extreme parties which are beyond a postulated region of acceptability (Rabinowitz and Macdonald, 1989:109–110). Without a clear theoretical definition of the location of this borderline of acceptability (which has so far not been provided in the literature), this element cannot be included other than by data fitting, which seems to us an inappropriate way to proceed. In any case, this chapter is not meant to provide either an elaborate discussion of the relative merits of these two approaches, nor to present a critical empirical test between them. We will present our views on this matter elsewhere. Suffice it to note, in the present context, that results presented below are hardly affected by substituting a directional measure for the distance measure which we use, except for a drop in explained variance of, on average, 0.09 per country.

... religious differences exert a much more pervasive impact than the presence of explicitly religious parties might indicate. Religious differences may also help to determine party choice in situations where the parties concerned are all ostensibly secular.

The exact manner in which religious differences between people are related to their choice of parties is, of course, a system-specific phenomenon which can only be understood in the light of the specific history of cleavages, party formation and politicization of issues related to religion in a particular country. What we are interested in, however, is not this specific history but rather the extent to which the preference of a voter for a specific party can be understood from the manner in which in their country religion and political choice have historically become intertwined. In order to capture this, we use a procedure which is similar to the one used to indicate the effects of socio-demographic variables on turnout in Chapter 19. For each of the parties separately (and hence for each of the countries separately) we conducted a regression analysis in which the preference score for that party was estimated from each voter's religious denomination and frequency of church attendance. The results indicate to what extent, in that specific country and for that specific party, religious differences between people determine their preference for that party. The effects of religion on preference are encapsulated in the predictions made for each respondent, which in statistical parlance are referred to as the y-hats ($\hat{y}$).

These y-hats are saved and added to the stacked dataset, yielding a variable which is comparable for all parties (and countries) and which can be referred to as the 'predicted religious effect', or, more briefly, 'religion'.[16]

The other independent variables mentioned earlier were operationalized by means of the same procedure. This yields cross-party (and cross-nationally) comparable measures of the effects on party preference of class, issues, (evaluation of) government performance, and approval of European integration (also referred to as 'EC-approval'). Additional independent variables will be introduced in the context of our multivariate analyses (see below).

---

16 The actual variable which is added to the stacked dataset is the deviation of the y-hats from their mean. This still encapsulates the variance in party preference caused by religious differences but prevents the average of these y-hats from being subsumed in this variable, an outcome to be avoided because in a stacked dataset these averages cause differences which cannot be attributed to religion and which would disturb subsequent analyses. It might be thought that this procedure (of centering), by introducing country-specific corrections to independent variables, might remove in later analyses the country-specific differences whose detection is one of our objectives (see Chapter 3, research question 6). However, later in this chapter we will elaborate a procedure involving interactions of these centered y-hats with country dummies that would have the effect of restoring any such differences.

Missing Data and Weighting

In the analyses reported below we have chosen to restrict ourselves to a specific group of cases characterized by the near-absence of missing data on relevant variables. We have done this in order to avoid changes in estimated coefficients (and hence the possibility of incompatibilities) when variables are added or deleted from a multivariate analysis. The following variables had to have valid values in order for the respective cases to be included in the analyses: party choice in a general election, probability to vote scores, and left/right self-placement. From our analysis we also excluded a number of very small parties which were not separately identified among the probability to vote questions. Each analysis conducted on this subset of respondents was repeated for all of those having valid data for the specific analysis concerned, and in no case were any significant differences found.

When analyzing the data for the various political systems separately we weighted them (just as we did elsewhere in this book) in such a way as to reflect the results of the European elections themselves (see Appendix B). In the Euro-wide analysis, these weights were multiplied by a constant which brings down the effective number of cases in the entire dataset to approximately 10,000 in order to reflect the real number of interviews obtained.

Explaining Preference for Parties

Table 20.2 displays the extent of variance in party preference (country-by-country and on average over the EC as a whole) that can be explained by the various theories outlined earlier, taken one at a time. On average the two ideological theories do best, followed by issue voting. All of these theories yield predictors that explain 12 percent or more, on average, of the variance in party choice, country by country, and no less than 6 percent in any country. Government approval follows closely, with 10 percent of variance explained on average, but with as little as 3 to 4 percent of variance explained in four countries. Other theories explain 6 percent or less on average, with negligible effects in one or more countries.

Except in Flanders, Britain and Northern Ireland, ideological proximity is the best predictor of party choice, performing nearly twice as well on average as any other predictor. In Flanders the best predictor is issue voting; in Britain it is government approval. Only in Northern Ireland is the best predictor a social cleavage: there, religious affiliation is among the highest coefficients in the table, and ideological proximity is not even the second most powerful predictor (as it is in Britain and Flanders). With few exceptions, the powerful predictors are powerful in all EC countries, and the weak predictors are weak

Table 20.2 Correlates of Party Preference, by Country (Coefficients are Variance Explained)

	Distance from Party on Left/Right Scale	Direction of Party on Left/Right Scale	Class	EC Approval	Government Approval	Issues	Postmaterialism	Religion
Den	0.31	0.25	0.08	0.14	0.14	0.18	0.02	0.03
Fla	0.09	0.05	0.06	0.00	0.04	0.15	0.01	0.06
Fra	0.32	0.21	0.04	0.02	0.08	0.09	0.02	0.06
Ger	0.31	0.14	0.04	0.01	0.13	0.09	0.05	0.06
GBr	0.19	0.16	0.04	0.00	0.24	0.10	0.05	0.02
Gre	0.34	0.17	0.04	0.06	0.25	0.14	0.03	0.02
Ire	0.17	0.12	0.05	0.02	0.08	0.07	0.01	0.03
Ita	0.19	0.12	0.03	0.00	0.03	0.06	0.02	0.08
Lux	0.19	0.07	0.04	0.01	0.03	0.18	0.05	0.03
NIr	0.15	0.14	0.05	0.08	0.06	0.20	0.03	0.28
Net	0.21	0.13	0.02	0.01	0.12	0.10	0.02	0.07
Por	0.22	0.07	0.03	0.04	0.10	0.09	0.02	0.03
Spa	0.23	0.15	0.06	0.03	0.13	0.10	0.03	0.06
Wal	0.19	0.10	0.10	0.01	0.04	0.18	0.02	0.05
EC	0.22	0.13	0.05	0.03	0.10	0.12	0.03	0.06

everywhere. The exceptions are unsurprising in the light of the country chapters. In addition to the three anomalies already mentioned, Denmark sees strong effects of EC approval and Greece sees strong effects of government approval.

As mentioned earlier in this chapter, these findings are important in two ways. They tell us something about how party preferences are grounded in the countries of the European Union, and also about the extent of similarity between these countries. Evidently, Downsean smallest distance theory works well in all countries. The directional variant does not work nearly as well,[17] though it still works better than other theories, on average. Of the other theories, the most helpful are issue voting and government approval. These are like the ideological theories in linking voting choice to policy outcomes rather than to

---

17 The reader should bear in mind the caveat mentioned earlier about our inability to specify boundaries of acceptability which might have made this variant perform better.

group loyalties, and can be seen as different ways of operationalizing the rational choice approach to electoral behavior. Only in a single country—Northern Ireland—do we see the dominance of any other basis for voting choice.

Though these implications of our findings are quite suggestive, they cannot be definitive. Our measures and procedures are not designed to establish which theoretical approach is absolutely best at explaining voting choice. Moreover, as they stand, these findings cannot even shed much light on the concern which they are primarily intended to illuminate. For while they indicate that there are remarkable similarities between countries of the European Union in the manner in which voters make their decisions as to which party to support, there are also significant differences between countries. Flanders, Britain, Denmark, Greece and Northern Ireland all stand out quite distinctly in one way or another; and close inspection of Table 20.2 will show other countries standing out in other respects, even if less markedly. How far does a country have to deviate in order for us to conclude that we are not dealing with a single basis for electoral choice in all countries? There is no baseline inherent in these bivariate comparisons that would enable us to settle this question. In order to determine whether the 1989 European elections were contested among one electorate or many, we have to adopt a different approach.

A Multivariate View of Party Preference

The bivariate approach needed in order to do justice to individual theories of voting choice provides us with no means to tell whether countries deviate significantly from one another in the manner in which these choices are made. To make progress with this question we need to adopt a variant of the procedure we employed in Chapter 19 when our attention was focussed on turnout. There it made sense to look at effects on the dependent variable of many characteristics taken together, and in that context we were able to devise measures of the extent to which individual countries deviated from the general pattern. In the present chapter we can do the same and employ the technique introduced in Chapter 19 to see whether there are differences between countries that cannot be accounted for by any of the theories.

Bringing the various measures together into a single model has a different theoretical status in this chapter than it had in Chapter 19 because most of the theories tested in Table 20.2 were intended by their authors as alternatives for each other rather than as complementary. However, to the extent that each of them contributes significantly to a total explanation of voting choice, a multivariate approach ensures that they are evaluated in the context of properly specified models with appropriate controls for contaminating influences. When we take all the theories together as defining an equation that can be employed in predicting party preference, we are effectively assuming that a proper causal structure could be specified in which to embed each theory. In this book we do not actually specify these causal structures—any specific structure would have to be justified with reference to other possible structures, a task beyond the scope of a single chapter (see Oppenhuis, 1995, for one attempt at defining and testing an appropriate causal structure). Instead, we leave unspecified how the elements of these various theories might be linked causally.

The coefficients that we estimate by means of multiple regression represent the direct causal effects of each independent variable on party preference when controlling for the impact of all other independent variables. Depending upon our ideas about the causal ordering of the elements of these various theories, we may suspect that their total effects will sometimes be larger than the coefficients that we estimate, since part of these total effects may operate via other variables. The maximum to which this could occur can be assessed from the zero-order correlation of the dependent with the respective independent variable, which is the same as the beta that would be obtained if no other variables were included in the regression to absorb part of its total causal effect. We will include this information in our tables.

As already stated, many of the controls we bring to bear are inherent in the competing theories. However, our research design makes it possible for us to bring to bear additional factors which conventional approaches of necessity ignore. How attractive a party is to voters may be affected by features which are more or less the same for all (or most) voters. Consider, for example, a party's strength. When having to choose between two parties which are equally attractive in all sorts of ways, but differ in the number of votes it receives, we may expect voters to prefer the larger over the smaller one because its strength puts it in a better position to be politically effective. When the choice would be between two parties which are not equally attractive, but almost so, with the smaller being the more attractive, it is still quite possible for voters to support, for tactical reasons, the slightly less attractive but more powerful party. To what extent such trade-offs take place is a matter for empirical assessment, which is only possible when preference scores for all parties are available.[18]

---

18 One might wonder whether relations between preference scores of parties and strength are tautological, as larger parties are large because many people prefer them, whereas only few people express strong preferences for small parties. This argument, however, applies only to ipsative party preference. There is no tautology between parties' strength and preferences scores when the latter also involve voters' second, third and following choices. Tillie (1995) investigates this relationship in more detail and concludes that the observed relationships cannot be interpreted as tautological artifacts, but as the consequence of considerations about 'power' or 'political impact' in voters' choice processes.

In addition to strength, one can think of other characteristics of parties that might explain variance in the stacked dataset. Incumbency is a case in point, reflecting the additional (dis)advantage that accrues to parties because of their role in government. An entire class of additional variables are derived from coding the 'party family' to which each party belongs, in case christian democracy or social democracy, for example, should be found to have advantages over and above the other factors we measure. Because our research design permits us to assess all parties simultaneously, we are able to characterize them in these and other ways and to use these characterizations, at the same time as we use the characteristics of individual voters, as predictors of why some parties are preferred more often than others. Taking these factors into account not only enables us to evaluate their importance relative to other factors but, more importantly, it enables us to measure the effects of other factors uncontaminated by these across-the-board effects. Thus, for example, if postmaterialists are less inclined to support green parties merely because of their electoral weakness, this will be taken into account in our multivariate analysis and the effects of postmaterialism will be able to show themselves uncontaminated by such factors.

In the event, incumbency did not add to variance explained in a model that already takes account of government approval. Of all the possible party characteristics evaluated, only two warranted inclusion in the first stage of our analysis. The first of these is strength. The second is one of the dummy variables which indicate the 'party family' of specific parties. Parties which belong to a group which can be referred to as 'new politics parties' differ systematically, and in the same way in all countries, from other parties.[19] So strength and 'new politics party' become the only ones among these variables that are included at this stage in our analysis in addition to the individual-level predictors derived from particular theories.

Table 20.3 summarizes the prediction equations that are found for each country when party preference is regressed on predictors derived from the various theories outlined earlier in this chapter, together with strength of party and 'new politics party'. Directional theory is not included there because of its extreme multicollinearity with smallest distance theory. As can be seen from the final column, these predictors explain 40 percent or more of the variance in party preference everywhere except in Flanders, Ireland and Italy. EC-wide, the proportion of variance explained approaches 42 per cent.

---

19 The same is not true for other party families. In a way, this variable is somewhat unsatisfactory, as it comes close to a theoretically unexplicated proper name. As we will show below, however, it represents a theoretically meaningful interaction which, however, cannot be measured directly because of inadequate operational indicators.

Table 20.3 Effects (b's) on Party Preference, by Country and EC-wide

	Size of Party (% of votes in last NE)	New Politics Party	Distance from Party on Left/Right Scale	Class	EC Approval	Government Approval	Issue Voting	Postmaterialism	Religion	Constant	R^2
Den	8.57	INAP	-0.57	0.45	0.20	0.32	0.39	0.38*	0.26*	4.43	44.2
Fla	5.51	2.15	-0.32	0.88	0.17*	0.45	0.78	0.26*	0.57	3.80	30.9
Fra	6.26	2.11	-0.54	0.40	0.40	0.48	0.49	0.32*	0.37	4.64	43.2
Ger	5.62	0.20*	-0.57	0.47	0.56	0.56	0.48	0.25	0.41	4.95	48.0
GBr	7.92	2.00	-0.40	0.34	-0.46*	0.69	0.56*	0.14*	0.29*	3.38	47.0
Gre	6.2	1.02	-0.43	0.17*	0.52	0.73	0.40	0.35	0.30*	3.39	61.6
Ire	5.18	1.50	-0.34	0.47	0.23*	0.79	0.68	0.36*	0.49	4.51	32.1
Ita	8.12	0.47*	-0.43	0.59	0.40*	0.46	0.72	0.42*	0.54	3.51	35.0
Lux	10.64	1.17	-0.36	0.69	0.59	0.60	0.75	0.28*	0.36	3.47	46.0
Net	9.15	0.98	-0.37	0.56	0.37*	0.51	0.49	0.27*	0.51	3.05	41.3
NIr	3.68	INAP	-0.27	0.54	0.33	0.21*	0.55	0.24*	0.66	4.42	44.8
Por	6.75	INAP	-0.40	0.36*	0.02*	0.55	0.57	0.20*	0.35	3.61	40.6
Spa	7.13	INAP	-0.37	0.39	0.34*	0.71	0.63	0.37*	0.47	3.41	50.1
Wal	8.29	1.98	-0.35	0.54	-0.18*	0.32	0.72	0.46	0.59	2.79	48.4
EC-wide	5.49	0.90	-0.41	0.49	0.24	0.55	0.58	0.27	0.50	4.06	41.9

* Not significant at p=0.05

The first column of coefficients shows the effects of strength on party preference having controlled for all the other factors in the table. In other words, these effects show how much more attractive a party is because it is large, over and above all the substantive motivations that would lead someone to vote for it. In all political systems of the EC there is a strong tendency for people to prefer large parties. On average the difference between a party that had 100 percent of the seats and one that had no seats would be 5.49 on the scale of preferences. Two parties that differed by 30 percent in terms of electoral strength (a difference that is easy to come by) would differ by nearly two points on the 10-point scale, on average, in terms of preferences, demonstrating the importance of tactical voting in all countries.

Except for the first three columns, all the coefficients are on the same scale and can be read as the increment (on a scale of 1 to 10) in the preference for a party that results from an increment (on the same scale) of one unit in the equivalent predictor. So an effect of 1.0 would mean that the predictor was moving absolutely in step with party preference. We cannot compare these effects with those represented by the coefficients in the first three columns (or those coefficients with each other) as long as we are comparing effects across different datasets; but in the next section of this chapter we will engage in an equivalent multivariate analysis across Europe as a whole in which standardization is feasible. At that stage we will be able to compare the magnitude of the effects better than we can in Table 20.3.

Perhaps the two most surprising coefficients in the table are the negative effects of EC-approval in Wallonia and Britain. The interpretation to be placed on these coefficients is that, once strength and other factors are taken into account, voters in these countries are slightly less likely to vote for the parties that are most attractive to them on the basis of their stance regarding the EC. These coefficients are, however, not statistically significant and should probably be interpreted as though they were zero, along with other starred coefficients in the table. The small importance of EC approval in determining voting choice is true of voters in all countries and emphasizes yet again the second-order nature of these elections.

The most remarkable feature of Table 20.3 is the similarity of the results for the various political systems in the EC. Despite their different party systems, electoral systems, and variations in the location of European elections in the natural cycle of political processes, the effects of the various predictors on preferences for parties are very similar, not only in direction, but with few exceptions also in magnitude. Nevertheless, we still need some means of assessing the importance of the few exceptions.

One Electorate or Many?

More important than the findings from the multivariate approach regarding the explanatory power of specific theories (which we have already said would have to be viewed in a causal perspective before they become really meaningful) is the help it provides in moving us towards our final objective of deciding whether the people of the European Union constitute one electorate or many. In order to decide this we have to take one final step and move from country-specific to EC-wide analyses, assessing whether a single equation can encapsulate these effects without modifications to do justice to specific countries. To the extent that modifications are necessary, because there remains country-level variance that can only be explained by the introduction of proper names, we cannot speak of a single European electorate.

We take this step by putting the 14 stacked datasets end-to-end and adding 14 country dummies as indicators of which country each respondent belongs to. These dummies can be used in two ways: in interaction with substantive variables in tests of differences between countries in the strength of effects, and on their own to test for differences in the average level of probability to vote, country by country. More importantly, the country dummies are accompanied by measures of systemic and compositional differences between countries, such as were employed in Chapter 19 to help account for differences in turnout. These variables can be employed, alone and in interaction with individual-level effects, to attempt to explain residual variance before we resort to the use of proper names.

Table 20.4 shows these effects in an EC-wide regression analysis where the dependent variable is the same measure of party preference as was employed in Tables 20.2 and 20.3 but in which a single equation incorporating contextual and systemic differences replaces the differentiation seen in those tables between 14 political systems. Because we are now dealing with a single dataset, we can also include standardized regression coefficients (betas) in the table along with unstandardized effects (b's).

The regression reported in Table 20.4 was constructed in two stages. We started by entering the variables included in previous tables into the equation. After this, we assessed a large number of theoretically meaningful interactions which would not necessarily add to variance explained, but rather to a proper specification of the equation.[20] Of all the dozens of possible interactions, only four were found to be statistically significant (at the .005 level), and were included in the equation and in Table 20.4.

Looking down the column of b's, we see that the EC-wide analysis tells pretty much the same story when systemic and compositional effects are included as when they were ignored (in the bottom row of Table 20.3). Variance explained

---

20   The following kinds of interactions were assessed: (a) interactions of individual with individual characteristics, such as between the variables included in Table 20.2, or between these on the one hand and variables such as education, political interest, age, or position in left/right terms; (b) interactions between the predictors included in Table 20.3 with systemic characteristics (like those used in Chapter 19) such as number of parties, proportionality of the electoral system, range of party positions on European integration, presence or absence of concurrent national elections; (c) interactions between individual variables (those included in Table 20.2) and party characteristics, such as electoral strength, ideological position or extremity, being in government or opposition, belonging to particular party families; and (d) various kinds of three-way interactions that can be constructed from those mentioned above. For a detailed account of this investigation of possible interactions, see Oppenhuis (1995).

Table 20.4 Predictors of Party Preference, EC-wide (Weighted N=9288)

Independent Variables	b	Beta	Sig. T	Correlation
Individual-level Effects				
EC-approval	0.244	0.044	0.0001	0.186
Postmaterialism	0.289	0.046	0.0001	0.165
Class	0.500	0.109	0.0001	0.219
Religion	0.502	0.126	0.0001	0.254
Government Approval	0.587	0.191	0.0001	0.329
Issue Voting	0.567	0.200	0.0001	0.351
Left-Right Distance	-0.421	-0.295	0.0001	-0.471
Individual-level Interactions				
Government Approval Where There is a				
Concurrent National Election	0.082	0.027	0.0032	-0.154
Left-right Distance with Extremity of Party	0.033	0.027	0.0007	-0.050
Issues with Structural Agreement	-0.010	-0.037	0.0001	-0.037
Left-right Distance with Structural Agreement	-0.006	-0.040	0.0001	-0.077
Party-level Effects				
Electoral Strength	6.614	0.284	0.0000	0.290
New Politics Party	1.023	0.105	0.0000	0.036
Constant	3.921			
Variance Explained	42.8%			

increases by just less than one percent and effects that appear in both tables are virtually unchanged. The column of betas permits us to more accurately evaluate the relative importance of explanations measured on different scales. Now we see that predicted left/right distance is one-and-a-half times as important as issue voting or government approval, and just about as important as parties' electoral strength (something that could not be judged from the coefficients in earlier tables). All these effects are significant well beyond the .001 level.

The interaction effects that were found to be relevant deserve some attention. As in Chapter 19, interaction terms are defined as deviation scores in order to minimize multicollinearity with the predictors with which they are associated. Thus, the interaction term between government approval and concurrent national elections must be added to that of government approval in the presence of such concurrent elections and subtracted from it otherwise. Substantively, this means that government approval is more important in generating party preferences when the allocation of power in the national political arena is directly at stake, a finding very much in line with our interpretation of aggregate level analyses in Chapter 18. The interaction between left/right distance and extremity of party implies that the importance of distance to a party becomes more important for a voter the less centrist a party is.[21] The two interactions involving structural agreement on left/right positions of parties are substantively more interesting. They imply that the contributions of left/right distances and issues on party preferences are both dependent on an aspect of the political culture in which voters make their choices. In countries with a comparatively strong consensus about the nature of the political world in left/right terms, ideological distance to parties acquires more weight, and issue considerations less weight in determining party preferences than in countries where such consensus is weaker.[22] Apparently, the more voters agree on how the political world is structured, the more those structuring dimensions contribute to party preferences.[23] As we are dealing here with the contrast between single issues and overarching ideological concepts, the implication is that the extent to which voters base their decisions on ideological notions is dependent on the likelihood that their choice will be interpreted by others in the same way they themselves intended it, a clear indication of a kind of meta-rationality on the part of voters.[24] At the same time, when there is less consensus on how the world is structured, it makes less sense for voters to base their own choice on ideological considerations, and separate issue considerations acquire more weight.[25] That additional weight is enough to raise the importance of issues to virtual equality with left/right distance (where structural agreement is lacking) in contrast to a situation in which left/right

---

21 This is probably a statistical artifact, generated by the greater range of left/right distances for extreme than for centrist parties, which is caused by the boundedness of the 10-point rating scale from which these distances have been derived.

22 This consensus involves the extent to which the entire sample perceives each political party to occupy the same location in an ideological continuum. The operationalization of the measure is described in Appendix B. For an interesting discussion about the relevance of this aspect of political culture, see, for example, Granberg and Holmberg (1988).

23 The increase in the importance of left/right distance in the context of high structural agreement is complemented by a reduction in the importance of issues in the same context, to an extent that is virtually identical (0.037 as opposed to 0.040). The fact that both these coefficients are negative must be understood in the light of the fact that the individual-level effect of left/right distance is negative, so the negative interaction increases its importance, while the individual-level effect of issues is positive, so the negative interaction reduces its importance.

24 This would not require any extraordinary perspicacity on the part of voters, since if their view of the world is widely shared it will be more likely to form the basis of political debate in the media and elsewhere.

25 The implication of thisinteraction is that, if only given an appropriate context, voters tend to be ideological (hence structured) in their decision-making. This suggests that mass publics may not be inherently limited in the extent to which they cognitively structure the political world, as has often been asserted since Converse's (1964) seminal contribution on the nature of belief systems, but rather that the cognitive and evaluative use of ideological dimensions (for example) may be encouraged or discouraged by the cultural context.

distance has more than twice the effect of issues (where structural agreement is widespread).[26]

In this context we can also comment on the meaning of the dummy 'new politics party'. When we omit this variable, two additional interaction effects become significant. The first arises from the greater effect of postmaterialism among postmaterialist voters. The second arises from the greater effect of this interaction among voters who prefer new politics parties. When, however, the dummy variable 'new politics party' is introduced, these two interaction terms lose their significance entirely, while the dummy variable still picks up some additional explained variance. The substantive meaning of these findings is simple: voters with new politics concerns are, ceteris paribus, more likely to prefer new politics parties. The reason why these effects are not as well indicated by our measure of postmaterialism has to be sought in the deficiencies of the often-used materialism/postmaterialism typology to adequately tap such concerns (cf. Clarke and Dutt, 1991; Duch and Taylor, 1993; van Deth, 1983a; Müller-Rommel, 1983; Flanagan, 1982a, 1982b, 1987).

The implications of the equation reported in Table 20.4 are unmistakable. Preferences among political parties are overwhelmingly determined by substantive political criteria involving parties' political stances and voters' preferences in terms of left/right ideology, issues and government approval. Along with these is a concern for parties' power (i.e., their ability to affect political outcomes). The additive nature of the equation implies that where people do not find an ideal party from among those on offer, these two kinds of considerations can compensate for one another: a large and acceptable party may be preferred to a small but more attractive one. How often such situations occur is mainly dependent on the options available in any particular political system, a matter which evidently differs from system to system.

The effects of people's positions in terms of cleavage lines are not entirely without consequence, but evidently such positions are of only minor importance; however, it would be plausible to assume that causal effects from these factors are mediated by other variables and are thus somewhat underestimated in our model, which contains only direct effects on party preferences. The coefficients in the final column of Table 20.4, which indicate the betas in models in which each factor in turn is the only predictor, suggest that in a more fully elaborated model the total effects of these cleavages would be greater.

The equation which is described in Table 20.4 contains no predictors defined in terms of proper names of countries or of parties. We use it to test in

---

26 Adding the two interaction terms in the absence of structural agreement yields a beta of 0.237 for issues as compared to −0.255 for left/right. Subtracting them in the presence of structural agreement yields a beta of 0.163 for issues as compared to 0.335 for left/right.

a more exhaustive manner the extent to which voters in different EU countries arrive at their party choice in the same way. To the extent that the process is not the same in different systems, this equation will be improved by adding terms which modify it to suit the different conditions pertaining in different countries. Such terms, where necessary, effectuate a change in the value of the coefficients for different countries. If, for instance, the regression coefficient of the class variable is too high in the Netherlands, this can be compensated for by adding a specific term which lowers its value for all cases in that country—an interaction of class with a dummy variable for the Netherlands. In this way we define 130 interaction terms.[27] Assessing the significance of these interactions provides the most direct and least equivocal test of the hypothesis that a single equation can predict party preferences in all systems without resorting to the use of proper names of countries. To the extent that this hypothesis fails (because interactions with country dummies prove significant) we will be able to specify how it fails, and how badly.[28]

The answer to this central question is very straightforward: none of the 130 ways in which the hypothesis could be rejected stands up empirically, since none of the interactions of predictors with country dummies comes even close to reaching significance. When we add all these 130 interactions with proper country names to the equation at once, the gain in explained variance is a meager 2.2 per cent, all of which is the evident consequence of capitalizing on chance.

The conclusion that a single equation fits the data equally well in all countries may appear at odds with the findings displayed in Table 20.3. The separate regressions for the various countries did appear to produce different coefficients. Religion appeared to be more important in Northern Ireland than elsewhere, just as did government approval in Britain and Greece. The contrast with the single equation in Table 20.4 is more apparent than real, however. First, in the equation of Table 20.4 interaction terms were added which do account for some of these differences. But, much more importantly, the distributions of the independent variables are not the same in the various countries. Northern Ireland clearly falls at one end of a distribution of salience of religious concerns, in having more voters with strong religious feelings than any other EC country. However, the fact that there are more such people does not imply that any of them behaves differently from equally zealous people elsewhere—

---

27 Of the 13 terms in the regression equation, three are constant within countries which leaves 10, each of which is combined with 13 system dummies (14 systems minus 1 for the base category).

28 This is the point at which, had there been any differences between countries that were removed in the process of centering the independent variables (see footnote 16) such differences would have been encapsulated in the interaction terms with country dummies, which therefore are the appropriate diagnostic for detecting whether inadvertently any country differences were removed by the procedures used.

there is nothing uniquely Northern Irish about their individual behavior. Voters in another country with equally politicized religious divisions would apparently make choices that were no different.

Omitted Effects

What of the 60 percent or so of variance that remains unexplained by our model? Is it possible that we have omitted variables that are important in determining party choice? If so, our tentative conclusion that country differences are unimportant might be found to be due to our focus on only some of the reasons why people make the choices that they do. In point of fact, much of the variance that remains unexplained by our model is of no substantive interest. We are very concerned, substantively, with differences in preferences between those parties that vie for primacy in the minds of particular individuals. We are not much concerned, substantively, with such differences between parties that particular individuals are unlikely to vote for. Especially when there are many parties, whether someone gives an unfavored party a score of 1 or 2 or 3 (on a 10-point scale) is of little substantive interest but strongly affects the amount of unexplained variance.[29] One way to set a benchmark for maximum explainable variance would be to insert dummy variables for all individual parties. If we do so (which involves introducing 105 additional dummy variables) these variables explain some 23.7 percent of the variance not explained by substantive variables, which is 13 percent of total variance. This may reflect party characteristics which we did not measure but which affect, as does strength of party, the preferences of voters. Arguably, when we do this we are focussing on variance which we just indicated was of little relevance, since it pertains to parties which do not really vie for these voters' actual choice. Consequently, using dummies to represent proper party names would probably overestimate the relevant attainable maximum of explicable variance.

Alternatively, we can employ as a surrogate for unmeasured effects the actual identity of the party voted for (as a single dummy variable in the stacked dataset). Evidently, knowing which party each voter chose will encapsulate much that we have been unable to measure about the reasons for their choice. This variable correlates highly with the highest probability to vote, as we saw in Table 20.1; yet it only adds 9.3 percent to the total variance explained when brought into the equation summarized in Table 20.4

---

29 If we select only those preferences from the stacked dataset that correspond to the party the respondent actually voted for, the equation of Table 20.4 explains over 67 percent of variance (calculated by 1 minus the ratio of residual to total sums of squares). This emphasizes the fact that unexplained variance is concentrated among preferences for parties that were not voted for.

as a surrogate for unmeasured effects. Evidently this variable discriminates well between the most preferred party and other parties, but provides no discrimination at all between the less preferred parties. As some of these other parties will nevertheless be serious contenders for a person's vote, this measure is bound to underestimate the relevant variance that might be explicable in a better specified model.

On the basis of these considerations we arrive at two benchmarks, neither of which is entirely satisfactory. The one, based on the use of party dummies, suggests that 55 percent (42 percent of the equation in Table 20.4 plus 13 percent extra from these dummies) is the maximum attainable explained variance—probably an overestimate. The other benchmark, based on the identity of the party actually voted for, suggests that 51 percent (42 percent of the model of Table 20.4 plus an additional 9 per cent) is the maximum to be attained—probably an underestimate. The margin between these two estimates is remarkably narrow—a four percent span centering on 53 percent explained variance.

On the basis of this estimate it seems that we have explained about 80 percent of what is available to be explained. Some of the unexplained variance would certainly be accounted for by our use of indirect measures of the effects of theories other than distance theory. We reported earlier that direct measurement of distance theory added some 3 percent to variance explained. Other theories explain less variance, so that direct measurement would add less, but with five directly measured indicators in lieu of the indirectly measured ones we use, some part of the missing variance would certainly be accounted for. Another part will presumably be found in considerations that we could not include in our model for lack of data: additional issues, economic concerns, and such like.

Given these considerations, it seems unlikely that missing variables can be having much effect of any kind, much less that such variables could skew the findings in such a way as to re-introduce country differences.

Replicability of the Findings

The findings reported above were obtained from the responses of European voters in 1989. To what extent are these findings unique to these elections or to the specific context within which they took place? Do the results derived from the 1989 data allow us to adequately model party preferences in 1994 as well? To answer these questions, we will employ the same strategy as in Chapter 19, and predict European voters' preferences for political parties on the basis of their observed scores on the independent variables listed in Table 20.4, in combination with the coefficients estimated in 1989, which are also listed in that table. These predictions may then be compared to the regression-predictions (y-hats) derived from re-estimating the equation of Table 20.4 on the 1994 data.[30] It turns out that the two predictions obtained in this manner are exceedingly similar, as is demonstrated by their correlation of 0.99. A straightforward re-estimation of the equation of Table 20.4 using 1994 data yields very similar, although not identical, coefficients.[31]

In terms of explained variance, the equation for 1994 is slightly weaker than that for 1989, which reflects the somewhat poorer operationalizations of independent variables in 1994 (see footnote 30 and Appendix C); it loses 3 percent of explanatory power. The crucial relation, however, between the multiple preferences that are analyzed in these multivariate analyses, and the exclusive party choice that voters are asked to make in most countries, is of the same strength in 1994 as it was shown to be in 1989 (see Table 20.1). Across Europe, over 90 percent of the respondents actually vote for the party to which they gave the highest preference score, in 1994 as in 1989. Obviously then, the pattern of empirical results is very much the same in 1989 and in 1994. Consequently, the substantive interpretations built upon our analyses of the 1989 data have a wider validity than only for that election.[32] The general insights derived from these analyses apparently pertain to basic foundations of party choice in European democracies.

Conclusion

Summing up the major implications of these analyses, we can state that, whatever may be different in the various political systems of the EC, it is not the way in which voters arrive at their electoral preferences for political parties. A Belgian who moved to Portugal, a Greek to Ireland, a Dane to Italy, once having had time to orient themselves to their new habitat (and given the right to vote), would not stand out as foreigners in terms of the manner in which

---

30 Obviously, just as was the case in Chapter 19, this procedure requires that the construction and weighting of data for 1994 is as far as possible identical to that of 1989. This is not entirely possible, particularly as the indicators for issue voting and government approval are in 1994 somewhat different from those in 1989.

31 Some differences in the estimated coefficients are only to be expected, because of (a) slightly different empirical information for some of the independent variables, (b) the somewhat more restricted set of parties for which the dependent variable—the probability to vote question—has been asked, and (c) because procedures which maximize variance explained unavoidably capitalize on chance to some extent. The most prominent difference between 1989 and 1994 is perhaps that the estimated coefficient of the dummy-variable representing new politics parties has lost in 1994 half of its 1989 weight, see also Appendix C.

32 As a further confirmation of the wider validity of these findings, it may be noted that many of them are also replicable in other studies, such as the Dutch Parliamentary Election Studies (see for example Tillie, 1995).

they made their choice between parties. In this sense, then, we can speak of a single European electorate which existed already at the time of the 1989 European elections, on the eve of the Single European Market and the Treaty of European Union. The division of this European electorate into separate national ones does not reflect differences in voting behavior but rather, from that perspective, might be considered to be irrelevant. The relative effects of cleavages, issues, ideology, and approval of government on the choices made by individual voters are quite similar in the various countries of the European Union, at least to the extent that they are operating in similar contexts. Opinions on European integration and (post)materialist value orientations hardly matter, although the failure of the latter is (given the effect of new politics parties in 1989) most likely to be predominantly the consequence of the failure of the traditional Inglehart typology to adequately capture relevant differences in value orientations. The (small, but significant) impact of new politics parties in that year does indicate that, where such parties do not exist, it is perhaps somewhat more difficult for voters to express their concerns in this area.[33]

The most important factors accounting for party choice are ideological and strategic considerations, followed at a considerable distance by issue concerns and government approval. New politics concerns trail far behind, at best on a level with, but possibly even weaker still than the effects of religion and class, which today are but shadows of their former selves.

The relative importance of these various determinants of party preference, which could be replicated in other elections as well, also allows us to address the question of the kind of motivations that underlie party preference. In Chapter 19 we distinguished two kinds of motivational factors, on the one hand those that are primarily affective and can be captured in terms of loyalty, habit, duty and identification with groups; and on the other those that are clearly instrumental in character. Of the various factors listed in Table 20.4, those relating to left/right distance, issues, government approval and EC-approval clearly belong to the instrumental category, as does strength, which generates strategic considerations in party preference. Their weights (together with those of the interactions associated with them) account for more than 70 percent of the variance explained in our analyses. Clearly, the strong signs of instrumental voter motivations that were visible in Chapters 18 and 19 are visible here as well.[34] Particularly in conjunction with the findings of those two previous

---

33 The reduced effect of this variable in 1994 is probably due to its lower priority (or status) on the political and media agenda of 1994 when compared to 1989, as is reflected by many election studies and opinion polls covering this time span.

34 Of course, our attribution of effects to instrumental or affective categories is based on a number of assumptions concerning the causal ordering of the factors included in the equation of Table 20.4. Elsewhere, these assumptions are explicitly modelled and tested (Oppenhuis, 1995);

chapters, we feel that not only do voters from various countries in the European Union use the same kind of decision-making process when choosing a party at the ballot box, but also that this process is overwhelmingly instrumental in nature. Voters are not merely reflecting myopic loyalties and identifications, but are reacting in a logical fashion to political stimuli. The lack of European content in European elections can therefore not be attributed to inherent limitations of European voters. The member countries of the European Union do differ from each other in terms of their institutions, political parties, and political contexts—and individual citizens do react to these differences—but there are no indications that the way in which they do so is itself different from one country to the next.

The findings of this chapter thus reinforce those of Chapter 19 which found no important country differences in the reasons why people turn out to vote, other than those that can be attributed to differences in political institutions and contexts. When it comes to voting choice only differences in political context are at issue. If such differences were removed, this would also remove the differences we observe in the manner in which party choices are made. Voters in different countries have not been socialized into country-specific modes of expressing at the ballot box their interests, hopes and fears. The answer to the question 'one electorate or many?' when interpreted in these terms is unequivocally in the singular.

So there is no reason to doubt that, once provided with leadership and political choices that allow a Europe-wide electoral verdict to be expressed, the voters that make up the European electorate would indeed render such a verdict, thereby transforming European elections into what they currently so obviously are not: mechanisms that contribute to legitimizing power, to holding politicians accountable for how they use that power and to representing citizens' interests. The question we are thus driven to ask is why are such leadership and choices lacking? That is the final topic we must address in this volume, and the one to which we now turn.

---

the results of those analyses support the interpretation of the findings presented here.

CHAPTER 21

Conclusions:
The Electoral Connection and
the Democratic Deficit

Mark Franklin, Cees van der Eijk and Michael Marsh

Direct elections to the European Parliament were supposed to provide the citizens of member countries with a mechanism for holding accountable those who rule over them, thereby supplying at least a modicum of democratic control over European affairs. Nowhere except perhaps in Denmark have we seen the slightest sign of this intention being realized. Why not?

One possible reason, mentioned in Chapter 1, would have been a degree of myopic parochialism on the part of European voters that would have precluded any possibility of representation other than on a country-by-country basis. Such parochialism, particularly in conjunction with a strong politicization of the dividing lines between national communities, would have been the equivalent on a Europe-wide scale of the segmentation that existed within some European countries until the 1960s (Lijphart, 1968). The borders of the different member-states of the European Union would in this view be the current equivalent of the traditional cleavage lines (based on class, religion, ethnicity, language, etc.) that in former days divided the populations of these states against themselves.[1] Such a segmented or 'pillarized' perspective on the political system of the European Union has often been used to argue the inevitability as well as the desirability of passive electorates and consociational elites rather than popular involvement in the conduct of politics (e.g. Lindberg, 1974; Busch and Puchala, 1976; Sloot, 1992). However, a principal finding of Chapters 19 and 20 in this book was that national boundaries do not appear to have any particular significance (independent of electoral system, party system, and the like) in dividing up what turns out to be a single European electorate. Europeans may speak many languages, but they evidently use the same forms of discourse when talking about politics.[2] This finding implies on the one

---

1 See, e.g. Lipset and Rokkan (1967) and Lijphart (1968) for theoretical perspectives on both the origins and the political consequences of these cleavages. See Crewe and Denver (1985), Dalton et al. (1984) and particularly Franklin, Mackie and Valen, et al. (1992) for accounts of the demise of these traditional cleavages.

2 And this rather common discourse is not framed in terms of animosities between nation-states

hand that the analogy with cleavage politics is not valid,[3] and on the other that the conditions are met within the countries of the European Union for a meaningful electoral contest transcending national borders. If parochialism is not the reason why citizens of the European Union do not enjoy even the modicum of control over European affairs that was supposed to result from the institution of direct elections to the European Parliament, then we must look for that reason elsewhere.

The Electoral Connection in European Elections

As pointed out in Chapter 1, notions of democratic accountability and control are associated with the existence of free elections; but in order for elections to fulfil these functions, a number of conditions must be met. In particular, electorates must know what various contenders stand for and have some awareness of their record in the arena under consideration. In the case of European elections the arena purportedly under consideration is that of European politics, and contenders for power are potential Members of the European Parliament. However, we have seen that in a European election, except in Denmark (or in France in 1989) there is virtually no discussion of what these contenders stand for or how they previously performed in the European arena.[4] Instead, European election campaigns focus on the national political arena in each member state. Indeed, in the country chapters of Part II, the single feature that most countries had in common was the fact that the election was seen to be relevant primarily to domestic matters;[5] and on the rare occasions when contenders made an effort to break out of this pattern (as in France and Spain in 1989) they either failed to make themselves heard (in Spain) or were not understood (in France).

Consistent with Reif and Schmitt's (1980) characterization of European elections as second-order national elections, the elections of 1989 and 1994 were generally treated as opportunities to discuss national political differences and to register support for, or opposition to, political parties on the basis of these differences. Occasionally, as in Britain in 1989, an issue from the European

---

or national interests, but rather in ideological terms that have a common, trans-European origin and content—see Chapter 20.

3 The analogy is not valid for a number of other reasons too, which will not be elaborated here.

4 In France, such discussions as occurred in 1989 were so totally divorced from any pre-existing public debate involving French voters as to have been virtually unintelligible to them—see Chapter 7).

5 This observation is in line with virtually all previous studies of European elections. See, for example Blumler (1983), Blumler and Fox (1982), Reif (1984b; 1985b), Lodge (1993).

arena might be injected into the campaign, but its salience only arose from its domestic significance, not its European significance.[6] It follows that the political decision encapsulated in the result of the European election had a different focus in each country. With different choices being made, it is clear that there can have been no single electoral verdict manifested in these elections over the European Union as a whole; and the European Parliaments elected in 1989 and 1994 had no mandate whatsoever in terms of the European arena. In particular, the incoming Parliaments on each occasion had no mandate to deal with the most important conflict dimension which operates in that arena, namely the future course of European integration. The electoral connection (Mayhew, 1974) that one expects to find in a functioning democracy was quite simply absent.

This lack of a European electoral mandate is entirely due to the segmentation of the European elections into separate national contests with national parties setting the agenda for each contest and determining the issues that were discussed. It is those parties that failed to give to the 1994, 1989 or earlier European elections any significant European content. One exception to the general rule has several times been mentioned (see especially Chapters 6 and 17). In Denmark, the presence of parties in European elections that do not compete in national elections makes it impossible for politicians or commentators to interpret the performance of any party in domestic political terms, and the fact that two parties put forward European policies encourages other parties to do the same.

The Role of Political Parties

The consequences of national elections in a Parliamentary regime derive from the existence of policy differences between political parties contesting those elections, and an electoral verdict arises from the perception that a choice has been made between those policies.[7] With few exceptions, the parties within the EU member states have no differences in regard to Europe (see van der Eijk and Franklin, 1991, for an elaboration of this theme). Most parties in most countries have long ago decided that European unification is good for

---

6 In France the lack of such linkages in 1989 prevented the discussion of European issues from having any impact on party choice.

7 The specificity of the policy differences involved may differ in different systems and periods. In systems characterized by strong cleavage politics the policy differences between parties may take mainly the form of associating different parties with the different (but not necessarily specified) interests of different cleavage groups. In systems or periods of strong ideological or issue polarization, the respective ideological or issue dimensions specify the nature of policy differences between parties.

their country. Differences over what is meant by unification are not allowed to surface for reasons we will explore below. The lack of inter-party policy differences on European matters makes it difficult for parties to fight elections on European issues; and, for lack of policy differences in the relevant arena, European elections are thus fought in terms of policy differences in each national arena, with the consequences we have already outlined.[8]

Of course, the really interesting question is why there are no manifest policy differences on European matters between the major parties. In other new areas of public policy, not part of the original conflicts between parties, problems have (if sufficiently important) tended to become aligned with existing dimensions of political conflict, even to the point where they eventually become one of the defining aspects of the party battle.[9] Why not on European matters?

The strange thing is that this lack of controversy over European affairs is not due to any lack of potentially divisive issues. Europe's politicians and voters do disagree (sometimes violently) on a whole range of European matters from the proper role of the European Commission in regulating national foodstuffs to the question of whether a single European currency would be desirable. Moreover, governments occasionally find themselves the objects of embarrassing scrutiny when the Commission promulgates new regulations that introduce production quotas for milk, olive oil or tomatoes, or forcefully open previously protected markets to competition. Sometimes they are even led to disassociate themselves from decisions that they did in fact participate in making (we will be citing one example of this later in the present chapter). Why could they not have taken public responsibility for their actions, defending them in terms of the interests, political principles, and ideologies underlying them, in much the same way as decisions in the domestic realm are normally defended, rationalized and explained? European elections would be good opportunities to present such overarching perspectives on what kind of Europe parties want to promote, but we have seen that this hardly happens. Why not?

Evidently the reason has nothing to do with European institutions. European elections are conducted at regular intervals and, while some policy initiatives possibly would arise between elections, many potentially contentious issues are known in advance. For example, the fact that there would soon be a debate over the desirability or otherwise of a single European currency was

---

8 It is exactly because of this emphasis on the politics of the national arena that these elections are characterized as second-order national elections.

9 See, for example Schattschneider's (1960) analysis of the displacement of conflicts and Silverman's (1985) discussion of gradual reorientations of dominant conflict dimensions.

known to political leaders long before the European elections of 1989; yet it was not discussed in any country—not even in Britain—during the European election campaigns of 1989. Nor was it discussed in 1994, despite the added salience that the issue gained from debates over ratifying the Maastricht Treaty. Why do political parties not use elections to the European Parliament as opportunities to generate a substantive public debate on European matters? Why do they not use them as platforms for articulating different 'visions' of Europe, or as venues for politicizing these differences and mobilizing citizen support?

The Importance of Party Unity

It seems to us that there is a very simple answer to these questions that springs directly from the findings of many of our country chapters. National political parties cannot easily put issues of this kind before their voters for fear of politicizing a latent (and sometimes manifest) division within their own ranks. These parties are almost all subject to such potential rifts. The party systems in European countries arose long before the process of European unification began, and are oriented around other issues: primarily religion, the proper role of government in the economy, and the limits of social welfare. Many of these domestic questions are hardly related to the central conflict dimensions which now operate in the European Parliament (cf. Bogdanor, 1989). Others could very well become important if they were politicized in a manner which transcends the boundaries of the member states. The questions, however, which currently are of central importance in the politics of the European Union cut across the divisions between national parties, with minorities even within nominally pro-European parties being often vociferously opposed to all things European.[10]

---

10 To a large extent this assertion is based on reasoning from what we know about the origins and development of party systems, supported by anecdotal evidence. Samuel Beer (1993) reaches the same conclusion on the basis of much the same evidence, though he uses it to develop a different argument. Harder evidence from the Maastricht referenda of 1992 will be cited below. The only evidence from our post-election surveys that can be brought to bear concerns the average extent of agreement among supporters of each political party on the question of European unity (see van der Eijk and Franklin, 1991, and Appendix B for details of these measures) as compared with the degree of agreement on left/right location—the only appropriate basis for comparison that is expressed in the same way numerically. On the left/right continuum, the average coefficient of agreement (party by party) in 1989 was 0.63, whereas on European unity it was 0.42. The equivalent coefficients for 1994 were of the same magnitude. On this basis, the internal agreement within European parties in terms of left/right ideological position is 50 percent greater (on average) than their internal agreement on questions of European integration. This is exactly what one would expect in view of the fact that left/right ideology embodies most of the politicized issues in a country, and is an important part of the

Because European political parties are highly disciplined, it follows that discordant voices are seldom heard during an election campaign—as long as issues are not raised that would provoke the potential dissidents within a party. An exception occurred in Britain in 1989. As we saw in Chapter 5, the politicizing of a European issue during that European election campaign in Britain brought to light a split in the Conservative party which was played out in full view of the electorate, gravely hurting the party's performance in the elections. It is easy to see why other parties would want to avoid the risk of similar embarrassments; and the easiest way to reduce such risks is to keep internally divisive (in this context, European) issues off the agenda.[11] In consequence national parties essentially 'hijack' European elections for partisan and national ends, thereby shutting out public discussion of European issues. This does not necessarily result from a conscious plan by national politicians, but rather from their awareness of the structure of opportunities and risks within which they operate. Quite simply, they avoid initiatives that risk creating such splits.

This hypothesis is ironically lent weight by the one major exception to the general rule that European issues were kept off the agenda of the 1989 election campaigns. In France, as we saw in Chapter 7, some politicians focussed on the European arena rather than on domestic issues. Under rather special circumstances, this was for them the 'safest' way to avoid damage to their future domestic political aspirations. Opposition and government parties alike could only anticipate a result which, when portrayed as their domestic political standing, would hurt them. Presidential and legislative elections had been held hardly a year earlier, and the incumbent administration was not unpopular, making it risky for the opposition to portray the election as a midterm 'test' election. At the same time, although their Presidential and legislative mandates were still fresh, the ruling socialists were engaged in an internal struggle for future leadership positions (see Charlot and Charlot, 1989). Bringing this struggle into the open could only hurt the standing of the entire party with the voters. Focussing on European issues in 1989 was therefore the best insurance for French parties in an election involving more risks than opportunities. But normally the risks and opportunities point the other way: towards playing down European issues.

---

basis on which parties acquire their support (see Chapter 20), whereas this is not the case for European integration.

11 We saw in Chapter 10 that the Irish Labour Party was careful to do exactly this when it changed its official position regarding Europe, and the British Conservatives, having learned from experience, managed to keep their internal divisions private during the 1994 campaign.

Political Parties and the Maastricht Treaty

This hypothesis, that parties have an interest in keeping European issues off the agenda for the sake of party unity, is hard to prove from data about voters. Only a study of party leaders could hope to convincingly establish its merit. Nevertheless, indirect evidence can be gleaned from an analysis of voting patterns in the referenda that were held in 1992 to ratify the Treaty of European Union. In that context, other research has shown that parties were internally divided on the question of ratification, and that these divisions were sometimes allowed to surface during the referendum campaigns, playing no small part in the ratification fiasco in France and Denmark (Franklin, Marsh and McLaren, 1994; Franklin, van der Eijk and Marsh, 1995a,b). Evidently, had the votes been votes for the parties rather than votes for a referendum question, the parties could not have been so sanguine about allowing dissent to surface and the results would have been very different. In an election where European issues were successfully prevented from coming onto the agenda we would see no dissension at all—as indeed we did not in most countries in 1989 or 1994. Meanwhile, the pernicious result in Denmark in 1992 was that the referendum failed to pass for reasons that apparently had not so much to do with the popularity or otherwise of the European Union among Danish voters as with the support for government and opposition parties on the basis of domestic political concerns (Franklin, Marsh and Wlezien, 1994).[12] The same pernicious process, in which the referendum vote was influenced to a considerable extent by the popularity of the incumbent government, could also be observed to operate in France and Ireland, although with less dramatic consequences (at least in Ireland).[13]

The insulation of European from domestic politics which the Danes succeed in maintaining in European elections could not be maintained in the face of the European Union issue, since the Treaty of European Union could not be ratified by the Danish government until popular consent had been obtained in a referendum. Here we see that the hybrid nature of the European institutional

---

12 This despite the fact that Europe is undoubtedly a more contested topic in Denmark than in most other member-states. With the referendum over, opinion in Denmark swung back in favor of the Treaty—even before the Edinburgh summit conference in which concessions were negotiated to make it more palatable to the Danes. The fact that opposition was greatest in the actual referendum emphasizes that the result of the referendum was contaminated by national political considerations. At any distance before or after the referendum the Danes showed themselves much more favorable towards the treaty.

13 Other research has shown that, in France, the close vote reflected the unpopularity not of Maastricht but of President Mitterrand; whereas in Ireland the clear majority in favor of Maastricht reflected the high standing of the Irish government (Franklin, Marsh and McLaren, 1994).

framework (with people being represented both in the European Parliament and by their governments) undercuts even the Danish solution, which insulates European matters from domestic political concerns only so long as European matters can be limited to European elections. Without that insulation, European matters are not necessarily decided on European grounds but can instead be decided on the basis of the popularity or otherwise of a national government and the vagaries of the domestic political process.

Very much the same mechanisms played out within the British House of Commons during the parliamentary process for ratifying the Maastricht Treaty. There, the British Labour Party managed to maintain unity in opposition to the government, and voted against the treaty despite the fact that most Labour MPs were in favor. The government thus had to obtain virtual unanimity in favor of the treaty from among its own supporters—a course of action that proved difficult because of the many strong opponents to Europe within the British Conservative Party.

These observations support our view that parties in Britain, Denmark, France and Ireland would have good reason to avoid speaking clearly on European questions in a European election because most of them would not wish to let European concerns become politicized. We are confident that the same would be true in other countries. Although failure to mobilize their voters in favor of the treaty hurt non-governing parties hardly at all in 1992, this would not be the case in a real election.

European Policy-making and the Permissive Consensus

Parties in parliamentary regimes do not adapt easily to new issues and concerns. Any new issue threatens to split existing parties, and party leaders thus become adept at either molding new issues in the image of existing party cleavages or of damping them down at every opportunity. Established parties have not had more difficulty with European issues than with environmental or gender or alternative lifestyle issues. All such issues are initially threatening to the unity of established parties and the position of their leaders. Where European issues have differed from all other new issues is in the fact that, as foreign policy issues, governments have been able to take advantage of the normal convention that gives democratic executives greater freedom of action in foreign than in domestic policy-making. Moreover, moves towards a united Europe are supported in general terms by a majority of the electorates of all European Union countries. The context of a truly popular foreign policy issue has provided governing parties with unusual freedom of maneuver, often referred to as a 'permissive consensus' (Inglehart, 1971b).

Given this permissive consensus, European unification has largely remained the fief of national political leaders carving out deals with each other behind closed doors and then asking for the support of their followers in ratifying the resulting agreements. While European unification was primarily a matter of reducing tariff barriers and regulatory complications, the notion that unification involved technical adjustments of little interest to the citizens of Europe was probably justified. To sell their products anywhere in Europe, automobile manufacturers (for example) had to be governed by standard regulations regarding safety glass and headlight glare—not subjects that might be thought likely to generate controversy. As long as these were the sorts of issues decided in Brussels, lack of popular debate and consultation did not often deprive European voters of anything they were likely to value.

However, unqualified support on the part of national political leaders for steps towards European Union continued long after the steps ceased to be purely technical and started to affect the daily lives of individuals. Integration, which initially involved the 'negative' activities of removing tangible barriers to trade and mobility, has now become more positive, involving the construction of joint policies in ever more salient areas. Nevertheless, European political parties were not led by these developments to present their voters with choices on EU matters. Rather, parties continued to act as they always had, taking credit for developments that would be popular with voters, like grants or bigger markets, and playing down or even blaming the EU for less popular ones, like pressures to reduce public sector debt. These habits still persist. In one case, the Economist (8th January 1993) pointed out how apparent attempts by EU bureaucrats to interfere with or ban a number of national foods were largely the result of the ineptitude or dishonesty of national governments in failing to take responsibility for decisions they had themselves taken behind closed doors in the Council of Ministers. Perhaps even worse, some politicians are not above setting up Brussels as a 'patsy' to take the blame for things that national political leaders want but do not have popular support for at home. For example a Dutch Minister of Transport, when her proposal to oblige truckers to install speed governors met with opposition in the Dutch Parliament, privately proposed to have the matter decided by the European Council of Ministers of Transport.[14]

Indeed, pro-European parties may well have contributed to the democratic deficit by perpetuating the illusion of national sovereignty over the years. Governing parties have tried to present themselves at one and the same time as 'bringing home the bacon' from the European cornucopia, and as defending the national interest against incursions from Brussels. The irony, however, is

---

14 As reported in the Dutch daily *De Volkskrant*, May 21, 1991.

that in maintaining the illusion of national sovereignty beyond the point at which the truth could be hidden from voters, politicians in European countries may have come to appear impotent to affect the course of events in Brussels. This in turn creates something of a credibility problem within the national political process of EU member-states, as governments are seen on the one hand to blame Brussels for unpopular policies while on the other they still proclaim the virtues of European unity. Moreover, to the extent that problems that are kept off the political agenda become more salient, the stratagem must contribute to declining trust in government and even to declining legitimacy of democratic institutions.

So the pattern of obfuscation by national governments on matters that pertain to Europe is not cost-free. The democratic deficit may appear a rather theoretical problem—a matter of concern for philosophers and constitutionalists—but it potentially has quite practical consequences for parties, governments and society. We will elaborate these consequences in greater detail below. However, first we wish to outline the steps we think could be taken to mitigate the problem.

The Democratic Deficit in European Elections

We are not the first to identify a democratic deficit in the conduct of European affairs. Indeed, the existence of such a deficit has periodically been used as an argument for making changes in institutional arrangements, either

(1) at the European level, for example by strengthening the European Parliament so as to give it 'real powers', with the objective of ensuring that no MEP would ever have to return to his or her constituents with the report that certain matters were beyond the Parliament's control; or

(2) at the national level, for example by strengthening the overview capacity of national parliaments and by restoring complete veto power to individual countries in the Council of Ministers, so that no Minister would ever have to return to his or her country with the report that he or she had been overruled.[15]

These two alternative proposals are evidently made from very different perspectives of how accountability and control of European affairs are supposed to be exercised. Those who would strengthen the European Parliament see accountability flowing through the European electoral process, with voters determining the complexion of the European Parliament and holding it

---

15 Note that member-states even today retain veto power in many areas.

accountable for its supervision of the policies instituted by the Commission and other bodies. They hope that by giving the Parliament additional powers (and by other measures as well) they can increase the salience of its decisions and ensure that its elections are taken seriously. On the other hand, those who would restore veto power to individual countries in the Council of Ministers, or strengthen the national parliaments in other ways, see accountability flowing through national elections with voters determining the complexion of their national parliaments and holding their national governments accountable for the behavior of members of the Council of Ministers. Components of the Treaty of Union that give additional powers to the European Parliament to approve the installation of a new Commission (and to be consulted in the choice of Commission President) seem quite one-sided in terms of this debate, and we will argue below that these reforms may actually have overreached the powers that the Parliament is currently able to exercise.

At first sight it might appear that because we have shown elections to the European Parliament to be largely devoid of European content, it follows that those who would enhance the role of national parliaments in their handling of European matters have a better chance of remedying the democratic deficit than those who would enhance the role of the European Parliament. In fact, our diagnosis suggests that both sets of proposals miss the point. The democratic deficit does not arise only from inadequate powers either of the European Parliament (in controlling the Commission) or of national parliaments (in controlling the Council of Ministers).[16] It arises because European decision-makers cannot be held accountable for their deeds by any portion of the European electorate—not even the part residing within a particular country. National elections are no more likely to see European matters discussed than are European elections. Indeed, it is because European elections resemble national elections in terms of the contending parties and the questions at issue that they have no European content. As a consequence, strengthening the powers of individual nations in the Council of Ministers will in no way increase the extent of democratic accountability and control over European decisions. Restoring the national veto might enable national Ministers to block certain developments, but the decision as to which developments to block would not result from democratic consultations unless changes also occurred in the nature of political debate within the member-states.

Above all, what is needed is for debates on European matters as seen to be salient for the allocation of power (either within countries or in the European Union, or both) by occurring in public view. Only then will voters become

---

16 Though if either type of institution were to receive a mandate on European matters, it might find that it required additional powers in order to carry that mandate out.

educated about what is at stake and about the arguments used by proponents of different courses of action. This is particularly relevant to decision-making by the Council of Ministers, which today takes place behind closed doors, so that it is often not known what process led to a particular decision, nor which (if any) of the ministers dissented. As long as this continues, no election (whether national or European) will produce a mandate for action on European matters, and without mandates for action on European matters the democratic deficit will persist. Indeed, as we argued in the first chapter of this volume, until elections provide mandates to govern Europe in some particular fashion, the democratic deficit will continue to fuel the crisis of legitimacy that the European Union now faces.

The problem of the democratic deficit thus rests not exclusively with institutional powers and prerogatives but to an important extent with the behavior of political parties, which in turn are constrained by their history, their traditions, and notably (in this context) by their domestic institutional setting. The fact that European elections are organized within member states rather than Europe-wide is an institutional arrangement. Once this parameter is set, party actors can be seen to be behaving perfectly rationally in the given institutional setting. So while the problem may rest with political parties, the solution does not. What is needed is to induce rational party actors to behave differently by reforming the institutional context. The institutional arrangements concerned may be national or European (or both)—our argument does not give primacy to one means of democratic accountability rather than another. In what follows we will focus on institutional arrangements which primarily affect each arena in turn.

Towards a European Polity

The low key nature of European elections can be seen, in the light of this discussion, as resulting from tacit collusion of a kind between party elites in individual countries, who do not even want to explore, let alone politicize, whatever differences of vision they may have on European matters because any discussion of Europe threatens the basis upon which they traditionally mobilize their voters around existing lines of political conflict—see Schattschneider's (1960) discussion of the 'displacement of conflict'. But why do we not see new parties taking advantage of the opportunity to mobilize voters on one side or the other of this neglected cleavage? It is evident that the party systems of European countries are open to new choices: regional parties, green parties and far-right parties have blossomed in recent years. Moreover, it seems plausible that European elections actually facilitate the birth and electoral breakthrough of such parties, as we have repeatedly seen in the country chapters of Part II.

So why do we not see the growth of parties that take positions for or against particular European concerns?

One possible reason why there have been few new parties with a (pro or anti) European orientation may be that new parties arise on the basis of national political discourses. With no public debates taking place about European issues, no activists come forward to create new parties with European orientations. This still leaves the possibility of new parties arising from splits in existing parties. Indeed, in many EU countries there are clear signs of intra-party debates about Europe expressed in national terms within national political parties, with pro-European factions generally carrying the day (though not always publicly) against anti-European factions. These factions might be seen as providing the bases for new parties—most new parties, after all, arise from splits in existing parties—but as yet this has not happened.

We can think of at least two reasons for this sclerosis, reasons that are consistent with our argument so far. First, established political entrepreneurs within the factions on the pro-European side already have a leadership position that would be put at risk by bringing up the European question, if European issues were to split the party and weaken its chances of (retaining) government power. Second, those on the anti-European side believe that voters are fundamentally pro-European and thus hesitate to go before them with an issue that they fear will lose. So those who could provide the leadership and focus for new parties, and the organizations which might provide the support, fear that the costs in the national political arena would outweigh the benefits.

Above all, the route taken so far—to de-politicize European issues as far as possible—has seemed a relatively risk-free strategy that has served political leaders well for thirty years. Why abandon this strategy now? Any party leader who decided to politicize a European issue would not only run the long-term risk of reducing the relative importance of national as opposed to European politics, thus sabotaging his or her own career prospects,[17] but much more immediately would run the risk of ceasing to be a party leader when replaced by someone willing to continue the softly-softly approach.

What happened to Margaret Thatcher in 1990 is instructive in this regard. Instead of being able to take her concerns to British voters, asking them to choose between a Europe that was unified purely in economic terms and one that was unified also in terms of the monetary and other policies that govern the economy, she found herself faced with a rebellion in her party that finally resulted in her being ousted from the Tory leadership. The reason why this happened is simple: Thatcher could not go to the voters with her concerns in

---

17 One criticism of the Maastricht Treaty made by French opponents is that it stood to cut the stature of the French Presidency to no more than that of the governor of Texas.

the context of a national election campaign because the resulting split in the Tory party would have drastically hurt its chances of re-election. So Thatcher was replaced, and the split within the party papered over in time for it to be able to face the election of 1992 with barely a mention of the issues that had caused such internal dissension only two years previously. Other parties have generally been more successful than the British Tories in avoiding publicity over their internal schisms, but only as a result of taking the problem seriously.

Eliminating the threat of party splits at European elections seems out of the question in the short run. The most viable alternative would be to generalize Denmark's success in 'containing' the effects of European elections. If other countries were to similarly develop a European party system for European elections, then national party leaders in those countries would not have to fear the politicization of European issues to the same extent as they do now. A legal requirement for parties to draw support from several different regions of the political territory does not seem at all practical; but, drawing on the experience of party development within European and other Western democracies, there are a number of possible institutional reforms which could promote the 'Europeanization' of parties by providing incentives for them to engage in pan-European election campaigns.

One incentive could be financial. The funding of European elections has been the source of much discussion and even litigation in the past. Currently there is little funding, and that which is available is given to European Parliament groups only for the purpose of publicizing the election. However, if significant European funding were to be made available to the parties campaigning in European elections, on condition that those parties ran a single, undifferentiated slate of candidates in more than one country, it would give parties an incentive to broaden their appeal, formulating programs and policy proposals with more than one country in mind, and focussing on issues which were not merely parochial. European elections would then be fought on a different basis from national elections, and the results of those elections could no longer be used as markers for the performance of domestic political parties (see Chapter 18 for such usage of elections). National party leaders would thus be insulated from the electoral consequences of debate over European issues. Such a development would probably require a common European electoral system in place of the nation-specific electoral systems that now govern European elections, but this too could help to insulate national politics from the consequences of European elections in countries that adopted different electoral systems for European elections. Results could not be taken as markers of what would happen under a different electoral system.

Even without accompanying financial incentives, a more uniform electoral system might have desirable consequences. Indeed, it has long been suggested that such a system is vital for an effective European Parliament (Jacobs, Corbett and Shackleton, 1992:24–28). In itself the point seems of only marginal importance unless the system chosen is one which provides incentives for cross-national parties to develop: one that encourages parties to adopt similar positions across all constituencies rather than tailoring their messages differently in different countries. As Katz (1980) pointed out, this is accomplished by proportional representation systems rather than by majoritarian ones. A system like that employed in Germany (now adopted with variations in Japan, Italy and New Zealand), with proportional allocation at the European level but individual candidacies in sub-national constituencies, would do this quite effectively.

A third suggestion stems from the US experience of party building, where the need to capture the presidency served to bring together political forces in the separate states. Bogdanor (1986) suggested that a 'Presidential model' might be more appropriate than a 'parliamentary model' for the European Union, with a directly elected president of the European Commission. The suggestion, which has a long pedigree, would necessitate a single Europe-wide contest which in itself would bridge country boundaries. If such a contest were to occur in tandem with elections to the European Parliament (a reasonable expectation now that the term of the president of the Commission is coterminous with that of the European Parliament) it would help to provide a European context for those elections too.[18]

Any of these reforms assumes that election campaigns can meaningfully be fought across the boundaries of EU member states. Opponents of reform will claim that this is impractical and expects too much of voters. The fundamental finding that this book brings to bear on these debates is that developments that link European voters across countries are not only desirable but also feasible. The fact that in terms of political discourse and in other important ways we do not have separate national electorates but only one European electorate is a precondition for any of the reforms listed above, but that precondition is in place, as was reflected in the findings of Chapters 18, 19 and 20. Another precondition, also in place, is that voters should be motivated to adapt to new political circumstances. Indeed, the evidence we have amassed that bears on the responsiveness of voters to changes in political and other contexts is a major contribution made by this book to our understanding of the mainsprings of voter rationality and motivation (see, again, Chapters 18 to 20, and the Coda to this volume).

---

18   For an alternative suggestion, that might lead to increased accountability of the presidency of the European Commission without introducing the need for Europe-wide presidential elections, see Ludlow and Ersbøll, 1994.

We do not propose in this book to do more than raise the question of what sort of reforms to European electoral institutions might achieve the desired objective; and our suggestions were chosen primarily as examples. It is likely that other reforms could achieve the same objectives, and it is possible that the ones we suggest overlook major flaws. But it seems evident that several different reforms would be needed in tandem in order to reinforce each other in ensuring the desired outcome, and the particular suggestions we have made were carefully chosen to work together towards the end we have in view. Nevertheless, the major problem is not with choosing a program of reforms but with finding the political will to carry them out.

Members of the European Parliament might not be hard to persuade; but the European Council consists of the leaders of the governments of EU member states who in turn are party leaders within those states. It is hard to see national party leaders voluntarily taking the steps that we hypothesize would be needed to remedy the democratic deficit. There are long-term risks in doing so, not only of reducing the stature of the offices they hold, but of an eventual showdown between an assertive European Parliament and a European Council serving as a last bastion of national interests.

One inducement would be to increase the costs of the present state of affairs by opening the Council of Ministers to public scrutiny, thereby making it more difficult for governments to hide the nature of their actions from parliamentarians and voters. This is our most important proposal for reform, to which we will return at the end of the chapter. But first we want to highlight existing costs exacted by the present system.

The Costs of European Elections

The democratic deficit in European elections (and in the government of the EU generally) is due to the lack of correspondence between the dimensions of competition among national parties and the dimensions of conflict within the European arena. The major cost resulting from this deficit is clear. It brings the risk of a breakdown in support for the European Union. Indeed, a decline in the number of people willing to support various aspects of European unification has been a recurring theme in Eurobarometers since 1990 (see Figure 21.1). It is not too strong to say that the future of a united Europe depends on halting (and if possible reversing) this decline. No doubt politicians in Brussels and in the capitals of member states hope that, if no new initiatives are brought forward, in time the decline may stop of its own accord and perhaps even be reversed. Certainly the return of economic prosperity and a decline in unemployment may help—mainly in reducing the opportunities to blame Brussels for economic problems.

**Figure 21.1 Support for European Integration and the Union,
Europe-wide 1990-1994**

Spring Fall Spring Fall Spring Fall Spring Fall Spring Fall
  90   90   91   91   92   92   93   93   94   94

Source: Eurobarometer Trends 1974-1993, EB41, EB42

The decline in popularity of the European Union may be halted, and even temporarily reversed, by developments like these; yet the situation is inherently unhealthy and can hardly fail to lead to further erosion of support for the European project in future years, particularly if any moves at all are made towards further integration. One thing that should have become clear in the aftermath of the Maastricht referenda, but seems to have largely escaped commentators and politicians of all stripes, is that European voters need to be involved in deliberations about the future of the European project. Yet the next initiative for strengthening the Union, an Intergovernmental Conference scheduled for 1996, pays no heed to this lesson. Instead, governments, bureaucrats and party leaders will get together with interest groups of various kinds to discuss the future of Europe with hardly a glance at the electorates of European countries.[19]

---

19 It is of course not certain that the decline in popularity of the European Union is linked to the emerging perception of a democratic deficit, but the link is theoretically plausible, and supported empirically by a quite strong relationship between the two variables in our 1989 post-election survey.

The most obvious way to remedy the perceived lack of democratic accountability and control would be to promote serious public debate about the future direction of European development. A natural forum for such debates might be provided by European election campaigns, were they to be employed for that purpose. It seems to us beyond question that the European costs of continuing the present system are potentially overwhelming.

What the findings of our country chapters have shown is that there are also clear national costs involved in a continuation of the present system. In their attempt to protect themselves from the effects of potentially divisive issues regarding European integration, parties and politicians often pay a price that is at least equally high when the consequences of neglecting those issues return to haunt them. Such consequences arise from the fact that it is not always possible to depoliticize an issue, and when the attempt fails the parties concerned risk losing both their European and their national stake, as almost happened to Britain's John Major over the ratification of the Maastricht Treaty.[20] The primary domestic consequence of trying to depoliticize European issues is that, by arranging things so that real (European or domestic) power is not at stake in a European election, these elections turn into occasions where voters can vote with the boot (see Chapter 18). This may have some benign effects, but it is clearly also a sword of Damocles that parties and politicians hang over their own heads; especially if they are misled by the electoral verdict into taking actions which they otherwise would not have taken, and which might damage their ability to successfully fight a more normal election. Moreover, protest voting is only one of several threats that national parties face in European elections as currently organized. At least as important is the possibility of a party's internal disarray on European matters becoming public. Nobody knows when their party will be struck by such developments, or in what manner. The only thing that is certain is that these things will happen again and again. This increases the

---

Among respondents who thought that the European Community worked "completely" or "to some extent" democratically, fully 64 percent gave it a good or excellent approval rating on a five-point scale in 1989. By contrast, of those who thought that the EC worked "very little" or "not at all" democratically, almost the same proportion (60 percent) rated it no better than medium on the same scale. The question was not asked in our 1994 survey, but given the general decline in approval for the EU shown in Figure 21.1, the results would almost certainly have been sobering.

20 After delaying the ratification process until Denmark's second referendum made further delays impossible, the British government submitted the treaty to Parliament where it initially failed to obtain a majority because so many members of the governing party voted against it. Only by making the issue a matter of confidence, and threatening his party with early elections (which it would certainly have lost for domestic political reasons) did the Prime Minister manage to carry the day on the second attempt.

unpredictability of the domestic political process, which in itself is certainly something that politicians would wish to avoid.

The country chapters have shown other consequences (summarized in Chapter 17) of treating European elections as purely national events. Some of these consequences were no doubt in the interests of some political actors; but overall there can be no question that they add uncertainty by injecting into national political life an apparent assessment of parties and policies that is easily perverted and often misunderstood. Such uncertainties exist even where European elections have as yet shown least effect. Because their intended purpose has been thwarted, unintended consequences can show up in any number of different ways.

Only in one country have we seen any degree of insulation of the national political scene from the consequences of European elections, and that country is Denmark. Not coincidentally, this is also the only country to have a European party system for European elections. This separate party system serves to contain the effects of European elections to the European arena. Even in Denmark the resulting election has no European consequences, but this is only because no other countries employ the same stratagem. If other countries were to copy the Danish means for containing European elections, the result could be a European party system capable of delivering a European mandate as the verdict of a Europe-wide election. This outcome, desirable from a European perspective, is thus desirable for national politics too, because it will protect national parties from the vagaries of European elections. The coincidence is not a happenstance. European elections get their undesirable national consequences from the fact that they do not function as proper elections. Give them a proper function of their own and they will cease to have unwanted repercussions in other spheres.

Why Reform?

Even though reform may be desirable both for European and national reasons, it will not be easily achieved. The difficulty standing in the way is the same difficulty that always stands in the way of reforming political institutions: those who have to agree to it have generally benefitted from the existing system. Politicians and parties are used to living with the uncertainties introduced into domestic politics by the regular occurrence of European elections. They are also used to a European Union that incorporates no effective electoral connection. By contrast, direct election of the Commission president, the development of a truly European electoral system, or campaign funding reform, would all introduce new contexts whose implications for each of the existing parties separately are not only less familiar but indeed unknown. It is not irrational to 'prefer the devil you know'.

As a counterweight to these concerns we would like to emphasize the dangers of the present situation which are much more serious than generally assumed. The warning we wish to sound in the final paragraphs of this book is close to home for national politicians, because it derives from the careful assessments of country experts in the chapters of Part II.

Familiarity has bred contempt, and politicians do not take sufficient account of the costs inherent in the present situation. In particular they ignore the havoc that will certainly be wreaked (at unpredictable times and occasions) by the increasing intrusion into national politics of EU-related issues. The potential embarrassments deriving from such intrusions are likely to get worse if the reforms incorporated in the Treaty of Union indeed lead (as many expect) to the establishment of a nexus of power between the European Parliament and the European Commission which consequently finds itself more frequently than in the past at odds with the Council of Ministers. It is bad enough for governments to have to explain to their electorates policy decisions over which they had some say in the Council of Ministers. Explaining decisions made by the Parliament and Commission can only be more difficult and more likely to cause credibility problems. Indeed, it is not fanciful to suggest that current institutional developments, if not accompanied by a politicizing of EU issues and proper debate of these issues in European election campaigns, will ultimately lead the crisis of legitimacy in the European Union to spread to national politics as well. From this perspective the Treaty of European Union can be seen as having set in train a developmental process that constitutes a time bomb at the heart of European democratic government. Doing nothing will not defuse it.

We do not wish to be alarmist, but it must be pointed out that lack of proper discussion of European issues could even result in one or more countries withdrawing from the EU, and even to the demise of the EU itself, if the failure to alleviate the democratic deficit were to lead in turn to a backlash by voters protesting lack of consultation. This would be a disaster that none of today's major party leaders could easily survive.[21] So if national politicians cannot be induced to embrace reform for Europe's sake, let them at least do so out of concern for their own professional skins.

---

21 The fate of politicians would be the least of our worries in such a circumstance. There is a real question whether our societies could survive the break-up of the European Union without real damage to the social and economic fabric, and perhaps major civil unrest.

The Council of Ministers as a Focus for Reform

One final mechanism can be suggested as a means for inducing politicians to adopt some version of the reforms suggested earlier. We have said that the main reason domestic party systems have been able to avoid confronting the issues involved in European unification has been the insulation of European decision-making from normal political processes within member-states. This insulation arises because European politics is treated as foreign policy, and governments are given a free hand to conduct foreign policy without the close supervision that parliaments provide in domestic matters. The most important feature of this insulation in the case of EU policy-making is the secrecy that surrounds the proceedings of the Council of Ministers and the European Council, even when these bodies are not performing an executive role (cf. Ludlow and Ersbøll, 1994). It is only because meetings are conducted in private that ministers can avoid giving a true picture of their actions—claiming to have done their best to protect the national interest when in fact the political wheeling and dealing that took place behind closed doors was of quite a different kind. If the veil of secrecy were lifted from meetings of the Council of Ministers (and preferably from meetings of the European Council as well) then ministers could no longer return to their own countries with freedom to mislead their parliaments about the positions they took and the factors that prompted them to take those positions.[22]

This change would have two consequences for the health of European democratic institutions: one immediate and one in the longer term. In the immediate aftermath of such a reform, national parliaments would gain new relevance in the conduct of European affairs. Instead of being faced with ministers who cast European negotiations as zero-sum games between the interests of member states, parliaments would instead be provided with knowledge of what had really taken place in Brussels, enabling them to hold ministers accountable for their actions in European affairs just as they do in regard to domestic matters. This might temporarily reduce the rate at which a unified Europe could develop, but that would be no bad thing. What the Maastricht fiasco indicated above all is that European voters need to become educated about European affairs. The sight of their parliaments properly discussing European issues, in full knowledge of the debates that had actually occurred in the Council of Ministers, would be educational as nothing else could be. European election campaigns taking place after this reform would be ones in which parties proposed policies that were already familiar to voters, because they would develop from debates that had already taken place in national

---

22   Ludlow and Ersbøll (1994) make the same suggestion from a more positive perspective.

parliaments. European elections could then be conducted in circumstances that permitted proper mandates to emerge.

In the longer term, the reform would give to governments a new incentive to accede to developments already promising to reduce the importance of the Council of Ministers. Since ministers would no longer be able to shrug off responsibility for decisions made there, they would have good reasons to permit decisions to be made elsewhere—hastening the transfer of decision-making power to the Parliament/Commission nexus. At the same time a European Parliament, newly legitimated by the mandates given at European elections in which European affairs were properly at issue, might be ready to take up its new burden of instructing the Commission and holding it accountable as though it were a proper political executive.[23]

We believe that, in this manner, the opening up of the Council of Ministers to public scrutiny will serve to promote other reforms such as those listed earlier in this chapter; reforms which will bring greater democratic accountability and control to European affairs by way of a more appropriate use of European elections, and which may give to national parties some respite from the intrusion into national politics of European affairs. But if national governments choose to retain control over European matters in this new context, at least that control will be subject to democratic scrutiny by way of national elections, which currently it is not. In this case the party systems of member states will be forced to adapt to the presence of European issues and concerns.

By making it more difficult for governments to leave their parliaments and voters in the dark about actions taken in the Council of Ministers, the reform would also remove a cancer from the heart of the body politic in most European countries. The Council of Ministers today often functions as a legislature, and a legislature that conducts its meetings in private has no place in a democracy. What would one make of a German Bundesrat that conducted its affairs in secrecy? Yet this is the body, as explained in Chapter 1, most analogous to the Council of Ministers today. The present system promotes deception, and deception puts democracy into disrepute.

At all events, the opening of the Council of Ministers to public scrutiny seems to us not only imperative from a normative democratic perspective but also a necessary prerequisite for any reforms whatsoever. Only if national parliaments are enabled to undertake proper debates about European matters

---

23 Any lessening of the role of the Councils of Ministers might have a further beneficial effect, as each of these operates in only a single policy domain, thereby reducing the possibilities for over-all bargaining and package dealing. In other words, the segmentation into policy areas enhances (and to some extent makes real) the perceptions of European politics as a zero-sum game between nation-states. Moving decision-making powers to the electoral and parliamentary arenas would reduce these perceptions.

will public opinion become educated to the point of being able to play its proper role at European or any other elections. Reforming the Council of Ministers will permit this development.

If this book has any single lesson to teach it is that elections conducted without proper debate of issues relevant to the arena concerned cannot function as real elections with consequences for the exercise of power in that arena. Instead such elections acquire alternative functions with consequences for other arenas—consequences that can be quite perverse. In this way, present-day European elections not only fail to function as proper elections to the European Parliament but also pervert the exercise of power in national parliaments as well. Only by allowing voters to choose between alternative visions of the future of Europe can a crisis of democratic legitimacy be averted. It is to be hoped that, given such choices, voters would choose the benefits of a more united Europe; but better a choice against further integration than no choice at all.

CODA
What We Have Learned About Voting Behavior and Elections

Cees van der Eijk and Mark Franklin

This book has presented analyses of European elections, their nature, and the forces that shape their outcomes. It examined their consequences for the national political arenas in which they are conducted, and their inability to perform in the European arena the functions that elections generally are expected to perform. It has drawn for the presentation of its major arguments heavily on analyses of two mass surveys, the European Election Studies of 1989 and 1994. Yet, the story of the book was not primarily one about voters and their behavior. As a consequence, much of what we have learned about voters has been reported only to the extent that it helped to develop the main themes of the book. The scope of these analyses, their comparative character, and their substantive significance for the study of electoral behavior warrants, however, a concise treatment of the most important substantive and methodological insights we have gained regarding voters, parties and elections.[1] This Coda is intended to present such an overview. In it we will focus in particular on findings which can be generalized across countries or contexts.

The structure of our presentation is as follows. First, for each of a number of themes we list one or several empirical propositions, numbered EP.1 et seq. These are general statements we believe to be justified by empirical analyses. The specific analyses that support the propositions are listed next, as sources. Finally, we discuss a number of implications under the general heading of corollaries: empirical statements which have not yet or only partially been tested—but which have not yet been falsified—and which we believe to hold

---

1 The surveys of the 1994 European Election Study have clearly not been fully analyzed as yet. Our use of them in this volume was exclusively intended to provide an independent test of hypotheses and insights derived from the 1989 European Election Study. Many other questions which might fruitfully be addressed with the 1994 study (and, indeed with the 1989 study as well) have not been pursued here. Consequently, this Coda relates only to knowledge acquired so far. A publication containing analyses from these studies, edited by Marsh and Schmitt, will be published in 1996 under the title *How Europe Voted 1994*.

true by logical deduction from the empirical propositions. Under corollaries we include also non-empirical statements which are of a prescriptive-methodological nature. This sequence of empirical propositions, sources and corollaries is repeated for each of the following themes:

- Individual-level determinants of electoral participation
- Systemic and contextual determinants of electoral participation and turnout
- Preferences for parties and party choice
- Determinants of such preferences
- Election results

Individual-level Determinants of Electoral Participation

Empirical Propositions

EP 1.0

Individual electoral participation is to a large extent a matter of random or politically irrelevant factors. It can only to a limited extent be explained by the kind of factors referred to in the literature as relevant explanatory phenomena.

EP 1.1

The contribution to explained variance in individual electoral participation of general political orientations—orientations that can be expected to be of importance irrespective the particular kind of election concerned—is larger than that of socio-demographic variables. This is even so when the latter are introduced first in an equation, and the former are only assessed in terms of their addition to R-square.

EP 1.2

The most important aspect of general political orientations is political interest, that is willingness to partake in communications concerning politics.[2]

EP 1.2.1

Willingness to expose oneself to media coverage of elections and election campaigns is an element of general political interest, not a separate empirical phenomenon.

---

2 This includes engaging actively or passively in personal communications—conversations and discussions—as much as in mass communications by reading, listening or viewing.

EP 1.3

In European countries without strong cleavage politics,[3] the most important socio-demographic characteristics in the explanation of electoral participation are age and education.

EP 1.4

The impact of (strength of) party attachment on electoral participation is quite limited once other factors are taken into account.

EP 1.5

Electoral participation in previous (national) elections—a proxy for independent variables omitted from an explanatory analysis—accounts for very little variance after socio-demographic and political orientational factors have been accounted for.

EP 1.6

Specific evaluative orientations towards the European Union hardly contribute at all to an explanation of electoral participation in European elections after the effects of socio-demographic characteristics and general political orientations have been taken into account.

EP 1.7

(Exposure to) Campaign information contributes to electoral participation only to the extent that it helps respondents to distinguish the positions of political parties or candidates.

EP 1.8

Electoral participation is promoted by the existence of at least one party that a voter finds really appealing.

Sources

The equivalents of Table 3.3 in the various country chapters; Table 17.2 and Appendix C for the comparable results in 1994; Chapter 19; also Schmitt and Mannheimer (1991a); Oppenhuis (1995).

Corollaries

C 1.1

Although different socio-demographic groups, or groups defined on the basis of political orientations can differ (sometimes considerably) in terms of their turnout, such groups will still exhibit considerable internal

---

3 In view of the decline of cleavage politics in western democracies, this condition can be expected to hold in an increasing number of political systems (see Franklin et al., 1992).

variance in electoral participation. In other words, such groups will neither participate nor abstain uniformly in elections.

(From EP 1.0)

C 1.2

No meaningfully defined stratum exists in the adult population (of European countries) that can be characterized as permanently disconnected from the electoral process.[4]

(From EP 1.0 and 1.5)

C 1.3

General political orientations (such as political interest) cannot be reduced to mere socio-psychological reflections of socio-demographic characteristics of voters (such as education, class, etc.).

(From EP 1.1)

C 1.4

Electoral participation is much more a motivationally directed act than a mere expression of habit or loyalty.

(From EP 1.4)

C 1.5

The existing scholarly literature on electoral participation has not omitted any major factors explaining electoral participation.

(From EP 1.5)

C 1.6

Electoral participation in European elections does not reflect support for or legitimacy of European integration, the European Union as a political system, or the institutions of the European Union. Consequently, neither turnout nor variations in turnout (from one European election to the

---

4 Two cautionary remarks have to made in this respect: (a) to the extent that specific groups or strata exist which are almost completely excluded from being interviewed (whether because of refusals, exclusion from interview frames, inaccessibility, or whatever) it is still possible that a stratum of permanent non-voters exists. No indications of the actual occurrence of such a condition are known to us, however. (b) the corollary does extend only to enfranchised citizens. An existing stratum of populations which is electorally disconnected, however, is the group of (permanent) residents that do not have the nationality of the country of their residence or of any other country of the EU. Such groups have no voting rights in European elections, nor in national elections. They are often not included in surveys because of a combination of formally not belonging to a target population (e.g. citizens), refusals, language problems in conducting interviews, etc. Such groups of non-indigenous residents may be quite numerous in certain regions, and may indeed be permanently and almost completely disconnected from the electoral process.

next) can be interpreted as reflecting changes in such support or legitimacy.

(From EP 1.6)

C 1.7

(Change in) turnout in national elections in the countries of the EU does in general not reflect (change in) popular support for or legitimacy of political community, regime (in Eastonian terms) or institutions.[5]

(From EP 1.5 and EP 1.6)

C 1.8

Efforts at mobilizing citizens to cast their vote which consist of general non-partisan appeals to citizen duty are ineffective.

(From EP 1.2.1 and EP 1.7)

C 1.9

The perception that an election involves having to pick 'the least of all evils' is not conducive to electoral participation.

(From EP 1.8)

Systemic and Contextual Determinants of Electoral Participation and Turnout

Empirical Propositions

EP 2.0

Compulsory voting has a strong (positive) effect on electoral participation in European elections, and hence on turnout. It does not, however, guarantee near-universal turnout.[6]

EP 2.1

Sunday voting has a positive impact on turnout in European elections.

EP 2.2

The degree of proportionality of the party system has a positive impact on turnout in European elections.

EP 2.3

The location of a European election in the interval between two adjacent national elections has an impact on turnout in the European election: the

---

5 See Easton, 1965.

6 'Near universal' turnout is meant to indicate turnout of virtually all those who are not (physically or psychologically) ill or handicapped, imprisoned, out of the country, off the electoral register because of delays in updating, etc. In practical terms, it is meant to indicate a level of turnout of at least 90 percent.

shorter the time period until the next national elections, the higher turnout will be (ceteris paribus). The case of concurrent European and national elections can be regarded as the limiting case of highest turnout.

Sources

Chapters 17 and 19; Oppenhuis (1995).

Corollaries

C 2.0

Systemic and contextual characteristics affect turnout in European elections because they either influence the cost of electoral participation for individual voters, or because they impinge on voters' participatory motivation through their perception of 'what is at stake'.

(From the logic of the interpretations in Chapter 19)

C 2.1

Propositions 2.0, 2.1 and 2.2 (pertaining to the effects of compulsory voting, Sunday voting and proportionality) hold for other kinds of elections as well.

(From the logic of the interpretations in Chapter 19)

C 2.2

Proposition 2.3 (on the impact of the temporal location of a second-order national election in the first-order election cycle) holds also for other second-order national elections than European elections (e.g., in most countries for local and regional elections, by-elections, etc.)

(From the interpretation of EP 2.3 in Chapters 2 and 19)

C 2.3

Systemic and contextual characteristics affect the relevance of motivational factors (i.e. political interest) for electoral participation.

(From EP 2.0, C 2.0)

C 2.3.1

Compulsory voting reduces, but does not entirely eliminate, the positive effects of motivational factors on electoral participation.

(From EP 2.0)

C 2.3.2

Informative election campaigns, i.e. campaigns that help people perceive what contending political parties and candidates stand for, promote turn-out and reduce (but do not eliminate) the effect of motivational factors on electoral participation.

(From EP 1.7, C 2.0)

Preferences for Parties and Party Choice

Empirical Propositions

EP 3.0

Preference for a party is a matter of degree, not a matter of presence or absence.

EP 3.1

Voters' preferences for parties are non-exclusive: strong preference for one party does not exclude a preference for other parties as well. The large majority of voters in each of the member states of the European Union holds medium to strong preferences for at least two different parties.

EP 3.2

Voters discriminate between parties in terms of degrees of preference they attach to them.

EP 3.3

Voters generally give their vote to the party for which they hold the strongest preference at the time of the election.[7]

EP 3.4

Voters' preferences for parties are structured: they reflect the similarity between voters and parties in a joint latent space.

EP 3.4.1

Voters preferences for any party are not constrained by their preferences for other parties.

EP 3.4.2

In the political systems of the European Union the relevant latent space that generates preferences for parties is largely one-dimensional, in line with the dominant political conflict dimension.

EP 3.4.3

The ordering of political parties on this dominant political conflict dimension corresponds largely with voters' perceptions of the parties in terms of left and right.

Sources

Chapter 20; the equivalents of Table 3.1 in the country chapters of Part II; van der Eijk and Oppenhuis (1991); Tillie (1995); Oppenhuis (1995).

---

7 In systems where voters can express more than one preference on the ballot (e.g., STV, the German second-ballot system, etc.) this proposition pertains to the first or politically most important preference expressed on the ballot.

Corollaries

C 3.1.

Party preference and party choice should conceptually and operationally be distinguished as separate phenomena.
(From EP 3.0, EP 3.1 and EP 3.2)

C 3.2

Determinants of party choice can be investigated empirically by analyzing party preferences.
(From EP 3.3)

C 3.3

Parties compete with each other for votes.
(From EP 3.1 and EP 3.3)

C 3.3.1

In addition to their actual electoral support in a particular election, parties can also be characterized by their potential electoral support.
(From EP 3.1 and EP 3.3)

C 3.3.2

Electoral competition takes place in the overlap between parties' potential electorates.
(From EP 3.1 and EP 3.3)

C 3.3.3

In view of the extent to which potential electorates in the member states of the European Union are shared between parties, few, if any, parties can take for granted in another election more than a fraction of the electoral support they receive in any given election.
(From EP 3.1 and EP 3.3)

C 3.4

For (most) voters no single party exists that can be considered the 'natural' and exclusive recipient of their votes.
(From EP 3.1)

C 3.4.1

Most voters are potential party switchers (i.e., will vote for different parties in different elections).
(From EP 3.1, EP 3.3)

C 3.4.1.1

Party switching is not restricted to 'exceptional' circumstances for most voters.
(From EP 3.1, C 3.3)

C 3.4.1.2

Party switching is not necessarily indicative of capriciousness, anomy or lack of political sophistication.[8]

(From EP 3.1, EP 3.3, C 3.3)

C 3.4.2

Few voters in the member states of the European Union could possibly be considered to be party identifiers in the Michigan sense of the concept.[9]

(From C 3.4, C 3.4.1 and C 3.4.1.1)

C 3.5

The extent of electoral competition between parties is a function of their similarity in the latent space underlying preferences: similarity promotes electoral competition.

(From EP 3.1 and EP 3.4)

C 3.5.1

The extent of electoral competition between parties varies positively with their similarity in terms of the dominant conflict dimension in a political system; in the political systems of the European Union this implies mainly their similarity in left/right terms.

(From EP 3.1 and EP 3.4)

Determinants of Party Preference

Empirical Propositions

EP 4.0

A single equation adequately describes variations in preferences for parties (variations between parties for each individual, and variations between individuals for each party) in each country of the European Union. With only minor adaptations a single equation describes such variation also for the countries of the European Union combined.

---

8   See also van der Eijk and Niemöller (1983:147–192).

9   We refer here to the conceptualization of party identification as proposed by Campbell et al., a conceptualization which contains a strong element of party-exclusiveness (see Campbell et al. 1960). The empirical propositions and corollaries listed in this section apply to a large extent also to those voters who would, on the basis of their responses to appropriate questions, commonly— but incorrectly—be classified by survey analysts as identifiers. For a detailed explanation of this phenomenon that is intimately related to the existence of multiple preferences as stated in EP 3.1, see also van der Eijk and Niemöller (1983:324–345).

EP 4.1

Among the strongest determinants of party preferences are the latent traits that define the structure of multiple preferences (see EP 3.4). Specifically, this implies that in European systems ideological (left/right) similarity between voters and parties is the strongest substantive determinant of party preferences.

EP 4.2

Besides ideological (left/right) similarity, preferences are also determined by other substantive political considerations and by factors relating to strategic considerations.

EP 4.2.1

Additional substantive political considerations are either instrumental (relating to issue preferences or to evaluation of government performance) or affective (relating to membership of or identification with groups based on class, religion, etc.) in nature.

EP 4.2.2

Strategic considerations pertain to the (perceived) ability of parties to significantly affect the course and contents of public policy. Electoral strength of parties captures most of these considerations and is one of the strongest determinants of party preferences: strong parties generate, ceteris paribus, more preference than weak ones.[10]

EP 4.3

The explanatory power of instrumental considerations—both of a substantive kind (ideology, issues, government approval) and of a strategic kind (power of parties as indicated by their electoral strength)—greatly outweighs that of affective considerations.

EP 4.4

Differences between electoral systems or between party systems are of little or no importance to the process that generates preferences for parties, except insofar as such differences affect the number and relative strength of parties.

EP 4.5

The process that generates preferences for parties is affected by those aspects of the political culture that relate to perceptual consensus of the political world.

---

10 At first sight, this statement may be mistaken as a mere tautology. It is not, however, when party preference is not equated with party choice (see C 3.1, above, and, for a fuller exposé, Chapter 20 and Tillie, 1995). Although the European Election Studies of 1989 and 1994 lack relevant indicators to demonstrate this, voters may differ in the weight they attach to such considerations. Some voters are more 'idealistic', whereas others are more 'pragmatic' in this respect (see Tillie, 1995:114–119).

EP 4.5.1

The contribution of ideological (left/right) considerations increases with the degree of consensus on the characterization of real-life political stimuli (e.g. political parties) in such ideological terms. At the same time, the contribution of issue considerations decreases with increasing consensus.

EP 4.6

The process that generates preferences for parties is affected by those aspects of the political context that define what is 'at stake' in or because of the elections.

EP 4.6.1

The contribution of evaluations of government performance (to the extent that these are not caused by general ideological affinity) to party preference is larger in contexts of first-order national elections than in the context of second-order elections (if the latter are not held concurrently with the former).

EP 4.6.2

The stronger the perception of voters that an election 'matters', the less likely voters are to vote sincerely.

EP 4.6.2.1

If the perception that an election 'matters' is based on the expectation that government power is at stake, strategic considerations that take the form of 'voting with the head' are strongest. Such considerations take into account expectations of the likelihood that various parties (or various coalitions) will attain government power.

EP 4.6.2.2

If the perception that an election 'matters' is based on the expectation that parties and media pay close attention to the result without the allocation of government power directly being at stake, strategic considerations that lead to the casting of protest votes are strongest. Such considerations take into account feelings of frustration and disaffection.

EP 4.7

Analyzing party preferences for each of the countries of the EU separately yields (sometimes rather strong) differences in the effects of explanatory variables. Such differences arise mainly from differences in the distributions of the variables involved between countries, not from differences in the process that generates preferences for parties.

Sources

Chapter 20; Oppenhuis (1995); Tillie (1995).

Corollaries

C 4.1

Voters behave more strongly as politically purposeful actors than as expressive or symbolic actors.
(From EP 4.2 and 4.3)

C 4.2

Voters are, in their preferences, sensitive to context. The contribution to party preferences of some political factors increases (decreases) when these factors are more (less) salient in the political context at the time.
(From EP 4.2.2, EP 4.5.1., EP 4.6.1)

C 4.2.1

Voters' party choice is sensitive to context.
(From EP 3.3, EP 4.5.1., EP 4.6.1)

C 4.3

The sensitivity of preferences to context is limited, and pertains only to the relative weight of various factors contributing to preferences, not to the substantive nature of those factors.
(From EP 4.0, EP 4.5.1, see also C 4.2)

C 4.3.1

The context-sensitivity of preferences does not undermine the interpretation of voters' behavior as largely purposeful.
(From EP 4.0, EP 4.5.1, C 4.2, C 4.3)

Election Results (Parties' Electoral Strength)

Empirical Propositions

EP 5.0

How well parties perform in second-order national elections in comparison with how they would have done in a first-order election (see also GC 2.1.3.1) is dependent on the interaction between party characteristics on the one hand and characteristics of the political context on the other.

EP 5.0.1

In contexts conducive to protest voting (see EP 4.6.2.2) small, ideologically extreme parties are likely to do better than they would in a first-order election held at the same time.

EP 5.0.2

In contexts conducive to sincere voting, small parties are likely to do better than they would in a first-order election held at the same time, with the exception of those that are seen as suitable vehicles for registering protest.

EP 5.1

Seemingly minor differences in electoral rules and procedures affect the performance of parties in second-order elections by comparison with their performance in first-order elections.

EP 5.1.1

Small parties suffer when the effective threshold is raised because of a smaller number of seats to be allocated.

EP 5.1.2

A reduction of the number of constituencies is beneficial to small parties by lowering the resources required for competing in all constituencies.

Sources

The country chapters of Part II; Chapter 17; Chapter 18; van der Eijk and Oppenhuis (1991).

Corollaries

C 5.0

Small parties will anticipate the effects of higher effective thresholds by engaging in electoral pacts or alliances.
(From EP 5.1.1)

C 5.1

In systems that have a larger number of constituencies in first-order than in second-order national elections, the latter offer relatively generous environments for new or small parties for breaking through on a national scale.
(From EP 4.6.2, EP 5.0 and EP 5.1.2)

General Corollaries

The following General Corollaries are derived from the empirical propositions and corollaries in the previous sections. They are set apart because they relate to more than just one of the earlier sections.

GC 1

Voters behave largely purposefully.
(From EP 1.2.1, EP 1.6, C 1.6, C 2.0, EP 4.2, EP 4.3, C 4.1, C 4.3.1)

GC 2

Voters are sensitive to the characteristics of the political context, and take those into account in their preferences and behavior.
(From EP 1.8, C 2.3, EP 4.2.2, EP 4.5.1, EP 4.6.1, C 4.2, C 4.3)

GC 2.1

Voters' preferences change in relation to changes in their political context. Whether or not their behavior will change depends on the stability of the ordering of their preferences.

(From GC 2)

GC 2.1.1

Stable preferences are indicative of either (a) stable contexts, or (b) strong affective, rather than instrumental bases of preferences.

(From GC 2.1)

GC 2.1.2

Stable choice behavior is indicative of either (a) stable preferences, or (b) such large differences between first and subsequent preferences that changing preferences do not affect the relative position of the most preferred choice option.[11]

(From GC 2.1)

GC 2.1.3

Analyses of changing electoral choice should take changing context into account.

(From GC 2.1)

GC 2.1.3.1

Comparisons of voter choices in different kinds of elections should distinguish between changes caused by differences in political context and differences between the kinds of election. This may require the construction of a relevant counterfactual (e.g., see Chapter 3 for such a procedure that employs the notion of 'quasi-switching' for this purpose).

(From GC 2.1.3)

GC 3

Whatever their differences may be in all sorts of other respects, in terms of their electoral behavior (including the motivations underlying it, and its sensitivity to systemic, contextual and political stimuli) the populations of the member-states of the European Union constitute a single electorate, and cannot be meaningfully be considered as distinct electorates.

(From Chapters 18, 19 and 20; EP 1.6, C 1.6, C 2.0, EP 4.0)

---

11 Stable choices may mask a slow erosion of preferences and preference orderings underlying those choices. Only when such erosion affects the top of the preference ordering will changes in overt choice occur, which may come as a surprise in the light of the apparent stability of earlier years. Such processes seem to have been at play in the decline of cleavage voting in many European countries (see Franklin, 1985; Franklin et al., 1992, Chapter 19; van der Eijk and Niemöller, 1983).

Appendices

Appendix A
The European Election Studies 1989 and 1994

Hermann Schmitt and Cees van der Eijk

Introduction and Study Design

The European Election Studies (EES) 1989 and 1994 were survey-based studies of the electorates of the 12 member states of the (then) European Community (in 1989), and of the European Union (in 1994). The member states were Belgium, Denmark, France, Germany, Greece, Ireland, Italy, Luxembourg, the Netherlands, Portugal, Spain and the United Kingdom. The studies focussed in particular on the third and fourth direct elections to the European Parliament, which were conducted in June 1989 and June 1994, respectively. It should be noted that these are the only European elections to date that were conducted in the same set of countries on more than one occasion. The elections of 1984 were conducted in only 10 countries, Spain and Portugal having acceded to the European Community only in 1986. The elections of 1979 were conducted in nine countries, Greece having acceded to the Community in 1981. Indeed the elections of 1989 and 1994 are likely to remain for some years the only two elections conducted in the same set of countries. The elections of 1999 will be held in at least fifteen countries, and the European Union is expected to be still larger by the time of the European elections of 2004. It is true that the European Union was enlarged, between 1989 and 1994, by the indirect accession of those German Länder that had been part of the former East Germany. Data for respondents from those areas are held in a separate file in the 1994 study (see below) and that file was not included in comparative analyses conducted for this volume.

The 1989 European Election Study

The 1989 study consisted of three waves of interviews, the first two of which took place before the European elections, in October-November 1988 and March-April 1989 respectively. The third wave was conducted immediately following the European elections, in June 1989. Though using the languages of each country, the questionnaires were otherwise identical in the various member states, apart from minor but unavoidable differences in the names of parties and other country-specific institutions. As a consequence, the study offers wide opportunities for the comparative study of voters.

The contents of the three waves of interviews partially overlapped. Many of the questions were included in two, some in all three of the waves, thus offering opportunities for longitudinal comparisons of voter behavior and orientations during the run-up to a European election. The three waves constitute a repeated cross-section study; that is, they were administered to three independently-drawn random samples of the populations of the member states of the (then) European Community. Consequently, longitudinal comparisons can only be made in terms of aggregates, not of individual respondents.

The number of interviews achieved in the different countries for each of the three waves was approximately 1000. For Luxembourg this number was lower, about 300. Sample size in the United Kingdom was approximately 1300, of which about 300 interviews were conducted in Northern Ireland. The total number of interviews conducted over all three waves in all member states of the European Union thus amounts to almost 34,000.

The 1994 European Election Study

The 1994 study consisted of a single wave of interviews, conducted immediately following the European elections of June 1994, with freshly drawn samples in all member states of the European Union. As in 1989, the questionnaires were identical in all member states (apart from unavoidable variations due to language and institutional differences) and a large number of the questions—including all those of central importance to the analyses reported in this volume—were identical to those used in the 1989 study, thus permitting over-time comparisons of voter behavior in the 1989 and 1994 elections.

Sample sizes were mostly of the same magnitude as in 1989, with a few exceptions. In most member-states approximately 1000 people were interviewed. In the United Kingdom, almost 1400 respondents took part in the survey, of which slightly over 300 came from Northern ireland. The Luxembourg sample contained just over 500 people, and the German sample slightly more than 2100, approximately half of whom were drawn from the area formerly known as East-Germany. The grand total of interviews in the study was just over 13,000.

Accessing the Data

The data of the studies have been organized as a set of interconnected files, one for each wave in each different political system. In view of the distinctiveness of Northern Ireland as a political system apart from the rest of the United Kingdom, the interviews from Northern Ireland were organized as a separate file. For 1994, the data from former East-Germany were likewise stored separately from those of West-Germany. Consequently, the data from the 1989 study comprise 39 files: 3 files (one for each of the 3 waves) for each of the 13 political systems.

In the 1994 data, 14 different systems are distinguished (one extra for the former East-German area). As a number of the questions in the immediate post-election survey (June/July 1994) were also included in surveys surrounding this study (i.e., in Eurobarometers 40, 41 and 42, conducted respectively in Fall 1993, Spring 1994 and Fall 1994), these Eurobarometers have been included as additional files, integrated with the main 1994 survey results.

The 1989 data have been archived at and can be obtained for secondary analysis from the Steinmetz Archive, Herengracht 510-512, 1017 BX Amsterdam, the Netherlands; and can also be obtained via the ESRC Data Archive at the University of Essex, the ICPSR at the University of Michigan, and other archives. The 1994 data will be archived in the same fashion. Note that the data just described are not the same as those catalogued under the title '1989 election study' in the ICPSR catalog, since that is simply the name given by the ICPSR to the Eurobarometer study that accompanied (and contained some of the questions used in) our election study in 1989 (see below). The same cataloguing problem may well occur in relation to the 1994 study. The Eurobarometer study contains data that has not been cleaned or rationalized in terms of the interlocking files mentioned above (see below), and which (above all) have not been weighted in such a way as to permit replication of our findings.

Organization and Funding

The European Election Studies of 1989 and 1994 were included as separately funded parts of the Eurobarometer surveys conducted for the European Community's/Union's Directorate-General Information, Communication and Culture, Unit Surveys, Research, Analyses. The Eurobarometer surveys in which the EES-89 questions were included were numbers 30, 31 and 31A, the Eurobarometer containing the EES-94 questions was number 41A. The data from these European Election Studies can therefore also be accessed as part of the regular Eurobarometer data files which are archived at the Zentralarchiv (ZA) in Cologne (Germany) and the ICPSR in Ann Arbor (USA). Major differences exist, however, between the way in which these data have been archived in their respective guises as Eurobarometers and European Election Studies. In their separate form, the EES datasets excel, when compared to regular

Eurobarometer data, in terms of documentation, cleaning, standardization of codings, transparency, embedded analytical tools (especially well-designed weight variables—see below), conciseness and possibilities for simple and effective merging of data across political systems or waves into customized files. In short, the EES datasets are superior in terms of completeness and user- friendliness.

The European Election Studies 1989 and 1994 were organized by an international group of researchers which came together for the first time in the corridors of the Joint Sessions of Workshops of the European Consortium for Political Research in Amsterdam in April 1987. The group consisted originally of Roland Cayrol (CEVIPOF, Paris), Cees van der Eijk (University of Amsterdam), Mark Franklin (then University of Strathclyde, now University of Houston), Manfred Kuechler (then Florida State University, now City University of New York), Renato Mannheimer (then University of Milan, now University of Genova) and Hermann Schmitt (University of Mannheim). Although prevented from being a formal member of the group, Karlheinz Reif (Commission of the European Communities and University of Mannheim) has to be regarded as its prime initiator and continuing supporter. As of 1990 the group was extended with Colette Ysmal (CEVIPOF, Paris), Pilar del Castillo (UNED, Madrid), Erik Oppenhuis (University of Amsterdam) and Michael Marsh (Trinity College Dublin). In 1992 Manfred Kuechler left the group. The design and funding strategies for the 1989 study were worked out during the course of 1987. For the 1994 study this work was done in the course of successive meetings held between 1991 and 1994.

The studies could not have been conducted without generous support from a variety of sources. Data-collection was made possible first of all by the Commission of the European Communities which agreed to the use of the Eurobarometer as a vehicle on which to 'piggy-back' the European Election Studies. The costs of the (large numbers of) questions added to the Euro-barometers for the EES-89 were covered by a generous grant from the British Economic and Social Research Council (ESRC), and an additional grant from the Office of the French Prime Minister. Remaining costs were paid by selling prospective reports of analyses of the (yet to be collected) data to interested media and other institutions throughout Europe. Media institutions which sponsored the project in this manner were: Corriere de la Sera (Italy), ITN/ITV (Great Britain), De Morgen (Belgium), Le Soir (Belgium), Tageblatt (Luxembourg), Nouvel Observateur (France), Politiken (Denmark), EL Periodico (Spain), Radio Athens (Greece), El Dia 16 (Spain), Sunday Independent (Ireland), O Seculo (Portugal), WDR (Germany), and PRETI (Greece). Other institutions which sponsored the project in similar fashions were: VDA and Bundespresseamt (both Germany), CIS (Spain), PvdA (the Netherlands),

MORI (Ireland) and EMNID (Germany). The costs of the EES-94 were covered by a large grant from the Deutsche Forschungs Gemeinschaft (DFG), a smaller grant from the Dutch National Science Foundation (NWO), and additional support from the European Parliament.

For both studies, the University of Mannheim created a special position, occupied by Hermann Schmitt, which functioned as a communications and coordination center for the group—a position that assumed special significance in the light of all the different sources of funding that had to be coordinated.

Non-fieldwork costs for data cleaning, data production, and documentation were covered by the Dutch National Science Foundation (NWO, the Netherlands), the University of Amsterdam, the University of Mannheim, and the Steinmetz Archive (Amsterdam, the Netherlands). Costs for meetings of the international group of researchers which designed and carried out the study were met by Volkswagen Stiftung (Germany), Thyssen Stiftung (Germany), the Dutch National Science Foundation (NWO, the Netherlands), the University of Mannheim, the CNRS (Paris) and a consortium of Italian local governments.

Additional Developments

After completing the 1989 European Election Study, the research group devoted part of its attention to designing follow-up studies. Given the increasing visibility and salience of EU policy-making after the completion of the Single Market and ratification of the Maastricht Treaty, the group decided to conduct a study of electoral representation in the new European Union, inquiring into the so-called democratic deficit of European Union politics. The European Election Study 1994 therefore included a Voter Study based on a post-election survey of those entitled to vote in the 1994 elections to the European Parliament (as described above), and an Elite Study which surveyed candidates standing for office in these elections and, in 1996, the elected Members of the European Parliament. Primary responsibility for the Elite component of the study was born by Jacques Thomassen (University of Twente, the Netherlands), Richard Katz (first at Johns Hopkins University, Baltimore, U.S.A., then at the State University of New York at Buffalo) and Pippa Norris (Harvard University).

Central portions of the questionnaire instruments were equivalent (if not totally identical) in both the Voter and the Elite parts of the study. Taken together with the replication in the 1994 Voter Study of many questions from the 1989 European Election Study, these interconnected datasets permit a multitude of cross-level and over-time comparisons.

Related Publications

In addition to the present volume, a number of publications have already arisen from the European Elections Studies. Additional work is still in progress. In mid-1995, publications of the European Elections Study research group included (apart from numerous papers and smaller publications):

Books, edited volumes, monographs and reports
Swyngedouw, de Winter and Schulpen (1990), Schmitt and Mannheimer (1991b); Rüdig and Franklin (1991); van der Eijk, Oppenhuis and Schmitt et al. (1993); Niedermayer and Schmitt (1994); Oppenhuis (1995).

Articles in professional journals, chapters in edited volumes
Cayrol (1991); van der Eijk (1996); van der Eijk and Franklin (1991, 1994); van der Eijk, Franklin and Marsh (1996); van der Eijk and Oppenhuis (1990, 1991); van der Eijk and Schmitt (1991); Franklin (1991, 1996); Franklin, van der Eijk and Oppenhuis (1996); Franklin and Rüdig (1992a,b; 1995); Keatinge and Marsh (1990); Kuechler (1991, 1994); Marsh (1991, 1992); Niedermayer (1994); Rüdig and Franklin (1991, 1992); Rüdig, Franklin and Bennie (1993, 1995); Schmitt (1989, 1990b, 1994a,b); Schmitt and Mannheimer (1991a); Schulz and Blumler (1994).

Appendix B
Variables Employed and Methods of Analysis

Cees van der Eijk and Erik Oppenhuis

Contents

B1: Weighting

The analyses reported in this volume have been performed, if not specified otherwise, on data which have been weighted in such a manner as to reflect the results of the European elections of 1989 and 1994. This section describes the weighting procedure employed.

The first step of the weighting procedure consists of applying (fractional) weights which ensure that in each of the member states of the European Community/Union the sample distribution of reported voting behavior and party choice in the European elections is rendered identical to the official election result. This weighting assigns equal weights to all non–voters, i.e. assumes all kinds of non–voters to be equally under– or over–represented in the sample. This assumption may be implausible in the light of the low level of turnout in most countries. A more plausible assumption would be that over– or underrepresentation of groups with specific party preferences affects both voters and non–voters. This assumption allows utilizing the close resemblance that exists in all countries between European vote and national vote intention. In other words, the assumption is that when preferences for a particular party are overrepresented among the voters in the sample (as can be gauged from their European party choice), it is also overrepresented among the European non–voters (for whom party preferences are gauged by their intended party choice in national elections).

Table B1.1 illustrates the procedure by means of a hypothetical example, which describes the distributions in a fictional sample from a country with three parties A,B and C.

The cell–entries in this table (aa, nb, C_{tot}) are frequency counts. The quantities A_{EE} etc. are target frequency counts, i.e. the numbers of observations which should occur in each row, were the sample to reflect the election result exactly.

For those who voted in the European elections the weighting procedure is quite simple. Respondents who voted for party A, were assigned a weighting coefficient $w_a = A_{EE} / A_{tot}$. For respondents voting for party B this coefficient is $w_b = B_{EE} / B_{tot}$ and for those who voted for party C it is $w_c = C_{EE} / C_{tot}$.

For European non–voters the procedure consists of two stages. In the first stage preliminary weights are calculated: European non–voters who indicated a national party preference for party A are assigned a first–stage weighting coefficient w_p as follows:

$$w_p = (aa*w_a + ba*w_b + ca*w_c) / (aa+ba+ca)$$

Likewise for European non–voters who intended to vote for party B or C in national elections first–stage coefficients w_q and w_r are defined:

$$w_q = (ab*w_a + bb*w_b + cb*w_c) / (ab+bb+cb)$$
$$w_r = (ac*w_a + bc*w_b + cc*w_c) / (ac+bc+cc)$$

European non–voters who expressed no intended party choice for national elections are assigned a first–stage coefficient w_s as follows:

$$w_s = (an*w_a + bn*w_b + cn*w_c + nn*(N_{EE} / N_{tot})) / (an+bn+cn+nn)$$

Table B1.1 Example of weighting

European party choice	National vote intention					Target distribution
	A	B	C	Novote	Total	
A	aa	ab	ac	an	A_{tot}	A_{EE}
B	ba	bb	bc	bn	B_{tot}	B_{EE}
C	ca	cb	cc	cn	C_{tot}	C_{EE}
No vote	na	nb	nc	nn	N_{tot}	N_{EE}

The second stage is necessary to ensure an identical proportion of non–voters in the weighted sample as in the population. The final weights are:

For European non–voters with a national vote intention for A: $w_u = w_p * w_t$
For European non–voters with a national vote intention for B: $w_v = w_q * w_t$
For European non–voters with a national vote intention for C: $w_w = w_r * w_t$
For European non–voters with no national vote intention: $w_x = w_s * w_t$

where

$$w_t = NEE / (na * w_p + nb * w_q + nc * w_r + nn * w_s)$$

B2: Calculation of Potential Electorates and their Overlap

The questionnaires of the European Election Studies contained a set of questions which has been referred to in various chapters of this volume as 'probability to vote' questions: for each of the parties in a political system the respondents are asked to indicate how likely it is that they will "ever" vote for it. The responses range on a 10–point scale from "I will never vote for this party" (score 1) to "I will certainly vote for this party at some time in the future" (score 10). The responses to this question indicate (non–ipsative) electoral party preferences, as has amply been demonstrated by Tillie (1995).[1] Therefore, these responses can be utilized to estimate the size of a party's potential electorate (expressed as a proportion of the entire electorate), namely as the weighted average of the responses of all voters. The higher the subjective probability, the larger the weight. Those who indicate that they "certainly" will vote at some time for the party in question (score 10) can be considered to belong to the potential electorate of the party and are assigned a weight of 1. Those who indicate that they will "never" vote for it (score 1), do not belong to the party's potential electorate and are assigned a weight of 0. The weights for intermediate scores can be derived from a monotone non–decreasing relationship between scores and weights. The character of this relationship determines the weights to be assigned to the intermediate scores between 1 and 10. Tillie (1994) has compared the responses to these questions with those yielded by magnitude estimation techniques, and concluded that the relationship between

---

1 Tillie's analyses pertained to the Netherlands. As far as the data of the European election studies allow, his validating analyses have also been conducted for the political systems of the European Community/Union, yielding substantively the same results.

scores and intensities of preference is a linear one.[2] Consequently, a linear function can also be used to derive the weights, yielding the following weights for the scores 1 to 10: 0, 0.11, 0.22, 0.33, 0.44, 0.56, 0.67, 0.78, 0.89 and 1.0.

To the extent that voters express electoral preferences for more than one party, the sum of the potential electorates of the various parties sums to more than 100 per cent. This indicates the existence of electoral competition. Competitive relations between parties can be expressed in several ways. In the country chapters the overlap of potential electorates of pairs of parties is reported, which indicates the extent to which two parties vie for the votes of the same voters (see also the discussion of such overlaps in Chapter 2, particularly on the basis of Table 2.1). This overlap can simply be calculated from the sizes of the potential electorates of the two parties and the size of their combined potential. The latter can be calculated by using the highest of the probability to vote scores of the parties whose combined potential is to be assessed. To the extent that parties' electoral potentials overlap, the size of their combined potential is smaller than the sum of their separate potentials:

Overlap between A and B = Potential of A + Potential of B – Potential of (A and B)

A more formalized analysis of overlaps involves not only pairs of parties, but all k–tuples (k > 2). This can be done by way of unfolding analysis. Without reporting such analyses in detail here, extensive stochastic unfolding analyses using the MUDFOLD algorithm devised by van Schuur (van Schuur, 1984; van Schuur and Wierstra, 1987) show that in all countries of the European Community/Union the responses to the probability to vote questions are to a large extent structured in terms of the left/right dimension. This means that electoral competition between parties varies largely as a function of their distance on this ideological continuum. Consequently, tables of overlap of electoral potential in the country chapters have been ordered by parties' position on the left/right scale. This position was measured by the interpolated median of the perceptions of all respondents of the parties' position on a 10–point left/right scale. This particular measure of location was used rather than the more commonly employed mean, as the latter is more vulnerable to centripetal bias which exists to the extent that responses are generated by (more or less random)

---

2 The calibrating analyses reported by Tillie (1995) yield weights that run from a value slightly larger than 0 to a value of approximately 0.9. He interprets the differences from 0 and 1 respectively as the consequence of measurement error. In this volume a range of 0 to 1 is used nonetheless, as the absence of similar possibilities for calibration leaves open the question whether the estimated lower and upper boundaries established for the Netherlands apply in other countries as well.

guessing, which may occur particularly for smaller and lesser–known parties.

In some instances the probability to vote question pertained to separate political parties which did not participate in the European elections on their own, but as part of a combined list with other parties. In those cases the electoral potential of the combination list was computed in the manner discussed above. For the 1989 European elections this was done in France for the Union as combination of RPR, PR–UDF and Rad–UDF. In Italy the potential electorate of the PRI–PLI combination was assessed from the maximum of the separate probabilities to vote for PRI and PLI. In the Netherlands the same was done for the Green Left combination by using the separate responses pertaining to PPR and PSP (other parts of the Green Left combination list had not been included as separate items in the set of probability to vote questions), and for the SGP/GPV/RPF combination by using the separate items for SGP, GPV and RPF.

B3: Calculation of Turnout Effects and Effects of Quasi–switching

This section pertains to the decomposition of the difference between the result of the European elections and that which would have been yielded by a (hypothetical) concurrent national election. These comparisons of European and concurrent (hypothetical) national election results, and the decomposition of the differences, were reported in the country chapters of Part II, after an initial discussion in Chapter 2, particularly on the basis of Table 2.2.

To perform the decomposition, three different relative frequency distributions are required: party choice in European elections (EE), intended national party choice of the entire sample (NE) and intended national party choice of those who turned out to vote in the European Elections (NE2). Intended national party choice is derived from responses to the question "If there were a 'General Election' tomorrow which party would you support?."

The net effect of quasi–switching is the difference between EE and NE2 (EE–NE2). The net effect of turnout is the difference between NE2 and NE (NE2–NE). The difference between the results of the European elections and concurrent, if hypothetical, national elections (EE–NE) equals the sum of the quasi–switching and turnout effects.

B4: Independent Variables in Analyses of Electoral Participation

This section describes the independent variables which were used in the analyses of electoral participation reported for 1989 in the country chapters of Part II (and for 1994 in Appendix C). A general discussion of the background of these analyses was presented in Chapter 3 (pages 50-51).

Demographic and socio–economic characteristics
This block of independent variables comprised in each country the following four variables: frequency of church attendance; home ownership; age and union membership.

In addition it comprised a country–specific selection (arrived at by means of a stepwise regression on electoral participation after the previous four variables were included) from the following variables: marital status (represented by two dummies: divorced/seperated/widow(er) and single); education; objective social class of household (represented by three dummies: farmers/fishers, managers, and workers); religious denomination (dummied); dummies for head of household or respondent being unemployed or not; dummy for respondent being employed in public sector or not; gender; subjective social class; income (quartiles); size of town (subjective).

Civic Attitudes and General or national political orientations
This block consists of two (sets of) indicators, the first representing measures of political interest, the second attitudes and orientations of a general nature, not related to substantive attitudes, orientations or preferences on European policies or European integration.

Indicators of political interest include in all countries the scale scores for campaign interest (see section B5, this Appendix) and political interest (see section B5, this Appendix). In addition this block comprised a country–specific selection of additional indicators of political interest which were not included in the cross–national comparative scales. This selection was made by means of a stepwise regression on electoral participation (after the previous two scale scores were included) from the following dichotomous variables: did or did not make use of each a large series sources of campaign information (newspapers and news magazines; radio; televison; polls; personal discussions; other); did or did not participate in each of a series of campaign activities (talked about European election with friends; with family or workmates; with party worker; attended a meeting or rally; read European election material sent by a party or a candidate; read election poster; read advertisement about the list of candidates; read election news in newspaper; watched election programmes on television; listened to radio programme on European election; persuaded others to vote for a specific candidate or party in the European election).

Attitudes and orientations of a general nature, not related to substantive attitudes, orientations or preferences on European policies or European integration comprise:
  • score on scale measuring importance of elected institutions (see for details section B5, this Appendix)

- maximum score on probability to vote question
- strength of party attachment
- satisfaction with democracy
- national issue saliency (number of four national issues rated as important)
- transnational issue saliency (number of issues rated as important from the following: unemployment, stable prices, arms limitation and environment)
- score on scale measuring campaign interest (see for details section B5, this Appendix). This is a different variable than the one used in the comparative analyses of Chapter 19, referred to as campaign mobilization (see footnote 17 on page 315). This dichotomous variable was scored 1 if, in response to a set of questions on how the European election campaign was covered on television, the respondent answered affirmatively to at least one of the following statements: "it helped me to make up my mind how to vote", "it showed me where my party stands on European questions" and "it brought out well the differences between the parties on European matters". If the respondent did not agree with any of these three statements, this variable was scored 0.

Habitual voting
Did vote in last (or concurrent) national election

European orientations
This block consists of two measures of substantive orientation and attitudes on European policies and European integration:
- score on scale measuring EC approval (see for details section B5, this Appendix)
- EC issue saliency (number of the following issues rated as important: European unification, Agricultural surpluses, application of Turkey for membership in the EC and realization of Single European Market).

B5: Construction of Scale Scores

A number of variables employed in the analyses in this volume have been measured by scores of uni–dimensional cumulative scales, each of which comprises several items. These variables are: Political interest, Importance of elected institutions, EC Approval and European informedness. The homogeneity (that is unidimensionality) of the items comprised in the scale has been assessed by a cumulative scaling model known as 'Mokken scaling' (Mokken 1971; Niemöller and Van Schuur 1983), which is a stochastic generalization of the well–known Guttman scale. All indicators of a scale were dichotimized.

The resulting scales all satisfy rather stringent requirements of unidimensionality in each of the political systems of the European Community/Union.

The results of the scale analyses were obtained by means of the computer
program MSP (Mokken Scale analysis for Polychotoumous items, Debets and
Brouwer 1989). Reported below are — for each country separately — the 'difficulty' of each of the scale–items (i.e., the proportion of the sample providing the
response which has been designated by the analyst as 'positive', that is, as indicative of the underlying trait to be measured) and the scalability coefficients H and
Hi. The first of these coefficients (i.e., H) yields information about the (unidimensional) scalability of the entire set of indicators, the second (Hi) reports the
scalability of each item vis–a–vis the other items of the scale combined. Tables
B5.1 through B5.4 pertain to the data from the 1989 European Election Study.
The 1994 European Election Study allows replication of these assessements of
unidimensionality for the scales measuring Political Interest and EC Approval.
Doing so yields exceedingly similar results as those reported in Tables B5.1 and
B5.3. For the sake of brevity, these replicated results are not reported separately.

In general, the following guidelines are used for the interpretation of the size
of these coefficients. H (or H_i) < .30 indicates that a set of items is no scale, or
that an item is not a scale-item. .30 =< H, H_i < .40 : weak scale (scale item), .40
=< H, H_i < .50: medium scale (scale-item), H, H_i >=.50: strong scale (scale-item).

Table B5.1 Political Interest

	Pol. Discussion with Friends		Interested in EC Politics		Interested in Politics		
	dif	H_i	dif	H_i	dif	H_i	H
Fla	0.07	0.78	0.32	0.81	0.33	0.82	0.81
Wal	0.06	0.90	0.27	0.81	0.19	0.80	0.83
Den	0.17	0.60	0.52	0.71	0.69	0.82	0.73
Fra	0.17	0.61	0.46	0.58	0.45	0.62	0.60
Ger	0.15	0.60	0.48	0.72	0.62	0.81	0.73
Gre	0.47	0.53	0.42	0.65	0.53	0.74	0.64
Ire	0.15	0.53	0.37	0.66	0.40	0.69	0.64
Ita	0.11	0.63	0.19	0.61	0.25	0.72	0.65
Lux	0.18	0.64	0.40	0.66	0.46	0.70	0.67
Net	0.16	0.50	0.38	0.66	0.59	0.79	0.66
Por	0.04	0.55	0.12	0.63	0.08	0.64	0.61
Spa	0.06	0.60	0.28	0.69	0.27	0.71	0.68
Bri	0.16	0.58	0.46	0.65	0.54	0.72	0.66
NIr	0.09	0.49	0.36	0.65	0.43	0.70	0.64

Positive answers: Political Discussion with Friends: 'frequently'
Interested in EC Politics: 'very interested'; 'interested'
Interested in Politics: 'very interested'; 'interested'

Table B5.2 Importance of Elected Institutions

	European Parliament		Local Assembly		National Parliament		
	dif	H_i	dif	H_i	dif	H_i	H
Fla	0.22	0.56	0.35	0.50	0.28	0.62	0.56
Wal	0.25	0.42	0.36	0.40	0.29	0.50	0.44
Den	0.28	0.51	0.52	0.40	0.65	0.51	0.46
Fra	0.24	0.50	0.44	0.36	0.33	0.50	0.45
Ger	0.19	0.64	0.41	0.42	0.53	0.48	0.50
Gre	0.38	0.72	0.37	0.71	0.59	0.91	0.77
Ire	0.23	0.61	0.31	0.16	0.10	0.61	0.57
Ita	0.25	0.51	0.39	0.34	0.35	0.45	0.43
Lux	0.24	0.41	0.37	0.47	0.43	0.57	0.49
Net	0.12	0.50	0.35	0.37	0.46	0.47	0.44
Por	0.30	0.70	0.29	0.56	0.47	0.77	0.67
Spa	0.24	0.86	0.38	0.76	0.32	0.80	0.80
Bri	0.20	0.48	0.24	0.35	0.40	0.53	0.45
NIr	0.12	0.65	0.37	0.43	0.18	0.48	0.52

Positive answers: All items: 'very important'

Table B5.3 EC Approval

	EC Dissolution		EC Beneficial		EC Membership		European Unification		
	dif	H_i	dif	H_i	dif	H_i	dif	H_i	H
Fla	0.26	0.77	0.55	0.67	0.56	0.70	0.68	0.77	0.72
Wal	0.31	0.72	0.50	0.65	0.48	0.70	0.73	0.81	0.71
Den	0.31	0.74	0.52	0.66	0.45	0.68	0.49	0.47	0.63
Fra	0.50	0.53	0.50	0.47	0.62	0.61	0.83	0.74	0.57
Ger	0.45	0.71	0.50	0.65	0.56	0.74	0.73	0.74	0.71
Gre	0.44	0.86	0.74	0.79	0.71	0.78	0.76	0.70	0.78
Ire	0.53	0.74	0.70	0.65	0.70	0.65	0.69	0.48	0.62
Ita	0.45	0.71	0.68	0.67	0.79	0.72	0.88	0.72	0.70
Lux	0.48	0.66	0.62	0.51	0.66	0.58	0.70	0.46	0.55
Net	0.50	0.65	0.67	0.53	0.78	0.64	0.78	0.50	0.58
Por	0.30	0.75	0.53	0.55	0.57	0.65	0.62	0.63	0.64
Spa	0.40	0.71	0.30	0.68	0.63	0.69	0.70	0.67	0.69
Bri	0.35	0.75	0.48	0.62	0.54	0.70	0.69	0.65	0.68
NIr	0.28	0.75	0.49	0.57	0.52	0.63	0.60	0.58	0.63

Positive answers: EC Dissolution: 'very sorry'
EC Beneficial: 'beneficial for ones own country'
EC Membership: 'a good thing'
European Unification: 'very much in favor'; 'in favor'

Table B5.4 Campaign Interest

	Interested in EE Campaign[a]		Watched TV on EE Campaign[b]		Watching EE news on TV[c]		
	dif	H_i	dif	H_i	dif	H_i	H
Fla	0.25	0.45	0.27	0.57	0.56	0.77	0.59
Wal	0.19	0.69	0.38	0.77	0.56	0.86	0.78
Den	0.27	0.51	0.58	0.71	0.77	0.87	0.70
Fra	0.31	0.53	0.52	0.68	0.71	0.81	0.67
Ger	0.42	0.37	0.60	0.42	0.90	0.90	0.49
Gre	0.31	0.41	0.48	0.61	0.72	0.85	0.62
Ire	0.29	0.42	0.49	0.55	0.76	0.85	0.59
Ita	0.27	0.48	0.49	0.60	0.75	0.85	0.63
Lux	0.31	0.44	0.47	0.63	0.66	0.77	0.62
Net	0.29	0.39	0.48	0.52	0.78	0.83	0.56
Por	0.30	0.50	0.55	0.58	0.78	0.78	0.61
Spa	0.19	0.34	0.50	0.48	0.80	0.77	0.53
Bri	0.33	0.55	0.50	0.63	0.75	0.84	0.66
NIr	0.28	0.48	0.38	0.60	0.62	0.85	0.64

Positive answers: a: "very interested", "quite interested"; b: "yes"
c: "from time to time"; "almost every day"; "every day"

B6: Country Characteristics

In the comparative analyses reported in Chapters 17, 18, 19 and 20 political systems are characterized by their scores on a number of variables. For the analyses pertaining to 1989 these scores are reported in Table B6.1, the conceptual status of these variables is discussed indetail in Chapters 17 to 20.

The variables listed in Table B6.1 are categorized into five clusters. The first one consists of characteristics of electoral systems or other aspects relating to the organization of elections. The second cluster consists of the supply side in elections: the parties on offer, their variety and characteristics. The third cluster contains a number of characteristics of electorates. The fourth cluster consists of variables describing in a number of ways the composition of society, and the final cluster relates to the distribution of materialist and postmaterialist values in the population.

Table B6.1 Characteristics of Countries, 1989

Country Characteristic	Fla	Wal	Den	Fr	Ger	Bri	Gre
Characteristics of Elections							
Compulsory voting	1	1	0	0	0	0	1
Proport. Represent.	1	1	1	1	1	0	1
Single Transf. Vote	0	0	0	0	0	0	0
Candidacy	1	1	1	1	1	2	1
Concurrent Nat. Elect.	0	0	0	0	0	0	1
Voting on Workday	0	0	1	0	0	1	0
Proportionality	92	92	95	81	99	79	93
Time since Last NE (Months)	30	30	13	12	29	24	48
Characteristics of Party Systems							
# of parties in EE	8	9	9	15	22	21	21
# of eff parties in NE	3.38	2.34	3.81	2.81	2.26	2.38	2.06
Competitiveness	1.8	1.4	2.1	2.2	1.8	1.7	1.1
Presence of chr. dem. pty	1	1	0	0	1	0	0
Presence of green pty	1	1	0	1	1	1	0
Range of EC pty positions	0.3	0.4	2.8	1.4	1.5	1.0	2.7
Range of l/r pty positions	3.5	6.1	7.1	8.5	7.2	5.5	8.5
Average l/r-extremity	1.61	2.04	1.87	1.91	1.59	1.61	2.02
Agreem. l/r perceptions of parties	40	40	63	65	56	55	71
Dimensionality: R^2 1st PC	28.9	30.1	44.3	38.2	39.6	33.1	38.6
Dimensionality: R^2 1st + 2nd PC	53.8	52.4	60.0	59.5	62.7	58.1	60.4
Characteristics of Electorate							
% subject to intense competition	22.9	22.9	38.3	45.5	25.5	16.3	19.4
% to whom no party appeals	7.3	10.0	4.6	7.6	4.1	9.8	3.2
Turnout last NE - EE	2.7	2.7	38.3	17.4	22.0	38.8	3.8
Importance NP - Imp. EP	10.3	10.4	33.0	10.5	32.3	20.0	13.6
% satisfied with democracy	68.6	57.2	62.6	54.4	76.1	57.5	53.3
Composition of Society							
% farmers and fishers	1.0	2.9	4.1	7.1	2.0	0.2	20.7
% workers	43.4	52.6	46.9	44.3	39.3	48.9	26.5
% managers	27.7	26.9	29.4	32.9	43.2	26.5	32.2
% union member	26.2	23.9	60.4	6.5	13.7	21.4	11.4
% middle class (subj.)	42.9	28.5	53.8	47.9	42.8	26.6	51.7
% lowest education	25.2	27.6	23.4	27.6	14.4	18.1	46.1
% no religion	24	38	24	30	10	36	1
% largest religious group	96	95	96	96	52	71	100
% strong religious	21.5	15.3	3.1	10.7	15.2	12.7	21.7
Values							
Mat/postmat (% mixed)	49.9	50.5	60.6	54.8	53.4	45.0	35.7
Mat/postmat (% postmat)	21.9	17.8	21.3	19.3	30.0	34.5	27.7

Table B6.1 Characteristics of Countries, 1989 (continued)

Country Characteristic	Ire	Ita	Lux	NIr	Net	Por	Spa
Characteristics of Elections							
Compulsory voting	0	1	1	0	0	0	0
Proport. Represent.	1	1	1	1	1	1	1
Single Transf. Vote	1	0	0	1	0	0	0
Candidacy	3	1	1	3	1	1	1
Concurrent Nat. Elect.	1	0	1	0	0	0	0
Voting on Workday	1	0	0	1	1	0	1
Proportionality	95	95	91	95	96	91	87
Time since Last NE (Months)	28	24	60	24	24	23	36
Characteristics of Party Systems							
# of parties in EE	9	14	10	10	10	12	32
# of eff parties in NE	2.07	3.11	2.86	2.38	3.07	1.64	2.06
Competitiveness	2.4	2.0	2.2	2.6	1.8	1.9	1.4
Presence of chr. dem. pty	0	1	1	0	1	1	0
Presence of green pty	1	1	1	0	1	0	0
Range of EC pty positions	1.5	1.0	0.8	1.7	1.2	1.8	2.2
Range of l/r pty positions	6.5	8	6.7	6.5	6.5	7.9	7.2
Average l/r-extremity	1.80	2.02	1.47	1.62	1.76	1.61	2.14
Agreem. l/r perceptions of parties	48	60	52	36	54	63	48
Dimensionality: R^2 1st PC	28.0	25.9	35.4	36.8	29.4	32.6	28.1
Dimensionality: R^2 1st + 2nd PC	50.9	45.2	54.3	56.2	56.2	55.9	49.4
Characteristics of electorate							
% subject to intense competition	42.8	26.5	34.2	53.9	28.8	24.9	10.3
% to whom no party appeals	6.5	7.5	4.5	8.8	6.0	7.5	16.5
Turnout last NE - EE	5.0	10.1	2.6	26.6	38.3	21.5	15.9
Importance NP - Imp. EP	15.1	11.6	25.8	10.9	34.6	11.4	13.2
% satisfied with democracy	61.0	27.5	77.5	39.5	74.8	59.1	53.5
Composition of Society							
% farmers and fishers	14.9	4.0	2.8	2.9	3.0	9.5	6.0
% workers	52.4	44.1	33.0	56.9	42.4	50.1	54.8
% managers	16.9	27.5	49.0	21.8	31.5	21.3	21.5
% union member	14.2	17.6	19.1	15.7	15.6	7.3	3.5
% middle class (subj)	32.8	44.8	44.3	23.8	40.5	47.4	51.3
% lowest education	21.8	54.7	9.3	22.4	18.2	65.2	56.4
% no religion	3	7	9	7	45	11	12
% largest religious group	95	98	99	59	54	98	98
% strong religious	75.1	36.8	22.2	50.5	18.4	30.0	27.9
Values							
Mat/postmat (% mixed)	41.9	39.9	46.3	46.2	58.4	32.4	41.6
Mat/postmat (% postmat)	31.0	29.4	33.0	27.9	25.1	14.7	14.8

B7: Parties Included in Comparative Analyses

In the comparative analyses reported in Chapters 18 and 20 political parties are characterized by their scores on a number of variables. These scores are reported in Table B7.1, the conceptual status of these variables is discussed in the respective chapters.

In most cases, the same parties are analysed in Chapters 18 and 20. In a few cases, however, differences exist owing to the differences between the dependent variables analyzed in both chapters. Parties (or combinations of parties) which have only been used in Chapter 20 are denoted in Table B7.1 with an asterisk (*), those which have only been used in Chapter 18 by the symbol #. All parties without these symbols have been used in the same fashion in both chapters.

The variables on which the parties are characterized are the following (corresponding with the respective columns of Table B7.1):

A percent of (intended) votes in a concurrent national election

B proportion of seats in national parliament since last National election

C position of party on left/right dimension (expressed as interpolated median of perceptions of the entire sample)

D agreement of perception of left/right position of party (expressed by value of agreement coefficient A, see section B9, this Appendix)

E extremity of left/right position of party (expressed as absolute difference between E and the interpolated median of respondents' self-location)

F position of party in terms of support for European integration (see van der Eijk and Franklin, 1991)

G coefficient of electoral competition (ranges between 0 and 1; 0: party is not affected by electoral competition, 1: party's potential overlaps entirely with that of other parties; see also van der Eijk and Oppenhuis, 1991; Tillie, 1994).

H government party (code 1) or opposition party (code 0)

I new politics party (code 1) or not (code 0)

J green party (code 1) or not (code 0)

K social democratic party (code 1) or not (code 0)

L christian democratic party (code 1) or not (code 0)

M extreme left party (code 1) or not (code 0)

N extreme right party (code 1) or not (code 0)

Table B7.1 Characteristics of Parties, 1989

	A	B	C	D	E	F	G	H	I	J	K	L	M	N
Flanders														
PVV	19.4	0.20	6.95	0.44	1.24	1.74	0.43	0	0	0	0	0	0	0
SP	17.6	0.26	3.50	0.48	2.22	1.83	0.48	1	0	0	1	0	0	0
CVP	30.6	0.35	7.03	0.36	1.32	1.60	0.44	1	0	0	0	1	0	0
Volksunie	5.8	0.13	6.84	0.39	1.12	2.06	0.64	1	0	0	0	0	0	0
Vlaams Blok	5.4	0.02	@	@	@	2.50	@	0	0	0	0	0	0	1
Agalev	17.3	0.05	4.59	0.30	1.13	2.02	0.46	0	1	1	0	0	0	0
Wallonia														
PRL	20.9	0.26	7.31	0.41	1.79	1.80	0.28	0	0	0	0	0	0	0
PS	41.5	0.45	2.68	0.55	2.84	1.71	0.19	1	0	0	1	0	0	0
PSC	22.0	0.22	7.45	0.40	1.93	1.81	0.28	1	0	0	0	1	0	0
FDF-RW	2.4	0.03	6.30	0.40	0.77	2.08	0.50	0	0	0	0	0	0	0
ECOLO	10.2	0.03	4.96	0.32	0.56	1.89	0.33.	0	1	1	0	0	0	0
PCB*	1.31	4.21	@	@	@	@	0.48	0	0	0	0	0	1	0
Denmark														
Social Democrat	31.8	0.31	4.48	0.63	1.22	1.84	0.26	0	0	0	1	0	0	0
Radical	4.0	0.06	5.43	0.64	0.27	1.96	0.49	0	0	0	0	0	0	0
Conservative	15.0	0.20	8.28	0.59	2.58	1.05	0.39	1	0	0	0	0	0	0
Centre Democrat	4.9	0.05	6.64	0.56	0.94	1.13	0.48	0	0	0	0	0	0	0
Soc. Peop's Pty	15.6	0.14	2.44	0.67	3.25	3.80	0.29	0	0	0	0	0	1	0
Liberals	10.7	0.13	7.94	0.57	2.24	1.05	0.41	1	0	0	0	0	0	0
Progress Pty	11.7	0.09	9.56	0.73	3.86	1.78	0.40	0	0	0	0	0	0	1
Chr. Peop. Pty	1.8	0.02	@	@	@	2.00	@	0	0	0	0	1	0	0
Peopl.Movemem.	0.0	0.00	@	@	@	3.80	@	0	0	0	0	0	0	0
France														
PC	9.0	0.04	1.49	0.81	3.54	2.76	0.38	0	0	0	0	0	1	0
PS	30.6	0.47	3.45	0.58	1.57	1.58	0.34	1	0	0	1	0	0	0
Ecologiste	15.2	0.00	4.78	0.63	0.25	1.90	0.40	0	1	1	0	0	0	0
FN	9.9	0.00	9.83	0.77	4.80	2.96	0.39	0	0	0	0	0	0	1
UNION#	26.7	0.46	7.58	0.59	2.55	1.80	0.48	0	0	0	0	0	0	0
Centre (CDS-UDF)	5.10	0.23	6.91	0.56	1.89	1.76	0.51	0	0	0	0	0	0	0
PR-UDF*	@	0.23	7.24	0.58	2.21	1.76	0.48	0	0	0	0	0	0	0
Rad-UDF*	@	0.23	7.14	0.54	2.11	1.76	0.55	0	0	0	0	0	0	0
RPR*	@	0.22	8.31	0.65	3.29	1.84	0.41	0	0	0	0	0	0	0
MRG*	@	0.00	3.49	0.52	1.53	1.58	0.52	0	0	0	0	0	0	0

*: These parties have only been used in the analyses reported in Chapter 20
#: These parties have only been used in the analyses reported in Chapter 18
@: missing data; data not required for respective analyses

Table B7.1 Characteristics of Parties, 1989 (continued)

	A	B	C	D	E	F	G	H	I	J	K	L	M	N
Germany														
CDU/CSU	36.4	0.45	7.34	0.53	2.05	1.51	0.24	1	0	0	0	1	0	0
SPD	39.2	0.37	3.64	0.58	1.65	1.72	0.29	0	0	0	1	0	0	0
FDP	5.6	0.09	5.65	0.59	0.36	1.73	0.49	1	0	0	0	0	0	0
Greens	8.5	0.09	2.44	0.59	2.85	2.35	0.57	0	1	1	0	0	0	0
Republikaner	7.4	0.00	9.62	0.72	4.33	3.00	0.50	0	0	0	0	0	0	1
Britain														
Conservative	37.5	0.59	8.58	0.57	3.06	1.41	0.40	1	0	0	0	0	0	0
Labour	39.9	0.36	3.11	0.53	2.41	2.38	0.35	0	0	0	1	0	0	0
Liberal Democr	8.6	0.03	4.83	0.61	0.68	1.99	0.37	0	0	0	0	0	0	0
Nationalists	2.5	0.01	3.91	0.02	1.61	2.50	0.50	0	0	0	0	0	0	0
Green	8.5	0.00	4.57	0.46	0.95	2.50	0.51	0	1	1	0	0	0	0
SDP*	1.9	0.01	4.89	0.53	0.62	2.02	0.53	0	0	0	1	0	0	0
Greece														
PASOK	39.1	0.54	4.82	0.68	0.62	1.46	0.13	1	0	0	1	0	0	0
New Democracy	44.3	0.42	8.77	0.72	3.34	1.10	0.13	0	0	0	0	0	0	0
DIANA	1	0.0	7.85	0.68	2.41	2.50	0.37	0	0	0	0	0	0	0
KKE-I-RL	0.3	0.0	1.86	0.79	3.57	2.50	0.44	0	0	0	0	0	1	0
EPEN	0.3	0.0	9.96	0.98	4.52	2.50	0.44	0	0	0	0	0	0	1
Left Coal.	13.1	0.04	1.72	0.82	3.72	3.40	0.22	0	1	0	0	0	1	0
Ireland														
Fianna Fail	44.1	0.49	7.86	0.47	1.64	1.21	0.35	1	0	0	0	0	0	0
Fine Gael	29.3	0.31	7.65	0.44	1.43	1.22	0.42	0	0	0	0	0	0	0
Labour	9.5	0.07	3.32	0.52	2.90	2.09	0.50	0	0	0	1	0	0	0
Workers' Pty.	5.0	0.02	2.31	0.61	3.92	2.75	0.53	0	0	0	0	0	1	0
Green	1.5	0.0	4.62	0.39	1.61	2.30	0.48	0	1	1	0	0	0	0
PDP	5.5	0.08	6.84	0.34	0.61	1.41	0.52	0	0	0	0	0	0	0
Sinn Fein	1.2	0.0	1.40	0.74	4.83	2.50	0.58	0	0	0	0	0	1	0
Italy														
PCI	28.8	0.28	1.77	0.76	2.89	1.93	0.23	0	0	0	0	0	1	0
PSI	14.5	0.15	3.63	0.52	1.03	1.64	0.33	1	0	0	1	0	0	0
PSDI	2.8	0.03	4.32	0.52	0.35	1.71	0.49	1	0	0	0	0	0	0
DC	31.7	0.37	6.22	0.52	1.56	1.43	0.23	1	0	0	0	1	0	0
MSI	5.0	0.06	9.63	0.71	4.97	2.47	0.36	0	0	0	0	0	0	1
DP	2.0	0.01	1.68	0.63	2.99	2.03	0.41	0	0	0	0	0	1	0
Verdi	7.2	0.02	4.31	0.43	0.36	1.57	0.33	0	1	1	0	0	0	0
PLI/PRI#	3.8	0.05	5.91	1.22	0.57	1.69	0.48	1	0	0	0	0	0	0
PR*	@	0.02	3.73	0.36	0.93	1.74	0.53	0	1	0	0	0	0	0
PLI*	@	0.02	6.52	0.47	1.85	1.69	0.51	1	0	0	0	0	0	0
PRI*	@	0.03	5.31	0.51	0.65	1.69	0.48	1	0	0	0	0	0	0

*: These parties have only been used in the analyses reported in Chapter 20
#: These parties have only been used in the analyses reported in Chapter 18
@: missing data; data not required for respective analyses

Table B7.1 Characteristics of Parties, 1989 (continued)

	A	B	C	D	E	F	G	H	I	J	K	L	M	N
Luxemburg														
CSV	32.4	0.39	8.00	0.49	2.73	1.30	0.35	1	0	0	0	1	0	0
LASP	26.2	0.33	3.96	0.55	1.31	1.44	0.41	0	0	0	1	0	0	0
DP	17.2	0.22	5.65	0.55	0.38	1.33	0.45	1	0	0	0	0	0	0
KP	4.4	0.03	1.92	0.70	3.35	2.83	0.68	0	0	0	0	0	1	0
GAP	2.9	0.03	3.88	0.56	1.39	2.06	0.55	0	1	1	0	0	0	0
GLEI	4.1	0.0	4.26	0.54	1.01	2.06	0.56	0	1	1	0	0	0	0
NAT-BEW	1.4	0.0	8.61	0.23	3.35	2.50	0.70	0	0	0	0	0	0	1
Northern Ireland														
Alliance	5.4	0.0	5.02	0.42	0.45	1.63	0.43	0	0	0	0	0	0	0
Ulster Unionist	25.7	0.29	7.55	0.32	2.08	2.07	0.34	0	0	0	0	0	0	0
Democr.Unionist	22.6	0.47	7.93	0.31	2.46	2.38	0.33	0	0	0	0	0	0	0
Sinn Fein	8.4	0.06	1.28	0.64	4.19	3.29	0.27	0	0	0	0	0	0	0
SDLP	19.9	0.18	3.82	0.31	1.65	1.68	0.32	0	0	0	0	0	1	0
Workers' Pty	1.4	0.0	2.28	0.53	3.18	2.26	0.40	0	0	0	1	0	0	0
Conservative	7.3	0.0	7.78	0.30	2.31	1.40	0.41	0	0	0	0	0	1	0
Labour	7.9	0.0	2.76	0.47	2.71	2.37	0.40	0	0	0	0	0	0	0
Other Unionists	0.3	0.0	7.08	0.30	1.61	2.19	0.44	0	0	0	1	0	0	0
The Netherlands														
PVDA	31.9	0.35	3.19	0.61	2.11	1.49	0.23	0	0	0	1	0	0	0
CDA	37.4	0.36	6.81	0.46	1.51	1.34	0.23	1	0	0	0	1	0	0
VVD	11.9	0.18	7.53	0.49	2.23	1.33	0.31	1	0	0	0	0	0	0
D66	8.3	0.06	4.67	0.60	0.64	1.59	0.33	0	1	0	0	0	0	0
Green Left#	4.0	0.01	2.31	0.67	2.99	2.13	0.47	0	1	1	0	0	0	0
SGP/GPV/RPF#	4.4	0.02	8.43	0.48	3.13	2.50	0.60	0	0	0	0	0	0	0
PPR*	@	0.01	2.52	0.65	2.78	2.13	0.47	0	1	1	0	0	0	0
PSP*	@	0.01	2.10	0.68	3.21	2.37	0.48	0	1	0	0	0	1	0
SGP*	@	0.02	8.61	0.48	3.31	2.50	0.60	0	0	0	0	1	0	0
GPV*	@	0.01	8.42	0.49	3.12	2.38	0.54	0	0	0	0	1	0	0
RPF*	@	0.01	8.26	0.46	2.96	2.43	0.58	0	0	0	0	1	0	0
Portugal														
CDU	14.4	0.12	1.40	0.83	3.78	3.25	0.24	0	0	0	0	0	1	0
CDS	8.7	0.01	9.26	0.70	4.07	1.91	0.35	0	0	0	0	0	0	1
PPM	0.6	0.0	8.03	0.45	2.85	2.37	0.51	0	0	0	0	0	0	0
PS	36.2	0.24	4.84	0.61	0.34	1.64	0.21	0	0	0	1	0	0	0
PSD	33.6	0.59	7.15	0.52	1.97	1.61	0.24	1	0	0	0	0	0	0
UDP	2.0	0.0	1.40	0.82	3.78	3.40	0.49	0	0	0	0	0	1	0
MDP/CDE	0.3	0.0	1.90	0.73	3.28	3.22	0.57	0	0	0	0	0	1	0
PDC	0.7	0.0	8.68	0.55	3.49	@	0.57	0	0	0	0	0	0	0
PRD*	@	0.03	4.00	0.53	1.18	2.30	0.46	0	0	0	0	0	0	0

*: These parties have only been used in the analyses reported in Chapter 20
#: These parties have only been used in the analyses reported in Chapter 18
@: missing data,;data not required for respective analyses

Table B7.1 Characteristics of Parties, 1989 (continued)

	A	B	C	D	E	F	G	H	I	J	K	L	M	N
Spain														
PSOE	43.5	0.53	4.14	0.38	0.16	1.12	0.14	1	0	0	1	0	0	0
PP	18.7	0.30	8.39	0.59	4.09	1.40	0.20	0	0	0	0	0	0	0
CDS	8.4	0.05	5.91	0.58	1.61	1.38	0.26	0	0	0	0	0	0	0
IU	8.6	0.02	2.13	0.69	2.16	1.75	0.25	0	0	0	0	0	1	0
HB	2.3	0.01	1.21	0.72	3.08	3.34	0.37	0	0	0	0	0	1	0
CIU	4.4	0.05	5.53	0.25	1.23	1.60	0.36	0	0	0	0	0	0	0
PNV*	@	0.02	5.25	0.19	0.95	1.60	0.54	0	0	0	0	0	0	0
EA*	@	0.01	4.10	0.26	0.19	1.60	0.52	0	0	0	0	0	0	0

*: These parties have only been used in the analyses reported in Chapter 20
#: These parties have only been used in the analyses reported in Chapter 18
@: missing data; data not required for respective analyses

B8: Logit Analysis of Electoral Participation

As reported in Chapter 16, the multivariate analyses of electoral participation and turnout have been conducted by means of OLS regressions. In the case of bounded dependent variables (such as individual electoral participation, or turnout percentages bounded by the limits 0 and 100) non–linear regression methods, such as for instance multinomial logistic regression, are often considered to be preferable in order to avoid model misspecifications (for example, Aldrich and Nelson, 1984). We were inclined to forego the alleged methodological superiority of non–linear regression in order to avoid the problems of how to report results from those methods in intelligible and simple terms — OLS is clearly superior in this respect. Yet, we did not want to risk model misspecification either. Consequently, we decided to run logistic regressions, just to be certain of the validity of our substantive conclusions. In addition to yielding a validation of the results presented in the chapters of this volume, this comparison of methods also yielded an unexpected methodological conclusion which we will come to in a moment. We will describe our findings (which are quite general to all the analyses conducted in this book) in terms of a single example—that given by the analyses we conducted in Chapter 16.

The validation of the substantive conclusions presented in chapter 16 can easily be seen in Table 16.4, where the final column contains estimates of the effects on the dependent variable of a one–unit change in each independent variable computed from logistic regression when all other independent variables are held at their mean values. Comparing these with the first column of coefficients in Table 16.4 (the b's from OLS regression) we see that the two sets are remarkably similar in their selection of main effects (systemic, contextual and individual) to be included in the equation as well as in the estimation of the magnitude of these main effects.

It is when we turn to the handling of interaction effects that we find a great and potentially damaging difference between the two estimation procedures, and it is a difference that raises questions about the utility of the logistic approach (which would apply equally to any other analysis that involved a logarithmic transform of the data—such as probit analysis). Logistic regression and OLS differ in the way in which the effects of independent variables are interpreted. In ordinary regression, the effect on the dependent variable of moving one unit in any of the independent ones is reflected by the b–coefficient. In logistic regression, the impact of a change in an independent variable depends on the values of all other independent variables. This particular trait of logistic regression implies that all of the interactions which logically can be specified between independent variables are automatically included in the model, and that they are fitted when the parameters of the model are estimated. In the OLS approach, by contrast, interactions have to be specified explicitly by the analyst in order to be empirically assessed (cf. Jaccard, Turrisi and Wan, 1990). As the model we reported in Table 4 includes 10 independent variables (5 at the systemic level and 5 at the individual level), the logistic model implicitly fits thousands of interaction terms, corresponding to the different combinations of values on all independent variables. Only a subset of these were scanned by our procedure for detecting interaction effects between systemic and individual variables. Still, in a large number of cases we found no empirical justification whatsoever for including them in the model. So the question arises whether logistic methods, by fitting unnecessary (implicit) interaction terms, are not just as prone to specification errors, albeit of a different kind, as OLS. Stated differently, logistic regression rules out the possibility of across–the–board effects of independent variables (at least in the empirical range of values of those variables), whereas in practice such fixed effects may very well exist. This is not the place to elaborate this argument, but it must be addressed somewhere.

Furthermore, the logistic model assigns equal status to all variables, whereas we have argued in Chapter 16 for taking into account a 'causal' order between them to do justice to the inherent multi–level character of the multi-variate analyses reported in Chapter 16. In the logistic model the effect of compulsory voting is equally dependent on values of political interest as the other way around, which strikes us as theoretically implausible.

As long as these questions are not settled, the justification for the alleged superiority of logistic models over OLS must be considered to be unproven.

Irrespective of how one wants to weigh the respective advantages and disadvantages of both OLS and multinomial logistic regression, it is remarkable that as far as the main effects of systemic, compositional and individual variables are concerned, no substantively different conclusions emerge from one method when compared to the other (compare Table 16.4). Furthermore, the two methods concur entirely with respect to variables not included in the equation reported in Table 16.4: both methods find them to be equally not significant.

B9: Measuring Agreement

In Chapter 19 (footnote 6) the extent of homogeneity of groups of voters is reported in terms of their ideological positions and substantive preferences. These positions and preferences are expressed as values on bounded and ordered rating scales (such as a left/right rating scale—in our case running from 1 to 10—on which respondents can indicate where they locate themselves). Customarily standard deviations and other dispersion measures (such as inter–fractile distances) are used to express how homogeneous or heterogeneous the scores on such a scale are. Such indices or coefficients are problematic however, because they may misrepresent what they are supposed to measure: the 'peakedness' of a distribution. When bounded rating scales are used, as is almost invariably the case in standardized survey research, standard deviations (and similar measures) do not yield comparable information for distributions which differ in terms of central tendency. A highly–peaked (i.e. homogeneous) distribution in which the median is far from the center of the rating scale will generally yield a larger standard deviation (i.e. suggesting less homogeneity) than a considerably less–peaked distribution in which the median is located near the center of the scale. Therefore, the homogeneity of the ratings given by a group has been expressed in terms of a different measure, van der Eijk's coefficient of agreement (A), which does not suffer from this deficiency.

Distributions can be decomposed in a unique manner into simple parts, 'layers', parts of a frequency distribution which comprise all categories and which are characterized by each of the categories either being empty (i.e. containing no cases at all) or containing exactly the same number of cases as each of the other non–empty categories of the layer. The agreement represented by a uniform distribution (a layer in which no category is empty) is defined as 0, the agreement of a layer in which only one category is non–empty is 1. For patterns which are characterized by contiguous non–empty cells (which are therefore patterns in between these two ideal types) the extent of agreement can be expressed in terms of a ratio of the number of empty and the total number of categories. Patterns which are characterized by non–contiguous non–empty cells can be considered as representing parts of multi–modal distributions, representing to some extent lack of agreement. How serious the breach of unimodality is can be assessed by the same method which is used in unfolding models to quantify deviations from unidimensionality (see van Schuur, 1984). In the extreme case of an equal number of cases in the two most extreme categories of mthe scale with all intermediate categories being empty, the coefficient of agreement reaches the value of –1. After decomposing a distribution in its component parts (the layers) and expressing the agreement represented by each of these, the agreement of the entire distribution is calculated by the weighted average of the agreement coefficients of each of the layers, where the weights to be used are the proportions of cases observed in each of the layers. The result is a measure of agreement which attains the value 1 in the case of complete consensus (all cases located in one category of the rating scale), which attains the value 0 in the case of a uniform distribution, and –1 in the case of a perfect polarized split of responses. For further details see van der Eijk (1996).

Appendix C
Replications of 1989 Findings using
1994 Election Study Data
Erik Oppenhuis and Cees van der Eijk

Contents

C1: Introduction

This Appendix presents findings from analyses (referred to in Chapter 17) that replicate, on data from the 1994 European Election Study, analyses (of 1989 data) reported in the country chapters of Part II. The methods and rationale of these analyses has been discussed in Chapter 3 (pages 43 to 51).

The first set of replications, one table per country, reports the magnitudes of the potential electorates of political parties and the extent of their overlap. These tables also include each party's share of the votes in the 1994 European election, expressed as a percentage of the valid vote and as a percentage of the population eligible to vote. Finally, each party's place on the left/right continuum is reported, measured by the interpolated median of the perceptions of all respondents of the party's position on a 10-point left/right scale.

The second set of replications (section C3 of this Appendix) concerns the estimation of quasi-switching and turnout effects. The corresponding figures for 1989 were reported in the country chapters. A comparative analysis of these quasi-switching and turnout effects was reported in Chapter 18.

The final set of replicated analyses (section C4), again resulting in one table per country, involves the explanation of differences in individual participation in the 1994 European elections. As described in Chapter 3, these analyses consist of regressions with stage-wise inclusion in the equation of blocks of explanatory variables. Analogous analyses (not separately reported here) were conducted by means of logit analysis, yielding no substantive differences (see also the discussion on regression and logit analyses in Appendix B, section B8).

C2: Potential Support and Overlap Between Parties in 1994

Table C.1 Potential Support and Overlap Between Parties in Flanders in 1994

	SP	Agalev	VU	PVV	CVP	VB
SP	1.00	0.56	0.59	0.42	0.47	0.44
Agalev	0.57	1.00	0.77	0.49	0.58	0.51
VU	0.41	0.52	1.00	0.34	0.44	0.51
PVV	0.55	0.62	0.65	1.00	0.61	0.43
CVP	0.47	0.56	0.63	0.46	1.00	0.51
VB	0.26	0.30	0.45	0.20	0.31	1.00
Pot. Support (% of Elect.)	32.7	33.2	22.5	42.4	32.3	19.7
Votes as % of Electorate	15.6	9.4	6.3	16.2	24.2	11.1
% of Valid Vote	17.7	10.7	7.1	18.4	27.4	12.6
L-R Median (1–10)	3.75	4.25	5.44	5.96	6.06	8.75

Table C.2 Potential Support and Overlap Between Parties in Wallonia in 1994

	PS	Ecolo	PSC	PRL	FN
PS	1.00	0.59	0.53	0.46	0.50
Ecologiste	0.40	1.00	0.48	0.42	0.32
PSC	0.44	0.60	1.00	0.53	0.44
PRL	0.41	0.56	0.57	1.00	0.48
FN	0.18	0.17	0.19	0.19	1.00
Pot. Support (% of Elect.)	37.7	25.6	31.5	33.9	13.4
Votes as % of Electorate	22.5	9.6	13.9	18.0	5.8
% of Valid Vote	30.4	13.0	18.8	24.3	7.9
L-R Median (1-10)	2.85	4.81	6.27	7.14	9.87

Table C.3 Potential Support and Overlap Between Parties in Britain in 1994

	Labour	SNP	Pl.Cymru	Greens	Lib.Dem.	Cons
Labour	1.00	0.76	0.75	0.74	0.67	0.41
SNP	0.13	1.00	0.66	0.30	0.16	0.10
Plaid Cymru	0.08	0.39	1.00	0.22	0.09	0.07
Greens	0.24	0.56	0.67	1.00	0.30	0.20
Liberal Democrats	0.55	0.76	0.74	0.77	1.00	0.53
Conservatives	0.29	0.41	0.46	0.46	0.46	1.00
Pot. Support (% of Elect.)	48.5	8.3	5.0	15.5	39.6	35.0
Votes as % of Electorate	16.1	1.2	0.4	1.2	6.1	10.2
% of Valid Vote	44.2	3.2	1.1	3.2	16.7	27.9
L-R median (1–10)	3.44	4.16	4.12	4.62	5.13	7.98

Table C.4 Potential Support and Overlap Between Parties in Denmark in 1994

	SPP	SD	Rad	CPP	CD	Cons	Lib	PP
Socialist People's Party	1.00	0.49	0.57	0.53	0.46	0.24	0.22	0.31
Social Democrats	0.78	1.00	0.80	0.68	0.68	0.41	0.38	0.45
Radicals	0.47	0.41	1.00	0.63	0.58	0.34	0.30	0.32
Christian People's Party	0.24	0.20	0.35	1.00	0.50	0.27	0.26	0.31
Centre Democrats	0.29	0.26	0.44	0.68	1.00	0.40	0.36	0.44
Conservatives	0.29	0.31	0.51	0.72	0.78	1.00	0.72	0.66
Liberals (Venstre)	0.29	0.32	0.48	0.74	0.75	0.78	1.00	0.73
Progress Party	0.19	0.18	0.25	0.43	0.45	0.35	0.36	1.00
Pot. Support (% of Elect.)	29.9	47.2	24.5	13.6	18.5	36.0	39.0	18.9
Votes as % of Electorate	4.5	8.2	4.4	0.6	0.5	9.2	9.9	1.5
% of Valid Vote	8.6	15.8	8.5	1.1	0.9	17.7	19.0	2.9
L-R median (1–10)	2.43	4.64	5.10	5.83	6.17	7.95	8.26	9.46

Table C.5 Potential Support and Overlap Between Parties in France in 1994

	PC	PS	MRG	Verts	Gen. Eco	Union	FN
PC	1.00	0.36	0.37	0.32	0.32	0.15	0.17
PS	0.77	1.00	0.84	0.63	0.64	0.36	0.30
MRG	0.58	0.62	1.00	0.55	0.56	0.33	0.30
Les Verts	0.52	0.48	0.57	1.00	0.94	0.40	0.39
Gen. Ecolo.	0.50	0.47	0.56	0.91	1.00	0.40	0.38
Union	0.36	0.41	0.52	0.60	0.62	1.00	0.70
FN	0.18	0.14	0.20	0.25	0.25	0.30	1.00
Pot. Support (% of Elect.)	16.3	34.9	25.6	26.5	25.6	39.8	17.0
Votes as % of Electorate	3.3	7.2	6.0	1.5	1.0	12.8	5.2
% of Valid Vote	6.7	14.5	12.0	3.0	2.0	25.6	10.5
L-R median (1–10)	1.39	3.09	3.41	4.69	4.76	7.50	9.82

Table C.6 Potential Support and Overlap Between Parties in (West) Germany in 1994

	PDS	Grünen	SPD	FDP	CDU	Rep
PDS	1.00	0.20	0.13	0.17	0.09	0.39
Grünen	0.88	1.00	0.58	0.61	0.36	0.54
SPD	0.84	0.82	1.00	0.78	0.52	0.61
FDP	0.59	0.47	0.42	1.00	0.45	0.52
CDU/CSU	0.55	0.48	0.48	0.78	1.00	0.62
Republikaner	0.54	0.17	0.13	0.21	0.15	1.00
Pot. Support (% of Elect.)	7.9	35.4	50.0	27.1	46.5	11.0
Votes as % of Electorate	0.3	6.4	19.8	2.4	23.6	2.4
% of Valid Vote	0.6	11.0	34.0	4.2	40.5	4.2
L-R median (1–10)	2.12	3.22	4.06	5.93	7.27	9.76

Table C.7 Potential Support and Overlap Between Parties in Greece in 1994

	KKE	Left Coal	PASOK	PA	ND
KKE	1.00	0.52	0.22	0.20	0.11
Progr.Left Coalition	0.69	1.00	0.34	0.28	0.16
PASOK	0.63	0.71	1.00	0.50	0.29
Politiki Anixi	0.39	0.40	0.34	1.00	0.54
New Democracy	0.27	0.29	0.25	0.69	1.00
Pot. Support (% of Elect.)	13.9	18.5	39.0	26.4	33.7
Votes as % of Electorate	4.3	4.3	26.0	5.9	22.5
% of Valid Vote	6.3	6.3	37.7	8.6	32.7
L-R median (1–10)	1.30	2.42	4.95	7.86	9.09

Table C.8 Potential Support and Overlap Between Parties in Ireland in 1994

	SF	Dem. Left	Labour	Greens	PDP	FG	FF
Sinn Fein	1.00	0.49	0.24	0.22	0.25	0.19	0.16
Democratic Left	0.57	1.00	0.37	0.35	0.39	0.27	0.25
Labour	0.62	0.82	1.00	0.66	0.67	0.60	0.57
Greens	0.63	0.85	0.73	1.00	0.74	0.60	0.57
PDP	0.52	0.70	0.54	0.54	1.00	0.55	0.45
FG	0.52	0.65	0.64	0.58	0.74	1.00	0.56
FF	0.52	0.69	0.73	0.65	0.71	0.67	1.00
Pot. Support (% of Elect.)	13.6	15.9	34.9	38.7	28.2	37.6	44.5
Votes as % of Electorate	1.3	1.5	4.7	3.3	2.7	10.3	14.8
% of Valid Vote	3.0	3.5	11.0	7.9	6.5	24.3	35.0
L-R median (1–10)	2.12	2.36	4.50	5.11	6.24	7.23	7.31

Table C.9 Potential Support and Overlap Between Parties in Italy in 1994

	Rif. Comm	PDS	Verdi	PPI	Lega N	Forza Italia	AN
Rif. Comm	1.00	0.53	0.40	0.32	0.31	0.15	0.19
PDS	0.82	1.00	0.55	0.46	0.39	0.22	0.25
Verdi	0.67	0.59	1.00	0.57	0.58	0.37	0.42
PPI	0.41	0.38	0.44	1.00	0.42	0.33	0.38
Lega Nord	0.33	0.27	0.38	0.36	1.00	0.33	0.40
Forza Italia	0.36	0.34	0.53	0.61	0.73	1.00	0.84
All. Nat.	0.30	0.25	0.40	0.46	0.59	0.55	1.00
Pot. Support (% of Elect.)	18.0	27.8	29.7	23.0	19.3	42.7	28.0
Votes as % of Electorate	4.2	13.2	2.2	6.9	4.6	21.2	8.7
% of Valid Vote	6.1	19.1	3.2	10.0	6.6	30.6	12.5
L-R median (1-10)	1.26	2.20	3.97	5.03	6.79	7.72	9.46

Table C.10 Potential Support and Overlap Between Parties in Luxembourg in 1994

	LSAP	Green	DP	CSV
LSAP	1.00	0.72	0.67	0.65
Green	0.53	1.00	0.56	0.46
DP	0.52	0.59	1.00	0.56
CSV	0.67	0.65	0.74	1.00
Pot. Support (% of Elect.)	47.0	34.7	36.6	48.4
Votes as % of Electorate	19.8	8.7	15.1	25.0
% of Valid Vote	24.8	10.9	18.9	31.4
L-R median (1–10)	4.06	4.44	5.85	6.62

Table C.11 Potential Support and Overlap Between Parties in The Netherlands in 1994

	GL	PVDA	D66	CDA	VVD	Orth.Chr	CD
Green Left	1.00	0.43	0.43	0.32	0.33	0.47	0.48
PVDA	0.80	1.00	0.68	0.56	0.54	0.58	0.69
D66	0.82	0.69	1.00	0.61	0.70	0.62	0.67
CDA	0.53	0.50	0.52	1.00	0.63	0.74	0.61
VVD	0.57	0.50	0.63	0.66	1.00	0.62	0.68
Orthodox Christian	0.32	0.21	0.22	0.31	0.24	1.00	0.49
CD	0.12	0.09	0.09	0.09	0.10	0.18	1.00
Pot. Support (% of Elect.)	24.3	45.4	46.5	40.0	42.0	16.5	6.0
Votes as % of Electorate	1.3	8.2	4.2	11.0	6.4	2.8	0.4
% of Valid Vote	3.7	22.9	11.7	30.8	17.9	7.8	1.0
L-R Median (1–10)	2.44	3.88	5.05	6.29	7.21	7.30	9.72

Table C.12 Potential Support and Overlap Between Parties in Northern Ireland in 1994

	SF	SDLP	Alliance	UUP	DUP
Sinn Fein	1.00	0.30	0.10	0.02	0.02
SDLP	0.77	1.00	0.55	0.19	0.18
Alliance	0.23	0.53	1.00	0.40	0.37
Ulster Unionist	0.07	0.28	0.61	1.00	0.90
Dem. Unionist	0.08	0.22	0.47	0.76	1.00
Pot. Support (% of Elect.)	13.0	33.1	31.5	47.8	40.3
Votes as % of Electorate	4.8	14.1	2.0	11.6	14.2
% of Valid Vote	9.9	28.9	4.1	23.8	29.2
L-R median (1–10)	1.85	3.49	5.15	7.89	8.37

Table C.13 Potential Support and Overlap Between Parties in Portugal in 1994

	CDU/PCP	PS	PSD	CDS/PP
CDU/PCP	1.00	0.28	0.19	0.34
PS	0.80	1.00	0.60	0.77
PSD	0.45	0.49	1.00	0.76
CDS/PP	0.55	0.44	0.53	1.00
Pot. Support (% of Elect.)	17.2	49.4	40.5	28.3
Votes as % of Electorate	3.8	11.5	11.7	4.1
% of Valid Vote	11.6	35.5	36.0	12.8
L-R median (1–10)	1.81	4.45	5.14	7.57

Table C.14 Potential Support and Overlap Between Parties in Spain in 1994

	IU	PSOE	PP	CIU	PNV
IU	1.00	0.60	0.37	0.63	0.60
PSOE	0.56	1.00	0.26	0.56	0.50
PP	0.38	0.30	1.00	0.48	0.59
CIU	0.23	0.22	0.17	1.00	0.62
PNV	0.13	0.11	0.12	0.36	1.00
Pot. Support (% of Elect.)	35.3	33.1	37.1	13.0	7.5
Votes as % of Electorate	7.9	18.0	23.6	2.8	1.6
% of Valid Vote	13.5	30.7	40.2	4.7	2.8
L-R median (1–10)	2.02	4.36	8.65	5.87	6.03

C3. Quasi-switching and Turnout Effects in the 1994 European Elections

Table C.15 Quasi–switching and Turnout Effects in the 1994 European Election in Flanders

	EE	NE	EE-NE	Quasi–switching	Turnout Effect
VLD	18.5	16.9	1.5	1.5	0.0
CVP	27.4	30.7	-3.4	-3.3	-0.1
SP	17.6	16.3	1.4	1.2	0.2
Agalev	10.8	11.1	-0.4	-0.7	0.3
Vlaams Blok	12.6	14.0	-1.5	-1.2	-0.3
VU	7.1	4.7	2.4	2.5	-0.1
Other	6.1	6.2	-0.2	-0.1	-0.1

Table C.16 Quasi–switching and Turnout Effects in the 1994 European Election in Wallonia

	EE	NE	EE-NE	Quasi–switching	Turnout Effect
PS	30.5	33.8	-3.3	-3.0	-0.3
PRL-FDF	24.3	25.2	-0.9	-1.3	0.5
PSC	18.8	18.3	0.6	1.4	-0.8
Ecolo	13.0	12.4	0.6	0.7	-0.1
FN	7.9	0.0	7.9	7.9	0.0
Other	5.5	10.3	-4.9	-5.7	0.8

Table C.17 Quasi–switching and Turnout Effects in the 1994 European Election in Britain

	EE	NE	EE-NE	Quasi-switching	Turnout Effect
Conservatives	27.8	28.3	-0.5	0.3	-0.9
Labour	44.1	48.7	-4.5	-7.5	2.9
Liberal Democrats	16.6	16.6	0.0	1.1	-1.1
SNP	3.3	2.0	1.3	0.6	0.7
Plaid Cymru	1.1	1.1	0.0	0.0	0.0
Green	3.3	2.1	1.1	2.2	-1.0
Other	3.8	1.1	2.7	3.3	-0.6

Table C.18 Quasi–switching and Turnout Effects in the 1994 European Election in Denmark

	EE	NE	EE-NE	Quasi-switching	Turnout Effect
Social Democrats	15.8	31.8	-16.0	-10.4	-5.6
Radicals	8.4	5.3	3.1	2.2	0.9
Conservatives	17.6	14.3	3.2	0.1	3.1
Center Democrats	1.0	0.3	0.7	0.6	0.2
Socialist People's Party	8.6	12.8	-4.2	-5.5	1.4
Christian People's Party	1.2	1.2	0.0	-0.5	0.5
Liberals (Venstre)	18.9	24.0	-5.0	-7.0	2.0
Progress Party	2.9	6.5	-3.6	-0.6	-3.0
People's Movement	10.4	0.0	10.4	10.4	0.0
June Movement	15.2	0.0	15.2	15.2	0.0
Other	0.0	3.8	-3.8	-4.4	0.6

Table C.19 Quasi–switching and Turnout Effects in the 1994 European Election in France

	EE	NE	EE-NE	Quasi-Switching	Turnout Effect
PC	6.7	8.6	-1.8	-1.9	0.1
PS	14.5	23.5	-9.0	-8.1	-0.9
MRG	12.0	7.9	4.2	4.2	0.0
FN	10.4	8.7	1.7	1.5	0.1
Les Verts	3.1	3.7	-0.7	-0.4	-0.3
Gen. Ecolo	2.0	2.7	-0.7	0.2	-0.9
Union	25.5	32.5	-6.9	-8.9	2.0
de Villiers	12.2	0.0	12.2	12.2	0.0
Other	13.5	12.4	1.0	1.2	-0.1

Table C.20 Quasi–switching and Turnout Effects in the 1994 European Election in Germany

	EE	NE	EE-NE	Quasi-switching	Turnout Effect
CDU/CSU	40.5	42.5	-2.1	-4.7	2.6
SPD	34.0	35.7	-1.7	-0.3	-1.4
FDP	4.2	4.8	-0.6	-0.5	-0.1
Bundnis/Grunen	11.0	10.3	0.7	1.1	-0.4
Republikaner	4.2	3.6	0.63	0.8	-0.2
PDS	0.6	0.6	0.0	0.0	0.0
Other	5.5	2.4	3.1	3.6	-0.4

Table C.21 Quasi–switching and Turnout Effects in the 1994 European Election in Greece

	EE	NE	EE-NE	Quasi-switching	Turnout Effect
PASOK	37.6	13.6	1.1	0.1	1.0
New Democracy	32.7	33.9	-1.2	-0.9	-0.3
Politiki Anixi	8.7	10.3	-1.6	-0.7	-0.9
KKE	6.3	6.3	0.1	0.1	0.0
Left Alliance	6.3	7.0	-0.7	-0.9	0.2
Other	8.4	5.9	2.4	2.4	0.0

Table C.22 Quasi–switching and Turnout Effects in the 1994 European Election in Ireland

	EE	NE	EE-NE	Quasi-switching	Turnout Effect
Fianna Fail	35.0	38.6	-3.5	-6.0	2.5
Fine Gael	24.4	22.0	2.4	-0.3	2.6
Labour	10.9	11.6	-0.7	-0.5	-0.2
Green	7.9	7.2	0.7	3.2	-2.5
Progressive Democrats	6.6	4.9	1.7	0.1	1.5
Sinn Fein	3.0	8.0	-5.0	-1.1	-3.9
Democratic Left	3.6	2.4	1.2	1.8	-0.6
Workers' Party	1.8	1.7	0.1	0.3	-0.2
Independents	6.3	3.6	2.8	1.9	0.8
Other	0.5	0.0	0.5	0.5	0.0

Table C.23 Quasi–switching and Turnout Effects in the 1994 European Election in Italy

	EE	NE	EE-NE	Quasi-switching	Turnout Effect
Forza Italia	30.6	31.9	-1.2	-1.2	0.0
PDS	19.1	20.7	-1.7	-1.6	-0.1
PPI	10.0	10.7	-0.7	-1.2	0.5
All. Nat.	12.5	13.9	-1.4	-1.9	0.5
Rif. Comm.	6.2	5.9	0.3	0.2	0.1
Lega Nord	6.6	6.3	0.3	0.9	-0.6
Verdi	3.2	3.4	-0.2	-0.2	0.0
Other	11.9	7.3	4.6	4.9	-0.4

Table C.24 Switching in the Concurrent 1994 Luxembourg Elections

	EE	NE	EE-NE
CSV	31.4	32.3	-0.9
LSAP	24.7	25.2	-0.5
DP	19.1	19.6	-0.5
Green	10.8	9.0	1.8
ADR	7.2	7.6	-0.4
Nat. Bewegong	0.5	1.0	-0.5
Other	6.2	5.4	0.8

Table C.25 Quasi–switching and Turnout Effects in the 1994 European Election in The Netherlands

	EE	NE	EE-NE	Quasi-switching	Turnout Effect
CDA	30.8	19.6	11.2	2.4	8.9
PvdA	23.0	21.9	1.1	2.3	-1.2
VVD	18.0	23.0	-5.0	-1.2	-3.7
D66	11.6	19.6	-7.9	-4.5	-3.5
GreenLeft	3.8	3.7	0.1	-0.5	0.6
CD	0.9	0.9	0.0	0.9	-0.9
Orthodox Christian	7.8	6.0	1.9	1.5	0.3
Other	4.1	5.5	-1.4	-0.8	-0.6

Table C.26 Quasi–switching and Turnout Effects in the 1994 European Election in Northern Ireland

	EE	NE	EE-NE	Quasi-switching	Turnout Effect
Alliance	4.2	5.9	-1.6	-1.0	-0.6
Ulster Unionist Party	23.9	26.1	-2.2	1.6	-3.8
Democratic Unionist Party	28.9	23.9	5.0	3.9	1.1
Sinn Fein	9.9	9.0	0.9	-1.3	2.2
SDLP	28.9	24.3	4.5	3.2	1.3
Other	4.2	10.8	-6.6	-6.3	-0.2

Table C.27 Quasi–switching and Turnout Effects in the 1994 European Election in Portugal

	EE	NE	EE-NE	Quasi-switching	Turnout Effect
PSD	36.0	35.8	0.2	-0.6	0.9
CDU/PCP	11.7	9.3	2.4	-0.5	3.0
CDS/PP	12.7	8.2	4.5	4.2	0.3
PS	35.4	45.8	-10.4	-6.3	-4.1
PSN	1.0	0.0	1.0	1.0	0.0
Other	3.2	0.9	2.3	2.3	0.0

Table C.28 Quasi–switching and Turnout Effects in the 1994 European Election in Spain

	EE	NE	EE-NE	Quasi-switching	Turnout Effect
PSOE	30.6	27.5	3.2	2.1	1.1
PP	40.2	39.5	0.7	-0.2	0.9
IU	13.6	16.7	-3.2	-1.8	-1.4
CIU	4.7	4.1	0.6	0.2	0.4
PNV	2.7	1.9	0.8	0.4	0.4
HB	0.0	0.1	-0.1	0.0	-0.1
CDS	1.1	1.5	-0.4	-0.2	-0.2
Other	7.1	8.7	-1.6	-0.5	-1.1

C4: Predictors of 1994 Participation in the European Elections

Table C.29 Predictors of 1994 Participation in the European Election in Flanders

	R^2	Added R^2
Demographics	0.02	
General Political Orientations	0.04	0.02
Habitual Voting	0.08	0.04
European Attitudes	0.08	0.00

Table C.30 Predictors of 1994 Participation in the European Election in Wallonia

	R^2	Added R^2
Demographics	0.09	
General Political Orientations	0.15	0.06
Habitual Voting	0.27	0.12
European Attitudes	0.28	0.01

Table C.31 Predictors of 1994 Participation in the European Election in Britain

	R^2	Added R^2
Demographics	0.08	
General Political Orientations	0.15	0.07
Habitual Voting	0.17	0.02
European Attitudes	0.18	0.01

Table C.32 Predictors of 1994 Participation in the European Election in Denmark

	R^2	Added R^2
Demographics	0.10	
General Political Orientations	0.24	0.14
Habitual Voting	0.24	0.00
European Attitudes	0.24	0.01

**Table C.33 Predictors of 1994 Participation in the European
Election in France**

	R^2	Added R^2
Demographics	0.15	
General Political Orientations	0.21	0.06
Habitual Voting	0.26	0.05
European Attitudes	0.26	0.00

**Table C.34 Predictors of 1994 Participation in the European
Election in Germany**

	R^2	Added R^2
Demographics	0.12	
General Political Orientations	0.20	0.08
Habitual Voting	0.22	0.03
European Attitudes	0.24	0.02

**Table C.35 Predictors of 1994 Participation in the European
Election in Greece**

	R^2	Added R^2
Demographics	0.17	
General Political Orientations	0.21	0.04
Habitual Voting	0.63	0.42
European Attitudes	0.63	0.00

**Table C.36 Predictors of 1994 Participation in the European
Election in Ireland**

	R^2	Added R^2
Demographics	0.11	
General Political Orientations	0.18	0.07
Habitual Voting	0.22	0.04
European Attitudes	0.22	0.00

Table C.37 Predictors of 1994 Participation in the European Election in Italy

	R^2	Added R^2
Demographics	0.02	
General Political Orientations	0.05	0.03
Habitual Voting	0.18	0.13
European Attitudes	0.18	0.00

Table C.38 Predictors of 1994 Participation in the European Election in Luxembourg

	R^2	Added R^2
Demographics	0.06	
General Political Orientations	0.17	0.11
Habitual Voting	1.00	0.83
European Attitudes	1.00	0.00

Table C.39 Predictors of 1994 Participation in the European Election in The Netherlands

	R^2	Added R^2
Demographics	0.15	
General Political Orientations	0.21	0.06
Habitual Voting	0.25	0.04
European Attitudes	0.25	0.00

Table C.40 Predictors of 1994 Participation in the European Election in Northern Ireland

	R^2	Added R^2
Demographics	0.11	
General Political Orientations	0.19	0.08
Habitual Voting	0.31	0.11
European Attitudes	0.32	0.01

Table C.41 Predictors of 1994 Participation in the European Election in Portugal

	R^2	Added R^2
Demographics	0.07	
General Political Orientations	0.16	0.09
Habitual Voting	0.20	0.04
European Attitudes	0.20	0.00

Table C.42 Predictors of 1994 Participation in the European Election in Spain

	R^2	Added R^2
Demographics	0.11	
General Political Orientations	0.23	0.12
Habitual Voting	0.31	0.08
European Attitudes	0.32	0.01

Appendix D
The Results of the 1989 and 1994
European Parliament Election

Tom Mackie

This Appendix is in two parts. The first describes the electoral systems used in the 12 countries of the European Community for the 1989 and 1994 European Parliament elections and compares them with the systems used for elections to the lower (or only) house of the national parliament. Summaries of European and national election laws are provided in Tables D1 to D3. The second part of the chapter reports the results of the 1989 and 1994 European Parliament elections for each country in 13 tables with a common format. Separate tables are provided for Great Britain and Northern Ireland. Each table reports the percentage turnout, the percent vote and number of seats won by parties or lists contesting the election. Party or list names are recorded in the same way as in the country chapters of Part II.

For full details of national electoral laws see Mackie and Rose (1991) and Hand et al. (eds) (1979).

Belgium

Seats in the Chamber of Representatives (*Kamer der Volksvertegenwoordigers, Chambre des Représentants*) are allocated by proportional representation in two stages. An initial distribution is made in each of the 30 constituencies (arrondisements) using a Hare quote. Any seat unallocated at the first stage is allocated at the provincial level (Belgium has nine provinces). All constituency votes are transferred to a provincial pool where a second allocation is made using the d'Hondt highest average formula. Electors may vote for a party list or a preferred individual candidate.

For the 1989 European Parliament election there were three constituencies and two electoral colleges which together returned 24 MEPs. The Flemish constituency comprised the provinces of Antwerpen, Limburg, Oost-Vlaanderen and West-Vlaanderen and the arrondissement of Leuven (which is part of the province of Brabant). The Walloon constituency comprised the provinces of Hainaut, Liège, Luxembourg and Namur and the arrondissement of Nivelles (part of the province of Brabant). The Brussels constituency consisted of the remainder of the province of Brabant, namely the arrondissement of Brussels-Hal-Vilvorde). For the` allocation of seats Belgium was divided into two electoral colleges, one Flemish with 13 seats and one Francophone with 11 seats. Electors resident in the Flemish and Walloon constituencies could vote only for a Flemish or a Francophone electoral college list respectively. Electors resident in the Brussels constituency could vote for either a Flemish or a Francophone list. Electors could vote either for a party list as a whole or for a preferred individual candidate. Seats were allocated between lists using the d'Hondt highest average formula. Seats were allocated within lists according to the number of votes received by individual candidates.

In 1994 the Flemish constituency had 14 MEPs and the Francophone constituency had ten. The extra seat given to Belgium at the 1992 Edinburgh summit was used to create a new single-member constituency for the German-speaking minority.

Denmark

Seats in the *Folketing* are allocated by proportional representation in two stages. One hundred and thirty five seats are allocated in 17 constituencies using a modified Sainte-Laguë formula (with an initial division of 1.4). To ensure greater overall proportionality 40 seats are allocated at national level using the d'Hondt highest average formula. Electors may vote either for a party list or for a preferred individual candidate.

For European Parliament elections Denmark forms a single national constituency which returns 16 MEPs. Seats are allocated between lists using the d'Hondt highest average formula. Alliances between party lists are permitted. Electors can vote for either a party list as a whole or for a preferred individual candidate.

France

The 577 members of the *Assemblée Nationale* are elected in single-member constituencies. An absolute majority of the valid votes cast is required for victory in the first round of the election. If no candidate wins an absolute majority a second round is held week later in which only first round contestants winning votes equivalent to at least 12.5 per cent of the number of registered electors in the constituency may participate. In the second round a plurality suffices for election.

For European Parliament elections all of France forms a single national constituency which returns 81 MEPs (87 in 1994). Seats are allocated between lists winning at least five per cent of the national voting using the d'Hondt highest average formula. Electors can choose only between party lists and not between individual candidates.

Germany

The 656 seats in the *Bundestag* are allocated by a mixture of proportional representation and plurality. Half of the deputies are elected by plurality from single-member constituencies and half from party lists presented in each of the 16 *Länder*. At *Land* level seats are allocated between parties using the Niemeyer formula (a variant of the largest remainder system). Only parties winning at least five per cent of the national vote or three single-member constituencies are allowed to participate in the *Land* seat allocation process. For single-member constituencies electors choose an individual candidate. For *Land* lists electors choose between party lists and may not express a preference for an individual candidate.

For elections to the European Parliament in 1989 Germany formed a single national constituency returning 78 MEPs. In addition West Berlin's three MEPs were chosen indirectly by the West Berlin Chamber of Deputies. Parties could present either a single national list or separate list for each land. All the parties put forward national lists except the Christian Social Union which stood only in Bavaria and the Christian Democratic Union which contested the remaining 15 *Länder*. Seats were allocated between lists winning at least five per cent of the national vote using the Niemeyer formula. Electors could choose only between party lists and not individual candidates. After reunification the number of seats was increased to 99.

Greece

The electoral system used for the 1993 elections to the *Vouli* was a relatively simple form of proportional representation. Two hundred and eighty eight deputies were elected in three stages from 56 constituencies. In the first stage deputies were chosen using the Hagenbach-Bischoff formula. Leftover seats are allocated in a second stage in 13 larger electoral districts where another allocation took place using the Hare formula. Any seats still unallocated were distributed to the party (ies) in a three step third distribution. Another 12 seats were allocated at national level using a Hare quota. Any unallocated seats were distributed using the d'Hondt quota. To be entitled to any seats at any stage, a party must win three percent of the national vote.

For elections to the European Parliament Greece forms a single national constituency which returns 24 MEPs (25 in 1994). Seats are allocated by proportional representation in three stages. In the first stage seats are allocated by a Hare quote. In the second stage the sum of the remainder (unused votes) of all the parties' votes are divided by the number of unallocated seats plus one to calculate a Hagenbach-Bischoff quota. This quota is then divided into the remainders, of the various parties list votes. Any seat or seats not filled by this procedure are distributed amongst the parties using the largest remainder formula. Voters could choose only between party lists, not between individual candidates. For 1994 a three percent nationwide threshold rule was introduced.

Ireland

The 166 members of the *Dáil* are elected in 41 constituencies by single transferable vote. European Parliament Elections use the same formula, but there are only four constituencies returning together 15 MEPs in 1989 and 16 MEPs in 1994.

Italy

Until 1994 the 635 members of the *Camera de Deputati* were elected from 32 multi-member constituencies using the Imperiali formula (a variant of the d'Hondt formula with an initial divisor of two rather than one). If, as was customarily the case, all seats were not allocated at the constituency level, remainders (unused votes) are collated into a national pool, where a second allocation took place, using the largest remainder system. In addition to casting a vote for a party list each elector could cast either three or four preference votes (depending on the size of the constituency) for individual candidates on the same list. In June 1991 a national referendum approved a proposal to limit the number of preference votes to one.

In 1993 a new system was introduced. Three quarters of all deputies were to be elected by simple plurality in single-member districts. The remainder were to be chosen by Nationwide PR using the Hare largest remainder system. Only parties winning at least four per cent of the nationwide vote can participate in the PR allocation.

The electoral system for the European Parliament is very similar to the pre 1994 system, except that there are only five constituencies which together return 81 MEPs (87 in 1994). Electors can vote both for a list as a whole and cast preference votes for between one and three individual candidates (the number varying between constituencies).

Luxembourg

The 60 members of the *Chambre des Deputés* are elected in four constituencies. Each elector has as many votes as there are seats in his/her constituency. The elector can vote either for a party list (which is equivalent to giving one preference vote to each candidate) or give one or two votes to individual candidates. The elector may divide his/her votes between candidates on different party lists. Seats are allocated between parties using the Hagenbach-Bischoff formula. Within the parties seats go to the candidates with the largest number of preference votes.

The six Luxembourg MEPs are chosen from a single national constituency. Each elector has six votes. The elector may vote either for a list or for individual candidates but, unlike national elections, may cast no more than one vote per candidate. Seats are allocated between lists using the Hagenbach-Bischoff formula and within lists using the votes cast for individual candidates.

The Netherlands

The 150 members of the Second Chamber (*Tweede Kamer*) are chosen from party lists presented in 19 electoral districts, but the overall division of seats between party lists is made at the national level using the d'Hondt formula. For European Parliament elections there is a single national constituency which returns 25 MEPs (31 in 1994). Seats are allocated using the d'Hondt formula. As in *Tweede Kamer* elections the voter casts his or her ballot by choosing one of the candidates on a party list.

Portugal

The 250 members of the *Assembleia de República* are elected from 22 constituencies using the d'Hondt formula. Portugal's 24 MEPs (25 in 1994) are chosen from a single national constituency where seats are also allocated by the d'Hondt formula. As in national elections electors may choose only between party lists and not between individual candidates.

Spain

The 350 members of the *Congreso de los Diputados* are chosen from 52 constituencies each of which comprise a single province. Seats are allocated between lists using the d'Hondt formula, except for two single member constituencies where the plurality system is used. Spain's 60 MEPs (64 in 1994) are chosen in a single national constituency. Seats are allocated between lists using the d'Hondt formula and, as in national elections, voters may choose only between party lists and not individual candidates.

The United Kingdom

The 651 members of the House of Commons are elected by plurality from single-member constituencies. The same procedure is used for electing the 78 MEPs from Great Britain. For European Parliament elections Northern Ireland forms a single three member constituency whose MEPs are elected by single transferable vote.

Table D.1 European Parliament Electoral Systems, 1989

Countries	Consti-tuencies	MEP's	Electors Per MEP	Votes per MEP	Electoral Formula Constit. / Higher Level
Belgium	3	24	296,000	268,000	PR d'Hondt
Denmark	1	16	245,000	114,000	PR d'Hondt
France	1	81	473,000	231,000	PR d'Hondt
Germany	1	81	565,000	353,000	PR Niemeyer
Greece	1	24	349,000	279,000	PR Hare / L. Remainder
Ireland	4	15	164,000	70,000	STV
Italy	5	81	564,000	460,000	PR Hare / L. Remainder
Luxembourg	1	6	36,000	31,000	PR Hagenbach-Bischoff
The Netherlands	1	25	444,000	211,000	PR d'Hondt
Portugal	1	24	338,000	173,000	PR d'Hondt
Spain	1	60	488,000	267,000	PR d'Hondt
Great Britain	78	78	539,000	197,000	Plurality
Northern Ireland	1	3	369,000	180,000	STV

Table D.2 European Parliament Electoral Systems, 1994

Countries	Constituencies	MEP's	Electors Per MEP	Votes per MEP	Electoral Formula Constit. / Higher Level
Belgium	3	25	346,677	261,519	PR
Denmark	1	16	249,634	132,111	PR
France	1	87	448,503	236,402	PR
Germany	1	99	610,311	366,594	PR
Greece	1	25	341,985	272,155	PR
Ireland	4	15	175,438	75,833	Single transferable vote
Italy	5	87	556,008	409,828	PR
Luxembourg	1	6	37,339	33,062	PR
The Netherlands	1	31	374,796	134,762	PR
Portugal	1	25	342,467	121,814	PR
Spain	1	64	486,630	289,917	PR
Great Britain	84	84	506,669	182,214	Plurality
Northern Ireland	1	3	383,435	186,349	Single transferable vote

Table D.3 National Parliament Electoral Systems, 1994

Countries	Constituencies	MP's	Electors Per MP	Votes per MP	Electoral Formula Constit. / Higher Level
Belgium	30	212	33,000	31,000	PR Hare/d'Hondt
Denmark	13/1	175	22,800	19,000	Ste Lagu'/Largest Remainder
France	577	577	66,000	43,000	Two Ballot: Majority/Plurality
Germany	16/328	656	92,000	71,000	Plurality/Niemeyer
Greece	56/13	300	26,000	22,000	PR Hagenbach-Bischoff/Lgst Remndr
Ireland	41	166	15,000	10,000	Single Transferable Vote
Italy	232/26	630[1]		65,000	Plurality/PR
Luxembourg	4	60	4,000	3,000	PR Hagenbach-Bischoff
The Netherlands	1	150	72,000	61,000	PR d'Hondt
Portugal	20	250	31,000	22,000	PR d'Hondt
Spain	52	350	85,000	58,000	PR d'Hondt
United Kingdom	651	650	66,000	50,000	Plurality

1: 475 deputies elected in single-member districts by plurality and 155 deputies elected in 26 multi-member districts by PR.

Table D.4 Belgium

List	1989 % Votes	1989 MEPs	1994 % Votes	1994 MEPs
Flemish Christian People's Party (CVP)[1]	21.1	5	17.2	5
Francophone Socialist Party (PS)	14.5	5	11.4	3
Flemish Socialist Party (SP)	12.4	3	11.0	3
Flemish Liberal Party (PVV/VLD)[2]	10.6	2	11.4	3
Francophone Social Christian Party (PSC)	8.1	2	7.0	2
Flemish Ecologists (AGALEV-GROEN)	7.6	1	6.6	1
Francophone Liberal Party (PRL/PRL-FDF)[3]	7.2	2	9.1	3
Francophone Ecologists (ECOLO-VERTS)	6.3	2	5.0	1
Flemish People's Union (Volksunie)	5.4	1	4.4	1
Flemish Block (Vlaams Blok)	4.1	1	7.8	1
Brussels Democratic Front (ERE-FDF)	1.5	0	-	-
Red-Green European Alliance	0.4	0	0.2	0
Flemish Workers' Party (PVDA)	0.3	0	0.7	0
Socialist Workers' Party (POS)	0.2	0	0.3	0
Francophone Workers' Party (PTB)	0.2	0	0.2	0
Workers and Democracy in Europe (LETD)	0.1	0	0.3	0
Humanist Party (PHHP)	0.1	0	0.1	0
National Front (Front National)	-	-	3.0	0
Protection for Elderly People (Waardig ouder Worden)	-	-	2.1	0
Agir (To Act)	-	-	4.7	0
United Left (Gauches Unies)	-	-	0.6	0
Belgium Europe (België-Europe-Belgique)	-	-	4.4	0
Natural Law Party (Natuurwetpartij)	-	-	0.3	0
Solidarity (Solidarité, Universitalité, Droits de l'Homme)	-	-		
Party of German-Speaking Belgians (Partei der deutschsprachiger Belgier)	-	-	0	0
Young Europe (Junges Europa)	-	-	0	0
Total	100.0	24	100.0	25
Electorate:	7,096,273		7,211,311	
Valid Votes:	83.1%		82.7%	
Invalid Votes:	7.6%		7.9%	

1 Including one MEP elected in the German-speaking constituency.
2 In November 1992 the PVV changed its name to VLD..
3 Federation of the Parti Réformateur Libéral (PRL) and the Front Démocratique des Francophones (FDF).

Table D.5 Denmark

List[1]	1989 %Votes	1989 MEPs	1994 %Votes	1994 MEPs
Social Democrats (Socialdemokratiet)	23.3	4	15.8	3
Radical Liberal Party (Det radikale Venstre)	2.8	0	8.5	1
Conservative People's Party (Det konservative Folkeparti)	13.3	2	17.7	3
Centre Democrats (Centrum-Demokraterne)	8.0	2	0.9	0
Socialist People's Party (Socialistisk Folkeparti)	9.1	1	8.6	1
People's Movement (Folkebevægelsen mod EF)	18.9	4	10.3	2
Christian People's Party (Kristeligt Folkeparti)	2.7	0	1.1	0
Liberal Party (Venstre, Danmarks Liberale Parti)	16.6	3	19.0	4
Progress Party (Fremskridtspartiet)	5.3	0	2.9	0
June Movement (Juni Bevægelsen mod EF-Unionen)	-	-	15.2	2
Total	100.0	16	100.0	16
Electorate:	3,923,549		3,944,200	
Valid Votes:	46.2%		52.1%	
Invalid Votes:	1.2%		0.8%	

1 In 1989 four electoral alliances were formed: (1) Social Democrats and Radical Liberal Party; (2) Conservative Peoples' Party and Liberal Party; (3) Centre Democrats and Christian People's Party; (4) Socialist People's Party and the People's Movement Against the European Community.
In 1994 three electoral alliances were formed: (1) Radical Liberals and Christain People's Party; (2) Conservative Peoples' Party, Centre Beaurocrats and Liberal Party; (3) Peoples' Movement and June Movement.

Table D.6   France

List	1989 %Votes	1989 MEPs	1994 %Votes	1994 MEPs
Union (L'Union UDF-RPR)	28.9	26	25.6	28
Majority of Progress for Europe (PS)[1]	23.6	22	14.5	15
Europe and Fatherland (FN)[2]	11.7	10	10.5	11
Greens (les Verts, Antoine Waechter)	10.6	9	2.9	0
Centre for Europe (CDS, Simone Veil)	8.4	7	-	-
Communist Party (PCF)	7.7	7	6.7	7
Hunting, Fishing Tradition (Chasse, Pêche Tradition, André Goustat)	4.1	0	4.0	0
Workers' Struggle (Lutte Ouvrière, Arlette Laguiller)	1.4	0	2.3	0
Animal and Environmental Protection	1.0	0	-	-
Alliance (Defenseurs de la famille et de l'Enfants)	0.8	0	-	-
Movement for a Workers' Party	0.6	0	-	-
Generation Europe[3]	0.3	0	0.6	0
List of the Majority for Another Europe (Philippe de Villiers)	-	-	12.3	13
Radical Energy (Bernard Tapie)	-	-	12.0	13
L'Autre Politique	-	-	2.5	0
Generation Ecologie (Brice Lalonde)	-	-	2.0	0
L'Europe commence a Sarajevo	-	-	1.6	0
Others	0.9	0	2.5	0
Total	100.0	81	100.0	87
Electorate:	38,297,496		39,019,797	
Valid Votes:	47.4%		49.9%	
Invalid Votes:	1.4%		2.8%	

1 In 1994 L'Europe Solidaire
2 In 1994 Liste contre l'Europe de Maastricht, Allez la France!
3 In 1994 L'Emploi d'abord!

Table D.7   Germany

	1989		1994	
List	%Votes	MEPs	%Votes	MEPs
Social Democratic Party (SPD)	37.3	31[1]	32.2	40
Christian Democratic Union (CDU)	29.5	25[1]	32.0	39
Greens (Die Grünen)	8.4	8[1]	10.1	12
Christian Social Union (CSU)	8.2	7	6.8	8
Republicans (Die Republikaner)	7.1	6	3.9	0
Free Democratic Party (FDP)	5.6	4	4.1	0
German People's Union (DVU)	1.6	0	-	0
Ecological Democratic Party (ÖDP)	0.7	0	0.8	0
Bavaria Party (BP)	0.3	0	0.3	0
Communist Party (DKP)	0.2	0	-	0
Party of Democratic Socialism (PDS)	-	-	4.7	0
League of Free Citizens (Bund freier Bürger)	-	-	1.1	0
Grey Panthers	-	-	0.8	0
Car Drivers and Citizens' Interest Party (APD)	-	-	0.7	0
'Instead Of' Party – The Independents	-	-	0.5	0
Others	1.1	0	2.0	0
Total	100.0	81	100.0	99
Electorate:	45,773,179		60,420,775	
Valid Votes:	61.6%		58.6%	
Invalid Votes:	0.7%		1.50%	

1 Including one MEP nominated by the West Berlin House of Deputies.

Table D.8   Greece

List	1989 %Votes	1989 MEPs	1994 %Votes	1994 MEPs
New Democracy (ND)	40.4	10	32.7	9
Panhellenic Socialist Movement (PASOK)	36.0	9	37.7	10
Coalition of Left and Progress (Synaspismos)	14.3	4	6.3	2
Democratic Renewal (DIANA)	1.4	1	2.8	0
National Political Union (EPEN)	1.2	0	0.8	0
Alternative Ecologists	1.1	0	-	-
Greek Democratic Ecological Movement	1.1	0	-	-
Greek Socialist Party (ESK)	0.7	0	-	-
KKE Interior-Renewal Left	0.6	0	-	-
Greek radical Movement	0.6	0	-	-
Political Spring (Politiki Anixi)[1]	-	-	8.6	2
Communist Party of Greece (KKE)[2]	-	-	6.3	2
Centre Union (Enossi Kentroon)	-	-	1.2	0
Kollatos	-	-	0.7	0
Other Green Lists	-	-	0.8	0
Others	2.6	0	2.1	0
Total	100.0	24	100.0	25
Electorate:	8,377,904		8,459,636	
Valid Votes:	78.5%		77.2%	
Invalid Votes:	1.5%		3.2%	

1 Split off from New Democracy.
2 In 1989 part of Coalition of Left and Progress.

Table D.9 Ireland

	1989		1994	
List	%Votes	MEPs	%Votes	MEPs
Fianna Fáil	31.5	6	35.0	7
Fine Gael	21.6	4	24.3	4
Labour Party	9.5	1	11.0	1
Sinn Féin	2.3	0	3.0	0
Workers' Party	7.5	1	1.9	0
Green Party	3.7	0	7.9	2
Independents	11.9	2	6.9	1
Progressive Democrats	11.9	1	6.5	0
Democratic Left [1]	-	-	3.5	0
Total	100.0	15	100.0	16
Electorate:	2,453,451		2,631,575	
Valid votes:	66.5%		43.2%	
Invalid votes:	1.7%		0.8%	

1 Founded by six of the seven Workers' Party TDs following a split in the party in 1992.

Table D.10 Italy

List	1989 %Votes	1989 MEPs	1994 %Votes	1994 MEPs
Christian Democracy (DC)/Popular Party (PPI)	32.9	26	10.0	8
Communist Party (PCI)/Democratic Party of the Left (PDS)	27.6	22	19.1	16
Socialist Party (PSI)/National Alliance (Alleanza Nazionale - AN)	14.8	12	12.5	11
Social Movement (Movimento Sociale Italiano (MSI)/Northern League (Lega Nord)	5.5	4	6.6	6
Liberal & Republican Parties (PLI and PRI) [1]	4.4	4	0.9	1
Green List (Lista Verde)	3.8	3	-	-
Social Democrats (PSDI)	2.7	2	0.7	1
Rainbow Greens (Verdi Arcobaleno)[2]	2.4	2	-	-
Lombard League (Lega Lombarda - Alleanza Nord)	1.8	2	-	-
Proletarian Democracy (DP)	1.3	1	-	-
Anti-Prohibitionists (Lega Antiproibizionisti Droga)	1.2	1	-	-
Federalism (Federalismo - Europa dei Popoli)[3]	0.6	1	-	-
South Tyrol People's Party (Süd-Tiroler Volks-partei SVP)	0.5	1	0.6	1
Pensioners' Party (Partito dei Pensionati)	0.5	0	-	-
Forza Italia	-	-	30.6	27
Communist Refoundation (RC)	-	-	6.1	5
Segni Pact (Patto Segni)	-	-	3.3	3
Greens (Federazione dei Verdi)	-	-	3.2	3
Pannella - Reformers (Pannella - Riformatori)	-	-	2.1	2
The Network (La Rete)	-	-	1.1	1
League for Southern Action (Lega d'Azione Meridionale)	-	-	0.7	0
Alpine Lombard League (Lega Alpina Lumbarda)	-	-	0.3	0
Solidarity (Solidarietà)	-	-	0.0	0
Total	100.0	81	100.0	87
Electorate:	45,722,791		48,372,726	
Valid Votes:	75.7%		68.3%	
Invalid Votes:	5.7%		5.4%	

1 In 1994 the Republicans and Liberals ran separately, winning 0.7 and 0.2 per cent of the vote, respectively.
2 One successful candidate was from the Radical Party.
3 Alliance of regional parties comprising two parties from the Val d'Aosta, the Union Valdotaine and the Alliance Democratique Progressiste, the Partito Sardo d'Azione, the Movimento Meridionale, Süd-Tirol (a label for Alfons Benedikter, formerly a leading figure in the Süd-Tiroler Volkspartei), the Union del Popolo Veneto, the Unione Slovena-Slovenska Skupnost, the Mouvement Autonomiste Occitan and independents representing the Franco-provencal, Albanian, Greek and Ladin linguistic minorities. The successful candidate was from the Radical Party.

Table D.11 Luxembourg

List	1989		1994	
	%Votes	MEPs	%Votes	MEPs
Christian Social Party (CSV)	34.9	3	31.5	2
Socialist Workers' Party (LSAP)	25.4	2	24.8	2
Democratic Party (DP)	20.0	1	18.9	1
Communist Party (KPL)	4.7	0	1.6	0
Green List Ecological Initiative (GLEI)	6.1	0	-	-
GLEI/GAP electoral alliance	-	-	10.9	1
Green Alternative (GAP)	4.3	0	-	-
Luxembourg for the Luxembourgers (National Bewegong)	2.9	0	2.4	0
Green Alternative Alliance (GRAL)	0.9	0	-	-
Revolutionary Socialist Party (RSP)	0.6	0	-	-
Why Not? (Firwat nët?)	0.2	0	-	-
Democratic Action Committee for Pension Rights (ADR)[1]	-	-	7.0	0
Group for Luxembourg Sovereignty (GLS)[2]	-	-	1.2	0
New Left (Nei Lènk)[3]	-	-	0.9	0
Independent and Neutral Party of Human Right (NOMP)[4]	-	-	0.9	0
Total	100.0	6	100.0	6
Electorate:	218,940		224,031	
Valid Votes:	87.4%		77.8	
Invalid Votes:	8.8%		8.8%	

1 Previously 5/6 Action Committee.
2 Founded by a former Christian Social Party Member. Opposed to voting rights for European Union Citizens.
3 Breakaway from the Communist Party.
4 Splinter from the ADR.

Table D.12 The Netherlands

List	1989 %Votes	1989 MEPs	1994 %Votes	1994 MEPs
Christian Democratic Appeal (CDA)	34.6	10	30.8	10
Labour Party (PVDA)	30.7	8	22.9	8
People's Party for Freedom and Democracy (VVD)	13.6	3	17.9	6
Rainbow (Regenboog) / Green Left[1]	7.0	2	3.7	1
Democrats 66 (D66)	6.0	1	11.7	4
Calvinist Political Parties[2]	5.9	1	7.8	2
Centre Democrats (CD)	0.8	0	1.0	0
Socialist Party (SP)	0.7	0	1.3	0
Initiative for a European Democracy (IED)	0.4	0	-	-
God With Us (God Met Ons)	0.4	0	-	-
Greens (De Groenen)	-	-	2.4	0
A Better Future (Een Betere Toekomst)	-	-	0.3	0
List de Groen	-	-	0.2	0
Total	100.0	25	100.0	31
Electorate:	11,099,123		11,618,677	
Valid Votes:	47.2%		35.6%	
Invalid Votes:	0.3%		0.4%	

1 1989: Alliance of the Communist Party (CPN), the Radical Political Party (PPR), the Pacifist Socialist Party (PSP) and the Evangelical People's Party (EVP). 1994: Party formed by merger of the parties forming the Rainbow Alliance in 1989.
2 Alliance of the Political Reformed Party (SGP), the Reformed Political Union (GPV) and the Reformed Political Federation (RPF).

Table D.13 Portugal

List	1989 %Votes	1989 MEPs	1994 %Votes	1994 MEPs
Social Democrat Party (PSD)	33.7	9	35.5	9
Socialist Party (PS)	29.5	8	36.0	10
United Democratic Coalition (CDU)[1]	14.9	4	11.6	3
Democratic-Social Centre (CDS)	14.6	3	12.8	3
Popular Monarchist Party (PPM)	2.1	0	0.3	0
Portuguese Democratic Movement (MDP)	1.4	0	-	-
Popular Democratic Union (UDP)	1.1	0	0.6	0
Revolutionary Socialist Party (PSR)	0.8	0	0.6	0
Christian Democratic Party (PDC)	0.7	0	-	-
Communist Party of the Portuguese Workers (DPCTP/MRPP)	0.7	0	0.8	0
Labour Party of Socialist Unity (POUS)	0.3	0	-	-
Front of the Revolutionary Left (FER)	0.2	0	-	-
Movement and Party of the Land	-	-	0.4	0
Party of National Solidarity (PSN)	-	-	0.4	0
Movement for the Solidarity of the Workers (MUT)	-	-	0.1	0
Politics XXI (Politica XXI)	-	-	0.4	0
Democratic Party of the Atlantic (PDA)	-	-	0.2	0
Party of Democratic Renewal (PRD)	-	-	0.2	0
Total	100.0	24	100.0	25
Electorate:	8,107,694		8,561,677	
Valid Votes:	49.5%		34.4%	
Invalid Votes:	1.6%		1.1%	

1 An electoral alliance of the Communist Party (PCP), the Greens (Os Verdes') and Democratic Intervention.

Table D.14 Spain

List	1989		1994	
	%Votes	MEPs	%Votes	MEPs
Spanish Socialist Workers' Party (PSOE)	40.2	27	31.0	28
Popular Party (PP)	21.7	15	40.7	22
Democratic and Social Centre (CDS)	7.3	5	1.0	0
United Left (IU)[1]	6.2	4	13.6	9
Convergence and Union (CiU)	4.3	2	4.7	3
Herri Batasuna (IIB)	1.7	1	1.0	0
For the Europe of the Peoples[2]	1.5	1	1.3	0
Left of the Peoples[3]	1.9	1	-	-
Nationalist Coalition[4]	1.9	2	2.8	2
Workers' Party of Spain (PTEDUC)	1.3	0	-	-
Andalusian Party (PA)	1.3	1	0.8	0
Ruiz-Mateos Electors' Association	3.9	2	0.4	0
Nationalist Block of Galicia (BNG)	0.3	0	0.8	0
Green List (LV)[5]	1.1	0	-	-
Ecological Greens (VE)	1.0	0	-	-
Federation of Regional Parties (FPR)	1.0	0	-	-
Communist Party of the Peoples of Spain (PCPE-PCC)	0.5	0	0.2	0
Others	2.8	0	3.4	0
Total	100.0	60	100.0	64
Electorate:	29,283,982		31,144,343	
Valid Votes:	53.5%		58.6%	
Invalid Votes:	1.2%		0.9%	

1 An electoral alliance of which the leading members, are the Spanish Communist Party (PCE) and its Catalan affiliate, PSUC).

2 In 1989 an alliance of three nationalist parties: Basque Solidarity (EA) a breakaway party from the mainstream Basque Nationalist Party, the Republican Left of Catalonia (ERC) and the Nationalist Party of Galicia (PNG) a 1987 breakaway from Coalición Galega. In 1994, Basque Solidarity, Republican Left of Catalonia, Tierra Comunerà, Partido Nacionalista Castellana, Entersa Nacionalista, Ecologista (in Catalonia) and Acció Catalana.

3 An electoral alliance of left-wing nationalist parties comprising nine parties and some independent candidates. The parties were: Basque Left (EE), the Galician Left (PSG-EE), a leftist Catalan party the Left Nationalist Agreement (ENE); the Socialist Party of Majorca (PSM); the Socialist Party of Minorca (PSM); the Aragonese Union (Unión Aragonesista); Unity of the Valencian People (UPV, itself and alliance of the Agrupamento del Pais Valencia and the Partit Nacionalista del Pais Valencia), Canary Islands Assembly (AC) and the Socialist Party of the Asturias (PSA).

4 In 1989 an alliance of the Basque Nationalist Party (EAJ/PNV), the Canary Islands Assembly (AIC), the Nationalist Party of Castille and Leon (PANCAL) and the Galician Coalition. In 1994 the Basque Nationalist Party Galicia Coalition, Coalición Canaria, Partido Aragones and Unio Mallorquina.

5 Electoral alliance of regional and local green parties comprising Los Verdes and in addition to some independent candidates, two Madrid Groups the Alternative Greens (LVAM) and Natural Culture (DCN), Ecological Alternative of Galicia (AEG) and the Ecologist Party of Euskadi (PEE).

Table D.15 Great Britain

	1989		1994	
List	%Votes	MEPs	%Votes	MEPs
Labour Party[1]	40.1	45	44.2	62
Conservative Party	34.7	32	27.9	18
Green Party	14.9	0	3.2	0
Social and Liberal Democrat	6.2	0	16.7	2
Scottish National Party	2.6	1	3.2	2
Plaid Cymru	0.8	0	1.1	0
Social Democrat Party	0.5	0	-	-
Independents and Others	0.1	0	2.5	0
Natural Law Party	-	-	0.6	0
Liberal Party	-	-	0.6	0
Total	100.0	78	100.0	84
Electorate:	42,603,716		42,293,640	
Valid Votes:	57.2%		56.8%	
Invalid Votes:	0.1%		0.1%	

1 Including votes for Labour/Cooperative Party candidates.

Table D.16 Northern Ireland

List	1989 %Votes	1989 MEPs	1994 %Votes	1994 MEPs
Democratic Unionist Party	29.9	1	29.2	1
Social Democratic and Labour Party	25.5	1	28.9	1
Ulster Unionist Party	22.2	1	23.8	1
Sinn Féin	9.1	0	7.9	0
Alliance Party	5.2	0	4.1	0
Conservative Party[1]	4.8	0	1.0	0
Green Party[2]	1.2	0	-	-
Workers' Party	1.0	0	0.5	0
Labour for Representative Government	0.7	0	-	-
Labour Party '87	0.2	0	-	-
Ulster Independence Movement	-	-	1.4	0
Independent Labour Party	-	-	0.5	0
Natural Law Party	-	-	0.3	0
Peace Coalition	-	-	0.2	0
Independent Ulster	-	-	0.1	0
Constitutional Independence for Northern Ireland	-	-	0.1	0
Total	100.0	3	100.0	3
Electorate:	1,106,852		1,150,304	
Valid Votes:	47.7%		48.8%	
Invalid Votes:	1.0%		0.5%	

1 The Conservative Party candidate in Northern Ireland was not endorsed by Conservative Central Office in 1989, but was affiliated with the Party in 1994.
2 The Green Party in Northern Ireland is affiliated to the Green Party in Great Britain.

List of Contributors

Johan Ackaert
  Limburg University Centre

Mário Bacalhau
  Lisbon

Roland Cayrol
  Fondation Nationale des Sciences
  Politiques, Paris

Pilar del Castillo
  Universidad Nacional de
    Educacion a Distancia, Madrid

John Curtice
  University of Strathclyde

Panayote Elias Dimitras
  Communication & Political
    Research Society, Athens

Cees van der Eijk
  University of Amsterdam

Mark Franklin
  Universities of Houston
    and Strathclyde

Colin Knox
  University of Ulster

Tom Mackie
  University of Strathclyde

Renato Mannheimer
  University of Genova

Michael Marsh
  Trinity College, Dublin

Erik Oppenhuis
  University of Amsterdam

Dolores O'Reilly
  University of Ulster

Hermann Schmitt
  University of Mannheim

Marc Swyngedouw
  Catholic University of Brussels

Lieven de Winter
  Catholic University of
    Louvain-la-Neuve

Torben Worre
  University of Copenhagen

Colette Ysmal
  Fondation Nationale des Sciences
    Politiques, Paris

References

Author Index

Subject Index

References

Achen, C. H. 1979. The Bias in Normal Vote Estimates. *Political Methodology.* 6:343–356.

Ackaert, J., L. De Winter, A.-M. Aish, and A.-P. Frognier. 1992. L'Abstentionnisme Electoral et Vote Blank et Nul en Belgique. *Res Publica.* 2:209–226.

Adonis, A. 1989. Great Britain. *Electoral Studies.* 8:262–269.

Aldrich, J. H., and F. D. Nelson. 1984. *Linear Probability, Logit and Probit Models.* Beverly Hills: Sage.

Alen, A., ed. 1992. *Treatise on Belgian Constitutional Law.* Deventer: Kluwer.

Andersen, K. 1979. *The Creation of a Democratic Majority 1928–1936.* Chicago: University of Chicago Press.

Anker, H. 1991. *Normal Vote Analysis.* Amsterdam: Het Spinhuis.

Anker, H., and E. V. Oppenhuis. 1989. De Partij van de Arbeid en de Ziektewet: Een Empirisch Onderzoek naar de Invloed van de Ziektewetplannen op de Electorale Aanhang van de PvdA in 1982. *Acta Politica.* 24:287–299.

———. 1990. De Breker Betaalt: De Kabinetscrisis van 2 Mei 1989. *Jaarboek Documentatie-centrum Nederlandse Politieke Partijen 1989.* Groningen: DNPP.

Asher, H. 1988. *Polling and the Public: What Every Citizen Should Know.* Washington, D.C.: CQ Press.

Astorkia, J. M. 1992. *Evolución y Tipologías de los Abstencinismos en España.* Madrid: Paper Prepared for the Jornadas Sobre Comportamiento Poltico y Electoral. UNED.

Aughey, A., P. Hainsworth, and M. J. Trimble. 1989. *Northern Ireland in the European Community: An Economic and Political Analysis.* Coleraine: Northern Ireland Policy Research Institute.

Baker, K. L., R. J. Dalton, and K. Hildebrandt. 1981. *Germany Transformed: Political Culture and the New Politics.* Cambridge, Mass. and London: Harvard University Press.

Barnes, S.H., and M. Kaase et al. 1979. *Political Action: Mass Participation in Five Western Democracies.* Beverly Hills, Calif.: Sage.

Barnes, S. H., P. McDonough, and A. Lopez Pina. 1986. Volatile Parties and Stable Voters in Spain. *Government and Opposition.* 21:56–75.

Bardi, L. 1985. Il Voto di Preferenza in Italia e la Legge Elettorale Europa. *Rivista Italiana di Scienze Politiche.* 15:293–312.

———. 1990a. *Il Voto Nelle Elezioni Eropee del Hiugno 1989: Implicazioni Nazionali e Propettive Comunitarie.* Working Papers Instituto per gli Studi di Politica Internazionale.

———. 1990b. Le Terze Elezioni del Parlamento Europeo: Un Voto per L'Italia o un Voto per l'Europa? In R. Catanzaro, and F. Sabbetti, eds., *Politica in Italia: Edizione 1990.* Bologna: Il Mulino.

Bartolini, S., and P. Mair. 1990. *Identity, Competition and Electoral Availability: The Stabilisation of European Electorates 1885–1985.* Cambridge: Cambridge University Press.

Bauer, P., and H. Schmitt. 1990. *Die Republikaner: Eine Empirische Analyse von Wähler-potential und Wahlmotiven.* Mannheim: ZEUS (Mimeo).

Beck, P. A. 1986. Choice, Context and Consequence: Beaten and Unbeaten Paths Toward a Science of Electoral Behavior. In H. F. Weisberg, ed., *Political Science: The Science of Politics.* New York: Agathon.

Beer, S. 1993. What's wrong with the Politics of European Federalism? In S. Hill, ed., *Visions of Europe.* New York: Duckworth.

Berelson, B. R., P. F. Lazarsfeld, and W. N. McPhee. 1954. *Voting: A Study of Opinion Formation in a Presidential Campaign.* Chicago: University of Chicago Press.

Betz, H.-G. 1990. Value Change and Postmaterialist Politics: The Case of West Germany. *Comparative Political Studies.* 23:239–256.

Billiet, J., A. Carton, and R. Huys. 1990. *Onbekend maakt Onbemind: Een Sociologisch Onderzoek naar de Houding van Belgen tegenover Migranten.* Leuven: Sociologisch Onderzoeksinstituut.

Blais, A., and R. K. Carty. 1990. Does Proportional Representation Foster Voter Turnout? *European Journal of Political Research.* 18:167–181.

Blumler, J. G., ed. 1983. *Communicating to Voters: Televison in the First European Parliament Elections.* London: Sage.

———. 1984. European Voters' Response to the First Community Elections. In K. Reif, ed., *European Elections 1979/81 and 1984: Conclusion and Perspectives from Emperical Research.* Berlin: Quorum.

Blumler, J. G., and A. D. Fox. 1982. *The European Voter: Popular Responses to the First European Community Elections.* London: Policy Studies Institute.

Bogdanor, V. 1986. The Future of the European Community. *Government and Opposition.* 21:161–176.

———. 1989. Direct Elections, Representative Democracy and European Integration. *Electoral Studies.* 8:205–216.

Borella, F. 1991. *Les Parties Politiques Français.* Paris: Le Seuil.

Brody, Richard A. (1978) The Puzzle of Political Participation in America. In Anthony King, ed., *The New American Political System.* Washington D. C.: American Enterprise Institute.

Brown, M. C., and C. N. Halaby. 1982. *Pooling Time Series and Cross–Sectional Data: Estimating the 'Cost' of Political Machines.* Denver: Paper Prepared for the Annual Meeting of the American Political Science Association.

Budge, I., I. Crewe, and D. Farlie, eds. 1976. *Party Identification and Beyond: Representations of Voting and Party Competition.* London: Wiley.

Budge, I., and D. Farlie. 1976. A Comparative Analysis of Factors Correlated with Turnout and Voting Choice. In I. Budge, I. Crewe, and D. Farlie, eds., *Party Identification and Beyond: Representations of Voting and Party Competition.* London: Wiley.

———. 1977. *Voting and Party Competition: A Theoretical Critique and Synthesis Applied to Surveys from Ten Democracies.* London: John Wiley and Sons.

———. 1983. *Explaining and Predicting Elections: Issue Effects and Party Strategies in Twenty-Three Democracies.* London: George Allen and Unwin.

Bürklin, W. 1987. Governing Left Parties Frustrating the Radical Non-Established Left: The Rise and Inevitable Decline of the Greens. *European Sociological Review.* 3:109–126.

Busch, P., and D. Puchala. 1976. Interest, Influence and Integration: Political Structure in the European Communities. *Comparative Political Studies.* 9:235–254.

Campbell, A. 1966. Surge and Decline: A Study of Electoral Change. In A. Campbell, P. E. Converse, W. E. Miller, and D. E. Stokes, eds., *Elections and the Political Order.* New York: Wiley.

Campbell, A., P. E. Converse, W. E. Miller, and D. E. Stokes. 1960. *The American Voter.* New York and London: Wiley.

Campbell, J. E. 1987. The Revised Theory of Surge and Decline. *American Journal of Political Science.* 31:165–183.

———. 1992. *The Presidential Pulse of Congressional Elections.* Lexington: University Press of Kentucky.

Carty, R. K. 1981. Towards a European Politics: The Lessons of the European Parliament Election in Ireland. *Journal of European Integration.* 4:211–241.

del Castillo, P. 1991. Elecciones 91: Continuidades y Cambios en el Mercado Electoral. *Nueva Revista.* 16:12–16.

del Castillo, P., and M. L. Morán. 1989. *The 1987 European Election in Spain.* Paris: Paper prepared for the ECPR Joint Sessions of Workshops.

del Castillo, P., and G. Sani. 1986. Las Elecciones de 1986: Continuidad sin Consolidación. In J. J. Linz, and J. R. Montero, eds., *Crisis y Cambio Electores y Partidos en la España de los Anos Ochenta.* Madrid: Centro de Estudios Constitucionales.

Castles, F. G., and P. Mair. 1984. Left-right Political Scales: Some 'Expert' Judgements. *European Journal of Political Research. 12:73–88.*

Cayrol, R. 1983. Media Use and Campaign Evaluations; Social and Political Stratification of the European Electorate. In J. G. Blumler, ed., *Communicating to Voters: Television in the First European Parliament Elections.* London: Sage.

———. 1989. Le Centrisme: une Petite Famille Politique. *Politique Aujourd'hui.* Numero spécial.

———. 1991. European Elections and the Pre-electoral Period: Media Use and Campaign Evaluations. *European Journal of Political Research.* 19:17–30.

Charlot, J., and M. Charlot. 1989. France. *Electoral Studies.* 8:246–253.

Clarke, H. D., and N. Dutt. 1991. Measuring Value Change in Western Industrialized Societies: The Impact of Unemployment. *American Political Science Review.* 85:905–920.

Clarke, H.D., N. Dutt, and A. Kornberg. 1993. The Political Economy of Attitudes towards Polity and Society in Western European Democracies. *Journal of Politics.* 55:998–1021.

Coakley, J., M. Holmes, and N. Rees. 1991. *Patterns of Opposition to European Integration in Ireland.* Limerick, University of Limerick (mimeo)

Collinge, M. 1989. Noir, Bleu, Orange, Vert, Rouge... Belges Strasbourg. *La Revue Nouvelle.* 9:28–38.

———. 1990. Elections Européennes en Belgique: Géographie des Voix de Préférence. Courrier Hebdomadaire du CRISP. 266:1–37.

Conover, P. J., and S. Feldman. 1984. How People Organize the Political World: A Schematic Model. American Journal of Political Science. 28:95–126.

Converse, P. E. 1964. The Nature of Belief Systems in Mass Publics. In D. Apter, ed., *Ideology and Discontent.* New York: Free Press.

———. 1975. Determinants of Individual Voting Choice. In F. I. Greenstein, and N. W. Polsby, eds., *Handbook of Political Science vol. 4.* Reading, Mass.: Addison-Wesley.

Cotgrove, S. 1982. *Catastrophe and Cornucopia.* New York: Wiley.

Cotgrove, S., and A. Duff. 1980. Environmentalism, Middle Class Radicalism and Politics. *Sociological Review.* 28:333–351.

Courtois, S. 1988. Parti Communiste: les Dernière Cartouches. In P. Habert, and C. Ysmal, eds., *Les Elections Legislative de 1988.* Paris: Le Figaro/Etudes Politique.

Couttenier, I. 1990. Belgian Politics in 1989. *Res Publica.* 2–3:208–227.

Crepaz, M. M. L. 1990. The Impact of Party Polarization and Postmaterialism on Voter Turnout: A Comparative Study of 16 Industrial Democracies. *European Journal of Political Research.* 18:183–205.

Crewe, I. 1981. Electoral Participation. In D. Butler, H. R. Penniman, and A. Ranney, eds., *Democracy at the Polls: A Comparative Study of Competitive National Elections.* Washington D. C.: American Enterprise Institute.

Crewe, I., and D. Denver, eds., 1985. *Electoral Change in Western Democracies: Patterns and Sources of Volatility.* London: Croom Helm.

Crewe, I., and A. King. 1994. Did Major Win? Did Kinnock Lose? In A. Heath, R. Jowell, and J. Curtice, eds., *Can Labour Win?* Aldershot: Gower.

Curtice, J. 1989. The 1989 European Election: Protest or Green Tide? *Electoral Studies.* 8:217–230.

Curtice, J., and M. Steed. 1986. Proportionality and Exaggeration in the British Electoral System. *Electoral Studies.* 5:209–28.

———. 1992. The Results Analysed. In D. Butler, and D. Kavanagh, eds., *The British General Election of 1992.* London: Macmillan.

Daalder, H. 1987. The Dutch Party System: From Segmentation to Polarization—and then? In Hans Daalder, ed., *Party Systems in Denmark, Austria, Switzerland, The Netherlands, and Belgium.* London: Frances Pinter.

Dalton, R. J. 1984. Cognitive Mobilization and Partisan Dealignment in Advanced Industrial Democracies. *Journal of Politics.* 46:264–284.

Dalton, R. J., S. C. Flanagan, and P. A. Beck. 1984. Electoral Change in Advanced Industrial Democracies. In R. J. Dalton, S. C. Flanagan, and P. A. Beck, eds., *Electoral Change in Advanced Industrial Democracies: Realignment or Dealignment?* Princeton, N. J.: Princeton University Press.

Dalton, R. J., and R. Rohrschneider. 1990. Wählerwandel und die Abschächung der Parteineigung von 1972 bis 1987. In M. Kaase, and H.-D. Klingemann, eds., *Wahlen und Wähler: Analysen aus Anlaß der Bundestagswahl 1987.* Opladen: Westdeutscher Verlag.

Dalton, R. J., and M. P. Wattenberg. 1993. The Not So Simple Act of Voting. In A. W. Finifter, ed., *Political Science: The State of the Discipline II.* Washington D. C.: APSA.

Das, E. 1989. *De Campagne voor de Europarlementsverkiezingen van 17 juni 1984 in België.* Leuven: Afdeling Politilogie.

———. 1992. De Personale Keuze bij de Parlementsverkiezingen van 24 November 1991. *Res Publica.* 2:155–173.

Das, E., and W. Dewachter. 1991. *Overdadig! Overtollig? De Verkiezingscampagne van December 1987. Leuven: Afdeling Politologie.*

Debets, P., and E. Brouwer. 1989. *MSP: A Program for Mokken Scale Analysis for Polychotomous Items. Groningen: IEC ProGAMMA.*

Denver, D. 1992. The Centre. In A. King, ed., *Britain at the Polls 1992.* Chatham, N.J.: Chatham House.

De Ridder, M., and L. R. Fraga. 1986. The Brussels Issue in Belgian Politics. *West European Politics.* 9:376–392.

Deschouwer, K. 1987. *Politieke Partijen in België.* Antwerpen: Kluwer.

van Deth, J. W. 1983a. Ranking the Ratings: The Case of Materialist and Post-Materialist Value Orientations. *Political Methodology.* 10:407–431.

———. 1983b. The Persistence of Materialist and Post-Materialist Value Orientations. *European Journal of Political Research.* 11:63–79.

Deweerdt, M. 1984. Het Gebruik van de Voorkeurstem bij de Europarlementsverkiezingen. *Res Publica.* 5:603–614.

———. 1990. Overzicht van het Belgisch Politiek Gebeuren in 1989. *Res Publica.* 2–3:168–206.

Dewachter, W. 1987. Changes in a Particratie: The Belgian Party System from 1944 to 1986. In H. Daalder, ed., *Party Systems in Denmark, Austria, Switzerland, The Netherlands and Belgium.* London: Pinter.

Dewachter, W., and L. De Winter. 1979. Het Verlies van het Machtspotentieel van een Zwak Parlement: Onderzoek aan de Hand van de Belgische Afgevaardigden in het Europees Parlement (1952–1979). *Res Publica.* 1:746–755.

De Winter, L. 1978. Officiële en Reële Omvang van het Absenteïsme bij de Na-oorlogse Parlementsverkiezingen. *Res Publica.* 4:685–692.

———. 1988. Analyse van een Afwendbare Afgang *Nieuw Links.* 5:4–7.

———. 1990. Les Motivations de Votes de l'Electeur Belge. *Etudes et Documents.* 4:1–22.

———. 1991. Parliamentary and Party Pathways to the Cabinet. In J. Blondel, and J.-L. Thibault, eds., *The Profession of Government Minister in Western Europe.* London: Macmillan.

———. 1993a. The Selection of Party Presidents in Belgium: Rubber-stamping the Nominee of the Party Elites. *European Journal of Political Research.* 24:233–256.

———. 1993b. *Socialist Parties in Belgium and the Catch-all Thesis.* Barcelona: Working Papers of the Institut de Ciencies Politiques i Socials.

De Winter, L., J. Ackaert, A.-M. Aish, and A.-P. Frognier. 1991. *L'Abstentionnisme Electoral et le Vote Blank ou Nul en Belgique.* Louvain-la-Neuve: Point d'Appui Interuniversitaire sur l'Opinion Publique et la Politique.

De Winter, L., and L. Janssens. 1988. De Stemmotivatie van de Belgische Kiezer. Brussel: Dimarso.

Dimitras, P. E. 1984a. Greece. *Electoral Studies.* 3:385–289.

———. 1984b. Elections to the European Parliament in Greece. In K. Reif, ed., *European Elections 1979/1981 and 1984.* Berlin: Quorum Verlag.

———. 1989a. Greece. *Electoral Studies.* 8:270–280.

———. 1989b. The 1989 Electoral Law. *Greek Opinion* (special issue). 2–17.

———. 1992. Greece. In M. Franklin, T. Mackie, and H. Valen et al., *Electoral Change: Responses to Evolving Social and Attitudinal Structures in Western Countries.* Cambridge: Cambridge University Press.

———. 1994. Electoral Systems in Greece. In S. Nagel, ed., *Eastern Europe: Development and Public Policy.* London: Macmillan.

Dinan, D. 1994. *Ever Closer Union? An Introduction to the European Community.* London: Macmillan.

Dinkel, R. 1977. Der Zusammenhang zwischen Bundes- und Landtagswahlergebnissen. *Politische Vierteljahresschrift.* 18:348–359.

Dittrich, K., J. Cohen, and V. Rutgers. 1983. *Het Einde van een Tijdperk: Verslag van de Kabinetsformaties van 1981 en 1982.* Maastricht: Rijksuniversiteit Limburg.

Di Virgilio, A. 1991. A che Servono le Elezioni Eropee? In M. Caciagli, and A. Sreafico, eds., *Vent'Anni di Elezioni in Italia. 1968–1987.* Padova: Liviana.

DNPP. 1978–1990. *Jaarboeken Documentatiecentrum Nederlandse Politieke Partijen 1978–1990.* Groningen: DNPP.

Downs, A. 1957. *An Economic Theory of Democracy.* New York: Harper and Row.

Duch, R., and M. Taylor. 1993. Postmaterialism and the Economic Condition. *American Journal of Political Science.* 37:747–779.

Easton, D. 1965. *A System's Analysis of Political Life.* New York: Wiley.

Economist. 1989. Countying it up. 13 May:39–43.

van der Eijk, C. 1984a. The Netherlands. *Electoral Studies.* 3:302–305.

———. 1984b. Dutch Voters and the European Elections of 1979 and 1984. In K. Reif, ed., *European Elections 1979/1981 and 1984.* Berlin: Quorum Verlag.

———. 1987. Testing Theories of Electoral Cycles: The Case of The Netherlands. *European Journal of Political Research.* 15:253–270.

———. 1989. The Netherlands. *Electoral Studies.* 8:305–312.

———. 1990. *Ideology, Party Systems and Voting in Europe.* San Francisco: Paper Prepared for the Annual Meeting of the American Political Science Association.

————. 1995. Protest-, Strategisch en Oprecht Stemmen: Observaties naar Aanleiding van de Verkiezingen in 1994. In: *Jaarboek 1994.* Groningen: DNPP.

————. 1996. Measuring Agreement in Ordered Rating Scales. In C. van der Eijk, M. Fennema, and H. Schijf, eds., *In Search of Structure: Essays in Methodology and Social Science.* Amsterdam: Het Spinhuis.

van der Eijk, C., and M. Franklin. 1991. European Community Politics and Electoral Representation: Evidence from the 1989 European Elections Study. *European Journal of Political Research.* 19:105–128.

————. 1994. Europäische Integration und Elektorale Repräsentation. In O. Niedermayer and H. Schmitt, eds., *Wahlen und Europäische Einigung.* Opladen: Westdeutscher Verlag.

van der Eijk, C., M. Franklin, T. Mackie, and H. Valen. 1992. Cleavages, Conflict Resolution and Democracy. In M. Franklin, T. Mackie, H. Valen et al. *Electoral Change: Responses to Evolving Social and Attitudinal Structures in Western Countries.* Cambridge: Cambridge University Press.

van der Eijk, C., M. Franklin, and M. Marsh. 1996. What Voters Teach us about European Elections / What European Elections Teach us about Voters. *Electoral Studies.* 15 (in press).

van der Eijk, C., and B. Niemöller. 1983. *Electoral Change in the Netherlands: Empirical Results and Methods of Measurement.* Amsterdam: CT Press.

————. 1984. Het Potentiële Electoraat van de Nederlandse Politieke Partijen. Beleid en Maatschappij. 7–8:192–204.

————. 1985. *Voter Behavior in the European Elections: Suggestions to Investigate the Effect of 'European' Factors.* Barcelona: Paper Prepared for the ECPR Joint Sessions of Workshops.

————. 1987. Electoral Alignments in the Netherlands. *Electoral Studies.* 6:17–30.

van der Eijk, C., B. Niemöller, and J. Tillie. 1986. *The Two Faces of 'Future Vote': Voter Utility and Party Potential.* Göteborg: Paper Prepared for the ECPR Joint Sessions of Workshops.

van der Eijk, C., B. Niemöller, and E. Oppenhuis. 1988. *Ideological Domains and Party Systems in Europe.* Washington, D. C.: Paper Prepared for the XIVth World Congress of the International Political Science Association.

van der Eijk, C., and E. Oppenhuis. 1989. *Parties' Attitudes Toward the European Community: A Cross-national Exploration of Voter Perceptions and their Usefulness in Electoral Research.* Paris: Paper Prepared for the ECPR Joint Sessions of Workshops.

————. 1990. Turnout and Second-order Effects in the European Elections of June 1989: Evidence from the Netherlands. *Acta Politica.* 25:67–94.

————. 1991. European Parties' Performance in Electoral Competition. *European Journal of Political Research.* 19:55–80.

van der Eijk, C., E. Oppenhuis, H. Schmitt et al. 1993. *EES-89: European Election Study 1989: Data Description and Preliminary Documentation.* Amsterdam: Steinmetz Archive/Swidoc.

van der Eijk, C., and H. Schmitt. 1990. The Role of the Eurobarometer in the Study of European Elections and the Development of Comparative Electoral Research. In K. Reif, and R. Inglehart, eds., *Eurobarometer: The Dynamics of European Public Opinion.* London: Macmillan.

Elklit, J., and N. Petersen. 1973. Denmark Enters the EC. *Scandinavian Political Studies.* 8:198–213.

Elliott, S. 1990. The 1989 Election to the European Parliament in Northern Ireland. *Irish Political Studies.* 5:93–100.

Enelow, J. M., and M. J. Hinich. 1984. *The Spatial Theory of Voting: An Introduction.* Cambridge: Cambridge University Press.

Erikson, R. 1988. The Puzzle of Midterm Loss. *Journal of Politics.* 50:1011–1029.

Ferrera, M., ed., 1991. *Le Dodici Europe: I Paesi della Comunità di Fronte ai Cambiamenti del 1989–1990.* Bologna: Il Mulino.

Fiorina, M. P. 1981. *Retrospective Voting in American National Elections.* New Haven: Yale University Press.

Fishbein, M., and I. Ajzen. 1975. *Belief, Attitude, Intention and Behavior: An Introduction to Theory and Research.* Reading, Mass.: Addison-Wesley.

Fitzgerald, R. 1992. The 1991 Local Elections in the Republic of Ireland. *Irish Political Studies.* 7:99–104.

Flanagan, S. C. 1982a. Changing Values in Advanced Industrial Society. *Comparative Political Studies.* 14:403–44.

———. 1982b. Measuring Value Change In Advanced Industrial Societies. *Comparative Political Studies. 15:99–128.*

———. 1987. Value Change in Industrial Society. *American Political Science Review.* 81:1303–19.

Flickinger, R., and D. Studlar. 1992. The Disappearing Voters? Exploring Declining Turnout in Western European Elections. *West European Politics.* 15(2):1–16.

Forschungsgruppe Wahlen. 1987. *Bundestagswahl 1987: Eine Analyse der Wahl zum 11. Deutschen Bundestag vom 25 Januar 1987.* Mannheim: Berichte der Forschungsgruppe Wahlen e.V. Nr. 45.

———. 1990a. Sieg ohne Glanz: Eine Analyse der Bundestagswahl 1987. In M. Kaase, and H.-D. Klingemann, eds., *Wahlen und Wähler: Analysen aus Anlaß der Bundestagswahl 1987.* Opladen: Westdeutscher Verlag.

———. 1990b. *Bundestagswahl 1990: Eine Analyse der Ersten Gesamtdeutschen Bundestagswahl am 2 Dezember 1990.* Mannheim: Berichte der Forschungsgruppe Wahlen e.V. Nr. 61.

Fraeys, W. 1979. Les Elections Européennes de 1979: Analyse des Résultats. *Res Publica.* 3:411–426.

———. 1984. Les Elections Européennes de 1984: Analyse des Résultats pour la Belgique. *Res Publica.* 5:587–601.

———. 1988. Les Elections Législatives du 13 Décembre 1987: Analyse des Resultats. *Res Publica.* 30:3–24.

———. 1989. Les Elections Européennes de 1989: Analyse des Résultats pour la Belgique. *Res Publica.* 4:551–564.

———. 1992. Les Résultats des Elections Législatives du 24 Novembre 1991: Analyse des Résultats. *Res Publica.* 2:131–153.

Franklin, M. 1982. Demographic and Political Components in the Decline of British Class Voting. *Electoral Studies.* 1:195–220.

———. 1984. How the Decline of Class Voting Opened the Way to Radical Change in British Politics. *British Journal of Political Science.* 14:437–462.

———. 1985. *The Decline of Class Voting in Britain: Changes in the Basis of Electoral Choice, 1964–1983.* Oxford: Oxford University Press.

———. 1991. Getting out the Vote: Social Structure and the Mobilization of Partisanship in the 1989 European Elections. *European Journal of Political Research.* 19:129–148.

———. 1996. European Elections and the European Voter. In J. Richardson, ed., *Policymaking in the European Union.* London: Longman's.

Franklin, M., C. van der Eijk, and M. Marsh. 1995a. Referendum Outcomes and Trust in Government: Public Support for Europe in the Wake of Maastricht. *West European Politics.* 18:101–117.

———. 1995b. Referendum Outcomes and Trust in Government: Public Support for Europe in the Wake of Maastricht. In J. Hayward, ed., *The Crisis of Representation in Europe.* London: Cass.

Franklin, M., C. van der Eijk, and E. Oppenhuis. 1996. Turnout Decline and the Motivational Basis of British Participation in the European Elections of 1994. In C. Rallings, D. Farrell, D. Broughton, and D. Denver, eds., *British Elections and Parties Yearbook 1995.* London: Harvester Wheatsheaf.

Franklin, M., T. Mackie, H. Valen et al. 1992. *Electoral Change: Responses to Evolving Social and Attitudinal Structures in Western Countries.* Cambridge: Cambridge University Press.

Franklin, M., M. Marsh, and L. McLaren. 1994. Uncorking the Bottle: Attitudes to Europe in the Wake of Maastricht. *Journal of Common Market Studies.* 32:455–472.

Franklin, M., M. Marsh, and C. Wlezien. 1994. Attitudes Towards Europe and Referendum Votes: a Response to Siune and Svensson. *Electoral Studies.* 13:117–121.

Franklin, M., R. Niemi, and G. Whitten. 1994. The Two Faces of Tactical Voting. *British Journal of Political Science.* 24:549–556.

Franklin, M., and W. Rüdig. 1992a. The Green Voter in the 1989 European Elections. *Environmental Politics.* 1:129-159.

———. 1992b. The Green Voter in the 1989 European Elections. In D. Judge, ed., *A Green Dimension for the European Community.* London: Frank Cass.

———. 1995. On the Durability of Green Politics: Evidence from the 1989 European Election Study. *Comparative Political Studies.* 28:409–439.

Frognier, A.-P. 1974.*Vote, Clivages Socio-politiques et Develloppement Régional en Belgique.* Leuven: Vanden.

———. 1976. Party Preference Spaces and Voting Change in Belgium. In I. Budge, I. Crewe, and D. Farlie, eds., *Party Identification and Beyond: Representations of Voting and Party Competition.* London: John Wiley and Sons.

Fuchs, D., and H.-D. Klingemann. 1989. The Left-Right Schema. In M. Kent Jennings, J. W. van Deth et al., eds., *Continuities in Political Action: A Longitudinal Study of Political Orientations in Three Western Democracies.* Berlin/New York: De Gruyter.

Gallagher, M. 1986. The Political Consequences of the Electoral System in the Republic of Ireland. *Electoral Studies.* 5: 253–275.

———. 1988. The Single European Act Referendum. *Irish Political Studies.* 3:77–82.

———. 1991. Proportionality, Disproportionality and Electoral Systems. *Electoral Studies.* 10:33–51.

Gallagher, M., M. Laver, and P. Mair. 1992. *Representative Government in Western Europe.* New York: McGraw-Hill.

Gallagher, M., and M. Marsh. 1991. Republic of Ireland Presidential Election: 7 November 1990. *West European Politics.* 14:169–173.

Ginsberg, W. 1982. *The Consequences of Consent: Elections, Citizen Control and Popular Acquiescence.* Reading, MA: Addison-Wesley.

Ginsberg, W., and A. Stone. 1986. *Do Elections Matter?* Armonk, N. Y.: M. E. Sharpe.

Goldey, D. B. 1972. The Portuguese Elections of 1987 and the Presidential Election of 1991. *Electoral Studies.* 11:171–176.

Granberg, D., and S. Holmberg. 1988. *The Political System Matters: Social Psychology and Voting Behavior in Sweden and the United States.* Cambridge: Cambridge University Press.

Gunther, R. 1986. El Hundimiento de UCD. In J. J. Linz, and J. R. Montero, eds., *Crisis y Cambio: Electores y Partidos en la España de los Anos Ochenta.* Madrid: Centro de Estudios Constitucionales.

Gunther, R., G. Sani, and G. Shabad. 1986. *Spain after Franco: The Making of a Competitive Party System.* Berkeley: University of California Press.

Habert, P., P. Perrineau, and C. Ysmal,. eds., 1992. *Les Elections Locale de Mars 1992: Le Vote Eclaté.* Paris: Presses de la Fondation Nationale des Sciences Politique.

Hainsworth, P. 1989. Northern Ireland. *Electoral Studies.* 8:313–316.

————, ed. 1990. *Towards 1992: Europe at the Crossroads.* Ulster: University of Ulster.

————, ed. 1992. *Breaking and Preserving the Mould: The Third Direct Elections to the European Parliament in the Irish Republic and Northern Ireland.* Coleraine: Policy Research Institute.

Hand, G., J. Georgel, and C. Sasse, eds., 1979. *European Electoral Systems Handbook.* London: Butterworth.

Hearl, D. 1989. Luxembourg. *Electoral Studies.* 8:296–304.

Heath, A., and S.-K. MacDonald. 1988. The End of Party Identification Theory. *Electoral Studies.* 8:95–107.

Heisler, M. O. 1974. Institutionalizing Societal Cleavages in a Cooptive Policy: The Growing Importance of the Output Side in Belgium. In M. O. Heisler, ed., *Politics in Europe: Structural Processes in some Postindustrial Democracies.* New York: McKay.

Herrero y Rodriguez de Miñón, M. 1992. De Europa Ambigua. *Nueva Revista.* 26:26–30.

Hill, K. 1974. Belgium: Political Change in a Segmented Society. In R. Rose, ed., *Electoral Behavior.* New York: Free Press.

Hinkley, B. 1981. *Congressional Elections.* Washington D. C.: Congressional Quarterly Press.

Hirczy, W. 1992. *Electoral Participation.* Ph.D. Diss., University of Houston. Ann Arbor: University Microfilms.

————. 1994. The Impact of Mandatory Voting Laws on Turnout: A Quasi–Experimental Approach. *Electoral Studies.* 13:64–76.

————. 1995. Explaining Near-Universal Turnout: The Case of Malta. *European Journal of Political Research.* 27:255–272.

Hirsch, M. 1984. Luxembourg. *Electoral Studies.* 3:299–301.

————. 1985. Luxembourg. In K. Reif, ed., *Ten European Elections: Campaigns and Results of the 1979/81 First Direct Elections to the European Parliament.* Aldershot: Gower.

Holmes, M. 1990. The 1989 Election to the European Parliament in the Republic of Ireland. *Irish Political Studies.* 5:85–92.

Hunneus, C. 1985. *La Unión de Centro Democrático y la Transición a la Democracia en España.* Madrid: Centro de Investigaciónes Sociológicas.

Huyse, L. 1983. Breuklijnen in de Belgische Samenleving. In L. Huyse, and J. Berting, eds., *Als in een Spiegel? Een Sociologische Kaart van België en Nederland.* Leuven: Kritak.

Inglehart, R. 1971a. The Silent Revolution in Europe: Intergenerational Change in Post-Industrial Societies. *American Political Science Review.* 65:991–1017.

————. 1971b. Public Opinion and European Integration. In L. N. Lindberg, and S. Scheingold, eds., *European Integration.* Cambridge, MA: Harvard University Press.

————. 1977. *The Silent Revolution: Changing Values and Political Styles among Western Publics.* Princeton, N. J.: Princeton University Press.

————. 1984. The Changing Structure of Political Cleavages in Western Society. In R. J. Dalton, S. C. Flanagan, and P. A. Beck, eds., *Electoral Change in Advanced Industrial Democracies: Realignment or Dealignment?* Princeton, N. J.: Princeton University Press.

————. 1990. *Culture Shift in Advanced Industrial Society.* Princeton: Princeton University Press.

Inglehart, R., and H.-D. Klingemann. 1976. Party Identification, Ideological Preference and the Left-Right Dimension among Western Mass Publics. In I. Budge, I. Crewe, and D. Farlie, eds., *Party Identification and Beyond: Representations of Voting and Party Competition.* London: John Wiley and Sons.

Inglehart, R., and J.-R. Rabier. 1979. Europe Elects a Parliament. Cognitive Mobilization and Pro-European Attitudes as Influences on Voter Turnout. *Government and Opposition.* 14:479–507.

Jaccard, J., R. Turrisi, and C. K. Wan. 1990. *Interaction Effects in Multiple Regression.* Newbury Park, Calif: Sage.

Jackman, R. W. 1987. Political Institutions and Voter Turnout in the Industrial Democracies. *American Political Science Review.* 81:405–423.

Jacobs, F., and R. Corbett with M. Shackleton. 1992. *The European Parliament.* Harlow, Essex: Longman.

de Jong, J. P., and J. A. Verduyn Lunel. 1983. Rode Politiek: PPR Samen Verder! *Radikale Notities.* 1983:7–16.

Justel, M. 1990. Panorámica de la Abstención Electoral en España, Madrid. *Revista de Estudios Políticos.* 68:343–396.

Kaase, M., and H.-D. Klingemann, eds., 1990. *Wahlen und Wähler: Analysen aus Anlaß der Bundestagswahl 1987.* Opladen: Westdeutscher Verlag.

Kalogeropoulou, E. 1989. Election Promises and Government Performance in Greece: PASOK's Fulfillment of Its 1981 Election Pledges. *European Journal of Political Research.* 17:289–311.

Katz, R. 1980. *A Theory of Parties and Electoral Systems.* Baltimore: Johns Hopkins University Press.

———. 1985. Measuring Party Identification with Eurobarometer Data: A Warning Note. *West European Politics.* 8:104–108.

Keatinge, P., and M. Marsh. 1990. The European Parliament Election. In M. Gallagher, and R. Sinnott, eds., *How Ireland Voted 1989.* Galway: PSAI Press.

Kerkhofs, J., K. Dobbelaere, L. Voy, and B. Bawin-Legros. 1992. *De Versnelde Ommekeer: De Waarden van Vlamingen, Walen en Brusselaars in de Jaren Negentig.* Tielt: Lannoo.

Kerlinger, M. 1984. *Liberalism and Conservatism.* Hillsdale, N. J.: Lawrence Erlbaum.

Kim, J., J. Petrocik, and S. Enokson. 1975. Voter Turnout among the American States: Systemic and Individual Components. *American Political Science Review.* 69:107–123.

King, D. 1984. The Interaction between Foreign and Domestic Policy in the 1979 European Election in Ireland. *Irish Studies in International Affairs.* 1:62–80.

Kitschelt, H. 1988. Left-Libertarian Parties: Explaining Innovation in Compatitive Party Systems. *World Politics.* 40:194–234.

Kok, W. J. P., I. Lipschits, and Ph. van Praag Jr. 1985. The Netherlands. In K. Reif, ed., *Ten European Elections: Campaigns and Results of the 1979/81 First Direct Elections to the European Parliament.* Aldershot: Gower.

Kuechler, M. 1991. Issues and Voting in the European Elections 1989. *European Journal of Political Research.* 19:81–104.

———. 1994. Problemlösungskompetenz der Parteien und Wahlverhalten bei den Wahlen zum Europäischen Parlament 1989. In O. Niedermayer and H. Schmitt, eds., *Wahlen und Europäische Einigung.* Opladen: Westdeutscher Verlag.

Ladner, M. 1996. *Economic Expectations and the Political Business Cycle.* Ph.D.Diss., University of Houston. Ann Arbor: University Microfilms.

Laffan, B. 1989. When You're Over There in Europe Get Us a Grant: the Management of the Structural Funds in Ireland. *Irish Political Studies.* 4:43–58.

Lakeman, E. 1990. Elections to the European Parliament 1989. *Parliamentary Affairs.* 43:77–90.

Lancelot, A. 1986. *L'Abstentionnisme Electoral.* Paris: Presses de la Fondation Nationale des Sciences Politique.

Laver, M., and W. B. Hunt. 1992. *Party and Policy Competition.* London: Routledge.

Laver, M., and N. Schofield. 1991. *Multiparty Government.* Oxford: Oxford University Press.

Lazarsfeld, P. F., B. R. Berelson, and H. Gaudet. 1944. *The People's Choice: How the Voter Makes up his Mind in a Presidential Campaign.* New York: Columbia University Press.

Lazarsfeld, P. F., and H. Menzel. 1969. On the Relation between Individual and Collective Properties. In A. Etzioni, ed., *A Sociological Reader on Complex Organizations.* New York: Free Press.

Leighley, J., and J. Nagler. 1992 Individual and Systemic Influences on Turnout: Who Votes? *Journal of Politics.* 54:718–740.

Lijphart, A. 1968. *The Politics of Accommodation: Pluralism and Democracy in the Netherlands.* Berkeley: University of California Press.

———. 1981a. *Conflict and Coexistence in Belgium: The Dynamics of a Culturally Divided Society.* Berkeley: Institute of International Studies.

———. 1981b. Introduction: the Belgian Example of Cultural Coexistence in Comparative Perspective. In A. Lijphart, ed., *Conflict and Coexistence in Belgium: The Dynamics of a Culturally Divided Society.* Berkeley: Institute of International Studies.

———. 1984. *Democracies: Patterns of Majoritarian and Consensus Government in Twenty-one Countries.* New Haven: Yale University Press.

Lindberg, L. N., 1974. The Political System of the European Community. In M. O. Heisler, ed., *Politics in Europe.* New York: McKay.

Linz, J. J. 1980. The New Spanish Party System. In R. Rose, ed., *Electoral Participation: A Comparative Analysis.* London: Sage.

Linz, J. J., and J. R. Montero. 1986. *Crisis y Cambio: Electores y Partidos en la España de los Años Ochenta.* Madrid: Centro de Estudios Constitucionales.

Lipset, S. M., and S. Rokkan. 1967. Cleavage Structures, Party Systems and Voter Alignments. In S. M. Lipset, and S. Rokkan, eds., *Party Systems and Voter Alignments: Cross-National Perspectives.* New York: Free Press.

LLera, P., 1985. El Sistema de Partidos en la Comunidad Autónoma del Pais Vasco. *Revista de Estudios Politicos.* 1985:46–47.

Lodge, J. 1993. EC Policy Making: Institutional Dynamics. In J. Lodge, ed., *The European Community and the Challenge of the Future.* New York: St.Martin's.

Lorwin, V. R. 1966. Belgium: Religion, Class and Language in National Politics. In R. Dahl, ed., *Political Oppositions in Western Democracies.* New Haven: Yale University Press.

Lopez Pintor, R. 1982. *La Opinión Pública: del Franquismo a la Democracia.* Madrid: Centro de Investigaciones Sociológicas.

Lucardie, P. 1991. Fragments from the Pillars: Small Parties in the Netherlands. In F. Müller–Rommel and G. Pridham, eds., *Small Parties in Western Europe: Comparative and National Perspectives.* London: Sage.

Ludlow, P. with N. Ersbøll. 1994. *Towards 1996: The Agenda of the Intergovernmental Conference.* Brussles: Centre for European Policy Studies.

MacDonald, S., O. Listhaug, and G. Rabinowitz. 1991. Issues and Party Support in Multiparty Systems. *American Political Science Review.* 85:1107–32.

Mackie, T., ed. 1991. *Europe Votes 3.* Aldershot: Dartmouth.

Mackie, T., and F. W. S. Craig. 1980. *Europe Votes 1.* Aldershot: Gower.

———. 1985. *Europe Votes 2.* Aldershot: Gower.

Mackie, T., R. Mannheimer, and G. Sani. 1992. Italy. In M. Franklin, T. Mackie, and H. Valen et al., *Electoral Change: Responses to Evolving Social and Attitudinal Structures in Western Countries.* Cambridge: Cambridge University Press.

Mackie, T., and R. Rose. 1991. *The International Almanac of Electoral History.* London and Washington D. C.: CQ Press.

MacKuen, M., R. Erikson, and J. Stimson. 1989. Macropartisanship. *American Political Science Review.* 83:1125–42.

Maddens, B. 1992. Agenda Setting in de Verkiezingscampagne van November 1991 in Vlaanderen. *Res Publica.* 2:175–208.

Maes, M. 1990. De Formele Aanstelling van de Partijvoorzitters in België. *Res Publica.* 1:3–62.

Mannheimer, R., and G. Sani. 1987. *Il Mercato Elettorale.* Bologna: Il Mulino.

Maravall, J. M. 1981. Los Apoyos Partidistas en España: Polarización, Fragmentación y Estabilidad. *Revista de Estudios Políticos. 23:9–33.*

———. 1984. *La Política de la Transición.* (2nd edition) Madrid: Taurus.

Marquand, D. 1979. *Parliament for Europe.* London: Cape.

Marsh, M. 1991. Accident or Design: Non-voting in Ireland. *Irish Political Studies.* 6:1–14.

———. 1992. *Neutrality, European Union and the Irish Public.* Dublin: Report for Irish Institute for European Affairs.

———. 1995. *Testing the Second–order Election Model after Four European Elections.* Bordeaux: Paper presented at ECPR Joint Sessions.

Matthews, D., and J. Prothro. 1963. Political Factors and Negro Voter Registration in the South. *American Political Science Review.* 57:355–67.

Mayhew, D. 1974. *Congress: The Electoral Connection.* New Haven: Yale University Press.

McAllister, I., and S. Nelson. 1979. Modern Developments in the Northern Ireland Party System. *Parliamentary Affairs.* 32:279–316.

McRae, K., ed. 1986. *Conflict and Compromise in Multilingual Societies: Belgium.* Waterloo, Ont.: Wilfred Laurier University Press.

Menke, K. 1985. Germany. In K. Reif, ed., *Ten European Elections: Campaigns and Results of the 1979/81 First Direct Elections to the European Parliament.* Aldershot: Gower.

Menke, K., and I. Gordon. 1980. Differential Mobilisation for Europe: A Comparative Note on Some Aspects of the Campaign. *European Journal of Political Research.* 8:63–90.

Merriam, C., and H. Gosnell. 1924. *Non-Voting: Causes and Methods of Control.* Chicago: University of Chicago Press.

Milbrath, L. W., and M. L. Goel. 1977. *Political Participation: How and Why Do People Get Involved in Politics?* 2nd ed. Chicago: Rand McNally.

Miller, W., and M. Mackie. 1973. The Electoral Cycle and the Assymetry of Government and Opposition Popularity. *Political Studies.* 21:263–279.

Minkenberg, M., and R. Inglehart. 1990. Neoconservatism and Value Change in the USA: Tendencies in the Mass Public of a Postindustrial Society. In J. R. Gibbins, ed., *Contemporary Political Culture.* London: Sage.

Mitchell, G., and C. Wlezien. 1995. The Impact of Legal Constraints on Voter Registration, Turnout and the Composition of the American Electorate. *Political Behavior* (in press).

Mitchell, P. 1991. Conflict Regulation and Party Competition in Northern Ireland. *European Journal of Political Research.* 20:67–92.

Mokken, R. J. 1971. *A Theory and Procedure of Scale Analysis.* The Hague: Mouton.

Molins, J. M. 1989. *Los Partidos de Ambito no Estatal y las Elecciones al Parlamento Europeo.* Paris: Paper Prepared for the ECPR Joint Sessions of Workshops.

———. 1992. *Las Elecciones al Parlamento Europeo de 1987 y 1989 en Cataluña.* Paper prepared for the Jornadas Sobre Comportamiento Político y Electoral, UNED.

Montero, J. R. 1986. La Vuelta a las Urnas: Participación, Movilización y Abstención. In J. J. Linz, and J. R. Montero, eds., *Crisis y Cambio: Electores y Partidos en la España de los Años Ochenta.* Madrid: Centro de Estudios Constitucionales.

———. 1990. *Non-voting in Spain: Some Quantitative and Attitudinal Aspects.* Barcelona: Institut de Ciencies Polítiques i Socials.

Morlino, L., and P. V. Uleri. 1989. *Le Elezioni nel Mondo 1982–1989.* Osservatorio Elettorale Regione Toscana/Giunta Regionale Dipartimento Statistica, Elaborazione dati Documentazione.

Mughan, A. 1979. Modernization and Ethnic Conflict in Belgium. *Political Studies.* 27:21–37.

———. 1983. Accommodation or Defusion in the Management of Linguistics Conflict in Belgium. *Political Studies.* 31:434–451.

Müller-Rommel, F. 1983. Die Postmaterialismusdiskussion in der Empirischen Sozialforschung: Politisch und Wissenschaftlich überlebt oder noch immer zukunftweisend? *Politische Vierteljahresschrift.* 24:251–269.

———, ed. 1989. *New Politics in Western Europe: The Rise and Succes of Green Parties and Alternative Lists.* Cambridge, Mass.: MIT Press.

Müller-Rommel, F., and G. Pridham, eds., 1991. *Small Parties in Western Europe: Comparative and National Perspectives.* London: Sage.

Niedermayer, O. 1990. Turnout in the European Elections. *Electoral Studies.* 9:45–50.

———. 1991. European Elections 1989. *European Journal of Political Research.* 19:149–156.

———. 1994. Europäisches Parlament und öffentliche Meinung. In O. Niedermayer and H. Schmitt, eds., *Wahlen und Europäische Einigung.* Opladen: Westdeutscher Verlag.

Nielsen, H. J. 1993. *EF på valg.* Copenhagen: Columbus.

Niemi, R., and H. F. Weisberg, eds. 1993. *Controversies in Voting Behavior.* 3rd ed. Washington, D. C.: Congressional Quarterly Press.

Niemi, R., G. Whitten, and M. Franklin. 1992. Constituency Characteristics, Individual Characteristics and Tactical Voting. *British Journal of Political Science.* 22:229–254.

Niemöller, B., and W. H. van Schuur. 1983. Stochastic Models for Unidimensional Scaling: Mokken and Rasch. In D. McKay, N. Schofield, and P. Whiteley, eds., *Data Analysis and the Social Sciences.* London: Francis Pinter.

Norris, P. 1990. *British By-elections: The Volatile Electorate.* New York: Oxford University Press.

van Schuur, W. H. 1984. *Structure in Political Beliefs: A New Model for Stochastic Unfolding with Applications to European Party Activists.* Amsterdam: CT Press.

van Schuur, W. H., and T. Wierstra. 1987. *MUDFOLD Manual.* Groningen: IEC ProGAMMA.

O'Sullivan, E. 1991. The 1990 Presidential Election in the Republic of Ireland. *Irish Political Studies.* 6:85–98.

Offe, C. 1984. *Contradictions of the Welfare State.* Cambridge, Mass.: MIT Press.

Oppenhuis, E. 1995. *Voting Behavior in Europe: A Comparative Analysis of Electoral Participation and Party Choice.* Amsterdam: Het Spinhuis.

Page, B. I., and C. C. Jones. 1979. Reciprocal Effects of Policy Preferences, Party Loyalties and the Vote. *American Political Science Review.* 73:1071–1089.

Pappi, F. 1984. The West German Party System. In S. Bartolini, and P. Mair, eds., *Party Politics in Contemporary Western Europe.* London: Frank Cass.

Parry, G., G. Moyser, and N. Day. 1992. *Political Participation and Democracy in Britain.* New York: Cambridge University Press.

Pedersen, M. N. 1979. The Dynamics of European Party Systems: Changing Patterns of Electoral Volatility. *European Journal of Political Research.* 7:1–26.

———. 1987. The Danish Working Multiparty System: Breakdown or Adaptation? In H. Daalder, ed., *Party Systems in Denmark, Austria, Switzerland, The Netherlands and Belgium.* London: Pinter.

Perrineau, P. 1989. Les Etapes d'une Implantation Electorale 1972–1988. In N. Mayer, and P. Perrineau, eds., *Le Front National à Découvert.* Paris: Presses de la Fondation Nationale des Sciences Politique.

Platone, F., and J. Ranger. 1981. L'Echec Electorale du Parti Communiste. In A. Lancelot, ed., *Les Elections de l'Alternance.* Paris: Presses de la Fondation Nationale des Sciences Politique.

Poguntke, T. 1992. *An Alternative Politics? The German Green Party.* Edinburgh: Edinburgh University Press.

Poguntke, T., and H. Schmitt. 1990. Die Grünen: Entstehungshintergrund, Politisch-programmatische Entwicklungen und Auswirkungen auf andere Parteien. In J. Schmif, and H. Tiemann, eds., *Aufbrüche: Die Zukunftsdiskussion in Parteien und Verbänden.* Marburg: SP Verlag.

Powell, G. B., Jr. 1980. Voting Turnout in Thirty Democracies: Partisan, Legal and Socio-Economic Influences. In Richard Rose, ed., *Electoral Participation: A Comparative Analysis*. Beverly Hills/ London: Sage.

————. 1986. American Voter Turnout in Comparative Perspective. *American Political Science Review*. 80:17–43.

Przeworski, A., and H. Teune. 1970. *The Logic of Comparative Social Inquiry*. New York: Wiley.

Rabinowitz, G., and S. MacDonald. 1989. A Directional Theory of Issue Voting. *American Political Science Review. 83:93–121.*

Reif, K. 1984a. National Electoral Cycles and European Elections 1979 and 1984. *Electoral Studies. 3:244–255.*

————, ed. 1984b. *European Elections 1979/81 and 1984: Conclusion and Perspectives from Emperical Research*. Berlin: Quorum.

————. 1985a. Ten Second-Order National Elections. In K. Reif, ed., *Ten European Elections: Campaigns and Results of the 1979/81 First Direct Elections to the European Parliament*. Aldershot: Gower.

————, ed. 1985b. *Ten European Elections: Campaigns and Results of the 1979/81 First Direct Elections to the European Parliament*. Aldershot: Gower.

Reif. K., and R. Inglehart, eds. 1990. *Eurobarometer: The Dynamics of European Public Opinion*. London: Macmillan.

Reif, K., and H. Schmitt. 1980. Nine Second-order National Elections: A Conceptual Framework for the Analysis of European Election Results. *European Journal of Political Research*. 8:3–44.

Rose, R. 1974. *Electoral Behavior*. New Haven: Free Press.

————. 1980. *Electoral Participation: A Comparative Analysis*. Beverly Hills/ London: Sage.

Rüdig, W. 1990. *Explaining Green Party Development: Reflections on a Theoretical Framework*. Glasgow: University of Strathclyde Papers on Government and Politics.

Rüdig, W., and M. Franklin. 1991. *The Greening of Europe: Ecological Voting in the 1989 European Elections*. Glasgow: University of Strathclyde Papers in Government and Politics.

————. 1992. Green Prospects: the Future of Green Parties in Britain, France and Germany. In W. Rüdig, ed., *Green Politics Two*. Edinburgh: Edinburgh University Press.

Rüdig, W., M. Franklin, and L. Bennie. 1993. *Green Blues: The Rise and Decline of the British Green Party*. Glasgow: University of Strathclyde Papers on Government and Politics.

Sani, G., and G. Shabad. 1986. ¿Adversarios o Competidores?: la Polarización del Electorado. In J. J. Linz, and J. R. Montero, eds., *Crisis y Cambio: Electores y Partidos en la España de los Años Ochenta*. Madrid: Centro de Estudios Constitucionales.

Sartori, G. 1976. *Parties and Party Systems: A Framework for Analysis*. Vol 1. Cambridge: Cambridge University Press.

Schacht, K. 1991. Der Rechtsextremismus hat eine Zukunft. *Die Neue Gesellschaft/Frankfurter Hefte*. 38:152–158.

Schattschneider, E. E. 1960. *The Semi-Sovereign People*. New York: Holt Rinehart and Winston.

Schmidt, O. 1981. Opkomst. In A. Th. J. Eggen, C. van der Eijk, and B. Niemöller, eds., *Kiezen in Nederland: 26 mei 1981: Wat de Kiezers Deden en Waarom*. Zoetermeer: Actaboek.

————. 1983. Kiezersopkomst van 1971 tot 1982. In C. van der Eijk, and B. Niemöller, eds., *In het Spoor van de Kiezer: Aspecten van 10 Jaar Kiezersgedrag*. Meppel: Boom.

Schmitt, H. 1987a. *Das Parteiensystem der Bundesrepublik Deutschland: Eine Einführung aus Politik-soziologischer Perspektive*. Hagen: Studienkurs der Fernuniversität Hagen.

————. 1987b. *Neue Politik in Alten Parteien: Zum Verhältnis von Gesellschaft und Parteien in der Bundesrepublik*. Opladen: Westdeutscher Verlag.

———. 1989. Was war Europäisch am Europawahl-Verhalten der Deutschen? Eine Analyse der Europawahl 1989 in der Bundesrepublik. *Aus Politik und Zeitgeschichte.* B43/89. Oct. 20:39–51.

———. 1990a. Die Sozialdemokratische Partei Deutschlands. In H. Oberreuter, and A. Mintzel, eds., *Parteien in der Bundesrepublik Deutschland.* München: Olzog.

———. 1990b. Party Attachment and Party Choice in the European Elections of June 1989: A Cross-national Comparative Analysis of the Post Electoral Surveys of the European Voters Study 1989. *International Journal of Public Opinion Research.* 2:169–184.

———. 1994a. Was war 'Europäisch' am Europawahlverhalten der Deutschen? Eine Analyse der Europawahl 1989 in der Bundesrepublik. In O. Niedermayer und H. Schmitt, eds., *Wahlen und Europäische Einigung.* Opladen: Westdeutscher Verlag.

———. 1994b. Parteibindungen und Issuekometenz der Parteien als Determinanten der Wahlentscheidung: Eine Vergleichende Analyse von Wahlverhalten in zehn Ländern der EG. In O. Niedermayer und H. Schmitt, eds., *Wahlen und Europäische Einigung.* Opladen: Westdeutscher Verlag.

Schmitt, H. and S. Holmberg. 1995. Political Parties in Decline? In H.–D. Klingemann and D. Fuchs, ed., *Citizens and the State.* Oxford: Oxford University Press.

Schmitt, H., and R. Mannheimer. 1991a. About Voting and Non-voting in the European Elections of June 1989. *European Journal of Political Research.* 19:31–54.

———, eds. 1991b. The European Elections of June 1989. *European Journal of Political Research* (special issue). 19(1).

Schram, A. J. H. C. 1989. *Voter Behavior in Economic Perspective.* Alblasserwaard: Kanters.

Schulz, W. 1983. One Campaign or Nine. In J. G. Blumler, ed., *Communicating to Voters: Television in the First European Parliament Elections.* London: Sage.

Schulz, W., and J. G. Blumler. 1994. Die Bedeutung der Kampagnen für das Europa–Engagement der Bürger. Eine Mehr–Ebenen–Analyse. In O. Niedermayer und H. Schmitt, eds., *Wahlen und Europäische Einigung.* Opladen: Westdeutscher Verlag.

Senelle, R. 1990. The Current Constitutional System. In M. Boudart, M. Boudart, and R. Bryssinck, eds., *Modern Belgium.* Palo Alto: SPOSS.

Silverman, L. 1985. The Ideological Mediation of Party–political Responses to Social Change. *European Journal of Political Research.* 13:69–93.

Sinnott, R., and B. J. Whelan. 1992. Turnout in Second-Order Elections: The Case of the EP Election in Dublin 1984 and 1989. *Economic and Social Review.* 23:147–166.

Sloot, T. J. M. 1992. Verzuiling en Pacificatie. In M. Wolters, ed., *Democatie en Beleid in de Europese Gemeenschap.* Alphen a.d. Rijn: Samson Tjeenk Willink.

Smith, E. 1989. *The Unchanging American Voter.* Berkeley: University of California Press.

Stimson, J. A. 1985. Regression in Space and Time: A Statistical Essay. *American Journal of Political Science.* 29:914–947.

Stokes, D. 1974. Compound Paths: An Expository Note. *American Journal of Political Science.* 18:191–214.

Swyngedouw, M. 1986. Verkiezingen en Partijvoorkeur tijdens de Parlementsverkiezingen van 13 Oktober 1985. *Res Publica.* 2:261–282.

———. 1992a. *Waar voor je Waarden: De Opkomst van het Vlaams Blok en Agalev in de Jaren Tachtig.* Leuven: Sociologisch Onderzoeksinstituut.

———. 1992b. L'Essor d'Agalev et du Vlaams Blok. *Courrier Hebdomadaire du CRISP.* 1362.

———. 1992c. National Elections in Belgium: The Breakthrough of the Extreme Right in Flanders. *Regional Politics and Policy.* 2:62–75.

Swyngedouw, M., and J. Billiet. 1988. Stemmen in Vlaanderen op 13 December 1987: Een Statistische Analyse. *Res Publica.* 1:25–50.

Swyngedouw, M., J. Billiet, and A. Carton. 1992. *Van waar komen Ze, Wie zijn Ze? Stemgedrag en Verschuivingen op 24 November 1991.* Leuven: Interuniversitair Steunpunt Politiek Opinie-onderzoek.

Swyngedouw, M., L. De Winter, and L. Schulpen. 1990. *De Europese Verkiezingen van 17 Juni 1989.* Brussels: Dimarso.

Teixeira, R. 1992. *The Disappearing American Voter.* Washington, D. C.: Brookings.

Thatcher, M. 1993. *The Downing Street Years.* London: Harper Collins.

Thomsen, B. N. 1993. *The Odd Man Out. Denmark and European Integration 1948–92.* Odense: Odense University Press.

Tillie, J. 1995. *Party Utility and Voting Behavior.* Amsterdam: Het Spinhuis.

Thomassen, J. J. A. 1976. Party Identification as a Cross–national Concept. In I. Budge, I. Crewe, and D. Farlie, eds., *Party Identification and Beyond.* London: Wiley.

Tindemans, M. L. 1976. European Union. Report to the European Council. *Bulletin of the European Communities.* Supplement 1/76.

Tingsten, H. 1937. *Political Behavior: Studies in Election Statistics.* London: King and Son.

Treiber-Reif, H., and H. Schmitt. 1990. *Structures in European Attitudes.* Report Prepared on Behalf of the Commission of the European Communities. Mannheim: University of Mannheim/ZEUS (mimeo).

Tufte, E. R. 1975. Determinants of Outcomes of Midterm Congressional Elections' *American Political Science Review.* 69:812–826.

Urwin, D. 1970. Social Cleavages and Political Parties in Belgium: Problems of Institutionalization. *Political Studies. 18:320–340.*

———. 1995. *The Community of Europe: A History of European Integration Since 1945.* 2nd ed. London: Longman.

Van den Brande, A. 1967. Elements for a Sociological Analysis of the Impact of the Main Conflicts on Belgian Political Life. *Res Publica.* 3:437–470.

———. A. 1974. *Ontwerp van een Macro-Sociologisch Model voor het Belgisch Politiek Systeem 1945–1968.* Gent: Rijksuniversiteit Gent (Doctoraat).

Van den Berghe, G. 1979. De Nationale Kieswetten voor de Europese Verkiezingen. *Res Publica.* 1:3–28.

Vedel, G. 1975. *The Role of the Parliamentary Institution in European Integration.* Luxembourg: Symposium on European Integration and the Future of Parliaments in Europe.

Verba, S., and N. Nie. 1972. *Participation in America: Political Democracy and Social Equality.* New York: Harper and Row.

Verminck, M. 1985. Le Parlement Européen de 1979–1984: La Perte en Potentiel du Pouvoir d'une Institution Faible. *Res Publica.* 2–3:287–296.

Voerman, G. 1990. Van Klein Links naar Groen Links: Hoe CPN, PSP en PPR van kleur verschoten. *Namens.* 5:34–39.

Weiler, J. 1982. *Supranational Law and the Supranational System.* Florence: European University Institute (Ph.D. Dissertation).

Whyte, J. 1983. How much Discrimination Was There under the Unionist Regime 1921–68? In T. Gallagher, and J. O'Connell, eds., *Contemporary Irish Studies.* Manchester: Manchester University Press.

Wilder, P. 1990. The British Elections to the European Parliament June 1989. *Representation.* 29:27–31.

Wirth, R. S. 1977. *Cleavage, Conflict and Parliament: Patterns of Legislative Coping in Belgium.* Ph.D. Diss. University of Tennessee. Ann Arbor: University Microfilms.

Woldendorp, J., J. Keman and I. Budge. 1990. Political Data 1945–1990. *European Journal of Political Research* (special issue). 24:1–120.

Wolfinger, R. A., and S. J. Rosenstone. 1980. *Who Votes?* New Haven: Yale University Press.

Worre, T. 1981. The 1979 European Election in Denmark: An Analysis of Participation, Choice of Party, and Attitude Towards Europe. *Cooperation and Conflict.* 16:73–89.

———. 1987. The Danish Euro-Party System. *Scandinavian Political Studies.* 10:79–85.

———. 1988. Denmark at the Crossroads: The Danish Referendum of 28 February 1986 on the EC Reform Package. *Journal of Common Market Studies.* 26:361–88.

———. 1989. Denmark. *Electoral Studies.* 8:237–245.

Ysmal, C. 1986. D'une Droite en Sursis à une Droit Défaite 1974–1981. In A. Lancelot, ed., *Les Elections de l'Alternance.* Paris: Presses de la Fondation Nationale des Sciences Politique.

———. 1989. *Les Partis Politiques sous la Cinquième République.* Paris: Dormat/Monchrestien.

———. 1990. *Le Comportement Electoral des Français.* Paris: Le Seuil.

———. 1992. L'UDF en Proie à ses Contradictions. In SOFRES, *L'Etat de l'Opinion.* Paris: le Seuil.

Author Index

Subject Index